Teaching Argument in the Composition Course

Background Readings

Timothy Barnett

Northeastern Illinois University

Bedford/St. Martin's Boston ◆ New York

For Bedford/St. Martin's
Developmental Editor: Joanne Diaz
Production Editor: Deborah Baker
Production Supervisor: Maria Gonzalez
Marketing Manager: Brian Wheel
Editorial Assistant: Emily Goodall
Copyeditor: Sarah Doerries
Text Design: Claire Seng-Niemoeller
Cover Design: Donna Lee Dennison
Composition: Karla Goethe, Orchard Wind Graphics
Printing and Binding: Haddon Craftsmen, Inc., an R. R. Donnelley & Sons Company

President: Charles H. Christensen
Editorial Director: Joan E. Feinberg
Editor in Chief: Karen S. Henry
Director of Marketing: Karen Melton
Director of Editing, Design, and Production: Marcia Cohen
Managing Editor: Elizabeth M. Schaaf

Manufactured in the United States of America.

9   8
f   e

For information, write: Bedford/St. Martin's, 75 Arlington Street, Boston, MA 02116
(617-399-4000)

ISBN-10: 0–312–39161–7
ISBN-13: 978–0–312–39161–4

Acknowledgments
Roger C. Aden, "The Enthymeme as Postmodern Argument Form: Condensed, Mediated Argument, Then and Now." *Argumentation and Advocacy* 31 (Fall 1994): 54–63. Reprinted with permission of the American Forensic Association.
Aristotle, excerpt from *Rhetoric.* Translated by W. Rhys Roberts. Copyright ©1954 by Random House. Reprinted by permission of Oxford University Press.
James S. Baumlin, "Persuasion, Rogerian Rhetoric, and Imaginative Play," *Rhetoric Society Quarterly* 17 (1987). Reprinted with permission of *Rhetoric Society Quarterly.*
Doug Brent, "Rogerian Rhetoric" from *Argument Revisited, Argument Redefined.* Edited by Emmel, Resch, and Tenney. ©1996 Sage Publications, Inc. Reprinted by permission of Sage Publications, Inc.
A. E. B. Coldiron, *"Refutatio* as a Prewriting Exercise," *TETYC* 18 (February 1991): 40–42. ©1991 by the National Council of Teachers of English. Reprinted with permission.

Preface

To teach students to argue knowledgeably, thoughtfully, and ethically is to equip them to participate effectively in the formal institutions of a large democracy as well as in smaller organizations, such as religious groups, school boards, or community action projects. Therefore, instructors using this book are encouraged to help their students learn to think of argument not as a method of confrontation, but as an engaged form of symbolic action (to borrow from Kenneth Burke) useful for solving problems with others.

The essays in this volume suggest that argument is a comprehensive and challenging form of writing, and that teaching such writing involves helping students to develop a variety of abilities. For example, students must learn to evaluate their own reading, writing, and thinking processes as well as the processes of others; to question personal and cultural assumptions about simplistic binaries such as right/wrong and good/bad; and to consider how cultural difference affects argumentation. Such efforts in the classroom can reconnect argument to rhetoric, a discipline with deep ties to philosophy and one heavily invested in the relationship between theory and practice. They can also help students understand that argumentation, at its most effective, is a process of working with others toward greater understanding, rather than a competitive game that one either "wins" or "loses" — and that every argument, no matter how simple or polarized, is subject to multiple viewpoints and a variety of resolutions.

Readers will note that certain theorists — Aristotle, Stephen Toulmin, Chaim Perelman, and Carl Rogers — figure prominently throughout this book. These theorists are the ones most often cited by argument textbooks in general (and, in particular, by the Bedford/St. Martin's argumentation textbooks this resource supports: *Current Issues and Enduring Questions* by Sylvan Barnet and Hugo Bedau, *Everything's an Argument* by Andrea Lunsford and John Ruszkiewicz, and *Elements of Argument* by Annette T. Rottenberg). Even the most oft-cited theorists, however, are interpreted in various ways in this text, and none are final authorities on the subject of argument. Many of the selections in this book question and reformulate the dominant ideas espoused by the theorists mentioned above, even as they use them to build new theories of argument. In this way, *Teaching Argument in the Composition Course: Background Readings* supports a central tenet of argumentation theory: the importance of recognizing the influence of theories from the past while also questioning the cultural, historical, and individual assumptions that guide all theories of argumentation, no matter how dominant.

I have divided this book into two main sections: "Major Theories of Argumentation" and "Teaching Argument." This is not to suggest that teachers should separate the theory and history of argument from classroom practices. They should instead draw on the theoretical essays from the first section of the book to stimulate thought about general philosophies of teaching and to create specific classroom assignments and practices. At the same time, readers should understand the essays in the "Teaching" section of the book in light of the historical and theoretical perspectives that inform them. In this way, they will be able to adapt the powerful writing assignments in this section for a variety of student populations.

Finally, to orient readers and provide contexts for understanding the readings, I have written introductions to both parts of the book and headnotes for each selection. I have also prepared a bibliography that should help readers extend their investigations into the literature and theory of argument.

Two additional, editorial notes: In a few of these readings, the authors use the formerly traditional masculine referent pronoun 'he'. This usage has been left unedited to maintain the integrity of the originals but should not be considered an endorsement of sexist language. Also, the original citation style has been maintained for each essay. Therefore no one bibliographic method unifies the book, although the majority of the essays use either the MLA or APA styles.

Acknowledgments

I would like first and foremost to thank my editor, Joanne Diaz, for providing invaluable advice throughout the process of creating this book. I learned a great deal from her linguistic sensitivity and her eye for clarity. At Bedford/St. Martin's I would like to thank Maura Shea for her expert guidance in the initial stages of this project, Emily Goodall for her editorial assistance throughout, Steve Scipione for his suggestions and insights, Deborah Baker for her adept production of the book, and president Charles Christensen for initially conceiving the project. My reviewers — Davida Charney, Vorris Nunley, Michelle Ballif, and three anonymous readers — provided exceptionally detailed and thought-provoking comments to early drafts of the book, and I greatly appreciate the seriousness with which they reviewed this work.

I would like to thank the faculty members and students with whom I worked on my doctorate at the Ohio State University, and who have given me so much. In particular Andrea Lunsford, as a scholar and person, continues to inspire me in all that I do; I would like to acknowledge her role as my primary mentor and teacher. I thank my colleagues at Northeastern Illinois University — particularly the English Department, the CAC, my book group, and the many faculty interested in writing — for all their support and talent. They provide extraordinary models of clear, insightful thinking and teaching every day.

Many students have shared their writing, wisdom, and lives with me over the past eleven years, and I thank them for contributing a great deal to this book and to all my thinking about writing. Finally, I owe a great deal to my friends and family who have had to hear about this project for almost a year, and who have always believed in me. Without them, little else matters.

I want to dedicate this book to current and future students, especially Adam, Sarah, Clara, George, Griffin, and the newest Barnett on the way. I hope that they will help create a world that values communication and difference in ways we only dream about today.

Timothy Barnett
Northeastern Illinois University

Contents

CHAPTER

1

Some Classical Influences on Argument

There is some debate over the exact dates of the classical period of rhetoric, but most scholars focus on the Greek and Roman era from the sixth century B.C.E. to the third century C.E. The classical period began with the rise of the Greek Sophists, a group of philosopher-educators, and includes the work of such notable figures as Aristotle, Plato, Cicero, and Quintilian, all of whom have had an immeasurable impact on the study and production of argument in Western culture.

In fact, it is not an overstatement to note that most of the primary issues under consideration in argumentation theory today (in composition, speech communications, legal studies, and other disciplines) were first broached in such texts as Plato's *Phaedrus* and *Gorgias*, Aristotle's *Rhetoric*, Cicero's *De Inventione,* and Quintilian's *Institutes of Oratory.* Plato's work is perhaps best known for its disparaging critiques of rhetoric, while Aristotle's, Quintilian's, and Cicero's works offer highly theorized and pedagogically useful ways of dealing with rhetorical issues such as imitation and audience analysis. Classical rhetoricians have also provided such lasting concepts as the canons of speechmaking — invention, arrangement, style, memory, and delivery — which have been adapted to the writing process and continue to be the object of analysis and debate today.

As this legacy suggests, the dominant intellectual movements and figures in the West have regularly "rediscovered" classical ideas about persuasion and adapted them to different time periods and changing cultures. Medieval rhetoricians such as St. Augustine, for example, depended on the ideas of Cicero to adapt rhetoric to an emerging Christian culture. Similarly, Renaissance rhetoricians such as Erasmus patterned the idea of the humanist intellectual on a classical model, insisting that students read original texts in Greek and Latin and that they study ethics, civic responsibility, and literary forms and texts, all staples of a classical education. In contemporary composition studies, Edward P. J. Corbett's *Classical Rhetoric for the Modern Student,* originally published in 1965, was the vanguard text proclaiming composition's intellectual, ethical, and pedagogical links to the Greeks and Romans. Since the 1960s, Corbett's text has been embraced by teachers eager for a philosophically rich system to help them teach argumentation and explore composition's deep roots in the Western intellectual tradition.

In addition, the twentieth century has seen an increased interest — after many years of neglect — in the Sophists, in part because postmodernism has raised questions about the construction of knowledge and the nature of objectivity that also concerned these early educators. The Sophists included philosophers such as Gorgias, who believed that language was central to knowledge construction and that knowledge and human nature were, at least in part, dependent on context. The Sophists were particularly skeptical of any claims to absolute knowledge that came from religion or early efforts at science. The Western tradition has historically emphasized Aristotle's concerns with empirical truth and Plato's belief in metaphysical truth over Sophistic beliefs in contingent truths, and, as a result, many Sophistic texts have been lost and their ideas minimized. However, as Sophistic ideas have increasingly been seen to support contemporary rhetorical theory (by scholars such as Sharon Crowley and Susan Jarratt), this attitude is slowly changing.

The revival of Sophistic thought has been only one component of a general renewed interest in the relationship between classical rhetoric and contemporary argumentation theory and pedagogy. The differing philosophical, ethical, and political beliefs of the Sophists, Plato, Aristotle, and others have offered scholars opportunities to explore historically competing notions of rhetoric. For instance, scholars such as Jasper Neel continue to debate Plato's attitudes toward rhetoric and writing (which have traditionally been characterized as negative) and the significance of these attitudes to contemporary theories of language. In addition, Andrea Lunsford and Lisa Ede have defended Aristotle's comprehensive scheme of rhetoric as appropriate to our time in spite of critiques that Aristotle promotes an agonistic rhetoric aimed at persuading a passive audience by any means necessary. More recently, Cheryl Glenn, Lunsford and others have explored the contributions women such as Aspasia have made to the classical tradition, offering new opportunities for considering how male-dominated scholarship has defined the Western rhetorical tradition.

Debates such as these suggest that classical rhetoric must continue to receive careful attention from scholars, teachers, and students. Though today's cultural and political contexts are extraordinarily different from those of the early Greeks and Romans, we face similar challenges. Early Greece saw a movement from a tribal system to a system of city-states that explored the possibility of government run at least somewhat democratically (rather than by kings or unquestioned rulers). The new economic and governmental systems necessitated the development of new forms of rhetoric, which were distinctive elements in the rise of Athenian culture and the eventual formation of the Roman Empire. Early Greek rhetoricians were also responding in part to a rise in alphabetic writing, which changed early cultures' ways of understanding themselves, knowledge, and the idea of communication. Though Eric Havelock's ideas about the impact of literacy have been rigorously (and rightfully) interrogated, there is little doubt that the rise of writing in the classical era created new possibilities for the development of education and knowledge and signaled a pivotal moment in intellectual history.

Like the early Greeks and Romans, we live in an unstable political time, symbolized dramatically by the dismantling of the Soviet Union and the destruction of the Berlin Wall in the last decades of the twentieth century. We also are witnessing a dramatic change in the ways we gather and disseminate information. In fact, some scholars (such as Jay David Bolter and George P. Landow) contend that computer technology is contributing to an epistemological shift similar to the one brought about by the early rise of literacy, a shift resulting in changes to the way we understand authorship, textuality, audience, and citizenship. As contemporary cultures reconfigure themselves in a "new world order"; deal with changing communication technologies; witness the rise of "free" trade, "open" borders, and a growing gap between rich and poor; and consider the possibilities and perils of English as an international language, we must consider how to use rhetoric in a changing world. If contemporary individuals and communities are to help shape a culture in flux, it is imperative that teachers and students foster appropriate and theoretically sound notions of rhetoric. Such work will depend on our ability to look carefully at the successes of the classical rhetoricians and to consider why and how even these extraordinarily sophisticated rhetorics failed, for example, to sustain the best elements of Athenian and Roman cultures.

Classical rhetoric will not provide every answer to contemporary questions about rhetoric. However, since rhetoricians such as Gorgias, Aristotle, and Cicero asked questions about persuasion and culture that we continue to ask today, and since the schemes they created to answer these questions are still fundamentally useful in the twenty-first century, contemporary argument teachers need to be acquainted with the Greeks and Romans. More than anything else we need to be reminded of our most basic debt to Cicero, who wrote that "the one point in which we have our very greatest advantage over the brute creation is that we hold converse one with another, and can reproduce our thought in word. Who therefore would not rightly admire this faculty, and deem it [their] duty to exert [themselves] to the utmost in this field, that by so doing

[they] may surpass [humans] themselves in that particular respect wherein chiefly [humans] are superior to animals?" (*Ad Herennium,* 204). If, as Cicero believed, the ability to recreate our thoughts in words is the primary attribute separating humans from "brutes," then it would seem that teaching students to argue effectively, ethically, and humanely — often considered the highest form of language use — is an appropriate way to extend the legacy of the classical rhetoricians to the twenty-first century.

NOTE: The classical rhetoricians mentioned here, as well as many others, have all contributed greatly to contemporary writing instruction. However, the figure most often called upon in argument textbooks and in contemporary theories on argumentation is Aristotle, and it is for this reason that his work is emphasized in the following section (as well as other parts of this book). For further understanding of the classical era and the multiple ways it has influenced argumentation theory and writing instruction, readers should refer to the section in the bibliography titled "Classical Argumentation — And Its Updates" (p. 454).

From *Rhetoric*, Books I and II

Aristotle (translated by W. Rhys Roberts)

Although he was born approximately 2,400 years ago, Aristotle's influence on the theory and practice of rhetoric remains powerful. For Aristotle, rhetoric was intimately connected to argument, a connection made concrete by his famous definition of rhetoric as "the faculty of observing in any given case the available means of persuasion" (p. 5).

Aristotle's Rhetoric *— which most experts believe to be a collection of teaching notes and which, in part, may be a compilation of student notes from his lectures (Bizzell and Herzberg, 144)* — was one of the first texts to codify many of the fundamentals of persuasion. Following are just a few Aristotelian principles that have influenced twentieth-century argumentation theory:*

1. *In-depth audience analysis is critical to the success of argument. Aristotle's work makes clear the importance of intimately understanding individual and cultural psyches and building on an audience's already established beliefs in order to effect persuasion.*
2. *Rhetoric is especially important for political (deliberative), legal (forensic), and ceremonial (epideictic) events.*
3. *The enthymeme (or rhetorical syllogism) and the example are the most important vehicles for applying logic to situations that depend on probabilities rather than on absolute fact.*
4. *The canon of invention is essential to the rhetorical process.*

---

* See bibliography for all parenthetical source citations.

While Aristotle's influence has been extraordinary, his work has also been critiqued for fostering a masculinist and exclusionary notion of rhetoric with a "win-at-all-costs" attitude. Such critiques (from feminist, Rogerian, multicultural, and other scholars) deserve ongoing and careful consideration because there is no doubt that Aristotle was exploring the potential of rhetoric for only a select group of upper-class men. Aristotle's comprehensive scheme of rhetoric, however, needs to be understood in all its complexity (as Lisa S. Ede and Andrea A. Lunsford demonstrate in their essay, "On Distinctions Between Classical and Modern Rhetoric") since his ideas have had an impact on virtually every textbook and scholarly work on argument in Western culture, whether in composition, rhetoric, speech, law, or other fields.

The following selection includes excerpts from Books I and II of the Rhetoric. *These selections include many of Aristotle's most influential ideas on rhetoric (including those listed above) and suggest the kind of interdisciplinary analysis that successful teachers of argument continue to demand today. Readers interested in further exploration should read Aristotle's entire work, including the complete* Rhetoric, Nichomachean Ethics, Poetics, *and* Topics.

From Book I

Rhetoric may be defined as the faculty of observing in any given case the available means of persuasion. This is not a function of any other art. Every other art can instruct or persuade about its own particular subject matter; for instance, medicine about what is healthy and unhealthy, geometry about the properties of magnitudes, arithmetic about numbers, and the same is true of the other arts and sciences. But rhetoric we look upon as the power of observing the means of persuasion on almost any subject presented to us; and that is why we say that, in its technical character, it is not concerned with any special or definite class of subjects.

Of the modes of persuasion some belong strictly to the art of rhetoric and some do not. By the latter I mean such things as are not supplied by the speaker but are there at the outset — witnesses, evidence given under torture, written contracts, and so on. By the former I mean such as we can ourselves construct by means of the principle of rhetoric. The one kind has merely to be used, the other has to be invented.

Of the modes of persuasion furnished by the spoken word there are three kinds. The first kind depends on the personal character of the speaker; the second on putting the audience into a certain frame of mind; the third on the proof, or apparent proof, provided by the words of the speech itself. Persuasion is achieved by the speaker's personal character when the speech is so spoken as to make us think him credible. We believe good men more fully and more readily than others: This is true generally whatever the question is, and absolutely true where exact certainty is impossible and opinions are divided. This kind of persuasion, like the others, should be achieved by what the speaker says, not by what people think of this character before he begins to

speak. It is not true, as some writers assume in their treatises on rhetoric, that the personal goodness revealed by the speaker contributes
nothing to his power of persuasion; on the contrary, his character may
almost be called the most effective means of persuasion he possesses.
Secondly, persuasion may come through the hearers, when the speech
stirs their emotions. Our judgments when we are pleased and friendly
are not the same as when we are pained and hostile. It is towards producing these effects, as we maintain, that present-day writers on rhetoric direct the whole of their efforts. This subject shall be treated in
detail when we come to speak of the emotions.[1] Thirdly, persuasion is
effected through the speech itself when we have proved a truth or an
apparent truth by means of the persuasive arguments suitable to the
case in question.

There are, then, these three means of effecting persuasion. The man
who is to be in command of them must, it is clear, be able (1) to reason
logically, (2) to understand human character and goodness in their various forms, and (3) to understand the emotions — that is, to name them
and describe them, to know their causes and the way in which they are
excited. It thus appears that rhetoric is an offshoot of dialectic and also
of ethical studies. Ethical studies may fairly be called political; and for
this reason rhetoric masquerades as political science, and the professors of it as political experts — sometimes from want of education, sometimes from ostentation, sometimes owing to other human failings. As a
matter of fact, it is a branch of dialectic and similar to it, as we said at
the outset.[2] Neither rhetoric nor dialectic is the scientific study of any
one separate subject: Both are faculties for providing arguments. This
is perhaps a sufficient account of their scope and of how they are related to each other.

With regard to the persuasion achieved by proof or apparent proof: 1356[b]
Just as in dialectic there is induction on the one hand and syllogism or
apparent syllogism on the other, so it is in rhetoric. The example is an
induction, the enthymeme is a syllogism, and the apparent enthymeme
is an apparent syllogism. I call the enthymeme a rhetorical syllogism,
and the example a rhetorical induction. Everyone who effects persuasion through proof does in fact use either enthymemes or examples:
There is no other way. And since everyone who proves anything at all is
bound to use either syllogisms or inductions (and this is clear to us
from the *Analytics*[3]), it must follow that enthymemes are syllogisms
and examples are inductions. The difference between example and
enthymeme is made plain by the passages in the *Topics*[4] where induction and syllogism have already been discussed. When we base the proof
of a proposition on a number of similar cases, this is induction in dialectic, example in rhetoric; when it is shown that, certain propositions
being true, a further and quite distinct proposition must also be true in
consequence, whether invariably or usually, this is called syllogism in
dialectic, enthymeme in rhetoric. It is plain also that each of these types
of oratory has its advantages. Types of oratory, I say: For what has
been said in the *Methodics*[5] applies equally well here; in some oratori-

cal styles examples prevail, in others enthymemes; and in like manner, some orators are better at the former and some at the latter. Speeches that rely on examples are as persuasive as the other kind, but those which rely on enthymemes excite the louder applause. The sources of examples and enthymemes,[6] and their proper uses, we will discuss later.[7] Our next step is to define the processes themselves more clearly.

A statement is persuasive and credible either because it is directly self-evident or because it appears to be proved from other statements that are so. In either case it is persuasive because there is somebody whom it persuades. But none of the arts theorize about individual cases. Medicine, for instance, does not theorize about what will help to cure Socrates or Callias, but only about what will help to cure any or all of a given class of patients: This alone is its business: Individual cases are so infinitely various that no systematic knowledge of them is possible. In the same way the theory of rhetoric is concerned not with what seems probable to a given individual like Socrates or Hippias, but with what seems probable to men of a given type; and this is true of dialectic also. Dialectic does not construct its syllogism out of any haphazard materials, such as the fancies of crazy people, but out of materials that call for discussion; and rhetoric, too, draws upon the regular subjects of debate. The duty of rhetoric is to deal with such matters as we deliberate upon without arts or systems to guide us, in the hearing of persons who cannot take in at a glance a complicated argument, or follow a long chain of reasoning. The subjects of our deliberation are such as seem to present us with alternative possibilities: About things that could not have been, and cannot now or in the future be, other than they are, nobody who takes them to be of this nature wastes his time in deliberation. 1357a

It is possible to form syllogisms and draw conclusions from the results of previous syllogisms; or, on the other hand, from premises which have not been thus proved, and at the same time are so little accepted that they call for proof. Reasonings of the former kind will necessarily be hard to follow owing to their length, for we assume an audience of untrained thinkers; those of the latter kind will fail to win assent, because they are based on premises that are not generally admitted or believed.

The enthymeme and the example must, then, deal with what is in the main contingent, the example being an induction, and the enthymeme a syllogism, about such matters. The enthymeme must consist of few propositions, fewer often than those which make up the normal syllogism. For if any of these propositions is a familiar fact, there is no need even to mention it; the hearer adds it himself. Thus, to show that Dorieus has been victor in a contest for which the prize is a crown, it is enough to say "For he has been victor in the Olympic games," without adding "And in the Olympic games the prize is a crown," a fact which everybody knows.

There are few facts of the "necessary" type that can form the basis of rhetorical syllogisms.[8] Most of the things about which we make decisions, and into which therefore we inquire, present us with alternative possibilities. For it is about our actions that we deliberate and inquire, and all our actions have a contingent character; hardly any of them are determined by necessity. Again, conclusions that state what is merely usual or possible must be drawn from premises that do the same, just as "necessary" conclusions must be drawn from "necessary" premises; this too is clear to us from the *Analytics*.[9] It is evident, therefore, that the propositions forming the basis of enthymemes, though some of them may be "necessary," will most of them be only usually true. Now the materials of enthymemes are Probabilities and Signs, which we can see must correspond respectively with the propositions that are generally and those that are necessarily true. A Probability is a thing that usually happens; not, however, as some definitions would suggest, anything whatever that usually happens, but only if it belongs to the class of the "contingent" or "variable." It bears the same relation to that in respect of which it is probable[10] as the universal bears to the particular. Of Signs, one kind bears the same relation to the statement it supports as the particular bears to the universal, the other the same as the universal bears to the particular. The infallible kind is a "complete proof" (τεκμήριον); the fallible kind has no specific name. By infallible signs I mean those on which syllogisms proper may be based: And this shows us why this kind of Sign is called "complete proof": when people think that what they have said cannot be refuted, they then think that they are bringing forward a "complete proof," meaning that the matter has now been demonstrated and completed (πεπερασμένον); for the word πέρας has the same meaning (of "end" or "boundary") as the word τέκμαρ in the ancient tongue. Now the one kind of Sign (that which bears to the proposition it supports the relation of particular to universal) may be illustrated thus. Suppose it were said, "The fact that Socrates was wise and just is a sign that the wise are just." Here we certainly have a Sign; but even though the proposition be true, the argument is refutable, since it does not form a syllogism. Suppose, on the other hand, it were said, "The fact that he has a fever is a sign that he is ill," or, "The fact that she is giving milk is a sign that she has lately borne a child." Here we have the infallible kind of Sign, the only kind that constitutes a complete proof, since it is the only kind that, if the particular statement is true, is irrefutable. The other kind of Sign, that which bears to the proposition it supports the relation of universal to particular, might be illustrated by saying, "The fact that he breathes fast is a sign that he has a fever." This argument also is refutable, even if the statement about the fast breathing be true, since a man may breathe hard without having a fever.

It has, then, been stated above what is the nature of a Probability, of a Sign, and of a complete proof, and what are the differences between them. In the *Analytics*[11] a more explicit description has been given of these points; it is there shown why some of these reasonings can be put into syllogisms and some cannot.

1357ᵇ

The "example" has already been described as one kind of induction; and the special nature of the subject matter that distinguishes it from the other kinds has also been stated above. Its relation to the proposition it supports is not that of part to whole, nor whole to part, nor whole to whole, but of part to part, or like to like. When two statements are of the same order, but one is more familiar than the other, the former is an "example." The argument may, for instance, be that Dionysius,[12] in asking as he does for a bodyguard, is scheming to make himself a despot. For in the past Peisistratus[13] kept asking for a bodyguard in order to carry out such a scheme, and did make himself a despot as soon as he got it; and so did Theagenes[14] at Megara; and in the same way all other instances known to the speaker are made into examples, in order to show what is not yet known, that Dionysius has the same purpose in making the same request: all these being instances of the one general principle, that a man who asks for a bodyguard is scheming to make himself a despot. We have now described the sources of those means of persuasion which are popularly supposed to be demonstrative.   1358ᵃ

There is an important distinction between two sorts of enthymemes that has been wholly overlooked by almost everybody — one that also subsists between the syllogisms treated of in dialectic. One sort of enthymeme really belongs to rhetoric, as one sort of syllogism really belongs to dialectic; but the other sort really belongs to other arts and faculties, whether to those we already exercise or to those we have not yet acquired. Missing this distinction, people fail to notice that the more correctly they handle their particular subject the further they are getting away from pure rhetoric or dialectic. This statement will be clearer if expressed more fully. I mean that the proper subjects of dialectical and rhetorical syllogisms are the things with which we say the regular or universal Lines of Argument[15] are concerned, that is to say those lines of argument that apply equally to questions of right conduct, natural science, politics, and many other things that have nothing to do with one another. Take, for instance, the line of argument concerned with "the more or less."[16] On this line of argument it is equally easy to base a syllogism or enthymeme about any of what nevertheless are essentially disconnected subjects — right conduct, natural science, or anything else whatever. But there are also those special Lines of Argument which are based on such propositions as apply only to particular groups or classes of things. Thus there are propositions about natural science on which it is impossible to base any enthymeme or syllogism about ethics, and other propositions about ethics on which nothing can be based about natural science. The same principle applies throughout. The general Lines of Argument have no special subject matter, and therefore will not increase our understanding of any particular class of things. On the other hand, the better the selection one makes of propositions suitable for special Lines of Argument, the nearer one comes, unconsciously, to setting up a science that is distinct from dialectic and rhetoric. One may succeed in stating the required principles, but one's science will be no longer dialectic or rhetoric, but the science to which the principles thus discovered belong. Most enthymemes are in fact based upon these particular or special Lines of Argument; comparatively few on the common or general kind. As in the *Topics,* [17] therefore, so in this work, we must distinguish, in dealing with enthymemes, the special and the general Lines of Argument on which they are to be founded. By special Lines of Argument I mean the propositions peculiar to each several class of things, by general those common to all classes alike. We may begin with the special Lines of Argument. But, first of all, let us classify rhetoric into its varieties. Having distinguished these we may deal with them one by one, and try to discover the elements of which each is composed, and the propositions each must employ.

Rhetoric falls into three divisions, determined by the three classes of listeners to speeches. For of the three elements in speech making — speaker, subject, and person addressed — it is the last one, the hearer, that determines the speech's end and object. The hearer must be either 1358[b] a judge, with a decision to make about things past or future, or an observer. [18] A member of the assembly decides about future events, a juryman about past events: while those who merely decide on the orator's skill are observers. From this it follows that there are three divisions of oratory — (1) political, (2) forensic, and (3) the ceremonial oratory of display. [19]

Political speaking urges us either to do or not to do something: One of these two courses is always taken by private counselors, as well as by men who address public assemblies. Forensic speaking either attacks or defends somebody: One or other of these two things must always be done by the parties in a case. The ceremonial oratory of display either praises or censures somebody. These three kinds of rhetoric refer to three different kinds of time. The political orator is concerned with the future: It is about things to be done hereafter that he advises, for or against. The party in a case at law is concerned with the past; one man accuses the other, and the other defends himself, with reference to things already done. The ceremonial orator is, properly speaking, concerned with the present, since all men praise or blame in view of the state of things existing at the time, though they often find it useful also to recall the past and to makes guesses at the future.

Rhetoric has three distinct ends in view, one for each of its three kinds. The political orator aims at establishing the expediency or the harmfulness of a proposed course of action; if he urges its acceptance, he does so on the ground that it will do good; if he urges its rejection, he does so on the ground that it will do harm; and all other points, such as whether the proposal is just or unjust, honorable or dishonorable, he brings in as subsidiary and relative to this main consideration. Parties in a law case aim at establishing the justice or injustice of some action, and they too bring in all other points as subsidiary and relative to this one. Those who praise or attack a man aim at proving him worthy of honor or the reverse, and they too treat all other considerations with reference to this one.

That the three kinds of rhetoric do aim respectively at the three ends we have mentioned is shown by the fact that speakers will sometimes not try to establish anything else. Thus, the litigant will sometimes not deny that a thing has happened or that he has done harm. But that he is guilty of injustice he will never admit; otherwise there would be no need of a trial. So too, political orators often make any concession short of admitting that they are recommending their hearers to take an inexpedient course or not to take an expedient one. The question whether it is not *unjust* for a city to enslave its innocent neighbors often does not trouble them at all. In like manner those who praise 1359ᵃ or censure a man do not consider whether his acts have been expedient or not, but often make it a ground of actual praise that he has neglected his own interest to do what was honorable. Thus, they praise Achilles because he championed his fallen friend Patroclus, though he knew that this meant death, and that otherwise he need not die: Yet while to die thus was the nobler thing for him to do, the expedient thing was to live on.[20]

It is evident from what has been said that it is these three subjects, more than any others, about which the orator must be able to have propositions at his command. Now the propositions of Rhetoric are Complete Proofs, Probabilities, and Signs. Every kind of syllogism is composed of propositions, and the enthymeme is a particular kind of syllogism composed of the aforesaid propositions.[21]

Since only possible actions, and not impossible ones, can ever have been done in the past or the present, and since things which have not occurred, or will not occur, also cannot have been done or be going to be done, it is necessary for the political, the forensic, and the ceremonial speaker alike to be able to have at their command propositions about the possible and the impossible, and about whether a thing has or has not occurred, will or will not occur. Further, all men, in giving praise or blame, in urging us to accept or reject proposals for action, in accusing others or defending themselves, attempt not only to prove the points mentioned but also to show that the good or the harm, the honor or disgrace, the justice or injustice, is great or small, either absolutely or relatively; and therefore it is plain that we must also have at our command propositions about greatness or smallness and the greater or the lesser — propositions both universal and particular. Thus, we must be able to say which is the greater or lesser good, the greater or lesser act of justice or injustice; and so on.

Such, then, are the subjects regarding which we are inevitably bound to master the propositions relevant to them. [. . .]

From Book II

The special forms of oratorical argument having now been discussed, we have next to treat those which are common to all kinds of oratory. These are of two main kinds, "Example" and "Enthymeme"; for the "Maxim" is part of an enthymeme.[22]

We will first treat of argument by Example, for it has the nature of induction, which is the foundation of reasoning. This form of argument has two varieties; one consisting in the mention of actual past facts, the other in the invention of facts by the speaker. Of the latter, again, there are two varieties, the illustrative parallel and the fable (e.g. the fables of Aesop, or those from Libya). As an instance of the mention of actual facts, take the following. The speaker may argue thus: "We must prepare for war against the king of Persia and not let him subdue Egypt. For Darius of old did not cross the Aegean until he had seized Egypt; but once he had seized it, he did cross. If therefore the present king seizes Egypt, he also will cross, and therefore we must not let him." 1393

The illustrative parallel is the sort of argument Socrates used: e.g. "Public officials ought not to be selected by lot. That is like using the lot to select athletes, instead of choosing those who are fit for the contest; or using the lot to select a steersman from among a ship's crew, as if we ought to take the man on whom the lot falls, and not the man who knows most about it."

Instances of the fable are that of Stesichorus[23] about Phalaris,[24] and that of Aesop in defense of the popular leader. When the people of Himera had made Phalaris military dictator, and were going to give him a bodyguard, Stesichorus wound up a long talk by telling them the fable of the horse who had a field all to himself. Presently there came a stag and began to spoil his pasturage. The horse, wishing to revenge himself on the stag, asked a man if he could help him to do so. The man said, "Yes, if you will let me bridle you and get on to your back with javelins in my hand." The horse agreed, and the man mounted; but instead of getting his revenge on the stag, the horse found himself the slave of the man. "You too," said Stesichorus, "take care lest, in your desire for revenge on your enemies, you meet the same fate as the horse. By making Phalaris military dictator, you have already let yourselves be bridled. If you let him get on to your backs by giving him a bodyguard, from that moment you will be his slaves."

Aesop, defending before the assembly at Samos a popular leader who was being tried for his life, told this story: A fox, in crossing a river, was swept into a hole in the rocks; and, not being able to get out, suffered miseries for a long time through the swarms of fleas that fastened on her. A hedgehog, while roaming around, noticed the fox; and feeling sorry for her asked if he might remove the fleas. But the fox declined the offer; and when the hedgehog asked why, she replied, "These fleas are by this time full of me and not sucking much blood; if you take them away, others will come with fresh appetites and drink up all the blood I have left." "So, men of Samos," said Aesop, "my client will do you no further harm; he is wealthy already. But if you put him to death, others will come along who are not rich, and their peculations will empty 1394ᵃ your treasury completely."

Fables are suitable for addresses to popular assemblies; and they have one advantage — they are comparatively easy to invent, whereas it is hard to find parallels among actual past events. You will in fact frame them just as you frame illustrative parallels: All you require is the power of thinking out your analogy, a power developed by intellectual training. But while it is easier to supply parallels by inventing fables, it is more valuable for the political speaker to supply them by quoting what has actually happened, since in most respects the future will be like what the past has been.

Where we are unable to argue by Enthymeme, we must try to demonstrate our point by this method of Example, and to convince our hearers thereby. If we *can* argue by Enthymeme, we should use our Examples as subsequent supplementary evidence. They should not precede the Enthymemes: That will give the argument an inductive air, which only rarely suits the conditions of speech making.[25] If they follow the enthymemes, they have the effect of witnesses giving evidence, and this always tells. For the same reason, if you put your examples first you must give a large number of them; if you put them last, a single one is sufficient; even a single witness will serve if he is a good one. It has now been stated how many varieties of argument by Example there are, and how and when they are to be employed.

We now turn to the use of Maxims, in order to see upon what subjects and occasions, and for what kind of speaker, they will appropriately form part of a speech. This will appear most clearly when we have defined a maxim. It is a statement; not about a particular fact, such as the character of Iphicrates,[26] but of a general kind; nor is it about any and every subject — e.g. "straight is the contrary of curved" is not a maxim — but only about questions of practical conduct, courses of conduct to be chosen or avoided. Now an Enthymeme is a syllogism dealing with such practical subjects. It is therefore roughly true that the premisses or conclusions of Enthymemes, considered apart from the rest of the argument, are Maxims: e.g.

> Never should any man whose wits are sound
> Have his sons taught more wisdom than their fellows.[27]

Here we have a Maxim; add the reason or explanation, and the whole thing is an Enthymeme; thus —

> It makes them idle; and therewith they earn
> Ill-will and jealousy throughout the city.[28]

Again, 1394ᵇ

There is no man in all things prosperous,[29]

and

There is no man among us all free,

are maxims; but the latter, taken with what follows it, is an Enthymeme —

For all are slaves of money or of chance.[30]

From this definition of a maxim it follows that there are four kinds of maxims. In the first place, the maxim may or may not have a supplement. Proof is needed where the statement is paradoxical[31] or disputable; no supplement is wanted where the statement contains nothing paradoxical, either because the view expressed is already a known truth, e.g.

Chiefest of blessings is health for a man, as it seemeth to me,[32]

this being the general opinion: or because, as soon as the view is stated, it is clear at a glance, e.g.

No love is true save that which loves for ever.[33]

Of the Maxims that do have a supplement attached, some are part of an Enthymeme, e.g.

Never should any man whose wits are sound, &c.[34]

Others have the essential character of Enthymemes, but are not stated as parts of Enthymemes; these latter are reckoned the best; they are those in which the reason for the view expressed is simply implied, e.g.

O mortal man, nurse not immortal wrath.[35]

To say "it is not right to nurse immortal wrath" is a maxim; the added words "O mortal man" give the reason. Similarly, with the words

Mortal creatures ought to cherish mortal, not immortal thoughts.[36]

What has been said has shown us how many kinds of Maxim there are, and to what subjects the various kinds are appropriate. They must not be given without supplement if they express disputed or paradoxical views: We must, in that case, either put the supplement first and make a maxim of the conclusion, e.g. you might say, "For my part, since both unpopularity and idleness, are undesirable, I hold that it is better not to be educated"; or you may say this first, and then add the previous clause. Where a statement, without being paradoxical, is not obviously true, the reason should be added as concisely as possible. In such cases both laconic and enigmatic sayings are suitable: Thus one might say what Stesichorus said to the Locrians, "Insolence is better avoided, lest the cicalas chirp on the ground."[37]   1395ª

The use of Maxims is appropriate only to elderly men, and in handling subjects in which the speaker is experienced. For a young man to use them is — like telling stories — unbecoming; to use them in handling things in which one has no experience is silly and ill bred: a fact sufficiently proved by the special fondness of country fellows for striking out maxims, and their readiness to air them.

To declare a thing to be universally true when it is not is most appropriate when working up feelings of horror and indignation in our hearers; especially by way of preface, or after the facts have been proved. Even hackneyed and commonplace maxims are to be used, if they suit one's purpose: Just because they are commonplace, every one seems to agree with them, and therefore they are taken for truth. Thus, any one who is calling on his men to risk an engagement without obtaining favorable omens may quote

One omen of all is best, that we fight for our fatherland.[38]

Or, if he is calling on them to attack a stronger force —

The War-God showeth no favor.[39]

Or, if he is urging people to destroy the innocent children of their enemies —

Fool, who slayeth the father and leaveth his sons to avenge him.[40]

Some proverbs are also maxims, e.g. the proverb "An Attic neighbor."[41] You are not to avoid uttering maxims that contradict such sayings as have become public property (I mean such sayings as "know thyself" and "nothing in excess"), if doing so will raise your hearers' opinion of your character, or convey an effect of strong emotion — e.g. an angry speaker might well say, "It is not true that we ought to know ourselves: Anyhow, if this man had known himself, he would never have thought himself fit for an army command." It will raise people's opinion of our character to say, for instance, "We ought not to follow the saying that bids us treat our friends as future enemies: much better to treat our enemies as future friends."[42] The moral purpose should be implied partly by the very wording of our maxim. Failing this, we should add our reason: e.g. having said "We should treat our friends, not as the saying advises, but as if they were going to be our friends always," we should add "for the other behavior is that of a traitor": or we might put it, "I disapprove of that saying. A true friend will treat his friend as if he were going to be his friend forever"; and again, "Nor do I approve of the saying 'nothing in excess': We are bound to hate bad men excessively."

One great advantage of Maxims to a speaker is due to the want of intelligence in his hearers, who love to hear him succeed in expressing as a universal truth the opinions which they hold themselves about particular cases. I will explain what I mean by this, indicating at the same time how we are to hunt down the maxims required. The maxim, as has been already said, is a general statement, and people love to hear stated in general terms what they already believe in some particular connection: E.g. if a man happens to have bad neighbors or bad children, he will agree with any one who tells him "Nothing is more annoying than having neighbors," or, "Nothing is more foolish than to be the parent of children." The orator has therefore to guess the subjects on which his hearers really hold views already, and what those views are, and then must express, as general truths, these same views on these same subjects. This is one advantage of using maxims. There is another which is more important — it invests a speech with moral character. There is moral character in every speech in which the moral purpose is conspicuous: And maxims always produce this effect, because the utterance of them amounts to a general declaration of moral principles: so that, if the maxims are sound, they display the speaker as a man of sound moral character. So much for the Maxim — its nature, varieties, proper use, and advantages.

1395[b]

We now come to the Enthymemes, and will begin the subject with some general consideration of the proper way of looking for them, and then proceed to what is a distinct question, the lines of argument to be embodied in them. It has already[43] been pointed out that the Enthymeme is a syllogism, and in what sense it is so. We have also noted the differences between it and the syllogism of dialectic. Thus we must not carry its reasoning too far back, or the length of our argument will cause obscurity: Nor must we put in all the steps that lead to our conclusion, or we shall waste words in saying what is manifest. It is this simplicity that makes the uneducated more effective than the educated when addressing popular audiences — makes them, as the poets[44] tell us, "charm the crowd's ears more finely." Educated men lay down broad general principles; uneducated men argue from common knowledge and draw obvious conclusions. We must not, therefore, start from any and every accepted opinion, but only from those we have defined — those accepted by our judges or by those whose authority they recognize: and there must, moreover, be no doubt in the minds of most, if not all, of our judges that the opinions put forward really are of this sort. We should also base our arguments upon probabilities as well as upon certainties.

1396[a]

The first thing we have to remember is this. Whether our argument concerns public affairs or some other subject, we must know some, if not all, of the facts about the subject on which we are to speak and argue. Otherwise we can have no materials out of which to construct arguments. I mean, for instance, how could we advise the Athenians whether they should go to war or not, if we did not know their strength, whether it was naval or military or both, and how great it is; what their revenues amount to; who their friends and enemies are; what wars, too, they have waged, and with what success; and so on? Or how could we eulogize them if we knew nothing about the sea fight at Salamis, or the battle of Marathon, or what they did for the Heracleidae,[45] or any other facts like that? All eulogy is based upon the noble deeds — real or imaginary — that stand to the credit of those eulogized. On the same principle, invectives are based on facts of the opposite kind: The orator looks to see what base deeds — real or imaginary — stand to the discredit of those he is attacking, such as treachery to the cause of Hellenic freedom, or the enslavement of their gallant allies against the barbarians (Aegina,[46] Potidaea,[47] &c.), or any other misdeeds of this kind that are recorded against them. So, too, in a court of law: Whether we are prosecuting or defending, we must pay attention to the existing facts of the case. It makes no difference whether the subject is the Lacedaemonians or the Athenians, a man or a god; we must do the same thing. Suppose it to be Achilles whom we are to advise, to praise or blame, to accuse or defend; here too we must take the facts, real or imaginary; these must be our material, whether we are to praise or blame him for the noble or base deeds he has done, to accuse or defend him for his just or unjust treatment of others, or to advise him about what is or is not to his interest. The same thing applies to any subject whatever. Thus, in handling the question whether justice is or is not a good, we must start with the real facts about justice and goodness. We see, then, that this is the only way in which any one ever proves anything, whether his arguments are strictly cogent or not: Not all facts can form his basis, but only those that bear on the matter in hand: Nor, plainly, can proof be effected otherwise by means of the speech. Consequently, as appears in the *Topics,*[48] we must first of all have by us a selection of arguments about questions that may arise and are suitable for us to handle; and then we must try to think out arguments of the same type for special needs as they emerge; not vaguely and indefinitely, but by keeping our eyes on the actual facts of the subject we have to speak on, and gathering in as many of them as we can that bear closely upon it: For the more actual facts we have at our command, the more easily we prove our case; and the more closely they bear on the subject, the more they will seem to belong to that speech only instead of being commonplaces. By "commonplaces" I mean, for example, eulogy of Achilles because he is a human being or a demigod, or because he joined the expedition against Troy: These things are true of many others, so that this kind of eulogy applies no better to Achilles than to Diomede. The special facts here needed are those that are true of Achilles alone; such facts as that he slew Hector, the bravest of the Trojans, and Cycnus the invulnerable, who prevented all the Greeks from landing, and again that he was the youngest man who joined the expedition, and was not bound by oath to join it, and so on.

1396ᵇ

Here, then, we have our first principle of selection of Enthymemes — that which refers to the lines of argument selected. We will now consider the various elementary classes of enthymemes. (By an "elementary class" of enthymeme I mean the same thing as a "line of argument.") We will begin, as we must begin, by observing that there are two kinds of enthymemes. One kind proves some affirmative or negative proposition; the other kind disproves one. The difference between the two kinds is the same as that between syllogistic proof and disproof in dialectic. The demonstrative enthymeme is formed by the conjunction of compatible propositions; the refutative, by the conjunction of incompatible propositions.

We may now be said to have in our hands the lines of argument for the various *special* subjects that it is useful or necessary to handle, having selected the propositions suitable in various cases. We have, in fact, already ascertained the lines of argument applicable to enthymemes about good and evil, the noble and the base, justice and injustice, and also to those about types of character, emotions, and moral qualities.[49] Let us now lay hold of certain facts about the whole subject, considered from a different and more general point of view. In the course of our discussion we will take note of the distinction between lines of proof and lines of disproof;[50] and also of those lines of argument used in what seem to be enthymemes, but are not, since they do not represent valid syllogisms.[51] Having made all this clear, we will proceed to classify Objections and Refutations, showing how they can be brought to bear upon enthymemes.[52]

1. One line of positive proof is based upon consideration of the opposite of the thing in question. Observe whether that opposite has the opposite quality. If it has not, you refute the original proposition; if it has, you establish it. E.g. "Temperance *is* beneficial; for licentiousness is hurtful." Or, as in the Messenian speech,[53] "If war is the cause of our present troubles, peace is what we need to put things right again." Or —

> For if not even evil-doers should
> Anger us if they meant not what they did,
> Then can we owe no gratitude to such
> As were constrained to do the good they did us.[54]

Or —

> Since in this world liars may win belief,
> Be sure of the opposite likewise — that this world
> Hears many a true word and believes it not.[55]

2. Another line of proof is got by considering some modification of the key-word, and arguing that what can or cannot be said of the one, can or cannot be said of the other: E.g. "just" does not always mean "beneficial," or "justly" would always mean "beneficially," whereas it is *not* desirable to be justly put to death.[56]

3. Another line of proof is based upon correlative ideas. If it is true that one man *gave* noble or just treatment to another, you argue that the other must have *received* noble or just treatment; or that where it is right to command obedience, it must have been right to obey the command. Thus Diomedon, the tax-farmer, said of the taxes: "If it is no disgrace for you to sell them,[57] it is no disgrace for us to buy them." Further, if "well" or "justly" is true of the person to whom a thing is done, you argue that it is true of the doer. But it is possible to draw a false conclusion here. It may be just that A should be treated in a certain way, and yet *not* just that he should be so treated by B. Hence you must ask yourself two distinct questions: (1) Is it right that A should be thus treated? (2) Is it right that B should thus treat him? and apply your results properly, according as your answers are Yes or No. Sometimes in such a case the two answers differ: You may quite easily have a position like that in the *Alcmaeon* of Theodectes:

1397[b]

And was there none to loathe thy mother's crime?[58]

to which question Alcmaeon in reply says,

Why, there are two things to examine here.

And when Alphesiboea asks what he means, he rejoins:

They judged *her* fit to die, not *me* to slay her.

Again there is the lawsuit about Demosthenes[59] and the men who killed Nicanor; as they were judged to have killed him justly, it was thought that he was killed justly. And in the case of the man who was killed at Thebes,[60] the judges were requested to decide whether it was unjust that he should be killed, since if it was not, it was argued that it could not have been unjust to kill him.

4. Another line of proof is the *a fortiori.* Thus it may be argued that if even the gods are not omniscient, certainly human beings are not. The principle here is that, if a quality does not in fact exist where it is *more* likely to exist, it clearly does not exist where it is *less* likely. Again, the argument that a man who strikes his father also strikes his neighbors follows from the principle that, if the less likely thing is true, the more likely thing is true also; for a man is less likely to strike his father than to strike his neighbors. The argument, then, may run thus. Or it may be urged that, if a thing is not true where it is more likely, it is not true where it is less likely; or that, if it is true where it is less likely, it is true where it is more likely: according as we have to show that a thing *is* or is *not* true.[61] This argument might also be used in a case of parity, as in the lines:

Thou hast pity for *thy* sire, who has lost his sons:
Hast none for Oeneus, whose brave son is dead?[62]

And, again, "if Theseus did no wrong, neither did Paris"; or "if the sons of Tyndareus did no wrong, neither did Paris"; or "if Hector did well to slay Patroclus, Paris did well to slay Achilles."[63] And "if other followers of an art are not bad men, neither are philosophers." And "if generals are not bad men because it often happens that they are condemned to death, neither are sophists." And the remark that "if each individual among you ought to think of his own city's reputation, you ought all to think of the reputation of Greece as a whole."

5. Another line of argument is based on considerations of time. Thus Iphicrates, in the case against Harmodius, said, "if before doing the deed I had bargained that, if I did it, I should have a statue, you would have given me one. Will you not give me one now that I *have* done the deed? You must not make promises when you are expecting a thing to be done for you, and refuse to fulfill them when the thing has been done."[64] And, again, to induce the Thebans to let Philip pass through their territory into Attica, it was argued[65] that "if he had insisted on this before he helped them against the Phocians, they would have promised to do it. It is monstrous, therefore, that just because he threw away his advantage then, and trusted their honor, they should not let him pass through now." 1398ᵃ

6. Another line is to apply to the other speaker what he has said against yourself. It is an excellent turn to give to a debate, as may be seen in the *Teucer*.[66] It was employed by Iphicrates in his reply to Aristophon. "Would *you*," he asked, "take a bribe to betray the fleet?" "No," said Aristophon; and Iphicrates replied, "Very good: if you, who are Aristophon, would not betray the fleet, would I, who am Iphicrates?"[67] Only, it must be recognized beforehand that the other man is more likely than you are to commit the crime in question. Otherwise you will make yourself ridiculous; if it is Aristeides[68] who is prosecuting, you cannot say that sort of thing to him. The purpose is to discredit the prosecutor, who as a rule would have it appear that his character is better than that of the defendant, a pretension which it is desirable to upset. But the use of such an argument is in all cases ridiculous if you are attacking others for what you do or would do yourself, or are urging others to do what you neither do nor would do yourself.

7. Another line of proof is secured by defining your terms. Thus, "What is the supernatural? Surely it is either a god or the work of a god. Well, any one who believes that the work of a god exists, cannot help also believing that gods exist."[69] Or take the argument of Iphicrates, "Goodness is true nobility; neither Harmodius nor Aristogeiton had any nobility before they did a noble deed." He also argued that he himself was more akin to Harmodius and Aristogeiton than his opponent was. "At any rate, my deeds are more akin to those of Harmodius and Aristogeiton than yours are."[70] Another example may be found in the *Alexander*.[71] "Every one will agree that by incontinent people we mean those who are not satisfied with the enjoyment of one love." A further

example is to be found in the reason given by Socrates for not going to the court of Archelaus. He said that "one is *insulted* by being unable to requite benefits, as well as by being unable to requite injuries."[72] All the persons mentioned define their term and get at its essential meaning, and then use the result when reasoning on the point at issue.

8. Another line of argument is founded upon the various senses of a word. Such a word is "rightly," as has been explained in the *Topics.*[73]

9. Another line is based upon logical division. Thus, "All men do wrong from one of three motives, A, B, or C: In my case A and B are out of the question, and even the accusers do not allege C."

10. Another line is based upon induction. Thus from the case of the women of Peparethus it might be argued that women everywhere can settle correctly the facts about their children. Another example of this occurred at Athens in the case between the orator Mantias[74] and his son, when the boy's mother revealed the true facts: and yet another at Thebes, in the case between Ismenias and Stilbon, when Dodonis proved that it was Ismenias who was the father of her son Thettaliscus, and he was in consequence always regarded as being so.[75] A further instance of induction may be taken from the *Law* of Theodectes:[76] "If we do not hand over our horses to the care of men who have mishandled other people's horses, nor ships to those who have wrecked other people's ships, and if this is true of everything else alike, then men who have failed to secure other people's safety are not to be employed to secure our own." Another instance is the argument of Alcidamas.[77] Every one honors the wise. Thus the Parians have honored Archilochus, in spite of his bitter tongue; the Chians Homer, though he was not their countryman; the Mytilenaeans Sappho, though she was a woman; the Lacedaemonians actually made Chilon a member of their senate, though they are the least literary of men; the Italian Greeks honored Pythagoras; the inhabitants of Lampsacus gave public burial to Anaxagoras, though he was an alien, and honor him even to this day. [It may be argued that peoples for whom philosophers legislate are always prosperous] on the ground that the Athenians became prosperous under Solon's laws and the Lacedaemonians under those of Lycurgus, while at Thebes no sooner did the leading men become philosophers than the country began to prosper.

11. Another line of argument is founded upon some decision already pronounced, whether on the same subject or on one like it or contrary to it. Such a proof is most effective if every one has always decided thus; but if not every one, then at any rate most people; or if all, or most, wise or good men have thus decided, or the actual judges of the present question, or those whose authority they accept, or any one whose decision they cannot gainsay because he has complete control over them, or those whom it is not seemly to gainsay, as the gods, or one's father, or one's teachers. Thus Autocles[78] said, when attacking Mixidemides, that it was a strange thing that the Dread Goddesses

1398[b]

could without loss of dignity submit to the judgment of the Areopagus, and yet Mixidemides could not. Or as Sappho said, "Death is an evil thing; the gods have so judged it, or they would die."[79] Or again as Aristippus[80] said in reply to Plato when he spoke somewhat too dogmatically, as Aristippus thought: "Well, anyhow, our *friend,*" meaning Socrates, "never spoke like that." And Hegesippus, having previously consulted Zeus at Olympia, asked Apollo at Delphi "whether his opinion was the same as his father's," implying that it would be shameful 1399ᵃ for him to contradict his father. Thus too Isocrates argued that Helen must have been a good woman, because Theseus decided that she was; and Paris a good man, because the goddesses chose him before all others; and Evagoras also, says Isocrates, was good, since when Conon met with his misfortune he betook himself to Evagoras without trying any one else on the way.[81]

12. Another line of argument consists in taking separately the parts of a subject. Such is that given in the *Topics*:[82] "What *sort* of motion is the soul? for it must be this or that." The *Socrates* of Theodectes provides an example: "What temple has he profaned? What gods recognized by the state has he not honored?"[83]

13. Since it happens that any given thing usually has both good and bad consequences, another line of argument consists in using those consequences as a reason for urging that a thing should or should not be done, for prosecuting or defending any one, for eulogy or censure. E.g. education leads both to unpopularity, which is bad, and to wisdom, which is good. Hence you either argue, "It is therefore not well to be educated, since it is not well to be unpopular": or you answer, "No, it is well to be educated, since it is well to be wise." The *Art of Rhetoric* of Callippus[84] is made up of this line of argument, with the addition of those of Possibility and the others of that kind already described.[85]

14. Another line of argument is used when we have to urge or discourage a course of action that may be done in either of two opposite ways, and have to apply the method just mentioned to both. The difference between this one and the last is that, whereas in the last any two things are contrasted, here the things contrasted are opposites. For instance, the priestess enjoined upon her son not to take to public speaking: "For," she said, "if you say what is right, men will hate you; if you say what is wrong, the gods will hate you." The reply might be, "On the contrary, you *ought* to take to public speaking: for if you say what is right, the gods will love you; if you say what is wrong, men will love you." This amounts to the proverbial "buying the marsh with the salt." It is just this situation, viz. when each of two opposites has both a good and a bad consequence opposite respectively to each other, that has been termed *divarication.*

15. Another line of argument is this: The things people approve of openly are not those which they approve of secretly: Openly, their chief praise is given to justice and nobleness; but in their hearts they prefer

their own advantage. Try, in face of this, to establish the point of view which your opponent has not adopted. This is the most effective of the forms of argument that contradict common opinion.

16. Another line is that of rational correspondence. E.g. Iphicrates, when they were trying to compel his son, a youth under the prescribed age, to perform one of the state duties because he was tall, said "If you count tall boys men, you will next be voting short men boys."[86] And Theodectes in his *Law*[87] said, "You make citizens of such mercenaries[88] as Strabax and Charidemus, as a reward of their merits; will you not make exiles of such citizens as those who have done irreparable harm among the mercenaries?"

1399[b]

17. Another line is the argument that if two results are the same their antecedents are also the same. For instance, it was a saying of Xenophanes that to assert that the gods had birth is as impious as to say that they die; the consequence of both statements is that there is a time when the gods do not exist.[89] This line of proof assumes generally that the result of any given thing is always the same: e.g. "you are going to decide not about Isocrates, but about the value of the whole profession of philosophy."[90] Or, "to give earth and water" means slavery; or, "to share in the Common Peace" means obeying orders. We are to make either such assumptions or their opposite, as suits us best.

18. Another line of argument is based on the fact that men do not always make the same choice on a later as on an earlier occasion, but reverse their previous choice. E.g. the following enthymeme: "When we were exiles, we fought in order to return; now we have returned, it would be strange to choose exile in order not to have to fight."[91] On one occasion, that is, they chose to be true to their homes at the cost of fighting, and on the other to avoid fighting at the cost of deserting their homes.

19. Another line of argument is the assertion that some *possible* motive for an event or state of things is the *real* one: e.g. that a gift was given in order to cause pain by its withdrawal. This notion underlies the lines:

> God gives to many great prosperity,
> Not of good will towards them, but to make
> The ruin of them more conspicuous.[92]

Or take the passage from the *Meleager* of Antiphon:

> To slay no boar, but to be witnesses
> Of Meleager's prowess unto Greece.[93]

Or the argument in the *Ajax* of Theodectes, that Diomede chose out Odysseus[94] not to do him honor, but in order that his companion might be a lesser man than himself — such a motive for doing so is quite possible.

20. Another line of argument is common to forensic and deliberative oratory, namely, to consider inducements and deterrents, and the
motives people have for doing or avoiding the actions in question. These
are the conditions which make us bound to act if they are for us, and to
refrain from action if they are against us: That is, we are bound to act
if the action is possible, easy, and useful to ourselves or our friends or
hurtful to our enemies; this is true even if the action entails loss, provided the loss is outweighed by the solid advantage. A speaker will
urge action by pointing to such conditions, and discourage it by pointing to the opposite. These same arguments also form the materials for   1400ᵃ
accusation or defense — the deterrents being pointed out by the defense, and the inducements by the prosecution. As for the defense, . . .
This topic forms the whole *Art of Rhetoric* both of Pamphilus and of
Callippus.[95]

21. Another line of argument refers to things which are supposed
to happen and yet seem incredible. We may argue that people could not
have believed them, if they had not been true or nearly true: even that
they are the more likely to be true because they are incredible. For the
things which men believe are either facts or probabilities: If, therefore,
a thing that *is* believed is improbable and even incredible, it must be
true, since it is certainly not believed because it is at all probable or
credible. An example is what Androcles of the deme Pitthus said in his
well-known arraignment of the law. The audience tried to shout him
down when he observed that the laws required a law to set them right.
"Why," he went on, "fish need salt, improbable and incredible as this
might seem for creatures reared in salt water; and olive-cakes need oil,
incredible as it is that what produces oil should need it."

22. Another line of argument is to refute our opponent's case by
noting any contrasts or contradictions of dates, acts, or words that it
anywhere displays; and this in any of the three following connections.
(1) Referring to our opponent's conduct, e.g. "He says he is devoted to
you, yet he conspired with the Thirty." (2) Referring to our own conduct, e.g. "He says I am litigious, and yet he cannot prove that I have
been engaged in a single lawsuit." (3) Referring to both of us together,
e.g. "*He* has never even *lent* any one a penny, but *I* have *ransomed* quite
a number of you."

23. Another line that is useful for men and causes that have been
really or seemingly slandered, is to show why the facts are not as supposed; pointing out that there is a reason for the false impression given.
Thus a woman, who had palmed off her son on another woman, was
thought to be the lad's mistress because she embraced him; but when
her action was explained the charge was shown to be groundless. Another example is from the *Ajax* of Theodectes, where Odysseus tells
Ajax the reason why, though he is really braver than Ajax, he is not
thought so.

24. Another line of argument is to show that if the *cause* is present, the *effect* is present, and if absent, absent. For by proving the cause you at once prove the effect, and conversely nothing can exist without its cause. Thus Thrasybulus accused Leodamas of having had his name recorded as a criminal on the slab in the Acropolis, and of erasing the record in the time of the Thirty Tyrants: to which Leodamas replied, "Impossible: for the Thirty would have trusted me all the more if my quarrel with the commons had been inscribed on the slab."[96]

25. Another line to consider whether the accused person can take or could have taken a better[97] course than that which he is recommending or taking, or has taken. If he has *not* taken this better course, it is clear that he is not guilty, since no one deliberately and consciously chooses what is bad. This argument is, however, fallacious, for it often becomes clear after the event how the action could have been done better, though before the event this was far from clear. 1400[b]

26. Another line is, when a contemplated action is inconsistent with any past action, to examine them both together. Thus, when the people of Elea asked Xenophanes[98] if they should or should not sacrifice to Leucothea and mourn for her, he advised them not to mourn for her if they thought her a goddess, and not to sacrifice to her if they thought her a mortal woman.

27. Another line is to make previous mistakes the grounds of accusation or defense. Thus, in the *Medea* of Carcinus[99] the accusers allege that Medea has slain her children; "at all events," they say, "they are not to be seen" — Medea having made the mistake of sending her children away. In defense she argues that it is not her children, but Jason, whom she would have slain; for it would have been a mistake on her part not to do this if she *had* done the other. This special line of argument for enthymeme forms the whole of the *Art of Rhetoric* in use before Theodorus.[100]

28. Another line is to draw meanings from names. Sophocles, for instance, says,

O steel in heart as thou art steel in name.[101]

This line of argument is common in praises of the gods. Thus, too, Conon[102] called Thrasybulus[103] *rash in counsel*. And Herodicus[104] said of Thrasymachus, "You are always *bold in battle*"; of Polus,[105] "you are always *a colt*"; and of the legislator Draco[106] that his laws were those not of a human being but of a *dragon*, so savage were they. And in Euripides, Hecuba says of Aphrodite,

Her name and Folly's (ἀφροσύνης) rightly begin alike,[107]

and Chaeremon writes

> Pentheus — a name foreshadowing grief ($\pi\acute{\epsilon}\nu\theta\text{os}$) to come.[108]

The Refutative Enthymeme has a greater reputation than the Demonstrative, because within a small space it works out two opposing arguments, and arguments put side by side are clearer to the audience. But of all syllogisms, whether refutative or demonstrative, those are most applauded of which we foresee the conclusions from the beginning, so long as they are not obvious at first sight — for part of the pleasure we feel is at our own intelligent anticipation; or those which we follow well enough to see the point of them as soon as the last word has been uttered.

Notes

1. ii, cc. 2–11.
2. i. 1. 1354ª1.
3. *Anal. Pr.* ii. 23, 24; *Anal. Post.* i. 1. Cp. 68ᵇ13.
4. *Top.* i. 1 and 12.
5. lost logical treatise of Aristotle. . . .
6. [An alternate and perhaps better reading would be "the reason of this."]
7. ii, cc. 20–4.
8. ["Material sources" or even "premises."]
9. *An. Pr.* i. 8, 12–14, 27.
10. i.e. bears the same relation to the conclusion to be reached: "to that to which its general probability is directed" — to the particular probable case which has to be proved.
11. *An. Pr.* ii. 27.
12. [Tyrant of Syracuse.]
13. [Tyrant of Athens.]
14. [Tyrant of Megara.]
15. Or Topics, Commonplaces.
16. i.e. the topic of *degree.* [Cp. 1397ᵇ12 ff.]
17. Cp. *Top.* i. 10, 14; iii. 5; *Soph. El.* 9.
18. θεωρός: a mere onlooker, present at a show, where he *decides* no grave political or legal issue (cp. 1391ᵇ16–20) and plays no higher role than that of speech taster or oratorical connoisseur. — *Political* has been preferred to *deliberative,* as being clearer to the English reader. The oratory of the "(parliamentary) counselor" is meant.
19. Or: deliberative (advisory), legal, and epideictic — the oratory respectively of parliamentary assemblies, of law-courts, and of ceremonial occasions when there is an element of "display," "show," "declamation," and the result is a "set speech" or "harangue."
20. Homer, *Iliad,* xviii. 97 ff.
21. i.e. of Complete Proofs, Probabilities, and Signs relating to the three subjects of the expedient, the just, and the noble.
22. i.e. not (as some think) a third main kind. Cp. 1394ª27–9.
23. [An early poet of choral lyrics, circ. 640–555 B.C.]
24. [Sixth-century tyrant of Acragas, famous for his cruelty.]

25. Perhaps, "which does not suit skilled orators except before a small audience."
26. [Cp. 1365^{a}28.]
27. Euripides, *Medea,* 295.
28. Ib. 297.
29. Euripides, fragm. 661, N.^{2}
30. Euripides, *Hecuba,* 864 f.
31. Surprising, startling, heretical, unorthodox.
32. Possibly a fragment of Epicharmus. . . .
33. Euripides, *Troades,* 1051.
34. Euripides, *Medea,* 295.
35. [From an unidentified tragedy.]
36. Epicharmus?
37. [Cp. 1393^{b}9.] . . . The cicalas would have to chirp on the ground if an enemy cut down the trees.
38. *Iliad,* xii. 243.
39. Ib. xviii. 309.
40. Cp. i, c. 15, 1376^{a}7.
41. ["An Attic neighbor" is a restless neighbor.]
42. Cp. ii, c. 13, 1389^b 23–5.
43. i, c. 2, 1356^{b}3, 1357^{a}16.
44. Cp. Euripides, *Hippolytus,* 989.
45. [These are some of the historical and mythical merits claimed by the Athenians mentioned in all praises of their city and their ancestors.]
46. Cp. Thucyd. ii. 27; iv. 57.
47. Cp. Thucyd. ii. 70.
48. Cp. *Top.* i, c. 14.
49. i, cc. 4–14; ii, cc. 1–18.
50. ii, c. 23.
51. ii, c. 24.
52. ii, c. 25.
53. Cp. 1373^{b}18. [A speech attributed to Alcidamas, a fifth-century sophist and orator.]
54. [From an unidentified tragedy.]
55. Fragm. of Euripides, *Thyestes.*
56. Cp. i, c. 9, 1366^{b}33.
57. i.e. the right of collecting them.
58. i.e. was there nobody who thought the slaying a just act? [Fragm. of the *Alcmaeon* of Theodectes. The tragedian and orator was a personal friend of Aristotle.]
59. [Probably not the famous orator. Nicanor is unknown.]
60. [Xenophon, *Hellen.* viii. 3.]
61. The reasoning in the text shows confusion, and the text is uncertain. We might rather have expected the following connection of thought: "The argument, then, may run thus — that if the less likely is true the more likely is true; or as before — that if the more likely is not true, the less likely is not true: according as we have to show, &c."
62. [Fragm. probably from a play about Meleager.]
63. [From a speech of the rhetorician Polycrates.]
64. [Iphicrates, the general, was granted a statue for his defeat of the Lacedaemonians in 392 B.C. He claimed his statue only after his retirement in 371 B.C. Harmodius, a political opponent, opposed the honor.]

65. [In 339 B.C. Philip of Macedonia sent an embassy to the Thebans requesting passage through their territory into Attica. An Athenian counterembassy persuaded the Thebans to refuse the request. The words here quoted are words of the Macedonian ambassadors, not of Philip.]
66. Of Sophocles; cp. iii, c. 15, 1416^{b}1.
67. [Aristophon, a celebrated orator of the century, prosecuted Iphicrates in 355 B.C. for a failure in a recent war.]
68. [An Athenian political leader of the fifth century, famous for his justice and integrity.]
69. Cp. Plato, *Apol.* 27 c–e.
70. [Another example taken from Iphicrates' speech against Harmodius (cp. 1397^{b}28 ff.) who claimed descent from Harmodius, the tyrannicide. The argument seems to have been: personal merit, not family relationship, conveys true nobility. On account of my merit I am closer to the tyrannicides than you, their descendant.]
71. From some rhetorical essay on Alexander (viz. Paris), possibly by Polycrates. [Cp. 1393^{b}23.] . . .
72. Cp. Xenophon, *Apol. Socr.* 17; Diog. Laert., *Vit. Socr.* ii. 5, 25.
73. . . . [Or,] "in the *Topics* the right use of words has been discussed." Cp. *Topics,* i, c. 15 and ii, c. 3.
74. [Possibly the person mentioned in Demosth. *Or.* xviii. 7, 10.]
75. [Nothing known of the case and the people.]
76. [The tragedian, rhetor, and friend of Aristotle.]
77. [The sophist and orator.]
78. [Autocles, an Athenian political figure and versatile orator, contemporary of Aristotle. Of the case and Mixidemides nothing is known. The reference is to the Erinys as seen in Aeschylus' play *The Eumenides* where they submit to the judgment of Areopagus.]
79. [Fragm. of Sappho.]
80. [Aristippus of Cyrene, pupil of Socrates, founder of the Cyrenaic school of philosophy and as such a rival of Plato.]
81. Isocrates, *Helen,* 18–38; Ibid., 41–8 . . . ; Isocrates, *Evagoras,* 51 ff.
82. Cp. *Top.* ii. 4; iv. 1.
83. [Fragm. of *Defense of Socrates* by Theodectes.]
84. [Calippus is quoted again in 1400^{a}4. Nothing is known of him or his work. He may have been an early pupil of Isocrates.]
85. ii, c. 19.
86. [For Iphicrates cp. 1397^{b}28 and 1398^{a}19.]
87. Cp. 1398^{b}6.
88. [The mercenaries were a problem for the Greek cities from the beginning of the fourth century. Charidemus, their celebrated leader in the middle of the century, served Athens and was rewarded by being made a citizen. Strabax is less well known but also was made an Athenian citizen.]
89. [Fragm. of Xenophanes the Eleatic philosopher. Cp. 1377^{a}20.]
90. [The manuscripts read "Socrates" but the passage has been identified in the *Antidosis* speech (173) of Isocrates.]
91. [From a speech of Lysias.]
92. [From an unidentified tragedy.]
93. [Fragm. from the *Meleager* of Antiphon.]
94. Cp. *Iliad,* x. 218–54.
95. [Both rhetoricians of the fifth century of whom nothing is known.]

96. [Thrasybulus freed Athens in 403 B.C. from the rule of the Thirty Tyrants. Leodamas is probably the famous orator.]
97. i.e. better suited to effect the evil purpose with which he is charged.
98. [Cp. 1399^{b}6.]
99. [A tragedian, contemporary of Aristotle.]
100. [Theodorus of Byzantium, outstanding teacher of rhetoric of fifth century.]
101. [Fragm. from the *Tyro* of Sophocles.]
102. [The victor of Cnidus (394 B.C.).]
103. [The liberator of Athens in 403 B.C.]
104. [The physician (cp. 1361^{b}5).]
105. [Thrasymachus and Polus, sophists and rhetoricians, are introduced by Plato in *Republic* I and in the *Gorgias.*]
106. [The almost mythical Athenian lawgiver of the seventh century.]
107. Euripides, *Troades,* 990.
108. [Fragm. of Chaeremon, a tragedian of the fourth century.]

The Enthymeme as Postmodern Argument Form: Condensed, Mediated Argument, Then and Now

Roger C. Aden

Roger C. Aden's essay is an important reminder of the links between the classical and contemporary worlds. Originally published in 1994 in Argumentation and Advocacy, *this piece suggests that today's postmodern age — which too often relies on sound bites and truncated arguments — is not unique. Instead, Aden argues, today's media-based political and social arguments draw from (often in an exaggerated way) Aristotle's notion of the enthymeme. Through his analysis of a* Donahue *show featuring David Duke, an ex-member of the Ku Klux Klan and former Louisiana State Representative, Aden illustrates some ways that public arguments presented in the media use enthymemes, often creating highly condensed and prejudicial arguments that defy easy decoding and yet remain persuasive. Through such analysis, Aden suggests that teachers and students critique the condensed arguments that have always been a part of the public sphere. Such work, he suggests, will optimize our ability to take part in a society still striving to be truly democratic.*

See Joseph Janangelo's "Joseph Cornell and the Artistry of Composing Persuasive Hypertexts" (p. 272) for further discussion of the way contemporary media builds on earlier forms of communication theory.

When Stephen Toulmin wrote *The Uses of Argument* in 1958, the modern age was in full bloom and television was in its infancy. Today, however, most scholars argue that we now live in a postmodern age, thanks in great part to the emergence of television as the primary communication medium in developed nations. Argumentation scholars have responded to these developments in a number of ways.

Goodnight, for instance, posits that our more complex contemporary world has spawned three spheres of argument: the personal, the technical, and the public. The erosion of public argument, he claims is due to the privileging of the technical and personal that occurs in a world fragmented with specialties. Willard (*Argumentation; Theory*), meanwhile, suggests that argumentation scholars should explore the multiple interpretations of argument made possible by the existence of multiple frames of reference in a postmodern age.

These and other responses, however, do not explore directly how public officials argue through the media to postmodern audiences. Jamieson (*Eloquence*) examines how the rhetorical style of public officials has changed in an electronic age, but she does not delve into the changes in argumentative style wrought by the new age. Her thesis, though, that whether it be through brief campaign commercials, decreasingly brief "sound bites" on the evening news, or appearances on talk shows in which topics change every few minutes, public figures' pronouncements are transmitted to audiences through media and in condensed forms, equally applies to the arguments found in those pronouncements. Understanding how these arguments are structured is an important step toward revising a conception of public argument that has evolved much more slowly than has public discourse itself. Such an exploration, which I initiate here, must begin with an understanding of how audiences in postmodern societies process condensed, mediated arguments. Ironically, today's postmodern audiences process arguments in a manner eerily similar to the classical audiences of ancient Greece. The implications of this notion on public argument raise some troublesome issues, only a few of which I can attempt to answer here. To develop these issues in further detail, I first compare the processing of postmodern and classical audiences. Next, I illustrate these theoretical similarities with a brief analysis of the rhetoric of David Duke. Then, I conclude with a discussion of the implications of this theoretical outlook.

The Convergence of Postmodern and Classical Theories

The postmodern condition, claims Collins, features a plethora of signs and symbols that circulate within a culture. "One of the key preconditions of the postmodern condition is the proliferation of signs and their endless circulation, generated by the technological developments associated with the information explosion (cable television, VCRs, digital recording, computers, etcetera)" (Collins 331). McGee calls these floating symbols "fragments," and argues that contemporary audiences primarily process new combinations of these previously articulated fragments. "The apparently finished discourse is in fact a dense reconstruction of all the bits of other discourses from which it was made" (McGee 279). Similarly, Collins calls this process the comprehension of the "already said" in new forms. "What is postmodern in all of this is the simultaneity of these competing forms of rearticulation — the 'already said' is being constantly recirculated, but from very different perspectives ranging from nostalgic reverence to vehement attack or a mixture of these strategies" (Collins 333).

Postmodernism appears on television in a variety of forms, from self-reflexive prime-time programming (S. Olson) to network news reporters dishing up stories about how politicians attempt to manipulate those stories. Television, as a less-than-linear medium, is an ideal vehicle for postmodern communication. Television requires less attention than other media (Luke), yet fosters a sense of involvement (Gozzi and Haynes). Furthermore, its immediacy produces snap judgments from viewers: "Yet there is a crucial difference between the oral and the electric: The electric epistemology functions with interactions often distant in both time and space, and the checks and validating experiences available to the face-to-face oral epistemology are not readily applied" (Gozzi and Haynes 221). As a result, television viewers must rely on their own store of fragments to decode, interpret, and evaluate televised arguments.

When public arguments are presented on television, then, both the content and the form of the arguments encourage postmodern processing. That is, the content of arguments presented to the public consist of "already said" fragments, from which individuals construct their own interpretations. The televised form of the arguments further encourages such processing: Viewers feel involved, but that involvement is more passive, fostering acceptance of the content more so than if the argument appeared in another medium. Both content and form suggest that arguments in postmodern cultures function deductively, relying upon audience agreement of what's already "known" to create further agreement.

Ironically, this form of argument processing mirrors that posited by Aristotle in his explanation of the deductive reasoning form he labeled an enthymeme. According to Aristotle, "to conclude from certain assumptions that something else follows from those assumptions . . . either universally or as a rule — this in Dialectic is called a syllogism, and in Rhetoric an enthymeme" (*Rhetoric* 10). Assumptions, Aristotle writes in *Prior Analytics,* can be either "probabilities" or "signs," but they depend upon audience acceptance of what the speaker takes for granted (158). This deductive form of reasoning is best suited for a "mass" audience since "the uneducated argue from their everyday knowledge," (*Rhetoric* 156), while educated persons such as scientists view induction as a superior form of reasoning (*Posterior Analytics* 199). Similarly, Aristotle's notions of topoi or commonplaces function as fragments to which speakers turn for agreed-upon examples. "Ideas or lines of argument, the students of antiquity learned, are things that can be stored in 'places.' By returning to that 'place' where a bit of information was filed, the information might later be retrieved" (Nothstine 152).

Relying on Aristotle's various descriptions of an enthymeme, Harper argues that "a complete enthymeme is constructed of (a) an observation, (2) a generalization, and (3) an inference" (306). Yet, most scholars of classical rhetoric agree, enthymemes are *incomplete* in that they omit at least one of the three parts — a part that is supplied by the audience. McBurney, for example, claims that "we can safely interpret Aristotle to mean that the enthymeme *usually* lacks one or more of the propositions of a complete syllogism" (67), while Bitzer argues that the missing premise is interjected by the audience "out of its stock of opinion and knowledge" (407). Even Harper agrees that "an enthymeme may be abbreviated, and when it is, it is usually the *generalization* which is omitted as a commonly accepted 'fact'" (306).

In a postmodern age, elements of an argument can be omitted easily since audience members possess and/or believe in a larger number of "commonly accepted facts" (or, "already said fragments"). Moreover, enthymemes — especially in postmodern cultures — encourage individual interpretations. As Medhurst and DeSousa illustrate in their analysis of the enthymematic nature of political cartoons, individuals create their own understandings of these abbreviated forms of public argument. And, as most public arguments in a postmodern age must be condensed to be carried by mediated channels, it stands to reason that public figures rely on audience members "filling in the blanks" of these abbreviated arguments.

Thus, audiences in postmodern cultures process public arguments, in theory, much the same as Aristotle suggested that classical audiences processed public arguments. Speakers offer arguments that use already accepted notions as foundations, knowing that audiences will take these notions for granted in constructing their understandings of the arguments. While Aristotle may have envisioned more interpretive convergence in his less complex culture, the *process* of comprehending public arguments in classical and postmodern cultures appears to be remarkably similar in theory.

To test this theory in practice, I examine David Duke's use of enthymeme in his 19 May 1989 appearance on the *Donahue* television show shortly after his election to the Louisiana State Assembly.[1]

David Duke's Enthymeme

David Duke relies on a number of cultural factors in constructing his enthymeme. First, he recognizes that a number of voters harbor strong prejudices toward people different than themselves. James J. Brady, chair of the Louisiana Democratic Party, told the *New York Times* during Duke's 1991 gubernatorial campaign: "Part of his vote is just a hardcore racist vote where if there was some candidate further to the right of Duke they'd be with him. That's probably 30 percent of his vote" (Toner A7). Second, Duke's constant bashing of welfare programs and affirmative action appeals to economically frustrated working class white voters (Toner A1). Pollster Stan Greenberg, for instance, reported finding during the gubernatorial campaign "great frustration among white men who have not gone to college, whose incomes are dropping in real terms . . ." (Toner A1). Finally, Duke's "candor" in discussing his beliefs sets him off as something of an anti-establishment figure. "GOP consultant Jim Innocenzi says Duke's success is no aberration. 'Everybody knows everything they want to know about Duke . . . from his sex life to face lift, and they don't care,' he says. 'Things are so bad down there that regardless of everything, he at least represents a change'" (Nichols, 1A; ellipses original).

Duke's success in planting himself in anti-establishment soil, I argue, is directly related to the first and second factors listed in the previous paragraph, for the establishment against which Duke rails is the government-sponsored program of incentives to promote equality. His anti-establishment rhetorical appeal is actually a sophisticated enthymeme that combines elements of populism, white supremacy, victimage, and mortification. On one level, Duke displays himself as a champion of the common person (populism) by attacking government programs like affirmative action and welfare, which supposedly limit economic opportunities for whites (victimage). At a second level, Duke's attacks on minority-targeted programs like welfare and affirmative action, along with his pride in his white heritage, promote prejudice (white supremacy) but he also accepts the blame for white supremacist feelings by repudiating the KKK and calling his past a "youthful indiscretion" (mortification). Together, these strategies constitute an enthymeme that allows Duke to appeal to prejudice without overtly doing so.

To illustrate Duke's layered message, I look briefly at his appearance on *Donahue*. I select this text for a number of reasons: It marks the beginning of Duke's political ascendance, it is public argument (Duke is put on the spot by Donahue and audience members), it is delivered to a national audience via the popular media forum of the talk show, and the format of the talk show (rapid question and answer) is reflective of the condensed rhetoric found in much political discourse (e.g., debates, talk show appearances, advertisements).

VICTIMAGE AND POPULISM.   Victimage and populism work in conjunction. Victimage, in Burke's explanation of societal guilt, "is the purging of guilt through a scapegoat that symbolizes society's guilt" (Brock 186). Victimage, ironically, is employed to promote "social cohesion" by eliminating the guilt possessed by a major portion of society (Burke 284). In this respect, victimage is a tool of the majority. Populism, on the other hand, chiefly maintains that elite forces stifle the wishes of the true majority, or the common people (Lee 274). Thus, a populist politician frequently utilizes victimage to provide a target for frustrated voters by convincing them that they, the "true majority," must take back what belongs to them.

Duke's audience certainly is ripe for populist appeals using victimage. Louisiana has suffered economically for a number of years and voters have looked unsuccessfully to the state capital for answers. Consequently, during the late 1980s "poor and working class whites have become deeply suspicious of state government" (Edsall 34). Duke uses victimage to play upon these suspicions. He targets government programs like affirmative action and welfare to tap into anti-government sentiment, and blames the recipients of those government programs for social and economic ills.

Duke argues that affirmative action eliminates opportunities for whites. And those missed opportunities, he suggests, account for some of the economic problems faced by whites: "That the best qualified person, the person that works harder, performs better, he's the one who should get the job or the scholarship or the promotion or whatever" (*Donahue* 4). Affirmative action, according to Duke, explains why whites are not improving economically — they are denied opportunities to advance their education or careers even when they are qualified.

Welfare, on the other hand, contributes both to economic and social problems faced by whites, says Duke. Economically, Duke claims that welfare recipients are freeloading off of hard-working whites. "And I think it's wrong for people to work hard to pay for children of their own, and to educate children of their own, to have to finance a massive illegitimate birthrate among welfare recipients" (*Donahue* 3). Additionally, Duke maintains, this "rising welfare underclass" is responsible for the social problems suffered by society. The group of welfare recipients is "the source of a tremendous amount of our crime, our economic disaster that we're having in terms of our fiscal responsibility. And it's also hurting our educational system" (*Donahue* 11). Crime, in particular, emanates from the so-called welfare underclass, says Duke. Accordingly, he pushes a bill "that will require drug testing for welfare recipients the same way we test policemen and firemen" (*Donahue* 6). In David Duke's world welfare is responsible for economic hardship, drugs, crimes, and problems in the education system.

To white voters frustrated by economic immobility and an uncertain future for their children, Duke's explanation of their worries may possess what Fisher calls "narrative fidelity," or whether the story rings true based upon a person's past experiences (Fisher 8). Also, by employing victimage, Duke absolves whites of any responsibility for their situation. Offering absolution by blaming both welfare and affirmative action programs *and* recipients is key for two reasons. First, it mitigates any feelings of guilt that may emanate from believing Duke's concurrent white supremacist claims; anonymous government *programs,* rather than individuals of color, can be outwardly blamed for society's ills. Second, it assures white individuals that they are doing plenty to improve their own lot. Affirmative action and welfare suggest to whites that minorities are permitted to take shortcuts to financial stability rather than exhibiting a work ethic; few if any white voters, on the other hand, would acknowledge that they are not working hard to succeed. The concept of common folk working hard, when contrasted with the perception of minorities receiving undeserved, government-sponsored shortcuts, reaffirms notions of populism through victimage. As Duke tells a questioner on *Donahue:* "You know how a man goes up in status, ma'am? He has to work hard, to study hard. And to produce, that's how you go up in status in America" (*Donahue* 12).

MORTIFICATION AND WHITE SUPREMACY. Duke's scapegoating of government programs limits to some degree the prejudicial feelings that may arise from blaming the recipients of those programs for social and economic problems. To supplement this guilt-reduction technique, and to mitigate his more blatant white supremacist claims, Duke engages in mortification. "Mortification," in Burke's societal analysis, "is an act of self-sacrifice that relieves guilt . . ." (Brock 186). This strategy complements Duke's white supremacist–oriented statements by supposedly demonstrating that since he is not a white supremacist now his statements cannot be taken as espousals of white supremacist beliefs.

Duke's mortification strategy has evolved even since his appearance on *Donahue*. Although he now "repudiates" the KKK, Duke was less unequivocal on *Donahue*. "I will not renounce everything I did, certainly, because I was responsible. But I'll certainly renounce any acts from any place, in any organization that is bound in racial hatred, or violence, or illegality. I will renounce that specifically" (*Donahue* 10).[2] Still, Duke offers the *Donahue* audience misgivings about his past. "I certainly am sorry for times in my youth, and I've been too strident to have shown any sort of intolerance" (*Donahue* 4).[3] Duke also points out that he has paid the price for his strident behavior, more so than other individuals who have succeeded in Democratic politics:

> The Senate Majority Leader of the United States Senate all during the Reagan years, Robert Byrd, was a former member of the Ku Klux Klan. If a liberal can be a former klansman and be accepted by the liberal Senate, I think there's nothing wrong with a conservative who might have been a former klansman. . . . Why should the Democratic Party embrace Jesse Jackson, who was quite a black radical in his youth? In fact, he admitted expectorating in white people's food, an act I would never consider. And yet when David Duke comes along, because in his youth he was strident, yes, that suddenly we have to get rid of him (*Donahue* 6, 7–8).

By pointing out his "youthful mistakes" and the sacrifices he has endured that others in similar circumstances have not felt, Duke suggests he suffers now for past white supremacist beliefs. That suffering indicates he has subsumed the sins of other individuals who have expressed prejudicial beliefs, and serves as a reaffirmation of his changed character. So even though he campaigns on minority-related issues, Duke uses mortification to suggest that he is a changed man who no longer possesses such radical beliefs.

Duke's white supremacist beliefs, however, also appear outside of issues like affirmative action and welfare. His strategy is to cast whites as victims rather than oppressors. In fact, he says, individuals of European descent are actually an oppressed minority. Arguing that "the

true minority on this planet is the European people, or the white peoples
of the planet" (*Donahue* 4), Duke laments the blame placed upon this
alleged minority group.

> I can't hardly pick up a newspaper or magazine, or turn on the televi-
> sion set without me seeing my heritage being attacked. I mean, the
> heritage of the European people were [sic] attacked as oppressing
> Indians, oppressing blacks, it's a continual recital, almost every day
> (*Donahue* 5).

Such white pride laments mesh well with Duke's mix of populism and
victimage. While blaming the government for granting shortcuts to
minorities, Duke hopes that voters see hypocrisy in government actions. Whites, Duke claims, are the true minority group but they are
denied opportunities in favor of members of the world's majority group,
people of color. Thus, the "common man" is left to suffer while those
with the true power continue to help themselves — a theme straight
out of old-time populism.

THE ENTHYMEME.   Because Duke's rhetoric features subjects deeply
ingrained in the American psyche — ethnic origin, work ethic,
government's role in society, etc. — I argue that he creates an
enthymeme that omits *both* a generalization and an inference.

> **Observation:** Government actions, especially welfare and affirmative
> action, hurt whites economically and socially.
> **Generalization:** Minorities are the cause, and recipients, of these
> government programs.
> **Inference:** Minorities are the cause of the social and economic prob-
> lems suffered by whites.

I claim that Duke's overall message is an enthymeme because he, like
most Americans, must know that some members of his target audience
of white voters will supply the missing generalization and inference.
The *generalization* is accepted as true by many white voters, especially
those younger voters who do not possess knowledge of the context that
led to the establishment of these programs. Even older white voters
can easily acknowledge that minorities "cause" these government programs to continue since the civil rights movement supposedly accomplished its objectives with the passage of the Civil Rights Act of 1964
over a quarter of a century ago. Recent debate over affirmative action,
for instance, seems to center on whether it has made up for past prejudice rather than whether it is needed to prevent present prejudice. The
inference, then, is a logical conclusion if one accepts as true the observation and generalization, so Duke need not utter it. Thus, Duke's only
chore in constructing this enthymeme is to persuade his potential supporters of the truth of the observation. Since observations require the
smallest inferential leap among the parts of an enthymeme, and since
dissatisfied white voters are looking for populist explanations of their

economic condition that provide outside entities as scapegoats, Duke's observation — and enthymeme — likely find a receptive audience. With voters young and old, Duke relies on the "already said" to provide both the political cover he desires and the political response he craves.

The political advantages of the enthymeme are numerous. Initially, Duke can appeal to frustrated white voters by illuminating an entity to blame for their current problems while offering a populist-tinged hope for the future. Next, he can appeal to latent and manifest prejudice without creating voter discomfort over their bigotry-tinged votes. Voters can resolve any cognitive dissonance in favor of high-mindedness: They are rebelling against government programs not people; they are not articulating the prejudicial inference of the enthymeme — it remains unstated; and Duke has accepted any remaining blame through mortification. Third, Duke assumes little political risk. He does not state the controversial portions of his enthymeme. He is not forced to argue the inferential leaps between its parts and thus risk exposure. He can also deny white supremacy because he has employed mortification. "And by the way, is David Duke creating the polarization [between ethnic groups], or are these unfair policies of racial discrimination — massive racial discrimination sponsored by the government against white people — is that what's causing the polarization?" Duke ingenuously queries the *Donahue* audience (*Donahue* 10).

Implications

The implications of considering the enthymeme as a postmodern argument form focus on the public sphere of argument. The primary implication is this: If the enthymeme is a postmodern argument form, then the explicit, reasoned decision making that Goodnight seeks to recover in the public sphere may never have existed. Classical democrats in Greece employed truncated arguments just as David Duke does. In U.S. history, Jamieson (*Packaging*) points out, "the ideal [of reasoned, deliberative selection of elected officials] unraveled rapidly. Only George Washington was chosen in a manner approximating that [ideal]" (5). Enthymemes are not the only truncated argument forms employed by public figures. Birdsell says that "tropes can condense arguments, which are then subject to recall in much the same manner as an enthymeme" (179), while Fritch and Leeper suggest that metaphor "is an important form of argument" (193).

That rhetorical forms take the place of explicit arguments in the public sphere suggests that what we have, and have always had, is a public sphere of *discourse* rather than a public sphere of *argument*. While classical democratic theory and modernism envision a public sphere of argument in which "individuals are conceptualized as free and responsible agents who innately seek the True and the Good . . . [where] [t]he natural abilities (i.e., reason and conscience) of individuals must be freed so that they can find Truth" (Davis and Jasinsky 142), that sphere is simply a vision, an ideal. As Willard ("Creation") notes, the public sphere similarly, and erroneously, assumes widespread participation among people possessing the specialized skills of argumentation and debate. In practice, public discourse is articulated in shorthand and relies on audience members knowing how to decode what is not said because, ironically, it has already been said. Public discourse is generated by individuals who spin symbols to manipulate public opinion. Therefore, to expect quality argumentation in the public sphere seems almost foolhardy when Aristotle's legacy of a managerial rhetoric has encouraged public figures throughout the ages to discover the available means of persuasion rather than the best decision (not that the two must be mutually exclusive; the former hopes for the success of the individual speaker, the latter for the success of the society).

Perhaps the most fruitful conceptualization of argumentation, then, is not as a form of rhetoric which can be recovered and used in the public sphere, but as a method of decoding the condensed, mediated discourse of the public sphere. Unpacking the arguments stuffed into enthymemes, tropes, and metaphors requires the skills of critics able to identify both the unsaid/already said and the means by which public figures attempt to further their own ends at the expense of what the critic sees as the societal good. For instance, Kathryn M. Olson illustrates how the Reagan and Bush administrations constrained open deliberation for political gain during the nation's recent wars in Grenada and the Persian Gulf. Public figures in both administrations, of course, managed discourse in a manner intended to make their policies appear appealing, so an expectation of open, reasoned deliberation is unwarranted even in a representative democracy. Yet, by critiquing the management of this public discourse, Olson offers lessons that can be applied to similar situations in the future.

Such criticism is necessary, for even if a public sphere of argument cannot be recovered/created, individuals generating public discourse must be watched by qualified critics. Two concerns, in particular, bear attention. First, speakers who use truncated arguments possess plausible deniability because of what is left unsaid. Second, audience members who fail to acknowledge their understanding of the already said may perpetuate their own cynicism.

Plausible deniability is not limited to David Duke's socio-economic analysis. The same year that Duke ran for governor, for example, then President George Bush offered a similar enthymeme in opposing the Civil Rights Bill of 1991.

> **Observation:** The bill will promote the use of quotas in the workplace.
> **Generalization:** Quotas give unearned opportunities to minorities.
> **Inference:** Whites' opportunities will be given to minorities if the bill passes.

The quota enthymeme contains an observation that can be defended as a logical discussion of a serious issue while its inference preys on prejudice. "Although [Bush's] rhetoric seems to suggest a principled conservative position, his maneuvering suggest a coolly calculated decision to divide the country on the fault line of racial fear" ("The Cynicism" 10). The hypocrisy of the quota enthymeme — Bush's alternative bill also encouraged quotas and his administration regularly utilized them in its hiring practices (Kinsley; "The Cynicism" 10) — marks the cynicism of the Bush technique, and suggests the ease with which speakers can proffer pernicious public arguments while denying malicious intent. Such situations demand the attention of argumentation critics, for most media personalities appear unable to respond effectively to the unsaid. Donahue, for example, sputtered and stammered throughout most of his interview with Duke, exasperated that he was unable to pin his guest down. That media forums generally preclude extended lines of questioning — talk shows take questions from the audience, debates feature reporters with one question per topic, etc. — exacerbates media personalities' inability to respond to the unsaid. Donahue's only extended series of questions produced Duke's only major gaffe of the hour-long program: a suggestion that whites are more intelligent than blacks.

Argumentation critics will serve a second function in performing such criticism: They can break the cycle of cynicism in which voters may find themselves. Voters who do not demand explicit argument on controversial issues know that public figures will not feel compelled to offer such argumentation on any public issue. Duke's "equal rights for all" rhetoric, for example, surely was not believed by even his supporters; therefore, they likely could not know what he was leaving unsaid on other issues. This wink-and-nod routine between elected and electorate does not engender closer ties between the two groups, it distances them. In this context, Taylor's report that fewer individuals are fulfilling the duties of citizenship is not surprising. Already, voters may even have reached the point of acceptance of such cynicism. For instance, one day after I read an account of Clinton administration officials playing "I have no recollection of . . ." before the Senate Banking Committee exploring the Whitewater imbroglio I saw a repeat of a *Wings* episode in which Oliver North proclaims that he has no recollection of how a hotel pen entered his possession. The postmodern cynicism reflected in these events is startling: A lie invented to avoid telling a lie — "a Kevlar jacket against perjury" (Kosova 16) — has become a form of humor. Exposing the unsaid as already said, however, may force audience members to realize that "business as usual" depends upon their acceptance of the usual/already said.

I want to conclude this essay with a question: What lies ahead for the theory and practice of public argumentation? In a postmodern culture the existence of more fragments than in previous eras — even if these fragments have already been said — may produce just a few more individual interpretations of public arguments, forcing public officials to clarify their arguments to gain a consensus among different public spheres. David Duke's emergence, after all, forced individuals to examine their beliefs about policies related to race. On the other hand, if individuals have heard it all before and possess keen televisual literacy skills, they may just rely on what they already take for granted rather than seek out new combinations of fragments. David Duke did, after all, emerge. In any event, and no matter how these issues are addressed, additional understanding of public argumentation in its condensed, mediated, and now ubiquitous, form is a vital project for teachers and scholars of argumentation.

Notes

1. Excerpts cited from Duke's *Donahue* appearance were taken from a transcript prepared by the firm Journal Graphics. I found two excerpts that I understood much differently than the firm's transcribers. My interpretations are elaborated in notes two and three.
2. My understanding of this segment is: "I will not renounce everything I did, certainly, *I acted responsibly.* But I certainly renounce any acts from *anybody in* any organization that *espouses* racial hatred, or violence, or illegality."
3. My understanding of this sentence is: "I certainly am sorry for times in my youth *when* I've been too strident *or* shown any sort of intolerance."

Works Cited

Aristotle. *Prior and Posterior Analytics.* Ed. and Trans. John Warrington. London: Dent, 1964.

———. *The Rhetoric of Aristotle.* Trans. Lane Cooper. Englewood Cliffs, NJ: Prentice-Hall, 1932.

Birdsell, David S. "Kenneth Burke at the Nexus of Argument and Trope." *Argumentation and Advocacy* 29 (1993): 178–85.

Bitzer, Lloyd F. "Aristotle's Enthymeme Revisited." *Quarterly Journal of Speech* 45 (1959): 399–408.

Brock, Bernard L. "Rhetorical Criticism: A Burkeian Approach Revisited." *Methods of Rhetorical Criticism.* 3rd ed. Eds. Bernard L. Brock, Robert L. Scott, and James W. Chesebro. Detroit: Wayne State UP. 183–95.

Burke, Kenneth. *Permanence and Change.* 1954. Berkeley: U of California P, 1984.

Collins, Jim. "Postmodernism and Television." *Channels of Discourse, Reassembled,* 2nd ed. Ed. Robert C. Allen. Chapel Hill: U of North Carolina P, 1992. 327–53.

"The Cynicism Thing." *The New Republic* 24 June 1991: 9–10.

Davis, Dennis K., and James Jasinski. "Beyond the Culture Wars: An Agenda for Research on Communication and Culture." *Journal of Communication* 43.3 (1993): 141–49.

Donahue. "State Representative David Duke." 19 May 1989: Transcript #2689. New York: Journal Graphics, Inc.

Edsall, Thomas B. "All the King's Men Can't Put Louisiana Back Together Again." *Washington Post National Weekly Edition* 22–28 May 1989: 34.

Fisher, Walter R. "Narration as a Human Communication Paradigm: The Case of Public Moral Argument." *Communication Monographs* 51 (1984): 1–22.

Fritch, John E., and Karla K. Leeper. "Poetic Logic: The Metaphoric Form as a Foundation for a Theory of Tropological Argument." *Argumentation and Advocacy* 29 (1993): 186–94.

Goodnight, G. Thomas. "The Personal, Technical, and Public Spheres of Argument: A Speculative Inquiry into the Art of Public Deliberation. *Journal of the American Forensic Association* 18 (1982): 214–27.

Gozzi, Jr., Raymond, and W. Lance Haynes. "Electric Media and Electric Epistemology: Empathy at a Distance." *Critical Studies in Mass Communication* 9 (1992): 217–28.

Harper, Nancy. "An Analytical Description of Aristotle's Enthymeme." *Central States Speech Journal* 24 (1973): 304–09.

Jamieson, Kathleen Hall. *Eloquence in an Electronic Age: The Transformation of Political Speechmaking.* New York: Oxford UP, 1988.

———. *Packaging the Presidency: A History and Criticism of Presidential Campaign Advertising.* New York: Oxford UP, 1984.

Kinsley, Michael. "Hortonism Redux." *The New Republic* 24 June 1991: 4.

Kosova, Weston. "True Lies." *The New Republic* 22 & 29 August 1994: 14+.

Lee, Ronald. "The New Populist Campaign for Economic Democracy: A Rhetorical Exploration." *Quarterly Journal of Speech* 72 (1986): 274–89.

Luke, Carmen. "Television Discourse Processing: A Schema Theoretic Approach." *Communication Education* 34 (1985): 91–105.

McBurney, James H. "The Place of the Enthymeme in Rhetorical Theory." *Speech Monographs* 3 (1936): 49–74.

McGee, Michael C. "Text, Context, and the Fragmentation of Contemporary Culture." *Western Journal of Speech Communication* 54 (1990): 274–89.

Medhurst, Martin J., and Michael A. DeSousa. "Political Cartoons as Rhetorical Form: A Taxonomy of Graphic Discourse." *Communication Monographs* 48 (1981): 197–236.

Nichols, Bill. "Past Follows Ex-Klansman on Campaign." *USA Today* 23 Oct. 1991: 1A+.

Nothstine, William L. "'Topics' as Ontological Metaphor in Contemporary Rhetorical Theory and Criticism." *Quarterly Journal of Speech* 74 (1988): 151–63.

Olson, Kathryn M. "Constraining Open Deliberation in Times of War: Presidential War Justifications for Grenada and the Persian Gulf." *Argumentation and Advocacy* 28 (1991): 64–79.

Olson, Scott R. "Meta-television: Popular Postmodernism." *Critical Studies in Mass Communication* 4 (1987): 284–300.

Taylor, Paul. "'A National Morale Problem.'" *Washington Post National Weekly Edition* 14–20 May 1990: 6–7.

Toner, Robin. "Ex-Klan Leader's Vote Sends Message to a Pained G.O.P." *New York Times* 22 Oct. 1991: A1+.

Toulmin, Stephen. *The Uses of Argument.* Cambridge: Cambridge UP, 1958.

Willard, Charles A. *Argumentation and the Social Grounds of Knowledge.* Tuscaloosa: U of Alabama P, 1983.

———. "The Creation of Publics: Notes on Goodnight's Historical Relativity." *Argumentation and Advocacy* 26 (1989): 45–59.

———. *A Theory of Argumentation.* Tuscaloosa: U of Alabama P, 1988.

Judgment, Probability, and Aristotle's *Rhetoric*

Barbara Warnick

Barbara Warnick's "Judgment, Probability, and Aristotle's Rhetoric,*"
originally published in 1989 in the* Quarterly Journal of Speech, *asks
teachers and scholars to consider how Aristotle's intellective categories
can help us define, produce, and analyze argument in a postmodern age.
Warnick argues that a strict reading of Aristotle does not support the idea
that rhetoric is a universal tool for creating and understanding all forms
of argument. Aristotle's comprehensive system of knowledge denies, for
example, that scientific and philosophical knowledge (which depend on
deductive logic) are subject to rhetorical study. Rhetorical argument,
according to Warnick, is only one kind of argument and is applicable only
in the pursuit of contingent, probable knowledge and therefore cannot
meet every discipline's needs.*

*Read this essay in conjunction with R. Allen Harris's "Assent, Dis-
sent, and Rhetoric in Science" (p. 242), Jeanne Fahnestock and Marie
Secor's "The Stases in Scientific and Literary Argument" (p. 58), and the
section on "Teaching Argument Across the Curriculum" (p. 389) to gain
further insight into this ongoing discussion among argumentation
theorists.*

In the *Uses of Argument,* Stephen Toulmin endeavors to show how
argumentation differs according to the field in which it is used. For
Toulmin, a field is a discipline or locus of inquiry and argumentation,
such as law, business, or mathematics.[1] Toulmin claims that the field
characteristics of argument include standards used in judging arguments, principles used to formulate inferences, sources of proof, and
modalities of argument.[2]

The thesis of the present paper will be that Aristotle, too, held a
"field theory" of inquiry and argument but that for him the source of
the differences between various forms was in *the means used,* not the
discipline of origin. In two passages, Aristotle explicitly identifies five
means humans use to inquire, deliberate, prove, produce, or make
choices. He calls these means "modes of thought" or "faculties by which
the soul expresses truth by way of affirmation and denial."[3] In this
essay, I shall call these capacities by which humans make choices about
true and false, right and wrong, and what action to take the "means of
judgment."[4]

Like Toulmin, Aristotle makes distinctions between these five means
in an effort to show how inquiry and argument differ in their various
applications. The means are intelligence (*nous* and *dianoia*), scientific
knowledge (*episteme*), theoretical wisdom (*sophia*), art (*techne*), and
practical wisdom (*phronesis*). Aristotle distinguishes each by its function (apprehending, proving, speculating, making or judging arguments,
and taking action), area of application (the physical world, metaphysics, and human affairs), starting points, form of discourse and products. As is well known, Aristotle identified rhetoric as a *techne,* and in

the *Rhetoric* he identified its unique function, uses, materials, forms, and purpose.

Viewing rhetoric within the context of this intellective system has many implications for rhetorical theory. First, it shows that those who attempt to assimilate Aristotelian rhetoric to argument and forms of proof in other fields such as philosophy and the natural sciences are erroneously interpreting Aristotle.[5] Second, it enables us to identify the unique characteristics of argument emergent in Aristotle's *Rhetoric*. Third, considering rhetoric's place within this system of means demonstrates how probability functions in Aristotle's account of rhetorical argument.

Two Case Studies in Mistaken Assimilation

The urge to elevate the logical element of rhetoric and to devalue its emotive dimensions has been irresistible to many theorists and critics. This type of move often eventuates in a theorist's claim that rhetoric is appropriately used in, or even indigenous to, the conduct of inquiry in philosophy, the sciences, and other fields where we do not normally situate Aristotelian rhetoric.[6] The tendency in contemporary rhetorical theory to emphasize *logos* and deprecate *pathos* and *ethos* has been well documented.[7] Problems arise, however, when commentators who are specifically examining Aristotle's *Rhetoric* interpret it in this way. Because such interpretations fail to take into account Aristotle's "field" theory of judgment and the place of rhetoric in the overall system of the Aristotelian corpus, they lead to confusion, error, and misinterpretation.

One example of such an error is the early work of William M. A. Grimaldi, who, in a 1972 commentary on the *Rhetoric*, takes a position so inconsistent that he seems to assume two personas.[8] Grimaldi$_1$ seeks to elevate rhetoric to the mode of discourse for the conduct of philosophy. He emphasizes the significance of the move Aristotle made in applying deductive logic (the syllogism) to argument and explanation by way of the enthymeme. He claims that "among other things the enthymeme introduces Aristotelian logic to rhetoric, i.e., the ways of inference and the axiomatic principles which for Aristotle are the tools enabling the mind to apprehend the true. . . . Furthermore, in bringing the syllogism into rhetoric, Aristotle acknowledges that there is an epistemology of the probable, namely that the mind can know and use the probable as well as the unconditioned in its attempt to understand the world of reality."[9]

A conclusion such as this would hardly be objectionable if Grimaldi$_1$ went on to illustrate the use of enthymematic reasoning in the construction of social reality or in political reasoning. Problems arise, however, from his desire to apply the *Rhetoric*'s theoretical contribution to areas quite different from those Aristotle intended. Grimaldi$_1$ goes so far as to claim that "from what Aristotle says . . . rhetoric is general and touches all areas of human knowledge wherein man attempts to convey understanding, whether it be philosophy, literature, or the physical sciences."[10] In a concerted effort to apply rhetoric to the conduct of discourse in philosophy, literature, and the sciences, Grimaldi$_1$ attempts to dissociate rhetoric from persuasion in the Aristotelian system. Rhetoric "does not effect persuasion as some of the technographers said . . . nor does it, as far as Aristotle is concerned, make persuasion in the same way as the artist makes his object."[11] Grimaldi$_1$ also endeavors to associate rhetoric with speculative rather than practical reasoning and with truth not belief: "Aristotle stresses the fact that rhetorical discourse is discourse directed toward knowing, toward truth not trickery. To one acquainted with Aristotle it should be evident that syllogism and induction are inextricably connected with the demonstration of truth. From the analogy drawn between 'enthymeme-example' as the rhetorical forms of 'deduction-induction,' Aristotle directs rhetoric toward the demonstration of the true."[12]

Grimaldi$_2$ implicitly realizes how far afield of the standard interpretations of the *Rhetoric* this construal has placed him. Beginning at midpoint in his treatise and continuing more or less on the same track until the end, he openly recognizes the uniqueness of rhetoric as an argumentative form of discourse and emphasizes the importance of credibility and emotion in the *topoi* and inferences of the enthymeme's elements. Unfortunately, by so doing he contradicts his earlier claims and reveals his own misinterpretations of Aristotle. The *Rhetoric* could be considered as primarily applicable to discourse in philosophy, literature, and the sciences only if Aristotle had not written other treatises concerning reasoning and discourse in those arts and sciences, if he had explicitly applied the principles of the *Rhetoric* to any one of those arts, if the three genres he stipulated (deliberative, epideictic, and forensic) were directly relevant to them, or if the topics he discussed (legislation, defense, commerce, personal character, an individual's past achievements, motives leading to just and unjust actions) constituted philosophical or scientific *topoi*.

By midway through his treatise, Grimaldi$_2$ retracts his earlier insistence on rhetoric as a primary means of coming to know the true by stressing the enthymeme's uniqueness. "The deductive process cannot be the simple scientific syllogism, the syllogism of pure reason. Not only does the modality of the subject matter in rhetoric prevent this, but the very object intended by rhetorical argumentation, i.e., personal conviction which will motivate personal action, does not permit it."[13] Further on, he openly acknowledges the differences between probability (*eikos*) and philosophical truth. "In his analysis of *eikos,* Aristotle validates probable truth and reasoning from probable sources. . . . It is not the way of first philosophy which works through absolute, unconditioned, and necessary principles to certain knowledge and certain truth. This second way works through premises (*eikota*) which may be false."[14] To argue that rhetoric is epistemic in the conduct of philosophy and other enterprises, then, Grimaldi$_1$ has had to feature senses in which the *Rhetoric* may be construed as endorsing the universal rather than the contingent, speculative rather than practical reasoning, and the certain and unconditioned rather than the probable and contingent. The resultant interpretation confuses the reader and distorts the unique nature of Aristotle's original project.

Similarly, Christopher Lyle Johnstone follows Grimaldi's lead in viewing rhetoric as the appropriate mode of discourse for the conduct of philosophy.[15] Like Grimaldi, Johnstone attempts to dissociate rhetoric from persuasion and instead argues that Aristotle's is a "dialectical rhetoric" intended to direct the recipient to a reasoned judgment. "The immediate goal of the art is to perceive in a given subject, problem, or situation those elements that may be used to influence the process of judging. While this conception has sometimes been construed to mean that rhetoric 'effects persuasion,' this characterization does not describe Aristotelian rhetoric. He does not speak of 'effecting persuasion' but rather of 'affecting judgment.'"[16]

Johnstone then moves on to argue that, insofar as rhetoric promotes reasoned judgment in deliberation, it can be used by a single, private mind, in dialogue with oneself, as it were. "The 'man of practical wisdom,' when he deliberates about conduct with a view toward choosing among competing alternatives, employs a kind of internal rhetoric. . . . If we can reasonably visualize deliberation as a sort of internal dialogue, then the practically wise person, when he or she deliberates, functions as both rhetor and auditor."[17] An assimilation of rhetoric to internal reasoning and dialogue such as this one suppresses or omits many of the unique elements of rhetorical argumentation identified in the *Rhetoric*. The need to incorporate audience convictions and values, to simplify argument structures for the comprehension of the multitude, and to direct one's claims toward decisions affecting the state and the *polis* are all neglected when Aristotelian rhetoric is applied to forums and situations that Aristotle himself did not consider in the *Rhetoric*.[18]

In the account that follows, the uniqueness of rhetoric as a *techne* for producing arguments will be recovered by contrasting it with capacities for proving and judging evinced by other modes of thought. In Aristotle's system, what is known, demonstrated, produced, or chosen is settled upon by procedures and criteria arising from the sort of means employed, be it intuition, speculative reasoning, practical reasoning, or skill in choice making. As Martin Ostwald observed, "while Plato's work is characterized by a passionate conviction of the unity and interdependence of all branches of human knowledge, . . . Aristotle is more concerned with finding what differentiates one branch of learning from the other and what is particular to each."[19] Let us, then, examine, the processes of reasoning, proof, argument, and choice making in *nous, dianoia, episteme, sophia, techne,* and *phronesis*. By examining the areas of application, products, modalities, methods, starting points, and forms of discourse unique to each, we will acquire a differentiated and refined understanding of the place of rhetoric in Aristotle's system of intellection. The major differences between these five modes of thought are displayed in figure 1.

Figure 1. Five Means by Which the Soul Affirms or Denies

	Examples	Products	Method	Starting Points	Form of Discourse
INTELLIGENCE	Nous — Grasps sense data; "intuitive apprehension of simple, uncomposite realities" Dianoia — Connects subject and attribute; coherent thinking	Apprehended sense data: first principles Associative inferences that make syllogism possible		Sense impressions Perceived qualities and characteristics	
EPISTEME "scientific knowledge"	Mathematics Physics	Objective knowledge based on principles produced by demonstrative reasoning	Move from what is better known to a lesser known conclusion through demonstrative syllogism	Axioms Definitions	Description Instruction
SOPHIA "theoretical wisdom"	Metaphysics Philosophy Theology	Eternal, universal truths	Internal dialectic; identify contradictions and fill in aporias	Opinions accepted by everyone or by the wise	Often done in solitude; any discourse would be an expository discussion

Figure 1. Five Means by Which the Soul Affirms or Denies (continued)

	Examples	Products	Method	Starting Points	Form of Discourse
TECHNE "art"	Sculpture Music	Statues Musical Compositions	Discover available means of production to produce products used in *phronesis*	Marble Notes, chords	Finished sculpture Symphony, etc.
	Rhetoric	Arguments		Opinions acceptable by particular audience	Continuous persuasive discourse
	Dialectic	Arguments		Opinions acceptable by universal audience	Interactive argument
PHRONESIS "practical wisdom"	Ethics Politics	Action which results in a virtuous life Action which results in a well-ordered state	Use experience, good sense, intelligence, & understanding to secure right action by deliberation	Initiating motive for action	Social action read as a text

Judgment in Intellection, *Episteme,* and *Sophia*

Intelligence is not really a locus for judgment as we normally think of the term, but rather for perception and coherent thinking, which are propadeutic to judgment by the other faculties. *Nous* and *dianoia,* the components of intelligence, provide the starting points of all cognition. In his commentary on the *Nicomachean Ethics,* J. A. Stewart described these two components. *Nous* is the intuitive intellect, or direct apprehension of the indemonstrable, whereas *dianoia* is discursive reason or coherent thinking. In regard to particular uses of the two terms, Stewart concluded that "we may say that *nous* grasps the end immediately, and *dianoia* reviews the means."[20]

Nous, then, is sense perception or intuitive reason. *Dianoia* occurs when the mind makes connections between concepts, for example, by the transitivity of the middle term in a syllogism. At *Post. An.* 100a10–b16, Aristotle describes the importance of intelligence, the source of first principles, as embodied in these two components. Sense perception, which we share with animals, persists in us in memory. Although we perceive particulars, the sum of sense perceptions coming to rest in the soul and taken together enables us to form categories or genera. These categories, when combined with the connective thinking of *dianoia,* then comprise the elements of the indemonstrable first principles that form the bases of scientific knowledge. Aristotle reasons that if "first principles" are indeed "first," they should not themselves be demonstrable; they must be immediate and unmediated. Only when humans are described as percipients in whom perception rests, preserved by memory and assimilated and interpreted by intuition, is apprehension of first principles possible. This effort to avoid infinite regress, undeveloped though it may be, presages similar views expressed in the faculty psychology of the eighteenth century and in contemporary philosophy.[21]

The term *"episteme"* has two uses in Aristotle's corpus. In one it refers to "knowledge" in general and in the other to "objective knowledge" or "scientific knowledge." It is this second specific usage that is referred to here. As discussed in *Posterior Analytics* and *Physics,* *episteme* refers to knowledge grounded in first principles, axioms, and definitions that characterize inquiry and proof in mathematics and physics. The reasoning used in *episteme* is demonstrative and apodeictic because "it is impossible to know what is contrary to fact" (*Post. An.* 71b26). The truth discovered arises from descriptions that are stated so as to correspond fully and completely to physical reality. As Joachim observed, "Aristotle held that the demonstrations of science were completely true — true in the sense that the premises and the conclusion faithfully represent the real. A judgment . . . is true in so far as the subject and predicate exactly reflect thing and property and their union or separation."[22]

The purpose of *episteme* is to discover knowledge of general rules that can apply invariably to all instances within the rubric for which the rule is intended. If exceptions were admitted, the rationale for the entire enterprise would be undermined. The modes of discourse in science are instruction and explanation. Emotive elements, probable proof, and considerations of moral choice are inappropriate in *episteme*.

Sophia or theoretical wisdom is another means the soul uses for affirmation or denial. Whereas *episteme* is concerned with necessary truths and connections as evidenced in physical reality, *sophia* is directed toward those elements of being that are eternal and changeless. *Sophia* considers metaphysical questions and theology. It may also deal with questions of being or reality in the world, such as the axioms of science, but only insofar as they exhibit the essential attributes of all being.[23]

Sophia is the highest kind of knowledge because its objects are the highest form of reality. It is superior to *phronesis* and politics, which study human affairs. *Sophia* comprises both scientific knowledge and intelligence and is science in its consummation — the science of things that are valued most highly (*Nic. Eth.* 1141a20). Since the contemplative life and possession of *sophia* are virtuous, theoretical wisdom produces happiness. Aristotle maintained that "of all activities that conform with virtue, activity in conformity with theoretical wisdom is the most pleasant" (*Nic. Eth.* 1177a24).

The purpose of *sophia,* then, is to arrive at a true conception of the eternal and unchanging elements of being. While the means to be used toward this end are not explicitly discussed, a connection is clearly made between the contemplative life, use of our highest faculties, and *sophia* (*Nic. Eth.* 1177a12–1179a31). *Sophia* is not therefore usually arrived at through intercourse with others. Rather, it presumably involves applying one's intellect so as to discover fundamental principles. We may get a better idea of what is involved here by watching Aristotle at work than by noting what he says. At *Topica* 101a35, he claims that dialectic is useful in the philosophical sciences because it enables one to consider difficulties on both sides of an issue and to discover the ultimate basis of each science. His own method seems to be the result of some sort of internal dialectic. He collects and juxtaposes principles and beliefs on a topic, uncovers the contradictions and problems they give rise to, and attempts to resolve them logically. Dialectic is thus used by him as a *techne* in the conduct of philosophy, and its function is to produce and test claims and theses.[24]

Judgment in *Techne* and *Phronesis*

Whereas *episteme* deals with physical reality and *sophia* with the divine and eternal, *techne* is immersed in the realm of human affairs. At *Nic. Eth.* 1140a21, a *techne* is defined as "a certain habit of producing under the guidance of true reason." An art or *techne* therefore has a theoretical as well as a practical dimension, and thus is to be distinguished from a mere skill. An "art" in this sense consists in *observing* the means available and *considering* how best to use them to promote virtue. This is what is meant by "under the guidance of true reason." Artistic knowledge consists of awareness of the general principles underlying an activity as well as of an ability to give an account of them.[25]

An art consists also of the capacity to produce something, and its end is the production of products intended to serve human needs. The uses to which these products are put in activity and living are the concern of *phronesis,* and so the producer's task ends as soon as the product is made. All productive activities are forms of *techne.* The *techne* of the sculptor is to produce statuary, of the harpist to produce music. Insofar as he promotes good health, the physician is engaged in a *techne,* although medical science as the study of anatomy and physiology is an *episteme.* The source of a *techne* is its producer; its starting points are the raw materials out of which the product is made; and its realm is the world of process, of coming-to-be (*Nic. Eth.* 1140a12–14).

Dialectic and rhetoric are both *technai,* whose function is to produce and judge arguments. In their mode of discourse and the forms of their reasoning, they differ from *episteme* and from each other. *Episteme* communicates by means of instruction and reasons by way of the demonstrative syllogism that eventuates in apodeictic conclusions. Dialectic assumes the form of interactive discourse with small groups of interlocutors who are learned and capable of following intricate chains of reasoning, and so its inferences may be complex.

Rhetoric consists of continuous discourse with large groups who are not capable of following complex reasoning, so its reasoning forms (the enthymeme) are often collapsed and simplified and its starting points are accepted opinions rather than conclusions reached through earlier arguments. In the *Rhetoric,* Aristotle emphasizes these characteristics: "We have already said that the enthymeme is a kind of syllogism, what makes it so, and in what it differs from the dialectical syllogism; for the conclusion must neither be drawn from too far back nor should it include all the steps of the argument. In the first case its length causes obscurity, in the second, it is simply a waste of words, because it states much that is obvious."[26] The enthymeme often leaves one or more of its premises unexpressed and is stated as opinion because of the nature of the situation in which rhetorical argument occurs; audiences already know or recognize opinions contained in the unexpressed premises and find extensive restatement of all the steps leading to the conclusion tedious. But because they are incapable of following intricate reasoning chains, argumentation must be simplified and use convictions derived from common experience as its starting point.

The means by which a *techne* is applied arise from the producer's "know how" as evidenced in the strategies for production employed. A craftsman learns these in apprenticeship; a rhetor acquires them through experience, observation, and study of the art. In the Aristotelian system, rhetoric is an "art," and not merely a knack or a skill because, as Aristotle envisioned it, rhetoric consisted of observing the available means of persuasion and considering how they could be applied so as to achieve good for the state and its citizenry through *phronesis*. His aim in the *Rhetoric* was to lay out the principles of the art and render an account of it so that it could be studied systematically.

In achieving the public good, rhetoric plays only a partial role. Only when it reaches its fruition in *phronesis* is rhetoric made effective. *Phronesis* is practical wisdom, or wisdom applied to and made manifest in action. Aristotle believed that *phronesis* was intrinsically good by definition, and in the *Rhetoric* (1364b21) he stated that the good was "that . . . which everything, if possessed of practical wisdom, would choose." The functions of *phronesis* are to use the products of *techne* wisely, to deliberate well about what is good and advantageous, and to command right action. Its starting points are the initiating motives or first causes of the action to be undertaken (*Nic. Eth.* 1151a15–20).

In order for *phronesis* to occur, certain conditions must be present. The agent taking the action must know what he or she is doing, must act voluntarily, and must be of firm and unchangeable moral character. The virtuous character of the action comes from the virtuous character of the person acting; Aristotle's criterion for virtuous action is basically circular. He maintains that "acts are called just and self controlled when they are the kind of acts which a just and self-controlled man would perform; but the just and self-controlled man is not he who performs those acts, but he who also performs them in the way just and self-controlled men do" (*Nic. Eth.* 1105b5–9). The person of high moral standards is for Aristotle the standard and measure that makes the normative and the actual coincide.

Right action in *phronesis,* then, must result from experience. The *phronimos* must "be a competent student of what is right and just, and of politics generally" (*Nic. Eth.* 1095b5). The *phronimos* must have had a proper upbringing in moral conduct and be a person of experience. For that reason, the person of practical wisdom must be mature; Aristotle observes that young men may make good geometricians and mathematicians because these sciences deal only with universals and abstraction. *Phronesis,* on the other hand, is concerned with particulars and with action, and knowledge of its fundamental principles is the result only of prior experience that enables wise judgment (*Nic. Eth.* 1142a11–21.).

Although experience and character are the determining factors in right action, deliberation is also highly desirable. *Phronesis* is realized most assuredly in human affairs when reasons are given and considered about how and why one is obligated to act, to choose or avoid one course of action over another. In considering the merits of alternative courses of action, rhetoric plays a significant role. Because *phronesis* can be applied only in the particular case and because human affairs are intrinsically changeable and contingent, the standards for right action must be relative and applied to the case at hand rather than invariant and universal. In determining such standards and the effects of action, rhetoric plays a vital role. It deals in probabilities and considers regularities across situations. Since such regularities and the general convictions regarding them can be known, rhetoric possesses a kind of knowledge, but it is qualitatively different from that possessed by *episteme* or *sophia*. Aristotle makes this clear at *Nic. Eth.* 1094b13–26:

> Problems of what is noble and just, which politics examines, present so much variety and irregularity that some people believe that they exist only by convention and not by nature. The problem of the good, too, presents a similar kind of irregularity, because in many cases good things bring harmful results. . . . When the subject and the basis of a discussion consist of matters that hold good only as a general rule, but not always, the conclusions reached must be of the same order. . . . For a well-schooled man is one who searches for that degree of precision in each kind of study which the nature of the subject at hand admits: It is obviously just as foolish to accept arguments of probability from a mathematician as to demand strict demonstrations from an orator.

The implications of this passage are that each mode of thought, when applied, possesses its own unique characteristics. Rhetoric has its starting point in general opinions, its fruition in right action, its inferences in the common topics, and probability as its modality. *Phronesis* begins with initiating motives and desire, eventuates in the good of the state and the *polis,* uses deliberation and experience as means, and is applied in the particular case. If rhetoric works effectively to produce good deliberation and if the *phronimos* is a person of good character, then the decision reached and action taken will themselves be virtuous.

Probability and *Techne*

Dialectic and rhetoric operate only in the realm of the probable. As productive arts, the subjects of their concern are determined by the uses to which they are put, and they are applied only to issues about which one deliberates. This excludes the impossible, the certain, and the inadmissable. Aristotle states this clearly at *Topica* 105a3–9:

> It is not necessary to examine every problem and every thesis but only one about which doubt might be felt by the kind of person who requires to be argued with and does not need castigation or lack perception. For those who feel doubt whether the gods ought to be honored and parents loved, need castigation, while those who doubt whether snow is white or not, lack perception. We ought not to discuss subjects the demonstration of which is too ready to hand or too remote; for the former raise no difficulty, while the latter involve difficulties which are outside the scope of dialectical training.[27]

At *Rhetoric* 1357a14 and 1359b1–3, he says essentially the same about rhetoric as a *techne*. Therefore, these two faculties are applied only to subjects that admit of more than one outcome, about which various considerations must be weighed, and about which we must deliberate.

When Aristotle discusses the uses of these *technai,* he alludes to at least three senses of probability. One is the likelihood that a past or future event did or will occur. The second is the extent to which premises operative in the argument are accepted by the audience. And the third sense of probability emerges in the use of the common and special topics for inference making.[28]

The first and most straightforward sense of probability — likelihood of occurrence — is made clear at *Rhetoric* 1402b9–11, where Aristotle discusses the use of enthymemes in forensic speaking. He notes here that the probable is not what occurs invariably but only for the most part. Therefore, it is not enough to respond to an accusation that something probably happened by showing that it is not necessarily true. In Aristotle's view, the accuser is obligated only to show that the incident in question was much more likely to have occurred than not to have occurred. Respondents attempting to refute an accusation only by showing that an incident *might* not have occurred have failed to fulfill their argumentative obligation, and the judge should decide in favor of their opponents. Aristotle concludes that "this is what is meant by deciding according to the best of one's judgment. It is therefore not enough to refute an argument by showing that it is not necessary; it must also be shown that it is not probable." Therefore, the conclusion must be shown to apply in the majority of cases. This is the first sense of probability.

Probability in rhetoric and dialectic is more closely tied to what the audience or interlocutor accepts or takes as true than to what is necessarily true. In fact, at *Nicomachean Ethics* 1141a3, when Aristotle lists the faculties by which we attain truth, he includes *episteme, phronesis,* and intelligence but excludes *techne.* This is presumably because the *technai* are means to an end or tools. It is only when they are applied through practical wisdom and intelligence, that truth and right action are settled upon.[29]

That probabilities consist of what is believed rather than what *is* is made clear throughout the *Rhetoric.* Proverbs, maxims, and fables are all described as acceptable starting points for enthymematic premises. In the *Topica* (100b18), dialectical reasoning is said to proceed from "generally accepted opinions," which include those commending themselves "to all or to the majority or to the wise." At *Prior Analytics* 70a4, a probability is defined as "that which people know to happen or not to happen, to be or not to be, usually in a particular way." In the Greek courts, probabilities were often given more credence than physical evidence and the testimony of witnesses. Physical evidence could be corrupted or prearranged, and witnesses could be bribed, but probabilities were viewed as constant and universally acceptable (*Rhetoric* 1376a17–18). A second sense of probability, then, arises from its role as a premise formed from a generally accepted proposition.

The third use of probability in argument construction arises from the role of the common and special topics in providing inferences.[30] Here I mean inferences as the connections we make between facts and conclusions in everyday reasoning rather than only syllogistic inferences. These inferences are the sort of "leaps" Toulmin says we make from data to claim in practical argument.[31] Here the common topics of possibility and magnitude that are grounded in probabilities play a role; for example, "if the harder of two things is possible, [it is likely that] so also is the easier" (*Rhet.* 1392a11). If our accepted premise is that someone climbed a ten thousand foot mountain successfully, we may reasonably conclude that the same person can make a climb of lesser difficulty. Whether a topic actually functions in an argument as an inference depends on its context, but it is clear that topics are used in this way. For example, they provide the principles for making all *a fortiori* arguments.

Therefore, in the *technai,* probability operates in at least three ways. It is connected to the question of whether an argument's conclusion actually applies in a given case. It operates in the premises that can be put forward as a basis for arguments. And, by way of topics functioning as probabilities, it serves as the source for inferences in practical argument.

Conclusion

The intent of this essay has been to set Aristotle's theory of rhetorical argument within the context of his overall view of human judgment. Aristotle believed that each of the five means "specialized in" different enterprises. Like the other modes of thought (intellection, *episteme, sophia,* and *phronesis*), the *technai* had their own unique characteristics and uses. When interpreting Aristotle, ad hoc assimilation of rhetoric to judgment in fields where the other modes of thought are dominant is ill advised.

The function of *episteme* is to discover and establish scientific and mathematical truths. Its starting points lie in empirically based perception provided by *nous* and connections made between objects and their characteristics by *dianoia,* or coherent thinking. These stimuli and the cognitive operations connecting them provide fundamental axioms and definitions that form the first principles of mathematics and the physical sciences. The reasoning producing knowledge in these fields is reductive and associative. Based on the assumptions that any statement that corresponds precisely and consistently with reality and that any demonstrative syllogism whose inferences are valid is "true," *episteme* produces conclusions that are invariably and necessarily true. The discourse of *episteme* is expository and instructive, and its product is knowledge about the structure and contents of physical reality.

Sophia, or theoretical wisdom, is applied in metaphysics, theology, and speculative philosophy. The objects of *sophia*'s contemplation are those things that are valued most highly, and in its operation *sophia* evinces the highest intellectual excellence of which the human mind is capable.[32] The kind of reasoning characterizing *sophia* is best shown in Aristotle at work as a philosopher. His starting points arise from the refined opinions of wise persons who preceded him; his method is to isolate apparent confusions and contradictions, to clarify and refine points of agreement and disagreement, and thereby to discover the kernel of truth in each opinion.[33] This process might proceed in intercourse with select groups of interlocutors through dialectic, or it might be conducted in isolation through extensive contemplation or internal dialogue. The form of reasoning required for *sophia* is the dialectical syllogism, which may be used in extensive, complicated forms of reasoning. The products of *sophia* take the form of metaphysical and ontological principles and the standard for judgment would include internal consistency and principles acceptable to the universal audience.[34]

A *techne* or true art is cognizant of the available means of production, considers how to best use them to produce virtuous outcomes, and can provide an account of its method. Rhetoric's aim as a *techne* is systematically to produce and judge arguments that can be applied by *phronesis* to produce right action. The mode of discourse of rhetoric is persuasive and its reasoning forms are collapsed and simplified so that the rhetor's appeals can be understood and accepted by large crowds. Applied to human affairs and adapted to changeable situations and exigencies, the argumentation of rhetoric perforce deals in probabilities and general opinion. However, since such matters are grounded in regularities and since that which is accepted can be known and acted upon, rhetoric produces a kind of knowledge. Principled use of rhetoric grounded in such knowledge produces high quality arguments and therefore excellent deliberation. Aristotle's aim in the *Rhetoric* was to articulate the logical principles of enthymematic reasoning and use of the topics so that rhetoric could be studied and practiced as a true art.

Phronesis is judgment applied directly to right action. The standards guaranteeing the rightness of the act are the moral character, experience, and knowledge of the actor. However, deliberation that makes use of the arguments produced by rhetoric and dialectic as *technai* can be conducive to right action. Products of *phronesis* are a virtuous life and a well-ordered state and its starting points are initiating motives directed toward these ends. Although argumentative discourse is productive of rather than produced by *phronesis,* the action the discourse produces could be read and judged as a social text. Examining the action of *phronesis* in this way involves considering the character of the *phronimos* and the effects of the action.

Considering the modes of judgment endemic to each of these means enables us to identify precisely the nature of Aristotle's contribution to rhetorical theory. In the *Rhetoric,* he developed principles intended to guide the construction of argumentative discourse in public affairs. In developing his theory of the enthymeme, in showing how special and common topics could be used as premises and inferences for arguments, and in demonstrating how arguments could be adjusted to audience expectations and the exigencies of the particular case, Aristotle developed rhetorical argument as a distinctive form, corresponding structurally to proofs in the sciences but incorporating nonrational components such as credibility and emotive appeals. Attempts to interpret the *Rhetoric* as applicable to philosophy and the sciences are therefore misdirected and suppress Aristotle's view of rhetoric as a unique argumentative form.

Notes

1. Stephen Toulmin, *The Uses of Argument* (Cambridge: UP, 1969), 14–15.
2. Stephen Toulmin, Richard Rieke, and Allan Janik, *An Introduction to Reasoning,* 2d ed. (New York: Macmillan, 1984), 272–273. For a number of provocative scholarly articles on the notion of argument fields, see *Journal of the American Forensic Association* 18 (1982).
3. Aristotle, *Posterior Analytics,* trans. Hugh Tredennick (Cambridge: Harvard UP, 1960); and *Nichomachean Ethics,* trans. Martin Ostwald (Indianapolis: Bobbs-Merrill, 1962). The passages are at *Post. An.* 89b7–9 and *Nic. Eth.* 1139b15. Subsequent citations to these editions will be included in the text.
4. "Judgment" in this essay is not to be taken as equivalent to the Greek *krisis,* which has more specific applications. In the two passages where Aristotle lists the five modes of thought by which the soul affirms or denies, he does not use a generic common noun to refer to them. In his subsequent discussion, he alludes to such processes as perceiving something in a certain way, evaluating an opinion, making a moral choice, or deciding on an action. In using the term "judgment" as globally synonymous with perception, discernment, and insight, I follow the practice of translators of the *Nicomachean Ethics.* See 1143a8–35 in Ostwald's translation and the same passages in *Nicomachean Ethics,* trans. H. Rackham (Cambridge: Harvard UP, 1962).
5. Two commentaries on the *Rhetoric* that avoid this error are J. Robert Olian, "The Intended Uses of Aristotle's *Rhetoric,*" *Speech Monographs* 35 (1968): 137–148; and Larry Arnhart, *Aristotle on Political Reasoning* (DeKalb: Northern Illinois UP, 1981).
6. For examples of this, in addition to the authors cited below, see Wilbur Samuel Howell, "Aristotle and Horace on Rhetoric and Poetics," *Quarterly Journal of Speech* 54 (1968): 328 and 331; and Arthur Miller and John Bee, "Enthymemes: Body and Soul," *Philosophy and Rhetoric* 5 (1972): 205.
7. Jane Sutton, "The Death of Rhetoric and its Rebirth in Philosophy," *Rhetorica* 4 (1986): 203–226.
8. William M. A. Grimaldi, S. J., *Studies in the Philosophy of Aristotle's "Rhetoric"* (Wiesbaden: F. Steiner, 1972).
9. Grimaldi, 16.
10. Grimaldi, 54.
11. Grimaldi, 27.
12. Grimaldi, 85.
13. Grimaldi, 82.
14. Grimaldi, 109.

15. Christopher Lyle Johnstone, "An Aristotelian Trilogy: Ethics, Rhetoric, Politics and the Search for Moral Truth," *Philosophy and Rhetoric* 13 (1980); 12.
16. Johnstone, 6.
17. Johnstone, 12.
18. Lawrence W. Rosenfield, in *Aristotle and Information Theory* (Hague: Mouton, 1971), 66, states very clearly the institutional contexts in which Aristotle intended the *Rhetoric* to be applied: "Plainly, rhetoric functions in the province of public behavior. . . . Deliberative oratory occurs in a legislative assembly, forensic speaking is found in the courts, and epideictic oratory takes place on ceremonial occasions. These are all public occasions which call for a speech much as a packed football stadium in the Fall calls for a football game. Aristotle can obviously imagine speaking taking place in contexts other than these, but he chooses not to treat them."
19. Ostwald's "Introduction" to the *Nicomachean Ethics,* xiii.
20. J. A. Stewart, *Notes on the Nicomachean Ethics* (Oxford: Clarendon P, 1892), 2:28. Elsewhere (p. 24), Stewart qualifies this distinction by observing that in some passages Aristotle uses the terms interchangeably or regards them as equivalent.
21. George Campbell, *The Philosophy of Rhetoric,* ed. Lloyd F. Bitzer (Carbondale: Southern Illinois UP, 1963), 37–42; and Ludwig Wittgenstein, *On Certainty,* ed. G. E. M. Anscombe and G. H. von Wright, trans. Dennis Paul and G. E. M. Anscombe (Oxford: Basil Blackwell, 1967).
22. H. H. Joachim, commentary on the *Nicomachean Ethics,* ed. D. A. Rees (Oxford: Clarendon P, 1951), 182.
23. Ostwald, xiv–xv.
24. The ambiguity of dialectic's role in the application of *sophia* arises largely from the multiple uses to which dialectic was put in Aristotle's day. Plato had elevated it in its pure form to a means of discovering the Good, whereas the sophists often used it as mere eristic — an effort to entrap or evade one's opponent in an intellectual sparring in dialogue. Aristotle believed dialectic could be fruitfully used in criticism, but he clearly rejected Plato's elevation of it and recognized the potential for abusing the dialectical method. Most commentators agree that Aristotle saw both dialectic and rhetoric as *technai.* See Eric Weil, "La Place de la logique dans la pensée Aristotelicienne," *Revue de metaphysique et de morale* 56 (1951): 245; Jeanne Croissant-Goedert, "La Classification des sciences et la place de la rhetorique dans l'oeuvre d'Aristote," *Proceedings of the Eleventh International Congress of Philosophy* 14 (1953): 269–75; Friedrich Solmsen, "Dialectic without the Forms," in *Aristotle on Dialectic: the Topics,* ed. G. E. L. Owen (Oxford: Clarendon P, 1968), 54; and Emile Janssens, "The Concept of Dialectic in the Ancient World," trans. Henry W. Johnstone, Jr., *Philosophy and Rhetoric* 1 (1968): 174–81.
25. Arnhart, 16 and 35.
26. Aristotle, *"Art" of Rhetoric,* trans. John Henry Freese (Cambridge: Harvard UP, 1926) at 1395b23–1396a3. All subsequent citations will be to this edition and included in the text.
27. Aristotle, *Topics,* trans. E. S. Forster (Cambridge: Harvard UP, 1960).
28. See Edward H. Madden, "Aristotle's Treatment of Probability and Signs," *Philosophy of Science* 24 (1957): 167–72. Madden describes three types of probability: (1) that which generally happens or which happens "for the most part," (2) that which is stated in the *endoxa* or opinions currently

accepted by most people, and (3) that which is more readily confirmable by evidence than its alternatives. Madden acknowledges Aristotle's recognition of the second type ("what most people believe"), but Madden himself seems very reluctant to accept it. He appears more inclined to link claims to factual reality than to what audiences find acceptable. Disregarding the persuasive role of *Endoxa* in argumentation concerning moral truths and action leads Madden to the following equivocal statement: "*Endoxa,* then, have a presumptive probability; and it is interesting to note that whatever the nature or analysis of the probability it does have, it is not the frequency one" (169).

29. Lois S. Self, "Rhetoric and *Phronesis:* the Aristotelian Ideal," *Philosophy and Rhetoric* 12 (1979): 130–145.
30. On the connection between the topics and inference making, see Arnhart, 141, Grimaldi, 17 and 131, and especially Eugene E. Ryan, *Aristotle's Theory of Rhetorical Argumentation* (Montreal: Bellarmin, 1984), 29–96.
31. Toulmin, 98–99.
32. Ostwald, 155.
33. Arnhart, 30.
34. Ch. Perelman and L. Olbrechts Tyteca, *The New Rhetoric: A Treatise on Argumentation,* trans. John Wilkinson and Purcell Weaver (Notre Dame: U of Notre Dame P, 1969), 31–35.

The Stases in Scientific and Literary Argument

Jeanne Fahnestock and Marie Secor

Jeanne Fahnestock and Marie Secor have written for several years on the value of stasis theory to argumentation. Their work extends both classical notions of stasis theory (from rhetoricians such as Cicero and Quintilian) and contemporary applications, such as Caroline Eckhardt's and David Stewart's efforts to understand argument in terms of definition, substantiation, evaluation, and recommendation.

The following essay, originally published in Written Communication *in 1988, asks teachers to consider the stases (questions of fact, questions of definition, questions of value, and, sometimes, questions of policy) as vehicles to teach invention and arrangement. Fahnestock and Secor also use the stases to explore conventions for writing arguments in science and literature. As their analysis demonstrates, these (and all) disciplines depend on the same stases to create arguments, even if they depend on them in different ways and to different degrees. Stasis theory, therefore, can provide students a fundamental grounding in argumentation across the disciplines as it asks them to consider the way disciplinarity subtly affects* all *argumentation.*

For more specific applications of teaching argument in the disciplines, refer to the last section of this text, "Teaching Argument Across the Curriculum" (p. 389).

The usefulness of classical rhetoric is often extolled but less often demonstrated. We tend to treat classical rhetoric as a source of basic rhetorical concepts rather than as an instrument capable of performing the kind of intricate analysis of audience and context for which we turn to modern rhetoricians. But the very specific forums and contexts explicitly addressed by classical rhetorical texts should not obscure their applicability to a wide range of discourse, even to situations and audiences undreamed of by their authors. After all, classical rhetoricians worked with the genres and types of discourse familiar to their audiences; so should we. Our purpose in this essay is to suggest some connections between a classical system of invention and the kind of sensitivity to audience and discourse community that we have come to expect in contemporary treatments of theory in rhetoric and composition.

The case in point is the classical system of invention known as the stases. It originated in the courtroom, where charge met countercharge and early rhetoricians found it useful to categorize the recurrent kinds of issues, or stases, in contention. The first substantial treatise on the stases was written by Hermagoras in the second century B.C., after which the stases were taken up and refined by every significant rhetorician until the Renaissance. The fullest and most familiar expositions are found in Cicero's *De Inventione,* Quintilian's *Institutio Oratoria* (Book III), and Hermogenes' *On Stases.* Although none of these works applies the stases outside the courtroom, they indicate in passing that such applications are possible (Fahnestock & Secor, 1983). We have found the stases not only useful as an invention tactic but also as a principle of arrangement and a probe for the analysis of audience and context. The stases are a particularly valuable construct in the study of the rhetoric of the disciplines; we will explore their usefulness in the analysis of scientific and literary discourse.

What Are the Stases and How Do They Function in Rhetorical Analysis?

In classical theory, the stases describe a series of three or sometimes four points at which certain types of questions arise about a subject; these questions constitute a taxonomy of arguments. They follow a logical, hierarchical order; the first, most basic question must be disposed of before more complex ones can be addressed. There are questions of fact, questions of definition, questions of value, and in some versions questions of procedure, which we will conflate with questions of policy. In our own version of the stases, we separate out questions of cause and assign them to a separate stasis. The ancients would have subsumed such questions under definition, for in the courtroom the notion of motive would help define actions; the rise of science has made questions of cause assume special importance (Fahnestock & Secor, 1985).

We have long been convinced of the power of the stases as a teachable invention tactic in the writing classroom. They are like a generating machine or device for extrusion molding; a topic dropped in the top hopper comes out in questions and potential theses. A student, for example, drops in the topic "food stamps" and creates a series of questions. "What are they?" is a definition question that, for this topic, searches for the operational definition, "Who is eligible?" Then comes a fact question, "How extensive is their use?"; next causes, "What brought them about or what is their history?" or "What are their effects?"; evaluation, "Are they a good or bad policy?"; and finally proposal, "Should they be continued, expanded, reduced, eliminated?" An attempt to provide a plausible answer to any of these questions gives the writer a thesis to support. The stasis pattern not only generates these questions but also determines the order in which they are asked. Questions of fact must be answered or assumed before questions of value or policy can be addressed. Most important, the stases tell the writer "where to think," not "what to think." They do not dictate or predict the precise claims that attempt to answer any of these questions; that will be a function of the particular arguer, audience, and available evidence. The stases simply describe the logic inherent in the development of an issue.

Another way to look at the stases is to see them as sitting between the general outline of an argument, applicable to all arguments regardless of field, described by the Toulmin model, and the very specific lines of argument engendered by the special topoi preferred by specific disciplines. The Toulmin model tells us that all arguments involve claims, warrants, grounds, and sometimes backing, qualification, and rebuttal (Toulmin, 1958). The special topoi of a field tell us what particular warrants are used in that field, such as the causal warrant of natural selection often appealed to in evolutionary biology or the value warrant of a preference for ambiguity assumed in literary criticism. Between these general and discipline-specific levels, the stases tell us that arguments may concern facts, definitions, causes, values, proposals, and that each kind of argument will employ its own peculiar kinds of warrants.

In addition to being a scheme of invention, the stases can also be regarded as a format for the arrangement of arguments, and thus as a corollary principle of rhetorical analysis. For example, the full stases, from fact to proposal, constitute the backbone or outline of articles in general-circulation magazines. Such articles introduce a topic by defining it and commenting on its extent, go on to consider causes and consequences, then evaluate the phenomenon, and finally turn to the future by predicting or recommending certain actions. We have seen this structure again and again in *Sports Illustrated,* the *New York Times Magazine,* the *Smithsonian.* It seems the inevitable format for a complete treatment of a subject. Of course there will be strategic differences in the way authors present these various components. The opening questions in the stasis of fact will often be rendered in narrative examples for the immediacy of "you were there" journalism, thereby endowing a topic with the "presence" so necessary in argument, as

Perelman and Olbrechts-Tyteca (1969, p. 116) have pointed out. Or instead of evaluating, an author will sometimes project a persona of objectivity by reporting contrasting viewpoints on an issue rather than a single judgment. Or, for the sake of effect, the order of stasis presentation might be inverted and an article begin with a salient question in the fourth stasis: "What should be done about X?" But after an attention-grabbing opening, the article addressed to a wide audience usually settles comfortably into the inevitable ontological pattern: What is it? What caused it? Is it good or bad? What should be done about it? — though any one of these sections may be extremely brief.

But to see the stases only as an invention technique and an all-purpose format for arrangement is to see them as rhetorical and somewhat sterile. A "logical" order of questions can help to generate arguments and events to arrange them in an effective order, but we seldom generate arguments in an intellectual vacuum, apart from considerations of audience and the expectations of a social or disciplinary context. The full stasis development of a subject is the exception in written arguments in the academic disciplines. Scholars usually focus on well-defined issues for limited audiences. In particular, arguments in disciplinary contexts often stay in one stasis.

For the rhetorician, the interesting question to ask then becomes, "Why is this audience being addressed in this stasis?" Our claim here is that the stases are even more useful for the analysis and generation of arguments when we consider them in relation to audience; indeed, they can be used as probes for the analysis of audience.

When an argument stays in one stasis rather than exploiting the full range of stasis development, the stasis it is in becomes a powerful indicator of the author's sense of audience. To begin with the least obvious relation between stasis and audience, the stasis in which an argument is pitched is not necessarily the stasis in which the arguer hopes to have an effect. Rather, the chosen stasis of an argument can be one of the arguer's rhetorical moves in response to the particulars of audience and situation, just like the choice of ethos-projecting devices or the use of pathetic appeals. For example, an arguer who wishes to move an audience to action may simply argue certain facts into place and allow the context of the argument and the audience's assumptions to do the rest.

The great template of the stases hovers above whatever piece of writing we are actually looking at; the stases represent a full set of possibilities from which an author, in a particular rhetorical situation, under a particular exigence, addressing a particular audience, selects. The author may stay in just one or two of the stases because that is where he or she can meet the intended audience, because that is where the audience's needs and interests lie, or because that is where they can be reached, no matter where the writer wants to take them. In other words, the stases are not only an invention device and a principle of arrangement; they can also become a sensitive tool of audience analysis.

Exactly how do the full stases operate on an audience? They operate as a set of potential assumptions or reactions. Their apparent logical order does not reflect an externally imposed requirement of validity; rather, that order anticipates the inevitable reactions of Western audiences. Arguments conducted in one stasis nudge audiences to either construct or assume arguments in other stases. An argument proposing action certainly assumes definitions and values; but less obviously, an argument at a lower stasis may move its audience to evaluation or even to action. For example, a proposal for housing the homeless may assume without support and carry its audience along to believe in the existence of a significant number of homeless people and the moral rightness of acting in their behalf. At the other end of the scale, the mere factual report of an attack on American shipping may outrage the public and cause them to clamor for action though no specific value or proposal arguments are directed at them.

Put another way: When we address an issue in one stasis, we may do so because of the preferred practices of our discipline. That does not mean, however, that the other stases are absent or irrelevant to the reactions of our readers or audience. As readers we push at arguments, testing the expressed and articulating the submerged assumptions of fact, definition, or value in order to accept or reject them. That is what it means to be sensitive to language in argument: to be aware of facts that are assumed significant, to notice definitions that might be slippery or inadequate, to pick out values that might be implicit in word choice and metaphor. Thus we often read arguments in the lower stases by pushing at their implications for action: If this is so, what follows from it? What positions or actions must I be committed to if I accept this argument? Such implications may not be expressed; members of a field understand them because they can read subtexts in ways that outsiders find difficult.

The Stases in Scientific Arguments

We can also look at the relation between stasis and audience from another perspective, one that emphasizes how arguments create audiences as well as respond to them. After all, the demographic or epistemological profile of an audience need not completely constrain an arguer. An argument conducted in the lower stases can actually begin to construct an audience that values an inquiry at that level. This point is most easily illustrated in the case of scientific articles. To begin with, scientific articles occupy the first two (or, depending on your scheme, three) stases. They are concerned with matters of fact, definition, and cause (Fahnestock, 1986). To test this generalization, we can look at one issue of *Science* (232/4751, May 9, 1986), the weekly journal of the American Association for the Advancement of Science, which publishes articles from diverse fields, though there is certainly a concentration in biochemistry and medical research.

Many of the articles and reports in *Science* in recent years concern the discovery and "definition" of biochemical compounds. A title like "Identification and Characterization of the Protein Encoded by the Human N-*myc* Oncogene" reveals its nature (Slamon et al., 1986); with relatively new techniques such as gene splicing, molecular biologists are still very much in the business of discovering and describing the entities in their domain. And there are disagreements in their discourse at this level. While we as outsiders may comfortably label the scientific article describing a protein as "information" relating matters of "fact," the scientists writing such an article are engaged in argument and controversy at this first stasis level. Establishing the sequence of base pairs in a gene is not so simple, and competing papers describing the same gene or its product will appear in the literature. Because mistakes are made, because individuals within a species vary in their genetic profiles, and because there are often stretches of "silent DNA" called introns in a gene, identifying the active stretches of DNA can be an artful act of interpretation, and research groups can differ in their "readings" in much the same way that competing schools of literary theory will produce different interpretations of a poem. (There is, however, a difference in the ultimate stability of the artifact interpreted, a way to judge ultimately between interpretations in molecular biology.)

More evidence of the nature of scientific reports as arguments in the first two stases comes from another article in a quite different field in the same May 1986 issue: "New Data on Northern Yukon Artifacts: Holocene Not Upper Pleistocene" (Nelson, Morlan, Vogel, Southon, & Harrington, 1986). Here obviously the issue engaged is definition or classification: Given our agreed-upon scheme of labeling prehistoric periods, which time slot does a particular artifact belong in? At the center of the controversy is one caribou tibia carved into a fleshing tool. The original carbon dating of this carved bone, based on inorganic carbon, indicated that it was 27,000 years old (Pleistocene). The recent dating reported in this issue, however, was based on the organic carbon in the tibia: the result, 1,200 to 1,500 years old (Holocene), or, not so old, not so remarkable at all. The association of the carved bone with the bones of extinct Pleistocene mammals had rendered the older date highly plausible, but this association at the site was fortuitous. So the 1986 *Science* article, coming thirteen years after the first, contradicts the classification argued for in the first. In the process, it weakens a superstructure of causal inferences based on the earlier dating about when prehistoric humans first appeared in the New World. The firmest evidence for human migration to the New World belongs to a date 11,500 years ago (Clovis); the caribou tibia was part of a small amount of evidence of earlier sites elsewhere, but it is now unmasked as a recent artifact. The two articles separated by twelve years constitute charge and countercharge in the first stasis.

Answers to questions about how something works are also represented in this issue of *Science:* "The Mechanism of Binding of a Polynucleotide Chain to Pancreatic Ribonuclease" (McPherson, Brayer,

Cascio, & Williams, 1986) and "Inorganic and Organic Sulfur Cycling in Salt-Marsh Pore Waters" (Luther, Church, Scudlark, & Cosman, 1986). Both of these articles describe processes and are therefore in the stasis of fact or definition. Cause is also represented in an article that isolates an active factor in a process: "Activation of Mouse T-Helper Cells Induces Preproenkephalen mRNA Synthesis" (Zurawski et al., 1986).

It would, however, be extremely naive to assume that the two higher stases, value and action, have no role in the formation of arguments in the lower stases. Now we can see the implications provided by a full stasis model. So far we seem to have left one critical question unanswered in our pursuit of a connection between the stases and rhetorical context: Why are arguments being addressed in these stases at all? Why is someone bothering to identify and characterize one particular protein out of the millions in nature, and why would someone redo the carbon dating on a carved caribou bone? We could simply assume that the mountain climber's answer will do: Because it is there. We cannot dismiss that answer, because "thereness" always does supply curious humans with exigence. A corollary exigence is "newness," and any undiscovered species of bee or fungi deserves its moment of notice. But "thereness" and "newness" may not be discriminating enough. What we are really after is what it takes to convince an audience to endow the stasis and hence the topic of an argument with significance. In a sense all arguers must justify the stasis they have chosen to argue in. Every topic or issue must have "won" an argument over value before it can be addressed at all. Such a preliminary value argument may not be addressed explicitly in the text of an actual argument, but it is a necessary part of the fit of argument to audience. If asked why he or she addressed a particular issue, the scientist is likely to answer, "Because it is interesting," framing this notion of "interest" as an awareness of where the cutting edge of a field is at the moment, what the exciting questions are. But this awareness of where the field is, is really an awareness of where the audience is (Fisher, 1981, p. 120; Gronbeck, 1981, pp. 1–20).

Back to the article on the caribou bone tool for illustration. The authors explicitly justify reopening an argument in the stasis of fact or definition: "Although many sites and study areas have been presented as providing evidence for pre-Clovis human occupation in both North and South America, the validity of this evidence is not accepted by all investigators" (Nelson et al., 1986, p. 749). In Kuhn's and Popper's terms, the first way to deal with anomalous evidence in a field is to refute it. Refutation had been attempted on the original Pleistocene dating. "Various arguments have also been advanced against these interpretations. It was suggested that the flesher could have been made recently on a bone that had already been fossilized, or that had been preserved by freezing" (Nelson et al., 1986, p. 749). The refutation undertaken in this *Science* article, the authors explain, is based on doubts about the original carbon dating. All of this prolegomenon amounts to a preliminary argument for the value or significance of the authors' undertaking. It is the first and a necessary move in the game.

Not all of the articles justify so explicitly the value of arguing a topic in a certain stasis. When such an explicit justification is absent, however, a very obvious one, based on audience addressed, can be inferred. Let's take as examples the articles "Amplification and Expression of Genes Associated with Multidrug Resistance in Mammalian Cells" (Scotto, Biedler, & Melera, 1986) and "Activation of the AIDS Retrovirus Promoter by the Cellular Transcription Factor" (Jones, Kadonaga, Luciw, & Tjian, 1986). Neither of these articles begins with a justification of establishing facts about the AIDS virus or drug resistance by discussing how lethal drug resistance or AIDS can be. Such evaluations are already firmly fixed in the intended audience. A popularization of either of these highly technical articles might begin with a rehearsal of the number of deaths traceable to either medical syndrome to remind a general audience that they would share the same evaluation.

To sum up, all arguments involve a prior value argument that establishes the significance of addressing an argument in a particular stasis to a particular audience. If no vestige of such a preliminary argument appears in the actual text, it is because the arguer has judged the audience already aware of the value of addressing a subject in a particular stasis. The brief mention of significance in the opening of an argument may serve simply as a reminder to the audience of the attention-worthiness of the subject, a way to endow the issue with "presence." Articles in the specimen issue of *Science* that were not in the dominating disciplines of molecular biology and medical biochemistry opened with a brief claim to significance betraying some uneasiness with the audience's acceptance of the value of the inquiry. For example, the article titled "Inorganic and Organic Sulfur Cycling in Salt-Marsh Pore Waters" begins, "The biogeochemical roles of sulfur in tidal wetlands is an area of intense research" (Luther et al., 1986, p. 746); an article titled "Geographic Origin of Benthic Foraminiferal Species" opens with the claim, "The centers of origin of species have been discussed in the literature of biogeography and evolution for over a century" (Buzas & Culver, 1986, p. 775). Both openings exploit the same appeal: This issue has value because many people have studied it. More to the point, the writers of both felt it necessary to justify their first stasis arguments explicitly.

The most difficult situation of all faces the arguer whose audience does not already recognize the value of opening an argument in a particular stasis. Then the job of creating the audience becomes especially challenging. A full preliminary argument is required in which certain discipline-specific lines of reasoning will appear, linking the subject under scrutiny to certain consequences or ethical principles already recognized by the intended audience as having value. Any arguer who cannot find a point of connection between his or her argument and the audience's interests may be left to various vain repetitions of the claim, "This is really interesting."

The Stases in Literary Criticism

To continue the analysis of arguments in a disciplinary field, we can turn to arguments in literary criticism. More specifically, we would like to look at the articles in a 1986 issue of *PMLA* (101/1, January 1986), a journal that, like *Science,* is directed broadly at people in its field rather than at specialists in one period or genre. Like *Science, PMLA* both assumes and creates an audience that shares certain values — one that has, for instance, read pretty much the same texts and recognizes what texts, authors, and approaches are worth talking about. The titles and topics of the articles will surprise no one familiar with literary studies: "From Allegory to Dialectic: Imagining Error in Spenser and Milton"; "The Genre and Place of the Intimations Ode"; "The Politics of Emerson's Man-Making Words"; "Of This Time, of *This* Place: Mrs. Alving's Ghosts and the Shape of Tragedy"; "'The Knowledge of the Line': Realism and the City in Howells's *A Hazard of New Fortunes.*" If, as Perelman and Olbrechts-Tyteca (1969, pp. 65–95) have pointed out, all argument begins in agreement, in shared assumptions of value, the literary canon offers such a value and even a general exigence for continuing argument: To come forward with something new to say about Spenser or Milton or Wordsworth or Emerson or Ibsen or Howells is to claim attention from a broadly literate professional audience. Even a Pope specialist belongs to a disciplinary community that is expected to comprehend a talk or read an article on many other figures. (Of course, merely to make such a claim is not to guarantee publication in *PMLA;* the claim must be made good in the judgment of *PMLA*'s reviewers and the argument must meet certain qualitative requirements.)

As in the *Science* articles, the arguments in the *PMLA* articles tend to be carried on at the stases of fact, definition, and cause. Although no direct policy recommendations are made, questions of value are much more noticeable than they are in the *Science* articles. The essays do not address questions about the value of treating their subjects, but they do debate the value of individual works, of the literary devices they use, and of the author's standing relative to others. Our discussion will focus on the first three articles, assuming that they are, in spite of their different approaches, fairly representative of *PMLA* essays and of contemporary literary criticism. In the order discussed, the essays are increasingly explicit about their value claims.

Gordon Teskey's article on Spenser and Milton is quite clearly a definition argument, as its title indicates, characterizing and comparing treatments of error by the two poets: "While Spenser associates error with the meanderings of narrative, Milton polarizes error and truth so that no ambiguous wandering can occur in the intervening space" (p. 6, abstract). Given the illustriousness of the two poets, the author does not overtly use the comparison as an instrument for establishing value, as he might if he were talking about Milton and an obviously minor poet whom he was attempting to elevate to canonical status. Rather, each poet's notion of error is used to illuminate unique aspects of the other's approach. Nevertheless, Teskey's language conveys strong indications of value that his readers will pick up as an essential though indirect part of his argument. When, for instance, Teskey writes that "Milton sought to teach by direct statement, Spenser to form character by engaging the reader in an interpretive game" (p. 6, abstract), clearly the second alternative is to be more highly valued by *PMLA* readers than the first. As literary critics, we would prefer to be engaged in an interpretive game where there are ambiguities rather than taught directly. Similarly, the last line of the article contrasts Milton, who is described as grasping the past by re-creating it, with Spenser, a "noursling of Dame *Memorie,*" who "has discovered the truth in a book" (p. 20). Again, an audience of literary critics is one that would naturally privilege the discovery of truth in a book.

Significantly, it is only in a footnote that Teskey tips his hand and announces that the usual consensus of value that there is "a tradition of apocalyptic epic in which Spenser fails and Milton succeeds is clearly one-sided" (p. 20). Thus the issue in the article is ostensibly engaged at the stasis of definition (the term at stake is *error*) using factual evidence from *The Faerie Queene* and *Paradise Lost.* But awareness of the assumptions about interpretation that the audience brings to the reading of the essay will uncover its implications at the stasis of value. The essay is actually a third stasis defense and canonical elevation of Spenser. Its exigence is an appeal to our interest in the further exploration of a familiar question: "In what sense was Spenser Milton's original?" Then Teskey tactfully reverses his readers' usual assumption of historical progression, by which we assume that Milton perfected a form or genre more primitively employed by Spenser. Instead, he offers his readers a vocabulary and a way of talking about Spenser that elevates the poet's canonical standing. One would not think that so canonical an author as Spenser would need any defense at all, but such questions of relative and specific value within the canon remain live issues. Even such a brief analysis suggests how awareness of audience and context thickens our understanding of the function of such a definition argument; conversely, awareness of the stases and the relation between them enriches our understanding of how audience and disciplinary field are addressed.

The second essay in *PMLA* is also an evaluation argument, more directly so than the first. Beginning with the fact that in editions of his poetry, Wordsworth always placed the Intimations Ode last and with the reported consensus that "for many readers the closure [of the poem] is forced and the final statement not very clear," (p. 24), Joseph Sitterson (1986) goes on to explore the implications these pieces of shared knowledge have for readers of Wordsworth. We may agree on the facts about the Intimations Ode that he brings to our attention; their significance is the subject of the essay, which he conducts by addressing a series of increasingly precise definitional questions: What is an ode? What did "ode" mean in Wordsworth's time? What did it mean to Wordsworth? The essay's title, "The Genre and Place of the Intimations Ode," suggests that its subject will be the definition of the Ode. But, again, even such an apparently straightforward issue is freighted with value. The "place" of the Intimations Ode at the end of collections of Wordsworth's poems is not a neutral fact; it is also a sign of Wordsworth's sense of the poem's importance (and presumably of his readers' acquiescence in that evaluation). Nor are we encouraged to assume that Wordsworth would use the term *ode* loosely and neutrally to refer to any long poem on an elevated subject. As Sitterson (1986, p. 25) says, "We may suspect that, however imprecise the terminology of second-rate poets, Wordsworth did not use the word *ode* carelessly." So even the poet's attribution of genre reflects assumptions of value.

The issue of value is addressed more directly in this essay than it is in the first, perhaps because the thesis is less controversial. Readers of *PMLA* may be more likely to accept the thesis that the Intimations Ode is unflawed than that Spenser is in any way to be preferred over Milton. Sitterson argues that understanding the genre and place of the Intimations Ode "helps us understand that its uneasy coexistence of statement and uncertainty" (what he elsewhere calls its deliberate suggestions and refusal of closure), "which many critics consider its greatest weakness is actually its greatest strength" (p. 6, abstract). Thus, although the argument is conducted by appeals to facts and definitions, its purpose, this time clearly stated, is to establish value. Sitterson wants readers to agree that the Intimations Ode is not weakened by its apparent lack of closure, and to conclude that Wordsworth "*deliberately* suggests and then refuses such closure" (p. 24; emphasis added). At this point we might again wonder what defense the Intimations Ode needs; indeed, it would be hard to name a more canonical poem of the nineteenth century or one more highly valued by Wordsworth scholars, nineteenth-century scholars, or readers of English poetry. Why should readers of *PMLA* need to be convinced that the Intimations Ode is a great poem? That's not news in the way that an accurate date for a piece of carved caribou bone is news.

To answer that question, it might be most helpful to think of essays such as this one and the Spenser-Milton essay less as arguing values into place than as celebrating and reinforcing the values already shared by their readers. They appeal to facts and definitions in order to confirm the previously held values of their readers and to shore them up at vulnerable points. Although readers of *PMLA* have no doubt about the canonical status of Spenser, Milton, or Wordsworth, questions of *relative* value are never dead. We can reaffirm our belief in shared values by reconsidering what we mean when we say that Spenser was Milton's original and by facing the implication that the Intimations Ode may be flawed by its incomplete closure. As we have said elsewhere, the arguments of literary criticism are fundamentally epideictic, celebrating the shared values of a community (Fahnestock & Secor, 1982). They do not usually move directly into the fourth stasis, that of procedure or policy; no recommendations or legislations follow at the conclusion of either Teskey's or Sitterson's arguments. Of course, that is not to say that none is implied: Canonical status denied or affirmed does eventually affect the classroom and the publication policies of journals such as *PMLA;* critical approaches are either acceptable or not, and, on a more practical level, careers are made (or unmade) by publication. But such political and institutional implications are not usually articulated in literary arguments. Like the scientific articles, they assume an audience that recognizes what questions are interesting and why.

The third article in this issue of *PMLA* differs from the first two. Its declared purpose is not to enhance the canonical status of an author or a work, but to destabilize a canonical figure — in this case Emerson. Its very title, "The Politics of Emerson's Man-Making Words," announces its political subject matter, and the article itself makes many direct references to a world outside of the texts under discussion, both to the political and social context of Emerson's time and to the politics of contemporary academia. Instead of celebrating or reaffirming Emerson's claim to the highest status, this article attacks it directly. The author, David Leverenz (1986), calls the self-transformations Emerson achieves through language "bizarre and sexist," and he judges negatively his "ideal of self-empowering" because it "reduces womanhood to spiritual nurturance while erasing female subjectivity" (pp. 39–40).

In this essay the thesis is frankly presented at the stasis of value: "Emerson's prose speaks to American expectations for becoming a man," but "To emphasize Emerson's class and gender politics deflates his reputation somewhat" (p. 6, abstract). Leverenz examines Emerson's writing and his life for evidence of his gender politics; he engages in some causal arguments accounting for the development of Emerson's attitudes; and he defines those attitudes as having political significance in Emerson's own time and, by implication, for us. The insistence that Emerson's language refers to a biographical, social, and political context is mirrored in Leverenz's own language, which makes reference to contexts familiar to today's readers.

But in spite of his highly critical, even subversive, thesis, Leverenz does not reject the methodology of literary criticism. Though his facts and definitions are adduced to serve an evaluative thesis, more negative than either of the other two articles, Leverenz does not abandon the preferred locus of literary criticism, which is to place the highest value on paradox and ambiguity, on that which cannot be resolved over that which is easily definable. Thus his essay ends not with the announcement of the level to which he wishes to reduce Emerson's stock but with the author's confession of paradox in his own attitude: "At times when I think I have cut through Emerson's fog or self, it is hard to disengage from his disengagements without wanting to dismiss him entirely. In other moods, the free play of his unselfconscious self-consciousness can seem endlessly absorbing" (p. 53). Which is it to be? Readers familiar with literary criticism know the answer the author chooses, not either of his responses to Emerson or neither but both: "not to take a stand within that paradoxical either-or but to see how his language resonates with the unresolved tensions of his life and time" (p. 53). Readers finally are not forced to choose between Spenser and Milton, or forced to decide whether the Intimations Ode is or ought to be more closed, or even whether to be intoxicated or exasperated by Emerson's language. The arguments of literary criticism seem to be notable for having it both ways. We can pose problems about literary works, uncover historical and biographical facts, sift evidence in the light of definitions, celebrate or question certain values. In doing so we come not to clear answers but to delight in the complexity of the process.

Discussion

What can we learn from this brief analysis of scientific and literary arguments according to their stasis? First, it is clear that arguments within a discipline usually assume the value of addressing certain subjects in certain stases. That is what it means to write within a discipline. Arguments in literary criticism do not spend time convincing readers that the works of Spenser, Milton, Wordsworth, and Emerson are worth reexamining. On the other hand, any argument that tried to make claims about an unrecognized author would have to justify itself. Similarly, arguments in science usually bypass explicit justification of the stasis and content of their approach. But in either science or literary studies, anyone who addresses a discipline in ways it does not recognize in effect tries to change that discipline or splinters off into a new one. Feminist criticism, for example, has challenged some basic assumptions of traditional literary studies, and it remains to be seen how institutions respond to the challenge.

Once we get beyond these initial arguments or assumptions about the value of the stasis of an inquiry, differences between arguments in science and arguments in literary criticism become apparent. As we pointed out above, arguments in science are quite clearly conducted in the lower stases. Researchers convince their readers that plants can be "genetically engineered to suppress symptoms due to viral infection" (Abel et al., 1986, p. 739), or that "salt marshes appear to be unique among marine systems in producing high concentrations of thiols" (Luther et al., 1986, p. 746). Arguments in literary studies are more problematic. If they are analyzed on the basis of what takes up the most space, arguments in literary studies (at least as they appear in *PMLA*) are also ostensibly arguments in the first stases. They support or dispute characterizations (i.e., interpretations of texts); they argue about what an "ode" is or what "error" was to a sixteenth-century poet.

But these preoccupations serve evaluative purposes that seem devoid of true exigence; that is, the stasis of these arguments seems without a compelling justification given the already-determined value of talking about a Spenser or Wordsworth or Emerson. Of course, questions may remain about the relative value of individual canonical writers or the relative merits of the individual canonical writers or the relative merits of their individual creations.

An even more striking difference between the two disciplines emerges when we ask what the implications of these arguments are in terms of the full stases. What happens when we ask what impact they are going to have on their disciplinary audiences? One can easily predict that the science articles will lead to specific proposals and altered actions (though perhaps not by the scientists who wrote the articles). The article on salt marshes, for example, primarily concerned with the techniques of a particular set of experiments, concludes that the process it has uncovered could have "profound consequences for the cycling of energy and material in wetlands" (Luther et al., 1986, p. 748). It would be hard to imagine a similar consequence for future action following a reevaluation of the Intimations Ode. It was read and admired before and it will be read and admired again; in fact, the function of the article may be simply to ensure that the Intimations Ode will continue to be read and admired. And Emerson will not be removed from the American literary canon, though critics may become aware of previously ignored complexities in his tone.

There is something more than a little artificial in the literary arguments that reopen such questions of relative value for authors who have long been so highly valued, and that have no implications for altered future action. But surely there is value in reminding an audience of its values. Literary articles may be in a sense artifactual, apparently conducted as knowledge-advancing arguments but concerned essentially with finding fresh ways to celebrate their subjects. Still, no rhetorician would deny that epideictic discourse serves an institutionally valuable function.

An analysis of the stasis of arguments in disciplinary contexts such as we have conducted above can reveal dimensions of the fit between argument and audience usually overlooked. Arguments such as those in science, which seem to concern nothing but getting arcane facts straight and which contain little more than elaborate backing for a warrant of verification, can be seen as having implications of value and action for their intended readers. Arguments in literary criticism can be seen as value arguments reinforcing and refining already-held values and thus solidifying their audience. An examination of the stasis of an argument and how that stasis is justified in a particular context is thus an important part of the rhetorical analysis of any argument.

Note

1. The works of Hermagoras have been lost, but twentieth-century historians of rhetoric have reconstructed the doctrine of the stases and explicated its uses. Otto Dieter (1950) discussed the philosophical origins of the term *stasis*, and Ray Nadeau (1964) translated a second-century A.D. manuscript on the stases by Hermogenes, adding an excellent historical introduction. Aristotle does not refer to the stases in any obvious way, but Wayne N. Thompson (1972) argues that he was indeed aware of the hierarchy.

References

Abel, P. P., Nelson, R. S., De, B., Hoffman, N., Rogers, S. G., Fraley, R. T., & Beachy, R. N. (1986). Delay of disease development in transgenic plants that express the tobacco mosaic virus coat protein gene. *Science, 232,* 738–743.

Buzas, M. A., & Culver, S. J. (1986). Geographic origin of benthic foraminiferal species. *Science, 232,* 775–777.

Cicero. (1949). *De inventione; de optimo genere oratorum; topica* (H. M. Hubbell, English trans.). Cambridge, MA: Cambridge University Press.

Dieter, O. (1950). Stasis. *Speech Monographs, 17,* 345–369.

Fahnestock, J. (1986). Accommodating science: The rhetorical life of scientific facts. *Written Communication, 3,* 275–296.

Fahnestock, J., & Secor, M. (1982, July). *The rhetoric of literary criticism.* Paper presented at the Penn State Conference on Rhetoric and Composition.

Fahnestock, J., & Secor, M. (1983). Grounds for argument: Stasis theory and the topoi. In D. Zarefsky, M. O. Sillars, & J. Rhodes (Eds.), *Argument in transition* (pp. 135–146). Annandale, VA: Speech Communication Association.

Fahnestock, J., & Secor, M. (1985). Toward a modern version of stasis theory. In C. Knuepper (Ed.), *Oldspeak / newspeak: Rhetorical transformations* (pp. 217–226). Arlington, TX: NCTE.

Fisher, W. R. (1981). Good reasons: Fields and genre. In G. Ziegelmueller and J. Rhodes (Eds.), *Dimensions of argument* (pp. 114–125). Annandale, VA: Speech Communication Association.

Gronbeck, B. E. (1981). Sociocultural notions of argument fields: A primer. In G. Ziegelmueller and J. Rhodes (Eds.), *Dimensions of argument* (pp. 1–20). Annandale, VA: Speech Communication Association.

Jones, K. A., Kadonaga, J. T., Luciw, P. A., & Tjian, R. (1986). Activation of the AIDS retrovirus promoter by the cellular transcription factor, spl. *Science, 232,* 755–759.

Leverenz, D. (1986). The politics of Emerson's man-making words. *PMLA, 101,* 38–56.

Luther, G. W., III, Church, T. M., Scudlark, J. R., & Cosman, M. (1986). Inorganic and organic sulfur cycling in salt-marsh pore waters. *Science, 232,* 746–749.

McPherson, A., Brayer, G., Cascio, D., & Williams, R. (1986). The mechanism of binding of a polynucleotide chaining to pancreatic ribonuclease. *Science, 232,* 765–768.

Nadeau, R. (1964). Hermogenes' *On Stases:* A translation with an introduction and notes. *Speech Monographs, 31,* 361–424.

Nelson, D. E., Morlan, R. E., Vogel, J. S., Southon, J. R., & Harrington, C. R. (1986). New dates on northern Yukon artifacts: Holocene not Upper Pleistocene. *Science, 232,* 749–751.

Perelman, C., and Olbrechts-Tyteca, L. (1969). *The new rhetoric: A treatise on argumentation.* Notre Dame, IN: University of Notre Dame Press.

Quintilian. (1920). *Institution oratoria* (Vol. 1) (H. E. Butler, trans.). Cambridge, MA: Harvard University Press.

Scotto, K. W., Biedler, J. L., & Melera, P. W. (1986). Amplification and expression of genes associated with multidrug resistance in mammalian cells. *Science, 232,* 751–755.

Sitterson, J. C., Jr. (1986). The genre and place of the Intimations Ode. *PMLA, 101,* 24–37.

Slamon, D. J., Boone, T. C., Seeger, R. C., Keith, D. E., Chazin, V., Lee, H. C., & Souza, L. M. (1986). Identification and characterization of the protein encoded by the human N-*myc* oncongene. *Science, 232,* 768–772.

Teskey, G. (1986). From allegory to dialectic: Imagining error in Spenser and Milton. *PMLA, 101,* 9–23.

Thompson, W. (1972). *Stasis in Aristotle's* Rhetoric. *Quarterly Journal of Speech, 58,* 134–141.

Toulmin, S. E. (1958). *The uses of argument.* Cambridge: Cambridge University Press.

Zurawski, G., Benedik, M., Kamb, B. J., Abrams, J. S., Zurawski, S. M., & Lee, F. D. (1986). Activation of mouse T-helper cells induces abundant preproenkephalin mRNA synthesis. *Science, 232,* 772–775.

From Formalism to Inquiry: A Model of Argument in *Antigone*

James Kastely

While argument theorists tend to focus on the theoretical and philosophical texts of the classical period, such as Aristotle's Rhetoric, James Kastely *argues that Greek tragedies are also rich sources for understanding the nature of argument. First published in* College English *in 1999, this essay considers* Antigone *as a model for understanding argument — not as a formal exercise of finding evidence to support a claim, but as a mode of inquiry that poses complex problems to democratic cultures.*

Tragedies such as Antigone, *Kastely argues, are especially useful for exploring the relationship between argument and contemporary issues of identity and difference. Tragedies can help redefine argument as a tool for understanding ourselves and our relations to others (rather than as a tool of domination), and this definition creates new political possibilities for individual students and teachers and their communities. Further, focusing on argument as political discourse illustrates the relevance of argument to students often numbed by the prospect of defending yet another position they do not believe in (or, conversely, that they believe in so absolutely that they cannot question) to a generic audience from whom they expect nothing.*

For another essay that considers the relationship between identity and argument, see James S. Baumlin's "Persuasion, Rogerian Rhetoric, and Imaginative Play" (p. 111) in the section on Rogerian Argument (p. 97).

Following Stephen Toulmin, many contemporary writing courses conceive of argument as a form of discourse used to justify a conclusion. To teach argument is to teach a form of practical reasoning or, at least, a form that represents the results of practical reasoning. One locates and examines claims, assesses support, and ultimately passes judgment on the worth of this support. The result is a justified claim that makes a legitimate demand on any reasonable member of a particular audience. It follows naturally from this understanding that teaching argument should focus primarily on learning the proper forms of support and the skills necessary to evaluate the force and relevance of particular support. The value of this approach is that it enables students to understand the relation of support to a conclusion, and such an understanding should then aid students as they produce well-formed arguments in which conclusions are appropriately supported.

The limitations of this approach to teaching argument are equally a consequence of its focus on the forms of inference. A formalist approach does not invite students to ask why one argues, so a concern about argument as a political or philosophical problem is precluded. Although the standard course in argument obviously recognizes political questions as legitimate concerns for student arguments, the larger question, spawned by the critical skepticism of theory, whether argument is possible is not asked. But given the current theatricalization of disagreement in such popular media as talk radio and in the dichotomized exchanges of political pundits and journalists as well as the blatant manipulation of discourse by various politicians and corporations, it is all too easy for students to see arguments as simply cynical exercises that never really intend to persuade another but that operate only as guises from which to attack opponents and defend positions that are not seriously open to question. By downplaying the aggression and pretense endemic in much contemporary political discussion, the concentration on form inadvertently aids a political depoliticalizing of a classroom. Because students are smart enough to understand that argument outside the classroom adheres to a different set of rules, a focus on form that does not address the aggression under the formal surface of an argument can become an empty formalism. When that happens, student arguments tend to become mere exercises in the construction of appropriate forms, and the serious engagement with alternative positions is limited to figuring out responses to counter gaps in one's support. Alternative positions never emerge in their difference as making serious demands that the arguer rethink his or her understanding; rather, these alternatives are seen only as raising points that need to be met in some way. The dismal consequence is that student arguments become rehearsals of unreflectively held positions or repetitions of unexamined banalities.

A second and more serious problem with a formalist approach to teaching argument is that it is unhelpful in investigating how race, gender, class, and age differences can be perceived as threats by those in power and how those who speak or write from a position of difference can be either ignored or rendered silent. Feminist writing teachers such as Susan Jarratt have argued for the importance of confronting difference in the classroom and of moving from a combative to a generative conception of argument (113, 117). Her formulation of an argument course, directed at an expressivist approach to writing, seeks to recontextualize individuality within a social frame. She fears that a too narrow focus on the individual leads to a misunderstanding of the ways that any identity is a social construction. But the danger posed by formalism is slightly different. Rather than valorizing the individual, a formalist approach assumes that reason as a universal form possesses the authority to negotiate the differences that arise within a collection of heterogeneous individuals or groups. When arguments threaten received understandings, this transpersonal or transcultural reason can be an important strategic device to rule out, on formalist grounds, issues raised by difference. But it is precisely such issues that are at the heart of democratic discourse, for such discourse should be an ongoing and creative invention of civic identity. If a democracy's vitality depends upon its citizens' abilities to engage deep and possibly irreconcilable disagreements, the teaching of argument must theorize both difference and resistance to difference. The theorizing of argument as a site of resistance to difference opens up the possibility of conceiving argument as a particular type of inquiry in which disagreement becomes a resource for exploring both personal and political identity.

If one takes the failure of and resistance to argument as starting points, it is possible to reframe a course in which argument itself is seen as problematic and hence in need of philosophical and political interrogation. The historical precedent for such a course is to be found in the Greek tragedies of the fifth century B.C.E. Jean-Pierre Vernant and Pierre Vidal-Naquet claim that tragedy was not simply an art form but also a social institution (9). Its civic function was not to provide ideological support for democracy but to offer its audiences an opportunity to critically engage the ideology embraced by democracy. By making the city's self-understanding a problem, tragedy presented the polis with an opportunity to reflect on itself (Goldhill 78; Vernant and Vidal-Naquet 9). Rhetoric was of particular interest to tragedy, for the holding and exercise of power in fifth century B.C.E. Athens had shifted from its basis in the aristocratic privilege of birth to the more democratic grounding in the ability to speak well. As civic poetry, tragedy interrogated this newly arising rhetoric and asked whether it did or could play a role in helping the city invent itself as a democracy.

What the Greek tragedians and audiences had discovered was the capacity for poetry to engage in a theoretical questioning of the possibility of civic discourse. This type of theoretical inquiry is by no means limited to Greek tragedy. Rather, as Deborah Britzman has argued in another context, both canonical and noncanonical texts which address the anxieties suppressed by dominant ideologies can serve a liberatory role by calling into question narratives offered in support of those ideologies (54–61). Such questioning challenges accepted understandings and reconceives the problems of a community as opportunities to take responsibility for that community and to make it more just. Writing courses that use literary works as instances of theory would seek to transform the teaching of argument from the always threatening evasiveness of an empty formalism into the active posing of argument as a problem.

I have chosen *Antigone* as a representative text for this approach because it challenges the very possibility of argument. Sophocles set the play in a situation in which discourse is essential if Thebes is to move from divisive conflicts to forge a new identity. This is a paradigmatic moment for a democracy because the capacity of a polis to discover or invent an identity through discourse is at issue. What makes *Antigone* a productive theoretical text is that it explores the failure of civic discourse. However much the characters congratulate themselves on their rationality or their piety, argument threatens them, for argument begins from and returns to the problem of an unassimilated diversity. The difficulties that argument encounters are not technical slips nor accidental obstructions but inhere in the very nature of argument.

Antigone begins in the aftermath of a civic cataclysm. Following a bitter and intense civil war that ended fittingly enough with the mutual fratricide of Polyneices and Eteocles, Creon assumes control of a shaken Thebes and seeks to reestablish civil order. Proclaiming a rule committed to fair and appropriate treatment of citizens, he appears to encourage a public discourse through which civic policy could be formulated. In his first speech, he announces:

> It is impossible to know any man —
> I mean his soul, intelligence, and judgment —
> until he shows his skill in rule and law.
> I think that a man supreme ruler of a whole city,
> if he does not reach for the best counsel for her,
> but through some fear, keeps his tongue under lock and key,
> him I judge the worst of any. . . . (193–99)

These seem to be the words of an enlightened leader who recognizes the importance of an open discourse in the conduct of political affairs. Events, however, quickly demonstrate otherwise, as Creon proves unwilling to hear or incapable of hearing any view that differs from his own. Part of what allows Creon to continue his contradiction of espousing public discourse while suppressing dissent is a convenient self-obfuscation in which he rejects as foolish any opinion that differs from his. After all, a commitment to public discussion is a commitment to rational speech and does not require one to entertain seriously the opinions of fools.

His son, Haemon, later characterizes Creon's delusion as an emptiness. In putting himself beyond the words of others, Creon has, in effect, destroyed the possibility of having a political or any kind of identity. His ever increasing isolation and his celebration of the strength of his resolve hide from him his fundamental fear of difference, which is propelling him on a course of personal and civic destruction. More than anything, Creon fears and resists argument, for argument entails a surrender of his personal authority and control.

Creon, of course, is not alone in his resistance to argument. Antigone, for other reasons, is equally unyielding. The fear of and resistance to argument by *Antigone*'s protagonists invite us to ask why we argue. The absence of argument makes argument a problem. *Antigone* is a play dominated by passionate and articulate verbal conflicts that never form into arguments, and its protagonists' intransigence demonstrates the impotence of argument, if the power of argument resides in force of reason. In *Antigone* argument seems a precarious enterprise in which even talented and concerned speakers such as Haemon are doomed to be ineffective. The intensity of the protagonists' resistance to argument raises a question about the viability of argument as a way of addressing serious disagreement. Behind the failure of argument is the problem of seeing difference as a threat that makes recognizing the other impossible to individuals who seek to protect the superficial coherence of their existing understanding.

This understanding of argument as a theoretical question is what puts *Antigone* at odds with the view that prevails in most contemporary writing courses. If the standard contemporary understanding of argument sees it principally as a practice of justification (Perelman 291–92; Zarefsky 53), *Antigone* suggests that developing logically adequate forms of justification may miss the crucial difficulties faced by argument. Prior to questions of justification are questions of the way that a serious exchange of understandings poses a threat to those who would argue. Thus *Antigone* challenges the possibility of argument that is so unproblematically assumed by much of contemporary pedagogy.

Histories of argument identify 1958 as an important year. In that year, two books were published that significantly changed the ways in which contemporary scholars thought about argument and eventually transformed the ways in which teachers organized courses in argument. One of these texts was Chaim Perelman and Lucie Olbrechts-Tyteca's *The New Rhetoric: A Treatise on Argumentation;* the other was Stephen Toulmin's *The Uses of Argument* (Johnstone, "Theory of Argumentation" 177). Both books challenged the appropriateness of formal logic as a model for the valid operation of reasoning in argument, and both sought ways of thinking about argument that addressed more adequately the actual practices of people when they offered reasons in support of various claims and conclusions. While the Perelman and Olbrechts-Tyteca text provided a more detailed and systematic discussion of an alternative approach to argument, it was Toulmin's *The Uses of Argument* that had the more serious impact on reforming the ways in which argument was thought about and taught at American universities (Conley 295; Fulkerson 45–46; van Eemeren 160). Part of the reason for Toulmin's influence was that he did not offer an elaborate set of distinctions; instead, he provided a straightforward and understandable account of how warranted data, when appropriately qualified, supported claims. The economy of his analysis lent itself to teaching. Teachers could move away from rehearsing lists of fallacies that seemed to have little or no benefit for students, and they were no longer restricted to teaching induction and deduction as if these modes of inference represented exclusively the forms of reasoning. Further, they were freed from the embarrassing fact that the application of induction and deduction to practical reasoning was often unclear or forced. In place of an unreflective use of formal logic as the paradigm for argument, Toulmin offered a simple and flexible account of practical reasoning. The pedagogical gain was clear, and it was complemented by a theoretical gain, as a curriculum that had originated at American universities for primarily nonacademic reasons and that had been pursued, for the most part, as a nonreflective practice (van Eemeren 193; Zarefsky 43) now, with the discovery or rediscovery of a distinct set of practices that constituted practical reasoning, became an appropriate subject for theoretical investigation.

But despite revolutionizing the ways in which argument as a strategic justification of belief could be understood and taught, Toulmin's *The Uses of Argument* did not raise the deeper question of the purpose of argument. Toulmin's focus was on assessing the support offered on behalf of claims:

> [W]e shall be interested in justificatory arguments brought forward in support of assertions, in the structures they may be expected to have, the merits they can claim and the ways in which we set about grading, assessing and criticizing them. It could, I think, be argued that this was in fact the *primary* function of arguments, and that the other uses, the other functions which arguments have for us, are in a sense secondary, and parasitic upon the primary justificatory use. (12)

The paradigmatic example of argument for Toulmin was the defense offered to support a challenged claim (11). Argument was defensive; it used warranted evidence strategically. Toulmin's concern was to develop an account of argument that would permit a better method of evaluation, one that would be able to specify "what features a logically candid layout of arguments will need to have" (95). His movement from a concern with form to a concern with formality was his attempt to articulate a method of evaluation more in line with the ways that arguments were actually deployed. This new account of argument would allow one to be candid about the structure of support. But in his reformulation of argument, he adopted uncritically the assumption that one argued because the other party either was ignorant of the truth or lacked some information relevant for understanding the force of the present claim. Such an assumption did not credit the misgivings of those who see the appeal to rationality as a guise for the operation of a will to domination, nor did it speak to the equally common feeling that argumentative rationality can be a not too subtle form of aggression. Rather, the issue for argument remained formal; it was simply that a more adequate account of the actual forms of practical reasoning was needed.

Part of the reason that Toulmin focuses on form is that, for him, argument is not a mode of inquiry but a way of presenting conclusions that have been discovered prior to the argument. More than anything else, Toulmin's examples in his third chapter, "The Layout of Arguments," reveal his commitments to what argument is and to what makes a good argument. His three chief examples of claims to be supported by argument are: (1) "Harry's hair is not black"; (2) "Peterson will not be a Roman Catholic"; and (3) "Wilkinson has committed an offense against the Road Traffic Acts" (97). Focusing more fully on the last of these examples, Toulmin develops his schema for a candid layout of an argument. The layout itself is quite simple. To support a claim, one provides data; to justify the force and appropriateness of data, one supplies warrants; to authorize a warrant, one supplies a context or backing that makes clear the reason for the warrant; to make sure that the claim is not too broad, one provides relevant qualifications; and, finally, to deal with possible objections, one offers apt refutations to these anticipated objections. Each of these moves represents a response to a challenge, and Toulmin analyzes the responses in terms of certain conventions or formalities. If one follows these formalities correctly, he or she will have a well-supported claim. And, most important, this claim will accord with a reality that exists independent of and prior to the argument. The assumption that legitimizes Toulmin's analysis of the structure of arguments is that a good argument lines up with a world that is determinant before the argument. It is this lining up that Toulmin's account allows one to get at. Arguments do not determine reality, but, if done well, they reflect or represent reality.

This assumption governs Toulmin's choice of examples. These examples bring with them key theoretical commitments, the most important being that a good argument is one that best corresponds to a reality that exists outside of, prior to, and independent of a particular dispute. But as soon as one looks seriously at these examples, they seem forced, for they offer types of disagreements that we do not normally turn to argument to settle. Instead, we seek other means to resolve these types of disputes. If we disagree over the color of Harry's hair, doesn't it make a lot more sense simply to go and inspect Harry's hair to see what color it actually is? Put another way, isn't this disagreement over a fact of the physical world best settled by an empirical investigation? If we then need to communicate these results, this communication will be aided if there exists a standard form in which to present evidence to back claims. The concern, then, is about strategies and conventions of presentation and not about particular problems that require a special form of inquiry. The final test of a presentation would be as Toulmin's examples suggest: Does the presentation effectively offer warranted data for an appropriately qualified claim about reality that exists independent of the argument? If Harry's hair is black, that fact becomes central to how we assess the success of the presented claim. To justify our claim, we present what we have discovered and add appropriate support when challenged. With slight variations, the same holds true for his other examples. The probability of Peterson, a Swede, being a Roman Catholic equally is determined prior to the argument. It is a simple matter of calculating the probability, which can be computed by consulting the relevant population statistics. And whether or not Wilkinson was speeding is also an empirical matter: What are the speed limits and what is the physical evidence for how fast he was going? In all three examples, it is possible to discover the particular truth at issue independent of an argument because each of these truths is about an already determinate world. The issue that determines for Toulmin how well an argument succeeds, then, is how well it presents and defends data that are arrived at independent of the argument and that reflect the actual conditions of this world. It is this reformulation of the reasoning structure as a series of challenges to a claim that makes candid the links between presentation and an already determinate world. But are such examples really paradigmatic for argument? Is this particular type of dispute instructive for an inquiry into the kinds of understanding that an argument seeks? Does it provide any way for dealing with the problems of resistance to argument or of the use of argument as a means for dominating or silencing an other?

The questions posed about argument by Sophoclean tragedy treat these questions seriously. Often Sophocles' dramas begin with a world at an impasse. It is not that information is lacking or that a claim is missing an appropriate warrant but that characters find themselves locked into a way of seeing the world that makes them unavailable for argument. The heroism of the protagonists develops out of their intransigence. In this unwillingness to attend to others, Creon and Antigone embody what Bernard Knox labels "the Sophoclean situation of resistance to persuasion and threat" (44). This personal intransigence ineluctably entails devastating political consequences. *Antigone* dramatizes how the preclusion of a genuine exchange over conflicting obligations endangers civic existence. In the disagreement between Creon and Antigone over which obligation should take precedence, political existence in Thebes is put into question. Even though the play eventually resolves the conflict by showing that the burial rights are the more important obligation, what gives it force as a tragedy and as philosophical inquiry into the conditions of persuasion is the failure of Creon and Antigone to sustain an argument, for it is their inability to argue that destroys them and denies the city a chance to reconstitute itself in response to an inherent tension.

Creon and Antigone disagree vehemently, not only with each other but with almost everyone else in the play. The tragedy arises because neither one ever listens to an objection or qualification. Because the protagonists cannot engage either each other or any of the other characters who speak to them, their competing monologues do not permit a discourse that could discover the complexity of the situation or move the protagonists to some sort of public discussion, especially one that recognized the full force of their differences. In their preemptive deafness, both characters foreclose argument and make a genuine political life impossible.

As Martha Nussbaum has commented, it is striking that the two protagonists do not feel tensions that we might expect in a community that has just survived a horrendous civil war (53). There is an eerie certainness about both characters. If the protagonists find themselves entangled in conflicts, they are themselves without conflict. Even more, they are incapable of imagining any honorable motive in a character who would oppose them. Conflicts for them serve only one purpose: to reveal loyalty. Because the rightness of their positions is self-evident to Creon and Antigone, their positions are not open for discussion or for any kind of modification. The only pertinent issues are: Whose side is somebody on and how does one make the larger world conform to a particular set of values? For such characters, the beliefs of others are not interesting, nor do they provide a possible resource to rethink values; rather, disagreement is considered only as an obstacle to action that is to be overcome through the assertion of will. This obsession with the strength of will and the ability to realize the dictates of this will makes the human race *deinos* (magnificent, awesome, awful, terrifying, powerful, clever). It is also what makes these characters inhuman, beyond the reach of others.

To be closed to the words and feelings of others is to place oneself beyond argument, and to be outside argument is to abandon one's humanity. Henry Johnstone, Jr., sees argument as a constitutive element of the human situation:

> Argument is a defining feature of the human situation. A being not capable of arguing or of listening to argument would simply not be human. Such a being would lack a self. Any reflective arguer knows, of course, that all of his arguments can be met by counterarguments. . . . The point of argument is not to provide effective control over others, as might be the case if there were some arguments that could not be met by counterarguments. It is rather to introduce the arguer into a situation of risk in which open-mindedness and tolerance are possible. ("Some Reflections" 7)

Essential to argument is the capacity to admit an other into one's world, to acknowledge a discourse that is other than one's own. The necessary precondition for argument is a serious respect for difference. But this is what Creon and Antigone, for different reasons, do not possess.

Creon's unavailability for argument is initially disguised by his espousal of a rationally ordered city. In abrogating the traditional laws that demand burial for the dead, he proclaims a new law that acknowledges and appropriately rewards the service or injury to the city done by the deceased. From Creon's perspective of a justice that is deter-mined rationally, the older, inherited view needs to be superseded be-cause it treats the loyal and the treacherous as one, and hence is deeply unjust to those who gave their lives in defense of the city (226–29). If such a view seriously misunderstands the fundamental obligation to bury the dead and collapses distinctions between how one treats the living and how one treats the dead, it has a superficial rationality and is not an unreasonable response to pressures that are part of any po-litical existence. If a city treats the loyal and the treacherous the same, its actions argue that loyalty is meaningless. If people view the city as indifferent to their loyalty, anarchy becomes a serious possibility, and the city, which is the protector of all, is imperiled. Creon seeks to counter this possibility by an edict that recognizes service to the city. The rigid-ity of the policy is part of its value, for it makes the world predictable, hence rational — subject to cost/benefit analysis. The price of loyalty or disloyalty is clear.

Creon himself, however, seems to perceive no conflict between pri-vate interests and public good that could endanger the state. As com-mentators have recognized, for Creon there is only political existence. It is impossible for him to imagine the independence of values such as friendship and love from political loyalty. He cannot conceive of there being a genuine conflict in these areas — someone who is disloyal to the city could never be a friend, and someone who does not place the city above all else would prove to be an unsatisfactory sexual partner. Nor can Creon imagine an honorable reason to disobey a law. The one nonpolitical and inherently private motive that he does recognize is greed (240). The problem is that one cannot dialectically engage or ar-gue with someone moved by greed; all that one can do is threaten, all that one can do is operate within the psychology of greed and make the cost of disobedience so onerous that it clearly outweighs any potential benefit from disloyal behavior.

Because Creon has a closed and self-validating narrative of pos-sible political motives, Antigone's devotion to her slain brother and her profoundly felt obligation to bury him are beyond Creon's ability to fathom. The only explanation available to Creon is that Antigone is mad, that she is someone who has a pathological resentment of civil authority or any authority — she is a woman who, if unchecked, would supplant a man. Creon's self-confirming rationality eliminates the pos-sibility of a motive incomprehensible to him, thus provoking him to reconsider his understanding. Antigone's actions may annoy him, but neither her actions nor her words cause him to question the adequacy of his understanding. Antigone is not someone with whom Creon be-lieves he can argue. His options are limited: first, threats, then, physi-cal suppression.

It is not Antigone alone whom Creon cannot hear. Equally he can-not listen to the chorus. Early in the play, the chorus of elders, whom Creon has assembled to hear his proclamation and whose loyalty and advice he purports to seek, take him at his word and most respectfully offer the suggestion that perhaps the burial of Polyneices signals that the gods think otherwise than Creon. Creon instantly dismisses this possibility. Given that the gods support justice and given that justice is based in rationality and requires that everyone receive appropriate treatment from the city, only a fool could suggest that the gods would endorse an equal treatment of loyal citizen and traitor. Given the self-confirming logic out of which he operates, the only reasonable response to such foolishness is a brusque dismissal. Buttressed by his faith in a rationality outside of custom, Creon has locked himself into a system of explanation that is impervious to criticism.

Because he cannot hear anything that contradicts his belief that all issues are ultimately political, Creon's faith in independent rationality hides from him his own need for control and does not allow him any purchase on the contradiction that structures his political policies. For even as Creon pronounces that the interests of the city dominate all private interests, he also believes, when pushed by Haemon, that the city exists to serve the interests of the ruler. For all his espoused rationality, Creon's political thought is incoherent. When challenged, he degenerates quickly to the assertion of his personal prerogative that he will back up by the use of physical force.

Haemon understands the contradiction that enables Creon to delude himself, and he equally understands how such a delusion empties a life of both personal and political content:

> Do not bear this single habit of mind, to think
> that what you say and nothing else is true.
> A man who thinks that he alone is right,
> or what he says, or what he *is* himself,
> unique, such men, when opened up, are seen
> to be quite empty. (760–66)

In contrast to such self-imposed isolation, Haemon suggests that a person needs to listen to and learn from others. Johnstone would label this listening and learning as mediation and would contrast a mediated life with a life of immediate and uncomplicated response ("Bilaterality" 98). He would further argue that it is in the process of mediation that reflection occurs and that such reflection is a necessary condition for a human being to understand himself or herself as an ethical agent. But Creon is not open to either reflection or mediation because he always has ready a defensive response to counter any challenge to his understanding. Questions cannot enter Creon's world because it is completely filled with preexisting answers. Since he lacks a reason to argue and feels no need to go beyond his understanding and its narrowly contained consistency, he can hide from his own incoherence.

If Creon shows how a commitment to rationality can, in fact, serve as a cover for a deeper commitment to control, Antigone reveals how even a praiseworthy commitment and strong sense of obligation can place a character outside the rich complexity of human existence by reducing the claims that others can legitimately make on her. Antigone does not seek to dominate others, only to fulfill her obligations. The single-minded intensity of her commitment to what she understands as her duty leaves no room for others. Antigone is obsessed with her duty to a brother who is dead but shows very little passion or concern for her betrothed. Until shortly before her death, Antigone appears indifferent to normal human concerns. She is unapproachable. Her sister's feeble attempt to raise the difficulties and complexities surrounding the forbidden burial of their brother is sufficient for Antigone to disown her. The instantaneousness and violence of Antigone's response suggest, as they did in Creon's identical refusal to countenance an other, the threat that complexity poses to such a character. A crucial condition of Antigone's purity is that she not acknowledge a complex world or even imagine a different yet honorable understanding of this obligation. If she is magnificent in her heroic resistance to Creon and in her dedication to her slain brother, she is also unfit for a normal life, which, subject to the exigencies of fortune and fated in its temporality to change, is necessarily impure and complex.

Knox sees this refusal to recognize the necessary limitations that time imposes on any human being as the condition that allows the Sophoclean hero to achieve greatness:

> Time is the condition and frame of our human existence, and to reject it is "to be in love with the impossible." But in Sophocles it is through this refusal to accept human limitations that humanity achieves its true greatness. It is a greatness achieved not with the help and encouragement of the gods, but through the hero's loyalty to his nature in trial, suffering, and death; a triumph purely human then, but one in which the gods, in time, recognize and in which they surely, in their own far-off mysterious way, rejoice. (27)

But if Vernant and Vidal-Naquet are correct that tragedy offers its dramas as problems, then maybe this greatness is itself troubling. Antigone is certainly ambivalent about her status. When the chorus tries to console her by comparing her impending death to that of Niobe's, Antigone can only hear such consolation or praise as mockery. Great renown but cold comfort. As she approaches her death, she becomes aware that she goes to her grave "unbedded, without bridal, without share / in marriage and in nurturing of children; / as lonely as you see me; without friends" (974–76). While she remains loyal to her obligations and defiant to Creon, she also, for the first time in the play, acknowledges what her act has cost her. She has not had an ordinary life, filled with the joys of love, motherhood, and friendship, and that is a reason to grieve. What is sad is not death but her being denied the experiences that make up more ordinary lives.

Antigone's sense of isolation and loss register how little political impact her words or actions have had. As Antigone approaches death, the chorus is not moved to reflect on the sanctity of family obligation but on the power of love. The choral ode prior to her entombment is a praise of Eros. The love that they praise is erotic and not fraternal. If Antigone is held in high esteem for her willingness to die, it is an honoring of her heroic temper but it is not an honoring or even endorsing of her position that one's obligations to family take precedence over one's obligations to the city. Antigone has persuaded no one of the rightness of her deed; her heroism, in its unyielding refusal to grant the possibility of an honorable, if incorrect, alternative, refuses to acknowledge a difference that could be engaged by argument.

The only speech that has an impact on another character is Teiresias's prophecy, which is sufficiently terrifying that it sets in motion the discussion that will advise Creon to yield. The theme of yielding is central to the resolution of the issues that structure this play (Nussbaum 79–81). Knox notes that *eikein* (to yield) appears to be Sophocles' favorite word, and that his plays are unusual to the extent that they make this particular demand on their protagonists (15–16). After warning his father that his need to dominate all the other citizens has created his emptiness, Haemon urges Creon to yield. He first draws an analogy between trees that stand too rigidly snapping in a storm and sailors capsizing their boats when they refuse to slacken their sails during a gale. The point of the analogies is that survival depends on an ability to adjust to situations and to know when to maintain a position and when to abandon one. If this were all there were to yielding, it would be easy to be sympathetic to both Creon's and Antigone's refusal to be disloyal to their fundamental commitments. Indeed, yielding would look very much like a policy of expediency, and as such, be bereft of any ethical worth. It would be anything but heroic. But Haemon follows his point with a second reason that is more telling and is especially relevant to argument as a method of inquiry. Haemon continues:

> Yield something of your anger, give way a little.
> If a much younger man, like me, may have
> a judgment, I would say that it were far better
> to be one altogether wise by nature, but,
> as things incline not to be so, then it is good
> also to learn from those who advise well. (774–79)

In this instance yielding is not a matter of expediency but a necessary action if one is to know or to understand. Haemon's claim is that no one is "altogether wise by nature," so everyone must learn from an other.

The question is: Why is no one altogether wise by nature? The chorus provides the beginning of an answer in an earlier ode:

> With wisdom has someone declared
> a word of distinction:
> that evil seems good to one whose mind
> the gods lead to ruin,
> and but for the briefest moment of time
> is his life outside of calamity. (673–78)

This is a disturbing insight, for it suggests the unreliability of one's perceptions. How is it possible to mistake good for evil? The answer is evident in Creon's behavior. To interpret the world, we need to start from some assumptions and values that allow us to frame our perceptions. Creon is paradigmatic of this. He sees all things in political terms. But Creon is blind to the ways in which his reductive account of human needs and desires, coupled to an inflexible sense of what counts as a rational explanation, leads him to disregard any view or opinion that contradicts his own. His assumption is that his mind can and does mirror the world. There is no reason to assume that he is duplicitous in his belief that he understands the best interests of the city or that he is acting in any way other than one that puts the city's best interests (as he understands them) first. He is someone who, in the chorus's terms, seeks good, but he does not understand that the good he perceives can be, or can, at least, entangle one in, an evil. His is a world without complexity or difference. He assumes that he can be wise by himself. Therefore, he need not and maybe cannot listen to another.

In this refusal to hear another, Creon is typical of Sophoclean protagonists. What these protagonists resist is argument. As Knox puts it, "[T]he assault on the hero's will usually takes the form of argument, of an appeal, not to emotion, but to reason" (12). The appeal from argument is an appeal to yield; it is an appeal that entails genuine risk, for it requires one to relinquish a defensive stance toward an established understanding. Yielding is what best enables creatures who cannot by themselves know good to negotiate the complexities of this world and to understand the fact of difference. In a complex world that encompasses serious difference, yielding is not a defeat but a path to knowledge or understanding. The heroes, of course, do not understand yielding in this way; rather, they see argument in terms of a test of their will and a challenge to their integrity, to their ability to maintain themselves. For them, to listen to the words of another would be to acknowledge that one is not self-sufficient.

In its obsession with autonomy, Sophoclean heroism dramatizes a fundamental fear of the individual that he or she can never achieve the kind of integrity that has been assumed to be essential to an autonomous individual. This obsession looks very much like a defense mechanism on a grand scale to deny human vulnerability. This heroism, then, is a magnificent, self-destructive, and finally mistaken attempt to maintain the integrity of the individual. In their mutual dependence, individuals are far more social than Creon or Antigone had ever imagined, and political life is necessary not simply as a form of mutual protection but as a condition of self-knowledge and knowledge of the world. Humans are not natural creatures whose immediate perceptions allow them to negotiate the larger world; they are instead interpretive creatures who will be either foolish or wise, depending on their abilities to subject their perceptions to criticism. That is the thrust of Haemon's second point. And given that humans are not naturally wise, the only path of wisdom then is through yielding, through attending seriously to the perceptions and values of others. Haemon's words lead back to Johnstone's insight that argument is a definitive aspect of the human condition. The human relationship to the world is a mediated one.

The fact that humans learn and know through the mediation of discourse does not imply that yielding is indiscriminate. On the contrary, the yielding is and must be discriminate without being rule-bound. There can be no calculus that can determine when and to whom one should yield and when one should resist. The demand to yield is a demand to risk oneself, and it is a demand that requires one to make a judgment. That judgment itself then becomes part of the path to self-knowledge. What kind of person yields here? Why yield or resist? What, if anything, was a threat? Why didn't the person initially see what the other saw? These and similar questions suggest how this decision to yield can initiate a process of self-knowledge.

The complexity of hearing an other and yielding appropriately also leads to knowledge of the larger world. First, the other stands before one in his or her otherness. If there is no otherness, there is no need to yield. Both Creon and Antigone begin from positions that have eliminated otherness from the world. For both, the world is imagined as singular; the only real obligations are to the city or to the family. Those who do not understand this do not differ from the protagonists; rather, those characters are instantly suspect and to be understood in terms of some moral failure that perverts their vision. They are not to be talked with, but opposed or controlled. This elimination of otherness creates a world of divisions in place of a world of differences. This world has no knowledge to offer; instead, it is populated by those interested only in dominating the otherness that is outside them. It offers only a normalizing discourse and makes critical discourse impossible. Creon's paranoid imagery of domination is evidence of the threat that he feels and to which he is responding. In contrast, Antigone's resistance is the self-protection of a marginalized individual challenged by a normalizing discourse.

Haemon, more than any other character, understands what is at stake in yielding to or resisting an other. When Creon accuses Haemon of arguing on behalf of Antigone, Haemon responds, "Yes, and [my argument is] for you and me — and for the gods below" (811). But Creon can hear him only as an advocate and fear that if Haemon's advocacy is successful, it will mean the defeat of Creon and the victory of Antigone. So the advocacy must be resisted. Creon's responses are never serious replies but only defensive repartees intended to ward off or hold at bay Haemon's points. He is not interested in either persuading or being persuaded; rather, he is interested only in maintaining his position and, more important, protecting his image of himself. Again, this is something that Haemon realizes when he charges that "you want to talk but never to hear and listen" (821).

Another way to put Haemon's point is that Creon listens only strategically. He listens only to attack or defend; he does not listen with the expectation that what the other says will have or can have any consequences for him. In this, his activity looks very much like the standard account of justification given in argument theory. The concern is with being effective (i.e., victorious) not with learning anything. In an important way, the words of an other are beside the point. The ultimate goal of such speech is certainly not to provoke an other to speak but to bring that person to silence by eliminating difference or otherness. Borrowing from Von Clausewitz, we might suggest that argument, in this view, is domination by other means. It is a way for an individual or a group to meet only itself, to dispose of otherness as a threat, and to have a world that reflects only the one position. To return to an earlier term, a person or group who is committed to such a strategy is *deinos*. Such a deliberate attempt to avoid enlarging or changing an understanding and instead to maintain that understanding in an ignorance that masks itself as knowledge or integrity is both awesome and awful. It is not surprising that Sophoclean protagonists so often end in isolation and that his tragedies are distinguished by the number of suicides. Part of the power of these tragedies is their recording of this basic drive to self-destruction as a response to the threat of a self-knowledge that would replace the purity of an absolute position with a complex, unstable, and fluid understanding. Actually listening to another has tremendous consequences. Susan Bickford lays out some of the consequences of listening and makes clear what is at stake:

> But our listeners are, paradoxically, like us — unique and active. It is the inevitable role that reception plays that makes the public action of citizenship a genuinely collective endeavor, one in which no individual can simply impose her or his will on another and insist on being heard in a particular way. The "who" that is formed by the story of my public actions and judgments is not necessarily the heroine of the story I would write, precisely because others' reactions are themselves *actions,* unpredictable and novel. This is the paradox of public appearance: Our very appearance as an active unique "who" relies on the attention of active others whose perceptions we do not control. (130)

Putting oneself in situations marked by real listening means giving up exclusive authorship over one's own account. Further, if such listening is possible, it suggests that individuals are not fixed and integral but inherently indeterminate. Who one is, is, in part, a consequence of with whom one talks. This insight is not particularly shocking given the various poststructuralist discourses of the last four decades, but it does suggest a very different role for argument. When listening or attending to the other is crucial to argument, the goal of argument moves from justifying claims to discovering conversations that encourage two apparently contradictory projects. One project is to promote the ongoing creation and revision of identity; the other is to explore the limits to what is or can be held in common. In its two goals argument is a dialectical interplay of the ancient polarity of same and different, and it remains creative to the extent that it can keep this pair in a productive tension.

Both of these projects carry a high degree of anxiety. In the first project we risk our understanding of our own history:

> The riskiness of listening comes partly from the possibility that what we hear will require change from us. A deliberative decision may mean real material change for the participants. But speaking and listening together may engender a change in consciousness. As Lorde says, "change means growth, and growth can be painful"; but "we sharpen self-definition by exposing the self in work and struggle." . . . This exposure, the possibility of sharpening, can be scary. In a sense, we fear being wrong, or being in the wrong. The opinions I have — views I have come to after imaginative work and struggle, perhaps — may be threatened by what you say. (Bickford 149)

What I may find out is that I am not who I think I am. This is a grave risk, especially since each of us is deeply invested in the understanding of who he or she is. We should anticipate that arguments will provoke resistance precisely because they attack a narcissism that we all possess.

The second project is equally scary. When I truly speak or listen, I may find that there are differences between us that cannot be resolved by an appeal to universality, common heritage, reason, or even a common situation. These differences can be of two kinds. Johnstone writes about the first kind of difference. He sees philosophically incompatible statements arising either from people attending to different problems or from them attending to different aspects of a common problem. In such cases, one cannot appeal to some notion of overarching rationality to solve philosophical disagreements, for the positions staked out are relative to the particular people involved and the particular values that they hold:

> The view that a valid philosophical argument obligates some individuals, but not all, to accept its conclusion serves as a reminder of the existence of genuine philosophical disagreement. It implies that any philosophical statement must be a source of disagreement between those obligated to accept it and those not so obligated. Such disagreement is radical, in the sense that it cannot be overcome through compromise. (*Philosophy and Argument* 52).

The point of philosophical argument, then, is not to seek agreement but to engage in criticism that allows one to see more clearly and more critically the understanding to which he or she has been led. It is an ongoing examination of commitments and the consequences of those commitments. Philosophical argument discloses what separates us intellectually.

The second instance of difference is social or political. In developing her account of an adversarial communication, Bickford locates several places from which differences arise: the distance between elites/ masses, the distinctiveness of individuals with their personal and particular histories, and the historical consequences from the injustices that surround and are dispersed through race, gender, and class. What these locations point to are differences that cannot simply be done away with by appeal to a universal or communal standard, since these differences mark/enable/injure individuals and groups in particular ways. Difference is the necessary condition for identity, and difference entails conflict, some of which can be resolved and some of which cannot. A full social harmony would inevitably signal domination and the clandestine import of certain particular norms of certain privileged groups or individuals as a specious representation of the whole (102). In an argument there is always the possibility that serious and attentive participation will not remove barriers between participants but rather encounter a difference that renders the participants, at least, partially opaque to each other.

The knowledge that argument can bring is not necessarily consoling: One is not who one thinks one is, and there is no single standard or viewpoint that all humans necessarily share. It is easy to understand why one might turn to an account of argument that postulates a less radical risk and directs attention to matters involving the support of claims, seeing an other only as one to be answered but not as one to be encountered seriously. The problem with such a view, though, is that a genuine or stable agreement cannot be reached between two parties who are seeking to control each other. In such a situation, the options are limited. I can become Creon-like and seek to dominate the opposition, eliminating difference and making particular claims hold as a matter of my will, even as I disguise my tyranny by appealing to rationality. In the background always lurks the threat of psychological, physical, or institutional violence. Or I can so wholly take over the other that there ceases to be a difference in viewpoints, and my claim becomes his or her claim. But as Bickford, following Hannah Arendt, argues, to eliminate other opinions is also to eliminate the possibility of opinion, since difference is a condition of being aware that something is an opinion (81). So the attempt to make all opinion agree is contradictory.

These are not simply theoretical difficulties; they are underlying pressures in any classroom discussion of or attempt at argument. Anyone who teaches argument must at times feel uncomfortable with what goes on in the class. How often are the student arguments successful in getting someone seriously to reconsider a position? In my experience students spend a great deal of time trying to make their case persuasive to either some universal or fictional audience, and hence they engage in an abstract exercise that they see as merely academic. If anything governs this work, it is the attention to the requirements of a particular form. Students dutifully present claims, back the claims with evidence and reasons, which they warrant as needed. They consider alternative positions to show that they have canvased all or most reasonable points of view and, further, that they have qualified their position in light of these other viewpoints. The result is a well-formed essay that, I suspect, has little if any impact on anybody. I suspect further that the students at some level sense this. And if they do, then the composition of an argument becomes primarily a formal exercise, and, more important, it inadvertently teaches a cynical lesson: The production of arguments is a charade, no one actually attends to them, and at best they are a mask for how real power operates — those who have power pretty much do what they want. There is a Creon-like commitment to the rhetoric of public reason because one knows in advance that this reason will have little impact on anyone or involve little risk to the one who argues. This is the dark vision that has haunted the rhetorical tradition. If students need confirmation of this view, all they have to do is look to the way that Congress and large corporations work. Serious argument is often impotent when it encounters the power of well-entrenched and well-financed interest groups. Reason and argument become the cover for the operation of powerful lobbying groups indifferent to the consequences of their actions for others.

If the operation of such power is the reality, what then are the consequences for teaching argument? This is an especially important question for a democracy and an even more important question for a democracy in which there is only limited citizen participation. Unlike fifth-century-B.C.E. Athens, we do not have a face-to-face democracy, so our courses in argument cannot pretend to be a straightforward preparation for a commonly available political life. Most of us are not leisured gentlemen free to attend to the direct business of governing our cities and states. Instead, we occupy a complex position toward current discourses of power, be they civic or corporate, and what we need is a rich and complex sense of the opportunities and limits of argument. What we need to explore is the value of argument given the way that power is held in the contemporary world.

Texts like *Antigone* offer an alternative to the current teaching of argument, for they see argument as problematic. They offer no easy or mechanical solutions but pose argument as a problem and offer it for serious reflection. Other scholars have argued for the value of teaching literature as argument (Fisher and Filloy), but I am advocating something else. What I am proposing is that literary texts such as *Antigone* be taught as theoretical works in argument. These works would allow us to teach argument as a philosophical or political problem and not as a mode of presenting evidence for purposes of justifying claims. Instead, they would raise questions as to why arguments so often fail, and they would open students to questions of why, given the unlikeliness of success, someone might argue. And a course based on such texts would train students to attend to their words and the words of others in a new way. Students could be taught that the point of serious exchange is not to assert a will at the cost of another or to seek domination or control but to risk understandings in the hope of discovering new understandings of themselves and others, recognizing that one of the uncomfortable understandings they will continually relearn is that not all limits can be exceeded.

The goal of this reconceived course in argument would be the pursuit of an understanding of identity and the articulation of difference. This would then lead to a new vocabulary of assessment that turned away from a language of victory and defeat and embraced other values. One would want to know, for example, if a particular argument was generative. Did it allow the students to learn something? Was it an argument that led to other or to unanticipated arguments? Did the argument encourage the student to take more risks in the future? The traditional concerns with rigor, with developing appropriate support, and with critically reviewing the positions of oneself or any other party to the argument would still be important, but they would now be directed by a goal of exploring identity and/or the articulation of difference and not be considered primarily as defensive strategies to be employed when a claim is challenged. Finally, it would make a course in writing a place to begin to ask the question, With whom can I converse? Education would then become in part a quest for people and texts with whom one could argue. Such education would not be technical but liberal and might help bring into place a discourse appropriate to a complex democracy in which the average citizen does not speak with the authority of the corporate lobbyist but in which a resigned silence is not a viable option. In arguing with an other or with ourselves, we would begin to discover new problems and possibilities. We would participate in allowing new discoveries to emerge that could contest standard or dominant understandings. Creon was right to fear citizens who can argue, for such citizens conduct a discourse that is unpredictable and that can lead to understandings that, in their articulation of difference, allow us to discourse with and respect others and to better understand ourselves.

Works Cited

Bickford, Susan. *The Dissonance of Democracy: Listening, Conflict and Citizenship.* Ithaca: Cornell UP, 1996.

Britzman, Deborah P. *Lost Subjects, Contested Objects: Toward a Psychoanalytic Inquiry of Learning.* Albany: State U of New York P, 1998.

Conley, Thomas M. *Rhetoric in the European Tradition.* New York: Longman, 1990.

Fisher, Walter R., and Richard A. Filloy. "Argument in Drama and Literature: An Exploration." *Advances in Argumentation Theory and Research.* Ed. J. Robert Cox and Charles Arthur Willard. Carbondale: Southern Illinois UP, 1982. 343–62.

Fulkerson, Richard. "The Toulmin Model of Argument and the Teaching of Composition." *Argument Revisited; Argument Redefined: Negotiating Meaning in the Composition Classroom.* Ed. Barbara Emmel, Paula Resch, and Deborah Tenny. Thousand Oaks: Sage, 1996. 45–72.

Goldhill, Simon. *Reading Greek Tragedy.* New York: Cambridge UP, 1986.

Jarratt, Susan C. "Feminism and Composition: The Case for Conflict." *Contending with Words: Composition and Rhetoric in a Postmodern Age.* Ed. Patricia Harkin and John Schilb. New York: MLA, 1991. 105–23.

Johnstone, Henry W., Jr. "Bilaterality in Argument and Communication." *Advances in Argumentation Theory and Research.* Ed. J. Robert Cox and Charles Arthur Willard. Carbondale: Southern Illinois UP, 1982. 95–102.

———. *Philosophy and Argument.* University Park: The Pennsylvania State UP, 1959.

———. "Some Reflections on Argumentation." *Philosophy, Rhetoric and Argumentation.* Ed. Maurice Natanson and Henry W. Johnstone, Jr. University Park: The Pennsylvania State UP, 1965. 1–9.

———. "Theory of Argumentation." *Contemporary Philosophy: A Survey.* Ed. Raymond Klibansky. Firenze: La Nuova Italia Editrice, 1968. 177–84.

Knox, Bernard M. W. *The Heroic Temper: Studies in Sophoclean Tragedy.* Berkeley: U of California P, 1964.

Nussbaum, Martha C. *The Fragility of Goodness: Luck and Ethics in Greek Tragedy and Philosophy.* Cambridge: Cambridge UP, 1986.

Perelman, Chaim. "Philosophy and Rhetoric." *Advances in Argumentation Theory and Research.* Ed. J. Robert Cox and Charles Arthur Willard. Carbondale: Southern Illinois UP, 1982. 287–97.

Perelman, Chaim, and Lucie Olbrechts-Tyteca. *The New Rhetoric: A Treatise on Argumentation.* Trans. John Wilkinson and Purcell Weaver. Notre Dame: U of Notre Dame P, 1969.

Sophocles. *Antigone.* Trans. David Grene. *The Complete Greek Tragedies, Sophocles I.* Ed. David Grene and Richmond Lattimore. 2nd ed. Chicago: U of Chicago P, 1991.

Toulmin, Stephen. *The Uses of Argument.* Cambridge: Cambridge UP, 1958.

van Eemeren, Frans H., et al. *Fundamentals of Argumentation Theory: A Handbook of Historical Backgrounds and Contemporary Developments.* Mahwah: Erlbaum, 1996.

Vernant, Jean-Pierre, and Pierre Vidal-Naquet. *Tragedy and Myth in Ancient Greece.* Trans. Janet Lloyd. Atlantic Highlands: Humanities, 1981.

Zarefsky, David. "Argumentation in the Tradition of Speech Communication Studies." *Logic and Argumentation.* Ed. Johan van Benthem, et al. North-Holland: Royal Netherlands Academy of Arts and Sciences, 1996. 43–60.

2

Argument in the Twentieth Century

In the twentieth century rhetorical theorists seeking to keep up with numerous cultural and linguistic changes have made important inquiries into many areas of discourse; two particularly important accomplishments will be discussed here. First, theorists sought to address the historical separation between rhetoric and invention, a separation resulting primarily from the work of the Renaissance scholar Peter Ramus (d. 1572). Most theorists after Ramus believed that knowledge was created through science and deductive logic and then transmitted by rhetoric. In the twentieth century, however, rhetorical theory challenged this view as too narrow and asserted the central role language plays in the invention of all knowledge. Twentieth-century theorists also examined the relationship between ethics and rhetoric, with significant scholarly efforts coming from analyses of the language of war, consumer culture, and racial and other differences. Ethical concerns have also been important to technical writing, computers and writing, and classroom pedagogy. The emphasis on invention and ethics has helped provide rhetoric with the philosophical and moral underpinnings to become, once again, a central concern in academic life.

Following is a brief sketch of some of the most important figures contributing to the revival of rhetoric in the twentieth century. These scholars have contributed directly to the scholarship on argumentation and persuasion even though their comprehensive inquiries into language often extended far beyond direct concerns with argumentation.

The turn of the twentieth century, according to many historians, saw a low point for rhetoric. First-year writing classes were mandatory at most institutions, but they held little institutional status. In response to the degraded state of rhetoric, speech-communications programs developed in the 1920s and 1930s. These programs helped reinstitutionalize the study of classical rhetoric and introduced new theories of persuasion. While the institutionalization of rhetoric at the university came primarily from scholars in speech at this time, three men from other fields were also reconsidering the connections among language, literature, philosophy, and persuasion: Kenneth Burke, I. A. Richards, and Mikhail Bakhtin. The work of these three has been particularly influential in English departments and has helped, among other things, to reconnect rhetoric and poetics in the second half of the twentieth century. These three scholars were particularly interested in the way discourse interacts with individuals, communities, and historical contexts to construct meaning. Burke in particular used his dramatistic rhetoric — an approach drawn from drama to understand the relationship between motives, language, and action — to explore the ethics of persuasion.

Burke's continued scholarship and the work of theorists such as Wayne Booth established stronger links between rhetorical and literary study in the 1950s and 1960s. The idea that literature was a form of rhetoric took hold for many scholars and further identified rhetoric with invention; if the creative act of writing literature was rhetorical, then invention had to be a central concern of the rhetorical process. Some of this century's most important influences on argument — Chaim Perelman, Lucie Olbrechts-Tyteca, and Stephen Toulmin — also contributed to the rise of rhetoric in the 1950s and 1960s. Perelman, Olbrechts-Tyteca, and Toulmin recognized that values and informal logic were critical elements of human life that could not be properly understood within positivist frameworks. They therefore developed comprehensive theories of argument that borrowed from and modified formal systems of logic and classical notions of rhetoric.

The late 1960s saw the rise of critical theorists such as Jacques Derrida and Michel Foucault, whose abstract theories and revisionist histories contributed to a thorough revaluation of language, reading, writing, and knowledge. At the same time, this period saw a rise in classroom-based rhetoric and argumentation theory. As the discipline of composition evolved in the era of the civil rights movement, student activism against the Vietnam War, and the women's movement, classroom practices and campus activities became as much a focus for argumentation scholars as did more abstract theory. In the face of such conflict, scholars such as Richard E. Young, Alton L. Becker, and Kenneth L. Pike sought to apply the notion of empathy (as promoted by psychotherapist Carl Rogers) to argumentation theory so that disputes could be resolved without violence and with respect for all concerned. Young, Becker, and Pike are also significant to contemporary composition because they helped institutionalize the idea that writing is a process of creating as well as transmitting ideas. Their use of tagmemics (heuristics to help writers create ideas) emphasized the importance of invention, and their work helped stimulate the growth of prewriting exercises in writing classes around the country.

Since the 1960s, the academy has seen rapid and unprecedented changes in the student body, as more women, students of color, older students, and others have fought not only for their place at the university but also for a curriculum that represents their needs and interests. Contemporary scholars in argumentation are particularly concerned with the conflicts created by such change and have sought to redefine the relationship between empathy, culture, and conflict. Chief among their concerns has been a recognition that the idea of "empathy" is limited when students and instructors alike are often ignorant of the multiple modes and methods of argumentation that take place in the world and on campus. However, formally studying with students the ways different cultures use language has helped denaturalize the supposedly universal mode of persuasion promoted by U.S. education. Such work has pushed scholars and students see that different rhetorical traditions use language to create meaning differently and that terms like "invention" and "rhetoric" are constructed and need to be considered carefully whenever argument takes place.

Studying difference, however, is limited unless scholars recognize the relationships between modes of argumentation and historical issues of power. Such a recognition does not mean teachers should stop teaching dominant forms of argumentation (models that depend on edited American English, for example); rather, respect for diversity means that the dominant forms should be taught alongside other forms of argument. More specifically, students should be taught argument as a contextualized, historical form of discourse that has always been embedded in structures of power, so that they can see how and why some forms of disputation have become entrenched, in Lisa Delpit's words, as the "codes of power," while others have remained marginalized. The connections between rhetoric and ethics, therefore, become increasingly complicated as we help students recognize that "ethics" themselves are also rhetorical constructs, situated in specific historical contexts and subject to multiple understandings.

Finally, it is important to close the introduction to this section with a qualification. Though the "Argumentation and Race, Class, Gender, and Culture" section (p. 154) includes readings that explore a variety of cultural influences on argumentation, it is impossible for any collection to represent fully the argumentative strategies of all groups and all contexts. Any attempt to be wholly inclusive would be misleading because it would imply that we can break down fluid forms of discourse (as well as the people who use them) into neat and complete subcategories. Instead, the essays in the "Argumentation and Race, Class, Gender, and Culture" section offer a sampling of informed ways to read argument in relation to cultural difference. Such ways of reading will help teachers and students analyze argument in terms of individual and cultural differences *and* demonstrate the dangers of relying on overly simplistic connections between identity and discourse.

Readers should consult the bibliography, especially those sections concerned with Stephen Toulmin, Chaim Perelman and Lucie Olbrechts-Tyteca, Carl Rogers, Philosophy and Rhetoric, and Culture and Rhetoric for further information about the role of argumentation in the twentieth century.

ROGERIAN ARGUMENT

From *Rhetoric: Discovery and Change* with Communication: Its Blocking and Its Facilitation

Richard E. Young, Alton L. Becker, Kenneth L. Pike,
Carl R. Rogers

The introduction of Carl Rogers's theories of communication to composition studies is accredited to Richard E. Young, Alton L. Becker, and Kenneth L. Pike, who included a chapter on Rogers in their influential 1970 text, Rhetoric: Discovery and Change. *Following is an excerpt from that chapter, including the transcript of Rogers's paper "Communication: Its Blocking and Its Facilitation," first delivered in 1951 at Northwestern University's Centennial Conference on Communications. From Young, Becker, and Pike's interpretation of Rogers, and from Rogers's words themselves, it is easy to see how important empathy and a specific kind of listening — listening to understand from another's point of view — are to this version of argumentation. In fact, Rogers's theories, which are taken from small-group therapy, reverse the traditional order of things in argumentation; instead of the writer or speaker being the primary focus, the listener or reader is given first priority. It is up to rhetors to fully understand their interlocutor's point of view, no matter how foreign or complex, and, more importantly, to state this point of view to the audience's satisfaction before explaining their own. Through this process, Rogers argues, true communication — communication aimed at solving a problem common to rhetor and audience rather than aimed at beating an opponent — can take place.*

Rogerian Argument

Rogerian argument rests on the assumption that out of a need to preserve the stability of his image, a person will refuse to consider alternatives that he feels are threatening, and hence, that *changing a person's image depends on eliminating this sense of threat.*[1] Much of men's resistance to logical argument seems explainable by this assumption. A strong sense of threat may render the reader immune to even the most carefully reasoned and well-supported argument. The Rogerian strategy seeks to reduce the reader's sense of threat so that he will be able to consider alternatives that may contribute to the creation of a more accurate image of the world and to the elimination of conflict between writer and reader. As Rogers suggests, a willingness to consider alternatives is evidence of the establishment of real communication, which greatly increases the chances that a reasonable solution can be reached.

The writer who uses the Rogerian strategy attempts to do three things: (1) to convey to the reader that he is understood, (2) to delineate the area within which he believes the reader's position to be valid, and (3) to induce him to believe that he and the writer share similar moral qualities (honesty, integrity, and good will) and aspirations (the desire to discover a mutually acceptable solution). We stress here that these are only tasks, not stages of the argument. Rogerian argument has no conventional structure; in fact, users of the strategy deliberately avoid conventional persuasive structures and techniques because these devices tend to produce a sense of threat, precisely what the writer seeks to overcome. We do not mean, of course, that the argument has no structure, but only that the structure is more directly the product of a particular writer, a particular topic, and a particular audience. The Rogerian strategy places a premium on empathy between writer and reader and on the peculiarities of the topic.

Conveying to the Reader That He Is Understood

Understanding here means something more than merely a grasp of the basic ideas of the opponent's position. It goes considerably beyond categorizing the opponent's position and noting its contrastive features. In "Communication: Its Blocking and Its Facilitation" Rogers explains that *understanding* means *"to see the expressed idea and attitude from the other person's point of view, to sense how it feels to him, to achieve his frame of reference in regard to the thing he is talking about."* It requires empathy, requires getting inside the other person's skin and seeing the world through his eyes, or, to speak less metaphorically, it requires considering the beliefs and perspectives of the reader in the context of his attitudes, values, and past experience.

The task of the writer is to induce the reader to consider his position and to understand it. The writer tries to make the reader understand this position as it is interrelated with the larger system of values and beliefs that compose the writer's image; he wants the reader to understand as an insider rather than an outsider. Curiously enough, one method of eliciting this response is to demonstrate that the *reader's* position has been understood. To do this, the writer states the reader's position as accurately, completely, and sensitively as he can, taking care not to judge it. Many conventional arguments fail either because the reader refuses to listen or because he distorts the argument, making it conform to his preconceptions of the writer and the writer's position. In either case, the reader is not trying to understand; he is trying to defend himself. He *will,* however, pay careful attention to a statement of his own position. The writer's first task, then, is to state the reader's position so carefully that the reader will agree that it has been well stated. If the writer "wins" this part of the argument, the reader is likely to continue listening. Furthermore, he is now motivated to understand the writer's position, for the reader too wants to score a victory. Demonstrating to the reader that a problem has been understood from *his* point of view is a powerful method of threat-reduction; not only can it induce the reader to listen to another position and try to understand it, but it can also create in him a willingness to pursue the argument, to reconsider his own position, and perhaps, finally, to change it.

Delineating the Area of Validity

When a person argues, he usually seeks to refute an opponent's position by evaluating it, pointing out what he considers to be its defective, or invalid, aspects. But [. . .] such a procedure is often threat-producing. The writer can mitigate this sense of threat by focusing on the aspects of the reader's position that clearly *are valid.* Just as isolating the invalid aspects of a position implies the existence of valid aspects, so isolating valid aspects implies that there are invalid ones. Logically, the two acts amount to much the same thing; their effects, however, are different psychologically. Focusing on the valid rather than the invalid reduces the reader's sense of threat and offers him further evidence that he is understood. It also encourages him to discover the valid aspects of the writer's position. When writer and reader discover validity in each other's positions, they discover important shared features that can form the basis of further interaction.

Generally speaking, a statement is neither entirely valid nor entirely invalid; its validity is relative to a context. [. . .] An awareness of this relativity makes it somewhat easier for the writer to understand opposing positions and to accept disagreement with his own position. Consider a trivial and obvious example: "Slate is hard." This statement is true if slate is being compared with talc, not true if it is being compared with diamond. Out of context, the statement seems an undeniable truth with which no reasonable person could disagree. In different contexts, however (i.e., if slate is compared with talc, with diamond, and so on), the statement is subject to rational discussion. Many people engaged in arguments ignore the effect that different contexts can have on a statement; they often say flatly, "It's true, and I can't imagine how any reasonable man could disagree with it." They might get further in an argument if they said, "If we consider it in such-and-such a context, or if we assume certain conditions, then it is true." Consider another example. Suppose someone says that underdeveloped countries should import Western technology. To most Americans, this proposal would seem entirely reasonable, for we would contemplate how technology can free people from hunger and disease. Thus we would place the statement in a context in which it is reasonable and true. But someone else, someone with a strong anthropological or historical bias, might disagree, arguing that artificially imposed technological development would destroy the cultural values of the society, those values that give it order and stability, or that the introduction of technology would lead to the kind of suffering that was experienced in sweatshops during the Industrial Revolution. Here is still another example: "Literature is important to national survival." This statement is not true if you consider it in a military context, for literature lacks the immediate force of arms. It may be true if you put it in a political or a sociological context, for literature can be a powerful propaganda instrument (e.g., much of modern Russian literature, or for that matter some of our own, particularly that written during times of national stress). The statement is also true in a psychological context: Literature can help people become more perceptive about human problems and human conflict, and as a result more willing and able to deal with them intelligently.

Opponents in an argument often, perhaps usually, disagree not because of fallacious reasoning or ignorance of the facts but because of the different contexts in which they see the problem. They may think that they are talking about the same subject when actually they aren't. [. . .] People "edit" experience in different ways; hence the same problem may well seem quite different to men on opposite sides of an argument. Facts will have different degrees of importance; attitudes and values, different weights. Perceptions and their meanings are to a great extent determined by the image of the observer.

Ignoring the contexts of statements leads opponents to make categorical denials or affirmations; positions in the argument then become polarized, and the chances for reaching an agreement are reduced. A statement of the conditions under which a position is valid, however, encourages discussion; the argument tends to become provisional, and a problem-solving orientation is developed. "The opposing views," says Anatol Rapoport,

> stem largely from different criteria for *selecting what to see, what to be aware of.* Therefore, the object in a debate is to induce the opponent to admit stimuli which he had not admitted before, in short to enlarge his vision. To do this, some feel, it is best to show him not the limits outside of which he is wrong, but, on the contrary, the limits inside of which he is right. They are, of course, the same limits! But putting it one way is likely to emphasize the threat to the image, while putting it the other way is likely to dilute the threat.

Definitions can be another source of disagreement. But the writer can often benefit from exploiting the fact that any definition is to some extent arbitrary. He usually loses little by agreeing to use his opponent's definitions (at least his denotative definitions) of key terms in the debate. And he may gain much, for he gives further evidence of his good will and understanding. Note, however, that before he can agree to use the reader's definitions, he must be aware of all the dimensions of their meaning. *Communist, worker,* and *capitalist* may have roughly similar denotations for a communist and a capitalist, but their connotations may differ radically. Ultimately, the meaning of a term is not its dictionary definition, nor even the meaning that people agree to assign to the word in a particular situation. The meaning arises from the living contexts within which the word occurs in connected speech or writing. A word is ultimately defined by its distribution in relation to the other words with which it is used. [. . .] The word *sincere,* for example, ordinarily refers to a correspondence between a person's inner and outer attitudes. Yet consider its meaning in the following context: "Always be sincere — whether you mean it or not."

Denotative definitions (e.g., the kind used in the scientific description of objects) are often easy to accept, and by doing so, the writer can clarify some of the issues of the debate. Connotative definitions, however, often encompass areas of genuine disagreement, for they carry with them evaluations of a situation — evaluations that may reflect profound differences in values, beliefs, and experience. For example, the writer may be able to grant to the communist his denotative definition of *capitalist* — that is, one or more of its economic meanings — but its connotation for the communist of ruthless exploiter or enemy of the worker may be precisely what the writer is trying to change by means of his argument. The most that the writer can do in this situation is recognize the definition's area of validity, accepting the truth that is there and hoping that the reader will come to see in what way the term is limited.

Rapoport explains that defining terms and delineating their area of validity is a necessary step in argument.

> If by changing definitions or properly delineating the area of validity, we can accept some of the opponent's assertions as true (whereas they had seemed false to us otherwise), let us do so. By doing so, we make it easier for him to do the same for us. If the issue of the debate evaporates on that account, then the debate was not really worth the effort.
>
> Most serious debates are *not* simply about words; so we cannot, as a rule, expect the issues to disappear as a result of semantic analysis and improved communication. But this preliminary job of understanding must first be done to make sure that it is not only words we are concerned with, and if it is not, to get down to the real business.

The techniques that we have been discussing in this section can help minimize irrelevant opposition and emotional explosion. They can also help the writer to distinguish the areas of real disagreement from the areas of agreement, which may provide bridges over which changes can take place.

Inducing the Assumption of Similarity

The immediate goal of the Rogerian strategy is to get the opponent to reciprocate — to induce him to understand the writer's position as the writer has understood his position. To some extent, demonstrating that the reader's position is understood and establishing where its area of validity lies are both techniques that encourage the reader to reciprocate. Inducing the reader to acknowledge that his position has been stated well constitutes a kind of victory; the reader realizes that he too can "win" if he studies the writer's position and states it equally well. He is also likely to become interested in pointing out the region of validity and invalidity in the writer's position, since it is to his advantage to demonstrate that this position too has its limitations. There are other reasons for a willingness to reciprocate. If he has been relieved of his sense of threat, it is to his advantage to reciprocate in order to prevent the writer's sense of threat from destroying the potential for cooperation that has begun to develop. Finally, a reader whose sense of threat has been reduced is more willing to consider alternative positions, including the writer's.

Attempts at persuading the reader to treat the writer as he himself has been treated are likely to fail if the reader thinks that the writer is different from himself in significant ways. He may not even try to understand the writer's position if he sees the writer as unreasonable, for example, refusing to grant what seem to the reader to be obvious, verifiable facts; or if he sees him as Machiavellian, deliberately using words as traps or employing arguments whose stated purposes mask different and unscrupulous ones. The Rogerian strategy requires that opponents confront each other as equals in an atmosphere of mutual trust. But how can the reader be brought to trust the writer, to regard him as worthy of being believed, and finally to understand his position?

The threat-reducing acts we have already discussed can help to create trust; a more explicit and direct method, however, is to show that writer and reader are similar in relevant ways. The writer can either build or discover bridges (e.g., shared attitudes, experiences, and values [. . .]) that will encourage trust and lead to further interaction. Consider the following imaginary debate between a Russian communist and an American liberal. In this excerpt, the liberal is pointing out historical, cultural, and ideological features that are shared by the two societies.

> Science is the common heritage in both our societies, and both societies are unquestionably adapted to utilizing the power which science confers on man over his environment — but only to a limited extent. The limitations of both sides stem from commitments to dogma, the antithesis of the scientific attitude. Dogma is that portion of one's outlook which is immune to modification.
>
> It will be futile for me to maintain that you as Communists are bound more rigidly by dogma than we, although it appears that way to us. Rather than try to measure the unmeasurable, I maintain from the start that both our societies are impeded by dogmatic attitudes from developing their full potentials. The difference is that you recognize dogma explicitly and call it Marxism (or dialectical materialism in the natural science sphere), while we deny that our fetishes (like "liberty")

are symptoms of dogma. The effects are similar. In the name of liberty we dare not undertake measures to safeguard minimum standards of economic security and health, which we can well afford. In the name of the "only correct philosophy" you have failed to extend the realm of scientific investigation to the nature of man and society, which you have unequaled opportunity to do.

I believe that taking refuge in dogma is a fear reaction. The irrational fear of planning, so conspicuous in the United States, stems from a dread of *overt* restraints on the activities of the individual. As so often happens, an overpowering fear incapacitates one in dealing with real dangers. In our pathological avoidance of overt restraints, we have succumbed to innumerable covert ones and have drifted into a drabness of conformity.

Your irrational fear stems from the dread of "idealism." You see "idealism" in any intellectual position which, however remotely, admits the perceptual or the cognitive structure of an individual in the start of a theoretical investigation. You keep fighting the intellectual battle of the nineteenth century, the battle against the hegemony of religious dogma, an issue which has since lost all significance in the intellectual sphere.

. . .

The witch hunts in the years of our McCarthy eclipse are well matched by the outbursts of intellectual lynching of the type the Russians call *razgrom*. . . .

Trust is encouraged by showing the opponent that he is trusted. There is considerable wisdom in one of the techniques used for bringing about a military truce: The initiator of the truce deliberately exposes himself to attack by laying aside his weapons and going to meet his opponent. His act implies that although the opponent distrusts him, he considers the opponent worthy of trust. It also suggests that they share certain values and interests that could form the basis for some sort of accommodation. In his argument with the Russian, the American liberal deliberately exposes the shortcomings of his own side: He acknowledges the existence of dogma in American political thought, our resulting inability to solve pressing social problems, the conformity pervading our social life, the political "witch hunts" of the early 1950s, and so on. He also makes explicit a definition of *dogma,* which, if left unstated, might inhibit understanding. And he lists the important features that both societies share: their common scientific heritage, the ability to utilize this heritage for human betterment, the burdens of dogmas. What could be better evidence of good faith and willingness to cooperate than letting down one's guard?

In situations involving great stress, where powerful values and beliefs clash, we tend to see our opponent as an extremist, as rigid, unreasonable, even dangerous; and no doubt we see ourselves as honest, reasonable, and responsible. But it is important to remember that our opponent is likely to hold the opposite view, to think that *he* is the one who is reasonable and that we are the unreasonable and rigid ones.

We may increase our chances of being listened to and understood by imagining that our opponent shares the qualities we attribute to ourselves and by behaving as if he did. As Rapoport points out, "Maybe he does not, but maybe this 'delusion' of ours will induce a similar delusion in him about us."

Rogerian Argument and Traditional Argument

Rogerian argument may at first seem somewhat puzzling and difficult to grasp. The cause of confusion may well be that traditional argument has been taught in schools so long and has been applied so extensively that it has shaped your image of what constitutes effective argument. The Rogerian strategy requires you to modify your image of effective argument; you may resist this change to some extent, since the characteristics of Rogerian argument may at times seem to contradict the techniques you are used to. In Rogerian argument, instead of stating your own case and refuting your opponent's, you state the opponent's case with as much care as your own, and you analyze the sound points of his argument. Instead of building up your own character and qualifications and attacking those of your opponent, you seek to gain your opponent's trust, even at the cost of acknowledging your own inadequacies. Logic, too, is used differently: In traditional argument it acts as a tool for presenting your case and refuting your opponent's; in Rogerian argument it serves an exploratory function, helping you to analyze the conditions under which the position of either side is valid. And language is used in different ways: Traditional argument often exploits language's capacity for arousing emotion in order to strengthen a position; Rogerian argument emphasizes the descriptive, dispassionate use of language. The goals of the two strategies also differ. The goal of traditional argument is to make your position prevail, to replace some feature of the opponent's image with one that you consider correct. The goal of Rogerian argument is to create a situation conducive to cooperation; this may well involve changes in *both* your opponent's image and your own. [. . .]

One last difference is worth noting. Traditional argument is highly conventional and draws on an armory of persuasive techniques [. . .]. Rogerian argument avoids conventional techniques and structures because they tend to be threat-producing. This absence of conventional structures, however, is more characteristic of oral argument than of written. Written argument excludes the possibility of continual readjustment of the discourse as the result of observing the opponent's reactions. Your opponent cannot show you where you have failed to state his position adequately and give you an opportunity to modify your statement before continuing the discussion. In written argument, then, especially great care must be taken to state his position well the first time. Furthermore, since the opponent is not present, he cannot state your position for you; you must state it yourself, pointing out its regions of validity and invalidity just as you did with his. Written argument thus lacks the flexibility of oral argument. And if the writer does not use a conventional, sharply defined structure, there are at least phases to his argument. These phases can be ordered as follows:

1) An introduction to the problem and a demonstration that the opponent's position is understood.

2) A statement of the contexts in which the opponent's position may be valid.

3) A statement of the writer's position, including the contexts in which it is valid.

4) A statement of how the opponent's position would benefit if he were to adopt elements of the writer's position. If the writer can show that the positions complement each other, that each supplies what the other lacks, so much the better.

We should here note that the assumption of similarity is best seen not as a phase of the argument but as an attitude revealed throughout the discourse.

If some people are puzzled by Rogerian argument, others react to it with skepticism. They grant its ethical attractiveness but object that it is impractical and self-deluding. Although reasonable, generous, and honest behavior under great stress is not to be dismissed lightly, Rogerian argument need not be defended exclusively on moral grounds. Its goal is an eminently practical one: to induce changes in an opponent's mind in order to make mutually advantageous cooperation possible. And its means, strange as they may seem at first, have been proven effective in a wide variety of social situations. Essentially, the writer induces his opponent to listen to his position, to understand it, and to see the truth in it, by demonstrating that he has done the same with the opponent's position. If we pause for a moment to consider how we would respond to someone who behaved in this way toward us, the strategy is not likely to seem so impractical after all. Reasonable, moral behavior can be a means to an end as well as an end in itself.

Communication: Its Blocking and Its Facilitation

Carl R. Rogers

It may seem curious that a person whose whole professional effort is devoted to psychotherapy should be interested in problems of communication. What relationship is there between providing therapeutic help to individuals with emotional maladjustments and the concern of this conference with obstacles to communication? Actually the relationship is very close indeed. The whole task of psychotherapy is the task of dealing with a failure in communication. The emotionally maladjusted person, the "neurotic," is in difficulty first because communication within himself has broken down, and second because as a result of this his communication with others has been damaged. If this sounds somewhat strange, then let me put it in other terms. In the "neurotic" individual, parts of himself which have been termed unconscious, or repressed, or denied to awareness, become blocked off so that they no longer communicate themselves to the conscious or managing part of himself. As long as this is true, there are distortions in the way he communicates himself to others, and so he suffers both within himself, and in his interpersonal relations. The task of psychotherapy is to help the person achieve, through a special relationship with a therapist, good communication within himself. Once this is achieved he can communicate more freely and more effectively with others. We may say then that psychotherapy is good communication, within and between men. We may also turn that statement around and it will still be true. Good communication, free communication, within or between men, is always therapeutic.

It is, then, from a background of experience with communication in counseling and psychotherapy that I want to present here two ideas. I wish to state what I believe is one of the major factors in blocking or impeding communication, and then I wish to present what in our experience has proven to be a very important way of improving or facilitating communication.

I would like to propose, as an hypothesis for consideration, that the major barrier to mutual interpersonal communication is our very natural tendency to judge, to evaluate, to approve or disapprove, the statement of the other person, or the other group. Let me illustrate my meaning with some very simple examples. As you leave the meeting tonight, one of the statements you are likely to hear is, "I didn't like that man's talk." Now what do you respond? Almost invariably your reply will be either approval or disapproval of the attitude expressed. Either you respond, "I didn't either. I thought it was terrible," or else you tend to reply, "Oh, I thought it was really good." In other words, your primary reaction is to evaluate what has just been said to you, to evaluate it from *your* point of view, your own frame of reference.

Or take another example. Suppose I say with some feeling, "I think the Republicans are behaving in ways that show a lot of good sound sense these days," what is the response that arises in your mind as you listen? The overwhelming likelihood is that it will be evaluative. You will find yourself agreeing, or disagreeing, or making some judgment about me such as "He must be a conservative," or "He seems solid in his thinking." Or let us take an illustration from the international scene. Russia says vehemently, "The treaty with Japan is a war plot on the part of the United States." We rise as one person to say "That's a lie!"

This last illustration brings in another element connected with my hypothesis. Although the tendency to make evaluations is common in almost all interchange of language, it is very much heightened in those situations where feelings and emotions are deeply involved. So the stronger our feelings, the more likely it is that there will be no mutual element in the communication. There will be just two ideas, two feelings, two judgments, missing each other in psychological space. I'm sure you recognize this from your own experience. When you have not been emotionally involved yourself, and have listened to a heated discussion, you often go away thinking, "Well, they actually weren't talking about the same thing." And they were not. Each was making a judgment, an evaluation, from his frame of reference. There was really nothing which could be called communication in any genuine sense. This tendency to react to any emotionally meaningful statement by forming an evaluation of it from our own point of view, is, I repeat, the major barrier to interpersonal communication.

But is there any way of solving this problem, of avoiding this barrier? I feel that we are making exciting progress toward this goal and I would like to present it as simply as I can. Real communication occurs, and this evaluative tendency is avoided, when we listen with understanding. What does that mean? It means *to see the expressed idea and attitude from the other person's point of view, to sense how it feels to him, to achieve his frame of reference in regard to the thing he is talking about.*

Stated so briefly, this may sound absurdly simple, but it is not. It is an approach which we have found extremely potent in the field of psychotherapy. It is the most effective agent we know for altering the basic personality structure of an individual, and improving his relationships and his communications with others. If I can listen to what he can tell me, if I can understand how it seems to him, if I can see its personal meaning for him, if I can sense the emotional flavor which it has for him, then I will be releasing potent forces of change in him. If I can really understand how he hates his father, or hates the university, or hates communists — if I can catch the flavor of his fear of insanity, or his fear of atom bombs, or of Russia — it will be of the greatest help to him in altering those very hatreds and fears, and in establishing realistic and harmonious relationships with the very people and situations toward which he has felt hatred and fear. We know from our research that such empathic understanding — understanding *with* a person, not *about* him — is such an effective approach that it can bring about major changes in personality.

Some of you may be feeling that you listen well to people, and that you have never seen such results. The chances are very great indeed that your listening has not been of the type I have described. Fortunately I can suggest a little laboratory experiment which you can try to test the quality of your understanding. The next time you get into an argument with your wife, or your friend, or with a small group of friends, just stop the discussion for a moment and for an experiment, institute this rule. "Each person can speak up for himself only *after* he has first restated the ideas and feelings of the previous speaker accurately, and to that speaker's satisfaction." You see what this would mean. It would simply mean that before presenting your own point of view, it would be necessary for you to really achieve the other speaker's frame of reference — to understand his thoughts and feelings so well that you could summarize them for him. Sounds simple doesn't it? But if you try it you will discover it one of the most difficult things you have ever tried to do. However, once you have been able to see the other's point of view, your own comments will have to be drastically revised. You will also find the emotion going out of the discussion, the differences being reduced, and those differences which remain being of a rational and understandable sort.

Can you imagine what this kind of an approach would mean if it were projected into larger areas? What would happen to a labor-management dispute if it was conducted in such a way that labor, without necessarily agreeing, could accurately state management's point of view in a way that management could accept; and management, without approving labor's stand, could state labor's case in a way that labor agreed was accurate? It would mean that real communication was established, and one could practically guarantee that some reasonable solution would be reached.

If, then, this way of approach is an effective avenue to good communication and good relationships, as I am quite sure you will agree if you try the experiment I have mentioned, why is it not more widely tried and used? I will try to list the difficulties which keep it from being utilized.

In the first place it takes courage, a quality which is not too widespread. I am indebted to Dr. S. I. Hayakawa, the semanticist, for pointing out that to carry on psychotherapy in this fashion is to take a very real risk, and that courage is required. If you really understand another person in this way, if you are willing to enter his private world and see the way life appears to him, without any attempt to make evaluative judgments, you run the risk of being changed yourself. You might see it his way, you might find yourself influenced in your attitudes or your personality. This risk of being changed is one of the most frightening prospects most of us can face. If I enter, as fully as I am able, into the private world of a neurotic or psychotic individual, isn't there a risk that I might become lost in that world? Most of us are afraid to take that risk. Or if we had a Russian communist speaker here tonight, or Senator Joe McCarthy, how many of us would dare to try to see the world from each of these points of view? The great majority of us could not *listen;* we would find ourselves compelled to *evaluate,* because listening would seem too dangerous. So the first requirement is courage, and we do not always have it.

But there is a second obstacle. It is just when emotions are strongest that it is most difficult to achieve the frame of reference of the other person or group. Yet it is the time the attitude is most needed, if communication is to be established. We have not found this to be an insuperable obstacle in our experience in psychotherapy. A third party, who is able to lay aside his own feelings and evaluations, can assist greatly by listening with understanding to each person or group and clarifying the views and attitudes each holds. We have found this very effective in small groups in which contradictory or antagonistic attitudes exist. When the parties to a dispute realize that they are being understood, that someone sees how the situation seems to them, the statements grow less exaggerated and less defensive, and it is no longer necessary to maintain the attitude, "I am 100% right and you are 100% wrong." The influence of such an understanding catalyst in the group permits the members to come closer and closer to the objective truth involved in the relationship. In this way mutual communication is established and some type of agreement becomes much more possible. So we may say that though heightened emotions make it much more difficult to understand *with* an opponent, our experience makes it clear that a neutral, understanding, catalyst type of leader or therapist can overcome this obstacle in a small group.

This last phrase, however, suggests another obstacle to utilizing the approach I have described. Thus far all our experience has been with small face-to-face groups — groups exhibiting industrial tensions, religious tensions, racial tensions, and therapy groups in which many personal tensions are present. In these small groups our experience, confirmed by a limited amount of research, shows that this basic approach leads to improved communication, to greater acceptance of others and by others, and to attitudes which are more positive and more problem-solving in nature. There is a decrease in defensiveness, in exaggerated statements, in evaluative and critical behavior. But these findings are from small groups. What about trying to achieve understanding between larger groups that are geographically remote? Or between face-to-face groups who are not speaking for themselves, but simply as representatives of others, like the delegates at Kaesong? Frankly we do not know the answers to these questions. I believe the situation might be put this way. As social scientists we have a tentative test-tube solution of the problem of breakdown in communication. But to confirm the validity of this test-tube solution, and to adapt it to the enormous problems of communication-breakdown between classes, groups, and nations, would involve additional funds, much more research, and creative thinking of a high order.

Even with our present limited knowledge we can see some steps which might be taken, even in large groups, to increase the amount of listening *with,* and to decrease the amount of evaluation *about.* To be imaginative for a moment, let us suppose that a therapeutically oriented international group went to the Russian leaders and said, "We want to achieve a genuine understanding of your views and even more important, of your attitudes and feelings, toward the United States. We will summarize and resummarize these views and feelings if necessary, until you agree that our description represents the situation as it seems to you." Then suppose they did the same thing with the leaders in our own country. If they then gave the widest possible distribution to these two views, with the feelings clearly described but not expressed in name-calling, might not the effect be very great? It would not guarantee the type of understanding I have been describing, but it would make it much more possible. We can understand the feelings of a person who hates us much more readily when his attitudes are accurately described to us by a neutral third party, than we can when he is shaking his fist at us.

But even to describe such a first step is to suggest another obstacle to this approach of understanding. Our civilization does not yet have enough faith in the social sciences to utilize their findings. The opposite is true of the physical sciences. During the war when a test-tube solution was found to the problem of synthetic rubber, millions of dollars and an army of talent was turned loose on the problem of using that finding. If synthetic rubber could be made in milligrams, it could and would be made in the thousands of tons. And it was. But in the social science realm, if a way is found of facilitating communication and mutual understanding in small groups, there is no guarantee that the finding will be utilized. It may be a generation or more before the money and the brains will be turned loose to exploit that finding.

In closing, I would like to summarize this small-scale solution to the problem of barriers in communication, and to point out certain of its characteristics.

I have said that our research and experience to date would make it appear that breakdowns in communication, and the evaluative tendency which is the major barrier to communication, can be avoided. The solution is provided by creating a situation in which each of the different parties come to understand the other from the *other's* point of view. This has been achieved, in practice, even when feelings run high, by the influence of a person who is willing to understand each point of view empathically, and who thus acts as a catalyst to precipitate further understanding.

This procedure has important characteristics. It can be initiated by one party, without waiting for the other to be ready. It can even be initiated by a neutral third person, providing he can gain a minimum of cooperation from one of the parties.

This procedure can deal with the insincerities, the defensive exaggerations, the lies, the "false fronts" which characterize almost every failure in communication. These defensive distortions drop away with astonishing speed as people find that the only intent is to understand, not judge.

This approach leads steadily and rapidly toward the discovery of the truth, toward a realistic appraisal of the objective barriers to communication. The dropping of some defensiveness by one party leads to further dropping of defensiveness by the other party, and truth is thus approached.

This procedure gradually achieves mutual communication. Mutual communication tends to be pointed toward solving a problem rather than toward attacking a person or group. It leads to a situation in which I see how the problem appears to you, as well as to me, and you see how it appears to me, as well as to you. Thus accurately and realistically defined, the problem is almost certain to yield to intelligent attack, or if it is in part insoluble, it will be comfortably accepted as such.

This then appears to be a test-tube solution to the breakdown of communication as it occurs in small groups. Can we take this small-scale answer, investigate it further, refine it, develop it and apply it to the tragic and well-nigh fatal failures of communication which threaten the very existence of our modern world? It seems to me that this is a possibility and a challenge which we should explore.

Notes

1. For an extended discussion and illustration of this idea, see Anatol Rapoport, *Fights, Games, and Debates* (Ann Arbor: University of Michigan Press, 1960), to which we are heavily indebted.

Persuasion, Rogerian Rhetoric, and Imaginative Play

James S. Baumlin

James S. Baumlin's essay suggests that argumentation theory should emphasize the multiplicity and constructed nature of the human self and the value of play to effective persuasion. In this essay, published first in Rhetoric Society Quarterly *in 1987, Baumlin reminds argumentation theorists that truly persuading listeners or readers involves asking them to change their notions of themselves. In order to make such a change, he continues, we must move beyond the still-dominant notion of the fixed and stable identity.*

Baumlin argues that Carl Rogers's work — especially Rogers's belief that interlocutors should give themselves over to each other's ideas in an attempt at absolute understanding — can help theorists conceptualize the kind of nonthreatening, imaginative play necessary for persuasion. Such imaginative play, Baumlin asserts, can help us move past an oppositional model of argumentation, one that does not allow for true change in individual selves and, therefore, for true freedom. Baumlin's essay offers the theoretical underpinnings for a pedagogy designed to promote deep understanding and offers provocative questions for discussion: Can anyone identify completely with another's ideas, feelings, and assumptions? If we assume we can, does that open the door for appropriation and domination of others? How can we promote empathy and imaginative play among students while also teaching them to be critical of the limits of such activities?

See Phyllis Lassner's "Feminist Responses to Rogerian Argument" (p. 406) and Doug Brent's "Rogerian Rhetoric: Ethical Growth through Alternative Forms of Argumentation" (p. 297) for other views on the application of Rogerian theories to argumentation.

deas can shape us, change us, and a change in beliefs enacts a change in self: witness, in an extreme literary case, Ebenezer Scrooge, or the man who admits, after years of self-deception, that he is an alcoholic. Yet teachers, preachers, politicians alike know that real change is rare and slow; we are, as a species, resistant to changes in our belief structures. Reasons for this resistance are easy to find. When beliefs become reflexes, habits of thought ingrained through a lifetime of unquestioned repetition, they become — as habits — hard indeed to change: So often we cling to a value or belief like the alcoholic to his bottle, afraid to question its effect on us, afraid of facing life without it. And logical appeal alone can never overcome such habit. There is yet another reason for this resistance, more subtle and more compelling: If we change with our beliefs, then surely our very identity, our sense of self, becomes threatened along with our belief structures. For whatever security and certainty and stability we perceive in ourselves and in the world rests on the stability of our network or web of beliefs. Right or wrong, our beliefs give us our comforting sense of security in a stable, predictable, understandable world; they also contribute to our sense of a fixed, stable self.

We choose, therefore, to live in a Newtonian, indeed Platonic universe of fixed laws and stable phenomena — a universe of fixed identities. Need we wonder why? The alternative ontology, the universe described by the modern physicist Werner Heisenberg — or, for that matter, the ancient Sophist Gorgias — denies certainty and fixture: Things change. And people change. And there is, for most of us, anxiety in such a recognition, a threat to our identities. Yet we have experienced the sad results when beliefs clash in their attempt to dominate, indeed define a "singular" reality: The more powerful ideology tyrannizes over the rest, treating them all rather as competitors for defining a single and stable reality than as collaborators in fashioning a world of greater complexity and potentiality. We fight for our beliefs as if our lives were at stake (and, since we define ourselves in accordance with our beliefs, in this real sense they are). We fight because in this arena we have not yet learned to play — I will explain this in later paragraphs — and we fight because we have forgotten that we *can* change ourselves, change each other, grow towards each other rather than apart. In this arena of beliefs and values, we can and should enjoy the capacity, at least, of persuading and being persuaded.

(1)

Speakers and audience alike rarely exercise their capacity for persuasion. Most speakers accept the resistance of an opposing audience as given, and changing the beliefs of such an audience is, in fact, rarely their goal. Many arguments do not even *attempt* to persuade but seek only to *confirm* an audience's adherence to beliefs they already hold. The strongest pleas often serve only to strengthen the believers — or alienate and anger more fully those who oppose. The strongest pleas may move our emotions and our wills to action (or reaction, if opposed); but rarely do they change us, converting those of no prior belief. This process of confirming an audience is not useless, of course. Most of us, on most issues, show a bored lack of concern, or show a bland, "intellectual" sort of adherence to a value or issue; we may agree "in principle" with philanthropy, but ignore the poverty in our midst, oppose apartheid "in principle" but not work toward its dismantling. Most of us, on most issues, at most times, live our lives in a passive state of disinterest toward issues, giving a numb sort of "yea" or "nay" — for we do not see our identities fully engaged and committed (or, conversely, threatened). And passive adherence must be turned to *acts,* involve our emotions and will — our whole self — in our beliefs. Catholicism provides an analogy: Once one is baptized, one must be confirmed in the faith. Confirmation, then serves an important purpose for the speaker: to move a convinced audience toward action. But how can a speaker succeed when his goal is to change minds?

If there is *confirmatio,* where, in our discourse, can there be *conversio* — literally, the change in belief, change in self? Certainly it cannot occur in a model for discourse that envisions only the three audience responses of opposition, disinterest, and identification. Note, however, the continuum these responses form. Separating opposition from identification is disinterest, the refusal to engage or identify with an issue; one might not disagree with a belief or value here as much as simply ignore it. If one does disagree, it is a disagreement of words — and not of the heart; a person reacting in disinterest typically says "No; but I don't care." Conversely, a person may agree with an argument, but not translate this agreement into a personal commitment or action. In either case, an emotional involvement is lacking. Emotional involvement occurs, rather, on the extreme ends of this continuum, in opposition and in identification. Here the whole man — mind, emotions, and will — is engaged in the argument and indeed *identifies itself* with the issue at hand. The world-views of speaker and audience become one: Kenneth Burke is right in equating persuasion with identification. Opposition, on the other hand, defines the self of the audience in its difference from the speaker's values and world-view. The audience's distinctive identity is asserted and preserved in its rejection of the speaker's argument.

The above model, though simplistic to the point of brashness, is a fairly traditional version of audience response. Its strength, if it has any, is that it observes two distinct features of this response: the extent of emotional engagement, and the way that the self is defined, either by identification with or in opposition to another's world-view. In each case, however, the self described by this model is fixed and singular, either this or that, and there seems to be no mechanism by which the self of the audience can be transformed from one of difference (or opposition) to one of identification with the speaker's world-view. Confirmation of belief remains possible — for the direction of movement in this traditional model is toward strengthened belief or opposition (and therefore towards an equal strengthening of one's self-identity). But in such a model the *direction* of one's belief appears unchangeable. Disinterest cannot mediate between the two poles of opposition and identification: It forms a chasm against rather than a bridge for change. True persuasion, in this particular model of audience response, is an impossibility.

There is another possible response, however, one in which the audience says — not "I agree" or "I disagree" (or "I don't care") — but, rather, "I understand." Understanding (or imaginative play, as I shall soon call it) turns this trinity into a quaternity of responses, offering an alternative that can in fact *mediate* between opposition and identification — that can become a mechanism, in other words, for change or true persuasion. Psychologist Carl Rogers, who was the first to explore the role of sympathetic understanding in persuasion, suggests that "the major barrier to mutual interpersonal communication is our very natural tendency to judge, to evaluate, to approve or disapprove, the statement of the other person" (284). Of course we evaluate and approve (or reject) another's discourse in comparison with our own world-view. But if we foster in ourselves an attitude of understanding, we will, according to Rogers, "see the expressed idea and attitude from the other person's point of view . . . sense how it feels to him . . . achieve his frame of reference in regard to the thing he is talking about" (285). As a result of such an attitude we "will find the emotion going out of the discussion, the differences being reduced, and those differences which remain being of a rational and understandable sort" (286). Paul Bator elaborates: "A necessary correlate of acceptance (of another's view) is understanding, an understanding which implies that the listener accepts the views of the speaker without knowing cognitively what will result."

> Such understanding, in turn, encourages the speaker to explore untried avenues of exchange. Rogers explains: "Acceptance does not mean much until it involves understanding. It is only as I *understand* the feelings and thoughts which seem so horrible to you, or so weak, or so sentimental, or so bizarre — it is only as I see them as you see them, and accept them and you, that you feel really free to explore all the hidden nooks and frightening crannies of your inner and often buried experience." (428–29)

The Rogerian strategy, in which participants in a discussion collaborate to find areas of shared experience, thus allows speaker and audience to open up their worlds to each other; and in this attempt at mutual understanding there is the *possibility,* at least, of persuasion. For in this state of sympathetic understanding we recognize both the *multiplicity* of world-views and our *freedom* to choose among them — either to retain our old or take a new.

To complete the model, then, and allow for the possibility of change in an audience, we must place as an alternative to disinterest and opposition the Rogerian attitude of receptive, sympathetic understanding. Given recent interest in Rogerian rhetoric, it should not be surprising to find understanding at the heart of any modern description of persuasion; through the rest of this essay, though, I shall explore some epistemological implications of Rogerian argument that have gone largely unnoticed by rhetorical theorists. For understanding, as I shall argue, can be achieved only in a world-view that conceives of self and reality as fluid and potentially multiple. And understanding demands not only a collaborative, as opposed to a combative or manipulative, rhetoric: It demands a rhetoric that is essentially playful or ludic in nature. Understanding, then, is possible only in a world of indeterminacy (and therefore of infinite potentiality), where the true *homo rhetoricus* is recognized as *homo ludens*. Thus, I would call understanding a realm of plural selves or identities. For we achieve this attitude when we sympathize with another's beliefs and world-view — when we role-play, in a sense, the life and values of another person. In a spirit of play and with suspended emotions we become that other person, taking on his value-system and trying out his world. Understanding requires, therefore, a temporary negation or effacement of self: We cease being only ourselves, cease reacting and thinking in ways we have become habituated to, and give ourselves over to an alien, often chaotic, inevitably unstable mixture of interests, values, desires. We mix another's values — we mix another's world — with our own. And out of the chaos we may see patterns of behavior and belief emerge that we can give fresh and perhaps full assent to. These beliefs were not originally our own; the self that emerges within these new patterns was not originally us — self invents itself anew in the free play of worlds.

Two of the above propositions — that rhetoric is a form of imaginative play, and that human personality consists of a dynamic multiplicity of selves — received not their first but surely their strongest formulation by Richard Lanham:

> Rhetorical man is an actor; his reality public, dramatic. His sense of identity, his self, depends on the reassurance of daily histrionic reenactment. He is thus centered in time and concrete local event. The lowest common denominator of his life is a social situation. And his motivations must be characteristically ludic, agonistic. He thinks first of winning, of mastering the rules the current game enforces. He assumes a natural agility in changing orientations. . . . he has dwelt not in a single value-structure but in several. He is thus committed to no single construction of the world; much rather, to prevailing at the game at hand. (4)

The multiplicity of value structures and indeed of worlds is the *sine qua non* of persuasion, and indeed of rhetoric as a mode of thinking and a way of living. Human values, and human roles, change — and rhetoric itself is the effecting of change through language. This multiplicity of perspectives, and the ludic nature of rhetoric, are aspects of

Lanham's thesis which I wholeheartedly espouse. But I hope to extend his thesis in a few significant ways. Lanham focuses almost exclusively on the speaker's ludic activity, ignoring the full impact of rhetorical play on audience. In addition, he emphasizes the antagonism and combativeness of rhetoric — elements that work, as I have argued, to *confirm* audience beliefs, but which cannot cause change. Actual persuasion occurs not through combat with an audience but through *collaboration* (though *collusion,* foregrounding *lusus* or play, is perhaps the more accurate term); as such, the notion of imaginative play can explain the workings of both Rogerian therapy and rhetorical persuasion. Finally, I would like to suggest an alternative to Lanham's model of human personality, which posits a number of dramatic, "rhetorical" selves arrayed around a serious, "central" self. I would argue (and I suspect Lanham would ultimately agree) that the central self, which each of us looks toward as the stable, unchanging core of our personality, is as much a "rhetorical" invention as the social roles/selves arrayed around it. The perceived stability and fixture of our central self becomes, in other words, an act of will, and not a part or an expression of our essence. A sense of fixed self provides us with a secure identity and with our sense of continuity, but this fixture and stability is nevertheless willed into existence — invented and maintained through patterns of language use and general behavior. As such the central self, our sense of a fixed identity, becomes susceptible to rhetoric, capable of change. The following paragraphs will show debts to others besides Lanham, to literary theorists (particularly in reader-response criticism) and contemporary hermeneuticians. This is itself worth noting: In past decades, the most exciting research into audience response has come not from students of rhetoric but from students of literature, philosophy, psychology. Rhetoric — traditionally the study of response and change — needs still to catch up with these disciplines.

(2)

In a recent *PMLA* article Marshall W. Alcorn and Mark Bracher survey critics "who argue that reading literature can influence if not actually mold the structure of the reader's self." They cite Georges Poulet on the idea that when one reads a text, "one's own identity is set aside and the text constitutes a new subjectivity within oneself." They quote Wolfgang Iser: "If reading removes the subject-object division that constitutes all perception, it follows that the reader will be 'occupied' by the thoughts of the author, and these in turn will cause the drawing of new 'boundaries.' . . . Every text we read draws a different boundary within our personality, so that the virtual background (the real 'me') will take on a different form, according to the theme of the text concerned" (342). We need simply add that this redrawing of psychic boundaries can result from an interaction with any kind of discourse — surely with persuasive discourse — and that hearing, as well as reading, can have this effect. But we must still ask ourselves: What allows for this re-experiencing, this re-creating of self — this meeting and intermixture of two worlds? Doesn't the very admission of alternative worlds confirm Heisenberg's principle of indeterminacy — and wouldn't this, in turn, foster the anxiety and insecurity that we all, very humanly, try at all costs to avoid in our lives? The realm of understanding is, after all, a realm of *potentiality,* and therefore of *uncertainty:* More than one course of action is admitted in understanding, more than one set of values — and this necessarily introduces contradiction, confusion. Indeed the realm of understanding (that is, of freely imagining and "trying on" another's beliefs) fosters at the same time a state of doubt (that is, of questioning the invincibility or even validity of one's own previously held world-view). Put otherwise, to understand — to imagine freely another's experience and to admit its validity and truth and goodness — is, in some degree, to doubt the self and its seemingly secure world-view. So if understanding breeds, at the same time, uncertainty, why do we not simultaneously feel threat and insecurity? — and why shouldn't an audience's opposition follow, therefore, from such a threat to identity?

A possible answer to such questions, one developed progressively by J. Huizinga, Hans-Georg Gadamer, and Richard Lanham, is that sympathetic understanding and persuasion result from imaginative play, and that by appealing vividly and directly to the imagination — by making one's case within the playground of the audience's mind — a speaker can control, even reduce the perception of threat. Perhaps rhetoric is best explained as a mental activity of "playing man" or *homo ludens,* as J. Huizinga describes our species. "Play," Huizinga notes, "creates order, *is* order. Into an imperfect world and into the confusion of life it brings a temporary, a limited perfection" (10). Play, in other words, is world-building, and allows for imaginative transport out of one's self "without, however, wholly losing consciousness of 'ordinary reality.'" Thus the playing child's — and I would add the rhetorician's — representation of a game-world "is not so much a sham-reality as a realization in appearance: 'imagination' in the original sense of the word" (14). Most significant, Huizinga observes that playing together fosters *identification:*

> A play-community generally tends to become permanent even after the
> game is over. . . . the feeling of being "apart together" in an exceptional
> situation, of sharing something important, of mutually withdrawing
> from the rest of the world and rejecting the usual norms, retains its
> magic beyond the duration of the individual game. (12)

Isn't this description of imaginative play — of voluntary imaginative activity taking place within prescribed limits of time and place, apart from the world but genuinely affecting the spirit of the participants — a description also of Rogerian and indeed of most methods of psychotherapy? Doesn't therapy allow one to "play out" otherwise threatening conflicts within the secure confines of a "game situation" (i.e., the analytic session)? Alcorn and Bracher have made this very claim for literature, which — like psychotherapy — can "promote greater tolerance of unfamiliar and potentially traumatic experiences. Meissner observes that experiencing potentially overwhelming emotions in a safe and supportive context 'can have an effect similar to desensitization, so that the patient is much better able to tolerate these affective experiences and to integrate them with the rest of his experiential life'" (344–45). Though their evidence comes from W. W. Meissner rather than Carl Rogers, the implication is the same: The controlled, game situation of therapy, like other forms of imaginative play, offers a "safe and supportive context" for exploring the "unfamiliar and potentially traumatic." And by freeing the patient from fear and habitual patterns of response, such play gives the patient freedom to accept what was once unfamiliar and perhaps even threatening, and to integrate it into the self.

Whether it occurs from our interaction with literature or with other forms of discourse — including the dialogue of psychotherapy — imaginative play reduces the threat we feel when facing alternatives; it does not, however, reduce the seriousness or the risk involved in the choices themselves. Paradoxically, play emphasizes the necessity of choice even as it affirms our freedom to choose among alternatives. As Hans-Georg Gadamer writes, a person engaged in the play of imagination

> still has the freedom to decide one way or the other, for one or the other possibility. On the other hand this freedom is not without danger. Rather the game itself is a risk for the player. One can only play with serious possibilities. This means obviously that one may become so engrossed in them that they, as it were, outplay one and prevail over one. The attraction of the game, which it exercises on the player, lies in this risk. (95)

The risk Gadamer speaks of is that game can become actuality, that choices made in play can become choices of life. The game can outplay us. In fact we do not play the game: The game plays us, taking over our world, making its rules of decision and conduct our own. And as Gadamer suggests, reading and response to literature enacts just such a serious game: "The work of art has its true being in the fact that it becomes an experience changing the person experiencing it" (92).

Once again, isn't this description of imaginative play also a description of rhetoric's impact upon an audience? Surely the first great rhetoricians of antiquity, Gorgias and the Sophists who followed him, recognized both the existence of a manifold reality and the ludic nature of persuasive speech. As Gorgias asserts in his "Encomium to Helen," speech "has the power to put an end to fear, to remove grief, to instill joy and increase pity" (8); what gives speech such power over an audience is its ability to create mental images — to substitute images in the mind for palpable phenomena — and in this way give imaginative reality to that which is as yet only possible. Play, being nonthreatening, allows the potential and hypothetical to come to temporary imaginative life in the mind of the audience. That which is imagined *is* only potential; it is up to the audience to give life to a thought — to embody a belief or adopt a course of action, ultimately, as its own. That which is "unthinkable" or perhaps even threatening to the rigidly defined, single self poses no danger to a fluid self engaged in imaginative play; that which one imagines *is,* once again, only *potential* — a vain bubble if rejected, an exciting prospect if we give it our assent. And we can explore issues more courageously in our imaginations than we are willing to do in the actions and thoughts of our daily lives. Thoughts freely and imaginatively pursued involve little threat, then, to the thinker — much less, at any rate, than the muzzle of a gun or a picket line, other more palpable, though generally failed means of persuasion. The classical rhetorical concept of *enargeia,* which Chaim Perelman resuscitated in the notion of "presence," is thus instrumental in establishing an attitude of understanding: Potentially new worlds, potentially new roles — potentially new selves — are given imaginative presence in the mind of the audience, revealing for examination and choice a new realm of experience. Again, the logic of discourse may *convince;* yet the extent to which discourse *invites such imaginative participation* and mixing of worlds will determine its success or failure as *persuasion.*

Like poetry, persuasive discourse can rely heavily on the compelling image to draw our imaginations into new worlds and new roles. It does not surprise, then, that the histories of rhetoric and poetry have been intertwined since antiquity. Gorgias, for example, looked upon his speeches as prose-poems, and both Isocrates and Cicero claimed a close kinship between the orator and poet. Undoubtedly, that kinship tie is their mutual grounding in imaginative play. For *poesis,* as Huizinga suggests, "is a play-function. It proceeds within the playground of the mind, in a world of its own which the mind creates for it. There things have a very different physiognomy from the other they wear in 'ordinary life,' and are bound by ties other than those of logic and causality" (119). Poetry, therefore, and fiction are among the most powerful tools in creating new worlds, and inviting understanding; so much so that there are, quite possibly, elements of *poesis* (and certainly of *enargeia*) in all truly persuasive discourse. Indeed the distinctions made throughout this essay between "literature" and "persuasive discourse" prove more apparent than real: The literary response, like the response to persuasion, rests squarely on imaginative play.

(3)

Finally, we exercise our freedom when participating in another's discourse — for otherwise we respond with disinterest or opposition, boredom or indignation. The realm of imaginative play, then, allows us to maintain our freedom while we explore new roles. More importantly, it is only in the realm of imaginative play, of understanding, that we actually make choices about who we shall be. In a state either of opposition or of identification the self is single and fully, indeed rigidly, defined. Only in a state of play, of unlimited potentiality, is the self equally fluid and changeable. In addition habit, emotion, and previous structures of belief — those elements of personality that sustain our illusion of a single, fixed self — become constraints upon our freedom, constraints upon our ability to create a new self and a new world to live in. Only in a world of play can such constraints be thrown off. Paradoxically, then, in our recognition of and sympathy toward the other we realize our own freedom to change — that is, to re-create our selves along new lines. The value of discourse itself lies ultimately in this ability to lead us into a realm of potentiality and of fluid, changeable identity, where we can actualize the limitless potential that man has for self-creation. I am arguing, in fine, that persuasion is impossible in any model of discourse that views the self as a single, fixed entity. This, rather, is persuasion: to open up a new world to the imagination of an audience and to free the audience from rigid structures of habit and belief. And while persuasion has often been connected with manipulation and coercion, it should in fact *return freedom* to an audience; it should return to them the ability to invent themselves and assume responsibility for creating their selves and their world.

References

Alcorn, Marshall W., and Mark Bracher. "Literature, Psychoanalysis, and the Re-Formation of the Self: A New Direction for Reader-Response Theory." *PMLA* 100 (1985), 342–54.

Bator, Paul. "Aristotelian and Rogerian Rhetoric." *College Composition and Communication* 31 (1980), 427–32.

Burke, Kenneth. *A Rhetoric of Motives.* Englewood Cliffs, NJ: Prentice-Hall, 1950.

Gadamer, Hans-Georg. *Truth and Method.* New York: Seabury P, 1975.

Gorgias. "Encomium of Helen." In *The Older Sophists.* Ed. Rosamund Kent Sprague. Columbia: U of South Carolina P, 1972.

Heisenberg, Werner. *Physics and Philosophy: The Revolution in Modern Science.* New York: Harper and Brothers, 1958.

Huizinga, J. *Homo Ludens: A Study of the Play-Element in Culture.* Boston: Beacon P, 1950.

Lanham, Richard. *The Motives of Eloquence: Literary Rhetoric in the Renaissance.* New Haven: Yale U, 1976.

Perelman, Chaim, and L. Olbrechts-Tyteca. *The New Rhetoric.* Notre Dame: U of Notre Dame, 1971.

Rogers, Carl. "Communication: Its Blocking and Facilitation." In Richard E. Young, Alton L. Becker, and Kenneth L. Pike, *Rhetoric: Discovery and Change.* New York: Harcourt, Brace, and World, 1970, pp. 284–89.

STEPHEN TOULMIN'S PHILOSOPHY OF ARGUMENT

From *The Uses of Argument*

Stephen Toulmin

Stephen Toulmin, along with Chaim Perelman, Lucie Olbrechts-Tyteca, and many others, helped revive argumentation as a mode of significant philosophical inquiry in the twentieth century. His work moved beyond the traditional syllogism into a model that does not depend on absolute truths. Instead, it takes into account probabilities and contingent circumstances to create a system of "practical reasoning." Toulmin's most influential work in rhetoric, The Uses of Argument *(excerpted here), was published in 1958, the same year as Perelman and Olbrechts-Tyteca's* The New Rhetoric. *Both have had a great impact on contemporary understandings of argumentation and informal logic, but Toulmin's work (in particular, his discussion of claims, data, warrants, qualifiers, rebuttals, and backings) has been especially useful for classroom teaching. In fact, many best-selling textbooks, including Annette Rottenberg's* Elements of Argument, *rely on Toulmin's scheme of argumentation, a scheme that is made clear in the visual models Toulmin provides to illustrate his ideas.*

Toulmin is also noted for his analysis of the ways in which arguments vary across fields and yet retain universal characteristics from field to field. Through such work, he helped set the stage for inquiries into the rhetoric of science (for one example, see R. Allen Harris's essay on page 242). Though his work has been celebrated by many scholars, Toulmin has also gathered critics, such as Richard Fulkerson, who believes that applications of Toulmin's ideas in composition are limited because they do not fully recognize argumentative writing as a process. As these few references suggest — and as even a brief review of the literature on argumentation confirms — Toulmin's work is omnipresent in contemporary theory and deserves careful analysis from students and teachers of argument.

For further discussion of Toulmin's ideas, see Gail Stygall's "Toulmin and the Ethics of Argument Fields: Teaching Writing and Argument" (p. 377) and Richard Fulkerson's "Technical Logic, Comp-Logic, and the Teaching of Writing" (p. 321).

The Layout of Arguments

An argument is like an organism. It has both a gross, anatomical structure and a finer, as-it-were physiological one. When set out explicitly in all its detail, it may occupy a number of printed pages or take perhaps a quarter of an hour to deliver; and within this time or space one can distinguish the main phases marking the progress of the argument from the initial statement of an unsettled problem to the final presentation of a conclusion. These main phases will each of them occupy some minutes or paragraphs, and represent the chief anatomical units of the argument — its "organs," so to speak. But within each paragraph, when one gets down to the level of individual sentences, a finer structure can be recognized, and this is the structure with which logicians have mainly concerned themselves. It is at this physiological level that the idea of logical form has been introduced, and here that the validity of our arguments has ultimately to be established or refuted.

The time has come to change the focus of our inquiry, and to concentrate on this finer level. Yet we cannot afford to forget what we have learned by our study of the grosser anatomy of arguments, for here as with organisms the detailed physiology proves most intelligible when expounded against a background of coarser anatomical distinctions. Physiological processes are interesting not least for the part they play in maintaining the functions of the major organs in which they take place; and micro-arguments (as one may christen them) need to be looked at from time to time with one eye on the macro-arguments in which they figure; since the precise manner in which we phrase them and set them out, to mention only the least important thing, may be affected by the role they have to play in the larger context.

In the inquiry which follows, we shall be studying the operation of arguments sentence by sentence, in order to see how their validity or invalidity is connected with the manner of laying them out, and what relevance this connection has to the traditional notion of "logical form." Certainly the same argument may be set out in quite a number of different forms, and some of these patterns of analysis will be more candid than others — some of them, that is, will show the validity or invalidity of an argument more clearly than others, and make more explicit the grounds it relies on and the bearing of these on the conclusion. How, then, should we lay an argument out, if we want to show the sources of its validity? And in what sense does the acceptability or unacceptability of arguments depend upon their "formal" merits and defects?

We have before us two rival models, one mathematical, the other jurisprudential. Is the logical form of a valid argument something quasi-geometrical, comparable to the shape of a triangle or the parallelism of two straight lines? Or alternatively, is it something procedural: Is a formally valid argument one *in proper form,* as lawyers would say, rather than one laid out in a tidy and simple *geometrical* form? Or does the notion of logical form somehow combine both these aspects, so that to lay an argument out in proper form necessarily requires the adoption of a particular geometrical layout? If this last answer is the right one, it at once creates a further problem for us: to see how and why proper procedure demands the adoption of simple geometrical shape, and how that shape guarantees in its turn the validity of our procedures. Supposing valid arguments can be cast in a geometrically tidy form, how does this help to make them any the more cogent?

These are the problems to be studied in the present inquiry. If we can see our way to unraveling them, their solution will be of some importance — particularly for a proper understanding of logic. But to begin with we must go cautiously, and steer clear of the philosophical issues on which we shall hope later to throw some light, concentrating for the moment on questions of a most prosaic and straightforward kind. Keeping our eyes on the categories of applied logic — on the practical business of argumentation, that is, and the notions it requires us to employ — we must ask what features a logically candid layout of arguments will need to have. The establishment of conclusions raises a number of issues of different sorts, and a practical layout will make allowance for these differences: Our first question is — what are these issues, and how can we do justice to them in subjecting our arguments to rational assessment?

Two last remarks may be made by way of introduction, the first of them simply adding one more question to our agenda. Ever since Aristotle it has been customary, when analyzing the micro-structure of arguments, to set them out in a very simple manner: They have been presented three propositions at a time, "minor premiss; major premiss; *so* conclusion." The question now arises, whether this standard form is sufficiently elaborate or candid. Simplicity is of course a merit, but may it not in this case have been bought too dearly? Can we properly classify all the elements in our arguments under the three headings, "major premiss," "minor premiss," and "conclusion," or are these categories misleadingly few in number? Is there even enough similarity between major and minor premisses for them usefully to be yoked together by the single name of "premiss"?

Light is thrown on these questions by the analogy with jurisprudence. This would naturally lead us to adopt a layout of greater complexity than has been customary, for the questions we are asking here are, once again, more general versions of questions already familiar in jurisprudence, and in that more specialized field a whole battery of distinctions has grown up. "What different sorts of propositions," a legal philosopher will ask, "are uttered in the course of a law case, and in what different ways can such propositions bear on the soundness of a legal claim?" This has always been and still is the central question for the student of jurisprudence, and we soon find that the nature of a legal process can be properly understood only if we draw a large number of distinctions. Legal utterances have many distinct functions. Statements of claim, evidence of identification, testimony about events in dispute, interpretations of a statute or discussions of its validity, claims to exemption from the application of a law, pleas in extenuation, verdicts, sentences: All these different classes of proposition have their parts to play in the legal process, and the differences between them are in practice far from trifling. When we turn from the special case of the law to consider rational arguments in general, we are faced at once by the question whether these must not be analyzed in terms of an equally complex set of categories. If we are to set our arguments out with complete logical candor, and understand properly the nature of "the logical process," surely we shall need to employ a pattern of argument no less sophisticated than is required in the law.

The Pattern of an Argument: Data and Warrants

"What, then, is involved in establishing conclusions by the production of arguments?" Can we, by considering this question in a general form, build up from scratch a pattern of analysis which will do justice to all the distinctions which proper procedure forces upon us? That is the problem facing us.

Let it be supposed that we make an assertion, and commit ourselves thereby to the claim which any assertion necessarily involves. If this claim is challenged, we must be able to establish it — that is, make it good, and show that it was justifiable. How is this to be done? Unless the assertion was made quite wildly and irresponsibly, we shall normally have some facts to which we can point in its support: If the claim is challenged, it is up to us to appeal to these facts, and present them as the foundation upon which our claim is based. Of course we may not get the challenger even to agree about the correctness of these facts, and in that case we have to clear his objection out of the way by a preliminary argument: Only when this prior issue or "lemma," as geometers would call it, has been dealt with, are we in a position to return to the original argument. But this complication we need only mention: Supposing the lemma to have been disposed of, our question is how to set the original argument out most fully and explicitly. "Harry's hair is not black," we assert. What have we got to go on? we are asked. Our personal knowledge that it is in fact red: That is our datum, the ground which we produce as support for the original assertion. Petersen, we may say, will not be a Roman Catholic: Why?: We base our claim on the knowledge that he is a Swede, which makes it very unlikely that he will be a Roman Catholic. Wilkinson, asserts the prosecutor in Court, has committed an offense against the Road Traffic Acts: In support of this claim, two policemen are prepared to testify that they timed him driving at 45 m.p.h. in a built-up area. In each case, an original assertion is supported by producing other facts bearing on it.

We already have, therefore, one distinction to start with: between the *claim* or conclusion whose merits we are seeking to establish (C) and the facts we appeal to as a foundation for the claim — what I shall refer to as our *data* (D). If our challenger's question is, "What have you got to go on?" producing the data or information on which the claim is based may serve to answer him; but this is only one of the ways in which our conclusion may be challenged. Even after we have produced our data, we may find ourselves being asked further questions of another kind. We may now be required not to add more factual information to that which we have already provided, but rather to indicate the bearing on our conclusion of the data already produced. Colloquially, the question may now be, not "What have you got to go on?" but "How do you get there?" To present a particular set of data as the basis for some specified conclusion commits us to a certain *step;* and the question is now one about the nature and justification of this step.

Supposing we encounter this fresh challenge, we must bring forward not further data, for about these the same query may immediately be raised again, but propositions of a rather different kind: rules, principles, inference-licenses or what you will, instead of additional items of information. Our task is no longer to strengthen the ground on which our argument is constructed, but is rather to show that, taking these data as a starting point, the step to the original claim or conclusion is an appropriate and legitimate one. At this point, therefore, what are needed are general, hypothetical statements, which can act as bridges, and authorize the sort of step to which our particular argument commits us. These may normally be written very briefly (in the form "If D, then C"); but, for candor's sake, they can profitably be expanded, and made more explicit: "Data such as D entitle one to draw conclusions, or make claims, such as C," or alternatively "Given data D, one may take it that C."

Propositions of this kind I shall call *warrants* (W), to distinguish them from both conclusions and data. [. . .] To pursue our previous examples: The knowledge that Harry's hair is red entitles us to set aside any suggestion that it is black, on account of the warrant, "If anything is red, it will not also be black." (The very triviality of this warrant is connected with the fact that we are concerned here as much with a counterassertion as with an argument.) The fact that Petersen is a Swede is directly relevant to the question of his religious denomination for, as we should probably put it, "A Swede can be taken almost certainly not to be a Roman Catholic." (The step involved here is not trivial, so the warrant is not self-authenticating.) Likewise in the third case: Our warrant will now be some such statement as that "A man who is proved to have driven at more than 30 m.p.h. in a built-up area can be found to have committed an offense against the Road Traffic Acts."

The question will at once be asked, how absolute is this distinction between data, on the one hand, and warrants, on the other. Will it always be clear whether a man who challenges an assertion is calling for the production of his adversary's data, or for the warrants authorizing his steps? Can one, in other words, draw any sharp distinction between the force of the two questions, "What have you got to go on?" and "How do you get there?" By grammatical tests alone, the distinction may appear far from absolute, and the same English sentence may serve a double function: It may be uttered, that is, in one situation to convey a piece of information, in another to authorize a step in an argument, and even perhaps in some contexts to do both these things at once. (All these possibilities will be illustrated before too long.) For the moment, the important thing is not to be too cut and dried in our treatment of the subject, nor to commit ourselves in advance to a rigid terminology. At any rate we shall find it impossible in *some* situations to distinguish clearly two different logical functions; and the nature of this distinction is hinted at if one contrasts the two sentences, "Whenever A, one *has found* that B" and "Whenever A, one *may take it* that B."

We now have the terms we need to compose the first skeleton of a pattern for analyzing arguments. We may symbolize the relation between the data and the claim in support of which they are produced by an arrow, and indicate the authority for taking the step from one to the other by writing the warrant immediately below the arrow:

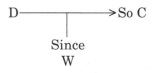

$$D \longrightarrow \text{So C}$$
$$\text{Since}$$
$$W$$

Or, to give an example:

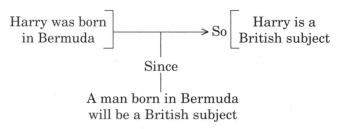

Harry was born in Bermuda ⟶ So Harry is a British subject

Since

A man born in Bermuda will be a British subject

As this pattern makes clear, the explicit appeal in this argument goes directly back from the claim to the data relied on as foundation: The warrant is, in a sense, incidental and explanatory, its task being simply to register explicitly the legitimacy of the step involved and to refer it back to the larger class of steps whose legitimacy is being presupposed.

This is one of the reasons for distinguishing between data and warrants: Data are appealed to explicitly, warrants implicitly. In addition, one may remark that warrants are general, certifying the soundness of *all* arguments of the appropriate type, and have accordingly to be established in quite a different way from the facts we produce as data. This distinction, between data and warrants, is similar to the distinction drawn in the law courts between questions of fact and questions of law, and the legal distinction is indeed a special case of the more general one — we may argue, for instance, that a man whom we know to have been born in Bermuda is presumably a British subject, simply because the relevant laws give us a warrant to draw this conclusion.

One more general point in passing: Unless, in any particular field of argument, we are prepared to work with warrants of *some* kind, it will become impossible in that field to subject arguments to rational assessment. The data we cite if a claim is challenged depend on the warrants we are prepared to operate with in that field, and the warrants to which we commit ourselves are implicit in the particular steps from data to claims we are prepared to take and to admit. But supposing a man rejects all warrants whatever authorizing (say) steps from data about the present and past to conclusions about the future, then for him rational prediction will become impossible; and many philosophers have in fact denied the possibility of rational prediction just because they thought they could discredit equally the claims of all past-to-future warrants.

The skeleton of a pattern which we have obtained so far is only a beginning. Further questions may now arise, to which we must pay attention. Warrants are of different kinds, and may confer different degrees of force on the conclusions they justify. Some warrants authorize us to accept a claim unequivocally, given the appropriate data — these warrants entitle us in suitable cases to qualify our conclusion with the adverb "necessarily"; others authorize us to make the step from data to conclusion either tentatively, or else subject to conditions, exceptions, or qualifications — in these cases other modal qualifiers, such as "probably" and "presumably," are in place. It may not be sufficient, therefore, simply to specify our data, warrant and claim: We may need to add some explicit reference to the degree of force which our data confer on our claim in virtue of our warrant. In a word, we may have to put in a *qualifier*. Again, it is often necessary in the law courts, not just to appeal to a given statute or common-law doctrine, but to discuss explicitly the extent to which this particular law fits the case under consideration, whether it must inevitably be applied in this particular case, or whether special facts may make the case an exception to the rule or one in which the law can be applied only subject to certain qualifications.

If we are to take account of these features of our argument also, our pattern will become more complex. Modal qualifiers (Q) and conditions of exception or rebuttal (R) are distinct both from data and from warrants, and need to be given separate places in our layout. Just as a warrant (W) is itself neither a datum (D) nor a claim (C), since it implies in itself something about both D and C — namely, that the step from the one to the other is legitimate; so, in turn, Q and R are themselves distinct from W, since they comment implicitly on the bearing of W on this step — qualifiers (Q) indicating the strength conferred by the warrant on this step, conditions of rebuttal (R) indicating circumstances in which the general authority of the warrant would have to be set aside. To mark these further distinctions, we may write the qualifier (Q) immediately beside the conclusion which it qualifies (C), and the exceptional conditions which might be capable of defeating or rebutting the warranted conclusion (R) immediately below the qualifier.

To illustrate: Our claim that Harry is a British subject may normally be defended by appeal to the information that he was born in Bermuda, for this datum lends support to our conclusion on account of the warrants implicit in the British Nationality Acts; but the argument is not by itself conclusive in the absence of assurances about his parentage and about his not having changed his nationality since birth. What our information does do is to establish that the conclusion holds good "presumably," and subject to the appropriate provisos. The argument now assumes the form:

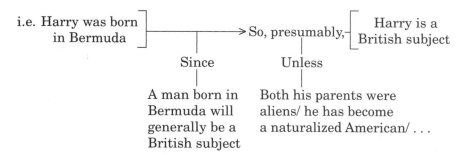

i.e. Harry was born in Bermuda ⟶ So, presumably, Harry is a British subject

Since

A man born in Bermuda will generally be a British subject

Unless

Both his parents were aliens/ he has become a naturalized American/ . . .

We must remark, in addition, on two further distinctions. The first is that between a statement of a warrant, and statements about its applicability — between "A man born in Bermuda will be British," and "This presumption holds good provided his parents were not both aliens, etc." The distinction is relevant not only to the law of the land, but also for an understanding of scientific laws or "laws of nature": It is important, indeed, in all cases where the application of a law may be subject to exceptions, or where a warrant can be supported by pointing to a general correlation only, and not to an absolutely invariable one. We can distinguish also two purposes which may be served by the production of additional facts: These can serve as further data, or they can be cited to confirm or rebut the applicability of a warrant. Thus, the fact that Harry was born in Bermuda and the fact that his parents were not aliens are both of them directly relevant to the question of his present nationality; but they are relevant in different ways. The one fact is a datum, which by itself establishes a presumption of British nationality; the other fact, by setting aside one possible rebuttal, tends to confirm the presumption thereby created.

One particular problem about applicability we shall have to discuss more fully later: When we set out a piece of applied mathematics, in which some system of mathematical relations is used to throw light on a question of (say) physics, the correctness of the calculations will be one thing, their appropriateness to the problem in hand may be quite another. So the question "Is this calculation mathematically impeccable?" may be a very different one from the question "Is this the relevant calculation?" Here too, the applicability of a particular warrant is one question: The result we shall get from applying the warrant is another matter, and in asking about the *correctness* of the result we may have to inquire into both these things independently.

The Pattern of An Argument: Backing Our Warrants

One last distinction, which we have already touched on in passing, must be discussed at some length. In addition to the question whether or on what conditions a warrant is applicable in a *particular* case, we may be asked why *in general* this warrant should be accepted as having authority. In defending a claim, that is, we may produce our data, our warrant, and the relevant qualifications and conditions, and yet find that we have still not satisfied our challenger; for he may be dubious not only about this particular argument but about the more general question whether the warrant (W) is acceptable at all. Presuming the general acceptability of this warrant (he may allow) our argument would no doubt be impeccable — if D-ish facts really do suffice as backing for C-ish claims, all well and good. But does not that warrant in its turn rest on something else? Challenging a particular claim may in this way lead on to challenging, more generally, the legitimacy of a whole range of arguments. "You presume that a man born in Bermuda can be taken to be a British subject," he may say, "but why do you think that?" Standing behind our warrants, as this example reminds us, there will normally be other assurances, without which the warrants themselves would possess neither authority nor currency — these other things we may refer to as the *backing* (B) of the warrants. This "backing" of our warrants is something which we shall have to scrutinize very carefully: Its precise relations to our data, claims, warrants and conditions of rebuttal deserve some clarification, for confusion at this point can lead to trouble later.

We shall have to notice particularly how the sort of backing called for by our warrants varies from one field of argument to another. The *form* of argument we employ in different fields

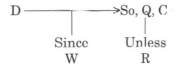

$$D \xrightarrow{\hspace{3cm}} \text{So, Q, C}$$

Since   Unless

W   R

need not vary very much as between fields. "A whale will be a mammal," "A Bermudan will be a Briton," "A Saudi Arabian will be a Muslim": Here are three different warrants to which we might appeal in the course of a practical argument, each of which can justify the same sort of straightforward step from a datum to a conclusion. We might add for variety examples of even more diverse sorts, taken from moral, mathematical or psychological fields. But the moment we start asking about the *backing* which a warrant relies on in each field, great differences begin to appear: The kind of backing we must point to if we are to establish its authority will change greatly as we move from one field of argument to another. "A whale will be (i.e. *is classifiable as*) a mammal," "A Bermudan will be (*in the eyes of the law*) a Briton," "A Saudi Arabian will be (*found to be*) a Muslim" — the words in parentheses indicate what these differences are. One warrant is defended by relating it to a system of taxonomical classification, another by appealing to the statutes governing the nationality of people born in the British colonies, the third by referring to the statistics which record how religious beliefs are distributed among people of different nationalities. We can for the moment leave open the more contentious question, how we establish our warrants in the fields of morals, mathematics and psychology: For the moment all we are trying to show is the *variability* or *field-dependence* of the backing needed to establish our warrants.

We can make room for this additional element in our argument pattern by writing it below the bare statement of the warrant for which it serves as backing (B):

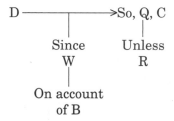

This form may not be final, but it will be complex enough for the purpose of our present discussions. To take a particular example: In support of the claim (C) that Harry is a British subject, we appeal to the datum (D) that he was born in Bermuda, and the warrant can then be stated in the form, "A man born in Bermuda may be taken to be a British subject": Since, however, questions of nationality are always subject to qualifications and conditions, we shall have to insert a qualifying "presumably" (Q) in front of the conclusion, and note the possibility that our conclusion may be rebutted in case (R) it turns out that both his parents were aliens or he has since become a naturalized American. Finally, in case the warrant itself is challenged, its backing can be put in: This will record the terms and the dates of enactment of the Acts of Parliament and other legal provisions governing the nationality of persons born in the British colonies. The result will be an argument set out as follows:

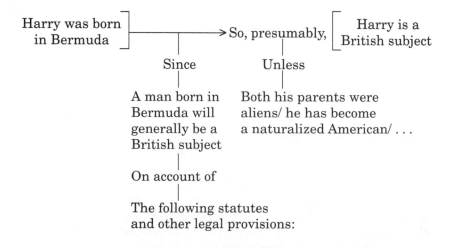

In what ways does the backing of warrants differ from the other elements in our arguments? To begin with the differences between B and W: Statements of warrants, we saw, are hypothetical, bridgelike statements, but the backing for warrants can be expressed in the form of categorical statements of fact quite as well as can the data appealed to in direct support of our conclusions. So long as our statements reflect these functional differences explicitly, there is no danger of confusing the backing (B) for a warrant with the warrant itself (W): Such confusions arise only when these differences are disguised by our forms of expression. In our present example, at any rate, there need be no difficulty. The fact that the relevant statutes have been validly passed into law, and contain the provisions they do, can be ascertained simply by going to the records of the parliamentary proceedings concerned and to the relevant volumes in the books of statute law: The resulting discovery, that such-and-such a statute enacted on such-and-such a date contains a provision specifying that people born in the British colonies of suitable parentage shall be entitled to British citizenship, is a straightforward statement of fact. On the other hand, the warrant which we apply *in virtue of* the statute containing this provision is logically of a very different character — "*If* a man was born in a British colony, he *may be presumed to be* British." Though the facts about the statute may provide all the backing required by this warrant, the explicit statement of the warrant itself is more than a repetition of these facts: It is a general *moral* of a practical character, about the ways in which we can safely argue in view of these facts.

We can also distinguish backing (B) from data (D). Though the data we appeal to in an argument and the backing lending authority to our warrants may alike be stated as straightforward matters of fact, the roles which these statements play in our argument are decidedly different. Data of some kind must be produced, if there is to be an argument there at all: A bare conclusion, without any data produced in its support, is no argument. But the backing of the warrants we invoke need not be made explicit — at any rate to begin with: The warrants may be conceded without challenge, and their backing left understood. Indeed, if we demanded the credentials of all warrants at sight and never let one pass unchallenged, argument could scarcely begin. Jones puts forward an argument invoking warrant W_1, and Smith challenges that warrant; Jones is obliged, as a lemma, to produce another argument in the hope of establishing the acceptability of the first warrant, but in the course of this lemma employs a second warrant W_2; Smith challenges the credentials of this second warrant in turn; and so the game goes on. Some warrants must be accepted provisionally without further challenge, if argument is to be open to us in the field in question: We should not even know what sort of data were of the slightest relevance to a conclusion, if we had not at least a provisional idea of the warrants acceptable in the situation confronting us. The existence of considerations such as would establish the acceptability of the most reliable warrants is something we are entitled to take for granted.

Finally, a word about the ways in which B differs from Q and R: These are too obvious to need expanding upon, since the grounds for regarding a warrant as generally acceptable are clearly one thing, the force which the warrant lends to a conclusion another, and the sorts of exceptional circumstance which may in particular cases rebut the presumptions the warrant creates a third. They correspond, in our example, to the three statements, (i) that the statutes about British nationality *have in fact* been validly passed into law, and say this: . . . (ii) that Harry *may be presumed* to be a British subject, and (iii) that Harry, having recently become a naturalized American, *is no longer covered* by these statutes.

THE NEW RHETORIC

From *The New Rhetoric: A Treatise on Argumentation*

Chaim Perelman and Lucie Olbrechts-Tyteca

The New Rhetoric *was published by Chaim Perelman and Lucie Olbrechts-Tyteca in 1958. This comprehensive study attempts to reintegrate theories of rhetoric into philosophy and to acknowledge the importance of informal logic to everyday and academic life. In particular, Perelman and Olbrechts-Tyteca believe that science is limited in its ability to make sense of the value judgments humans face every day; they sought to revive and revise classical concepts to accommodate life in the highly technological, abstract, and dualistic twentieth century.*

The New Rhetoric *has been exceptionally influential with writing and speech scholars. It helped lay the foundation for rhetoric as a serious subject with a long history (Perelman and Olbrechts-Tyteca provide an extremely thorough analysis of rhetoric in Western culture) and helped to adapt "old" ideas to modern times. For example, the New Rhetoric draws on classical theory to explore the way binary oppositions (e.g., reason and imagination) influence the way we create and use knowledge today. Such an emphasis presaged a great deal of important theory that questions the binary oppositions that have "naturally" developed in Western culture, languages, and argumentation.*

The following brief passages from The New Rhetoric *begin to discuss the ways values relate to argumentation. In addition, the authors summarize a term crucial to the New Rhetoric: "presence." For Perelman and Olbrechts-Tyteca, presence is an undertheorized and highly important element of argumentation that concerns — in its most basic form — rhetors' ability to make even abstract data "real" to an audience so that they can gain the audience's adherence to an argument. As argument teachers today continue to explore the difficulties of communicating across multiple value systems and of helping students to imbue texts with life and meaning, we would do well to explore all that* The New Rhetoric *continues to offer.*

For further study of Perelman and Olbrechts-Tyteca's ideas, consult the section in the bibliography titled "The New Rhetoric" (p. 461).

Agreement

18. Values

Values enter, at some stage or other, into every argument. In reasoning of a scientific nature, they are generally confined to the beginning of the formulation of the concepts and rules that constitute the system concerned and, insofar as the reasoning aims at the truth value, to the conclusion. As far as possible, the actual unfolding of the argument is free from values, and this exclusion is at a maximum in the exact sciences. But in the fields of law, politics, and philosophy, values intervene as a basis for argument at all stages of the developments. One appeals to values in order to induce the hearer to make certain choices rather than others and, most of all, to justify those choices so that they may be accepted and approved by others.

In a discussion, it is not possible to escape from a value simply by denying it. Just as someone who contests that something is a fact must give reasons for his allegation ("I don't see that," which is the same as saying, "I see something else"), so, when a value is in question, a person may disqualify it, subordinate it to others, or interpret it but may not reject all values as a whole: This would amount to leaving the realm of discussion to enter that of force. The gangster who rates his personal safety above anything else can do so without any need for explanation as long as he confines himself to the domain of action. But, if he wants to justify this primacy to others or even to himself, he must acknowledge the other values marshaled against it in order to be able to fight them. In this respect, values are comparable to facts: For, when one of the interlocutors puts forward a value, one must argue to get rid of it, under pain of refusing the discussion; and in general, the argument will imply that other values are accepted.

Various objections are raised to our conception that values are objects of agreement which do not claim the adherence of the universal audience.

In making this distinction, are not more fundamental differences overlooked? Is it not enough to say that facts and truths express the real, whereas values are concerned with an attitude toward the real? But, if the attitude toward the real were universal, it could not be distinguished from truths. It is only its nonuniversal aspect that makes it possible to confer on it a status of its own. It is indeed hard to see how purely formal criteria can be relevant. For a statement can be understood as relating to what is commonly considered a fact or to what is considered a value, depending on its place in the speech, on what it enunciates, refutes, or corrects. Also, the status of statements evolves: When inserted into a system of beliefs for which universal validity is claimed, values may be treated as facts or truths. In the course of the argumentation, and sometimes by a rather slow process, it may perhaps come to be recognized that one is dealing with objects of agreement that cannot make a claim to the adherence of the universal audience.

But if this is, as we claim, the characteristic of values, what about such things as the *True,* the *Good,* the *Beautiful,* and the *Absolute,* which are readily considered as universal or absolute values?

The claim to universal agreement, as far as they are concerned, seems to us to be due solely to their generality. They can be regarded as valid for a universal audience only on condition that their content not be specified; as soon as we try to go into details, we meet only the adherence of particular audiences.

According to E. Dupréel, universal values deserve to be called "values of persuasion" because they are

> *means of persuasion* which, from a sociological viewpoint, *are that and no more than that;* they are, as it were, spiritual tools which can be completely separated from the material they make it possible to shape, anterior to the moment it is used, and remaining intact after use, available, as before, for other occasions.[1]

This conception displays extremely well the role of these values in argumentation. These tools, as Dupréel calls them, can be used for all audiences: The particular values can always be connected to the universal values and serve to make the latter more specific. The actual audience will be able to consider itself all the more close to a universal audience as the particular value seems to fade before the universal value it determines. It is thus by virtue of their being vague that these values appear as universal values and lay claim to a status similar to that of facts. To the extent that they are precisely formulated, they are simply seen to conform to the aspirations of particular groups. Their role is accordingly to justify choices on which there is not unanimous agreement by inserting these choices in a sort of empty frame with respect to which a wider agreement exists. Though this agreement is reached over an empty form, it is nonetheless of considerable significance: It is evidence of the fact that one has decided to transcend particular agreements, at least in intention, and that one recognizes the importance attaching to the universal agreement which these values make it possible to achieve.

19. Abstract Values and Concrete Values

In argumentation concerning values, there is a fundamental, but too often neglected, distinction to be made between abstract values, such as justice or truth, and concrete values, such as France or the Church. A concrete value is one attaching to a living being, a specific group, or a particular object, considered as a unique entity. There is a close connection between the value attached to what is concrete and to what is unique: By displaying the unique character of something we automatically increase its value. By revealing to us the unique character of certain beings, groups, or moments in history, the romantic writers have brought about, even in philosophical thought, a reaction against abstract rationalism, a reaction characterized by the prominent position assigned to that preeminently concrete value — the human person. Though Western morality, insofar as it is based on Greco-Roman ideas, values most the obedience to rules that are valid for all people and under all circumstances, there exist virtues and forms of behavior that can be conceived only in relation to concrete values. Such notions as obligation, fidelity, loyalty, solidarity, and discipline are of this kind. Likewise Confucius' five universally binding obligations — between rulers and ruled, father and son, husband and wife, older brother and younger brother, friend and friend[2] — reflect the importance attached to personal relations among beings who constitute concrete values for one another.

Whatever the dominant values may be in a cultural milieu, the life of the mind cannot avoid relying on abstract values as well as concrete ones. It seems that there have always been people who attach more importance to one set than to the other; perhaps they form characterial families. In any case their distinctive trait would not be complete neglect of values of one kind, but subordination of these values to those of the other. We may contrast Erasmus who preferred an unjust peace to a just war with the man who rated the abstract value of truth higher than Plato's friendship.

Argumentation is based, according to the circumstances, now on abstract values, now on concrete values: It is sometimes difficult to perceive the role played by each. When a person says that men are equal because they are children of the same God, he seems to be relying on a concrete value to find an abstract value, that of equality; but it could also be said that really only the abstract value is expressed, by appealing, through analogy, to a concrete relationship; in spite of the use of *because,* the starting point would lie in the abstract value.

This motion back and forth from concrete to abstract values is nowhere better seen than in reasonings involving God, considered both as absolute abstract value and perfect Being. Is God perfect because he is the incarnation of all abstract values? Is a quality perfection because certain conceptions of God make it possible to grant perfection to that quality? In this matter it is difficult to establish any kind of priority. The contradictory positions taken by Leibniz on this question are very instructive. He knows God is perfect, but he wishes that this perfection should be justifiable and that all God's decisions should not be considered good solely for the very reason that they are God's decisions.[3]

The universality of the principle of sufficient reason requires that there be a sufficient reason, a conformity to a rule, justifying God's choice. On the other hand, belief in the perfection of God precedes any proof that Leibniz may be able to provide and is the starting point for his theology. For a great number of thinkers, God is the model who must be followed in all things. Thus Kenneth Burke was able to draw a lengthy list of all the abstract values which found their origin in the perfect Being.[4]

Some ideologies unwilling to recognize God as the foundation of all values have had to turn to notions of a different order, such as the State or Mankind. These notions also can be conceived either as concrete values of the personal type or as the outcome of reasonings based on abstract values.

The same reality, a social group, for instance, will sometimes be treated as a concrete value and as an entity and sometimes as a multiplicity of individuals which will be opposed to one or several others, by means of argumentation in terms of number which are completely removed from any idea of concrete value. That which is, under certain circumstances, a concrete value is not always such: For a value to be concrete, it must be envisaged in its aspect of unique reality; to say that a particular value is, once and for all, a concrete value is to take an arbitrary stand.

Concrete values are most frequently used as the foundation of abstract values, and conversely. In order to establish which conduct is virtuous, we often turn to a model whom we strive to imitate. The relationship of friendship and the actions it prompts provide Aristotle with a criterion for evaluation:

> Also, the things which we like to do to our friend are more desirable than those we like to do to the man in the street, e.g., just dealing and the doing of good rather than the semblance of them; for we would rather really do good to our friends than seem to do so, whereas towards the man in the street the converse is the case.[5]

Fénelon, on the other hand, is indignant that certain virtues are extolled over others because of the wish to praise a man who practiced them; in his view, "a hero must be praised only in order to teach his virtues to the multitude and to incite it to imitate them."[6]

The need for reliance on abstract values is perhaps essentially connected with change. They seemingly manifest a revolutionary spirit. We have seen the importance the Chinese attached to concrete values, and this attitude would tie in with China's imperviousness to change.

Abstract values can readily be used for criticism, because they are no respecters of persons and seem to provide criteria for one wishing to change the established order. On the other hand, where change is not wanted, there is no reason to raise incompatibilities. Now concrete values can always be harmonized; the very existence of the concrete implies that it is possible, that it achieves a certain harmony. Abstract values, on the other hand, when carried to extremes, are irreconcilable: It is impossible to reconcile, in the abstract, such virtues as justice and love. Perhaps in the West the need for change has been the stimulus for argument on abstract values, as such argument is better suited for raising incompatibilities. At the same time, the confusion of these abstract notions would allow us, after these incompatibilities have been raised, to form new concepts of these values. An intense activity in the realm of values is thereby made possible; they are constantly being recast and remodeled.

Leaning on concrete values would thus be much easier when one wishes to preserve than when one wishes to renovate. The reason conservatives consider themselves realists is perhaps that they put these values in the foreground. The notions of fidelity, loyalty, and solidarity, which are connected with concrete values, do in fact often characterize conservative argumentation. [. . .]

The Choice of Data and Their Adaptation for Argumentative Purposes

29. Selection of Data and Presence

One datum in argumentation consists of the agreements available to the speaker as supports for his argument. But this element is so large and capable of being used in so many different ways, that the manner in which one makes use of it is of paramount importance. Accordingly, before examining the use of this datum in argumentation, it is essential that we say something of the part played by preliminary selection of the elements that are to serve as the starting point of the argument and by the adaptation of these elements to its purposes.

We must make it clear, however, that being able to choose from among data does not imply that the elements which are not utilized can be totally disregarded. For each audience there is a set of things that are admitted, and all of them are liable to have an effect on its reactions. This set can be determined fairly easily if the audience is a specialized one: It will be the corpus of knowledge recognized by those trained in a scientific discipline;[7] it will be the whole juridical system within which a legal decision is fitted.[8] Except where a formalized field which can be completely isolated is involved, the aggregate of things admitted is fluid and remains open. Its boundaries are especially vague where the audience is not a specialized one, although at certain periods the elaboration of philosophical ideas may help to make its content slightly more definite. In any case, it provides each audience with a frame of reference by means of which arguments can be tested.

The part that is played by selection is so obvious that when facts are mentioned, we must always ask ourselves what it is that their use can strengthen or weaken. The press, whether it supports the government or is in opposition to it, has made us accustomed to this selection of the facts either for the purposes of explicit argument or for those of argument which it is hoped the reader will carry out himself. In the traditional systems of rhetoric under the heading of "narration," there is no dearth of advice on the methods of choosing the facts of the case.[9] But this choice is also a dominant factor in scientific debates: choice of the facts deemed relevant, choice of hypotheses, choice of the theories that should be confronted with facts, choice of the actual elements that constitute facts. The method of each science implies such a choice, which is relatively stable in the natural sciences, but is much more variable in the social sciences.

By the very fact of selecting certain elements and presenting them to the audience, their importance and pertinency to the discussion are implied. Indeed, such a choice endows these elements with a *presence,* which is an essential factor in argumentation and one that is far too much neglected in rationalistic conceptions of reasoning.

What we have in mind is illustrated by this lovely Chinese story:

> A king sees an ox on its way to sacrifice. He is moved to pity for it and orders that a sheep be used in its place. He confesses he did so because he could see the ox, but not the sheep.[10]

Presence acts directly on our sensibility. As Piaget shows, it is a psychological datum operative already at the level of perception: When two things are set side by side, say a fixed standard and things of variable dimensions with which it is compared, the thing on which the eye dwells, that which is best or most often seen, is, by that very circumstance, overestimated.[11] The thing that is present to the consciousness assumes thus an importance that the theory and practice of argumentation must take into consideration. It is not enough indeed that a thing should exist for a person to feel its presence. This is true even of the disputes of scholars, witness the role played in the Gassendist dispute by the book in which Jean de Launoy pointed out the variations in the Church's attitude toward Aristotle:

> To be sure, says the Abbé Lenoble in this connection, no one is unaware that the Church is much older than the Aristotelianism of the thirteenth century. All the protagonists know this, but nobody thinks of it.[12]

Accordingly one of the preoccupations of a speaker is to make present, by verbal magic alone, what is actually absent but what he considers important to his argument or, by making them more present, to enhance the value of some of the elements of which one has actually been made conscious.

In Bacon's view, rhetoric, envisaged as a technique making it possible "to apply reason to imagination, for the better moving of the will,"[13] is essentially connected with the effects of presence:

> . . . The affection beholdeth merely the present; reason beholdeth the future and sum of time. And therefore the present filling the imagination more, reason is commonly vanquished; but after that force of eloquence and persuasion hath made things future and remote appear as present, then upon the revolt of the imagination reason prevaileth.[14]

Bacon is expressing, in the philosophical language of his day, an idea not far removed from ours: Presence, at first a psychological phenomenon, becomes an essential element in argumentation.

Certain masters of rhetoric, with a liking for quick results, advocate the use of concrete objects in order to move an audience: Caesar's bloody tunic which Antony waves in front of the Roman populace, or the children of the accused brought before his judges in order to arouse their pity. The real thing is expected to induce an adherence that its mere description would be unable to secure; it is a precious aid, provided argumentation utilizes it to advantage. The real can indeed exhibit unfavorable features from which it may be difficult to distract the viewer's attention; the concrete object might also turn his attention in a direction leading away from what is of importance to the speaker. Presence, and efforts to increase the feeling of presence, must hence not be confused with fidelity to reality.

On the other hand, one should not either, as one might be tempted to by overrationalizing thought, want to reduce presence to certitude and treat events that are more remote from the present as less important because they are less probable. Lewis considers that this is the only solution that makes propinquity and remoteness — put forward by Bentham as a dimension of pleasures — compatible with utilitarian calculus.[15] However abnormal it may be in his system, the introduction by Bentham of this supplementary dimension is, for us who interpret it in terms of presence, perfectly justified since it conforms to undeniable psychical tendencies.

In an appendix to his work on rhetoric, Whately[16] reproduces a lengthy note by Campbell dealing with the conditions of time, place, relation, and personal interest by means of which an event affects us: These conditions are also those which determine presence. Presence is thus not exclusively linked to proximity in time, although such proximity is an essential element. It should also be observed that the effort to make something present to the consciousness can relate not only to real objects, but also to a judgment or an entire argumentative development. As far as possible, such an effort is directed to filling the whole field of consciousness with this presence so as to isolate it, as it were, from the hearer's overall mentality. And this is essential. If one finds that a properly developed syllogism, which was accepted by the hearer, does not necessarily induce him to act in accordance with the conclusions, it is because the premises, which were isolated during the demonstration, might have encountered obstacles once they entered the mental circuit of the person they were supposed to persuade.[17]

The importance of presence in argumentation has a negative as well as a positive aspect: Deliberate suppression of presence is an equally noteworthy phenomenon, deserving of detailed study. We will give only an indication, which we consider essential, of the unreal character of all that which is not a part of our actions, which is not connected with our convictions. Stephen Spender makes the following accurate remark:

> . . . Nearly all human beings have an extremely intermittent grasp on reality. Only a few things, which illustrate their own interests and ideas, are real to them; other things, which are in fact equally real, appear to them as abstractions. . . . Your friends are allies and therefore real human beings. . . . Your opponents are just tiresome, unreasonable, unnecessary theses, whose lives are so many false statements which you would like to strike out with a lead bullet. . . .[18]

Applying this conception to the reactions he felt during the civil war in Spain when confronted with the atrocities committed by the pro-Franco and Republican sides, he adds: "In the first case I saw corpses, in the second only words."

In the same book, Koestler, writing about executions required by the cause, makes this observation:

> Now these two individuals had become more real to me than the cause in the name of which they were to be sacrificed. . . .[19]

The individual whom one is ready to sacrifice to the system is not only unreal *de jure* because he has lost his ontological status, but also *de facto* because he is not present. Shock is experienced either because of theoretical doubts or when, in a concrete situation, the presence of the man one is going to sacrifice can no longer be kept out of the consciousness.

This notion of presence, which we are speaking of here and which we consider to be of paramount importance for the technique of argumentation, is not a philosophical formulation. A philosophy that considers presence as a cornerstone of its structure — that of Buber or Sartre, for example — would connect it with an ontology or an anthropology. That is not our purpose. We are interested only in the technical aspect of this notion, which leads to the inevitable conclusion that all argumentation is selective. It chooses the elements and the method of making them present. By doing so it cannot avoid being open to accusations of incompleteness and hence of partiality and tendentiousness. And we must bear this criticism in mind when we want argumentation to be convincing, that is, valid for the universal audience. A tendentious argument, deliberately put forward on behalf of a party it is one's interest or duty to favor, will have to be completed by the adverse argument in order to reach a balance in the appraisal of the known elements. The judge will not make a decision before he has heard both parties. But going beyond this requirement to the assertion that the totality of informational elements must be presented, giving to each element the emphasis it deserves, would imply the existence of a criterion for determining these relevant elements and would imply also that the totality defined in this way can be exhausted. We think this is an illusion and that passage from the subjective to the objective can be accomplished only by successive enlargements, none of which can be regarded as final. The person who effects a new enlargement will necessarily emphasize that the previous statements had involved a choice of data, and he will probably be able to show quite easily that this was indeed the case. We must add that in the social as well as in the natural sciences this choice is not mere selection, but also involves construction and interpretation.[20]

Notes

1. Dupréel, *Sociologie générale,* pp. 181–182.
2. Kou Hong Ming and Borrey, *Le Catéchisme de Confucius,* p. 69, following the *Tchoung-young,* chap. XX, § 7, Pauthier, *Confucius et Mencius,* p. 83. See also the *Hsiao King* or classic of filial piety in Legge, *The Sacred Books of the East,* vol. 3, p. 482.
3. Leibniz, *Discourse on Metaphysics,* pp. 2–3.
4. Burke, *A Rhetoric of Motives* (Braziller), pp. 299–301.
5. Aristotle, *Topics,* III, 2, 118a.
6. Fénelon, "Dialogues sur l'Eloquence," *Œuvres,* vol. XXI, pp. 24–25.
7. Cf. Kneebone, "Induction and Probability," *Proceedings of the Aristotelian Society,* 50 (1949–50), 35. In the field of mathematics, cf. Wilder, "The Origin and Growth of Mathematical Concepts," *Bulletin of the American Mathematical Society,* 59 (1953), 424–425.
8. Cf. Cosio, "Phenomenology of the Decision," in *Latin-American Philosophy,* p. 399. Cited by Goldschmidt, *Le Système Stoïcien et L'Idée de Temps,* p. 97, note 7.
9. *Rhetorica ad Herennium,* I, 12; Cicero, *De Inventione,* I, § 30; Quintilian, IV, II, especially § 57.
10. Pareto, *The Mind and Society,* vol. II, § 1135, p. 671, summarizing a story of Meng-Tseu, bk. I, § 7, in connection with his treatment of pity as a residue. Cited in Pauthier, *Confucius et Mencius,* pp. 230 et seq.
11. Piaget, *Introduction à l'épistémologie génétique,* vol. I, pp. 174–175.
12. Lenoble, "Histoire et physique," *Revue d'histoire des sciences et de leurs applications,* 1953, p. 125.
13. Bacon, *Advancement of Learning,* bk. II, XVIII, § 2, GBWW, vol. 30, p. 66.
14. *Ibid.,* bk. II, XVIII, § 4, p. 67.
15. Lewis, *An Analysis of Knowledge and Valuation,* p. 493.
16. Whately, *Elements of Rhetoric* (Harper), Appendix H, pp. 328 et seq.
17. Cf. § 6, supra: Persuading and Convincing.
18. Crossman, *The God That Failed* (Bantam), p. 257.
19. *Ibid.,* p. 72.
20. Cf. Aron, *Introduction à la philosophie de l'histoire,* p. 115.

Bibliography

Aristotle. *Aristotle,* Great Books of the Western World (GBWW), vol. 8 (Chicago, IL, Encyclopaedia Britannica, Inc.) 1952.

Aron, Raymond. *Introduction à la philosophie de l'histoire,* Essai sur les limites de l'objectivité historique, Bibliothèque des Idées (Paris, Gallimard) 1948.

Bacon, Francis. *Francis Bacon,* Great Books of the Western World (GBWW), vol. 30 (Chicago, IL, Encyclopaedia Britannica, Inc.) 1952.

Burke, Kenneth. *A Rhetoric of Motives* (Englewood Cliffs, NJ, Prentice-Hall, Inc.) 1950.

Cicero. *De l'Invention (De Inventione),* text revised and translated into French with an introduction and notes by Henri Bornecque (Paris, Garnier) 1932.

Cosio, C. "Phenomenology of the Decision," *Latin-American Legal Philosophy* (Cambridge, MA, Harvard University Press) 1948.

Crossman, Richard, ed. *The God That Failed* (New York, Bantam Books, Inc.) 1952.

Dupréel, Eugène. *Sociologie générale,* Travaux de la Faculté de Philosophie et Lettres, Université Libre de Bruxelles (Paris, Presses Universitaires de France) 1948.

Fénelon. *Oeuvres* (Paris, Lebel) 1824, vol. XXI, *Dialogues sur l'éloquence en général et sur celle de la chaire en particulier.*

Kneebone, G. T. "Induction and Probability," *Proceedings of the Aristotelian Society,* new series, vol. L, 1950, pp. 27–42.

Kou Hong Ming and Francis Borrey. *Le Catéchisme de Confucius, Contribution à l'étude de la sociologie chinoise* (Paris, Marcel Rivière) 1927.

Legge, James. *The Sacred Books of the East,* translated by various scholars and edited by F. Max Müller (London, Henry Frowde, Oxford University Press, Oxford, Clarendon Press) vol. III.

Leibniz, Gottfried Wilhelm. *Discourse on Metaphysics* (Chicago, IL, and London, Open Court Publishing Company) 1927.

Lenoble, Robert. "Histoire et Physique, à propos des conseils de Mersenne aux historiens et de l'intervention de Jean de Launoy dans la querelle gassendiste," *Revue d'histoire des sciences et de leurs applications* (Paris, Presses Universitaires de France) 1953, pp. 112–135.

Lewis, Clarence Irving. *An Analysis of Knowledge and Valuation* (La Salle, IL, The Open Court Publishing Company) 1946.

Pareto, Vilfredo. *The Mind and Society* (New York, Harcourt, Brace and Co.) 1935.

Pauthier, G. *Confucius et Mencius, Les quatre livres de Philosophie morale et politique de la Chine* (Paris, Charpentier) 1852.

Piaget, Jean. *Introduction à l'épistémologie génétique* 3 vol. (Paris, Presses Universitaires de France) 1950.

Rhetorica ad Herennium. Loeb Classical Library (New York, G.P. Putnam's Sons; London, Heinemann).

Whately, Richard D. D. *Elements of Rhetoric,* comprising the substance of the article in the *Encyclopaedia Metropolitana* with additions, etc. (London, John Murray; Oxford, J. Parker) 1828.

A Theory of the Rhetorical Audience: Reflections on Chaim Perelman

Alan Gross

Chaim Perelman and Lucie Olbrechts-Tyteca's considerations of the universal and particular audience have created interest and controversy among argument scholars. Alan Gross's essay, originally published in the Quarterly Journal of Speech *in 1999, attempts to clear up some of the controversies. Gross responds to incomplete readings of the universal and particular audience by noting that* The New Rhetoric's *theory of audience is comprehensive and can be understood clearly only in its entirety. He also demonstrates that both the universal and particular audience are rhetorical constructs that have particular relationships to facts and values, and that they complicate twentieth-century notions of objectivity and subjectivity.*

In The New Rhetoric, *Gross argues, the particular audience is a construct that relates to a "real" and easily labeled group. Arguments to particular audiences depend on values or nonuniversal beliefs and self-consciously recognize the limits of their scope. For* The New Rhetoric, *Gross notes, arguments made in philosophy and science epitomize appeals to a universal audience because they rely on appeals to facts and propose unchanging truths. What Gross points out, however, is that* The New Rhetoric *is not proposing that timelessly valid arguments appealing to all "rational" people actually exist. Instead, Perelman and Olbrechts-Tyteca's discussion of the universal audience recognizes that a universally like-minded community does not, and cannot, exist, and that appeals to fact depend on persuading an audience to believe in a "universal truth" more than they depend on the* existence *of such truth.*

Argument teachers should consider how Gross's description of audience in The New Rhetoric *relates to contemporary questions in composition about objectivity, subjectivity, and the role of discourse communities in constructing knowledge. It may also be useful to consider the ways Gross differentiates several of* The New Rhetoric's *key terms, including "fact," "truth," "presumption," and "value," and to consider how a discussion of such terms can help students understand various elements of argumentation. Maybe most important for teachers interested in using models for analysis, Gross examines the ways famous speeches (such as Abraham Lincoln's inaugural address) utilize appeals to universal and particular audiences in order to gain broad adherence to controversial ideas.*

[. . .]

Any discussion of Chaim Perelman's view of the rhetorical audience must acknowledge the deeply contested debate concerning the most original of his concepts, the universal audience. John Ray, Henry Johnstone, and Lisa Ede have all mounted arguments against the coherence, and the usefulness of this idea. Ede must stand for the rest when she says that Perelman is caught in a trap of his own making, a contradiction between his fundamental belief that any plausible theory of argumentation must assail the idea of self-evidence, and his assertion that "argumentation addressed to the universal audience must convince the reader that the reasons adduced are of a compelling character, that they are self evident, and possess an absolute timeless validity, independent of local or historical contingencies" (32). Indeed, Perelman himself pays tribute to the cogency of such criticisms when he says that "it is the notion of the universal audience which has created the most misunderstandings among my rhetorical readers" (*The New Rhetoric,* p. 190). It is my view, however, that Perelman uses the concept of universal audience consistently, and that it is part of a theoretically coherent concept of audience with considerable potential as a tool for rhetorical criticism.

Perelman believes that all rhetorical audiences are constructed by the speaker. Of course there are real audiences; of course their study poses a genuine problem; but it is a challenge, he feels, beyond the scope of rhetoric: The study of real audiences is the business of experimental psychology. "We shall proceed differently. We seek ... to characterize the different argumentative structures, the analysis of which must precede all experimental tests of their effectiveness" (9). This argument seems disingenuous at best: Speakers obviously need prior knowledge of their audiences. This necessity means that the rhetorician is dependent on, not independent of experimental psychology, and that it is experimental psychology, not rhetoric, that is cognitively prior. The use of poll results by American political candidates is an instance of this dependence and this priority.

But this defective argument does no damage to Perelman's central tenet that all rhetorical audiences must be constructed by the speaker: "The audience, as visualized by one undertaking to argue, is always a more or less systematized construction" (19). Moreover, this rhetorical audience is always composite: Since real audiences must consist of disparate individuals with differing convictions of differing intensity, and since no algorithm exists that can combine these differences conceptually, the achievement of a synthetic unity must be a consequence of the speaker's intuition. In their opening remarks — indeed throughout their speeches — speakers must embody their best guesses of their audiences' views of the two components of this systematical unity, the twin categories of fact and value, of the real and the preferable:

> An orator does not have to be confronted with several organized factions
> to think of the composite nature of his audience. He is justified in
> visualizing each one of his listeners as simultaneously belonging to a
> number of disparate groups. Even when an orator stands before only a
> few auditors, or indeed, before a single auditor, it is possible that he will
> not be quite sure what arguments will appear most convincing to his
> audience. In such a case, he will, by a kind of fiction, insert his audience
> into a series of different audiences. (22)

Perelman's example is from the novel *Tristram Shandy,* in which Tristram's father persuades his wife to have a midwife by arguing "like a Christian, like a heathen, like a husband, like a father, like a patriot, like a man" (22).

If all audiences are constructed, then their views of the real and the preferable, as imagined by the speaker, must form the initial common ground between speaker and audience, the starting points of any argumentation. To illustrate the real, I will use the exordium of the "Cooper Institute" Address of February 27, 1860, a beginning in which Abraham Lincoln rehearses the components of the real, the matters of fact and of truth that he believes he shares with his audience:

Mr. President and fellow citizens of New York: The facts with which I shall deal this evening are mainly old and familiar; nor is there anything new in the general use I shall make of them. If there shall be any novelty, it will be in the mode of presenting the facts, and the inferences and observations following that presentation.

In his speech last autumn, at Columbus, Ohio, as reported in the New York *Times,* Senator Douglas said: "Our fathers, when they framed the Government under which we live, understood this question just as well, and even better than we do now."

I fully indorse this, and I adopt it as a text for this discourse. I so adopt it because it furnishes a precise and an agreed starting point for a discussion between Republicans and that wing of the Democracy headed by Senator Douglas. It simply leaves the inquiry: "What was the understanding those fathers had of the question mentioned?"

What is the frame of government under which we live?

The answer must be: "The Constitution of the United States." That Constitution consists of the original, framed in 1787, (and under which the present government first went into operation), and twelve subsequently framed amendments, the first ten of which were framed in 1789.

Who were our fathers that framed the Constitution? I suppose the "thirty-nine" who signed the original instrument may be fairly called our fathers who framed that part of the present Government. It is almost exactly true to say they framed it, and it is altogether true to say they fairly represented the opinion and sentiment of the whole nation at that time. Their names, being familiar to nearly all, and accessible to quite all, need not be now repeated.

I take these "thirty-nine" for the present, as being "our fathers who framed the Government under which we live."

What is the question which, according to the text, those fathers understood "just as well, and even better than we do now"?

It is this: Does the proper division of local from federal authority, or anything in the Constitution, forbid our Federal Government to control as to slavery in our Federal Territories?

Upon this, Senator Douglas holds the affirmative, and the Republicans the negative. This affirmation and denial form an issue; and this issue — this question — is precisely what the text declares our fathers understood "better than we." (Basler 517–18)

Facts are true assertions about the world, assertions about which everyone must agree. It is a fact that Senator Douglas made the remark Lincoln attributes to him; it is a fact that the Constitution was ratified in 1787 and later amended; it is a fact that there were thirty-nine signers of the Constitution. But it is a truth, not merely a fact, that that document constitutes our government, a truth that must be the basis of any views concerning the extension of slavery to the territories. Truths transcend, but are in conformity with the facts of the world. Current scientific theories are truths; so are political theories that explain and justify our form of government.

Presumptions form a third category of starting points concerning the real. They are matters that can be taken for granted in regard to particular audiences, the presumption of innocence, for example. This does not mean that particular defendants are innocent, only that they are innocent until proven guilty, that, in criminal proceedings, it is the state, not the defendant, that bears the burden of proof. As Perelman asserts, presumptions are intimately connected with what particular audiences regard as normal: Moreover, "the existence of this connection between presumptions and what is normal is itself a general presumption accepted by all audiences" (71). It is a presumption that the New York *Times* is invariably accurate; it is a presumption that the views of the founders were representative of the nation at the time.

The speaker's idea of his audience must also include their idea of values, of the preferable. To illustrate the components of the preferable,[1] I will use the opening remarks in the fourth Lincoln-Douglas debate, in Charleston, Illinois, on September 18, 1858. In his beginning, Lincoln rehearses values, hierarchies of values, and the loci of quality or quantity that establish or intensify these values, components of the preferable he believes he shares with his audience:

> While I was up at the hotel to-day, an elderly gentleman called upon me to know whether I was really in favor of producing a perfect equality between the negroes and the white people. While I had not proposed to myself upon this occasion to say much upon that subject, as the question was asked me, I thought I would occupy, perhaps, five minutes, in saying something in regard to it.
>
> I will say then, that I am not nor ever have been in favor of bringing about in any way, the social and political equality of the white and black races, that I am not, nor ever have been in favor of making voters of the negroes, or jurors, or qualifying them to hold office, or having them marry with white people. I will say in addition, that there is a physical difference between the white and black races, which I suppose will forever forbid the two races living together upon terms of social and political equality, and inasmuch, as they cannot so live, that while they do remain together, there must be the position of superior and inferior, that I as much as any other man am in favor of the superior position being assigned to the white man. I say in this connection, that I do not perceive, however, that because the white man is to have the superior position, that it requires that the negro should be denied everything. I do not perceive because I do not court a negro woman for a wife, that I must necessarily want her for a [slave]. My understanding is that I can just leave her alone. I am now in my fiftieth year, and certainly have never had a black woman either for a slave or a wife, so that it seems to me that it is quite possible for us to get along without making either slaves or wives of negroes. (Holzer 189)

In this exordium, Lincoln assumes that he shares two values with the audience he imagines: the Constitutional imperative that all men are created equal, and social and political imperative that blacks are inferior. These values he arranges in a hierarchy in which the Constitutional imperative has the priority, constrained, of course, by the social and political imperative of black inferiority as a justification for the denial of full citizenship.

Values and hierarchies of values may merely be asserted on the basis of authority, but they may also be justified by means of general schemes of inference, which Perelman identifies with the classical loci or topics. Important in this connection are the loci of quantity and quality. According to the first, the preferable is to be preferred because it provides more of a good; according to the second, it is to be preferred because the good it provides is greater than some other, lesser good. It is a locus of quality that anchors Lincoln's nuanced racism in his debate with Douglas: A physical difference that is, presumably, a sign of mental inferiority is thus reconciled with a document that insists all men are created equal. The locus of quantity is specifically side-stepped: It does not matter how many black Americans there are: None is entitled to full citizenship. Along with this neglect one aspect of the locus of quality is also avoided: Even if the black race is generally inferior to the white, can it also be true that every black is inferior to every white?

I now come to the puzzle of Perelman's distinction between particular and universal audiences, a puzzle that can be solved now that we understand the difference between the real and the preferable. Since all rhetorical audiences are constructed, both particular and universal audiences are, equally, those imagined by the speaker. The difference is that speeches for the universal audience thematize the real; those for particular audiences thematize the preferable:

> The conceptions people form of the real can vary widely, depending on the philosophical views they profess. However, everything in argumentation that is deemed to relate to the real is characterized by a claim to validity vis-à-vis the universal audience. On the contrary, all that pertains to the preferable, that which determines our choices and does not conform to a preexistent reality, will be connected with a specific viewpoint which is necessarily identified with some particular audience, though it may be a large one (66).

It is only in the former case, according to Perelman, that the speaker is addressing a universal audience; that is, he is addressing the men and women actually before him, not as Americans or Republicans, as Catholics or Jews, but as rational human beings. He is presuming, through his argumentation, to convince, rather than to persuade,

> to gain the adherence of every rational being. The nuance involved is a delicate one and depends, essentially, on the idea the speaker has formed [of] the incarnation of reason. Every person believes a set of facts, of truths, which he thinks must be accepted by every "normal" person, because they are valid for every rational being. But is this really the case? Does not this claim to an absolute validity for any audience composed of rational beings go too far? On this point, even the most conscientious writer can do no more than submit to the test of facts, to

his readers' judgment. In any case he will have done all he can to convince, if he thinks he is validly addressing such an audience (28).

Clearly, at this point in our intellectual history it would be futile to argue that either philosophy or science is value-free. But Perelman's point is not that such discourse is value-free, but that it is a condition for making philosophical and scientific assertions that they be addressed to an audience of all rational beings, namely, to a universal audience: "The thesis defended in *The New Rhetoric* is that every philosopher addresses himself to the universal audience as he conceives it, even in the absence of an objectivity which imposes itself on everyone. The philosopher develops an argumentation thanks to which he aspires to convince any competent interlocutor whatsoever" (*The New Rhetoric,* 191). The universal audience is an ideal that must be assumed in such discourse. Discourse that emphasizes, that thematizes values, can never address a universal audience because particular values can never be plausibly asserted as binding on all human beings in all circumstances.

I can now place Ede's criticism of the universal audience in its proper context. It is true that "argumentation addressed to the universal audience must convince the reader that the reasons adduced are of a compelling character, that they are self evident, and possess an absolute timeless validity, independent of local or historical contingencies" (32). But this is not because such timeless validity exists; rather, it is because speakers arguing for the real in a particular case must assume its existence in the general case. All such arguments are subject to the paradox that speakers must presuppose a concept of timeless validity, a concept clearly subject to contingency. As Perelman puts it: "Each individual, each culture, has thus its own conception of the universal audience" (33).

We can see this paradox clearly if we look at philosophy, for Perelman paradigmatic of discourse addressed to a universal audience. To illustrate, we reproduce a speech of Socrates from Plato's dialogue *Phaedrus.* In this section of the dialogue, Socrates addresses a single interlocutor, Phaedrus, as if he were a universal audience of rational beings. Socrates is outlining the conditions that a science of rhetoric must satisfy:

> Since the nature of speech is in fact to direct the soul, whoever intends to be a rhetorician must know how many kinds of souls there are. Their number is so-and-so many; each is of such-and-such sort; hence some people have such-and-such character and others have such-and-such. Those distinctions established, there are, in turn, so-and-so many kinds of speech, each of such-and-such a sort. People of such-and-such a character are easy to persuade by speeches of such-and-such a sort in connection with such-and-such an issue for this particular reason, while people of such-and-such another sort are difficult to persuade for those particular reasons.
>
> The orator must learn all this well, then put his theory into practice and develop the ability to discern each kind clearly as it occurs in the

actions of real life. Otherwise he won't be any better off than he was when he was still listening to those discussions in school. He will now not only be able to say what kind of person is convinced by what kind of speech; on meeting someone he will be able to discern what he is like and make clear to himself that the person actually standing in front of him is just this particular sort of character he had learned about in school — to that he must now apply speeches of such-and-such kind in this particular way in order to secure conviction about such-and-such an issue. When he has learned all this — when, in addition, he has grasped the right occasions for speaking and for holding back; and when he has also understood that the time is right for Speaking Concisely or Appealing to Pity or Exaggeration or any other of the kinds of speech he has learned and when it is not — then, and only then, will he have finally mastered the art well and completely. But if his speaking, his teaching, or his writing lacks any one of these elements and he still claims to be speaking with art, you'll be better off if you don't believe him. (Nehamas and Woodruff 271D–272B)

In this speech, we recognize the contingency of Socrates' views. Few today would accept Socrates' vision of a science of rhetoric, one that depends on a precise knowledge of the constitution of particular "souls"; like all actual audiences, Socrates' is particular. At the same time, the *Phaedrus* is philosophical discourse, discourse in which Socrates imagines every member of his audience as a rational being, an embodiment of universal standards of rationality. It is this view of audience that accounts for the emphasis in philosophical discourse on logical as distinct from emotional appeals. It accounts also for the absence of symbols in such discourse, symbols which, like the flag or the eagle, are "characteristic of a particular culture" (335)[2]. While philosophy is Perelman's paradigm for discourse addressed to a universal audience, his definition applies as well to all scholarly discourse, including Perelman's own work.

Another sort of discourse that addresses the universal audience is that of the sciences. Like philosophy, it participates in the paradox that the actual audience is particular, while the audience the speaker addresses is universal: "The scientist addresses himself to certain peculiarly qualified men, who accept the data of a well-defined system consisting of the science in which they are specialists. Yet, this very limited audience is generally considered by the scientist to be really the universal audience, and not just a particular audience. He supposes that everyone with the same training, qualifications, and information would reach the same conclusions" (34). To illustrate the universal audience addressed by scientists, I cite a passage from the *Almagest* of Ptolemy, the great ancient astronomer. Ptolemy is arguing for the immobility of the earth at the center of the universe:

If the earth had a single motion in common with other heavy objects, it is obvious that it would be carried down faster than all of them because of its much greater size: Living things and individual heavy objects

would be left behind, riding on the air, and the earth itself would very
soon have fallen completely out of the heavens. But such things are
utterly ridiculous merely to think of. (p. 44.)

No one today would find Ptolemy's argument compelling, since no
one today would presuppose the Aristotelian physics that Ptolemy presupposes. But the fact that this passage is riddled with errors does not
affect the fact that Ptolemy was addressing a universal audience with
what he thought were compelling arguments, arguments so compelling that he believed that those who would disagree with him had a
burden of proof so heavy that it was "ridiculous" to try to discharge it.

Let us now turn from these relatively "pure" cases of discourse in
the sciences and philosophy — each in its own way addressed to a universal audience — to the mixed discourse of public address, discourse
Perelman refrains from analyzing. Let us look at a typical stretch of
public discourse, Lincoln's reply to Douglas at Galesburg, on October 7,
1858:

I suppose that the real difference between Judge Douglas and his
friends, on the one side, and the Republicans on the other hand is, that
the Judge is not in favor of making any difference between slavery and
liberty, that he is in favor of eradicating, he is in favor of pressing out of
view, and out of existence, all preference for free over slave institutions,
and consequently, every sentiment that he utters, discards the idea that
he is against slavery, every sentiment that emanates from him discards
the idea that there is any wrong in slavery. Every thought that he utters
will be seen to exclude the thought that there is anything wrong in
slavery. You will take his speeches and get the short pointed sentiment,
expressed by him, that he does not care if slavery is voted up, or voted
down, and such like, you will see at once that it is a perfectly logical
idea if you admit that slavery is not wrong, but if it is wrong, Judge
Douglas cannot say that he doesn't care for a wrong being voted up.
Judge Douglas declares that if any community wants slavery they can
have it. He can logically say that, if he admits that there is no wrong in
it, but he cannot say that, if he admits that there is wrong in it! He
insists, upon the score of equality, that the owner of slaves and the
owner of horses should be allowed to take them alike to new territory
and hold them there. That is perfectly logical if the species of property is
perfectly alike, but if you admit that one of them is wrong, then you
cannot admit any equality between right and wrong. I believe that
slavery is wrong, and in a policy springing from that belief that looks to
the prevention of the enlargement of that wrong, and that looks at some
time to there being an end to that wrong. The other sentiment is, that
there is no wrong, and the policy springing from it that there is no
wrong in its becoming bigger, and that there never will be any end of it.
There is the difference between Judge Douglas and his friends and the
Republican party. (Holzer 257–58)

I think that such discourse is typical of public address in that it
mixes arguments of fact with those of value. In so far as he is arguing

for the fact that Douglas has certain views, views that have definite ethical consequences, Lincoln is speaking to his audience at Galesburg as if they were the universal audience. Whether or not Douglas holds these views, and whether or not these views have these consequences are matters of fact and truth. But Lincoln is also discoursing about values. He is asserting slavery is wrong and that Douglas is wrong to endorse it. In arguing about values, Lincoln is addressing a particular audience, though one might more truly say, particular audiences, since the Galesburg audience is long dead, and his words speak to us as well, another particular audience. As wide as this audience may have been in Lincoln's time, however, as wide as it may be over time, nevertheless it does not speak to every rational human being.

Perelman feels that in the case of all persuasive discourse the audience alters in character as the discourse progresses. It is still, at the end of discourse, what it was at the beginning, a construction of the speaker. But it is a construction that has altered as a consequence of the degree to which the speaker feels that he has advanced the adherence of the audience he imagines from their initial views to those he would prefer them to have. This means that for the universal, as for the particular audience, the order of discourse is crucial:

> A speech does not leave the hearer the same as he was at the beginning. On the other hand, it does not change his beliefs irresistibly, as would the steps in a demonstration. If it did, order would not be of such importance. The order adopted is crucial precisely because the changes in the audience are both effective and contingent.
>
> This is true of the different incarnations of the universal audience as it is of particular audiences. At first sight, order does not matter in the universal audience. But the universal audience is no less than other audiences a concrete audience, which changes with time, along with the speaker's conception of it (491).

We can see change in the speaker's conception of his audience in operation by examining the beginning and ending of Lincoln's First Inaugural:

> Fellow-citizens of the United States:
>
> In compliance with a custom as old as the government itself, I appear before you to address you briefly, and to take, in your presence, the oath prescribed by the Constitution of the United States, to be taken by the President "before he enters on the execution of his office."
>
> I do not consider it necessary at present for me to discuss those matters of administration about which there is no special anxiety or excitement.
>
> Apprehension seems to exist among the people of the Southern States, that by the accession of a Republican Administration, their property, and their peace, and personal security, are to be endangered. There has never been any reasonable cause for such apprehension. Indeed, the most ample evidence to the contrary has all the while existed, and has been open to their inspection. It is found in nearly all

the published speeches of him who now addresses you. I do but quote
from one of those speeches when I declare that "I have no purpose,
directly or indirectly, to interfere with the institution of slavery in the
States where it exists. I believe I have no lawful right to do so, and I
have no inclination to do so." Those who nominated and elected me did
so with full knowledge that I had made this, and many similar declara-
tions, and had never recanted them.

. . . In your hands, my dissatisfied fellow countrymen, and not in
mine, is the momentous issue of civil war. The government will not
assail you. You can have no conflict, without being yourself the aggres-
sors. You have no oath registered in Heaven to destroy the government,
while I shall have the most solemn one to "preserve, protect and defend"
it.

I am loath to close. We are not enemies, but friends. We must not be
enemies. Though passion may have strained, it must not break our
bonds of affection. The mystic chords of memory, stretching from every
battle-field, and patriot grave, to every living heart and hearth-stone, all
over this broad land, will yet swell the chorus of the Union, when again
touched, as surely they will be, by the better angels of our nature.
(Basler 579–88)

The rhetorical audience at the end of Lincoln's address is very different from the one that forms its starting point. At the beginning of
his speech, Lincoln assumes only that he must calm southern appre-
hensions concerning his election by producing facts and arguments that
clarify his resolve not to interfere with slavery in the South. Only when
he has accomplished this task in the body of his speech does he feel
justified in arguing for the preservation of the Union. Only after these
latter arguments are completed does he attempt the direct emotional
appeals to the South with which he ends.

I may summarize by saying that Perelman has a complete and coherent theory of a rhetorical audience as a concept constructed by the
speaker. This audience is of two kinds, universal and particular. Universal audiences consist of all rational beings; persuasive discourse
addressed to these thematizes facts and truths. Particular audiences
consist of one segment or another of humanity: Americans, Republicans, Elks, Medicare recipients; discourse addressed to them thematizes
values. Discourse in public arenas is rarely addressed simply to particular audiences or to a universal audience; it rarely has as its goal
either adherence to facts and truths or adherence to values. Usually,
public address represents a mixture of goals, and therefore of rhetorical audiences. Finally, the concept of audience with which speakers
start differs from the concept with which speakers end the discourse.
By means of the discourse, step by step, speakers bring their rhetorical
audience to the desired adherence; at the same time, they hope that
their discourse brings their actual audience to the same point.

Notes

1. Epideictic is the genre of oratory most centrally concerned with values. This is a genre that Perelman thinks has been seriously misunderstood, a misconception stemming from Aristotle's view that the primary criterion for judging such discourse is aesthetic. For this reason, it is often called ceremonial discourse. Perelman thinks that nothing could be further from the truth. For him, an epideictic discourse is not peripheral, but rather "forms a central part of the art of persuasion" (49). It is designed "to strengthen the disposition toward action by increasing adherence to the values it lauds" (50).

2. Although elsewhere in the *Phaedrus,* Socrates makes extensive use of imaginative allegory, his "flights of fancy" are always under strict intellectual control.

Works Cited

Dearin, Ray D., ed. *The New Rhetoric of Chaim Perelman: Statement and Response.* Lanham, MD: UP of America, 1989.

Ede, Lisa S. "Rhetoric versus Philosophy: The Role of the Universal Audience in Chaim Perelman's *The New Rhetoric.*" In Dearin, 141–51.

Golden, James L. "The Universal Audience Revisited." In James L. Golden and Joseph J. Pilotta, eds., *Practical Reasoning in Human Affairs: Studies in Honor of Chaim Perelman.* Dordrecht: D. Reidel, 1986, pp. 287–304.

Johnstone, Henry W., Jr. "New Outlooks on Controversy." In *Validity and Rhetoric in Philosophical Argument: An Outlook in Transition.* University Park, PA: The Dialogue Press of Man & World, 1978, pp. 93–100.

Lincoln, Abraham. *Abraham Lincoln: His Speeches and Writings.* Ed. Roy P. Basler. New York: Da Capo P, 1946.

———. *The Lincoln-Douglas Debates: The First Complete, Unexpurgated Text.* Ed. Harold Holzer. New York: HarperCollins, 1994.

Perelman, Chaim. "The New Rhetoric and the Rhetoricians: Remembrances and Comments." *Quarterly Journal of Speech,* 70 (1984), 188–98.

Perelman, Chaim and Lucie Olbrechts-Tyteca. *The New Rhetoric: A Treatise on Argumentation.* Tr. John Wilkinson and Purcell Weaver. Notre Dame: Notre Dame P, 1969.

Plato. *Phaedrus.* Tr. and ed. Alexander Nehamas and Paul Woodruff. Indianapolis: Hackett, 1995.

Ptolemy, Claudius. *Ptolemy's Almagest.* Tr. G. J. Toomer. New York: Springer Verlag, 1984.

Ray, John W. "Perelman's Universal Audience." *Quarterly Journal of Speech,* 64 (1978), 361–75.

Scult, Allen. "Perelman's Universal Audience: One Perspective." In Dearin, 153–62.

ARGUMENTATION AND RACE, CLASS, GENDER, AND CULTURE

Other Voices, Different Parties: Feminist Responses to Argument

Catherine E. Lamb

*Many recent and diverse contributions to argumentation theory have
come from feminists. Catherine E. Lamb summarizes a few of these
contributions and develops her own notion of argument in the following
essay, first published in* Perspectives on Written Argument *in 1996. In
this piece, Lamb acknowledges that some feminists resist the traditional
oppositional model of argument, which sometimes results in the denial of
the conflicts that occur when people have different viewpoints and levels
of power. The feminist emphasis on expressivist, personal storytelling is
one — although, it is important to note, only one — by-product of this
response (see Susan Jarratt's "Feminism and Composition: The Case for
Conflict," in Patricia Harkin and John Schilb's* Contending with Words,
for another view). Lamb respects the expressivist tradition in feminist
composition but argues that disagreement and conflict can exist in a
feminist model — without an emphasis on adversarial discourse. She
suggests a feminist method of argumentation that maintains a subject-
subject relationship even when both parties have strong feelings about
and material investment in the issue under dispute.*

*Lamb advocates negotiation and mediation as effective techniques for
teaching feminist notions of argument in the writing class (see her
"Beyond Argument in Feminist Composition" for an in-depth description
of these ideas). In the following essay, she adds to these two strategies the
notion of "response," or "needing to honor the present tension, staying in
the moment of the disagreement, recognizing that resolution may never
occur but that continuing the conversation is still a legitimate way of
maintaining a relationship." Through techniques such as negotiation,
mediation, and response, Lamb suggests ways that feminist argumentation can address conflict productively and realistically while also respecting the tradition of feminist expressivism.*

*See Phyllis Lassner's "Feminist Responses to Rogerian Argument" (p.
406), Doug Brent's "Rogerian Rhetoric: Ethical Growth through Alternative Forms of Argumentation" (p. 297), and the section on Rogerian
Argument (p. 97) in this collection for further discussion of the relationship between understanding and conflict in argument.*

Imagine that you enter a parlor. You come late. When you arrive, others
have long preceded you, and they are engaged in a heated discussion, a
discussion too heated for them to pause and tell you exactly what it is
about. In fact, the discussion had already begun long before any of them
got there, so that no one present is qualified to retrace for you all the
steps that had gone before. You listen for awhile, until you decide that
you have caught the tenor of the argument; then you put in your oar.

---

* See the bibliography for all parenthetical source citations.

Someone answers; you answer him; another comes to your defense; another aligns himself against you, to either the embarrassment or gratification of your opponent, depending upon the quality of your ally's assistance. However, the discussion is interminable. The hour grows late, you must depart. And you do depart, with the discussion still vigorously in progress.

— Kenneth Burke (1967, pp. 110–111)

Kenneth Burke's description of the "unending conversation" of humankind probably appeals to most practitioners and scholars of composition, whether feminist or not. We want to see ourselves and our students as part of something valuable that is larger than any of us and that will continue indefinitely. When I read this passage as a feminist, however, I ask questions that make me less comfortable about it. The "you" in it takes it for granted that he is invited and can enter the parlor; he also seems to have no doubts about being able to speak, using the proper forms, and being listened to once he speaks. His challenges are only those of timing and strategy. I, on the other hand, ask who has been invited and who has been left out. Why should only these forms be used and not others? Must we assume an antagonistic relationship between participants? What other parties can we imagine that might continue the conversation?

Feminist composition — approaches to the teaching and practice of writing that draw on women's experience and theorizing about it for goals, pedagogy, and forms of discourse — offers new ways to answer these questions. For most of the past twenty years of this field's history, the emphasis has been on developing the personal voice. Argument, techniques of persuasion for gaining acceptance of one's point of view, if it was dealt with, was seen usually in pejorative terms, as an expression of patriarchy. Although the confrontation implicit in such a view does not reflect the attitudes of some of the most influential twentieth-century rhetorical theorists, including Kenneth Burke (in the essay from which I quoted earlier, he spoke, for example, of the value of "cooperative competition"), it remains popular both for our students and, judging from the orientation of most composition textbooks, for many teachers of composition. For practitioners of feminist composition, however, there are now suggestions that other alternatives are possible.

With recent changes in the place of argument in feminist composition, we have alternatives to argument that can enlarge our vision of possible responses to conflict. The goals are arrived at through theory and practice that return to women's experience in spite of the pitfalls of idealizing or overgeneralizing that experience. We have not had and do not wish to have the luxury of remaining in theory; because we cannot assume we will be heard, we have had to articulate concrete ways to respond when there appears to be little, if any, common ground from which to negotiate a relationship. Burke's image of the parlor suggests a spatial relationship between the participants — in this case, the writer and reader. Our concern as teachers and practitioners of feminist composition is how to enter that space and keep it open, developing a sense of spaciousness in the resolution of the conflict. As actors in that space, we exercise power in defining the nature of the space. We also enable others to do the same. Both actions change the texture and shape of the space.

Conflict and the Place of Personal Voice in Feminist Composition

Feminist composition has always been concerned with creating and maintaining a space from which women can speak and be heard. In 1971, *College English* published Howe's "Identity and Expression: A Writing Course for Women," which was her response to the feelings of inferiority she saw in women students and in their attitudes toward women writers. Or one could go back to Emig's article, "The Origins of Rhetoric: A Developmental View," which first appeared in 1969, in which she examined the mother's role in language learning as the first "co-speaker/co-writer" who "expands" on what the child says. Essays written in the intervening twenty years have continued the emphasis on developing women's voices, usually without considering the effects of race, class, or sexual orientation on the "difference" to which they are giving expression, although varieties of expression are valued (see, for example, Caywood & Overing, 1987; see also Annas, 1985; Flynn, 1988; Osborn, 1991). It seems reasonable to assume that the emphasis on women's personal voices reflects a continuing need to develop them — a need that I welcome and trust will continue.

Although the expressionist orientation in feminist composition need not have meant necessarily that responses to conflict would be avoided, that is what has happened. Feminist composition was developing at a time also of great idealism in the women's movement. In their commentary on their collection of essays, *Conflicts in Feminism,* Hirsch and Keller (1990) noted that the "'dream of a common language'" — the title of a collection of Adrienne Rich's poetry published in 1978 — was sustained "by the illusion of a domain internally free of conflict. For the most part, feminists of the seventies wrote, and tried to think, of conflict as operating between feminism and its alternatives" (p. 379). The title of Morgan's anthology, *Sisterhood Is Global* (1984), reflects a similar orientation. We should not be surprised that the variables of race, class, and sexual orientation were not a concern.

Another reason for the absence of a response to conflict is that the expressionist pedagogy accompanying an emphasis on developing a personal voice means there is no need to consider conflict; it may even be discouraged. As Jarratt demonstrates in "Feminism and Composition: The Case for Conflict," even though the teacher's authority is displaced, the emphasis on uncritically accepting what another has written means that real differences, whatever their source, are elided (pp. 108–111). The relationship to readers is also seen as unproblematic.

Audiences, when considered, are usually thought of as sympathetic (see, again, Caywood & Overing, 1987; Farrell, 1979; Flynn, 1988; Howe, 1971), or they are ignored, as in Juncker's discussion of how one can bring the spirit of French feminists, especially Hélène Cixous, into the classroom. At some point, voice is taken over by egocentrism. Nothing beyond self-expression seems to matter; readers may or may not be confused, angry, or delighted. Once again, the personal voice will always have a place in feminist composition. But any attempt to respond to conflict must also include with it a recognition of how one is to relate to an audience with whom one disagrees. Doing so is likely to call on the confidence engendered by attention to the personal voice and may test that confidence by requiring that the voice be modified.

If feminist composition has not typically developed responses to conflict, its practitioners and other feminists have been vocal in criticizing the "male mode" as the usual way we have been taught to respond to conflict — persuading someone else to one's way of thinking by making a claim and then supporting it. Many of the criticisms may best be called problem definitions, which actively invite alternatives. Shotter and Logan (1988) called for a new rhetoric in the social sciences that reflects feminist ways of knowing. Gearhart (1979), in speech communication, said simply, "Any intent to persuade is an act of violence" (p. 195). Moulton (1983), a philosopher, noted the prevalence of the "adversary method" in philosophical reasoning and the limitations it puts on thinking. And Frey (1990) demonstrated how widespread such an approach is in contemporary literary critical writing.

Feminist Responses to Argument

With our history of either ignoring conflict or criticizing others' attempts to respond to it, and our use of women's experience as a source for theorizing, we have not talked much about how it can be feminist to both at times be confrontational and at other times advocate approaches that minimize confrontation. It has been far easier for me to begin at the latter point, in which I assume I have a voice that will be heard; the question becomes how to reconcile it with an opposing voice. How one can speak and be heard where the spaciousness required for conflict resolution does not yet or may never exist is at least as complicated a question. I have avoided it because any response has appeared to require a use of force I found as unacceptable as the antagonism in argument.

In this discussion of feminist responses to argument, I begin with what has been easier for me, situations for conflict resolution in which one strives for an outcome that is acceptable to both parties. To return to Burke's metaphor, a person in such a situation assumes she is invited and can speak in the party in the parlor. She also believes she may be listened to: She is bold enough to want to change the rules by which the discussion is held. In "Beyond Argument in Feminist Composition" (Lamb, 1991), I advocated mediation and negotiation as alternatives to argument as it is often taught and practiced, in which the goal is to win, making confrontation virtually inevitable. Making this switch requires a contrasting view of power — that it is not something one can possess and therefore use on others in the manner that one applies force; rather, following Arendt in *The Human Condition* (1958) and more recent contemporary feminist theorists, power is present when a group comes together for a particular purpose. It can energize and enable, thus increasing competence and reducing hierarchy. (One implication of the line of thinking I am developing in this chapter is that the opposition between the two views of power I have just summarized is overdrawn — even though it is certainly convenient. Here, I am continuing to explore more aspects of Foucault's [1978] definition of power in *The History of Sexuality:* "Power is not something that is acquired, seized, or shared, something that one holds on to or allows to slip away; power is exercised from innumerable points, in the interplay of non-egalitarian and mobile relations" [p. 94]. A major difference, however, is Foucault's interest in analyzing power as it has been exercised historically or in existing societies and institutions and not in imagining new, positive ways in which it might be used, as I do here.)

In "Beyond Argument" I showed how an egalitarian orientation toward power can be exercised in an enabling way between writer and reader or, in collaborative work, between the writers who produce the writing and who are also its primary audience. To imagine how such a relationship would work, I began with Ruddick's (1988) notion of "maternal thinking" discussed in her book of the same name. Maternal thinking is thought and practice derived from reflecting on mother-child relationships, although Ruddick was careful to say that one need not be a biological parent or a woman in order to engage in it. A central notion is that of "attentive love or loving attention": "Loving attention is much like empathy, the ability to think and feel as the other. In connecting with the other, it is critical that one already has and retains a sense of one's self" (Lamb, 1991, p. 16). A writer-reader relationship characterized by loving attention reduces the inequality between writer and reader, inviting the reader into the act of making meaning. When writer and reader are in conflict, it can still permit them to remain connected "while also going through the giving and receiving necessary if they are to resolve their conflict" (p. 17). Techniques of mediation and negotiation provide concrete ways to resolve conflict when the goal is no longer winning but finding a solution in a fair way that is acceptable to both sides. Argument as it is usually taught has its place at the beginning of the process, not the end, where one usually finds it. Participants use it to be clear about their own positions before the negotiating or mediating begins. They also employ its tools — for example, identifying fallacies, evaluating the strength of the link between premises and conclusion in an inductive argument — in preparing the writing, which is the final outcome of the process. In the case of mediation, it is an agreement arrived at by the disputants and the mediator, stating what each party is willing to do to resolve the conflict. In negotiation, the outcome is a paper written by the disputants that records the process by which the two of them reached an agreement (Lamb, 1991, pp. 17–22).

Mediation and negotiation as I have described them and use them with my students are examples of what I think Dietrich would have us do if we take seriously the assumption that argument, like knowledge more generally, is socially constructed. First, the win-lose orientation of agonistic argument is quickly exposed as inadequate. In a positive way, we would look at the process of argumentation as problem solving rather than a contest; we would require students to seek out and understand perspectives other than their own; we would encourage students to acknowledge the place of emotions and personal experience in decision making; we would require that any solution advocated be seen as fair by all those with legitimate interests in solving the problem; and we would make the process of defining and developing the line of argument itself a social process, open to assessment and reformulation (Dietrich, 1992). We are thus acknowledging that writing is never "socially neutral" (Flynn, 1988, pp. 148–149), the same point made by a feminist critique of the conversation in Burke's parlor. Who can write, and why, using what forms, are always questions to ask.

The potential for nonadversarial approaches to conflict resolution in writing classes is great. And yet, if we think only in those terms, rich as they are, when we consider the place of argument in feminist composition, we are not exploring the full range of a healthy use of power in writer-reader relationships. Neither do we have a way to account for the variety of practices engaged in by feminists writing in response to situations of conflict. Advocating mediation or negotiation may also be seen as an emphasis on coming to closure. Although anyone who has mediated or negotiated knows the process can easily break down, the restrictions of using these techniques in the classroom can mean an artificial emphasis on finding a solution at the expense of really exploring the nature of the conflicts involved. Karis (1989) made the same point in discussing the place of conflict in collaboration from a Burkean perspective: "This *predisposition* for finding manageable solutions of the 'truth' in some middle ground before fully exploring the problem through dialectic can become a restrictive element in the collaborative process" (p. 113). As Karis stated later, it is possible to move too soon to identification, the point at which the parties in the conflict agree their interests are the same.

That my classroom uses of mediation and negotiation might be encouraging such an orientation was not something I gave much thought to until this past semester when, for the first time in the five years since I first began my experimenting along these lines, a mediation group (composed of the mediator and two disputants) informed me that they were unable to come up with an agreement. Their case was based on an actual disagreement with a member of the Student Life staff at Albion over what was to be done with unused college furniture in the suites of a fraternity house. The students describing the situation insisted that this staff person was rarely willing to negotiate on any issue. The student playing his role simply chose to stay in character. Two other groups were using the same scenario and did arrive at agreements, which they regarded as unrealistic because of their experience with this staff person.

If feminist responses to argument are to be viable, they must include in them a broader range of possibilities in their responses to conflict. Is it possible that power exercised can eventually be enabling? Surely there is a place for focusing on practices of writing or speaking that might end as well as begin in the giving and receiving of maternal thinking; resolution may or may not be possible or even desirable. Such an approach can be enabling if one is clear about one's goals and intentions. The goal is still for writer and reader to establish and maintain a subject-subject relationship, clearly the assumption if one is applying maternal thinking. The main feature of the relationship, however, may be needing to honor the present tension, staying in the moment of the disagreement, recognizing that resolution may never occur but that continuing the conversation is still a legitimate way of maintaining a relationship. The other party remains a subject, I think, if her or his views are still taken seriously, even if there appears to be no movement in the dialogue. Continuing to talk or to write may seem a small goal. But consider what too often happens when faculty (at least at Albion) have deep disagreements over matters of ideology — they just stop talking, and any possibility for movement and cooperation, let alone the new knowledge they might generate, is foreclosed. I believe the Palestinians and Israelis now participating in peace talks would say that talking at all is a miracle.

In expanding the space of feminist argument — the possibilities for how a practitioner of feminist composition can be in conflict — I am drawing on examples of recent discourse, not all of it specifically feminist, but feminist at least in spirit. There is first of all the question of how one even enters a tradition of discourse if the terms under which that discourse is conducted are antithetical to the assumptions under which one is operating, that is, if the system is closed and its adherents show no interest in an opening. We might, as with Cixous (1968) in "A Woman Mistress," not be particularly bothered if we gain a place in that space by simply playing the rules of the game as they have already been defined:

> I distrust the identification of a subject with a single discourse. First, there is the discourse that suits the occasion. I use rhetorical discourse, the discourse of mastery, orally, for example, with my students, and obviously I do it on purpose; it is a refusal on my part to leave organized discourse entirely in men's hands. I never fell for that sort of bait.
> (p. 136)

Or we might, as Frey (1990) did in "Beyond Literary Darwinism," use the adversarial method, exercise our power in this way, because we believe we have no other choice if we are going to be heard. Her hope is that the adversarial method is useful in her essay "if only as a means to its own destruction" (p. 524). Or we might, like hooks (1989), feel no necessity for justifying our use of it, but still take great care in how it is exercised. In her essay "Toward a Revolutionary Feminist Pedagogy," hooks talked about the place of confrontation in her classes in which her goal, as an African American modeling her pedagogy on African American teachers she had as a child, "is to enable all students, not just an assertive few, to feel empowered in a rigorous, critical discussion" (p. 53). My guess is hooks's classroom style is like her writing and her public appearances: When she criticizes, she is extremely focused, a practitioner of verbal laser surgery. Although her comments are intense, they are not personal, possessing a degree of lightness that makes it clear they apply only to the matter at hand.

hooks is doing what Nye (1990) in *Words of Power* called "responding"; both are instances of maternal thinking. *Words of Power*, as the book's subtitle indicates, is a "feminist reading of the history of logic." Noting that all the logicians of history have been men, who have tried to show how Truth can be arrived at, regardless of who speaks it or under what conditions, she wished instead to illuminate the social and historical conditions in which logic has been developed. Doing so requires, as she said, committing fallacies: the genetic fallacy, in which one claims that the source of an idea is relevant . . . whether or not it is true; or the ad hominem fallacy, in which one might claim that it is relevant to know who said something and why. A basic assumption for Nye is that "all human communication, including logic, is motivated" (p. 175). The answer to masculinist logic is not some new feminist version or a new women's language. Nye's answer — responding — is disarmingly simple, and yet, as her book demonstrates with eloquence, very powerful:

> But if a refutation can always be refuted, a response cuts deeper. A response might refashion the words of those in power into a serpent whose bite is exposure, the exposure that pricks inflated vanity, the exposure that weakens the resolve to continue on in ridiculous, imperious blindness to reality, the exposure that makes it impossible to continue to deny one's vulnerability and the limits of any human power, the exposure that shows all men to be mother's sons dependent on others. (p. 176)

The type of response that Nye advocates is one that cultivates the skills of reading, one that sounds much like the practice of maternal thinking: "attention, listening, understanding, responding" (p. 83). In the response that is her book, Nye is creating a new space or at least putting a new overlay on the old one. The principles of logic do not allow for mediation: A syllogism is or is not valid. (Hirsch & Keller [1990] made a similar point when they assessed the tactics used by the writers in their volume, *Conflicts in Feminism:* The writers "begin with an attempt to displace 'opposing views' by disputing their very delineations, and accordingly, to shift, or even refuse, the original ground of the discussion" [p. 372].) Nye is taking the power she has as a writer to name something new in which we as readers have the choice of participating, thus setting in motion a new circulation of power.

When I thought about how I could use negotiation and mediation in a writing class, the primary task I faced was how to adapt oral forms of discourse that depended for their success on the give and take of conversation. In the case of negotiation, I wanted a type of writing that reflected the process through which the two parties had gone. I was willing to sacrifice the forward momentum of a well-structured argument moving to its conclusion to get this sense of process. For mediation, the outcome — a mediation agreement — was definitely writing as product, but arrived at in a collaborative way. Having new forms of writing to which I can point makes it easier to say that here really are alternatives to argument as we have taught and practiced it.

If I am "responding," in Nye's sense of the word, what I or my students might be doing is less clear. My task as a teacher in this context is not to provide the clarity and security of a prescribed form. I believe it is to create the kind of atmosphere in which students can think honestly and openly about their position on an issue about which they care and then can reflect on the most generous response of which they are capable. In my upper-level expository writing course this semester, students will again be working in pairs as they do if the assignment is based on negotiation. The partners will agree on the topic on which they are writing (preferably something in which both of them have some emotional investment) and will each take contrasting positions. The first paper they will write individually; it could be recognized as traditional argument. Its function, however, will be primarily to enable them to be as clear as possible about their positions. The second paper can be written either together or separately. When I ask them for their most generous response to the conflict, they may feel they can negotiate; perhaps the most they will be capable of is a paper in which they respond to their partner's first paper, indicating what they think has been overlooked or misrepresented. One can see the conversation continuing from there.

Or they might choose to step back, as did the abbot of St. Gregory's Abbey, an Episcopal Benedictine abbey near Three Rivers, Michigan, in a recent article on gays and lesbians in the church, particularly on the question of whether homosexuals in a committed relationship should be ordained. Readers unfamiliar with current controversies in the Episcopal Church should know this question is as inflammatory as any it has faced in recent years. The governing body of the Church did not take any decisive action at its triennial meeting in July 1991; in the meantime, some bishops, applauded by some and attacked by others, have continued to ordain out homosexuals. I provide this background for some indication of the depth of feeling on both sides. It is also an issue on which I cannot see any compromise: Homosexuals in a committed relationship either can or cannot be ordained. (Most people I know in the Episcopal Church will agree that throughout its history it has been ordaining gay men. In theory at least, they have been celibate.) So it is in this atmosphere, and in the middle of a $5 million capital campaign for substantial new construction at the Abbey, that Abbot Andrew chose to write on homosexuality for the Fall 1991 issue of the *Abbey Letter* (Marr, 1991).

After some general comments on inclusiveness in the Episcopal Church, the abbot proceeded to consider Christian perspectives on homosexuality, noting it is "a mystery which does not lend itself to an easy explanation," and that our task is to learn to live with such mysteries constructively rather than fearfully. He noted the passages in Leviticus and Romans often used to attack homosexuality; without denying what they say, he also provided us with broader contexts in which to interpret them, thus showing that the primary issues may not be homosexuality. There is then the question of what is acceptable sexual behavior in the church. Abbot Andrew refused to rule out the possibility of a legitimate permanent union between homosexuals within a Christian context; he also noted, however, that we tend to believe too easily that "sexual contact is the only way to deepen a relationship" and to forget that "many caring relationships develop with the greatest depth when there is no physical sexual involvement." Later, he noted that we are to empty "ourselves of all that makes us want to push others away just because they are different. . . . If our identity is threatened by the difference of another that is a signal of our own need to empty ourselves of that identity, in the faith that we will discover ourselves more deeply in the other person and in God." I hope these selections suggest the balance and evenness of tone that run throughout the article. The abbot never took an explicit position; the emphasis instead was on broadening the context in which the discussion takes place, creating openings for anyone except possibly the most diehard on either side. From what I know, the abbot was successful. In a later letter to people associated with the abbey, he said he had never had so much correspondence on an article; most of the responses on both sides had been "constructive and rational," in spite of how "explosive" the subject has been in the church.

I want to be clear about how difficult it can be to respond, as I have been using the term. What is one to do with one's anger or, more generally, with the strong commitment felt toward an issue, and whatever emotion accompanies the commitment? Certainly the commitment must be there, or the response will sooner or later be exposed as a manipulative exercise. In the case of the abbot, he communicated his commitment by deciding to write and by using his authority as an abbot to gain an audience. His own position on the issue is less important than that the conversation continue. Responding is also not likely to be the only way anyone is or should be in conflict. Anger probably will come first, but with time and awareness, one can create a space in which it is possible to move toward the other. (A single writing assignment will not permit this evolution.) Is such an act persuasion and therefore violent, as Gearhart claims? Persuasion in the broadest sense, yes, as in this chapter, and not to be apologized for as long as we live in community. Violent? Only if any invitation to redefine oneself is seen as invasive. A person responding is thus claiming a legitimate authority, one to be exercised with openness, humility, even lightheartedness.

Mediation, negotiation, responding — all suggestions for what might characterize a feminist "unending conversation." It probably would not happen in a parlor; that way more people could come more easily. The people there would be able to tell from observing that they could speak, if they wished, from difference. There would be more silence because people would be listening more. Groups would be fluid, forming and dissolving around issues. This image is not impossibly idealistic: Each encounter would require that one again chooses with whom and how to speak, and toward what ends.

Note

1. I thank Patricia Bizzell, Gesa Kirsch, and Jody Norton for their thoughtful comments on this essay.

References

Annas, P. J. (1985). Style as politics: A feminist approach to the teaching of writing. *College English, 47,* 360–371.

Arendt, H. (1958). *The human condition.* Chicago: University of Chicago Press.

Burke, K. (1967). *The philosophy of literary form* (2nd ed.). Baton Rouge: Louisiana State University Press.

Caywood, C. L., & Overing, G. R. (Eds.). (1987). *Teaching Writing: Pedagogy, gender, and equity.* Albany: State University of New York Press.

Cixous, H. (1986). A woman mistress. In H. Cixous & C. Clement (Eds.), *The newly born woman* (B. Wing, Trans., Vol. 24, pp. 136–146). Minneapolis: University of Minnesota Press.

Dietrich, J. (1992). *Toward a social argumentation.* Unpublished paper.

Emig, J. (1983). The origins of rhetoric: A developmental view. In D. Goswami & M. Butler (Eds.), *The web of meaning* (pp. 55–59). Upper Montclair, NJ: Boynton/Cook. (Reprinted from *School Review,* September 1969)

Farrell, T. J. (1979). The female and male modes of rhetoric. *College English, 40,* 922–927.

Flynn, E. A. (1988). Composing as a woman. *College Composition and Communication, 39,* 423–435.

Foucault, M. (1978). *The history of sexuality, Vol. 1: An introduction.* (R. Hurley, Trans.). New York: Pantheon.

Frey, O. (1990). Beyond literary Darwinism: Women's voices and critical discourse. *College English, 52,* 507–526.

Gearhart, S. M. (1979). The womanization of rhetoric. *Women's Studies International Quarterly, 2,* 195–201.

Hirsch, M., & Keller, E. F. (1990). Conclusion: Practising conflict in feminist theory. In M. Hirsch & E. F. Keller (Eds.), *Conflicts in feminism* (pp. 370–385). New York: Routledge.

hooks, b. (1989). Toward a revolutionary feminist pedagogy. In *Talking back: Thinking feminist, thinking black* (pp. 49–54). Boston: South End.

Howe, F. (1971). Identity and expression: A writing course for women. *College English, 32,* 863–871.

Jarratt, S. A. (1991). Feminism and composition: The case for conflict. In P. Harkin & J. Schilb (Eds.), *Contending with words* (pp. 105–123). New York: Modern Language Association.

Karis, B. (1989). Conflict in collaboration: A Burkean perspective. *Rhetoric Review, 8,* 113–126.

Lamb, C. E. (1991). Beyond argument in feminist composition. *College Composition and Communication, 42,* 11–24.

Marr, A., O.S.B. (1991). Letter to Confraters. On being an inclusive church. *Abbey Letter,* No. 167, n.p.

Morgan, R. (1984). *Sisterhood is global: The international women's movement anthology.* New York: Anchor Press/Doubleday.

Moulton, J. (1983). A paradigm of philosophy: The adversary method. In S. Harding & M. B. Hintikka (Eds.), *Discovering reality: Feminist perspectives on epistemology, metaphysics, methodology, and philosophy of science* (pp. 149–164). Boston: D. Riedel.

Nye, A. (1990). *Words of power.* New York: Routledge.

Osborn, S. (1991). Revision/re-vision: A feminist writing class. *Rhetoric Review, 9,* 258–273.

Rich, A. (1978). *The dream of a common language.* New York: Norton.

Ruddick, S. (1988). *Maternal thinking.* Boston: Beacon.

Shotter, J., & Logan, J. (1988). The pervasiveness of patriarchy: On finding a different voice. In M. M. Gergen (Ed.), *Feminist thought and the structure of knowledge* (pp. 69–86). New York: New York University Press.

Class Ethos and the Politics of Inquiry: What the Barroom Can Teach Us about the Classroom

Julie Lindquist

As Julie Lindquist reminds us, the issue of social class remains undertheorized in composition studies. In the following essay, published originally in College Composition and Communication *in 1999, Lindquist argues that teachers who hope to persuade working-class students of the value of academic argument need to investigate how and why argument works in traditional sites of working-class culture. Lindquist provides an ethnographic study of a working-class bar where political argumentation is an important form of discourse. By analyzing sites of working-class argument next to sites of academic argument, Lindquist suggests, academics will better understand the alienation many working-class students feel toward critical pedagogies — alienation that exists in spite (and maybe because) of academics' often highly theorized efforts to persuade students of the necessity of argumentation.*

Lindquist's essay productively questions the connections between social class and the success or failure of critical pedagogies in argument classes. Perhaps most importantly, she also asks teachers to consider teaching as a rhetorical process — an argument — that can improve if we carefully analyze how we create ethos and use discourse in relation to dominant notions of capitalism. Lindquist asks us to recognize that all rhetorical forms are tied to notions of work, culture, and power and that, if we are to persuade students of the value of what we teach, we need to be more attentive to the complex relationships between class and discourse.

Before I was an English teacher, I was a bartender. When I tell my first-year composition students this as we take turns exchanging getting-to-know-you trivia during the first class session, they laugh — some, I suspect, struck by the improbability of the leap from one profession into the other; others, I know, amused by the irony of ending up with an ex-bartender for a teacher. For these others, sons and daughters of iron workers and auto mechanics and waitresses, my move from barroom to classroom traces the trajectory of their own lives.

When I first began teaching, I thought — or, I have to say, I hoped — that the university was the farthest point from the local tavern, and that teaching writing to college students was the furthest thing from opening bottles of Bud for laborers. So I was surprised to find myself, after three years of teaching writing, feeling compelled to return to the bar where I'd worked for several years to do community research into local rhetorical practices. In the ethnographic tale that was to grow out of this research, I wanted to map out connections between class, culture, and rhetoric by investigating how rhetorical genres — and in particular, arguments about politics — participated in the public construction of knowledge in, and ultimately in the production of, working-class culture. I was not, of course, surprised to see my data confirm what I'd already suspected: that this small blue-collar society at the bar differed significantly from the cultures of middle-class academics in orientations to word, work, and world. What did come as something of a surprise, however, were what I have come to recognize as functional parallels between the barroom and the classroom as institutional sites of rhetorical practice. When, as a teacher working in a public university, I question the nature of the service I provide and try to understand the dynamics of the relationship I have with my student "regulars," I am struck by how handily the questions I ask myself about my role in the classroom can be expressed in the same language I might use to reflect on the nature of my job at the bar: What am I selling? Who are my customers, and where do they come from? Why are they here? Do I get to decide what's on tap — and to decide when a customer has had enough? To what extent do I mediate the talk that goes on, and when should I attempt to contain or redirect it? Do I have the right to decide when someone's language is inappropriate and bounce him out? Such questions (suggestive as they are of parallels between the roles of bartender and teacher in their respective institutional contexts) have motivated me to further question how the barroom might compare to the classroom. What does each institution mean to the community it serves? What does each *do* for the populations it serves? And what discourse(s) are sanctioned by each?

I want to suggest that an examination of rhetorical practices at the local bar is instructive for two reasons: (1) The barroom is predictably different from the university writing classroom; and (2) The barroom is surprisingly similar to the university writing classroom. A look at how neighborhood bars are qualitatively different from classrooms can teach us about our working-class students' rhetorical motives, and a recognition of how they are functionally similar can teach us something about our own. As repositories of cultural values, the working-class bar and the university writing classroom are, of course, quite different. As institutional spaces where public knowledge is constructed according to private rules and where conventional discourses are routinely — even ritually — performed, they have much in common. Just as the university writing classroom is an institutional context within which rhetorics — ways of speaking and of knowing — of the middle-class academic community are sanctioned and performed, the neighborhood bar functions as an institution in which rhetorics of working-class communities are routinely transacted. Within each institution is an economy of discourse, and it is within the terms of that economy that rhetoric — the sum of the discourse-knowledge equation — is produced.

No longer do we assume that classrooms are happily homogenous and insular "communities" that are somehow exempt from the market forces of other linguistic economies. Thus in a recent article Virginia Anderson characterizes classrooms as "rhetorical situations, sites of complex interactions between speakers, audiences, subjects, and codes," a situation she trusts that "teachers all along the continuum between activism and neutrality recognize" (198). But I believe that having recognized these complexities, we still have plenty to learn about what *kinds* of rhetorical situations writing classrooms are — especially insofar as they are constituted by competing (academic and local) discourses. It would help, I think, to conceive of the classroom as a kind of rhetorical marketplace, one that constitutes a complex scene of rhetorical performances, performances that take on value as cultural capital and are symbolically meaningful as currency.[1] As middle-class writing teachers working with students from working-class communities, we need to make it a priority to cultivate an awareness of how our own class capital — *as well as* our institutional power — positions us as rhetors in such a marketplace. Such an awareness would serve us well in moving us closer to a resolution of the ethical problem (of ethics *and* of ethos) that Frank Farmer identifies as the problem of "knowing how to teach in manner that both respects our students' views and, at the same time, questions the complacencies which too often inform these views" (187). Thinking of the writing classroom as a marketplace where discourses operate as symbolic capital can help us to understand how the rhetorical strategies that we use to establish our class(room) identity may delimit our authority to influence belief even as they allow us to enforce belief; and further, to see why it may be unconvincing to sell what functions as capital in the private marketplace of the academy as a transcendent rhetoric of moral integrity or political empowerment.

The problematics of social class and higher education in the United States have received a good deal of attention by Marxist educators and proponents of critical teaching such as Ira Shor, Peter McLaren, Stanley Aronowitz, and Henry Giroux. The autobiographical narratives of working-class academics like Mike Rose and Victor Villanueva have further enriched conversations about confrontations between local working-class and middle-class academic ways of knowing. Researchers such as Tom Fox have conducted ethnographic investigations into the composing strategies of working-class students to understand what it means for these students to grapple with the (social and rhetorical) demands of university writing instruction. Still, inquiries into the class-based cultural affiliations of the students who turn up in our writing classrooms have lagged behind inquiries into the pedagogical implications of identity and difference based on race, ethnicity, or gender. Since Lynn Z. Bloom complained in the October 1996 issue of *College English* that her call for papers on "intersections of race, class, and gender in composition studies" for the 1993 meeting of the MLA drew one lone proposal on class in contrast to 12 on race and 94 on gender (657), little has changed. We continue to operate with a thin understanding of the social knowledge — by which I mean epistemological habits rooted in community practice and emerging from material conditions — working-class students bring with them to that space.

What is worse is that when we do recognize this social knowledge, we too often regard it as a bad habit to be broken. Thus Jeff Smith finds in the words of Marshall Alcorn powerful evidence for his complaint that we seriously undervalue students' social obligations, arguing that when Alcorn "speaks of disabusing students of their 'commitments' without seeming to realize, or care, that he is thereby admitting students *have* commitments (not just wishes, commitments!) different from the ones he would like them to have" (303). Though I have reservations about the kind of instrumental approach to writing instruction Smith appears to recommend, I share his concern that well-intentioned writing teachers — often those most concerned with issues of social justice — seem to give little attention to the material circumstances from which students' local knowledge emerges.

It is perhaps symptomatic of this problem of inattention to the meaning of students' commitments that the approach to writing instruction most concerned with investigating institutional rhetorics to uncover the formative processes of social knowledge seems at times to be so unwilling to consider the specifics of local practice or to acknowledge the ways in which even the most "critical" or "multicultural" classroom works as a site of cultural reproduction. Cultural studies–derived pedagogies aim to have students interrogate the material conditions of their lives, and thus to help them arrive at a fuller understanding of their own (and others') socioeconomic predicaments. While I see this as a worthy goal, I question the means, which seem not to put nearly enough energy into the enterprise of learning what is at stake (and in particular, what is at stake for working-class students) in assenting to such critiques, into figuring out what resistance to cultural-studies projects might mean. For these reasons, it is important that we look beyond the university to see what happens in institutions where working-class identities and values are publicly invented and ritually affirmed.

In what follows, I offer a view of rhetorical practice in one such community institution. I offer examples of the public discourse of the barroom to show that the rhetoric that is valued most highly in today's writing classroom — that is, the rhetoric of conjecture and speculation — not only operates differently as currency in the working-class institution of the barroom, but often becomes, in that rhetorical economy, a powerful class symbol, one that occasions expressions of the problematics of working-class identity. Since speculative rhetoric — the discourse of inquiry — tends to be highly valued as currency in the classroom (and especially in the cultural-studies classroom, where inquiry into social and institutional power structures is the explicit goal), my hope is that teachers of composition will be encouraged not only to examine their assumptions about what this rhetoric is worth and why, but to consider how their authority to teach it is a function of the ethos they create by their own claims of rhetorical capital. Such considerations will, I believe, better equip teachers not only to understand the terms of working-class resistance to their critical teaching agendas, but to understand the nature (and consequences!) of their own resistance to working-class agendas. It is imperative that we learn how to manage (if not transcend) these resistances if we wish to rescue the classroom from its current predicament as the site of a standoff between working-class students' goals of entry into institutions of power and teachers' goals of critique of these same institutions.

"The Problem with You Is That You Ask So Many Questions!"

The Smokehouse Inn,[2] the bar where I both worked as a bartender and conducted ethnographic research into working-class rhetoric, is more than just a place for the locals to get good barbecue and cold beer: It is a neighborhood institution. The barroom of the Smokehouse, though it functions in part to service the adjoining family-style restaurant, serves the local community as a kind of public forum where members of this suburban Chicago community — laborers, machinists, Teamsters — can congregate to meet with friends and fellow workers, to drink, and to participate in conversation and debate with others about how to make sense of current issues and political events.

Though a relatively small sample of the larger population participates in the social life of the Smokehouse, the bar nonetheless plays an important role in the life of the community. In many working-class neighborhoods, local bars like the Smokehouse have long served as public spaces where private rhetorics are enacted. Historian Roy Rosenweig points out, for example, that barrooms have historically functioned as sanctuaries for expressions of working-class identity, and came to represent an institutional articulation of working-class resistance to middle-class values (145). Despite changes in the industrial landscape, the barroom persists as a site where working-class concerns are given voice. Writes Stanley Aronowitz:

> We live in a postindustrial service society in which the traditional markers of working-class culture survive — especially, the barroom, where waves of male industrial workers have congregated to share their grievances against the boss, their private troubles, their dreams of a collective power and individual escape. (204)

Ethnographic studies of working-class communities have, as well, demonstrated the importance of taverns to the production of knowledge and flow of information in these communities. In E. E. Le Masters's study of lifestyles in a working-class bar in a Midwestern town, for example, the author concludes early on that "the tavern in this small community was the center of social life," to the extent that "the proprietor had an amazing amount of knowledge about the residents of the town" such that "he could predict election results with great accuracy" (17). While neighborhood demographics have changed since the time of Le Masters's study, it remains true that bars continue to function as public forums in many working-class communities. (Though there are many people in such communities who have no direct involvement with bars, local taverns nonetheless act as important sites for the construction of working-class identity.) As such, they are likely to serve as a general point of reference for others in the community, including those who are (legally) considered too young to patronize them. Given the status of bars as neighborhood institutions, young working-class adults — even adolescents — are likely to feel the influence of local bars even if they have never set foot in one. Yet given as well the tendency of working-class adolescents to assume adult roles earlier on, chances are that they will in fact have had direct experience with bars.[3] As a teenager growing up in a blue-collar neighborhood, I experienced bars as an important rite of passage from childhood to adulthood — one that has as a functional parallel, I would venture, the passage undertaken by young middle-class adults first going "away" to college. My experience, while perhaps not universal, is far from unique.

The Smokehouse, where working people come together to publicly invent a private culture, is not in fact situated in what one thinks of as a traditional white-ethnic enclave. However, the community it serves largely comprises working whites who moved from such southside enclaves to flee the southward migrations of urban African Americans. One could argue, in fact, that the Smokehouse is all the more important as a community institution now that the community itself has been geographically "displaced." Most of the men and women who participate regularly in the social life of the Smokehouse work in traditional blue-collar jobs: The men are skilled laborers (telephone linemen, woodworkers, plumbers, truck drivers, machinists) and the women work in service jobs (as waitresses, bartenders, clerks, child-care providers, and hairdressers).

The voices who have featured most prominently in my story of Smokehouse rhetoric belong to the men and women who were "regulars" at the bar: that is, to those who treated the bar as a kind of home-away-from-home and who enjoyed an established role in the social network there. Many of these "regulars" spent several hours a day, several days a week at the bar. Though at the time I conducted my research most of the regular bar patrons were men, the bar did have its share of women who enjoyed status as regulars, as well.[4] The regular Smokehousers who are at the core of my study are Walter, a retired foreman for a farm equipment manufacturer; Arlen, a sixty-year-old cook and bar manager; Joe, a forty-year-old machinist; Maggie, a young mother who has worked at the Smokehouse as waitress, hostess, and bartender; Roberta, waitress and fifteen-year Smokehouse veteran; and Jack, entrepreneur and former steelworker. There have been constellations of others as well, regulars and droppers-in who have moved in and out of the Smokehouse scene, and with whom I have chatted, joked, commiserated, and contended.

Since I had lived in the area for many years and was well-connected in the community, I got the Smokehouse job through a friend of a friend who had been a bartender there. Within a week from the day I first showed up to work the bar at the Smokehouse, I found (or rather, was relegated to) my niche in the small society of the barroom. My prior commitment to the neighborhood meant that I was regarded by the Smokehouse "establishment" as an insider, even as my status (then) as a graduate student clearly marked me as an outsider. This ambiguous identity earned me a distinctive place in the social structure of waitresses, bartenders, and regular customers. I like to describe my role at the Smokehouse as that of friendly antagonist, since my status as insider and place in the network depended on my willingness to provide occasions for argument by challenging conventional values and beliefs. To be an insider, in other words, I had to cultivate a performative persona as outsider. It was in my capacity as bartender that I worked as ethnographer, using my position behind the bar to record the political arguments that took place with such frequency, and such apparent fury.[5]

As bartender/ethnographer — and, as worker/graduate student — I often found myself to be a central actor in these speech events. My own presence at the Smokehouse offered a reference point in terms of which Smokehousers could express themselves as a coherent sociopolitical body by articulating who and what they were not. For this reason, my own conversations and confrontations with others at the Smokehouse were responsible for generating data that is richly suggestive of Smokehouse orientations to truth and language, and of the relationship between rhetorical practice and class identity. Often quite against my will, I "helped" those at the Smokehouse to articulate the conventional wisdom of the community by taking part in arguments in which oppositions to middle-class rhetorics (and in particular, academic rhetorics) were ritually dramatized.

I expect that the terms of my place among others at the Smokehouse will sound (perhaps painfully) familiar to anyone who has ever found himself or herself struggling to negotiate the space between local working-class and middle-class academic social spheres. Smokehousers publicly spoke about my associations with the university in ways that revealed that I came to represent an orientation to work and knowledge that was vastly different from local norms. Any mention of my "other life" as student and teacher of English, for example, invariably inspired much lively commentary from the regulars at the bar, much of it derisive: Wendell, a union laborer and Smokehouse regular, would often ask me if I was "done with school yet," and would remark on my status as a "professional student." On one occasion, he leaned over the bar to me and demanded to know if I was *still* in school." When I assured him that I was, Wendell turned his attention to the others at the bar, and addressing them, remarked, "This one here's the only one I know gonna be collecting her social security checks from a goddamn *college!*" Though he does not articulate my transgression against community norms in terms of social class, his quip suggests that as a graduate (and therefore "professional") student, I symbolize an unnatural, or at least unhealthy, identification with the university — and a defection to middle-class values and lifestyle. For Wendell, and presumably for the audience he addresses in his commentary, I clearly represent a departure from local norms which dictate that public identities are built on the fundamental values of work and community. My involvement and identification with the university meant that what I came to signify for others in Smokehouse society was an orientation to all things academic, pedantic, and ultimately without value in the everyday life of the "real world" of work. Once, in a conversation about race relations in the aftermath of the Rodney King verdict, Walter threw up his hands in exasperation and complained, "The problem with you is that you ask so many questions that sooner a later, a guy runs out of answers!" My rhetorical habit of speculating and raising questions, a strategy that is so richly rewarded within the academic institution, was apparently seen by Walter and others at the Smokehouse as both unproductive and manipulative. However (as I shall argue), the contempt Smokehousers such as Wendell and Walter show for the habit of "asking so many questions" has at least as much to do with (what they perceive to be) my *use* of it as a status claim as it does with their attitudes toward this rhetoric more generally. That is, the Smokehousers' responses to me have less to do with any negative assessment of my personal integrity or with wholesale rejection of a particular rhetorical practice than with their critique of the public self they saw me as trying to invent in my arguments with them.

Social scientists have long struggled to describe the class situation in the United States quantitatively, in terms of material conditions. But the place of political argument in the everyday life of the Smokehouse community indicates the extent to which "working-class" is a cultural category, and hence, a rhetorical construct. Richard Ohmann, taking as an example his own class experience, describes class "membership" as a discursive process: "In all my doing from day to day I and the people I mingle with and am affected by constantly *create* my class position. . . . From this perspective, class is not a permanent fact, but something that continually *happens*" (qtd. in Fox 73–74). Though of course the everyday realities of people in traditional blue-collar jobs are shaped by material conditions, these conditions are always subject to (and the subject of) invention and interpretation; the barroom at the Smokehouse is just one example of a site where working-class identity is under construction. This collective identity is, however, conflicted and problematic: In a sense, contentions about how it should be named are what define the group as a social unit. In the absence of an articulated consensus about how the class to which they belong should experience itself as a sociopolitical body — people at the Smokehouse tend to believe that they can claim neither the established power that accrues to those at the top of the socioeconomic hierarchy, nor the emergent power of historically marginalized "minority" groups — their social identity comes, in large part, from managed dissent.

One important way the Smokehousers express class solidarity is through participation in performances of agonistic discourse. Political argument at the bar functions as a conventional speech genre, knowledge of the conventions of which establishes one's place among others — at the Smokehouse, and in the world. Further, ritual performance of conventional speech genres establishes and authorizes the "official" discourse of the institution. *Topoi* for barroom debates are shaped in relation to that official discourse, which functions as a conservative but negotiable public epistemology, one that maps out the rhetorical territory on which contenders in performed arguments position themselves in staging their disputes. Though individuals may occupy different positions on this discursive terrain, the official discourse serves as the heuristic *in terms of which* class identity is invented. My presence as a dissenter helps to resolve the tension between individuating and consolidating functions of rhetoric — that is, it both opens possibilities for inquiry (thus freeing individuals to claim distinctive positions) and inscribes the parameters of social knowledge (thereby allowing the Smokehousers to articulate what they have in common). In their arguments with me, that is, the Smokehousers could show dissent without showing themselves to be *dissenters*.

One topic that functions as a site for — and implicates me as "teacher" in — the process of invention and identification is that of education. Though most people who work and play at the Smokehouse have not attended college, they urge their children to "stay in school and work hard," seeing higher education as a means to economic opportunity. Many at the bar have been quietly supportive of my academic career, have congratulated me on my efforts to "make something of myself." Yet this valorization of my success in achieving whatever economic mobility my education makes possible — often by the very people who publicly devalue it — bespeaks a deeply ambivalent attitude toward the kind of capital higher education has to offer. Smokehousers privately approve of those who strive to join the middle class, but publicly disapprove of those who embrace the rhetoric of its institutions: Earning a degree is seen as a route to upward mobility even as identification with the university is perceived as a kind of cultural abandonment.

Attitudes about the role of education are connected in complex ways to views regarding the value of work; attitudes about the meaning of work are an essential component of the institutional discourse. In the terms of that discourse, work tends to be defined in opposition to play or leisure, a distinction that reflects a deeper structural opposition in Smokehouse conventional wisdom between doing and thinking, producing and philosophizing. Speaking to me one-to-one in an interview, Walter articulates an investment in practice as the distinctive feature of Smokehouse sociopolitical identity.[6] His response to a question I posed about what is to be learned from institutional versus experiential education suggests that he sees the world of formal education as a world of artifice, one that sets itself in opposition to the "real" world of work. Walter explains that you "learn more" outside of school than in it:

> The first thing they [employers] almost always — everyone'll tell you: First thing you gotta do is, forget what you learned in school! 'Cause you're out in the so-called real world — that's where it's at. There's more to be learned outside of college than there is inside of college . . . with the exception, now, of, ah, let's say, uh, engineering, ah, medical professions, uh, some disciplines like chemistry . . . you just can't do without college . . . there's where you learn, you learn the basics. Uh, the real test comes when you get out in the field . . . uh, I, um, here I go again — you're gonna think I'm really hung up on this subject — but I am! Ah, I judge an educated man by his ability to *do*. You understand? That really says it all.

Walt will concede the value of higher education, but only if it doesn't come with indoctrination into middle-class values, values here represented by identification with rhetoric-for-its-own-sake. He speaks for many at the Smokehouse in insisting that the value of formal education lies in its ability to convey immediately applicable, practical knowledge — not in training in speculative rhetoric.

Though the official discourse serves as a heuristic for public debate, the conventional wisdoms it encodes are by no means professed with equal enthusiasm by all. Rather, one's position with respect to the official discourse has everything to do with how one is positioned within the group. Walter, who describes himself as "working class," does in fact identify strongly with the conventional wisdom, and in public arguments, tends to perform views that affirm group solidarity. Walt is the voice of consensus at the Smokehouse, and he is often called upon to give voice to the public view in response to challenges from "outside." In this sense, he occupies a much different role in the Smokehouse network from that of Perry, the owner of the Smokehouse. In private interviews with me, Perry clearly attempted to position himself *against* what he perceived to be working-class cultural habits and Smokehouse conventional wisdom. He told me that he thought of himself as "lower middle class," and his commentaries on the uses of higher education are suggestive of his middle-class identification and his approval of upward mobility. Perry spoke to me of the humanistic potential of a college education, and remarked often on its capacity to allow for social mobility. He remembered his own college experience, for example, as a time when he was free to break from local norms:

> I think that the friends I made, the ah, black friends that I had in college that were my best friends, had something to do with shaping my life . . . so yeah, in some respects you learn a tolerance, that you can't pick up if you don't get an education . . . if you don't spend time with a variety of people, and around learned people. If you're just gonna be — you know, if your life is sitting around a bar, entirely, then that's all you're gonna know . . . is those people, it's those *rednecks* out there, that you're gonna be doing most of your learning from. Unless you really are a person who can rise above it. . . .

In looking at the conflicting responses of Walter and Perry, it becomes clear that Smokehousers' attitudes toward the value of higher education have much to do with how it is claimed as an identification strategy. To simply attend college is not enough to set one apart: To inhabit its philosophical world, however, is.

For Walter — himself a skilled rhetorician — to claim the rhetorical is suspect, because it confuses the practical with the theoretical, mixes work with play. Walter voices this attitude in valorizing those who "do," while devaluing those who merely "talk." As an illustration of the preferable former type, he holds up as an example another Smokehouse regular, Joe:

> You got people around here that — and I don't want to mention any names — but, uh, that are very quick, and very responsive, and uh uh blah blah blah, they got the floor all the time, but they, uh, when it comes to the ability to *do,* earn a living and take care of yourself — Joe is head and shoulders above 'em.

Walt's sly reference to my own rhetorical posturing sets me up as a point of reference against which to contrast Joe as a man of action. For Walt (who doesn't always agree with Joe, and who frequently tries to bait him into arguments) Joe's refusal to play rhetorician and to claim rhetorical prowess as a source of prestige marks him as someone who exemplifies class loyalty and with whom it is appropriate to identify. Walt's praise of Joe is consistent with a view, expressed by Smokehousers time and time again, that doing rhetoric — performing and philosophizing at the same time — is essentially dishonest, is a play for status motivated by personal vanity, and not necessarily by concern for truth or for the public good. While Smokehousers regularly use the barroom as a place to stage elaborate verbal performances demonstrating individual prowess in agonistic rhetoric, they hold in suspicion those performers who are obviously adept at the game — the better one speaks, in other words, the less he or she can be trusted. (Not surprisingly, Walter himself was often accused of being a "bullshitter" by other Smokehousers who suspected *him* of enjoying argument as a rhetorical exercise.)

Though the official discourse of the Smokehouse serves a solidarity function in setting itself in opposition to the middle-class practice of speculative rhetoric, in arguments individuals stage performances to distinguish themselves as rhetoricians in the group even as they publicly declaim skepticism about the usefulness of rhetoric-as-inquiry. In barroom arguments I was consistently scripted into the role of one who, as teacher (and therefore as one who asks questions for a living), cannot therefore *do* (anything *really* productive). This was the part in which I was cast even though people at the Smokehouse knew me first in my capacity as worker: My alliance with the university and its ways of knowing worked to divest me of the authority to speak the truth on matters of "real life" and to provide meaningful commentary on the world of work and action. In performed arguments, I was consistently cast by others at the Smokehouse into the role of "teacher" — that is, I was called upon to give dramatic voice to what, in terms of orientation to discourse and knowledge, the academic institution represented to the Smokehouse community.

An excerpt from one argument in particular illustrates how argument operates in the domain linking rhetorical practice to class identity. The argument from which these data are taken took place among several Smokehouse regulars and workers on a Friday evening as I worked behind the bar, and features Walter and me as primary players. The exchange began as a discussion about then-candidate Bill Clinton's qualifications for the office of president given his history as a "draft dodger," and quickly grew into a more philosophical debate about the general morality of refusing to serve in the military during wartime. I held that there were indeed circumstances under which one might refuse to participate in war; others at the bar, and most notably Walter, argued that the duty to serve one's country is an absolute moral imperative:

> *Walt:* [indicating a man seated across at the bar] I wanna talk about this young man, here. Next year we get involved in a war — and he's ripe. Do you think that he's got the prerogative to say, "I don't *like* this war, so I'm not going!"?

Me: It depends entirely on the circumstances. Now why don't you ask him what *he* thinks?

Walt: There's no *circumstances!* The law says — the law says, we've declared war on . . . ah . . . Mesopotamia . . .

Me: So what if we declared war, and it . . . it did not seem like a just cause?

Walt: We didn't declare war on anybody! Well, this is why I say I can't ever discuss anything with you, because here you always say, "What if, what if?" *Bullshit on "What if"!* When our country says we're at war, it's his [points again at the man across the bar] job to go!

A Voice from Across the Bar: That's what *I* say!

Me: So you should do *whatever* your country says to do, regardless —

Walt: That's right!

Me: So what if you lived in Germany —

Walt: Same thing! I don't care *where* it is! If your country says you go, *you go!*

Me: But who makes these decisions? Aren't — aren't you, the people — this is a democracy — aren't —

Walt: Ooooh, *fungu* on your goddamn *bullshit!* Now you're changin' the argument — who makes the laws, who done this, who done that. . . . I wanna ask you one —

Me: You said —

Walt: [pounding on the bar to punctuate each word] I wanna ask you *one* question, and *one question only!* Do you think that each man has an individual right to obey the law or disobey it?

Me: Sure, but I *also* think people — since this is a *democracy* —

Walt: I don't want to hear it! I want a yes or no answer.

Me: [with exasperation] Wal-ter . . . !

Roberta: Wait, wait — I gotta ask one question —

Me: You're imposing all these conditions —

Roberta: Do you think —

Me: — and you won't let me impose my own!

What is most immediately striking about this exchange is how operatic the argument is in its exaggerated rendering of moral opposites, and how much it depends for dramatic effect on the performances of individual actors. While individuals work to display their talents to the audience of others (each player functions by turns as performer and as audience), they also work together to express the thematic structure of a unified dramatic composition. As performance, the argument is in effect cordoned off as ceremonial space where the script of public knowledge is enacted. Within this generic dramatic structure, however, Walter performs a role that gives voice to the deep assumptions that are fundamental to the institutional discourse of the Smokehouse. What is dramatized by Walt in his performance for the larger audience of people at the Smokehouse bar is his (and, by implication, the audience's) contempt for my privileging of theory over practice — that is, for my investment in the hypothetical *what-if* at the expense of the constative *it-is*. Walt's dramatization of the importance of practice over theory, then, enacts the institutional philosophy regarding the place of *what-if* in the cultural marketplace in which the Smokehouse participates.

And *yet* — while it tends to be something of a commonplace among middle-class academics that the working class is characterized as a group by a kind of stubborn literal-mindedness — it is important to understand that Walt's rejection of my rhetorical strategy *does not mean that Walter and others at the Smokehouse do not practice what-if rhetoric.* Notice how Walter himself proposes a hypothetical scenario immediately prior to his grand dismissal of my own what-if question. (In fact, the barroom — as a place for leisure, a place apart from work — is the official site, the appropriate institutional space for *what-if.*) It means, rather, that in this particular rhetorical economy, I will not be granted the authority to claim the rhetoric of *what-if* as capital. As illocution, Walt's declamation can be understood to mean something like "bullshit on people who use what-if to show they're better than me!" While the bar is seen as a place of *play* and therefore as an appropriate place for what-if games, my status as one who takes part in a marketplace where *what-if* has actual value as *work* — in which theory *is* practice — undermines my persuasive ethos and makes me an occasion for cultural performance. In other words, at the Smokehouse it is appropriate to practice what-if rhetoric only *if* one neither publicly claims (or proclaims) it as a way to make knowledge nor identifies with institutions where theory *is* practice, where talk *is* action. *What-if* is particularly suspect when it becomes clear that someone outside the community is trying to use it as a way to claim a position of privilege: In the absence of an alternative rhetoric which makes it possible to conceive class in other than crudely economic terms, *what-if* becomes the site of agonistic performance when it is suspected to activate claims of symbolic capital. (Consider, if you will, another example of how *what-if* is linked to persuasive authority: Almost without exception, those at the Smokehouse supported the presidential candidacy of Ross Perot, an anti-politics politician whose persuasive ethos was predicated on his wholesale rejection of all things political. Having demonstrated a commitment to *getting things done,* Perot was free to spin hypothetical scenarios illustrating just *what* would be different *if* he were president. In other words, Perot can be forgiven for his material capital — he can still be *real* — as long he doesn't claim rhetorical capital.) To use *what-if,* and to publicly advocate its uses, is predicated on the ethos one can only establish by refusing to use it to claim class privilege. This powerful association of *what-if* with cultural capital has obvious implications for middle-class teachers working in middle-class institutions to teach middle-class rhetorics to working-class students.

Teachers, Students, and the Politics of Inquiry

Of course, Walter doesn't speak for all working-class students, or even for most. How students will receive the critical agenda of the writing classroom has to do with how they perceive rhetoric to work as currency in marketplaces in which they currently trade, on the one hand, and aspire to claim membership, on the other. The population of a writing class is not a mere random sample of the larger population, as Jeff Smith points out. "For," he says, stating the obvious but often overlooked truth, "students have *already* passed through gates en route to our classrooms." He goes on to remind us that as different as our students may be from us and from each other, what they have in common is that they have chosen to come to college (102). Clearly, the writing students who show up in our classrooms have — unlike Walter — demonstrated a commitment to the middle-class enterprise of higher education. But though the very presence of a working-class student at the university would seem to indicate his or her belief in the virtue of upward mobility (or at least, if such a desire is not fully realized, an ambivalence toward identification with the working class), such a student may not be equipped to trade in the kind of rhetorical currency we're offering. The place of *what-if* in the rhetorical economy of the Smokehouse suggests that it is not learning the habits and conventions of inquiry that is troublesome for working-class students — since, as we have seen, what-if rhetoric *does* happen in working-class institutions — but rather, that the politics of identification in the use of this rhetoric is what these students find truly problematic.

Quite obviously, the barroom differs from the classroom in the social values it sanctions. As institutional sites, barroom and classroom embody different sets of cultural prerogatives. In "Freshman Composition as a Middle-Class Enterprise," Lynn Z. Bloom argues that whatever else we may think we're doing in the writing classroom, we are promoting — through teaching style, writing assignments, evaluation, everything — a set of clearly identifiable middle-class virtues. She goes on to list some of the values university writing instruction promotes: respectability, decorum and propriety, moderation and temperance, thrift, efficiency, order, cleanliness, punctuality, delayed gratification; and, finally, critical thinking. It is easy to see how working-class bars represent the violation, indeed the antithesis, of this middle-class value structure: The typical corner bar appears to be a place of fierce solidarity, vice, aggression, drunkenness, profligacy, leisure, chaos, sloth, and excess. But it is the final item in Bloom's list, the one that does not participate quite so neatly in the above list of oppositions, that we as writing teachers use most often, and most insistently, to define ourselves and our classroom discourses against local institutions and local rhetorics: the virtue of critical thinking.

Though we still haven't reached a consensus about the means and ends of freshman writing instruction, I think it's fair to say that most teachers — and particularly those who see themselves as working to advance the aims of a "critical pedagogy" — are committed to teaching the transformative power of rhetoric both for self-discovery and social change. This would include any writing teacher who participates in current conversations in composition studies, from process-approach specialists to proponents of Freireian liberatory pedagogy to those who take a cultural-studies approach to the teaching of writing. In other words, it implicates anyone who believes that an important goal of first-year writing instruction should be to educate students in ways to approach discourse "critically;" — that is, to both interpret and invent strategic uses of text. Marilyn Cooper articulates this common philosophical ground in noting that most compositionists "believe in the value of critical thinking, cognitive dissonance, and adopting different perspectives — all of which are based on the central value of coming to know through reading and writing" (55).

What is productive as an educational goal, however, is likely to be counterproductive when claimed as a moral virtue. I would go so far as to argue that the rhetorical habits Cooper describes are habits in which we as compositionists not only believe, but identify — that is, we claim their practice as a moral virtue which we then use to locate ourselves in relation to our students and the institutional rhetorics they represent. While addressing the needs of working-class students demands that we become aware of the ways in which the classroom is different from the barroom in the rhetorical gestures it rewards, it would also serve us well to note that as a rhetorical marketplace, the classroom has much in common with the barroom. Like the barroom, the classroom is a place where (though different market values may obtain) insiders trade in cultural currencies and claim their places in the institution through generic cultural performances.

While it's important that we remain aware that we speak from a position of institutional power and therefore have a moral obligation to speak responsibly to students in our classrooms, the difficulty as I see it has as much to do with how to be persuasive *at all* as with how to decide what kind of influence to have. As politically sensitive instructors, we worry endlessly about the ideological messages we convey to our students, but my work and field experiences at the bar have given me to suspect that we're giving ourselves rather too much credit.[7] In her recent work exploring the meaning of authority in the postmodern composition classroom (1996), Xin Liu Gale argues that teachers working within institutions of higher education have always had coercive power, a power that derives from their associations with the institutions themselves, but she gives rather less attention to the question of what kind of coercion this power implies, and to how it actually affects students' ways of thinking about their lives. I do think it is safe to assume that, just as persuasive authority is unevenly distributed among rhetoricians at the Smokehouse, the academic institution does not wholly, unequivocally, or unproblematically determine the authority of individuals working within it. If working-class students have had limited participation in marketplaces in which intellectual capital holds currency, then what is to say that they will regard writing teachers — who are often rich in symbolic capital but do not display signs of material capital — to have the kind of *ethos* that effectively persuades them of the value of *what-if* as a resource?

It seems doubtful that we will be able to make the necessary ethical appeals to convince students to engage in the kind of writing-as-inquiry we value when we claim *what-if* as capital at the same time we fail to demonstrate social and economic power.[8] In this discussion of the nature of authority in the writing classroom, Mortensen and Kirsch call into question the idea that authority as it functions in the classroom "community" is a linear process or static condition that works independently of particular discursive contexts, observing that "relations in communities are in part defined by differences in knowledge, experiences, and status — differences in power that endlessly shift with and across social contexts" (557–58). To identify different kinds of authority in the social dynamic of the classroom, Mortensen and Kirsch suggest that a functional distinction be made between the power to enforce belief and the power to influence belief, calling the former "authority of office" and the latter "authority of expertise" (559). In one sense, what we lack when we fail to persuade of the value of *what-if* is the authority of expertise — i.e., we have somehow failed to demonstrate the profitable uses of our knowledge-as-capital, even as the authority we enjoy by virtue of our office within the institution gives us the power to dictate classroom policies and procedures. From another perspective, the crisis of persuasive authority can be located in the relation between the authorities of office and expertise, insofar as our failure to persuade of the value of *what-if* originates in our failure to make apparent to our students the specificity of the relationship between the authorities of office and of expertise. In other words, what we have failed to demonstrate is that the kind of expertise we are selling — the capacity to engage speculative rhetoric — does in fact have something to do with the authority of offices outside the academy. When we display a kind of capital that appears to be without value in the larger social economy, we have not succeeded in persuading students from working-class communities that expertise in *what-if* confers power in socioeconomic institutions that exist in (as such a student might put it) "the real world."

Writing about problems feminist teachers face in attempting to persuade students to ally themselves with feminist concerns, Virginia Anderson calls upon the Burkean idea of identification to explain that such attempts fail because they misapprehend the rhetorical situation in which they operate, and misunderstand the role of ethos in the process of identification. In her critique of Dale Bauer's tactics for persuading students to realign themselves with her feminist agenda, Anderson argues that it is Bauer's own ethos that is largely responsible for her failure to persuade. Explains Anderson: "[Bauer] presents herself as an embodiment of her political agenda, and hence as a site, intrinsically valid and appealing in itself, where students will one day decide they want to end up . . . [But] sites are seldom intrinsically persuasive; identification is created. We induce it through the tactical choices we make — our own moves in the rhetorical alignment and the types of arguments we construct" (200). She speculates that feminist teachers go wrong in that "they align themselves with [what] those students hope never to become, and they depict themselves as enemies of what many students are" (203). I am suggesting that a similar dynamic is at work in the attempts of middle-class teachers to persuade working-class students to identify with the practice of *what-if* — that teachers who claim *what-if* as capital while encouraging critique of other symbols of middle-class capital do not themselves embody persuasive sites. In making conventional symbols of middle-class capital the subject of our critical performances, we not only set ourselves in opposition to the discourse of working-class institutions but also demonstrate class privilege by aligning ourselves with an economic predicament working-class students are trying desperately to transcend. In a recent issue of *CCC*, Frank Farmer confesses that his students, upon being asked for their responses to essays critical of popular culture forms for an advanced composition course, were more interested in figuring out what the *critics* stood to gain in their rhetorical performances than they were in evaluating the validity of the critiques themselves. Far from accepting the claims of the pop-culture critics uncritically, Farmer's students suspected that the critics were motivated by an urge to assert class distinction at the expense of the average, unenlightened reader (190–92).

What I have come to understand since Walter pounded his fist on the bar at the Smokehouse and declared "*bullshit* on 'what if'!" is that he was right in suspecting me of trying to win the game by claiming *what-if* as capital. I was, admittedly, more concerned with characterizing myself as something other than the ill-informed, literal-minded working stiff I imagined (and constructed) him to be — was more concerned, that is, with showing myself to be middle-class — than I was with trying to move the conversation into a place where we could engage in mutual inquiry into the truth of the matter. I knew immediately that Walter was using me as a foil against which to construct a public persona, but it took me longer to see that I was just as eagerly doing the same.

I worry that what we are doing is convincing students who have strong local ties that the only use of *what-if* is as a strategy for identification with something they don't necessarily want to be. While some students (those who, like Perry, are driven by a desire to set themselves apart from "those rednecks out there") might be persuaded to identify with us and with the institutional rhetorics for which we speak, this hardly encourages critique of dominant institutions, nor does it produce humane, informed citizens. It merely teaches working-class students a trick of achieving class distinction, a trick that entails seeing those in their home communities — and worse, those parts of themselves that remain at home — as dupes. I worry that when we construct *what-if* as class capital and ourselves as examples of successful investors in such capital, students who wish to buy into *what-if* must necessarily identify *against* the "rednecks."

What, then, can we do to create an *ethos* that is persuasive to students who may be inclined, like Walter, to say, "bullshit on 'what if'"? We need to make the uses and powers of *what-if* the very subject of deep inquiry in the writing classroom — to focus, for example, on the relationships between the practice of *what-if* and socioeconomic power, and to pose such questions as, Who has the "right" to engage in *what-if,* and under what circumstances? What is the relationship between the ability to perform speculative rhetoric and capacity to achieve one's social, economic, and political goals? At the same time that we work to understand students' reasons for their resistance to us and to what we stand for, we should also interrogate the terms of our resistance to what *they* stand for. We need to communicate our efforts in both respects. We can begin, for one, by responding not with contempt or derision for such students' vulgar instrumentalism, but by demonstrating a willingness to open a space in the classroom for inquiries into the relationship between academic writing and *what-if,* to interrogate the different instrumentalities *what-if* might have. It is important, I think, that we as teachers remain open to what sometimes may strike us as the (distressingly) utilitarian motives of first-year students, and to work to open a dialogue between writing-as-critical-inquiry and writing-as-instrument; between means and ends. When students invested in acquiring practical knowledge want to know what learning to write in the ways we sanction will *do* for them, we should take the question seriously.

The way to persuade working-class students of the value of *what-if,* then, is to openly acknowledge functional parallels between the rhetoric of the barroom and that of the classroom. This means that we would make the nature of institutional discourse the focus of our pedagogy, and would encourage students to think about how speculative rhetoric can be of value to them as capital, how it can be useful as currency in the marketplaces in which they wish to participate. Examining how *what-if* can be useful as an instrument in the academic marketplace might then invite inquiries into how much philosophical and instrumental rhetorics are differences in kind, and to what degree they suggest differences in context. The language of *action* and *use* may help to invest us with the authority to persuade students that writing has important uses even when it isn't being *useful.*[9] I am not arguing that we should be concerned only with teaching students how to fill out job applications; I believe that we should encourage them to write in ways that are critical and exploratory. But I *am* suggesting that we need to make it a priority to raise questions about how each text performs, in which domain, and to what ends. This seems essential if we are to demonstrate to students that we are aware of what we are up to in our performances.

Every so often I hear one or another of my colleagues invoke the white-male-in-a-baseball-cap-who-wants-just-the-facts as a symbolic focus for his or her resentment toward student resistance to *what-if* (and to critical pedagogy more generally). Just as Walter publicly identifies me as a symbol of the kind of middle-class intellectual one must not claim to be, teachers construct such students as symbols that are ritually invoked for political ends. Such rhetorical strategies bring to mind the profoundly troubling what-if question Virginia Anderson poses: "What if the real solidarity that appeals to activist teachers is not that solidarity we might achieve with our students, but rather the unity and satisfaction we find in our radical stance?" (212). It is certainly true that working-class students' obvious lack of (middle-class) cultural capital, combined with their apparent political conservatism, may tend to frustrate and alienate teachers whose political views and teaching philosophies work together as valuable symbolic resources within the institution. But while white working-class students may seem to offer a safe opportunity to express such resentments, surely these students are not themselves unaware of their status as the focus of such teacherly frustrations. In setting ourselves in opposition to such students we may succeed in expressing our own class distinction, but we succeed neither in showing solidarity with their needs, nor in constructing an *ethos* that might help us to persuade them of the value of *what-if* in their writing and in their lives.

While it is certainly true that learning about rhetorical practices in working-class institutions helps us to understand the nature of working-class students' (social and rhetorical) commitments, it may also be true that an awareness of the politics of inquiry in our own institutional context better equips us to persuade our more traditional students of the value of inquiry, as well. That *what-if* is so problematically linked to class identification does, of course, mean that working-class students have more to gain, and more to lose, in buying stock in the rhetorical capital of the academic institution. But I am convinced that knowing our own rituals and performances is a way of becoming intimately familiar with who we are as rhetors, with our powers and limitations, with our motives and agendas. If we are truly concerned with teaching the transformative power of writing for political empowerment and social change, then we must understand that our first and most critical task is to assess, and commit ourselves to working within, the rhetorical economy of the writing classroom itself — even when this entails taking an honest look at the terms of our own investments in *what-if.*

Notes

1. Joseph Harris complained years ago of the tendency of compositionists to accept the notion of *discourse community* uncritically, and cautioned that "theories have tended to invoke the idea of community in ways at once sweeping and vague: positing discursive utopias that direct and determine the writings of their members, yet failing to state the operating rules or boundaries of these communities" (12). Harris's caveat has encouraged me to see

that the complex sociocultural dynamics of the classroom "community" might better be understood in Bourdieu's terms, whereby specific social scenes operate as marketplaces within a larger social economy in which products of culture function as currency and take on value as capital (1991).

2. A pseudonym. Since the bar services a barbecue restaurant and is usually filled with a dense haze of cigarette smoke, "the Smokehouse" seemed like the obvious choice of name.

3. In her study of social categories in a suburban Detroit high school, sociolinguist Penelope Eckert demonstrates how working-class students tend to assume adult roles much earlier than their middle-class counterparts, for whom adolescence is preparation for an adult life characterized by stages of upward mobility. Eckert explains that because working-class adolescents tend to look to local networks for social and economic resources, they are not necessarily set off categorically from the social world of adults. "Continuity between high school and early adulthood," writes Eckert, "resides in different spheres [for middle- and working-class adolescents]" (139).

4. It has been noted by linguists and anthropologists who have studied bar-room cultures (Le Masters, Spradley and Mann, Bell) that bars have traditionally functioned as spaces where rituals of masculinity are given ceremonial treatment. At the Smokehouse, women are active participants in the social life at the bar — though they earn the right to claim membership by taking part in male-solidarity rituals (such as buying rounds of drinks and participating in performances of agonistic discourse), they nonetheless are an important part of the Smokehouse scene. This participation extends beyond the domain of work, since women who are employed as waitresses and bartenders often spend much of their leisure time at the bar. As a bartender — that is, as one in a central position in Smokehouse social routines — I enjoyed a position of high visibility and status in Smokehouse society.

5. Because of the bar's status as private-space-within-a-public-space, the mechanics of data collection presented particular challenges. My general method for gathering data was to switch on a small, hand-held tape recorder I kept behind the bar as episodes of conversation happened. Though I did not remind people of the presence of the tape recorder as I recorded each episode of talk, I did discuss my plan to record conversations with the owner of the Smokehouse as well as with those regulars who are featured most prominently in the study. In other words, regulars knew I was working on a research project about "how people talked about politics in the real world," and that I was likely to tape conversations (even if I did not announce my intent to record particular stretches of discourse). Generally speaking (though many at the bar said that they were glad I was going to write something about the way things *really* were among people who worked), my *research* project was regarded as an eccentricity, as further evidence of the peculiar habits of academics.

6. It is, of course, important to bear in mind that even though I conducted interviews with individuals at a remove from the arena of public performance, interviews are themselves performances to an audience — me — perceived to be skeptical of the truth of working-class values.

7. In his research on first-year writing students' responses to critical pedagogy, David Seitz observed that working-class students in a cultural-studies research writing class at the University of Illinois at Chicago learned how to render convincing performances of the kinds of critical discourses

sanctioned by teacher and institution. In conducting a series of follow-up interviews with these students, however, Seitz found that the students remained unpersuaded of the truth (or usefulness) of these discourses, and that the architecture of their local knowledge had managed to remain more or less intact (65–73).

8. That teachers operate as signs in the assemblage of texts that is the discursive world of the writing classroom is no great revelation, but it is nonetheless a crucial point in considering what kind of persuasive authority we have with students. No matter what else we may be doing in the classroom at a given moment, we are busily signifying our social allegiances. I am made uncomfortably aware how much I work as signifier beyond (and perhaps in spite of) the more explicit messages I wish to convey each time a student informs me that I don't "*look* like an English teacher." That students perceive my physical self to signify something other than what they've come to expect an English teacher to represent tells me that the signified "English teacher" is associated with a particular and conventional set of signifiers. Clearly, what for middle-class academics functions as valuable currency in their cultural economy — the capital of tastes, manners, language, and style that signals to insiders the power to *reject* the very kinds of material capital to which working-class students aspire — may have no cultural meaning for students "outside," or worse, may be read as signs of failure to achieve socioeconomic success.

9. In William Covino's rhetoric for writing students, *Forms of Wondering*, reader-writers are drawn into a conversation about the means and ends of writing. The book opens with an assignment entitled "What's the Use of Writing?" a dialogue designed to get the writer to create a dialectic between the philosophical and utilitarian functions of writing. While some of the writing tasks in Covino's book may be too generically esoteric to be persuasive to students seeking to learn forms of writing that perform conventional functions in nonacademic marketplaces, *Forms'* ongoing dialogue about the goals and uses of writing is an excellent model for teachers wishing to structure classroom activities around such a discussion.

Works Cited

Anderson, Virginia. "Confrontational Teaching and Rhetorical Practice." *CCC* 48 (1997): 197–214.

Aronowitz, Stanley. "Working-Class Identity and Celluloid Fantasies in the Electronic Age." *Popular Culture: Schooling and Everyday Life.* Eds. Henry Giroux and Roger Simon. New York: Bergin, 1989.

Bell, Michael J. *The World from Brown's Lounge: An Ethnography of Black Middle-Class Play.* Urbana: U of Illinois P, 1983.

Bloom, Lynn Z. "Freshman Composition as a Middle-Class Enterprise." *College English* 58 (1996): 654–75.

Bourdieu, Pierre. *Distinction: A Social Critique of the Judgment of Taste.* Trans. R. Nice. Cambridge: Harvard UP, 1984.

Cooper, Marilyn. "Unhappy Consciousness in First-Year English: How to Figure Things Out for Yourself." *Writing as Social Action.* Marilyn Cooper and Michael Holzman. Portsmouth: Boynton, 1989. 28–60.

Covino, William. *Forms of Wondering.* Portsmouth: Boynton, 1991.

Eckert, Penelope. *Jocks and Burnouts: Social Categories and Identity in the High School.* New York: Teachers College P, 1989.

Farmer, Frank. "Dialogue and Critique: Bakhtin and the Cultural Studies Writing Classroom." *CCC* 49 (1998): 186–207.

Fox, Tom. *The Social Uses of Writing.* Norwood: Ablex, 1990.

Gale, Xin Liu. *Teachers, Discourses, and Authority in the Postmodern Composition Classroom.* New York: State U of New York P, 1996.

Harris, Joseph. "The Idea of Community in the Study of Writing." *CCC* 40 (1989): 11–22.

Le Masters, E. E. *Blue-Collar Aristocrats: Lifestyles at a Working-Class Tavern,* Madison: U of Wisconsin P, 1975.

Lindquist, Julie. "'Bullshit on "What If"!' An Ethnographic Rhetoric of Political Argument in a Working-Class Bar." Diss. University of Illinois at Chicago, 1995.

Mortensen, P., and Gesa Kirsch. "On Authority in the Study of Writing." *CCC* 44 (1993): 556–72.

Ohmann, Richard. "Reflections on Class and Language." *College English* 44 (1982): 1–17.

Rosenweig, Ray. "The Rise of the Saloon." *Rethinking Popular Culture: Contemporary Perspectives in Cultural Studies.* Eds. Mukerji and Schudson. Berkeley: U of California P, 1991: 121–56.

Seitz, David. "Keeping Honest: Working Class Students, Difference, and Rethinking the Critical Agenda in Composition." *Under Construction: Working at the Intersections of Composition Theory, Research, and Practice.* Ed. Christine Farris and Chris Anson. Logan: Utah State P, 1998.

Smith, Jeff. "Students' Goals, Gatekeeping, and Some Questions of Ethics." *College English* 59 (1997): 299–320.

Spradley, James, and Brenda Mann. *The Cocktail Waitress: Women's Work in a Man's World.* New York: Knopf, 1975.

Opening the Composition Classroom to Storytelling: Respecting Native American Students' Use of Rhetorical Strategies

Karen Redfield

Karen A. Redfield's essay, ostensibly about Native American storytelling in the composition class, was originally published in Perspectives on Written Argument *in 1996. Redfield's goal is to ask teachers to expand their definitions of argument and of the linguistic competencies students and others need in order to persuade an audience. Redfield advocates reading student essays, especially those that seem to be missing elements of the traditional academic format, for what they accomplish rather than for what they lack. More specifically, in this essay she relies on a contrastive model (adapted from linguistics) to reread the rhetorical strategies used by two Native Americans who wrote essays that, at first glance, appear to fail.*

The kind of reading Redfield advocates encourages teachers to explore multiple rhetorical traditions and to better understand the importance of context and culture to persuasion. The benefits of such work are multiple, but Redfield stresses two:

1. *When teachers respect student voices and cultures, they allow students the opportunity to create arguments that are meaningful to them and the cultures from which they come.*
2. *When teachers care enough to learn about multiple rhetorical traditions, they will be more persuasive in their attempts to ask students to learn the argumentative strategies that teachers are most comfortable with, strategies that will also assist students' success in the university and in the dominant culture.*

An ultimate value of oral tradition was to create a situation for someone who had not lived through it so that the listener could benefit directly from the narrator's experience. . . . The persistence of stories and storytelling suggests that oral narrative is central to an indigenous intellectual tradition and provides the core of an educational model. (Cruikshank, with Sidney, Smith, & Ned, 1990, p. 340)

The problem of cognitive competence — the ability to recognize and use higher order thinking — may be more in the eye or ear and brain of the interpreter than in the mouth and brain of the speaker of a culturally nonstandard way of speaking. This is a problem of ethnocentric bias in the study of relations between language and thought, a problem of which much educational research on students' reasoning seems to be unaware. (Erickson, 1988, p. 213)

About midway through the spring semester of 1993, a courageous and articulate Native American student confronted me about my demands and her frustrations in our Composition I course. I, too, was frustrated: All my detailed comments on the deficiencies in her essays were having little effect except on surface grammatical errors. The gulf between the student's rhetorical form and the acceptable college essay I was so sincerely trying to teach was widening. After much intense discussion — I am paraphrasing what I remember as faithfully as possible — the student said: "I don't understand what you want. I told the story in my own way and you say this is not how they write in college. I've been writing stories for a long time. This is my way of using language. How can I write for white people who won't understand me anyway?"

I had no answer for her. Indeed, it took me a while to truly understand her question. Having taught English as a second language both here and abroad, I was accustomed to looking for the problems arising from first language transfer errors and culturally based rhetorical differences in my students' essays. What I had clearly not considered in my Native American student's essay, however, was that similar principles were at work. I had been reading her writing from the perspective of a deficit model, seeing only what it lacked when compared to a "standard" form. To draw on Catherine Lamb's use of Kenneth Burke's parlor metaphor (p. 154), I was assuming that once I gave the student the proper academic forms, she would be able to speak — and others would listen and understand. What I found out was that I had not been listening at all.

Why a Chapter on Storytelling Is Not Out of Place in a Book on Argument

As the argument is believed to reflect cognitive and rhetorical competence in Western intellectual tradition, storytelling reflects similar qualities in Native American intellectual tradition (Cruikshank et al., 1990, p. 340). The story form is historically significant, rhetorically complex, sociologically powerful, and educationally effective, teaching everything from community moral standards to mathematical principles (Hankes, personal communication, June 1, 1994). This use of stories is not uncommon; stories are also symbolically important teaching events among Pacific Islanders, as Watson-Gegeo shows.

Although the argument per se does not seem to exist as a separate Native American rhetorical genre, listeners are expected to learn something useful from a story (Cruikshank et al., 1990, p. 340). Bartelt (1982) noted that redundancy of lexical items is often used by Navajo and Apache politicians: "When trying to persuade community members to support a particular policy. This feature of rhetorical redundancy for persuasion is, of course, also a likely part of the discourse resources available to most Navajo and Western Apache speakers" (p. 167).

Although exploring the possible existence of argument as a traditional Native American rhetorical form would be fascinating, my intentions here are slightly different. Through a review of current research and a close reading of two Native American students' essays, I hope to prove at least that a culturally based structure underlies my students' work. Both pieces — which I called essays and they called stories — have a main point that is supported through thoughtful, logically organized detail. As Berrill [1996] suggested [. . .] we do need "a different word for reasoning processes which are 'logical' in non-hierarchical ways." Such new terminology would free Native American student writers from the burden of being labeled *basic* or *deficient* writers. Such labels combine with a lack of clarity about writing competencies to produce sad results for students.

As Farr noted (1993, pp. 6–7): "To render essayist literacy problematic, we must first make explicit the style of discourse that now underlies most expository writing instruction. Currently this is a poorly understood but nevertheless real construct" (Walters, in press). Coming up against this very real construct, students often lose.

Writing about the University of New Mexico, which has the highest Native American population of any four-year institution in the United States, Gregory (1989) stated that the attrition rate is 77 percent — the highest of any group on campus. She theorized that "the inability to produce acceptable academic writing serves as one of the major stumbling blocks for academic success among Native Americans" (p. 1). McLaughlin (1988) painted a similarly dismal picture; based on his research, the dropout rate for Native American students is from three to ten times the national average. Informal interviews I conducted in Madison, WI, tend to support such figures, although it should be stressed that this is not true for all Native American students. For Native American students in general, though, writing college assignments is an especially trying task.

Using Contrastive Analysis in the Classroom

What choices do students make when faced with such a daunting task? A logical assumption is that they use forms that are already familiar. Such culturally influenced rhetorical forms may not be conscious, so it is difficult for the students to explain their explicit, surface features. As I suggest at the end of this chapter, the work of contrastive analysis can and should become a partnership between the teacher and students from different cultures — extending to other students in the classroom.

I began my search for culturally distinctive Native American rhetorical forms in my students' writing — as I had begun research into ESL students' writing previously (Redfield, 1987) — with the hypothesis of Kaplan (1966, p. 2). "Logic (in the popular, rather than the logician's sense of the word) which is the basis for rhetoric, is evolved out of a culture; it is not universal. Rhetoric, then, is not universal either, but varies from culture to culture."

To support his hypothesis, Kaplan used the essays of his English as a second language college students from various cultural and linguistic backgrounds. These students had done well in mastering the syntactic and lexical forms of English, but their writing still suffered from a lack of focus. The main and supporting points were arranged differently than "the expected sequence of thought in English . . . essentially a Platonic-Aristotelian sequence" (p. 3). Although Kaplan stressed the need for more research and more accurate descriptions, he offered the following diagrams of the paragraph movement in various language groups (see Figure 1).

In general, English essays are arranged in a linear pattern; Semitic language essays are constructed along parallel lines of themes or images; Oriental language essays begin in a more global sphere and wind down into the particular; and Romance and Russian language essays tend to contain what an English reader would deem digressions to the main point.

Assuming that an underlying logical pattern exists, I approached my students' writing with the intention of making this pattern more visible to non–Native American readers like myself. By contrasting actual student writing with an expected Western cultural model, I was employing the "weak" version of contrastive analysis, a theory that seeks to explain similarities and differences between language systems (Wardhaugh, 1983). Because Native American culture is not monolithic, it would be inappropriate to apply the strong version of contrastive analysis that would attempt to predict patterns in a given student's writing based on the discovered patterns in another student's work.

Figure 1.   Contrasting rhetorical patterns
From "Cultural Thought Patterns in Inter-Cultural Education," by R. B. Kaplan, Language Learning, 1966, Vol. 16, Nos. 1 and 2, p. 15. Reprinted by permission.

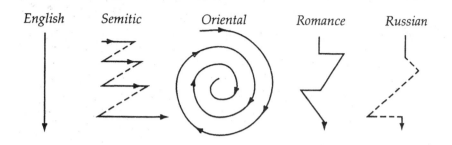

However, the knowledge that certain patterns might exist gives me a framework from which to work. Using this hypothesis of weak contrastive analysis, I must always begin with evidence "provided by linguistic interference," as Wardhaugh noted (1970, p. 10). Such evidence can then be used:

> To explain the similarities and differences between the systems . . . systems are important because . . . the approach does [not] result in merely classifying errors in any way that occurs to the investigator. . . . The starting point in the contrast is provided by actual evidence . . . and the reference is made to the two systems only in order to explain actually observed interference phenomena. (1983, p. 10)

The implications of such hypotheses on Native American writing have recently been explored by several researchers such as Bartelt (1982), Basso (1979), Bataille and Mullen Sands (1984), and Ghezzi (1993). Before looking at broader implications, however, I turn to Sarah and Cheryl's stories.

Sarah's Story

Sarah entered a general equivalency diploma (GED) course of study through Madison Area Technical College's Homeless Basic Skills Program in 1989. The essay that follows was written in response to my directions to "write something of interest, perhaps a story about your life." Our goal was to work toward the GED essay requirement eventually; Sarah moved on before we came to that stage.

Sarah's story follows:

> This is a story about my Mom and Dad and my Grandma who lived on the Chippewa Reservation.

> The Chippewa Reservation was up in Red Lake Minnesota.

I was very little at the time when I was there.

My Dad used to get up real early and go out hunting for deer or whatever he could get for my Mom and Grandma to fix for dinner.

He would leave way before anyone in the house awoke.

When my Mom awoke she would fix a hot breakfast made from corn meal and fried bread.

She would boil the corn meal and pour it in a cup and we would drink it from the cup.

After breakfast and dishes were done we would go outside and enjoy the warm sunshine.

Now my Grandma she would sit and work on her Indian beads or whatever she was working on.

I would sit and watch her.

She would always tell me stories about herself when she was a little girl while she was sitting and working.

In the winter she made Indian blankets to keep us warm and they were made from deer or bear fur.

They would keep us warm in the winter.

My Dad he would go out and bring plenty bear meat, deer meat, fish and hang them on a tree where the wolves couldn't get ahold of them.

Then he would take the meat and put the meat in a hot little house and keep it warm and dry for the winter.

My Dad was a hard working man.

My Grandma kept busy making warm clothes for us.

My Mom she did what she could to take care of all of us.

When school started we went to school and learned to do Indian dances and talk in our own language.

The school was very different then the schools we have now.

The school was 5 miles out of the reservation.

Mom got up and got us dressed warm and had us off every morning at 6:00 AM unless it was really snowing hard and it was really cold then she had our deer coats and the boots my Grandma made to keep my feet warm.

Early day like that we started off at 5:00 in the morning and be to school at 8:00.

Late in the afternoon my Dad met me at the end of the road leaving from the school to walk home.

It would be just getting dark when we reached home.

But supper was waiting all nice and warm.

But after a long while we had to move.

Now where our home used to be is all flat land and farmers have their crops there.

How I miss my people.

The Chippewas remain together and are all settled here in Wisconsin.

There are over 400 Chippewas here in Wisconsin.

We may be apart but we are all family brothers and sisters in spirit.

We never forget our old ways we used to live.

The new ways are very different for us but we will get used to them.

We were used to living on the reservation just all Indians but to some of us it is very strange and different to live in a mixed world.

The clothes are different and shoes and boots are different but we are used to them.

Even the schools are different we are also used to them.

I like living this way but I miss the old way I used to live among my Indian brothers and sisters.

One day I hope we will all get together again and live like we used to.

I was moved by Sarah's story on a first reading; however, I was also concerned about the long road it seemed we would have to travel from this story to an acceptable GED essay. Viewed in this way, the essay lacked several "standard" features such as paragraph structure, a thesis statement, supporting points, and a conclusion. It was not even clear "whose" story this was — Sarah's or her family's. What I was missing — along with the rhetorical strategies inherent in supporting Sarah's main point — was that her sense of self within a community was the main point.

In writing of the Dune-za/Cree people of British Columbia, Canada, Ridington (1990) foregrounded the connection between storytelling and a person's place in the community:

> You are a character in every other person's story. You know the stories of every person's life. You retain an image or model of the entire system of which you are a part. Each person is responsible for acting autonomously and with intelligence in relation to that knowledge of the whole. Each person knows how to place his or her experience within the model's meaningful pattern. Each person knows the stories that connect a single life to every other life. People experience the stories of their lives as small wholes, not as small parts of the whole. (p. 192)

Both the student essays included in this chapter clearly demonstrate this. Although one writer is Chippewa and one Menominee, and although the topics are as seemingly disconnected as a family history and a women's softball league, the main themes are community: How a "single life" is connected "to every other life," in Ridington's words.

Sarah began by saying that the story was about her parents and grandmother; it was equally about herself. She did not make herself part of the introduction, though; instead she wove her own reflections and memories into the story. The story of Sarah's family was also woven into the larger story of the Chippewa family in Red Lake and the sadness Sarah felt at being separated from those "brothers and sisters." The main point of Sarah's essay, embedded two-thirds of the way into her piece, and shortened for dramatic effect, was, "How I miss my people." Her conclusion echoed the sentiment, and the hope that she would one day be able to live with her people again.

Community as a central focus in a broader world view is also found, as Dorothy Perry Thompson noted [. . .] in African American storytelling. Values such as interdependence, groupness, and communality are reflected in much the same way as they are in Native American stories. In Sarah's story, such "groupness" had been rent by outside forces. The site of her community had been appropriated: "Now where our home used to be is all flat land and farmers have their crops there."

This line signals a shift in theme and tone; it functions as an "argument," if you will, that life on the reservation was much preferable to life off the reservation, in which a sense of real community did not exist.

Reading backward from the second half of Sarah's main point — "How I miss my people" — and then forward, a rhetorical method of support becomes clear: repetition. Sarah used 10 repetitions of the words *warm* or *hot* throughout the first half of her story. No references to warmth were made in the second half of the story.

As noted earlier in this chapter, Bartelt (1982, p. 171) explained that redundancy may be used for persuasion. Deliberate emphasis in a first tribal language appears as redundancy in oral or written English:

$$\begin{bmatrix} \text{Discourse} \\ \text{[+ emphasis]} \end{bmatrix} ----> \begin{bmatrix} \text{Apachean English Discourse} \\ \text{[+ redundancy]} \end{bmatrix}$$

Ghezzi (1993) also examined the traditional uses of rhetorical devices such as repetition, markers such as "now presently" and "and then," and "truncated, staccato-like" lines for emphasis in her article "Tradition and Innovation in Ojibwe Storytelling: Mrs. Marie Syrette's 'The Orphans and Mashos.'" All of these devices appear in Sarah's story, pointing to a living consistency in contemporary Chippewa/Ojibwe storytelling.

Sarah's story is most compelling when read aloud as I did at a recent conference. When I reached Sarah's main point — "How I miss my people" — an audible sigh arose from the audience. The images of a happy childhood inside of a warm family and community circle did not seem to lead to such a statement. Through her impressive use of traditional storytelling forms, Sarah was able to make the audience feel the sadness of one woman and her community. And yet, such clear rhetorical competence would likely receive a low grade for "deficiencies" such as paragraph structure.

Cheryl's Story

It was Cheryl's question — paraphrased at the beginning of this chapter — that guided my research.

The following essay was written in response to an assignment to write a cause-and-effect essay in a university transfer Composition I class at Madison Area Technical College. Though it did not seem to reflect the traditional cause and effect rhetorical form, it did answer the title question and gave, I realized upon subsequent readings, causes for why Cheryl enjoys softball. My comments after a first reading, however, caused Cheryl's frustration with a deficit-model grading scale to become articulate. After my discussions of this piece, I suggest possible grading strategies.

Why I like to play softball? Cheryl Dodge (Menominee):

1 Playing softball every summer for 10 weeks is very invigorating and exciting.

2a Every year, around the middle of February when the snow is knee deep and the temps are still quite cold, the Madison Recreation Dept. sends out to all softball managers, the "blue cards" to be filled out and returned usually by the end of February.

2b It is still difficult during this time of the year to get people thinking of "softball" but in order to have a team you need to turn in the amount of 12 "blue cards".

3 So as one or two people run around getting players out of "hibernation", the excitement grows and one can start visualizing the softball diamonds in their natural state instead of covered with "snow".

4 Playing on a all women's slow pitch softball team is fun as well as competitive, considering our team is in the 7th league and we do quite well every summer.

5 I personally like the "high" I get from playing 3rd base, because playing that particular position one has to be quick and have a strong throwing arm. I like the fact that when the ball is hit, whether it be on the ground or a line drive in the air, it is coming at you full speed.

6 I also enjoy playing this sport because it is an all "women's" team and that is how we play. There is no "classroom" study to go through, no having to be a "Mom", just simply playing softball.

7   The "fans" are another reason I like to play, they are very supportive and fun. It's exciting to stand out there, on that diamond, under
the lights and perform in front of about thirty people.

8   Hitting a "home run", with the bases loaded, has to be one of the
most "happy" "exciting" feelings one can experience while playing a
game.

9   There are many "good" reasons why I like to play this sport but
mainly it is just "simply fun" and relaxing and I get to be a "hero"
every now and then, it also brings together about fifteen "women of
color" the only "minority" women's team registered with the rec.
dept. in the city of Madison.

10 So for one whole "hour", once a week, I get to leave the student/
Mom world and be in the best fantasy I can think of and just what I
love doing and that is "play softball"!

Cheryl began with a question — "Why I like to play softball?" —
that was "answered" throughout her essay with elements and themes
also evident in Sarah's writing: repetition and the theme of community. The implicit tone here was to justify rather than simply state that
Cheryl had "good" reasons to enjoy this sport. By the end of the essay
the reader was in a sense persuaded to see the positive aspects of
Cheryl's participation in the sport, as if the reader might feel that a
"student/Mom" should not have time to play.

Leaving the episodic structure aside for the moment, I focus on
Cheryl's sense of self within a group. The "I" of the title question did
not reenter the story until section 5: "I personally like the 'high' I get
from playing 3rd base." Until this point there was no clear sense of
agency; many sentences were in the passive voice. Cards were sent out
and received, but Cheryl did not clarify if she was one of the team's
managers receiving the blue registration cards. What was very clear,
however, was the importance of the team. "Team" was used repeatedly,
as were "people," "women of color," and "fans" — ten plural nouns or
noun phrases referring to a community punctuated the essay. Being an
actively contributing member of this community — a quick third-base
player with a strong throwing arm — was one half of the main point of
the essay. The personal enjoyment and sense of satisfaction of being on
this team was the second half: Playing on an all-women "minority" softball team was exciting and fun.

The softball team was Cheryl's community here, as Sarah's
Chippewa family was hers. This theme is not uncommon for a broader
context. Ghezzi (1993) reminded us that, although "There are differences in the narrative traditions between tribes [and] . . . differences
between the creative acts of individuals within a tribal group" (p. 47),
community acts as a major theme and as a rhetorically shaping force
in much Native American writing. In a discussion on Louise Erdrich's
novel *Love Medicine* (1993) the following semester, Cheryl said that
she saw similarities in theme and style between her writing and that

of Erdrich. This connection allowed Cheryl to take pride in her own writing — a bonus of doing such contrastive analysis in class. This issue will be discussed further at the end of this chapter.

Also, like Sarah, Cheryl employed the rhetorical strategy of contrast. Cheryl also used cold and warmth. Although she could speak only of summer games, she began with winter and images of "hibernation," a time when people do not often form groups. The softball diamonds themselves seemed unhappy, covered in snow, rather than being in "their natural state."

McLaughlin and Leap (1991) pointed out similar use of contrast as a common Native American rhetorical strategy in their Navajo students' writing. They also commented on the coherence of the episodic format, once it was perceived to support a main point. They began to see "much more coherence in the construction of this text and in its presentation of message. . . . Seemingly random comments . . . turned out to be elements within a tightly connected, closely ordered statement" (p. 9).

This was also the case with Cheryl's essay on softball. She framed her essay as an answer to a reader's or listener's (in this case the teacher's) question, using rhetorical devices of contrast and repetition as strategies. The emphasis on herself as part of a community of softball players is both a common theme in Native American writing — both published and private — and an element in standard essayist literacy, which presents "a rationalization of one's own position and a consideration of alternative positions while arguing one's own" (Farr, 1993, p. 10). Any reader should be convinced of the importance of playing on an all woman-of-color softball team by the end of Cheryl's essay, regardless of whether or not the reader is a woman of color, a regular player, or a watcher of softball.

Once I was able to see the rhetorical strategies underlying Cheryl's work, I was able to explain the expected academic forms of future assignments more clearly. I adopted a more flexible portfolio method of grading, using progress as my measure rather than grades on individual assignments. Cheryl has been successful in writing assignments for subsequent college transfer courses. She has also written new stories in the context of a Native American literature class, suggesting that she now has mastery over two distinct forms of writing.

The Value of Classroom-Based Contrastive Analysis

This brief analysis of two students' essays cannot hope to delineate the complex, varied, or historical storytelling strategies of Native American writers. I sincerely hope, however, that I have been able to persuade you that both Sarah and Cheryl are exhibiting cognitive competence and culturally based rhetorical forms in their writing. Clearly more work is needed on our part. As Farr (1993) stressed:

> To understand and, one would hope, to teach students more effectively, researcher and educators must identify and describe the range of discourse styles they bring to the classroom and to treat this range of styles as contrastive models to essayist literacy. (p. 13)

This perspective should apply to all students, as Dorothy Perry Thompson [. . .] demonstrated with African American students [. . .]. That students speak English as a first language does not mean — and really has never meant — that students naturally write Western academic discourse. Much work that has been done in applied linguistics can be adapted for use with Native American students, such as Sarah and Cheryl, if we broaden our definition of *target language* to include mainstream academic discourse as well as English as a second language. As Houghton and Hoey (1982) pointed out, factors of linguistic and cultural relativity are at work within a framework of contrastive rhetoric (see Figure 2).

Doing this kind of contrastive rhetoric research should provide fascinating relative implications in the field of discourse analysis. More classroom-based contrastive analysis will also yield several benefits for the student writers, the class as a whole, and the field of composition theory. Such research foregrounds students' individual forms of communicative competence and allows students to explain their forms to other students and the teacher. Such explanations fit naturally into the well-established peer review format and its reliance on concrete points in the genuine, insightful, and constructive exchange of com-

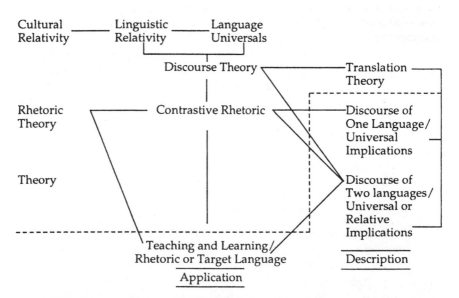

Figure 2. Linguistic and cultural factors in rhetorical forms
From Linguistic and Written Discourse: Contrastive Rhetorics, by Diane B. Houghton and Michael M. Hoey, *Annual Review of Applied Linguistics*, 1982. Reprinted with permission.

ments between students. Contrastive analysis will also force us to clarify all implicit and often personal expectations of "good writing" as we expand our notions of essayist literacy and the boundaries of argument to fit the demands made on education in the late twentieth century. Farr (1993) advocates a debate on what traditional characteristics of essayist literacy should continue to be taught — a debate supported by this volume.

To engage in an honest and truly lively debate, we have to allow our students to debate in their own voices. In *Literacy: Reading the Word and the World* (1987), Freire and Macedo remind us of the importance of the student voice:

> As Giroux elegantly states, the students' voice "is the discursive means to make themselves 'heard' and to define themselves as active authors of their world." The authorship of one's own world, which would also imply one's own language, means what Mikail Bakhtin defines as "retelling a story in one's own words." . . . The students' voice should never be sacrificed, since it is the only means through which they make sense of their own experiences in the world. (p. 151)

Ridington (1990) also reminds us that culture — of which writing is a part — is never fixed or static. Reflecting Bakhtin and Giroux's feelings on the importance of all voices, Ridington wrote:

> Discourse is only a problem when we talk past each other or worse use talk to suppress another person's ability to express him- or herself freely. Discourse is as old as language. It is as fundamental to human experience as culture. It is also as new and as fragile as each new breath of life. We create our culture in the act of speech and the intersubjectivity of discourse. (p. 190)

Finally, this debate is also heralded by Hill (1990), in her book *Writing from the Margins*. Coming out from behind old definitions and old barriers between standard forms and new possibilities puts teachers on "the margin between self and other, old ideas and new" (pp. vii–viii). It is, she feels, an invigorating place to be:

> There one can read things better, see how lines get drawn, tell new stories, create different kinds of spaces, live at the risky critical edges between one's own values and those of others, have a say perhaps in generating changes in people's minds.
>
> Such a job. But such an exciting idea of writing to give our students. (pp. vii–viii)

Conclusion

Assuming an underlying cognitive competence and culturally based rhetorical form whenever I come to a student paper has not only opened me to expanded notions of essayist literacy and the boundaries of argument, it has also made reading compositions a good deal more enjoyable. Being able to first share a genuine sense of the strengths in a piece of student writing with the writer makes it easier and more effective to then discuss other form and style options. Respecting a Native American student's knowledge first also allows the student to be more open to what I need to teach — and together we can start building a bridge between Native American culture and the halls of Western academic discourse.

This bridge, once built, may enable Native American students to more easily cross over to academic success without feeling that their cognitive competences have been totally left on the other side. We, as educators, have an exciting chance to learn new ways of reasoning and to rethink what we now so rigidly define as logic and argument.

In conclusion, I invite you to reread your own Native American student essays from this "bridge." Where you once saw no thesis statement, there may be an embedded but clear main point. Where you once saw unclear pronoun references, there may be a writer who is framing his or her sense of self within a larger sense of community. You may see supporting points where you first saw disjointed ramblings. Overall, you may see culturally influenced rhetorical devices where you once saw only a deficient college essay.

Our views may not be dramatically different, but even small differences in our perspectives will make a difference to the writers. We need to engage our colleagues in discussions on how logic, reasoning, and argument may be reflected in the writing of all of our students. Then we can discuss how our own teaching and writing can reflect what we have learned.

References

Bartelt, H. G. (1982). "Rhetorical redundancy in Apachean English interlanguage." In H. G. Bartelt, S. P. Jasper, & B. L. Hoffer (Eds.), *Essays in Native American English* (pp. 157–172). San Antonio: Trinity University Press.

Basso, K. H. (1979). *Portraits of the Whiteman: Linguistic play and cultural symbols among the Western Apache.* Cambridge, UK: Cambridge University Press.

Bataille, G. M., & Sands, K. M. (1984). *American Indian women: Telling their lives.* Lincoln: University of Nebraska Press.

Cruikshank, J. with Sidney, A., Smith, K., & Ned, A. (1990). *Life lived like a story: Life stories of three Yukon native elders.* Lincoln: University of Nebraska Press.

Dodge, C. (1993). *Louise Erdrich's Love Medicine: A Native American student's reading.* Unpublished paper, Madison Area Technical College.

Erdrich, L. (1993). *Love medicine* (New, expanded ed.). New York: Harper Perennial.

Erickson, F. (1988). School literacy, reasoning, and civility: An anthropologist's perspective. In E. R. Kintgen, B. M. Kroll, & M. Rose (Eds.), *Perspective on literacy* (pp. 205–226). Carbondale: Southern Illinois University Press.

Farr, M. (1993). Essayist literacy and other verbal performances. *Written Communication, 10(1),* 4–38.

Freire, P., & Macedo, D. (1987). *Literacy: Reading the word and the world.* New York: Bergin and Garvey, Critical Studies in Education Series.

Ghezzi, R. W. (1993). Tradition and innovation in Ojibwe storytelling: Mrs. Marie Syrette's "The Orphans and Mashos." In A. Krupat (Ed.), *New voices in Native American literary criticism* (pp. 37–76). Washington and London: Smithsonian Institution Press.

Gregory, G. A. (1989). Composing processes of Native Americans: Six case studies of Navajo speakers. *Journal of American Indian Education, 28*(2), 1–6.

Hankes, J. Personal interview. June 1, 1994.

Hill, C. E. (1990). *Writing from the margins: Power and pedagogy for teachers and composition.* New York: Oxford University Press.

Houghton, D., & Hoey, M. (1982). Linguistics and written discourse: Contrastive rhetorics. *Annual Review of Applied Linguistics, 3,* 23–37.

Kaplan, R. B. (1966). Cultural thought patterns in inter-cultural education. *Language Learning, 16*(1 and 2), 1–20.

McLaughlin, D. (1988, April). Curriculum for cultural politics: Lessons from literacy program development in a Navajo school setting. Paper presented at the Conference of the American Educational Research Association, New Orleans.

McLaughlin, D., & Leap, W. L. (1991, April). What Navajo students know about written English. Paper presented at the Conference of the American Educational Research Association, Chicago.

Redfield, K. A. (1987, April). *The need for a contrastively based theory of rhetoric.* WITESOL Conference (Wisconsin Teachers of English to Speakers of Other Languages), University of Wisconsin-Madison.

Ridington, R. (1990). *Little bit know something: Stories in language of anthropology.* Iowa City: University of Iowa Press.

Thompson, D. P. (1996). Rescuing the failed, filed away, and forgotten: African Americans and eurocentricity in academic argument. In D. P. Berrill (Ed.), *Perspectives on written argument* (pp. 221–240). Cresskill, NJ: Hampton Press.

Walters, K. (1993). Writing and its uses. In H. Gunter & O. Ludwig (Eds.), *Schrift und schriftlicheit* [Writing and its uses].

Wardhaugh, R. (1983). The contrastive analysis hypothesis. In B. W. Robinette, B. Wallace, & J. Schacter (Eds.), *Second language learning: Contrastive analysis, error analysis, and related aspects* (pp. 3–14). Ann Arbor: University of Michigan Press.

Watson-Gegeo, K. A. (1996). Argument as transformation: A pacific framing of conflict, community, and learning. In D. P. Berrill (Ed.), *Perspectives on written argument* (pp. 189–204). Cresskill, NJ: Hampton Press.

Logic in the Black Folk Sermon: The Sermons of C. L. Franklin

Gary Layne Hatch

Gary Layne Hatch's essay brings forth several critical questions for teachers of argument. Originally published in the Journal of Black Studies *in 1996, it asks readers to consider the relationship between argumentation and the art of preaching (*ars praedicandi*), a relationship most famously codified in St. Augustine's* On Christian Doctrine *and addressed by rhetorical theorists such as Pope Gregory the Great, Alain de Lille, and Robert of Basevorn. The sermon has been a particularly important act of rhetoric throughout African American history, serving as a source of spiritual solace and a call to political action.*

Hatch's essay considers the history of logic in the black sermon so that readers can reexamine the relationship between logical and emotional appeals in argument. In particular, he is responding to the work of critics such as William Harrison Pipes, who suggest that sermons in the African American church have traditionally offered appeals of limited logic, relying primarily on emotion to sway their audiences. Hatch argues that the Western rhetorical tradition's narrow definition of logic excludes analogical, metaphorical, and poetic logics, and he calls attention to the logic we have failed to see in significant sites of public argumentation such as the African American church. By arguing for a broader understanding of logical appeals and a more inclusive history of rhetoric, Hatch's essay highlights the links between history, oppression, and argumentative "standards" and recognizes the importance of the oral tradition to all argumentative forms.

In his rhetorical analysis of old-time Black preaching in Macon County, Georgia, William Harrison Pipes (1951) classifies and ranks the persuasive techniques used by various preachers. He concludes that the main persuasive strategy of these preachers is the emotional appeal. Pipes argues that folk preachers "excite the emotions of the audience" to help the audience "escape from an 'impossible world'" (p. 156). Pipes admits that the ethical appeal is also important for the Black folk preacher but argues that the logical appeal only appears in the sermons of "more highly-educated ministers" in "the less emotional points of the sermon" (p. 157). Pipes is not alone in assigning the emotional appeal predominance. Cowley (1966), in his study of Bahamian folk preaching, argues that the main strategy of the Black folk sermon is "to play upon the emotions of the hearers" (p. 16). Davis (1985) points out that the emotional element of Black folk sermons has traditionally presented a problem to some scholars. He notes that both Pipes and Davis see the emotional nature of preaching as evidence of "a lack of sophistication and education" (p. 41). (Pipes sees education as the means of providing Black worshipers with a "normal" means of religious expression [1951, p. 158].)

One problem with Pipes's analysis is that he does not specify what criteria he uses to categorize persuasive strategies. Pipes gives plenty of examples of the emotional and ethical strategies of the sermons, but he does not tell how he isolated these examples. This flaw is particularly significant in his discussion of logic. Because Pipes does not outline what he means by logic, it is impossible to validate Pipes's claim that logical persuasion is largely absent from Black folk preaching. Pipes also talks about the presence of "inductive and deductive reasoning" in the sermons of more highly educated ministers, but he does not define these categories any further or cite any examples.

I will argue that the traditional definition of logic as inductive and deductive reasoning is much too confining for analyzing Black folk sermons. These sermons contain appeals to reason, but these appeals are not presented explicitly as a thesis with support or as claims backed by reasons and evidence. Nor does the preacher reason from individual instances to a general truth. The appeals to reason in Black folk sermons are embedded in the narratives, examples, comparisons, and biblical references chosen by the preacher. These narratives establish a series of relationships that appeal to the intellect and imagination as well as to the emotions. These relationships constitute a type of "poetic" logic in which reasoning is neither inductive nor deductive, but rather analogical, proceeding from one particular instance to another particular instance of the same relationship. I find this type of poetic logic in the sermons of Rev. C. L. Franklin, a preacher that is clearly within the tradition of "old-time religion" outlined by Pipes.

Clarence LaVaughn Franklin was born in Sunflower County, Mississippi, January 22, 1915. His stepfather, Henry Franklin, was a poor sharecropper. At the age of twelve, Franklin joined the St. Peter's Rock Baptist Church; he began preaching at the age of fourteen. For a while, Franklin worked as a full-time circuit preacher in Mississippi, preaching at one of four different churches each Sunday. From his circuit in Mississippi, Franklin moved to the New Salem Baptist Church in Memphis, Tennessee, and then to the Friendship Baptist church in Buffalo, New York. For the greatest part of his career, Franklin pastored the New Bethel Baptist Church in Detroit, Michigan, a church with a congregation numbering in the thousands.

In 1953, Franklin began recording sermons with Chess Recording Company. He recorded a total of 76 albums, many of which sold millions of copies. Franklin also had a successful radio ministry in Nashville. Through his record sales and radio ministry, Franklin's sermons reached millions of listeners. Franklin was a member of the Southern Christian Leadership Conference, and with Dr. Martin Luther King, helped organize the Detroit area Great Freedom March in June 1963. At this march, King first delivered his famous speech, "I Have a Dream."

Despite his family's difficult economic position, Franklin had numerous opportunities for education. After graduating from high school in Cleveland, Mississippi, Franklin finished a course of instruction at the Howe School of Religion, in Memphis. He received a B.A. from

LeMoyne College and studied briefly at the University of Buffalo and at the Extension School of the University of Michigan. He received his divinity degree through the tutorship of Dr. R. B. Gayden. (For a more detailed account of Franklin's life, see Titon, 1987, pp. 86–105.)

Franklin's education had little effect, however, on the folk pulpit style he learned as a young man. Pipes (1951) characterizes this pulpit style in his study of preaching in Macon County, a style that Pipes argues is typical of Black preaching from slave times:

> The style of Macon County preaching is basically simple: short words which are familiar to the audience (with a long word thrown in occasionally for effect). Sentences are often elliptical (without complete subject and predicate). . . . . Slang and Negro dialect (the language of the audience) form the level of expression. But the style is figurative, with the use of metaphor, based on the experiences of the audience or drawn from the Bible, taking the lead. The style is narrative — for the listener rather than the reader. (p. 157)

Franklin's style fits the model of Black preaching described by Pipes. Although Franklin does not use much slang in his sermons, his recorded sermons show that he does use traditional Black speech patterns. Franklin uses words his audience will understand and carefully defines any scholarly or unfamiliar terms he introduces to the audience. In "Ye Must Be Born Again," Franklin discusses the visit of Nicodemus to Christ by night. He is careful to define *Pharisee, Sadducee,* and *Sanhedrin* in terms that his audience will understand, comparing the Sanhedrin, for example, to the Supreme Court and calling Nicodemus a "court justice" (Franklin, 1989, p. 115). Franklin's sentences are often elliptical. Typically, after reading his scriptural text, Franklin will make a brief, elliptical statement that functions as a title or theme for his sermon. In "How Long Halt Ye between Two Opinions?" Franklin reads the text from I Kings 18:21 relating to Elijah and the priests of Baal and then says, "Israel in the throes of indecision. Israel in the throes of indecision" (Franklin, 1989, p. 71). In "Moses at the Red Sea," Franklin reads the text describing the children of Israel at the borders of the Red Sea, and he then says, "Facing a crisis with God. Facing a crisis with God" (p. 107). The largest number of elliptical sentences are found in the second half of each sermon, the half characterized by intoned chanting or "whooping." Consider this passage from "Without a Song":[1]

> O Lord.
> > Everywhere,
> > > everywhere,
> > ah everywhere
> > (I don't believe you know what I mean,)
> > oh everywhere,
> > > I said everywhere I go,
> > every,

```
         yes
   ah everywhere,
       I said everywhere
   ohh!
       yes.
```
                    (Titon, 1987)

Because this passage comes near the end of the sermon, where Franklin and his audience typically join in an enthusiastic emotional outpouring, it is not surprising that traditional syntax is ignored. Franklin's style is figurative. In "The Eagle Stirreth Her Nest," Franklin provides an extended comparison of God and an eagle. He also compares the members of the congregation to eaglets. In "Ye Must be Born Again," Franklin compares the process of being born again to the metamorphosis of a tadpole into a frog. And in "Moses at the Red Sea," Franklin compares the Red Sea to adversity and the rod of Moses to the power of faith within each human being. He also compares Moses to Abraham Lincoln, Frederick Douglass, and George Washington Carver (1989, p. 107).

I will discuss figurative language at greater length later in this essay because the essential difference between my analysis and Pipes's analysis lies in how we each view figurative language. Pipes sees metaphor and comparison as an aspect of style, as a type of ornamentation. I see metaphor as an example of poetic logic, a type of concrete reasoning.

Franklin's sermons also fit the structure of the old-time sermons described by Pipes. According to Pipes, the sermon has four parts: the introduction, statement, discussion, and conclusion. The introduction often involves the reading of a scripture passage. The statement usually comes from the Bible. Pipes (1951) argues that the discussion "merely has the appearance of organization, for it is often a series of digressions aimed to arouse the emotions of the audience" (p. 157). He notes that "the more highly-educated minister" typically uses a more logical organization. The conclusion, according to Pipes, is often absent when the emotional climax of the sermon is so intense as "to make articulate speech impossible" (p. 157).

Franklin typically begins by reading a passage from the scripture. He then makes a statement of his theme, usually in the form of a phrase taken from the passage or a phrase that refers to the passage. His discussion is divided into two parts: a spoken part and a part that involves intonation or whooping. He does not have a logical organization of the type imagined by Pipes, that is to say that he does not set forth a thesis and defend that thesis with reasons and evidence. Nor does he divide his sermon into logical parts. His sermons contain what Pipes might consider numerous digressions: narratives, comparisons, and examples that all relate in some way to the theme or subject set forth in the statement. In other words, Franklin's sermons are usually organized around a central image. Titon (1987) provides an example of how

Franklin envisioned his own organization in the sermon "Without a Song":

Singers
Introduction
Singing a distinguishing characteristic of man
The effects that enslavement has upon oppressed peoples
Israel should have sung
The Negro sung in the night

The text of this sermon as it was performed shows that Franklin follows this organization of ideas. He begins by presenting his biblical text:

By the rivers of Babylon, there we set down, yea, we wept when we remembered Zion. We hanged our harps upon the willows in the midst thereof, for they that carried us away captive required of us a song; and they that wasted us required of us mirth, saying, Sing us one of the songs of Zion. How shall we sing the Lord's song in a strange land? (Psalms 137:1–4; quoted in Franklin, 1989, p. 89)

The statement follows this text: "The subject that we're using tonight is, Without a song. Without a song" (1989, p. 89).

The discussion consists of a series of anecdotes and general observations. Franklin follows his outline, but he also includes a number of anecdotes and illustrations that are not part of his outline. He tells of the inhabitants of the West Indies who campaign for office through singing. He relates the story of Roland Hayes singing in front of the Nazis in Berlin. He tells the story of Mary, an old woman who is rejected by an English Methodist minister, and tells how the congregation comforts her by singing. "Without a Song" is organized in a topical and anecdotal fashion. Each "digression" or example relates back to the statement, "Without a song." I hope to show later that each example also has a logical progression that continues through both parts of the sermon to the emotional climax.

Pipes would most likely say that "Without a Song" lacks a conclusion because the sermon ends in an emotional climax.

Franklin does occasionally end in a spoken conclusion (in "How Long Halt Ye Between Two Opinions?" "Hannah, the Ideal Mother," "The Preacher Who Got Drunk," "A Bigot Meets Jesus," and "Meeting Jesus in the Dawn"). There is still a sense of closure, however, in the sermons that lack a spoken conclusion at the end of the intoned section. Pipes misses the fact that the emotional climax itself is a type of conclusion. In fact, the "calm to storm" format is one of the most common organizational patterns in Black folk preaching.

Because Franklin's sermons are so typical of what Pipes calls the old-time style of Black preaching, these sermons provide an opportunity for testing Pipes's claim that the logical appeal is largely absent from this style of preaching.

Consider "Without a Song" (Franklin, 1989). The scriptural passage describes the children of Israel captive in Babylon, far from their homeland. Their captors ask them to sing one of the songs of Zion. The psalmist asks, "How shall we sing the Lord's song in a strange land?" Franklin contextualizes the passage for his audience, describing how the children of Israel must have felt in this situation. Franklin takes the position that the children of Israel should have sung the songs of Zion in their captivity. He then moves to what might appear to be a series of digressions. First of all, Franklin discusses how it is natural for humans to want to sing and how humans can convey many messages through song. He gives the particular instance of the West Indians who campaign for office by singing. This example is not merely an illustration, however. Franklin mentions that the West Indians are under British rule. They are a people subject to a foreign government. They cannot get up on stage and speak, so they communicate their political views through music. Franklin's next story relates the visit of Black singer Roland Hayes to Berlin. Because Hayes is a Black man, the German audience refuses to be silent so that Hayes can sing. Hayes begins to sing above the noise of the audience, and his voice is so enthralling that the audience grows quiet and listens to him sing, "Lord, thou art my peace, thou art my peace." After his performance, many of the audience members rush to the stage and join in his song. Hayes is a Black man in a foreign land with an oppressive government. He wins their favor by singing one of the songs of Zion. Franklin then tells how the slaves sang for their White oppressors in the South. These illustrations are not mere digressions designed to hold the interest of the audience. Each story parallels the scriptural passage and establishes a set of correspondences that advance Franklin's argument:

Bible Text	Illustration	Illustration
Israel	Roland Hayes	African slaves
Babylon	Nazi Germany	slave owners
captivity	prejudice	slavery
did not sing	sang	sang

This matrix shows the relationships among Franklin's illustrations. Each column lists the essential components of each individual illustration. Each row shows the correspondences among the illustrations. Israel, Roland Hayes, and the African slaves represent those who are oppressed. Babylon, Nazi Germany, and the slave owners are the oppressors. Captivity, prejudice, and slavery are the types of oppression each group suffers. The final row indicates how each group responds to oppression.

Franklin's illustrations show how oppressed people should handle their oppression. The children of Israel are a negative example. Roland Hayes and the African slaves provide positive examples.

Franklin continues this argumentative strategy through the remainder of the sermon. His next story is about an old woman who goes to hear Charles Wesley preach. She is moved by his preaching and responds to his invitation for baptism. He rejects her because she is Black and tells her to go join a church for Black people. The other Black people, who are forced to remain outside during the sermon, respond by singing:

> Oh Mary, don't weep, don't mourn;
> Pharaoh's army got drowned;
> Mary, don't weep, and then don't mourn.

In this case, Mary and the Black members of the congregation are oppressed by the White Christian church. The oppression takes the form of religious segregation. This story shows that the proper response to this segregation is singing a song of Zion. Mary and the Black Christians correspond to the children of Israel captive in Babylon. The White Christian church corresponds to Babylon. The verse from the spiritual also establishes a correspondence between Mary and the Children of Israel captive in Egypt and between the White church and Pharaoh's army.

Franklin continues the spoken part of the sermon with an extended discussion of the Black people in slavery. The slaves were prevented from wearing nice clothes, but they gained hope by singing, "I'm going to put on a long, white robe, one of these days." They could not ride in chariots, but they could sing "Swing low, sweet chariot, coming for to carry me home." They were not allowed to meet together for worship, so they had to meet secretly at night. They sang, "Steal away, steal away to Jesus. We ain't got long to stay here." With each example, Franklin shows how the slaves would sing one of the songs of Zion to give them hope in their oppressed condition. At the conclusion of the spoken part of the sermon, Franklin returns to the scriptural text, arguing that Israel should have sung the songs of Zion in Babylon because these songs would have helped Babylon to understand God's relationship with his people. Franklin then applies the text to his congregation, arguing that they should take the songs of Zion wherever they go and that they should not exclude themselves from others. In the intoned section of the sermon, Franklin repeats this theme and sings snatches from religious songs such as "Amazing Grace" and "On Jordan's Stormy Banks I Stand."

In "Without a Song," Franklin (1989) certainly appeals to the emotions of his audience. The story of Roland Hayes is designed to evoke feelings of pride and admiration just as the story of Mary calls forth feelings of pity. But the main function of these illustrations is to advance Franklin's logical argument that the members of his congregation should meet oppression and prejudice with songs that engender hope and understanding. This logical progression is not really deductive or inductive. It does not move vertically along the ladder of abstraction from general truths to specific instances or from specific instances to general truths. The logical progression in "Without a Song" is horizontal, from one specific instance to another. It is analogical. Each illustration provides a parallel instance of the same general truth that reverberates throughout the sermon.

This type of reasoning is present in other sermons by Franklin. Consider "Dry Bones in the Valley" (Franklin, 1989). Franklin begins with his text:

> The hand of the Lord was upon me, and carried me out in the Spirit of the Lord, and set me down in the midst of the valley which was full of bones, and caused me to pass by them round about: and, behold, there were very many in the open valley; and, lo, they were very dry. And he said unto me, Son of man, can these bones live? And I answered, O Lord God, thou knoweth. And again he said unto me, Prophesy from these bones, and say unto them, O ye dry bones, hear the word of the Lord. (Ezekiel 37:1–4, quoted in Franklin, 1989, p. 80)

The controlling images in this sermon are Ezekiel as "son of man" and the valley of the bones. Franklin compares the valley to Babylon:

> So to Israel, we see in this vision, Babylon was a desolate place. Babylon represented a valley to Israel, a valley of depravity, a valley of disfranchisement, a valley of hopelessness, a valley of dry bones, a valley of lifelessness. (p. 81)

Franklin then compares the United States during the time of slavery to a valley:

> But to the Negro, when he embarked upon these shores, America to him was a valley: a valley of slave huts, a valley of slavery and oppression, a valley of sorrow. (p. 81)

The sermon also ties Babylon and Israel to African American slavery through the spiritual "Ezekiel Saw the Wheel."

The valley of bones in Babylon is surrounded by a ring of "obstructing mountains": "Economic mountains, social and political mountains, religious mountains enclosed her in. And she was down here in the stagnant air of a valley in Babylon" (Franklin, 1989, p. 82). Franklin also compares this valley of the dry bones to life's problems:

> We know what the human problems are, we know men are mean, we know men are prejudiced, we know that men are narrow-minded, and we know they are selfish. We know men are unkind, ruthless, and cruel. We know men are murderers and sinful. But what we don't know is what to do about it! (p. 82)

As in "Without a Song," Franklin establishes a set of correspondences: Babylon, valley of dry bones, United States during slavery, life's problems.

The answer to each of these problems lies in the word of God preached by Ezekiel. Franklin says a number of things about Ezekiel. First of all, Franklin emphasizes Ezekiel's training:

> When we study his minute descriptions of the temple order and of the temple liturgy, when we read of his intimate knowledge of things directly or indirectly concerned with Judaism, we must conclude that he had formal training as a priest. (p. 80)

Franklin also stresses the importance of Ezekiel's role as a prophet or a preacher:

> You know, and the word *prophet* can be interchanged with the word *preacher,* for a prophet is a preacher, and a preacher ought to be a prophet. (p. 81)

The prophet is also one who receives visions. He has "sight, insight, and foresight" (p. 81). Franklin tells of Ezekiel's vision of the three wheels. According to Franklin, one wheel represents Israel. The wheel enclosing Israel's wheel represents Babylon, and the wheel enclosing both the other two wheels represents God's plan. Franklin's mentioning of this vision stresses Ezekiel's role as prophet and his knowledge of God's providence. But Franklin also stresses Ezekiel's role as "son of man," as a man limited in his vision and ability because he cannot answer the question, "Can these bones live?" Franklin equates Ezekiel's limitations as a "son of man" with human limitations in general:

> Son of man, you are a scholar, you are an educator. Son of man, you are a scientist: Can these bones live? Son of man, you are an engineer: Can these bones live? Son of man, you are a heart specialist; son of man, you are a geologist, you are a botanist, you are a specialist in various phases of the human body, you are a psychologist and psychiatrist, you know all about drives and reactions and responses and tendencies. I want to know with all of this knowledge can you tell me: Can these bones live? (p. 82)

Even though Ezekiel is a prophet/preacher and has received formal education, and even though he has had visions of the providence of God, he cannot comprehend how the valley of bones can live again. Franklin points out that the Lord even takes Ezekiel around the valley so that Ezekiel has a full understanding of Israel's problems, but Ezekiel, with his human limitations, still cannot come up with a solution. The answer lies in preaching the word of the Lord to the bones.

The captivity of Israel in Babylon, slavery in the United States, and the obstacles faced by Franklin's congregation in the mid-1950s are all instances of the same problem — they each represent impossible situations that can be overcome only through the word of God:

My Lord.
   Tell those bones,
   "Hear my words."
   And that's my solution tonight,
   that's my answer tonight
   to every problem that we have:
   that is to hear God's words.
   Hear God's words.
   It's all right
      to go to the United Nations,
   it's all right
      to preach on international fellowship,
   it's all right
      to call on the scholars,
      to call on our businessmen,
      it's all right,
   but I tell you what you had better do:
   hear God's words,
   hear God's words.   (Franklin, 1989, p. 87)

This passage shows the conflation of Israel's problems in Babylon with the problems faced by Franklin's congregation. It's all right to attempt to solve political problems through political means. In other words, it's all right for Ezekiel in his role as "son of man" to survey the valley of the dry bones to try to find a solution to the problem. But the only way out of an impossible situation is to hear the word of God.

"Dry Bones in the Valley" shows another instance of Franklin's use of analogical reasoning. He does not use Ezekiel's story merely as an example of his thesis; he presents the valley of the bones, slavery, and the problems of his congregation as parallel instances of the same problem. Again, the logical progression moves horizontally from one specific instance to the next.

The final sermon I will discuss is considered by many to be Franklin's greatest: "The Eagle Stirreth Her Nest" (Franklin, 1989). The controlling image in this sermon is the eagle. Franklin presumably begins by reading Deuteronomy 32:11–12 (the text is not included on the recording):

As an eagle stirreth up her nest, fluttereth over her young, spreadeth abroad her wings, taketh them, beareth them on her wings: so the Lord alone did lead him, and there was no strange god with him.

Franklin states that the eagle symbolizes God and God's care and concern for his people. Franklin equates the nest with history and the eaglets with God's children. The stirring of the nest refers to God's changing people's circumstances to make them better:

Some of the things that have gone on in your own experiences have merely been God stirring the nest of your circumstances. Now the Civil War, for example, and the struggle in connection with it, was merely the promptings of Providence to lash man to a point of being brotherly to all men. In fact, all of the wars that we have gone through, we have come out with new outlooks and new views and better people. (p. 47)

Early in the sermon, Franklin establishes a series of correspondences:

Eagle	God
Eaglets	God's children, human race
Nest	History, human circumstances
Stirring the nest	Adversity, changing human circumstances

The bulk of the spoken section of the sermon describes the attributes of the eagle that make it a fit symbol for God. Franklin points out that the eagle is regal, that the eagle is "king of the birds." This makes the eagle a fitting symbol for God because God is the king of kings. The second attribute of the eagle is strength. Franklin states that God is also strong. He compares God to a fortress or citadel that protects against the enemy. He also compares God to a leaning post that numerous people can lean on. The eagle's third attribute is swiftness. Franklin describes God's swiftness in freeing Daniel from the lion's den and in helping Peter to get out of prison. The eagle also has tremendous vision. The eagle can see a storm coming that is still far away. God has the same type of extraordinary sight:

He can see every ditch that you have dug for me and guide me around them. God has extraordinary sight. He can look behind that smile on your face and see that frown in your heart. (p. 48)

In this section, Franklin is not merely enumerating God's attributes; he is also extending the system of correspondences he has already established:

Eagle	God	God	God	Citadel
Eaglets	God's children	Peter	Daniel	God's people
Stirring	Adversity	Jail	Lions	Enemy

Again, each column represents the narrative progression of a story or set of examples. Each row shows the correspondences between elements of each of these narratives. Through these correspondences, Franklin demonstrates that God has control over the circumstances of his people. He is able to deliver his people from their adverse circumstances whenever he sees fit.

Franklin then addresses the issue of why God sometimes chooses not to deliver his people from adversity. He returns to the image of the eagle. He tells his audience that the eagle has an unusual way of building a nest. The eagle lines the nest with soft materials. After the eaglets are born, the eagle gradually removes the soft lining from the nest. The nest grows uncomfortable, so the eaglets want to leave the nest and learn to fly. Franklin compares this "stirring" of the nest to the adverse conditions humans frequently face:

> I believe that God has to do that for us sometimes. Things are going so well and we are so satisfied that we just lounge around and forget to pray. . . . God has to pull out a little of the plush around us, a little of the comfort around us, and let a few thorns of trial and tribulation stick through the nest to make us pray sometime. (p. 49)

Franklin then tells the story of the eagle that grew up in a chicken coop thinking it was a chicken. A man who knows about eagles comes to the farm, sees the eagle, and instructs the farmer to build a cage for the eagle. As the eagle grows larger, the farmer is to build bigger and bigger cages until the eagle becomes fully grown. At this point the cages would grow so uncomfortable that the eagle would want to fly with the other eagles and would leave the chicken coop. This story ends the spoken section of the sermon and continues into the intoned section. At first, this story may appear to be a digression, an afterthought on Franklin's part. But the story fits perfectly into the matrix of correspondences that Franklin has already established:

Eagle	Man who knows eagles	God
Eaglets	Eagle	God's people
Nest	Chicken coop	Comfort
Stirring	Cage	Adversity

Toward the end of the intoned section, Franklin adds one more set of correspondences based on the following passage:

> My soul
>   is an eagle
> in the cage that the Lord
>   has made for me. . . .
> my soul
>   is caged in,
>   in this old body,
>   yes it is,
> and one of these days
> the man who made the cage
> will open the door
> and let my soul
>   go.   (Franklin, 1989, p. 53)

In this passage, God is the man who knows eagles and the man who made the cage. The eagle is Franklin's soul. The body is the cage. In accordance with the story, at some point, Franklin's soul will be set free from the body and will return to God.

"The Eagle Stirreth Her Nest" is more complex than the other two sermons I have discussed. In this sermon, Franklin's argument really has two parts. He has one matrix of correspondences to show that God has power to deliver his people from adversity. He has another matrix to show that God frequently does not deliver his people from adversity, so that they can experience growth. These two arguments are linked through the image of the eagle, the central image in the sermon. Part of the complexity of this sermon comes from the fact that Franklin uses the same image to describe both God and humans. The difference is one of degree: God is the grown eagle, and humans are eaglets. The double reference of this image implies that by relying on God and enduring adversity, humans can acquire some of the attributes of God and become like him.

Pipes's attempt to construct a hierarchy of persuasive strategies in Black folk preaching presents a number of difficulties. First of all, one must question the reasonableness of attempting to construct such a hierarchy in the first place. Pipes obviously favors the preaching style of educated ministers and the use of inductive and deductive reasoning. He uses his hierarchy to disparage old-time Black preaching. He sees this old-time style of preaching as the efforts of a frustrated and oppressed people to express itself. (The subtitle to Pipes's book is *A Study in American Frustration.*) His solution is to educate Blacks, to provide them with able leadership, and to extend to them all the opportunities of a democratic society (1951, pp. 158–161). Pipes predicts that once Blacks are removed from their frustrated condition, old-time Black preaching will disappear (1951, p. 158). One must admire Pipes's desire to improve social conditions in the Black community, but at the same time, one must reject his condescending attitude toward traditional Black folk preaching.

There is another problem with Pipes's hierarchy. He argues that Black folk preachers rely predominately on the emotional appeal because, in his analysis of the sermons, he has counted more instances of the emotional appeal than of the other appeals. He gives no consideration, however, to the degree of persuasive power that each instance carries. There could, for example, be only one instance of logical reasoning in a sermon, but that one instance could carry enormous persuasive power. It is difficult to see how one could measure the relative strength of a given strategy. This problem of intensity again calls into question the reasonableness of undertaking the task of ranking persuasive strategies in the first place.

The final problem I see with Pipes's study is that he does not specify the criteria he uses for his classification. Pipes's notion of logic is much too restrictive. The appeal to reason probably plays a much more significant role in Black folk sermons than Pipes imagines, but this appeal may often take the form of analogical rather than deductive or inductive reasoning. C. L. Franklin, a preacher in the old-time preaching tradition, uses systems of analogical reasoning that are often quite complex, systems that integrate logic, imagination, and emotion. I am not suggesting that the type of logical matrices Franklin establishes can be found in all Black folk sermons. There is the possibility that this type of reasoning is unique to Franklin. Some consider Franklin the master of the genre. He had more opportunities for education than some of his fellow preachers and admits that he consciously tried to make a logical appeal in his sermons (Titon, 1987, pp. 94–95). It would be useful, therefore, to test the sermons of other Black folk preachers for the presence of analogical reasoning — especially in those sermons studied by Pipes.

Note

1. In his edition of selected sermons by Franklin, Jeff Todd Titon divides the sermon into two parts: a spoken part (represented in prose) and a chanted part (represented in poetry). Titon makes a line break whenever Franklin pauses for breath. The lines are indented to show musical pitch levels in Franklin's chant.

References

Crowley, D. J. (1966). *I could talk old-story good: Creativity in Bahamian folklore.* Berkeley: University of California Press.

Davis, G. L. (1985). *I got the word in me and I can sing it, you know.* Philadelphia: University of Pennsylvania Press.

Franklin, C. L. (1989). *Give me this mountain* (J. T. Titon, Ed.). Urbana: University of Illinois Press.

Pipes, W. H. (1951). *Say amen, brother! Old-time Negro preaching: A study in American frustration.* New York: William-Frederick.

Titon, J. T. (1987). Reverend C. L. Franklin: Black American preacher-poet. *Folklife Annual,* pp. 86–105.

The Classroom and the Wider Culture: Identity as a Key to Learning English Composition

Fan Shen

Shen's essay, originally published in 1989 in College Composition and Communication, *illustrates some of the differences between writing in Chinese and English. Shen's experiences, which concern the writing process in general, raise particularly important questions about the cultural norms that influence argumentation in the West. While Westerners tend to think of argumentative writing as one of the most objective modes of communication available, Shen suggests strong links between our notions of a thesis statement and topic sentence, for example, and the dominant ideologies informing our sense of self and community. Shen's essay raises critical questions about the way argument is tied to cultural logics and asks argument teachers to work with students to reconsider these logics. Such deconstruction will offer students from all backgrounds a better understanding of the argumentative process, a greater number of strategies for argument, and the understanding that argumentative*

language is always tied to issues of identity and context. This knowledge
will help students understand how their cultural backgrounds contribute
to all their writing — even academic argument — and give them a greater
respect for how complicated and important audience analysis is to
persuasion.

One day in June 1975, when I walked into the aircraft factory where
I was working as an electrician, I saw many large-letter posters
on the walls and many people parading around the workshops shouting slogans like "Down with the word 'I'!" and "Trust in masses and the
Party!" I then remembered that a new political campaign called "Against
Individualism" was scheduled to begin that day. Ten years later, I got
back my first English composition paper at the University of Nebraska-
Lincoln. The professor's first comments were: "Why did you always use
'we' instead of 'I'?" and "Your paper would be stronger if you eliminated
some sentences in the passive voice." The clashes between my Chinese
background and the requirements of English composition had begun.
At the center of this mental struggle, which has lasted several years
and is still not completely over, is the prolonged, uphill battle to recapture "myself."

In this paper I will try to describe and explore this experience of
reconciling my Chinese identity with an English identity dictated by
the rules of English composition. I want to show how my cultural background shaped — and shapes — my approaches to my writing in English and how writing in English redefined — and redefines — my *ideo-*
logical and *logical* identities. By "ideological identity" I mean the system
of values that I acquired (consciously and unconsciously) from my social and cultural background. And by "logical identity" I mean the natural (or Oriental) way I organize and express my thoughts in writing.
Both had to be modified or redefined in learning English composition.
Becoming aware of the process of redefinition of these different identities is a mode of learning that has helped me in my efforts to write in
English, and, I hope, will be of help to teachers of English composition
in this country. In presenting my case for this view, I will use examples
from both my composition courses and literature courses, for I believe
that writing papers for both kinds of courses contributed to the development of my "English identity." Although what I will describe is based
on personal experience, many Chinese students whom I talked to said
that they had had the same or similar experiences in their initial stages
of learning to write in English.

Identity of the Self: Ideological and Cultural

Starting with the first English paper I wrote, I found that learning to
compose in English is not an isolated classroom activity, but a social
and cultural experience. The rules of English composition encapsulate
values that are absent in, or sometimes contradictory to, the values of

other societies (in my case, China). Therefore, learning the rules of English composition is, to a certain extent, learning the values of Anglo-American society. In writing classes in the United States I found that I had to reprogram my mind, to redefine some of the basic concepts and values that I had about myself, about society, and about the universe, values that had been imprinted and reinforced in my mind by my cultural background, and that had been part of me all my life.

Rule number one in English composition is "Be yourself." (More than one composition instructor has told me, "Just write what *you* think.") The values behind this rule, it seems to me, are based on the principle of protecting and promoting individuality (and private property) in this country. The instruction was probably crystal clear to students raised on these values, but, as a guideline of composition, it was not very clear or useful to me when I first heard it. First of all, the image or meaning that I attached to the word "I" or "myself" was, as I found out, different from that of my English teacher. In China, "I" is always subordinated to "We" — be it the working class, the Party, the country, or some other collective body. Both political pressure and literary tradition require that "I" be somewhat hidden or buried in writings and speeches; presenting the "self" too obviously would give people the impression of being disrespectful of the Communist Party in political writings and boastful in scholarly writings. The word "I" has often been identified with another "bad" word, "individualism," which has become a synonym for selfishness in China. For a long time the words "self" and "individualism" have had negative connotations in my mind, and the negative force of the words naturally extended to the field of literary studies. As a result, even if I had brilliant ideas, the "I" in my papers always had to show some modesty by not competing with or trying to stand above the names of ancient and modern authoritative figures. Appealing to Mao or other Marxist authorities became the required way (as well as the most "forceful" or "persuasive" way) to prove one's point in written discourse. I remember that in China I had even committed what I can call "reversed plagiarism" — here, I suppose it would be called "forgery" — when I was in middle school: willfully attributing some of my thoughts to "experts" when I needed some arguments but could not find a suitable quotation from a literary or political "giant."

Now, in America, I had to learn to accept the words "I" and "Self" as something glorious (as Whitman did), or at least something not to be ashamed of or embarrassed about. It was the first and probably biggest step I took into English composition and critical writing. Acting upon my professor's suggestion, I intentionally tried to show my "individuality" and to "glorify" "I" in my papers by using as many "I's" as possible — "I think," "I believe," "I see" — and deliberately cut out quotations from authorities. It was rather painful to hand in such "pompous" (I mean immodest) papers to my instructors. But to an extent it worked. After a while I became more comfortable with only "the shadow of myself." I felt more at ease to put down *my* thoughts without looking over my shoulder to worry about the attitudes of my teachers or the

218 Chapter 2 • Argument in the Twentieth Century

reactions of the Party secretaries, and to speak out as "bluntly" and "immodestly" as my American instructors demanded.

But writing many "I's" was only the beginning of the process of redefining myself. Speaking of redefining myself is, in an important sense, speaking of redefining the word "I." By such a redefinition I mean not only the change in how I envisioned myself, but also the change in how *I* perceived the world. The old "I" used to embody only one set of values, but now it had to embody multiple sets of values. To be truly "myself," which I knew was a key to my success in learning English composition, meant *not to be my Chinese self* at all. That is to say, when I write in English I have to wrestle with and abandon (at least temporarily) the whole system of ideology which previously defined me in myself. I had to forget Marxist doctrines (even though I do not see myself as a Marxist by choice) and the Party lines imprinted in my mind and familiarize myself with a system of capitalist/bourgeois values. I had to put aside an ideology of collectivism and adopt the values of individualism. In composition as well as in literature classes, I had to make a fundamental adjustment: If I used to examine society and literary materials through the microscopes of Marxist dialectical materialism and historical materialism, I now had to learn to look through the microscopes the other way around, i.e., to learn to look at and understand the world from the point of view of "idealism." (I must add here that there are American professors who use a Marxist approach in their teaching.)

The word "idealism," which affects my view of both myself and the universe, is loaded with social connotations, and can serve as a good example of how redefining a key word can be a pivotal part of redefining my ideological identity as a whole.

To me, idealism is the philosophical foundation of the dictum of English composition: "Be yourself." In order to write good English, I knew that I had to be myself, which actually meant not to be my Chinese self. It meant that I had to create an English self and be *that* self. And to be that English self, I felt, I had to understand and accept idealism the way a Westerner does. That is to say, I had to accept the way a Westerner sees himself in relation to the universe and society. On the one hand, I knew a lot about idealism. But on the other hand, I knew nothing about it. I mean I knew a lot about idealism through the propaganda and objections of its opponent, Marxism, but I knew little about it from its own point of view. When I thought of the word "materialism" — which is a major part of Marxism and in China has repeatedly been "shown" to be the absolute truth — there were always positive connotations, and words like "right," "true," etc., flashed in my mind. On the other hand, the word "idealism" always came to me with the dark connotations that surround words like "absurd," "illogical," "wrong," etc. In China "idealism" is depicted as a ferocious and ridiculous enemy of Marxist philosophy. Idealism, as the simplified definition imprinted in my mind had it, is the view that the material world does not exist; that all that exists is the mind and its ideas. It is just the opposite of

Marxist dialectical materialism which sees the mind as a product of the material world. It is not too difficult to see that idealism, with its idea that mind is of primary importance, provides a philosophical foundation for the Western emphasis on the value of individual human minds, and hence individual human beings. Therefore, my final acceptance of myself as of primary importance — an importance that overshadowed that of authority figures in English composition — was, I decided, dependent on an acceptance of idealism.

My struggle with idealism came mainly from my efforts to understand and to write about works such as Coleridge's *Literaria Biographia* and Emerson's "Over-Soul." For a long time I was frustrated and puzzled by the idealism expressed by Coleridge and Emerson — given their ideas, such as "I think, therefore I am" (Coleridge obviously borrowed from Descartes) and "the transparent eyeball" (Emerson's view of himself) — because in my mind, drenched as it was in dialectical materialism, there was always a little voice whispering in my ear "You are, therefore you think." I could not see how human consciousness, which is not material, could create apples and trees. My intellectual conscience refused to let me believe that the human mind is the primary world and the material world secondary. Finally, I had to imagine that I was looking at a world with my head upside down. When I imagined that I was in a new body (born with the head upside down) it was easier to forget biases imprinted in my subconsciousness about idealism, the mind, and my former self. Starting from scratch, the new inverted self — which I called my "English Self" and into which I have transformed myself — could understand and *accept,* with ease, idealism as "the truth" and "himself" (i.e., my English Self) as the "creator" of the world.

Here is how I created my new "English Self." I played a "game" similar to ones played by mental therapists. First I made a list of (simplified) features about writing associated with my old identity (the Chinese Self), both ideological and logical, and then beside the first list I added a column of features about writing associated with my new identity (the English Self). After that I pictured myself getting out of my old identity, the timid, humble, modest Chinese "I," and creeping into my new identity (often in the form of a new skin or a mask), the confident, assertive, and aggressive English "I." The new "Self" helped me to remember and accept the different rules of Chinese and English composition and the values that underpin these rules. In a sense, creating an English Self is a way of reconciling my old cultural values with the new values required by English writing, without losing the former.

An interesting structural but not material parallel to my experiences in this regard has been well described by Min-zhan Lu in her important article, "From Silence to Words: Writing as Struggle" (*College English* 49 [April 1987]: 437–48). Min-zhan Lu talks about struggles between two selves, an open self and a secret self, and between two discourses, a mainstream Marxist discourse and a bourgeois discourse her parents wanted her to learn. But her struggle was different from mine. Her Chinese self was severely constrained and suppressed by mainstream cultural discourse, but never interfused with it. Her experiences, then, were not representative of those of the majority of the younger generation who, like me, were brought up on only one discourse. I came to English composition as a Chinese person, in the fullest sense of the term, with a Chinese identity already fully formed.

Identity of the Mind: Illogical and Alogical

In learning to write in English, besides wrestling with a different ideological system, I found that I had to wrestle with a logical system very different from the blueprint of logic at the back of my mind. By "logical system" I mean two things: the Chinese way of thinking I used to approach my theme or topic in written discourse, and the Chinese critical/logical way to develop a theme or topic. By English rules, the first is illogical, for it is the opposite of the English way of approaching a topic; the second is alogical (non-logical), for it mainly uses mental pictures instead of words as a critical vehicle.

THE ILLOGICAL PATTERN. In English composition, an essential rule for the logical organization of a piece of writing is the use of a "topic sentence." In Chinese composition, "from surface to core" is an essential rule, a rule which means that one ought to reach a topic gradually and "systematically" instead of "abruptly."

The concept of a topic sentence, it seems to me, is symbolic of the values of a busy people in an industrialized society, rushing to get things done, hoping to attract and satisfy the busy reader very quickly. Thinking back, I realized that I did not fully understand the virtue of the concept until my life began to rush at the speed of everyone else's in this country. Chinese composition, on the other hand, seems to embody the values of a leisurely paced rural society whose inhabitants have the time to chew and taste a topic slowly. In Chinese composition, an introduction explaining how and why one chooses this topic is not only acceptable, but often regarded as necessary. It arouses the reader's interest in the topic little by little (and this is seen as a virtue of composition) and gives him/her a sense of refinement. The famous Robert B. Kaplan "noodles" contrasting a spiral Oriental thought process with a straight-line Western approach ("Cultural Thought Patterns in Inter-Cultural Education," *Readings on English as a Second Language,* Ed. Kenneth Croft, 2nd ed., Winthrop, 1980, 403–10) may be too simplistic to capture the preferred pattern of writing in English, but I think they still express some truth about Oriental writing. A Chinese writer often clears the surrounding bushes before attacking the real target. This bush-clearing pattern in Chinese writing goes back two thousand years to Kong Fuzi (Confucius). Before doing anything, Kong says in his *Luen Yu (Analects),* one first needs to call things by their proper names (expressed by his phrase "Zheng Ming"正名). In other words, before touching one's main thesis, one should first state the "conditions" of composition: how, why, and when the piece is being composed. All of this will serve as a proper foundation on which to build the "house" of the piece. In the two thousand years after Kong, this principle of composition was gradually formalized (especially through the formal essays required by imperial examinations) and became known as "Ba Gu," or the eight-legged essay. The logic of Chinese composition, exemplified by the eight-legged essay, is like the peeling of an onion: Layer after layer is removed until the reader finally arrives at the central point, the core.

Ba Gu still influences modern Chinese writing. Carolyn Matalene has an excellent discussion of this logical (or illogical) structure and its influence on her Chinese students' efforts to write in English ("Contrastive Rhetoric: An American Writing Teacher in China," *College English* 47 [November 1985]: 789–808). A recent Chinese textbook for composition lists six essential steps (factors) for writing a narrative essay, steps to be taken in this order: time, place, character, event, cause, and consequence (*Yuwen Jichu Zhishi Liushi Jiang [Sixty Lessons on the Basics of the Chinese Language],* Ed. Beijing Research Institute of Education, Beijing Publishing House, 1981, 525–609). Most Chinese students (including me) are taught to follow this sequence in composition.

The straightforward approach to composition in English seemed to me, at first, illogical. One could not jump to the topic. One had to walk step by step to reach the topic. In several of my early papers I found that the Chinese approach — the bush-clearing approach — persisted, and I had considerable difficulty writing (and in fact understanding) topic sentences. In what I deemed to be topic sentences, I grudgingly gave out themes. Today, those papers look to me like Chinese papers with forced or false English openings. For example, in a narrative paper on a trip to New York, I wrote the forced/false topic sentence, "A trip to New York in winter is boring." In the next few paragraphs, I talked about the weather, the people who went with me, and so on, before I talked about what I learned from the trip. My real thesis was that one could always learn something even on a boring trip.

THE ALOGICAL PATTERN. In learning English composition, I found that there was yet another cultural blueprint affecting my logical thinking. I found from my early papers that very often I was unconsciously under the influence of a Chinese critical approach called the creation of "yijing," which is totally non-Western. The direct translation of the word "yijing" is: *yi,* "mind or consciousness," and *jing,* "environment." An ancient approach which has existed in China for many centuries and is still the subject of much discussion, yijing is a complicated concept that defies a universal definition. But most critics in China nowadays seem to agree on one point, that yijing is the critical approach that separates Chinese literature and criticism from Western literature and criticism. Roughly speaking, yijing is the process of creating a pictorial environment while reading a piece of literature. Many critics in China believe that yijing is a creative process of inducing oneself, while reading a piece of literature or looking at a piece of art, to create mental pictures, in order to reach a unity of nature, the author, and the reader. Therefore, it is by its very nature both creative and critical. According to the theory, this nonverbal, pictorial process leads directly to a higher ground of beauty and morality. Almost all critics in China agree that yijing is not a process of logical thinking — it is not a process of moving from the premises of an argument to its conclusion, which is the foundation of Western criticism. According to yijing, the process of criticizing a piece of art or literary work has to involve the process of creation on the reader's part. In yijing, verbal thoughts and pictorial thoughts are one. Thinking is conducted largely in pictures and then "transcribed" into words. (Ezra Pound once tried to capture the creative aspect of yijing in poems such as "In a Station of the Metro." He also tried to capture the critical aspect of it in his theory of imagism and vorticism, even though he did not know the term "yijing.") One characteristic of the yijing approach to criticism, therefore, is that it often includes a description of the created mental pictures on the part of the reader/critic and his/her mental attempt to bridge (unite) the literary work, the pictures, with ultimate beauty and peace.

In looking back at my critical papers for various classes, I discovered that I unconsciously used the approach of yijing, especially in some of my earlier papers when I seemed not yet to have been in the grip of Western logical critical approaches. I wrote, for instance, an essay entitled "Wordsworth's Sound and Imagination: The Snowdon Episode." In the major part of the essay I described the pictures that flashed in my mind while I was reading passages in Wordsworth's long poem *The Prelude.*

> I saw three climbers (myself among them) winding up the mountain in silence "at the dead of night," absorbed in their "private thoughts." The sky was full of blocks of clouds of different colors, freely changing their shapes, like oily pigments disturbed in a bucket of water. All of a sudden, the moonlight broke the darkness "like a flash," lighting up the mountain tops. Under the "naked moon," the band saw a vast sea of mist and vapor, a silent ocean. Then the silence was abruptly broken, and we heard the "roaring of waters, torrents, streams/Innumerable, roaring with one voice" from a "blue chasm," a fracture in the vapor of the sea. It was a joyful revelation of divine truth to the human mind: The bright, "naked" moon sheds the light of "higher reasons" and "spiritual love" upon us; the vast ocean of mist looked like a thin curtain through which we vaguely saw the infinity of nature beyond; and the sounds of roaring waters coming out of the chasm of vapor cast us into the boundless spring of imagination from the depth of the human heart. Evoked by the divine light from above, the human spring of imagination is joined by the natural spring and becomes a sustaining source of energy, feeding "upon infinity" while transcending infinity at the same time. . . .

Here I was describing my own experience more than Wordsworth's. The picture described by the poet is taken over and developed by the reader. The imagination of the author and the imagination of the reader are thus joined together. There was no "because" or "therefore" in the paper. There was little *logic*. And I thought it was (and it is) criticism. This seems to me a typical (but simplified) example of the yijing approach. (Incidentally, the instructor, a kind professor, found the paper interesting, though a bit "strange.")

In another paper of mine, "The Note of Life: Williams's 'The Orchestra,'" I found myself describing my experiences of pictures of nature while reading William Carlos Williams's poem "The Orchestra." I "painted" these fleeting pictures and described the feelings that seemed to lead me to an understanding of a harmony, a "common tone," between man and nature. A paragraph from that paper reads:

> The poem first struck me as a musical fairy tale. With rich musical sounds in my ear, I seemed to be walking in a solitary, dense forest on a spring morning. No sound from human society could be heard. I was now sitting under a giant pine tree, ready to hear the grand concert of Nature. With the sun slowly rising from the east, the cello (the creeping creek) and the clarinet (the rustling pine trees) started with a slow overture. Enthusiastically the violinists (the twittering birds) and the French horn (the mumbling cow) "interpose[d] their voices," and the bass (bears) got in at the wrong time. The orchestra did not stop, they continued to play. The musicians of Nature do not always play in harmony. "Together, unattuned," they have to seek "a common tone" as they play along. The symphony of Nature is like the symphony of human life: Both consist of random notes seeking a "common tone." For the symphony of life
>> Love is that common tone
>>> shall raise his fiery head
>>> and sound his note.

Again, the logical pattern of this paper, the "pictorial criticism," is illogical to Western minds but "logical" to those acquainted with yijing. (Perhaps I should not even use the words "logical" and "think" because they are so conceptually tied up with "words" and with culturally based conceptions, and therefore very misleading if not useless in a discussion of yijing. Maybe I should simply say that yijing is neither illogical nor logical, but alogical.)

I am not saying that such a pattern of "alogical" thinking is wrong — in fact some English instructors find it interesting and acceptable — but it is very non-Western. Since I was in this country to learn the English language and English literature, I had to abandon Chinese "pictorial logic," and to learn Western "verbal logic."

If I Had to Start Again

The change is profound: Through my understanding of new meanings of words like "individualism," "idealism," and "I," I began to accept the underlying concepts and values of American writing, and by learning to use "topic sentences" I began to accept a new logic. Thus, when I write papers in English, I am able to obey all the general rules of English composition. In doing this I feel that I am writing through, with, and because of a new identity. I welcome the change, for it has added a new dimension to me and to my view of the world. I am not saying that I have entirely lost my Chinese identity. In fact I feel that I will never lose it. Any time I write in Chinese, I resume my old identity, and obey the rules of Chinese composition such as "Make the 'I' modest," and "Beat around the bush before attacking the central topic." It is necessary for me to have such a Chinese identity in order to write authentic Chinese. (I have seen people who, after learning to write in English, use English logic and sentence patterning to write Chinese. They produce very awkward Chinese texts.) But when I write in English, I imagine myself slipping into a new "skin," and I let the "I" behave much more aggressively and knock the topic right on the head. Being conscious of these different identities has helped me to reconcile different systems of values and logic, and has played a pivotal role in my learning to compose in English.

Looking back, I realize that the process of learning to write in English is in fact a process of creating and defining a new identity and balancing it with the old identity. The process of learning to write in English is in fact a process of creating and defining a new identity and balancing it with the old identity. The process of learning English composition would have been easier if I had realized this earlier and consciously sought to compare the two different identities required by the two writing systems from two different cultures. It is fine and perhaps even necessary for American composition teachers to teach about topic sentences, paragraphs, the use of punctuation, documentation, and so on, but can anyone design exercises sensitive to the ideological and logical differences that students like me experience — and design them so they can be introduced at an early stage of an English composition class? As I pointed out earlier, the traditional advice "Just be yourself" is not clear and helpful to students from Korea, China, Vietnam, or India. From "Be yourself" we are likely to hear either "Forget your cultural habit of writing" or "Write as you would write in your own language." But neither of the two is what the instructor meant or what we want to do. It would be helpful if he or she pointed out the different cultural/ideological connotations of the word "I," the connotations that exist in a group-centered culture and an individual-centered culture. To sharpen the contrast, it might be useful to design papers on topics like "The Individual vs. The Group: China vs. America" or "Different 'I's' in Different Cultures."

Carolyn Matalene mentioned in her article (789) an incident concerning American businessmen who presented their Chinese hosts with gifts of cheddar cheese, not knowing that the Chinese generally do not like cheese. Liking cheddar cheese may not be essential to writing English prose, but being truly accustomed to the social norms that stand behind ideas such as the English "I" and the logical pattern of English composition — call it "compositional cheddar cheese" — is essential to writing in English. Matalene does not provide an "elixir" to help her Chinese students like English "compositional cheese," but rather recommends, as do I, that composition teachers not be afraid to give foreign students English "cheese," but to make sure to hand it out slowly, sympathetically, and fully realizing that it tastes very peculiar in the mouths of those used to a very different cuisine.

Unruly Arguments: The Body Rhetoric of Earth First!, ACT UP, and Queer Nation

Kevin Michael DeLuca

This essay demonstrates a long-standing method of political and social argument used by groups often left outside of "mainstream" society's boundaries. Leaders such as Mahatma Ghandi and Martin Luther King Jr., and groups such as the student protesters of the 1960s and unions, have long recognized the need to use the body as a form of argument. While most composition students will not be writing academic arguments that incorporate their bodies as text, students and teachers of argument need to understand how bodies have worked as argument throughout history and how they can and do become modes of persuasion. Kevin Michael DeLuca's essay, published first in Argumentation and Advocacy *in 1999, explores how bodies — as they are used to create arguments by the contemporary activist groups Earth First!, ACT UP, and Queer Nation — can operate almost as Aristotelian enthymemes, abbreviated arguments that ask audiences to call on a host of cultural paradigms to create loosely articulated but emotionally powerful calls for change.*

To save old growth forest, an Earth First! activist sits on a platform suspended 180 feet up in a redwood. Protester and platform are dwarfed by the ancient giant. Deep in the woods, a blue-capped, smiling, bearded head pokes up out of a logging road. The rest of the person is buried in the road. This attempt to stop logging by blockading the road extends the meaning of the term passive resistance.

To protest governmental and corporate policy with regards to AIDS research, ACT UP (AIDS Coalition to Unleash Power) activists chain their bodies to the White House gates and conduct kiss-ins in public spaces. ACT UP occupies St. Patrick's Cathedral and interrupts Mass with a "die-in." Police carry out the bodies of 134 "dead" demonstrators. Together, healthy bodies, emaciated bodies, and wheelchair-bound bodies stop traffic on Wall Street. Queer Nation activists "sit-in" Cracker Barrel restaurants to protest employment policies that discriminate against them for failing to practice "normal" values. They invade straight bars and shopping malls to kiss and otherwise display gay sexual identity.

These contemporary activist groups, whether termed new social movements or postmodern social movements, are particularly notable for three reasons. They reject traditional organizational structures while forming radically democratic disorganizations. They neglect conventional legislative and material goals while practicing the powers of naming, worldview framing, and identity making. Finally, and most significantly for this essay, they slight formal modes of public argument while performing unorthodox political tactics that highlight bodies as resources for argumentation and advocacy.

In terms of their stance towards organizational form, Earth First! is exemplary. It is an antihierarchical disorganization with no official leaders, no national headquarters, no membership lists, no dues, no board of directors, and no tax-exempt status (Setterberg, 1995, p. 70; Kane, 1987, p. 100). This was a conscious decision, as Earth First! co-founder Dave Foreman explains: "We felt that if we took on the organization of the industrial state, we would soon accept their anthropocentric paradigm, much as Audubon and the Sierra Club already had" (1991, p. 21). ACT UP and other groups are similarly radically democratic and decentralized. AIDS activist and writer David Feinberg's description of meetings is revealing: "ACT UP has no leaders. Meetings are run according to Roberta's Rules of Order and are democratic to the point of near anarchy. The facilitator's role is to try to allow as full a discussion as possible without letting things slide into complete chaos, and to lower the level of vituperative and personal aggrievement to an acceptable level" (1994, p. 10; for descriptions of Queer Nation's designed disorganization, see Cunningham, 1992, Berlant and Freeman, 1993).

Typical of these groups, ACT UP's aims are neither limited to nor centered on the conventional goals of electoral, legislative, legal, and material gains. As Sean Strub, founder and editor of the AIDS magazine *POZ* explains,

> Someone 25 years old, gay or straight, with AIDS or not, has a different view of their doctor than they would have 10 years ago. There's a reason ACT UP never incorporated, never sought to build a staff. The idea was not to build an institution with a budget and a bureaucracy. The objective was to change people's relationship to the epidemic and the health care system in general, to make us all players. To analyze its impact, don't look at how many people show up at ACT UP's meetings. Look at how many people took ACT UP's values into their lives (quoted in Schoofs, 1997, pp. 12, 44).

These groups, then, are eschewing conventional goals in favor of contesting social norms, deconstructing the established naming of the world, and suggesting the possibilities of alternative worlds.

In performing these goals, Earth First!, ACT UP, and Queer Nation are practicing a form of argumentation that is an important manifestation of what has become known as constitutive rhetoric: the mobilization of signs, images, and discourses for the articulation of identities, ideologies, consciousnesses, communities, publics, and cultures.[1] For all of these groups, formal public address and argumentation are not primary practices, as denoted by the absence of the eloquent orator of Earth First! or ACT UP.[2] Instead, these activist groups practice an alternative image politics, performing image events designed for mass media dissemination. Often, image events revolve around images of bodies — vulnerable bodies, dangerous bodies, taboo bodies, ludicrous bodies, transfigured bodies. These political bodies constitute a nascent body rhetoric that deploys bodies as a pivotal resource for the crucial practice of public argumentation.[3]

In considering the use of bodies by these groups as argument, it is important to consider such usage as in part an adaptation to the unique possibilities and constraints of television, the de facto national public forum of the United States at the close of the twentieth century. Unable to buy time like corporations and mainstream political parties do, groups such as Earth First!, ACT UP, and Queer Nation "buy" air time through using their bodies to create compelling images that attract media attention. Even when they have the media's eye, however, these groups' options remain severely restricted. First, the protocols of sound-bite journalism that dominate commercial news suggest that most issues will receive only precious seconds and that a few minutes are an eternity. Hardly the time to practice the methods of the Lincoln-Douglas debates. Second, since these groups do not own their time, they know neither if they will be allowed to speak nor for how long. In addition, as radical groups questioning societal orthodoxies, they can expect news organizations to frame them negatively as disrupters of the social order (Gitlin, 1980; Parenti, 1993). These groups are in hostile territory with little control. What they do have some control over, however, is the presentation of their bodies in the image events that attract media attention. Their bodies, then, become not merely flags to attract attention for the argument but the site and substance of the argument itself.

The aim of this essay is to explore the power and possibilities of bodies in public argumentation. After briefly chronicling the relative neglect of the body in criticism of social movement protests, I will perform close readings of the bodies in the performances of Earth First!, ACT UP, and Queer Nation. The purpose of this analysis is not to valorize these groups or to privilege body rhetoric, but, rather, to suggest that we must account for their bodies in order to understand the force of these groups' protests, for Earth First!, ACT UP, and Queer Nation have challenged and changed the meanings of the world not through good reasons but through vulnerable bodies, not through rational arguments but through bodies at risk.

The Argumentative Force of Unruly Bodies

Although there is beginning to be some attention to the argumentative and rhetorical potential of images,[4] bodies remain virtually invisible.

Even when the tumultuous street politics of the 1960s and the early 1970s forced rhetorical critics to look beyond the boundaries of conventional politics and formal argumentation and consider the implications of extralinguistic confrontational activities, the scope was limited and bodies escaped sustained attention.[5] As Brant Short points out, "Although critics acknowledged the rhetorical aspects of confrontation, protest, and agitation, these studies suggest that theoretical accounts of seemingly *nonrational* discourse remained linked to traditional notions of logic, rationality, and artistic proofs" (1991, p. 173). Contrary to this perspective, I propose that Earth First!, ACT UP, and Queer Nation's tactics are arguments in their own right and that their bodies are central to the force of their arguments.

To suggest that bodies and images of bodies argue is controversial and defies the traditional delimitation of argumentation as linguistic. Even those sympathetic to the argumentative force of body images hesitate. Celeste Condit's discussion (1990, pp. 79–95) of fetus images is illustrative of the hesitation yet demonstrative of the argumentative force of bodies. In a discussion of the role of images of fetuses in the public debate over abortion, Condit offers a nuanced account of the force of images in public argument. Although Condit starts by granting that images can replace narratives and offer a form of grounding, she asserts the primacy of words, contending that the power of images is dependent on their translation into verbal meanings (1990, p. 81). As Condit shouts, "Without verbal commentary, pictures DO NOT ARGUE propositions" (1990, p. 85; see also pp. 81, 86, 87, 88, 90). Despite such protestations, Condit's own argument remains conflicted. First, Condit admits that images can provide general substance for a ground (1990, pp. 81, 85, 91). In Condit's reading of the fetus images of the pro-Life movement, she asserts that "the pro-Life pictures bring us a weighty set of grounds and that those grounds substantiate the claim that fetuses are important and valuable and ought to be protected" (1990, p. 91). Second, Condit seems to be subtly stretching the bounds of public argument and tacitly suggesting that these fetus images *do* argue. For instance, Condit argues that images offer "a different kind of understanding" (1990, p. 81) and, in referring to images, Condit writes "like any other form of argument" (1990, p. 81). Most explicitly, Condit later declares, "I believe that the pictures argue forcefully for the substance and value of the fetus" (1990, p. 91). Finally, belying her earlier assertions privileging verbal commentary, Condit does not argue that the pro-Life argument was more persuasive than the pro-Choice argument due to superior verbal commentary. Rather, it was a battle of images. As Condit herself concludes, "The persuasive force of the image of the fetus, towering over the meager pro-Choice images, would powerfully influence the popular consciousness, eventually establishing elements of the pro-Life vocabulary deeply within popular culture and within the lives of polarized subcultures" (1990, p. 94). Significantly, then, not only were images, not words, decisive, but body images, those of fetuses, trumped other images, like those of a hanger.

I side with those who accept that the nonlinguistic can argue.[6] Indeed, in an age of mixed media dominated by a televisual discourse composed of visual, aural, and verbal codes, to cling to an anachronistic definition of argumentation risks rendering it irrelevant. That said, I am not suggesting that a naked, prediscursive body constitutes an argument. There are no a priori bodies. Bodies are enmeshed in a turbulent stream of multiple and conflictual discourses that shape what they mean in particular contexts. I am contesting, however, that bodies are in any simple way determined or limited by verbal frames. To think of bodies as crucial elements of arguments in a televisual public forum, then, requires imagining forms of argument that exceed the protocols of deliberative reasoning.

Bodies in Nature

Since their founding in 1980, Earth First!, a radical, no-compromise environmental group, has deployed an array of tactics as they attempt to change the way people think about and act toward nature. In their efforts to put onto the public agenda issues such as the clear-cutting of old-growth forests, over-grazing by cattle on public lands, depredations by oil and mineral companies on public lands, loss of biodiversity, and the general ravaging of wilderness, Earth First! activists have resorted to sitting in trees, blockading roads with their bodies, chaining themselves to logging equipment, and dressing in animal costumes at public hearings. As this brief listing of Earth First! image events makes clear, their tactics are dependent on their bodies. Although these direct actions sometimes succeed and often fail in their immediate goals, their effectiveness as image events can be partially measured by the emergence of clear-cutting, old-growth forests, spotted owls, cattle grazing, and the 1872 mining law as hot-button political issues. Earth First!, like Greenpeace before them, understands that the significance of direct actions is in their function as image events in the larger arena of public discourse. Although designed to flag media attention and generate publicity, image events are more than just a means of getting on television. They are crystallized argumentative shards, mind bombs, that shred the existing screens of perception and work to expand "the universe of thinkable thoughts" (Manes, 1990, p. 77).

The image events of Earth First! interrogate the fundamental beliefs of industrialism while contesting the actions such beliefs warrant. For analysis, let us look at a protester sitting on a platform one hundred feet up in a redwood and a protester buried up to his neck in a logging road.[7] What is striking about both of these images is the utter vulnerability of the protesters as they intervene on behalf of nature. Quite clearly, the Earth First!ers, human beings, are putting at risk their bodies, their lives for wilderness, for trees.[8] This is an almost incomprehensible act in a modern, humanist, secular culture. In Western culture nature has been displaced in numerous narratives, including Christian, Enlightenment, scientific, capitalistic, socialistic, and industrial, that place human reason and humans at the center. Humans risking their lives for animals shakes the a priori anthropocentric assumption of these narratives, breaks the Great Chain of Being, and disobeys the command in *Genesis* to "Be fruitful and multiply, and replenish the earth, and subdue it: and have dominion over the fish of the sea, and over the fowl of the air, and over every living thing that moveth upon the earth" (*The Holy Bible: King James Version,* 1974, Genesis 1:28, p. 9). In refuting human-centered world views, the protesters' bodies give presence (Perelman, 1982) to the proposition that humans are not apart from the natural world but a part of it. They disclose the possibility of an ecocentric world.

While lowering the position of humans in the hierarchy, by risking their bodies for trees the Earth First!ers simultaneously challenge the understanding of animals and nature as mere machines or matter in motion, a storehouse of resources for humans to exploit. These notions are the products of a centuries-long process that Berman felicitously calls "the disenchantment of nature" (1982). In short, by placing themselves at risk, Earth First!ers challenge the anthropocentrism of Western culture and proffer the humble thought that other animals have a right to live and have intrinsic value, not merely economic value.

Perhaps in identification with the forms of nature that they are attempting to save, trees and ecosystems, both protesters have rendered their bodies relatively immobile. The Earth First! activist on the eight-by-four platform one hundred feet up the tree is helpless if the loggers decide to cut the tree despite the protester's presence (this has happened). The Earth First!er buried up to his neck in the road is utterly helpless. He is exposed not only to the potential anger of loggers or law enforcement officers, but to the torturous immobility of not being able to use his hands, whether to swat away a mosquito or scratch an itch. In performing these image events, the activists translate their humanist bodies into ecocentric bodies. Perched high in the Douglas fir, the protester sees the world from the tree's point of view and "becomes" the tree. Rendered relatively immobile, his movements are limited to the swaying of the tree. The protester, like the tree, depends on nourishment to come to him. Finally, their fates are entwined as the protester depends on the tree for support and shelter while the tree depends on the protester's presence to forestall the chainsaw. This mutual dependence is particularly clear in the case of Julia "Butterfly" Hill, who has lived in a one-thousand-year-old redwood, Luna, since December 10, 1997. She has told of how the tree sheltered her during the worst El Niño storms in California's history. Her presence, meanwhile, has stopped Pacific Lumber from killing Luna. Butterfly's bodily presence is a direct response to Pacific Lumber's practice of clear-cutting old-growth forests. Her body *is* a NO. Indeed, it is the only "no" that Pacific Lumber respects. Often logging illegally (they were cited for over two hundred violations of California's logging laws in the past two years), Pacific Lumber cut the trees surrounding Butterfly and Luna.

In the road blockade, the protester buried in the earth becomes the earth. He adopts a ground-level view of the world. People and equipment tower over him. He is immobile and must be spoon-fed. But his vantage point allows him to speak for the earth: "Defending what's left of the wilderness, defending what's left of the world." In clinging to treetops and embedding themselves in the earth, the Earth First! protesters both literally perform and symbolically enact humanity's connection to nature. In dislodging the blinders of a human-centered world view, the protesters bring into being an ecocentric perspective. In identifying with the tree and the earth, the protesters invite viewers also to identify with the natural world.

As the protester buried in the road speaks, the camera zooms in on him. Technology brings his face and the face of the tree-sitter into my world. Their faces confront me, compel my attention. "A face turned to us is an appeal made to us, a demand put on us . . . there lies the force of an imperative that touches us, caught sight of wherever we see a face turned to us" (Lingis, 1994, p. 167). The weary face of the tree-sitter and the bespectacled, bearded, smiling face popping out of the road testify to their thoughtfulness, resolution mixed with resignation, and humanity. In my encounter with these faces, "I find all that I am put into question by the exactions and exigencies of the other. In the face of another, the question of truth is out on each proposition of which my discourse is made, the question of justice put on each move and gesture of my exposed life" (Lingis, 1994, p. 173). The imperative of these faces call to us and call us to account. They call us to account for proposing an anthropocentric world view that reduces the rest of the world to a storehouse of resources. They call us to account for industrial practices that destroy a natural world so intimately connected to their bodies, our bodies.

Being buried in the road is significant. In blocking a road, the protester is disrupting literally and symbolically a major artery of industrialism. Indeed, the restructuring of the economy, foreign policy, housing, and social practices around the needs of automotive transportation suggest that our society in the late twentieth century could be termed a "car culture." Although the blocked road is a dirt road, it is key to industrialism in that it is a road for resource extraction. In blocking this road, then, the protester confronts the productive and symbolic capital of the culture and violates social norms.

From an early age, all children are inculcated with a necessary respect: pedestrians should

> always *give way* to automobiles. Such rules are mostly concerned with letting road users "go about their (and capitalism's) business," and are intended to coerce those who might obstruct their "rights of way" or infringe on their liberty. . . . For these reasons, if no other, the advent of recent road protests marks a radical challenge to the instrumental, one-dimensional, and codified ethos of the modern road (Smith, 1997, p. 349).

This body in this road interrupts the industrialization and homogenization of time and space and calls us to slow down and consider this place. By forcing the industrial juggernaut to pause, if only for a moment, this body gives us pause. Such pause opens a space for refuting the oft-repeated assertion of industrialism that progress is inevitable. In pausing, we stop the clock for a moment. In the moment, we can take the time to notice this particular place.

In short, these images of bodies at risk are encapsulated arguments challenging the anthropocentric position granting humans dominion over all living creatures and implicitly advocating ecocentrism as an alternative. By arguing against reducing trees and ecosystems (old-growth forests) to economic resources and instead proposing that they have intrinsic value and inalienable rights, Earth First! contests the linking of economic progress with nature as a storehouse of resources, thus reconstructing the discourse of industrialism that warrants the use of technology to exploit nature in the name of progress.

The bodies of Earth First!, then, question the possibility of property and the definition of the land as a resource and, instead, suggest that biodiversity has value in itself and, following Leopold's land ethic, "[a] thing is right when it tends to preserve the integrity, stability, and beauty of the biotic community. It is wrong when it tends otherwise" (1949/1968, pp. 224–25). Progress, then, is not the increasing production of goods through the technological exploitation of nature as a storehouse of resources, but, rather, the recognition of the intrinsic value and fundamental importance of ecosystems and the need for humans to live within limits as a part of larger ecosystems. By implacing their bodies in a region through burying themselves in the ground, perching in trees, hugging trees, and living in these areas until forcibly removed, Earth First!ers constitute an ecocentric community. Through the care of a neighbor, a tree becomes *this* tree, a mountain *this* mountain. The formation of an ecocentric community argues for the possibility of an alternative to the dominant industrial consumer culture.

The inhabiting of trees and regions by Earth First! activists is important. As brief glimpses of camp sites suggest, Earth First!ers often live in the places they are trying to protect. They dwell in the woods. Trees sitters live with the trees. As mentioned, Julia "Butterfly" Hill has lived at 180 feet in one redwood for over a year now. Through inhabiting the tree, she feels, "I have become one with this tree and with nature in a way I would never have thought possible" (quoted in Hornblower, 1998). In dwelling in the woods, the activists compel us to dwell on our relation to nature, to meditate on our fundamental relation as dwelling on the earth. I am using the word "dwelling" in the sense suggested by Heidegger: "The way in which you are and I am, the manner in which we humans *are* on the earth is *baun,* dwelling. To be a human being means to be on the earth as a mortal. It means to dwell" (1993, p. 349). By placing their bodies in the woods, the Earth First! activists bring the wilderness to us and bring us to the wilderness. They make present a natural world too often obscured by the overlaid technosphere that envelops the majority of Americans as they go about their daily routines. In dwelling in the woods they strip away the technological veneer, they reveal nature, and encourage us to confront our fundamental relation to the world as that of dwelling on earth.[9]

The body rhetoric of Earth First!, besides being a sustained critique of the articulation of nature and progress in the discourse of industrialism, also interrogates the accepted universalization of humanity as "rational man," the Cartesian subject. In the image events discussed, we witness people acting passionately ("irrationally") on behalf of nature and place, commitments that owe as much to love and emotional connections as they do to instrumental reason. Indeed, often these image events are refuting the results of a scientific rationality that uses the methods of cost-benefit analysis and risk assessment to sanction environmental destruction and extinctions in exchange for profits. Earth First! is questioning the very possibility of "science" (a neutral universal practice based on reason) as it condemns the science of the U.S. Forestry Service that recommends clear-cutting and other practices that most clearly benefit the timber, oil, and mining industries. In putting their bodies on the line in solidarity with trees and ecosystems, the Earth First! activists enact an embodied and embedded defense of nature that belies anthropocentrism's abstraction of "man" from the natural world and contests science's contextless universalization of nature. Finally, in the acts of their bodies, the activists transgress a notion of subjectivity anchored in reason and proffer their bodies as the founding texts for an embodied subjectivity that radically expands the bounds of human identity. Importantly, in using their bodies to perform their arguments, Earth First!ers are enacting a mode of argument that supports the substance of their argument. That is, they are practicing a mode of argument that is less focused on an abstract, universalized reason and more attuned to the feelings that accompany lived experiences.

The most explicit proposition and refutation dynamic revolves around the network news' consistently negative framing of Earth First! The framing states two explicit propositions: 1) Earth First! is violent; 2) Earth First!ers are terrorists. These claims are presented by the reporters or Earth First! critics through direct charges or through descriptive language of Earth First! activities. ABC News titles the first in-depth national network news story on Earth First! "War in the Woods" (August 10, 1987). Peter Jennings's introduction begins, "Now, the war in the woods" and ends by claiming that Earth First! "is so angry . . . it has been particularly extreme fighting back." Later in the story, reporter Ken Kashiwahara claims Earth First! has turned the forests into "a battlefield for guerrilla warfare." Kashiwahara interviews a U.S. Forest Service official who warns against going "to war over it. . . . Ultimately somebody could be murdered in this whole event." Then-head of the National Wildlife Federation Jay Hair chillingly pronounces judgment and punishment: "I reject out of hand their being environmentalists. They're terrorists, they're outlaws. They should be treated as such." Kashiwahara's final description labels Earth First! "terrorists or freedom fighters." Though the terms carry different valences, both ensconce Earth First! in the terminology of war.

Other network news stories echo the terminology. Earth First!ers are "outlaws" or zealots" (NBC News, July 5, 1990). ABC's Sam Donaldson opens a report, "On the American Agenda tonight, what some people are calling civil disobedience, what others are calling a form of terrorism" (ABC News, August 19, 1993). The report goes on to describe a "battle over logging" and "running battles." Reporter Barry Serafin asserts that tourists "have been scared away by guerrilla war being waged by this country's most radical environmental group."

The verbal framing in these stories of Earth First! activists as violent terrorists is refuted by two sets of body images. The bodies of Earth First! immobilized in a tree or in the earth, chained to logging equipment, holding hands and sitting in front of a bulldozer, bloodied from attacks by loggers, peacefully submitting to arrest, are not violent but vulnerable. They embody the counterproposition: Earth First! practices nonviolent civil disobedience.

Many of the images of Earth First!'s opponents in action suggest that the violent framing has been misplaced. Law enforcement officials roughly arrest protesters. Loggers violently confront Earth First!ers. A logger in a pickup truck speeds toward men, women, and children sitting in rocking chairs blocking a road. A log truck inexorably pushes an Earth First! activist trying to block a road. A leading citizen of a small town sits astride his horse and threatens to rope an Earth First! demonstrator. He tells the sheriff, "I guarantee you're gonna have to arrest me to keep me from dragging that sucker down the street" (ABC News, 1993). The loggers who beat an Earth First!er follow their bloodied victim to camp. Though Earth First! members significantly outnumber the four loggers, all they do is talk with them. Overall, the bodies of the Earth First! activists and their opponents belie the verbal framing and attest to the nonviolence of Earth First!

Acting Up

Although ACT UP was founded in 1987 with the express purpose of improving care for AIDS patients by violating the veneer of civility that was shrouding the deaths of thousands, it is not too much to claim, as the headline on one article proclaims, that the members of ACT UP are THE AIDS SHOCK TROOPERS WHO CHANGED THE WORLD (Schoofs, 1997, p. 42). Besides speeding drug approval, challenging drug prices, and obtaining numerous changes in health care and policy, ACT UP has forced the United States to confront its homophobia on state, institutional, civil, and private levels. It also has given rise to many other gay and lesbian activist organizations, including Queer Nation. Thanks to these groups, mainstream politicians must acknowledge and deal with gay and lesbian issues, the idea of same-sex couples as parents and marriage partners is now imaginable and possible, and homosexuals are becoming a presence in popular culture.

Central to the success of ACT UP and Queer Nation has been an in-your-face body rhetoric. The body is front and center in their arguments for it is the body that is at stake — its meanings, its possibilities, its care, and its freedoms. In their protest actions, the activists use their bodies to rewrite the homosexual body as already constructed by dominant mainstream discourses — diseased, contagious, deviant, invisible. In order to explicate these body arguments, let us take a closer look at some of the actions mentioned in the opening of this essay.

The force of the body makes it a sublime and contested site in cultures, subject to feverish and multiple modes of disciplining and constructing (Foucault, 1977, 1978; Lingis, 1994). In our culture at this time, homosexual bodies are a particularly hot site for they serve as the necessary foil for heterosexuality and yet are evidence of the failure of discursive disciplining and the excess of bodies. Additionally, they are marked not due to physical features but sexual practices, which provokes erotophobia, "the terrifying, irrational reaction to the erotic which makes individuals and society vulnerable to psychological and social control in cultures where pleasure is strictly categorized and regulated" (Patton, 1985, p. 103). More specifically, homosexuality represents an especially potent boundary transgression that violates the hegemonic discourse of heterosexuality and threatens the social order. As Judith Butler explains, "Since anal and oral sex among men clearly establishes certain kinds of bodily permeabilities unsanctioned by the hegemonic order, male homosexuality would, within such a hegemonic point of view, constitute a site of danger and pollution, prior to and regardless of the cultural presence of AIDS" (1990, p. 132). Taking advantage of their liminal status, ACT UP and Queer Nation activists deploy their dangerous bodies in their tactics.

At a basic level, the presence of their openly homosexual bodies is stunning in a culture where gay bodies do not exist or, if they must, their proper place is still the closet. In many regions of the country, to refuse to be proper, to pass as straight, is to risk being bashed. The penalty for exposing one's gay body ranges from verbal abuse to physical beatings to death (with the horrific murder of Matthew Shepherd serving as a ghastly reminder). Thus, by their very presence at a protest the activists are enacting a defiant rhetoric of resistance.

This resistance is intensified in the context of a social field permeated by medical and homophobic discourses that constitute gay bodies as diseased plague carriers bearing the mark of God's disfavor. Germphobia constructs AIDS as a modern plague that calls for quarantine (Patton, 1985, pp. 51–66). The New Right and Christian fundamentalists read AIDS as a message from God and a warrant for oppressive social policies. As Patton observes, "AIDS is a particularly potent symbol for the hard-line radical right because it is evidence of sin, God's disfavor, and an ultimate solution: It is both a sign and a punishment embodied in one of the groups targeted for political decimation long before AIDS" (1985, pp. 86–87). Medical fears and religious prejudice merge in the comments of a doctor in the *Southern Medical Journal:* "Might it be that our society's approval of homosexuality is an error and that the unsubtle words of wisdom of the Bible are frightfully correct? Indeed, from an empirical medical perspective alone, current scientific observation seems to require the conclusion that homosexuality is a pathologic condition" (quoted in Patton, 1985, p. 87). In such a hostile context, the presence of gay bodies, sick, emaciated, and healthy, constitute an eloquent and courageous response to discrimination and hate. It is a refusal to be quarantined, isolated, marginalized, silenced. In making their bodies visible, present, exposed, the ACT UP activists call on society to care.

The same-sex kiss-in ups the ante. The romantic kiss, the portal to heterosexuality, marriage, children, and the family values that function as the ideological bedrock of patriarchy is subverted, made "bi." The same-sex kiss instantiates the claimed identity of homosexuality and provokes erotophobia. As a performance of gay or lesbian sexuality, it violates two taboos — the taboo on homosexuality and the backup taboo on visibility. The same-sex kiss-in, whether at a public protest, straight bar, or shopping mall, turns the normalized terrain of heterosexuality into an alien landscape. It embodies the Queer Nation slogan, "We're here. We're queer. Get used to it."

The kiss-ins of ACT UP were a specific response to the intensification of homophobic discourses as the AIDS crisis developed. As activist Douglas Crimp explains, a kiss-in was "a public demonstration of gay and lesbian sexuality in the face of homophobia" (1990, p. 50). A poster for an April 29, 1988, kiss-in, created by Gran Fury, "a band of individuals united in anger and dedicated to exploiting the power of art to end the AIDS crisis" (quoted in Crimp, 1990, p. 16), shows two male sailors french kissing. One sailor has his arms around his partner's waist. The other sailor's arms are around his partner's neck. In other words, it is a classic kiss, made famous in celluloid dreams and here transformed into a transgressive political act, charged freedom rhetoric. Part of the charge comes from the bodies of the sailors in uniform, since the armed forces represent the first and last purified bastion of masculinity. At the time, the military was an institution dedicated to weeding out homosexuality in its ranks. Even the Clinton Administration's "Don't Ask, Don't Tell" policy is simply an official version of The Closet. The poster of the sailors kissing is a symbolic coming out that refutes the twin assertions of nonexistence or at least invisibility. More than just a refutation, it also asserts the presence of gays and lesbians in the military. The artists know the argumentative force of the body, for the poster's caption simply says, "READ MY LIPS." Although ACT UP distributed a flier explaining "why we kiss," the force of a kiss-in rests with the body, not the linguistic rationale, which cannot compel attention and is not disseminated through mass media broadcasting.

The Catholic Church is another institution that does not accept the practice of homosexuality. Besides condemning homosexuality and not allowing gays to be priests (of course, the patriarchal Church does not allow straight or lesbian women to be priests), the Church also opposes AIDS education and safe sex. For ACT UP in New York City, the Church's positions and John Cardinal O'Connor's active lobbying against the availability of condoms in public schools "promotes violence against gays" (quoted in Bullert, 1997, p. 125). On December 10, 1989, ACT UP responded to these positions with a "die-in" during Mass in St. Patrick's Cathedral. The "die-in" is designed to violate the veil of sanctity that shrouds the Church and O'Connor. It makes present the fatal consequences of the positions of an institution that purports to preach love, compassion, and understanding. In presenting themselves as symbolic victims and potential actual victims of Church policies, the ACT UP activists practically embody the consequences of Church policies tied to dusty dogma and abstract principles. In interrupting the Mass, the bodies in the "die-in" refuse to be sacrificed on the altar of Church doctrine. In using their gay and lesbian bodies to intervene in a public policy debate over AIDS prevention, ACT UP injects an emotional urgency into the debate. The presence of their individual bodies personalizes the debate and gives faces to the statistics. As one protester shouts, "You're murdering us! Stop killing us! We're not going to take it anymore! Stop it!" (quoted in Bullert, 1997, p. 126).

Queer Nation, founded at a New York City ACT UP meeting in 1990, deploys the body arguments and other tactics of AIDS activists in the service of the more general aims of challenging heterosexism and queering public spaces. Cofounder Michael Signorile describes the group's tactics: "Utilizing ACT UP's in-your-face tactics to take on gay bashers and increase visibility, Queer Nation spawned chapters across the country. Its members invaded bars and restaurants to hold kiss-ins. Dressed in the most fabulous gay regalia, Queer Nation went into suburban shopping malls" (1993, p. 88). In reterritorializing the terrain of the straight bar or shopping mall through kiss-ins and "fashion shows," Queer Nation activists transgress heterosexist spaces, make them uncomfortable for taken-for-granted heterosexuality, transform these spaces into alien landscapes. This is only a first step. As Berlant and Freeman suggest, "Queer Nights Out" are acts of sexual desegregation that hope to broadcast the ordinariness of the queer body and the banality of same-sex kissing (1993, p. 207). Queering public spaces is a deconstructive rhetoric that does not reverse the heterosexual/homosexual hierarchy, but instead hopes to displace it and create public spaces that are safe for visible manifestations of multiple sexualities: "*Visibility* is critical if a safe public existence is to be forged . . . secure spaces of safe embodiment for capital and sexual expenditures . . . safe spaces, secured for bodies by capital and everyday life practices. . . . 'Being queer is not about a right to privacy: It is about the freedom to be public'" (Berlant and Freeman, 1993, p. 201) — the freedom to be visible, to exist.

Reterritorializing the mall is especially significant in an America where the mall has become the public space for the display of the normative ideals of its consumer culture. It is the contemporary version of Main Street. Teenagers hang out there and conduct the dating rituals of heterosexual adolescence. Families shop for the goods of the American Dream. Seniors power walk into their Golden Years. Into this mythic space Queer Nation activists assert their public place.

The body rhetoric of the kiss-ins also work to "normalize" homosexuality through denaturalizing the conventions of heterosexuality. In consciously imitating and thus parodying the ritual practices of heterosexuality in a bar or mall, the activists reveal in the possibility of imitation the constructedness and contingency of the practices of heterosexuality. As Butler suggests, "As imitations which effectively displace the meaning of the original . . . parodic proliferation deprives hegemonic culture and its critics of the claim to naturalized or essential gender identities" (1990, p. 138). In using their bodies as billboards to disrupt the straight spaces of these places, Queer Nation activists recreate these spaces as sites for multiple significations of sexuality.

Conclusion

The aim of this essay is fairly limited. This essay is not meant to offer a theory of the body and, indeed, is implicitly incoherent with respect to a theory of the body, for the body is a site of incoherence. Still, the discussions of bodies in this essay do suggest that the body is *both* socially constructed and excessive. That is, bodies simultaneously are constructed in discourses and exceed those discourses. This essay is not an argument about or for postmodern politics or new social movements, though others have made those arguments about ACT UP, Earth First!, and other contemporary social protest groups.[10] Still, if postmodern or new social movements are understood as being concerned with discursive issues relating to identity, social norms, ideologies, power, and world views; forming grass-roots groups practicing radical participatory democracy; and performing unorthodox rhetorical tactics; the interpretation of the groups in this essay is consonant with such a characterization of postmodern politics. Finally, this essay is not an argument about image politics, though since the focus is on bodies that often appear to people as images of bodies through mass media dissemination, the argument of this essay is supportive of what Mitchell (1994) terms "the pictorial turn" and provides further evidence of the need for a visual rhetoric.

This essay is an argument for the necessity of considering the body when attempting to understand the effects of many forms of public argument, especially social protest rhetoric in a televisual public forum. In close readings of the unruly acts of Earth First!, ACT UP, and Queer Nation, it is evident that both the meaning and force of their arguments are dependent on the deployment of their bodies. I would suggest that these groups are not atypical. Bodies are central to the activism of environmental justice groups, Operation Rescue, and other groups. In attempting to understand the dynamics of social change and the role of rhetoric in constituting identities, ideologies, communities, and cultures, critics must analyze bodies as a rich source of argumentative force. Such a task requires a reconsideration of argumentation so as to take account of public arguments that exceed the bonds of reason and words. Through its readings of body arguments, this essay makes a contribution to such a task.

Notes

1. Greene (1998) provides a compelling history of the development of constitutive rhetoric.
2. Dave Foreman and Larry Kramer are important speakers, but their speeches are mostly for internal group consumption and are unheard in the larger public sphere. These groups' primary public rhetoric is the body rhetoric of their image events.
3. In this essay I conflate bodies and images of bodies. My analysis largely focuses on images of bodies represented on televisual news. To get into issues of representation would take me far afield from the thrust of this essay. In addition, an argument could be made that images of bodies on television news are perceived transparently, that is as real bodies, in a way that bodies in Hollywood films, for example, are not.
4. See Olson (1987), Jamieson (1988, 1994), Condit (1990), Gronbeck (1992, 1993, 1995), Birdsell and Groarke (1996), Lucaites (1997), and Lake and Pickering (1998).
5. For examples, see Haiman (1967), McEdwards (1968), Scott and Smith (1969), Bowers and Ochs (1971), and Simons (1972).
6. See Jamieson (1988, 1994), Gronbeck (1992, 1993, 1995), Birdsell and Groarke (1996), and Lake and Pickering (1998).
7. These image events appeared on ABC World News' report "War in the Woods" (August 10, 1987) and are typical of the images of Earth First! bodies on the news. For an extended discussion of grass-roots environmental groups and the media, see DeLuca (1999).
8. For accounts of violent incidents against environmental activists, see Foreman (1991, pp. 124–127), Helvarg (1994), and Rowell (1996). On September 17, 1998, an irate logger felled a redwood with Earth First! protesters in the area. The falling tree killed Earth First!er David Chain. For a compelling account of the confrontation, see Goodell (1999).
9. For more on the importance of piercing the technological veil, plus a consideration of the paradoxical role of technology in making possible the environmental movement and a new understanding of nature, see DeLuca (1996).
10. See Aronowitz (1996), Cohen (1985), Crimp (1990), Offe (1985), Patton (1985, 1990), and Touraine (1985).

Works Cited

ABC News (1987, August 10). War in the Woods. New York: ABC.
ABC News (1993, August 19). American Agenda. New York: ABC. [ref.]
Aronowitz, S. (1996). *The death and rebirth of American radicalism.* New York: Routledge.

Berlant, I. and E. Freeman (1993). Queer nationality. In M. Warner (Ed.). *Fear of a queer planet: Queer politics and social theory,* pp. 193–229. Minneapolis: University of Minnesota.

Berman, M. (1984). *The reenchantment of the world.* Toronto, Canada: Bantam Books.

Birdsell, D. S. and L. Groarke (1996). Toward a theory of visual argument. *Argumentation and Advocacy, 33,* 1–10.

Bowers, J. W., and D. J. Ochs (1971). *The rhetoric of agitation and control.* Prospect Heights, Illinois: Waveland Press.

Bullert, B. J. (1997). *Public television: Politics & the battle over documentary film.* New Brunswick: Rutgers University Press.

Butler, J. (1990). *Gender trouble: Feminism and the subversion of identity.* New York: Routledge.

Cohen, J. L. (1985). Strategy or identity: New theoretical paradigms and contemporary social movements. *Social research, 52,* 663–716.

Condit, C. M. (1990). *Decoding abortion rhetoric: Communicating social change.* Urbana: University of Illinois.

Crimp, D. (1990). *AIDS demographics.* Seattle: Bay Press.

Cunningham, M. (1992, May). If you're queer and you're not angry in 1992, you're not paying attention; if you're straight it may be hard to figure out what all the shouting's about. *Mother Jones, 17:3,* pp. 60–68.

DeLuca, K. (1996). Constituting nature anew through judgment: The possibilities of media. In S. Muir and T. Veenendall (Eds.), *Earthtalk: Communication and empowerment for environmental action.* Westport, CT: Praeger.

——— (1999). *Image politics: The new rhetoric of environmental activism.* New York: Guilford Publications.

Feinberg, D. B. (1994). *Queer and loathing: Rants and raves of a raging AIDS clone.* New York: Penguin Books USA Inc.

Foreman, D. (1991). *Confessions of an eco-warrior.* New York: Harmony Books.

Foucault, M. (1977). *Discipline and punish: The birth of the prison.* New York: Vintage Books.

Foucault, M. (1978). *The history of sexuality: Volume I: An introduction.* New York: Random House.

Gitlin, T. (1980). *The whole world is watching.* Berkeley: University of California Press.

Goodell, J. (1999, January 21). Death in the redwoods. *Rolling Stone,* 60, 69, 86.

Greene, R. W. (1998, Summer). The aesthetic turn and the rhetorical perspective on argumentation. *Argumentation and Advocacy, 35,* 19–29.

Gronbeck, B. (1992, August). Negative narrative in 1988 Presidential campaign ads. *The Quarterly Journal of Speech, 78,* 333–346.

——— (1993). The spoken and the seen: Phonocentric and ocularcentric dimensions of rhetorical discourse. In J. F. Reynolds (Ed.), *Rhetorical memory and delivery: Classical concepts for contemporary composition and communication* (pp. 139–155). Hillsdale, NJ: Lawrence Erlbaum Associates.

——— (1995). Rhetoric, ethics, and telespectacles in the post-everything age. In R. H. Brown (Ed.), *Postmodern representations: Truth, power, and mimesis in the human sciences and public culture* (216–238). United States: University of Illinois Press.

Haiman, F. S. (1967). The rhetoric of the streets. *Quarterly Journal of Speech, 53,* 99–114.

Heidegger, M. (1993). Building dwelling thinking. In D. Krell (Ed.), *Martin Heidegger: Basic writings.* San Francisco: HarperSanFrancisco.

Helvarg, D. (1994). *The war against the Greens: The Wise-use movement, the new right and anti-environmental violence.* San Francisco: Sierra Club Books.

Hornblower, M. (1998, May 11). Five months at 180 ft.: An ecowarrior who calls herself Butterfly has set a tree-squatting record. *Time, 151:18.*

Jamieson, K. H. (1988). *Eloquence in an electronic age.* New York: Oxford University Press.

———— (1994, September 28). Political ads, the press, and lessons in psychology. *The Chronicle of Higher Education.* (A56).

Kane, J. (1987, February). Mother nature's army. *Esquire,* 98–106.

Lake, R. A. and B. A. Pickering (1998). Argumentation, the visual, and the possibility of refutation: An exploration. *Argumentation 12,* 79–83.

Leopold, A. (1949/1968). *A Sand county almanac.* Oxford: Oxford University Press.

Lingis, A. (1994). *Foreign bodies.* New York: Routledge.

Lucaites, J. L. (1997). Visualizing "The People": Individualism vs. collectivism in *Let Us Now Praise Famous Men. The Quarterly Journal of Speech, 83,* 269–288.

Manes, C. (1990). *Green rage, radical environmentalism and the unmaking of civilization.* Boston, MA: Little, Brown & Co.

McEdwards, M. G. (1968). Agitative rhetoric: Its nature and effect. *Western Speech, 32,* 36, 43.

Mitchell, W. (1994). *Picture theory.* Chicago: University of Chicago Press.

NBC News (1990, July 5). Assignment Earth: Earth First! New York: NBC.

Offe, C. (1985, Winter). New social movements: Challenging the boundaries of institutional politics. *Social Research, 52,* 817–868.

Olson, L. (1987). Benjamin Franklin's pictorial representations of the British Colonies in America: A study in rhetorical iconology. *Quarterly Journal of Speech, 73,* 18–42.

Parenti, M. (1993). *Inventing Reality.* New York: St. Martin's.

Patton, C. (1985). *Sex and germs: The politics of AIDS.* Boston: South End Press.

Patton, C. (1990). *Inventing AIDS.* New York: Routledge.

Perelman, C. (1982). *The realm of rhetoric.* Notre Dame: University of Notre Dame.

Rowell, A. (1996). *Green backlash: Global subversion of the environment movement.* New York: Routledge.

Schoofs, M. (1997, March 25). ACT UP: 10 years and counting — The AIDS shock troopers who changed the world. *Village Voice, 42:12,* pp. 42, 44–47.

Scott, R. and Smith, D. (1969). The rhetoric of confrontation. *Quarterly Journal of Speech, 58,* 1, 8.

Setterberg, F. (1987, May/June). The wild bunch: Earth First! Shakes up the environmental movement.*Utne Reader,* 68–76.

Short, B. (1991). Earth First! and the rhetoric of moral confrontation. *Communication Studies, 42,* 172–88.

Signorile, M. (1993). *Queer in America: Sex, the media, and the closets of power.* New York: Random House.

Simons, H. W. (1972). Persuasion in social conflicts: A critique of prevailing conceptions and a framework for future research. *Speech Monographs, 39,* 227–47.

Smith, M. (1997, Winter). Against the enclosure of the ethical commons: Radical environmentalism as an "ethics of place." *Environmental Ethics, 18,* 339–353.

Touraine, A. (1985, Winter). An introduction to the study of social movements. *Social Research, 52,* 749–787.

ARGUMENT IN THE AGE OF SCIENCE AND TECHNOLOGY

Assent, Dissent, and Rhetoric in Science

R. Allen Harris

R. Allen Harris is one of many rhetoricians, scientists, and philosophers (other recent and influential examples include Michael Polanyi and Alan Gross) reevaluating the positivism claimed by some scientists and generally accepted as an attribute of science by the public. In this essay, first published in Rhetoric Society Quarterly *in 1990, Harris examines the tropes scientists use when making arguments and the ways scientific experiments and debates are situated within specific contexts. Harris uses rhetoric to understand science as an epistemic field, one that constructs knowledge through the interaction of rhetors (in this case, scientists), their audiences (including other scientists, the government, and the public), language, and the material world.*

Harris's detailed examination of this interaction revises the traditional paradigm of argument — which posits an individual writer or speaker addressing a more- or less-defined audience — by defining argument as an institutional function. In this sense, argument becomes the backbone of the institution of science as opposed to something individual scientists do. In addition, unlike many theorists in this book, Harris makes strong claims for the benefits of argument as a contestatory form of discourse, one that requires strong challenges in order to create new truths.

Harris's work reminds writing instructors that our students will engage in rhetoric regardless of their disciplinary interests, and that we need to analyze more carefully the rhetoric of disciplines such as science, religion, and philosophy, which have historically tried to elevate themselves above the consideration of rhetoric. Harris also points to the interdisciplinary nature of rhetorical studies, an idea that has the potential to significantly broaden the scope of the traditional first-year writing or second-year argument course.

In this text, see the section "Teaching Argument Across the Curriculum" (p. 389), Jeanne Fahnestock and Marie Secor's "The Stases in Scientific and Literary Argument" (p. 58), and Barbara Warnick's "Judgment, Probability, and Aristotle's Rhetoric*" (p. 42) for further discussion of rhetoric in the disciplines.*

1. Introduction

> Lo, a Spartan appears, and says that there never is or ever will be a real art of discourse which is unconnected with the truth.
>
> — Socrates

Socrates, of course, does not mean to venerate the art of discourse here. He is telling Phaedrus that there is discourse and there is truth. Once you have gone out and dug up the truth somewhere else, you apply the art of discourse to it and fashion a persuasive argument that will permit others to partake also of the truth. Two immediate implications follow from Socrates' position. First, only when the art of discourse, rhetoric, is put to the task of selling truth to the benighted does it become "real." Second, rhetoric is necessary in human affairs just to the extent that humans are unable to apprehend truth directly. It is an unfortunate evil, required because we are rationally degenerate creatures. Both positions have remained very popular over the intervening two millennia. Bitzer, for instance, can still say that "in the best of all possible worlds there would be communication perhaps, but not rhetoric;"[1] we get our truth and knowledge somewhere else, and only our lack of perfection prevents us from casting rhetoric out of the garden. But there is an important lesson in those two millennia that can help us to see the Spartan's words in another light: The sources of truth which rhetoric has been obliged to serve have changed dramatically — from Socrates' dialectic and Aristotle's apodeixis, to Christianity's biblical exegesis and divine revelation, to the current authority on matters of knowledge and truth, Science.

This rotation of leading roles while the supporting actress, Lady Rhetoric, remains constant indicates that the real art of discourse is connected with truth not because of human degeneracy, but because of precisely the reverse, because of our spark of perfection, because we are truth-seeking, knowledge-making creatures who sometimes get it right. We occasionally do something important with rhetoric: We find truth and we build knowledge out of it. When we manage the trick, though, we are so eager to dissociate it from all the foul and inane things we also do with rhetoric that we give the process another name. But these other names are clearly just aliases for rhetoric, or for some subset of rhetorical interests. Dialectic, for instance, is essentially questing debate. Apodeixis is distinguished only by the level of rigor Aristotle demands of the argumentation, not by any qualitative difference. Exegesis is rhetorical analysis. The only possible gap to this pattern is divine revelation, whose capacity to generate truth I will leave to more knowledgeable commentators, pausing only to notice that, true or not, reports of revelation usually involve a fair amount of persuasive machinery — burning bushes, hovering spirits, and the like. In any case, science is certainly no exception.

Scientists, although they are as fond of philosophers (from whom they come) of finding hard-boiled aliases for their rhetorical activities, traffic incessantly in suasion. They argue. They challenge and criticize. They appeal to form, to prestige, even to emotion. They build elaborate discursive structures out of loaded terms, topoi, and set pieces. They change each other's minds. They sway and are swayed.

Their aliases, however, have been very successful. Their acts of rhetoric when they "do science" are usually self-effacing in the extreme, covert enough that they appear to be out of the domain of rhetoric altogether. Their overt acts of rhetoric — polemics, Nobel acceptance speeches, grant proposals, and the like — they disclaim as something other, something which is wholly incidental to science. Like Socrates, they differentiate "real science" from all those other things they do with words, even when they do them as scientists. Consequently, while other humanist approaches to science (notably in history and philosophy) have venerable traditions, rhetoric of science is still a relatively new and quite apologetic discipline. The apologia can go overboard. Jerry, for instance, and McGuire trade on the curious perspective that "science is not truth but a form of lie"[2] to argue that rhetoric has a moral duty to act as "a counter-force"[3] against the inflated prestige of science. But, although it is not necessary to drag *science* down into the covinous muck where many relegate *rhetoric,* the impulse to let a little air out of the word is on the right track. In particular, scientists are said to deal in Truth and Certainty and Rationality, when, in fact, they deal with the same deflated phenomena that occupy most rhetoricians, truth and certainty and rationality. Where the two differ is at the intersection of these three discursive forces, knowledge. Scientists make it. Rhetoricians, for the most part, study it, and study the making of it.

Cutting to the chase: Scientists make knowledge because they are rhetors, and this paper looks at the twin paths scientist-rhetors break in pursuit of knowledge. One of these paths is dissent — the immensely productive, back-biting, barking way that scientists forge truth. The other is assent — the smoothly pervasive, communal, cooperative concert in which they arrange their truths into knowledge. These two paths give a distinctly non-Socratic meaning to the Spartan's observation: Truth and discourse are fundamentally inseparable. They are Siamese twins, sharing the same vital organs. They are weight and mass, chaos and order, wave and corpuscle. You can't have one without the other. And you can't have science without both.

2. Rhetoric in Science

> Please observe, gentlemen, how facts which at first seem improbable will, even on scant explanation, drop the cloak which has hidden them and stand forth in naked and simple beauty.
>
> — Galileo

Science is profoundly rhetorical. Ignoring the many intermediate patterns, take only the two extremes that Kuhn identifies: normal science and revolutionary science. Rhetoric permeates the one and constitutes the other. Rhetoric suffuses normal science so completely that it is impossible to find even the smallest corner without suasion, argumentation, topoi — without the nuclear ingredients of rhetoric with which we manage symbols, achieve consensus, and make knowledge. Normal science is unimaginable without agreement, and agreement is unimaginable without rhetoric. At least, to rhetoricians. Scholars with ostensibly opposing positions (that agreement occurs in spite, not because, of rhetoric), such as most philosophers and most scientists, have an impoverished view of rhetoric and simply use one of its aliases to talk about consensus. As for revolutionary science, even those who deny the deeply rhetorical nature of normal science drop the aliases here and concede that periods of scientific dissent are overtly rhetorical. They also usually concede that these periods are epistemically very productive.

As in all other domains, then, rhetoric has two principal reflexes in scientific argumentation, to achieve consent, and to galvanize dissent. Both reflexes have received a good deal of attention in the various humanist approaches to studying science. Traditional philosophies of science emphasize the criteria by which scientific communities reach agreement; traditional sociologies emphasize cooperative cohorts; traditional histories of science emphasize the steady accretion of knowledge. More recent philosophies of science emphasize dissonance; sociologies, the clash of incommensurate positions; histories, periods of upheaval. But it is important to realize that — as Kuhn captures in a rare eloquent phrase, *The Essential Tension*[4] — both sides of this dialectic rule science equally.

There is agreement. Scientists cooperate. Knowledge grows. Mitchell Feigenbaum, a physicist currently embroiled in the cooperation and anarchy that characterize the emergence of chaos studies, puts it this way: Today science "tells you how to take dirt and make computers from it."[5] Yesterday it told us how to take dirt and make lenses from it that brought the stars closer and made the micro-organic world grow bigger — close enough and big enough to enter our theories of the deepest mysteries, life and death. Tomorrow, if the men who play with the nastier fruits of science give us one, it will tell us how to take dirt and make eyes and hearts and consciousness from it. And this knowledge will be, as it is now, as it was in the past, the product of cooperation and consensus.

It will also be, as it is now, as it was in the past, the product of exclusion and dissensus. This is certainly true observationally: The accretion of knowledge is far from linear. Science is gangly. It takes two steps forward, one step back, another to the side. There are relatively long periods of stasis, but the equilibrium is punctuated by fierce, uncompromising, unruly debate, by rhetoric which only "enspirit[s] the already enspirited troops while further enraging the already enraged enemy."[6] But, more crucially, this punctuation is not an unfortunate interruption in the smooth flow of a single, grandly unfurling tapestry of truth, an epistemic hiccup. It is a necessity, an engine of knowledge and truth. Fierce, unruly debate is at least as productive as calm, orderly cooperation. Often, it is much more productive. Paul Feyerabend, for instance, has built a compelling cluster of ideas about scientific knowledge-making around the notion of counter-induction — in which a theory makes truth, earns its bacon, not primarily by amassing good evidence (induction), but by amassing good counterevidence to prevailing dogma. As is his own countervailing wont, where most commentators place this cluster of ideas in the province of philosophy of science, Feyerabend says it belongs to anthropology of science.[7] But Cook and Seamon are a good deal closer to the mark in classing it with rhetoric of science,[8] especially in light of Feyerabend's own connection of counterinductivity to what he sees as the sophistic goal, *"to make the weaker case the stronger."*[9]

Notice, however, that we are back to only one face of the dialectic. This is rhetoric, clearly, but it is a long way from the rhetoric of good reasons. Rather, it is a rhetoric of bad reasons — or, if there is a distinction, a rhetoric of good counter-reasons. It does not pursue consubstantiality, but dissubstantiality; it is not rhetoric of assent, but rhetoric of dissent.

Rhetoric of science, though it has not become sophisticated enough theoretically to bring Wallace or Burke or Booth to the task in any concerted manner, has made a number of very impressive sallies up both faces of rhetoric in science, the management of consensus and the productivity of dissensus. Campbell's several papers on Darwin,[10] for instance, demonstrate how he engineered agreement by plugging into the most powerful currents in the ethos of Victorian England — chauvinistic nationalism, bootstrap capitalism, and natural theology. Halloran shows much the same about Watson and Crick, for a strikingly different and much more local community.[11] Lyne and Howe scale the other face of the dialectic, exploring the epistemic fruitfulness of the phyletic gradualism-punctuated equilibria controversy in the neo-Darwinian synthesis.[12] Anderson shows the same with respect to Lavoisier, who redirected the course of science, in large part by manufacturing a dispute with phlogiston chemistry.[13] And Gross spends time on both faces, exploring first how Newton failed to affect the science of optics when he approached it trying to pick a fight with Descartes, and then how he revolutionized it several years later with a conciliatory offering of the same ideas.[14]

Although these papers, and others of varying quality,[15] clearly demonstrate the capacity of rhetoricians to make important contributions to humanist studies of science, and although there has been a good deal of talk in the last decade or so about the epistemic consequences of rhetoric, most rhetoricians still have a sneaking wariness about the legitimacy of their colleagues speaking about how scientists make knowledge. The reticence is understandable, since *science* is such a swollen and honored word in our culture, and *rhetoric* is such a small, ignoble one. The god-term and the weasel-word parcelled together in a construction like *rhetoric of science* still seems incongruous, even for professional rhetoricians, and leads to a fair amount of squirming at rhetoric conferences.

A more appropriate reaction to that construction, however, would be to observe that it is virtually redundant, on a par with *rhetoric of politics*. Like politics, science is so thoroughly saturated with rhetoric there is very little room for anything else. More pointedly, just as in politics, that is not a bad thing. Rhetoric is not an unfortunate social disease corrupting an otherwise robust and virtuous activity. Quite the opposite, as even extremely hard-nosed theories of science, like most varieties of positivism, tacitly admit. Positivism is, after all, a semantic theory, concerned exclusively with building words into explanatory structures and with closely monitoring meaning within those structures — two fundamentally rhetorical pursuits. It is also a theory of how to build words into arguments that produce conviction, an idealized and unreal variant of the central notion in rhetoric, persuasion.

Still, the acknowledgement is far from overt and, although more flexible and genial notions of science are currently the top sellers in philosophy, a few observations to smooth this discomfort are in order. In particular, we need to consider how thoroughly rhetoric permeates the bones of science, and how, like calcium, it strengthens those bones, giving science a spine sturdy enough to support the back-breaking work of digging up truth and building knowledge.

2.1 The Pervasiveness of Rhetoric in Science

> In all eternity it is impossible for me to compel a person to accept an opinion, a conviction, a belief. But one thing I can do: I can compel him to take notice.
>
> — Soren Kierkegaard

Most rhetoricians are hindus in one essential regard. Hinduism holds that everybody is a hindu, but most people are just too unenlightened to know it, and rhetoricians hold that everybody is a rhetor, but that most people are just too unenlightened to know it. Certainly some of us feel this way with regard to those people who constitute the various sciences. But even rhetoricians often fail to see that the relationship between rhetoric and science is not one of involvement, but of commitment. (To illustrate the distinction, in a bacon and egg breakfast: The chicken is involved; the pig is committed.) Science is rhetorical, leaf to root, but most scientists and many rhetoricians regard it as a dispassionate, objective activity, and, replete with upper-case reverence, an eminently Rational one. They regard science as fundamentally above the reach of the petty suasions that govern life in other, less rational, spheres. But the evidence is compelling that scientists are deluded rhetors.

As a deep example of the pervasiveness of suasion in science, consider the well-known but little discussed "experimenter effect" in research with human subjects. Even when the experiments are conducted and the data gathered by "blind" assistants (researchers who are deliberately left ignorant of both the hypothesis being tested and the predicted outcome), there is measurable bias in the results, and the bias is uniformly in favor of the predicted outcome. Indeed, even the much vaunted "double blind" technique exhibits the experimenter effect in a significant number of investigated cases.[16] Clearly, there is a marked, if subliminal, amount of persuasion at work here. The experimental designer conveys her expectations to her assistant, who conveys them to the subject, who behaves in accordance with the designer's wishes, unbeknownst to all.

Or, consider a less opaque example of this pervasiveness. Consider the impact that names have on gaining adherence for, and shaping, a position. Stephen Hawking, for instance, considers John Wheeler's name for a certain class of celestial and theoretical phenomena a "masterstroke" because *black hole* "conjures up a lot of human neuroses"[17] and consequently focuses a great deal of attention on those phenomena, determining the concerns of scientists and their theories. In Kierkegaard's terms, it compels them to take notice. Noam Chomsky's *deep structure,* though he has since repudiated it for causing "confusion . . . at the periphery of the field,"[18] was a similarly compelling masterstroke. Because of the blurring between *deep* and *profound,* Chomsky's term helped garner a staggering amount of scholarly attention to his theories, as well as a fair amount of unscholarly attention. The greater part of a very vibrant decade of linguistic research hinged on competing interpretations of the term; it is difficult to imagine a denotatively comparable but connotatively more neutral term (say, *initial phrase marker*) determining the flow of so much energy. Gell-Mann's famous borrowing of *quark* from Joyce also generated a great deal of attention, and helped shape the ethos of an entire discipline in the bargain — a discipline which now rejoices in generating terminology like *charm* and *strangeness* and *color* to code properties of the quark. Even more strikingly, consider how the tyrannizing image of language has determined molecular biology, where they talk of *codes* and *translations* and *semantics* as if molecules really traffic in meaning. The entire science would be unthinkable without the metaphor and the terminological baggage it brings along. Nor is this a new phenomenon. Particle physics of the midcentury, for instance, is saturated with the language "of disintegration, violence, and derangement,"[19] language which was very compelling for the existential intellectuals of the period. The Devonian controversy in Victorian geology saw the introduction of terms like *Silurian* (after a British tribe) and *Cambrian* (from the Roman name for Wales),[20] reflecting the chauvinism of nineteenth-century Britain. Even further back, Enlightenment scientists extended their reverence for individual men of genius to the naming of celestial objects, the Romans extended their religious concerns, the Babylonians their kinship preoccupations.

Still more clearly, consider the amount of argumentation in science. Even the desiccated remnants of these arguments that make it into the mainstream literature — where persuasion is said to be replaced by harder-edged notions, like demonstration, proof, and conviction — are rhetorical through and through. Although the rational processes behind the argument are often hidden, and the suasive intentions obscured, the style, the terminology, the construction of an exigence, even the use of citation in scientific articles, are all chosen more or less carefully (and, hence, more or less successfully) to sway the reader into the author's perspective. The format of the experimental paper, for instance, masks a great deal of the experiment it reports, while serving the latent rhetorical function of appealing to the power of induction.[21]

The level of readability in scientific prose also has suasive ends,[22] and even the lowly footnote is often wielded very deftly.[23] Scientific presentation "may be dressed up to resemble the policeman's deadpan testimony in the witness box; but the true analogy is with the barrister's advocacy, designed to sway the jury to a favorable verdict."[24] Even that model of rationality, Isaac Newton, illustrates this point clearly. He worked out most of his celestial mechanics with a mathematical tool he developed for the purpose, calculus, but he presented his conclusions in the language of geometry, to put them in a more common tongue, and to borrow from the authority of Euclid and Apollonius. He was also extremely adept at manipulating the fudge factor, and a large measure "of the *Principia*'s persuasiveness was its deliberate pretense to a degree of precision quite beyond its legitimate claim."[25]

And, of course, there is no shortage of less subtle rhetoric in science. Consider this little agonistic gem by Nobel laureate Sheldon Glashow:

> Until the string people can interpret perceived properties of the real world, they are simply not doing physics. Should they be paid by universities and be permitted to pervert impressionable students? Will young Ph.D.'s whose expertise is limited to superstring theory be employable if and when the string snaps? Are string thoughts more appropriate to departments of mathematics or even to schools of divinity than to physics departments? How many angels can dance on the head of a pin?[26]

All the stops are out here. Glashow is attacking a new theoretical school in physics with a whole range of *ad bacculums* — moral warnings, financial threats, threats of excommunication — which build toward a nose-thumbing flourish of ridicule that stretches back to Bacon's assault on the Schoolmen. Such manifest hostility is usually masked in the public face of science — though there are attested examples of public obscenity and even violence — but the fact that it occasionally breaks out so ferociously is clear evidence that there is always dissonance lying dormant in the sciences.

These examples could be multiplied at will: Rhetoric pervades science like a fart in a confessional. At least, the common perception is that rhetoric is as disruptive to the quiet, pristine halls of science and as malodorous as such excretions. Certainly Kuhn, the first man to draw attention to this pervasiveness with any degree of rhetorical force, was treated as though he had fouled the monastery. He was also treated as something of a traitor, a confessor of secrets, the one who let it out. And there turned out to be more than a grain of reality to these fears. Before Kuhn (and Lakatos, and Feyerabend) had any impact on the popular conception of scientists, they were seen as detached, ascetic authorities, untroubled by the egos, passions, and paranoia that characterized the rest of the human barnyard. At best, they were the priests of a new age, at worst, nerds. Now they are regularly portrayed as "howling, scrapping alley cats" in books like *Bones of Contention, Nobel*

Dreams: Power, Deceit, and the Ultimate Experiment, and *Betrayers of the Truth.*[27] But if Kuhn brought the bad news, the good news is that the deeply rhetorical nature of science also accounts for its phenomenal knowledge-making success.

2.2 The Productivity of Rhetoric in Science

> It is only through the clash of adverse opinions that the remainder of the truth has any chance of being supplied.
>
> — John Stuart Mill

Again, the number of events and episodes which illustrate the scientific productivity of rhetoric is, to all practical extents, limitless (and, in many cases of course, coextensive with illustrations of pervasiveness). But, changing tack a few degrees, one representative anecdote should establish the point firmly.

Richard Muller tells how he was quietly minding his own business in his office one day when Louis Alvarez burst in with "Rich, I just got a crazy paper from Raup and Sepkoski. They say that great catastrophes occur on the Earth every 26 million years, like clockwork. It's ridiculous."[28] Alvarez had been one of the prime movers and, thanks to a rich vein of native obstreperousness, one of the prime media figures, in the catastrophic extinction story about the dinosaurs. He and a small group of collaborators had suggested that the dinosaurs went missing because a huge comet plowed into the earth, kicked up vast clouds of debris, choked off the sun, and disturbed plant production so much that the biggest and most vulnerable members of the food chain couldn't get enough to eat. This hypothesis stirred up a great deal of rancor, with paleontologists yelling that Alvarez and his team didn't have the ethos to make these arguments, since they came from other disciplines (chemistry, geology, and physics), and Alvarez sneering back that "[paleontologists] aren't very good scientists. They're more like stamp collectors."[29] But the claim that this was only one of a regular series of extinctions, a claim coming from a pair of paleontologists no less (even though Raup had been sympathetic to the Cosmic Interruptus theory of dinosaur extinction), was too much.

Muller agreed. Periodic extinctions "*did* sound absurd," but he was cajoled into playing devil's advocate. Alvarez had written a letter to Raup and Sepkoski, pointing out the errors of their ways, but he wanted Muller to look it over first, with *look it over* as a euphemism for "study the paper, the letter, and all pertinent data, then work your damnedest to find holes in all three." Alvarez had an especially eristic view of how science should proceed, reflecting Mill's maxim about the fruitfulness of clashing opinions, and Muller had been his most promising apprentice at Berkeley; he went away fully expecting Muller to find some strong counterarguments to his case against Raup and Sepkoski.

When Alvarez came back a few days later, after Muller had thought carefully about the issues, Muller took his role reluctantly, "like a law-

yer, interested in proving my client innocent, even though I wasn't totally convinced myself." Alvarez quickly mounted a belligerent offence,
pulling authority, calling names, and refusing to grant any merit at all
to Muller's strongest and most obvious counterargument: that, assuming some arbitrary mechanism which could slam an asteroid into the
earth every 26 million years, the Raup and Sepkoski data held up.
Alvarez was completely obtuse to the point, repeatedly demanding,
"What is your model?" Muller said that he didn't need a model. The
mere possibility of such a model legitimated the data that Alvarez
wanted to discount. Muller argued that the shoe rightly belonged on
the other foot, that Alvarez would have to demonstrate the impossibility of such a model. They were at a particularly fierce *onus probandi*
loggerhead.

Alvarez turned up the heat. Muller became desperate ("Why couldn't
Alvarez understand what I was saying? He was my scientific hero. How
could *he* be so stupid?") and decided he would win the argument on
Alvarez's terms. He grasped at the first model that occurred to him:

> Suppose there is a companion star that orbits the sun. Every 26 million
> years it comes close to the Earth and does something, I'm not sure what,
> but it makes asteroids hit the earth. Maybe it brings the asteroids with
> it.

Alvarez lapsed into uncharacteristic silence. He had been deliberately baiting Muller to come up with a model, but only because he was
holding some damaging data up his sleeve with which he could shoot
down the obvious class of explanatory models; namely, that some agent
external to our immediate solar neighborhood intruded periodically.[30]
But, since the hypothesized companion star and its asteroids would
have the same chemical signatures as materials in our solar system,
Muller's model, though very outlandish, was not vulnerable to his
counterattack.

The argument cooled down almost immediately and the two of them
began working out the specifics of whether or not the orbit was fea-
sible, what effects nearby gravity fields would have on the stability of
the companion, how far it would have to be away from earth now, and
so on. Within minutes the baiting, the name-calling, the rank-pulling,
and the belligerence had evaporated:

> "It looks good to me. I won't mail my letter." Alvarez's turnaround had
> been as abrupt as his argument had been fierce. He had switched sides
> so quickly that I couldn't tell whether I had won the argument or not. It
> was my turn to say something nice to him, but he spoke first. "Let's call
> Raup and Sepkoski and tell them that you found a model that explains
> their data."

The moral of the story is that fierce, unconstrained argumentation
is productive. Muller's hypothesis has no directly empirical support
yet, but it is a very hot topic in astronomy and paleontology at the

moment — generating papers, conferences, and arguments of equally fevered tenor, and it has a large body of astronomers developing methods to comb the heavens, pursuing the star which Muller has dubbed *Nemesis,* and the Nobel prize that would almost certainly follow its discovery.[31]

The Alvarez-Muller story is far from unique. I chose a relatively circumscribed event to illustrate the point, and a relatively novel one to minimize the strain on your patience, but such examples can be multiplied *ad libitum.* The most immediate examples are the ones that Kuhn brought to widespread scholarly attention in 1962, revolutions: Two subcommunities go at it tooth and nail over rival explanatory programs for a class of data until, at least in the more sanguine versions of Kuhn's thesis, the remainder of the truth is supplied. In less sanguine versions (usually given as straw positions in polemics against Kuhn), there is no truth at all, since debates between competing programs "fail of objectivity" and resolutions without objectivity entail only "non-rational conversions."[32] In brief, the argument runs: Truth is an objective commodity; objectivity is unavailable in Kuhn's picture of scientific change; therefore, truth is unavailable. But such arguments manufacture their difficulties with Kuhn, by confusing truth with Truth.

3. Truth and Knowledge

> In characterizing an episode or a state as that of knowing, we are not giving an empirical description of that episode or state; we are placing it in the logical space of reasons, of justifying and being able to justify what one says.
>
> — Wilfrid Sellars

It has been clear since at least the turn of the century that if there is such a thing as Truth, its home is not in science. A profusion of logics, geometries, and physical hypotheses in the latter part of the nineteenth century led to the realization that scientific theories were not, as had long been the blithe assumption, "exact and exclusive duplicates of prehuman archetypes buried in the structure of things, [in]to which the spark of divinity hidden in our intellect enables us to penetrate."[33] An instrumentalist view of science precipitated around the dominant scientist-philosophers of the period — men like Maxwell, Ostwald, Boltzmann, Duhem, Hertz, and Mach — which recognized that theories were, necessarily, symbolic representations of nature, with no more claim to exact correspondence with nature than a string of letters (say, *theory*) has to the concept it evokes. In Boltzmann's paraphrase of Hertz,

> a theory cannot be an objective thing that really agrees with nature but must rather be regarded as merely a mental picture of phenomena that is related to them in the same way in which a symbol is related to the thing symbolized. It follows that it cannot be our task to find an absolutely correct theory — all we can do is to find a picture that represents phenomena in as simple a way as possible.[34]

It cannot be the scientists' task to find the Truth, but only the truth.

This instrumentalist turn in the philosophy of science had a profound and bracing, if short-lived, effect on epistemology. It gave rise to the pragmatism of Pierce, James, and Dewey — to "more flexible and genial" notions of knowledge and truth.[35] In essence, these more genial notions are updated variants of Protagoras' position that man is the measure of all things. They take the god-term status away from *truth,* stripping away its charismatic authority, and return it to the language a leaner, more functional term. Truth becomes a relation that pieces of language have with other pieces of language — measured and mediated by man — not a metaphysical status. Truth in this view is not doled out at Genesis, to reside as a stagnant property inherent in Ideas that float in another realm: "Truth *happens* to an idea. An idea *becomes* true, is *made* true by events."[36]

It is important to notice that these instrumentalists and pragmatists were writing during the absolute apex of classical physics — a time when it seemed so certain that a prestigious professor whom Planck approached could tell him that "Physics is a branch of knowledge that is just about complete. The important discoveries, all of them, have been made."[37] And while most philosophy quickly returned to exploring Platonic and Kantian notions about certainty (until the more flexible and genial developments of Sellars and Quine and Rorty), science became more instrumental and pragmatic, in deed if not always in word. Planck developed quanta, Einstein relativity, Bohr probabilistic models of subatomic behavior, Heisenberg the uncertainty principle — to stay only with physics. All of these developments, and a great many more, drove science further away from its allegiance to certainty, most explicitly in Heisenberg's case, and in Einstein's famous aphorism "as far as the laws of mathematics refer to reality, they are not certain; as far as they are certain, they do not refer to reality."[38] But a lack of absolute certainty did not suggest to these men that quantum mechanics or relativity was false — Einstein was so sure of relativity's truth that he was notoriously unfazed by empirical arguments one way or the other[39] —just that their truth was contingent. James points out that a Beethoven string-quartet can be accurately and exhaustively explained as the scraping of horses' tails over dried cat bowels, but there are other truths which hold for the same event.[40] And these additional truths can augment, modulate, or replace that account, depending on the criteria relevant to the describer and his audience.

Moreover, these scientists made truth the old fashioned way. They hurled adverse opinions at one another until the remainder was supplied. At various levels of hostility, and to various degrees of return fire, Boltzmann attacked Planck, Planck attacked Einstein, Einstein attacked Bohr and Heisenberg; Bohr and Heisenberg had fierce arguments.[41] But hurling adverse opinions is only half the story; the more dramatic half, to be sure, but half all the same. The step from truth to knowledge is agreement, and all of these disputes ended in agreement. The agreement was not always between the principals of the dispute

(Einstein and Bohr never did agree about quantum theory), though such resolutions are clearly possible (Bohr and Heisenberg did), but there is now very widespread consensus that quanta, relativity, probabilistic subatomic behavior, and the uncertainty principle are among the soundest, most robust, pieces of knowledge in our culture.

The fight we looked at in some detail, the one between Muller and Alvarez, serves to illustrate three things about the rhetorical dimensions of these notions — instrumentalism and pragmatism — and consequently about the rhetorical dimensions of science. First, although revolutions are the most spectacular manifestations of dissent in science, they are far from the only ones. Smashing ideas against one another, like neutrinos, is productive even at very small scales. The brief debate between Muller and Alvarez has sparked a great deal of work, which, even if the big idea at the center of their theoretical instrument fails to stand up, if Nemesis is not confirmed, will no doubt spin off a great many epistemic by-products, the way NASA gave us powdered drinks and nonstick frying pans. There will be subsidiary truths. Second, like those between Bohr and Heisenberg, the squabble ended in mutual agreement. If this agreement ripples out into the general scientific community, especially if it is consonant with other pockets of agreement, particularly the ones that concern the hermeneutics of the sky, it will make new knowledge. Alvarez, for one, is certain Nemesis will be in harmony with astronomical hermeneutics, but Muller is still hedging his bets.[42]

Third, and most crucially, it illustrates the fundamental epistemic function of rhetoric, which builds the theoretical instruments of science and finds their warrants. Muller gave Alvarez a good reason to believe that Raup and Sepkoski's data could be real (not just statistically artifactual). The reason it took to please Alvarez is curious, as is his initial intransigence, but when he was finally compelled to take sympathetic notice of the data, he granted his assent. The two of them then set off immediately, building a logical space of reasons to justify asserting that Muller's model was true. This job is not over, of course, and may not be for a very long time. The essential piece of support, the essential reason, is still missing. If Muller, or someone else, can successfully assign an interpretation to the sky that fits both a broader network of reasons, woven by the historical community of astronomers, and the specific demands of his model, if he can "find Nemesis," the bulk of the job will be over, astronomers will grant their assent, and we will have a new robust piece of knowledge. (Alternatively, someone could "find Planet X" and vitiate many of the reasons to believe in Nemesis.)[43]

The central feature of this process is unquestionably rhetorical. As the sophists argued two millennia ago,[44] and more recent scholars have tenuously echoed,[45] the business of making knowledge would not get very far without talk. Even the most sacred of our truths depend on what rhetoric can do for them:

> If we think of our certainty about the Pythagorean Theorem as our
> confidence, based on experience with arguments on such matters, that
> nobody will find an objection to the premises from which we infer it,
> then we shall not seek to explain it by the relation of reason to triangu-
> larity. Our certainty will be a matter of conversation between persons,
> rather than a matter of interaction with nonhuman reality.[46]

Rorty is quite explicit on this point, echoing a long line of clear
thinkers, running through Berkeley back at least to Heraclitus: It is
extremely difficult to root knowledge and truth directly in nonhuman
reality, in the ontology of notions like triangularity. It is also, of course,
extremely difficult to root it in discourse, a notoriously loose and shift-
ing soil. But discourse has the virtue that it houses our truths, shelters
our knowledge. And we can come to understand them better if we examine the architecture of that dwelling than if we stumble blindly outside searching for an ineffable triangle.

I hold with many of the sophists — as well as with James and Rorty
and others who use different terms — that rhetoric makes truth as
well as frames it (more particularly, that it makes it as a consequence
of framing it), and this paper argues from that position in several places.
But there is no need to grant this strong form of the rhetoric-as-
epistemic thesis to see that knowledge would be oarless up a creek
without rhetoric. Suppose that the Pythagorean Theorem is somehow
True, that it is a property of something, somewhere, an Immutable
Idea in the Realm of the Forms, and not solely an instrument of human
minds. Such a reaction is natural. "When you discover these things,"
says Feynman, "you get the idea that they were somehow true before
you found them. So you get the idea that somehow they existed somewhere." He also adds, however, that "there's nowhere for such things."[47]
But let's ignore him. Let's arbitrarily deny the first of Gorgias' three
epistemic-cum-ontological principles. We are still faced with two more.
Let's say there is such a place. How would we discover the Truths that
lie there? How would we grant Them our assent, share our warrants
about Them, teach or be taught? How would we *know* without the mea-
suring, mediating, human force of rhetoric?

We wouldn't.

3.1 Dissent

> Whereas unanimity of opinion may be fitting for a church, or for the
> willing followers of a tyrant, or some other kind of "great man," variety
> of opinion is a methodological necessity for the sciences.
> — Paul K. Feyerabend

Rhetoric and hostility have always been close traveling companions.
Plato, for all his suspect motives, hits pretty close to the mark when he
lampoons a group of sophists who used to be teachers of warfare,[48] and
more recent observers have noticed that martial language defines the

way we talk about argumentation.[49] Returning to science, and to a specific example, consider the vitriol from Glashow above. It is an unmistakable symptom of the Max Planck Effect — the phenomenon whereby two opposing camps divide over paradigmatic issues along generational lines. The young Turks propose some conceptual reorganization, and their elders in the field repress that reorganization. Acrimony wells up. Ridicule and political manipulation rapidly become the prime instruments of attack. The youngsters thumb their noses at the failures of the established program, and warn that anyone who tries to maintain "the old religion" will be swept away in the tide of historical change.[50] The elders sneer at the vast array of problems the new program can't address and oppose it on the grounds that it will strand the next generation of scientists up a blind alley with no map to guide them back to the real issues of the field. In this case, Glashow defends the standard quantum mechanical view of physics that he helped to build, against the heresy of a group of theorists who are attempting to build another view of physics around undimensional curves they call *strings*. They, of course, are fighting back, making a good deal of hay out of the inconsistencies of the standard quantum program (in particular, that all attempts to reconcile it with gravity generate absurdities). Glashow, in turn, is very frank in his repression: "I do everything in my power to keep this contagious disease — I should say far more contagious than AIDS — out of Harvard."[51] *Ad hominems* are the order of the day; the Turks suggest their elders don't have the intellectual chops to follow string theory because it depends on "real mathematics, not ersatz mathematics,"[52] and the Old Guard snaps back that "the mathematics is far too difficult for [the string theorists], and they don't draw their conclusions with any rigour. So they just guess."[53]

The Max Planck Effect is just one aspect of clashing opinions in science, which very frequently involves animosity, which always involves dissent, and which is one of the prime vehicles whereby scientists make knowledge. *Opinion,* though, is rarely the word that antagonists in such a dispute choose to characterize their positions; in fact, the preferred term is a word usually taken to be its virtual antonym, *truth.* Each side is convinced that it has the program which, in the terms it chooses to frame the debate, has the brightest spark of truth to it. Each side is Certain. Yet Certainty is only supposed to obtain, as Descartes told us, when there is no room for doubt, and it is an important maxim of epistemic investigations of science that there is always room for doubt. No theory is ever fully determined by the evidence. What the underdetermination thesis should lead to, in a perfectly rational world, is a high degree of skepticism, with each scientist placing bets on the approach that seems most fruitful at the moment. And, in effect, that's pretty much what goes on as a general trend in science. But in times of conflict, when disparate paradigms clash head on, scientists on either side of the schism suspend their skepticism for the fundamental principles of their own paradigm, and magnify it for the competing paradigm. From largely the same, necessarily impoverished, body of evidence, each side is certain about its own claims to truth.

Robert Thouless noticed this phenomenon much earlier in the century, and framed it, as was the positivist wont of social scientists at the time, as a law of social psychology:

> When, in a group of persons, there are influences acting both in the direction of acceptance and rejection of a belief, the result is not to make the majority adopt the belief with a low degree of conviction, but to make some hold the belief with a high degree of conviction while others reject it also with a high degree of conviction.[54]

Thouless called his maxim the *principle of certainty,* because it notices that in precisely those instances where doubt should intercede, when there are good reasons on both sides of a question, people tend to be most certain about their beliefs. Edward Witten, for instance, one of the "Princeton String Quartet," is so convinced of the truth of string theory that he calls it "a piece of twenty-first century physics that fell by chance into the twentieth century,"[55] while Glashow is equally certain that Witten's dates are vastly off target, suggesting rather that string theory is a sterile piece of thirteenth-century scholasticism that has infected twentieth-century physics.

Thouless attributes this impulse to cognitive dissonance — "doubt and skepticism are for most people unusual and, I believe, generally unstable attitudes of mind"[56] — and he connects the desire to avoid dissonance quite explicitly to the sorts of epistemic shifts now familiar in the study of science:

> It may be that the operation of this tendency is a considerable part of the explanation of sudden intellectual conversions, in which a new opinion comes into the mind with strong conviction as a result of the spontaneous tendency of the mind to pass from the unstable and painful condition of doubt to the stable and tensionless one of certain conviction.[57]

One of the interesting aspects of Thouless's position here is that it is shared by James, who says that when you have knowledge, "epistemologically, you are in stable equilibrium."[58] Agitation is valuable, then, because it compels people to pursue the stability of sure knowledge. But James differs in two essential points, both of which connect him with sophistic lines of thought, and both of which make very clear the epistemic exigence for rhetoric of science (and, incidentally, partially mark the boundaries between psychology of science and rhetoric of science). First, whatever the psychological drivers which career people toward knowledge, truth is more the trajectory than the destination, more process than product. The meeting of belief and reality is not a matter of "truth or consequences" for James, but of "truths are consequences." "True ideas" for him "are those we can assimilate, validate, corroborate and verify."[59] At its most idle, truth is a stored charge, an action potential. A belief must have, ever ready, a battery of corroborative and verificational arguments, or it is not true.

Second, and more important, James holds that it is right to be certain in such instances. Again, the argument involves a case deflation; this time from *Rationality* to *rationality*. If the stakes are high, it is rational to have conviction on partial evidence. If one only commits oneself to a position when it is Rational to do so, when the proposition expressing it is True, when Certainty obtains, then one misses out on the world. Since these grand upper-case concepts are never attainable, a man waiting for Certainty is like a man who hesitates

> indefinitely to ask a certain woman to marry him because he was not perfectly sure that she would prove an angel after he brought her home. Would he not cut himself off from that particular angel-possibility as decisively as if he went and married someone else?[60]

When the stakes are high, as they are in paradigm clashes and marriages, skepticism can be debilitating. Witten is right to believe that string theory is a gift from the twenty-first century, because if he didn't, if his collaborators didn't, if other scientists in parallel situations didn't, as Kepler believed his insights were the gifts of God, and Darwin the gifts of Induction, there would be very little progress. What progress there was would be piecemeal, following the simple, linear-function, accretionary model that Kuhn displaced. There would be no conceptual shake-ups, no passion. Astrophysicists would be trying still to get epicycles more and more predictively accurate. By exactly the same token, Glashow is right to retrench so deeply against string theory. If there wasn't a huge amount of inertia to overcome when new perspectives surface, our communal understanding of the cosmos would rise and fall with the hemlines, a situation just as epistemically debilitating as skepticism. Within the argument fields of science, as Popper tells us, "the dogmatic scientist has an important role to play. If we give in to criticism too easily, we shall never find where the real power of our theories lies."[61] Popper's student, Feyerabend, refracts dogmatism into his principle of tenacity, which, in concert with his proliferation principle, concisely describes epistemic progress as "the active interplay of various tenaciously held views."[62]

When these tenaciously held views clash head on over foundational issues, we call the events *revolutions,* after Kuhn's generalization of a long established term for the great period of intellectual upheaval that spun medieval epistemic assumptions into their modern shape, *the* scientific revolution. The word is apt, not the least because it makes clear that what happened to western intellectual culture in that period is played out regularly on a smaller scale in individual scientific fields. But scientific change is too heterogeneous, and dissent is too widespread, for the naive application of Kuhn's normal-science-to-revolution-back-to-normal-science paradigm. There are periods in every discipline when dissent forms along broad lines and voices get louder because they're shouting in unison — when disagreements spill out into other fields and into the newspapers — but there is always at least a slow boil, a background growl of dissonance, in every field productive enough to be awarded the honorific label of *science*. Even with those periods in the development of a field that fit the concept of normal science very closely, there are innumerable disagreements about individual problems and solutions, about the character and meaning of data, about the status of anomalies, about a whole welter of empirical, methodological, and philosophical issues — not to mention the more overt power struggles over institutional organs, publication, tenure, and all the social trappings of the field.

The crucial point for our purposes is that all of this dissent is immensely productive. Science is a knowledge-generating activity, and knowledge is too precious a commodity to lay fallow for long. Rhetoric — reasoned exchange, as well as bickering, back-stabbing, barking disputation — is the life's blood of science. The point is extremely easy to establish. It is illustrated by virtually any major dispute in any science. There is usually a clear team of winners and a clear team of losers in any controversy, but if you look closely at the winning position, it almost always includes elements introduced into the dispute by the losers, elements that the winners introduced expressly to meet challenges from the losers, and elements which are simply by-products of the scuffle. That is, much of what constitutes the triumphant program, the new packet of knowledge, was either (1) appropriated from the defeated program, (2) introduced to plug holes shot in it by the gunslingers from the losing side, or (3) generated in response to issues that arose spontaneously in the heat of battle. These elements are difficult to extract directly from the statements of the antagonists, because the winners are usually too bitter to acknowledge contributions from their enemies, and the losers are usually too bitter to discriminate. The winners (who usually write the histories) come to view their victory as an intellectual triumph over error, deceit, and pig-headedness. They are loath to see, let alone acknowledge, the portions of the other program they have swallowed. The losers, as their work and its defining context become marginalized, come to view the whole process in political, rather than intellectual, terms. They usually degenerate into crankiness, and claim the victorious program, where it is not flagrantly wrong, has stolen their truths. The resulting polemical stew follows the recipe that Kellen gives for propaganda, mixing clear truth with "half truth, limited truth, truth out of context."[63]

But careful study can disentangle the components of the successful program, uncovering the network of pressure and counterpressures which shaped it. Almost every rhetorical case study of a scientific dispute traces the development of the final positions in a dispute, revealing the sources and contexts of its constituents, but, by a vast margin, the most fine-grained study of this sort is Rudwick's map of the thrust and parry that constituted the Devonian controversy in nineteenth-century geology. Indeed, some of Rudwick's visual depictions go into so much detail, tracing the trajectories of individuals and positions in the dispute, that they resemble circuit board schematics.[64]

On a more general scale, it is often the case that periods of broad intellectual turmoil are extremely productive. Certainly for the paradigmatic case of this phenomenon, the period of epistemic wrangling so productive that it warrants a definite article, *the* scientific revolution, the correlation is indisputable. The scientific achievements of the sixteenth and seventeenth centuries are best seen as symptoms, rather than as causes of a steamy agonistic climate that included a gamut of disputes — personal and social, cultural and religious, political and economic.[65] And many of these controversies enter the scientific literature as themes and leitmotifs. Galileo, for instance, wrote in Italian, to enlist the clamoring mercantile classes, and he salted his arguments with analogies to the world of commerce.[66] He also made sure to appeal to the self-importance of that upwardly mobile group by contrasting their perspicacity to "the shallow minds of the common people."[67] Most of the Copernican-Galilean champions were also lay people, though some were Protestant clergy, and most of their opponents were Catholic. Throughout Europe, Copernicanism came to "be construed as antipapal and hostile to the power of the Catholic clergy,"[68] and rode the crest of Protestant reformation. A classic text on the scientific revolution (and an important antecedent for Kuhn and Feyerabend) comments frequently on the epistemically "healthy friction" of the period, and glowingly commends agitators like Marin Mersenne, "a man who provoked enquiries, collected results, set one scientist against another, and incited his colleagues to controversy."[69]

Or consider our own century. Whatever the relation to the overwhelming mood of pathological testiness that has produced two major wars, countless minor wars (if the phrase is not an oxymoron), and the recurrent clatter of jackboots, that has seen superpowers regularly explode entire islands in order to impress one another with weapons teetering on the brink of apocalypse, that daily pits state terrorism against populist terrorism — whatever the relation to this overall storm of violence, repression, and death, the twentieth century has also seen a moil of intellectual battles and an astonishing amount of new knowledge: The theory of relativity, quantum mechanics, plate tectonics, molecular biology, cognitive psychology, and an array of less spectacular epistemic achievements, were all born of conflict and had to struggle for survival. All fit Kuhn's *revolution* like the premise of received violence apparently fits arguments toward the conclusion of returned violence.

The knowledge produced by these revolutions comes right from the heart of the tumult. Take again the very local example of Muller's argument with Alvarez. It is a synecdoche of *the* scientific revolution, and of most scientific revolutions. Alvarez, here playing the epistemic status quo, bullies, ridicules, pulls rank, withholds data, and dismisses counterarguments without a hearing. He is an intolerant authoritarian, squelching dissent. Muller, holding the new position, pleads, cajoles, grasps at straws, and probably employs a number of strategies not quite so mild, which didn't stay in his memory or didn't make it into his book. He is an intolerant revolutionary, pressing for assent. Together, they forge a compelling new theory which is now in search of the empirical support needed to achieve the rank of truth. The epistemic status quo also brought Galileo before the Inquisition and threatened to burn Kepler's mother as a witch. Galileo, for his part, employed a wide range of "psychological tricks,"[70] and Kepler tried so many tacks that Holton calls his turbid style a "mirror [of] the many-sided struggle attending the rise of modern science."[71]

Science was born of strife. Copernicus had to fight for his theories. Kepler had to fight. Galileo had to fight. And none of these fights was the fight of clear and shining Truth against the dark repression of church bureaucrats that popular mythology portrays. The scholastic world picture was full and rich. It was a largely consistent, coherent, explanatory model of the planets, of motion, of what happened when someone dropped cannon balls from the tower of Pisa. The new models (and there was an abundance of new models) quite rightly had to prove their merit in a clash with the epistemic status quo. Together, these men, their advocates and their opponents, and the fierce dialectic they all propelled, laid the cornerstones of science and the modern world.

3.2 Assent

> A man is necessarily talking error unless his words can claim membership in a collective body of thought.
> -- Kenneth Burke

For all the barking disputations of science, the product is communal assent, knowledge. The point of every argument is to gain adherence, which is to say, adherents: to increase the membership of a body of thought, to pursue assent. The first of these points is the stated exigence of one of the most lauded recent books in the history of science — that the foundation of science is the rhetoric of assent. The book, which has already made a few appearances in this paper, is Martin Rudwick's *The Great Devonian Controversy* (which Stephen Jay Gould, for instance, has hailed as potentially "one of our century's key documents in understanding science"[72]). It is a laborious case study of a forgotten geological dispute in the nineteenth century, organized around the notion that, overwhelmingly, the most characteristic form of scientific dispute is exactly like the Devonian controversy — a dispute which ended in a satisfactory resolution for all the principals and a new piece of knowledge. Such disputes then quickly drop out of view, and only their residue, the new piece of knowledge, remains. Rudwick doesn't use Booth's phrase, of course, but he very deliberately sets his argument against the loose philosophic confederation that Laudan calls the dissensus theorists[73] — people like Kuhn and Feyerabend, who hold that full resolution is unobtainable for nontrivial scientific disputes, that opposing paradigms are incommensurate. Paradigm clashes, in the view of this school, can be dispatched by political maneuvering, by superior propaganda, or simply by waiting for the Max Planck Effect to run its course, when the new program's opponents "die off, and a new generation grows up that is familiar with it."[74] But they cannot be settled in any meaningful way. Rudwick uses this school's terms for his demonstration (which, not coincidentally, are also our terms), terms like *persuasion* and *influence,* even the nonpejorative use of *rhetoric.* But where Kuhn has a note of despair that a paradigm dispute is "not the sort of battle that can be resolved by proofs,"[75] and Feyerabend glories in the irrationality that necessitates rhetoric,[76] Rudwick regards rhetoric as not only a valuable ingredient in the scientific ragout, but fundamental to its rationality. Science for Rudwick is the human activity that takes an interpretation of the physical world and makes knowledge with it, as the interpretation is "forged into new shapes with new meanings, on the anvil of heated argumentative debate."[77]

The crucial notion here is what Rudwick calls the "social and cognitive topography," but which we can discuss with terms like *context,* and *frame,* and *circumference.*[78] Rudwick's case study is essentially the close analysis of how conflicting interpretations of data pressed upon one another within the confines of the 1830s geological frame, until they fused into an interpretation that could fit the frame without too many perturbations. These interpretations would have been incoherent without that frame (or another one with similar implications). They could have neither conflicted in the first place, nor fused in the second, without the meaning lent to them by the collective body of thought that constituted stratigraphical geology in the period.

Despite Rudwick's implicit opposition to Feyerabend, the two are in complete agreement on this point, though Feyerabend makes it a little more dramatically. He argues that Michelson's set of ether drift experiments are in fact two sets of experiments — at the least, two.[79] In one context, classical mechanics, they were a failure. They failed to generate empirical evidence of drifting ether, and to that extent they were relevant; they undermined (but not disconfirmed) the tenets of the framework that predicted luminiferous ether. (When Michelson was awarded his Nobel prize in the distinctly classical milieu of 1907 no mention was made of this work.) In another context, special relativity, they were a success, obviating the need for an absolutely stationary space and dovetailing smoothly with Einstein's alternative framework. The point is very straightforward: "Experimental evidence does not consist of facts pure and simple, but of facts analyzed, modeled, and manufactured according to some theory;"[80] that is, of facts circumscribed by some collective body of thought.

However straightforward the point is, absolute theories of science find it repugnant. Notice, though, that absolutists wouldn't have any trouble if Feyerabend's comments exclusively concerned words. We all recognize that *duck* is a noun in one context, a verb in another ("Fred gave Betty a duck" and "He was lucky to duck Wilma"), and we recognize that *rake* is two nouns, one which describes a dissolute cad, perhaps Fred, and one which names a yard implement. Uncontroversially, this multiplicity is also true of technical terms. Democritus and Lucretius' *atom,* for instance, is not Rutherford and Bohr's *atom.* Democritus' *atom,* by definition, codes absolutely the smallest possible bit of matter, something which is absolutely indivisible (rather like today's quark); Rutherford's *atom* codes an object with constituents. For that matter, Rutherford's *atom* is not Bohr's, and Bohr's *atom* of 1913 is not Bohr's *atom* of 1927.

Nor do we have any trouble with sentences. We know that the string of words "Nirmala saw the man from the library" is two sentences, two propositions, depending on whether Nirmala is looking out the library window at a man, or is walking down the street and spots a man she knows to work at the library. Put in the most elemental terms with which we discuss the semantics of these complex phenomena, sentences, one interpretation can be true while the other is false, depending on the frame of reference. Again, this is uncontroversially true of technical sentences. "Parallel lines never meet" is true in some geometries, false in others. Crick's central dogma — "Information flows one way and one way only, DNA to RNA" — is true under some interpretations, false under others.

But many of us balk when something as reified as a scientific experiment is said to be ambiguous, to have more than one meaning, to *be* more than one phenomenon. This is simply prejudice. Experiments are much more complex arrangements of words and readings and relationships than sentences.

Rudwick's principal point is exactly this one, that the Devonian interpretation of geological strata is crucially dependent on the context of its creation; namely, the controversy that raged in and around the Geological Society of London from 1832 to 1842. The principals of that controversy rangled bitterly. They lied. They cheated. They performed anatomically unethical manoeuvres, going behind each other's backs and over each other's heads. They also debated, negotiated, converged, and eventually agreed on a specific interpretation. In the course of this activity, the data changed incessantly. They had different meanings at different points to different people, as the arguments which defined them changed. The core data set warranted different configurations of assent at different points in the controversy. Meaning, and therefore truth, modulated.

When the assent of the principals converged on one interpretation, they had made a new piece of knowledge, and now that the squabble has long since faded into history (or had, before Rudwick resuscitated it), that fossilized knowledge plays its part in the current context of geological assent.

Rudwick's wider point is more problematic. He argues that his case study is "a *characteristic* piece of scientific debate,"[81] which it surely is, but as his italic histrionics indicate, he also argues that most other case studies "are *uncharacteristic.*" Science, he says, is full of innumerable disputes, the vast majority of which resolve into a solution that most of the principals can grant their warranted assent. The dispute then rapidly disappears into history, leaving only the remainder of the clashed opinions, the truth, as another brick in the epistemic wall of science. He adds that humanist approaches, however, usually ignore this vast majority and focus on only the more flamboyant episodes, the ones which don't resolve smoothly, a focus which gives rise to theories of dissent, mutually hostile cohorts, and incommensurability.

His remarks hold only for *recent* humanist approaches to science, of course, but even if they held more widely, there is no reason to believe that smoothly resolved debates are more characteristic of science than any other form of debate. Certainly there are plenty of bricks of fossilized knowledge in every science, and many of them came from debates long forgotten, but that is hardly evidence that the debates all generated single solutions that all the principals found satisfactory. In the Devonian controversy, the resolution came about when the "victor" finally modified his interpretation to fall closely enough to the "loser's" position that the compromise was agreeable. They settled on a price. But if the loser had remained pig-headed to the end, and the majority of the community still found the compromise position congenial, Rudwick would surely hold (as he should) that knowledge and truth had still been served in the encounter. Or, if the loser and a significant party of backers from the general community had all remained intransigent, but had died off or were otherwise marginalized, and the victor's solution slowly took hold in the community, Rudwick would again surely hold (as he should) that knowledge resulted from the clash. When the community has sufficient warrant to reach consensus, there is knowledge.

I am not arguing that Rudwick is wrong. On the contrary, he is right. The rhetoric of science, because it is epistemic, is a rhetoric of assent. But he is right in the limited case. Assent does not come in just one characteristic flavor. More generally, Rudwick is only interested in half the picture, and is antagonistic to the other half, the rhetoric of dissent and revolution. That, he discounts as anomalous.

It should be clear by now that the rhetoric of dissent is far from anomalous, but what is more interesting for our purposes is the point Thouless raises — that it is highly unstable and either rapidly evolves into arguments which seek broader adherence, or it just dies out. As Burke's observation about collective bodies of thought indicates, saying no to one body implies saying yes to another. Rejecting one circumference implies accepting another. This is perhaps one reason that scientific revolutionaries who kill off their fathers also resurrect their grandfathers; it is extremely difficult to draw up a new program *ab novo.* Moreover, the rhetoric of dissent has an especially galvanizing effect on a revolutionary cohort, which often has a level of internal assent that borders on religious devotion. Although history presents us with a pageant of great men — Copernicus, Galileo, Newton, Darwin — most intellectual revolutions can be traced to a small fervent group, banded together in the name of truth and light to battle the prevailing error of the day. The men in the pageant were certainly great, but three additional points need to be stressed. The first has already been tabled: As great as they were, they were not without their collaborators and disciples. Indeed, they had collaborators and disciples *because* of their greatness. Copernicus had Galileo, of course, and both of them had a wealth of supporters. Newton had the Royal Society virtually in his waistcoat pocket. Darwin had a brigade, headed by Huxley. Einstein had Eddington. Bohr had Heisenberg and Pauli and the Copenhagen Institute.

The second point has also made an appearance, that the sense of being privy to the truth in the face of indifference or hostility is a powerful determinant of group ethos, inducing members of the group to say yes more loudly and widely, to go forth and convert the heathens. Einstein and Schrödinger, and others, fought the Copenhagen interpretation fervently, often resorting to blatantly metaphysical appeals, like Einstein's "God does not play dice with the universe." Max Delbrück's objective in his evangelical Cold Spring harbor course in molecular biology is widely recalled as "frankly missionary: to spread the new gospel among physicists and chemists."[82] Robert May recalls his early chaos theory call-to-arms paper for *Nature* as "messianic."[83] Most of the early chaos papers, in fact "sounded evangelical, from their preambles to their perorations."[84]

The third point, however, has not yet been raised, and it is the most important aspect of winning adherents: Regardless of conviction and oratorical prowess, if the missionaries don't have a positive program to offer when they denounce the old religion, there is little hope for widespread assent. Indeed, there is only a very weak form of assent called for in an exclusively negative rhetoric — a consensus of dissent, a communal agreement that something is wrong, without a clear idea of how to put it right. Einstein and Schrödinger, as passionate, eloquent, and sharply reasoned as their assaults on probabilistic models were, had no remotely comparable program to offer if Bohr's work was overturned. By contrast, Delbrück did. May has. Molecular biology rapidly became the framework that most scientists said yes to, and chaos studies are burgeoning. Scientists need something to do, and as James points out with his angel analogy, inactivity is too steep a price to pay for the privilege of rejecting error. To be successful, a new program has to have a wide enough circumference to embrace recruits, and set them to work right away. Aaron Novick recalls precisely that sense of expansiveness in Cold Spring Harbour, 1947:

> In that three-week course we were given a set of clear definitions, a set of experimental techniques and the spirit of trying to clarify and understand. It seemed to us that Delbrück had created, almost single-handedly, an area in which we could work.[85]

Heinz-Otto Peitgen, one of the earliest chaos converts, describes the situation in more general terms, saying that in an established program the problems that are left to work on, the ones that don't already have consensually satisfactory solutions, have usually been passed over for a reason. They are hard. Moreover, the background required just to frame the solution is often staggering. But in a new program, like chaos theory, there are less demanding opportunities: "You can start thinking today, and if you are a good scientist you might come up with interesting solutions in a few days or a week or a month."[86]

This, of course, is precisely why the word *evangelical* comes up so often in accounts of successful epistemic shifts. The rhetor's purpose is, in Socrates' terms, to win souls,[87] to convert the heathens and the innocents. And to win souls, rhetoric must offer consubstantiality; it must map out a place where the auditor can join the rhetor in some mutual enterprise, where they can both say yes together, not just no.

4. Conclusion

A rhetoric which conceives of "truth" as a transcendent entity and requires a perfect knowledge of the soul as a condition for its successful transmission automatically rules itself out as an instrument for doing the practical work of the world.

— Douglas Ehninger

The structural equation woven through this paper looks a little too neat. In one line of the argument we have the productivity of rhetoric in science, the breeding of dissent, and the forging of truth. In the other line, we have the pervasiveness of rhetoric in science, the achievement of assent, and the construction of knowledge. And, of course, it is too neat. Falling back on James once again, he says about another, equally tidy, argument, "it seems *a priori* improbable that the truth should be so nicely adjusted to our needs and powers as that. In the great boarding-house of nature, the cakes and the butter and the syrup seldom come out so even and leave the plates so clean."[88] The productivity and pervasiveness of rhetoric in science are inextricably entangled. Dissent and assent are relative, in the most profound sense of that term. Nor are truth and knowledge easily disengaged; one is the efficacy of a belief, and the other is the consent we award a belief when our warrants convince us it is efficacious. But the two threads of the discussion, however interspliced, are two threads for all that.

As long as we have James back for a moment, in the same essay where he worries about the flapjacks of nature, he offers some help here. He identifies two deep psychological drivers which define these threads. There are two reactions we have, he says, whenever we confront the world looking for knowledge: Believe truth! and Shun error![89] We want to be right, but we are nervous of being dupes. You want to agree with me, but what if I'm wrong? I want to agree with James, but what if he's wrong? We yearn for truth and fear error. Rhetoric, with its twin prongs, assent and dissent, is the discursive manifestation of both impulses.

Both prongs are associated with epistemologies of very respectable lineage. The first descends from Aristotle, had its fiercest advocate in Bacon, and is now making something of a comeback as a new inductivism, which Hacking calls "a Back-to-Bacon movement."[90] The second descends from the skeptics and sophists, had its starkest formation in Gorgias' three epistemic principles, and has seen some latter day success under the banner of Popper's falsificationism and its various radical extensions (notably with Lakatos and Feyerabend). Feyerabend, in particular, makes the antithetical nature of these epistemologies clear, with the label he chooses for his side of the divide, *counterinduction.*

Science, the primary cultural expression of our deep epistemic urges, tries very hard to follow these two paths equally. It fails often, of course, but it also succeeds, far more often and far more spectacularly than any other cultural organ. One of the reasons that rhetoric has had such bad press for so long, and that it is regularly portrayed as the evil opposite of science (and its parent, philosophy) is that Plato successfully pinned the scarlet disquisitional letter to it, and disquisition is relentlessly faithful to only one of James's deep drivers, Believe truth! The exclamatory formulation of this impulse is especially appropriate to disquisition, since its principal exponents are preachers, politicians, and salesmen — people whose sole objective is to exhort their own brand of the truth, and eliminate enquiry. By contrast, science has always understood — even if many individual scientists have not — that no matter how true an idea "may be, if it is not fully, frequently, and fearlessly discussed, it will be held as a dead dogma, not a living truth."[91] Dogma has its function, as Popper, Feyerabend, and others have argued, but science has remained epistemically quite responsible because the rhetorical antidote of dissent, revolution, and renewal have always had equal play.

It has been a dogma of humanist studies of science since the 1950s that there is no such thing as *the* scientific method, but perhaps there is. Rhetoric.

Notes

1. Lloyd F. Bitzer, "The Rhetorical Situation," *Philosophy and Rhetoric* 14 (1968): 14; see also "Functional Communication: A Situational Perspective," *Rhetoric in Transition: Studies in the Nature and Uses of Rhetoric,* Eugene E. White, ed. (University Park: The Pennsylvania State UP, 1980): 27.
2. M. McGuire, "The Ethics of Rhetoric: The Morality of Knowledge," *Southern Speech Communications Journal* 45 (1980): 147.
3. E. Claire Jerry, "Rhetoric as Epistemic: Implications of a Theoretical Position," *Visions of Rhetoric: History, Theory and Criticism,* Charles W. Kneupper, ed. (Arlington: Rhetoric Society of America, 1987): 126.
4. Chicago: U of Chicago P, 1977.

5. Quoted by James Gleick, *Chaos: Making a New Science* (New York: Viking Books, 1987): 184.

6. Wayne C. Booth, "The Scope of Rhetoric Today," *The Prospect of Rhetoric: Report of the National Development Project,* Lloyd F. Bitzer and Edwin Black, eds. (Englewood Cliffs: Prentice-Hall, 1971): 97.

7. See, for instance, *Against Method: Outline of an Anarchistic Theory of Knowledge* (London: Verso, 1978 [1975]): 260.

8. Tom Cook and Ron Seamon, "Ein Feyerabenteur," *PRE / TEXT* 1 (1980): 126.

9. *Against Method,* 30.

10. John Angus Campbell, "Darwin and *The Origin of the Species.*" *Quarterly Journal of Speech* 37 (1970): 1–14, "The Polemical Mr. Darwin," *Quarterly Journal of Speech* 61 (1975): 375–90, "Scientific Revolution and the Grammar of Culture," *Quarterly Journal of Speech* 72 (1986): 351–76. See also Barbara Warnick, "A Rhetorical Analysis of an Episteme Shift," *The Southern Speech Communication Journal* 49 (1983): 26–42.

11. "The Birth of Molecular Biology," *Rhetoric Review* 3 (1984): 70–83.

12. John Lyne and Henry F. Howe, "Punctuated Equilibria," *Quarterly Journal of Speech* 72 (1986): 132–147.

13. Wilda Anderson, *Between the Library and the Laboratory: The Language of Chemistry in Eighteenth-Century France* (Baltimore: Johns Hopkins Press, 1984).

14. Alan G. Gross, "On the Shoulders of Giants: Seventeenth-Century Optics as an Argument Field," *The Quarterly Journal of Speech* 74 (1988): 1–17. Gross, however, does not pay sufficient attention to Newton's different public ethoi when he made his two offerings. The *Principia* came in between, giving his words on optical theory considerably more authority in 1704 than they had in 1672.

15. See James Zappen, "Historical Studies in the Rhetoric of Science and Technology," *The Technical Writing Teacher* 14 (1987): 285–98, for a good survey of this literature. Lyne and Howe, 145n2 contains a few additional references.

16. See Robert Rosenthal, *Experimenter Effects in Behavioral Research* (New York: Irvington, 1976), and "How Often Are Our Numbers Wrong?" *American Psychologist* 33 (1978): 1005–8.

17. Quoted in John Boslough, *Stephen Hawking's Universe: An Introduction to the Most Remarkable Scientist of Our Time* (New York: Quill, 1985): 66. See George Greenstein, *Frozen Star: Of Pulsars, Black Holes, and the Fate of Stars* (New York: New American Library, 1984): 362–6, for some interesting, not to say peculiar, meditations on these neuroses.

18. Noam Chomsky [with Mitsou Ronat], *Language and Responsibility* (New York: Pantheon Books, 1979): 171.

19. Gerald Holton, *Thematic Origins of Scientific Thought,* rev. ed. (Cambridge: Harvard UP, 1988): 79.

20. See James A. Secord, "King of Siluia: Roderick Murchison and the Imperial Theme in Nineteenth-Century Geology," *Victorian Studies* 25 (1982): 413–42, for an examination of, among other interesting issues, names in early Victorian geology.

21. Alan G. Gross, "The Form of the Experimental Paper: A Realization of the Myth of Induction," *The Journal of Technical Writing and Communication* 15 (1984): 15–26.

22. See the survey in J. Hartley, M. Trueman, and A. J. Meadows, "Readability and Prestige in Scientific Journals," *Journal of Information Science* 14 (1988): 67–75.

23. Alfred de Grazia, "The Scientific Reception System," *The Velikovsky Affair,* Alfred de Grazia, ed. (New Hyde Park, NY: University Books, 1966): 207.

24. Martin Rudwick, *The Great Devonian Controversy* (Chicago: U of Chicago P, 1985): 404.

25. Richard S. Westfall, "Newton and the Fudge Factor," *Science* (23 February) 179: 731–2.

26. Sheldon Glashow, "Tangled up in Superstring: Some Thoughts on the Predicament Physics is in," *The Sciences* (May/June): 25.

27. The quotation is from Robert Kanigel and Geoffrey Cowley, "The Seamy Side of Science," *The Sciences* (July/August) 28: 47. The books are: Roger Lewin, *Bones of Contention: Controversies in the Search for Human Origins* (New York: Simon and Schuster, 1987), Gary Taubes, *Nobel Dreams: Power, Deceit, and the Ultimate Experiment* (New York: Random House, 1988), William Broad and Nicholas Wade, *Betrayers of the Truth* (New York: Schuster and Schuster, 1983).

28. All unattributed quotations in the remainder of this section are from Richard Muller, *Nemesis, the Death Star: The Story of a Scientific Revolution* (New York: Weidenfeld & Nicolson, 1988): 3–9.

29. Quoted by Malcolm Browne, "The Debate over Dinosaurs Takes an Unusually Rancorous Turn," *The New York Times* (19 January 1988): C4.

30. Alvarez knew of a recent finding that the geological layer associated with the extinction of the dinosaurs has an isotopic signature (a rhenium-187/rhenium-185 ratio) that matches the rest of Earth's crust, indicating that whatever caused the catastrophe which eliminated the dinosaurs was formed at the same time as our solar system, hence was very likely formed as part of our solar system. Ironically, this is a pretty weak counterargument, since it is fairly easy to imagine a model in which some external agent disturbed asteroids or comets within the solar system which then plowed into the earth. Indeed, even if Muller's star was formed in another part of the galaxy altogether, at another time, and therefore didn't have the rhenium signature (if, say, it was passing by and was somehow trapped into a new orbit by our sun), Muller's theory would have exactly the same practical consequences (disturbing the Oordt comet belt and hurling some of those comets into the inner solar system).

31. Returning to an earlier theme for a moment, notice how the name, which quickly picked up an attendant epithet, *the death star,* is one of the reasons that Muller's hypothesis is such a hot topic. Here we also have clear evidence that Muller knew exactly what he was doing when he chose the name. He says that he was inspired by Gell-Mann's *quark* to pour over *Bulfinch's Mythology* looking for a name with just the right ring of classicism and violence. David Raup, *The Nemesis Affair: A Story of the Death of Dinosaurs and the Ways of Science* (New York: W. W. Norton, 1987): 145, attributes some of the theory's success to its name — which he wisely borrowed for the title of his own book on the catastrophic extinction controversies, to help ensure *its* success. Muller himself uses not only the name in his title, but also its Homerian epithet. Moreover, he admits that a competing hypothesis, based on a hidden tenth planet, is "even cleverer than the Nemesis theory," adding ingenuously, "Maybe it was even true, and we should be searching for Planet X rather than Nemesis. I hoped

not. I thought 'Nemesis' was a better name than 'Planet X'" (176). One of the principal opponents apparently recognizes the power of the name, since he refused to use it at a major conference on catastrophic extinction hypotheses, referring to it only as "the putative death star" (Muller, 154).

32. Israel Scheffler, *Science and Subjectivity* (Indianapolis: Bobbs-Merrill, 1967): 84.

33. William James, *The Meaning of Truth: A Sequel to "Pragmatism"* (Cambridge: Harvard UP, 1975 [1909]): 40.

34. Quoted in Paul K. Feyerabend, *Realism: Rationalism & Scientific Method, Philosophical Papers 1* (Cambridge: Cambridge UP, 1981): 9. Feyerabend's translation.

35. William James, *The Meaning of Truth,* 41. I am, of course, collapsing variations, uncertainties, controversies and developments in using terms like *instrumentalism* and *pragmatism,* just as when I use terms like *rhetoric* and *science.* Mach's instrumentalism, for instance, was not Boltzmann's, and Pierce had problems with James's treatment of truth. But, again like *rhetoric* and *science,* they are convenient pegs on which to hang important intellectual themes.

36. William James, *Pragmatism* (Cambridge: Harvard UP, 1975 [1907]): 97. James's italics.

37. Barbara Lovett Cline, *The Men Who Made a New Physics* (Chicago: U of Chicago P, 1983 [1965]): 34.

38. Albert Einstein, *Sidelights on Relativity,* G. B. Jeffrey and W. Perret, trans. (New York: Dover Books, 1983 [1922]): 28.

39. See, for instance, Ilse Rosenthal-Schneider, *Reality and Scientific Truth,* Thomas Braun, ed. (Detroit: Wayne State UP, 1983): 74, for Einstein's classic reaction to the news that Eddington had confirmed the effect of gravity on light.

40. William James, *The Will to Believe and Other Essays in Popular Philosophy* (Cambridge: UP, 1896): 76.

41. Virtually any text on the history of physics tells of these, and many other, confrontations. See, for instance, Lovett Cline, where they are discussed, respectively, on pages 49f, 120, 235–44, and 201.

42. See Alvarez's preface to Muller's book (esp., xiii), and Muller's remarks about Planet X in note 31 above.

43. There is at least one other point that Muller's discussion raises (as does the instrumentalist discussion above): that the depiction of scientists as deluded rhetors given earlier in the paper is something of a caricature. Muller is, however unequipped with the analytical machinery of rhetorical theory, quite aware of the discursive, argumentative, suasive aspects of his field. Raup's book on the same set of disputes reveals an even deeper awareness of the extent to which "science is basically an adversarial process" (147), and, in general, the closer a scientist is to controversy, the more aware he is of productive nature of dissent.

44. See, for instance, Richard Leo Enos, "The Epistemology of Gorgias' Rhetoric: A Re-examination," *Southern Speech Communication Journal* 42 (1976): 35–51.

45. For instance, Robert Scott's seminal "On Viewing Rhetoric as Epistemic," *Central States Speech Journal* 18 (1967): 9–17, and his reappraisal and survey, "On Viewing Rhetoric as Epistemic: Ten Years Later," *Central States Speech Journal* 27 (1976): 258–66.

46. Richard Rorty, *Philosophy and the Mirror of Nature* (Princeton: Princeton UP, 1979): 157.

47. Quoted in P. C. W. Davies and J. Brown's book of interviews, *Superstrings: A Theory of Everything?* (London: Cambridge UP, 1988): 208.
48. *Euthydemus,* 275^c.
49. George Lakoff and Mark Johnson, *Metaphors We Live By* (Chicago: U of Chicago P, 1980): 4ff.
50. The quotation is Muller's characterization of gradualist extinction theories, page 152.
51. In Davies and Brown, *Superstrings,* page 157.
52. Abdus Salam, in Davies and Brown, *Superstrings,* page 179.
53. Richard Feynman, in Davies and Brown, *Superstrings,* page 194.
54. Robert H. Thouless, "The Tendency to Certainty in Religious Belief," *British Journal of Psychology* 26 (1935): 24.
55. Quoted in K. C. Cole, "A Theory of Everything," *The New York Times Magazine* (18 October 1987): 28.
56. Thouless, 29.
57. *Ibid.*
58. William James, *Pragmatism,* 97.
59. *Ibid.,* 41.
60. William James, *The Will to Believe,* 26.
61. "Normal Science and its Dangers," *Criticism and the Growth of Knowledge: Proceedings of the International Colloquium in the Philosophy of Science, London 1965,* I. Lakatos and A. Musgrave, eds. (London: Cambridge UP, 1970): 55.
62. *Problems of Empiricism, Philosophical Papers 2* (London: Cambridge UP, 1981): 142.
63. Konrad Kellen, "Introduction," Jaques Ellul, *Propaganda: The Formation of Men's Attitudes,* Konrad Kellen and Jean Lerner, trans. (New York: Random House, 1965): v.
64. See especially, 412–3.
65. See, for instance, Margaret C. Jacob, *The Cultural Meaning of the Scientific Revolution* (New York: Alfred A. Knopf, 1988).
66. For instance, he compares an experimenter who lets errors creep into his work with "a calculator who does not know how to keep proper accounts," *Two Chief World Systems,* Stillman Drake, trans. (Berkeley: U of California P, 1967 [1632]): 207.
67. *Discoveries and Opinions of Galileo,* Stillman Drake, trans. (New York: Doubleday, 1957 [1610]): 200.
68. Jacob, 25.
69. Herbert Butterfield, *The Origins of Modern Science,* rev. ed. (New York: Macmillan, 1957): 83.
70. Feyerabend, *Against Method,* 81.
71. Holton, 54.
72. Stephen Jay Gould, "A Triumph of Historical Excavation," *The New York Review of Books* (27 February 1986): 9. For an even more extravagant appraisal, see Frank M. Turner, "Scientific Resolution," *Isis* 77 (1986): 508–11, where the book is "brilliant and probing," where the study of science is divided into "a pre- and a post-Rudwick era," and where Rudwick is compared favorably with Francis Bacon.
73. Larry Laudan, *Science and Values* (Chicago: U of Chicago P, 1984).
74. Max Planck, *Scientific Autobiography and Other Papers,* F. Gaynor, trans. (New York: Philosophical Library, 1949): 33–4.
75. *The Structure of Scientific Revolutions,* 2nd ed. (Chicago: U of Chicago P, 1970): 148.

76. For instance, consider this passage: "[the ideal scientist's] aims remain stable, or change as a result of argument, or of boredom, or of a conversion experience, or to impress a mistress," *Against Method,* 189.
77. Rudwick, 455.
78. Rudwick, 421. Karl Wallace, "The Substance of Rhetoric: Good Reasons," *The Quarterly Journal of Speech* (1963) 44, p. 242, is quite explicit about the conditioning effect of context in scientific argumentation: "The scientist cannot escape choices, whether he is addressing other scientists or a popular audience. His decisions are anchored in contexts governed by rules, conventions, and practices, whether they be those of the scientist or those of the non-scientist public."
79. *Problems of Empiricism,* 152f.
80. *Realism, Rationalism, and the Scientific Method,* 61.
81. Page xxii.
82. Gunther Stent, "That Was the Molecular Biology that Was," *Science* (26 April 1968): 363.
83. Quoted by Gleick, 80.
84. *Ibid.,* 39.
85. Aaron Novick, "Phenotypic Mixing," *Phage and the Origins of Molecular Biology,* John Cairns, Gunther Stent, and James Watson, eds. (Cold Spring Harbour: Cold Spring Harbour Laboratory of Quantitative Biology, 1966): 134–5.
86. Quoted by Gleick, 230.
87. *Phaedrus,* 261.
88. *The Will to Believe,* 22.
89. *Ibid.,* 17ff.
90. Ian Hacking, *Representing and Intervening* (Cambridge: Cambridge UP, 1983), 150.
91. John Stuart Mill, *On Liberty* (Indianapolis: Hackett Publishing, 1978 [1859]): 34.

Joseph Cornell and the Artistry of Composing Persuasive Hypertexts

Joseph Janangelo

Joseph Janangelo's essay calls attention to the constantly evolving nature of argumentative (and all) discourse. He begins his essay by drawing from Margaret Mead's notion of a prefigurative culture — one in which adults must learn from children as they teach them because the knowledge the adults grew up with is no longer fully useful. Janangelo asks argument teachers to consider this paradigm in light of the rapid technological changes happening in our culture. Specifically, he asks teachers to imagine a future in which large numbers of students are writing persuasive hypertexts. He suggests we prepare for such a moment by understanding the relationship between hypertext (texts created from a collection of linked screens on the computer) and postmodern culture, particularly the uniquely American artistic form of collage.

Drawing on the work of collage artist Joseph Cornell, Janangelo argues that persuasive hypertexts can conform to the academic desire for focus, coherence, and purpose. In order for this to happen, though, teachers must be willing and able to read students' hypertexts in new ways and, more importantly, to help students adapt traditional rhetorical standards of persuasion to these texts. This kind of give and take between student and teacher and between academic and popular cultures is inevitable, Janangelo suggests, in an age when technology and communication are changing at an unprecedented speed.

As our notions of the nature of text change, so must our means of composing it.
— George Landow ("Rhetoric of Hypermedia" 102)

And there's Joe Cornell who would pick things up and put them in boxes.
— a museum guide, The Art Institute of Chicago

In *Culture and Commitment,* anthropologist Margaret Mead identifies three cultural styles. They include the *"postfigurative,* in which children learn primarily from their forebears, *cofigurative,* in which both children and adults learn from their peers, and *prefigurative,* in which adults learn also from their children" (1). Mead argues that unprecedented technologies such as computers propel us into the prefigurative era where concepts "bound to the past, could provide no models for the future" (72). Drawing on Mead's work, Gail Hawishor and Cynthia Selfe discuss teachers' resistance to incorporating electronic writing into literacy instruction. Situating that resistance within a framework of cultural change, they use the term "prefigurative" to say that we teach at a time "where change is so rapid that adults are trying to prepare children for experiences the adults themselves have never had" (160).

The reality of having no models to teach by recently hit me when two students turned in persuasive hypertexts after I had assigned print-based term papers. By the terms "persuasive," I refer to hypertexts that students compose in order to show teachers that they have grasped the course content.[1] Both texts were turned in without drafts in order to fulfill incompletes. Hence, my help in drafting was not solicited. While I cannot replicate these texts in linear prose, I will try to describe them. The first text was written by a graduate student. It was supposed to be a ten- to twelve-page conference paper on composition theory. Instead, his project was a simulated hypertext — a linear text designed to represent linked screens. The text included an envelope of quotations and reflections. It also offered instructions for reading, showing how the envelope's texts could be "linked in diverse ways" so as to keep meaning in "continuous oscillation." The second text, written by a graduating senior who had access to his parents' software, was supposed to be a critical examination of two or three literary texts that meant the most to him. Instead of thesis-driven prose, I received dozens of linked screens. They featured the titles of novels, plays, poems, films, and compact discs. The author offered no prefatory comment or explanatory prose. Both of these texts struck me as elaborate, yet unsatisfying. They seemed to present much of what their authors had read and thought rather than to offer a focused response to a specific assignment. Due to their intertextuality, I found these texts to be much like poor print-based term papers where authors write in bulk (i.e., include lots of quotations) without specifying any rationale for the inclusion of quoted passages. Beyond that, both authors seemed to think that their texts could thrive on a juxtaposition, rather than integration, of readymade texts.

The desire to link texts seems endemic to hypertext — especially when we consider Richard J. Selfe's definition:

> A term coined by T. H. Nelson in the 1960s . . . hypertext refers to the non-sequential arrangement of text-based information. Hypertexts are broken down into *nodes,* small units of text (screens of text, of text and graphics, or scrolling screens of text and graphics, for instance), which are *linked,* or connected to other nodes in *webs,* or connected sets of information. (217)

To Selfe's definition, I would add Miller's and Knowles's explanation that "Electronic hypertexts are marked links that are highlighted in color or underlined or both" (177). I would also add Moulthrop's cue that "Invoking the link, by typing a phrase on a keyboard or sending some indication through a pointing device (or 'mouse') brings the indicated passage to the screen" (18–19). But while I had no trouble physically invoking my students' links, I experienced great difficulty discerning what those links meant. My inability to follow the intellectual connections behind the links led me to assign the texts low grades and to write to their authors about the communicative impasse I experienced. Mead might attribute my actions to my postfigurative orientation. She writes that as community elders, parents and teachers "still hold the seats of power and command" (74). Yet instead of changing and learning from our students, "we are making do with what we know" — in this case venerating the paradigms of linear prose — while "dwelling in [the security of] old patterns with new and better understood materials" (75).[2]

Although it is true that, given financial constraints and the power of print culture, most writing teachers will not be receiving many persuasive hypertexts any time soon, it interests me that some students are beginning to compose beyond print paradigms — even if they must simulate hypertextual format to do so. This experimentation is especially interesting because it took place at a school like mine, which is not especially technologically advanced. For example, at my school computer-assisted writing courses are the exception rather than the rule. We share a writing lab (not designed with composition courses in mind) with other departments, and when we teach hypertext it tends to be at the graduate level as a theoretical model, a discursive enactment of postmodern theory rather than as a prose model for students to emulate. To me, the fact that my institution is more invested in teaching print than electronic writing makes it especially suggestive and interesting that I am receiving such texts from students. It makes me wonder if the use of hypertext programs at the K–12 levels is leading students to compose with an understanding that linear argumentation is not the only credible form that academic writing can take.[3]

Yet, as a community elder, I am conscious of the paradox that the discourse features best suited to hypertext are difficult to use in composing academic discourse as it is traditionally conceived. I also suspect that the presentational and rhetorical possibilities offered by hypertext invite us to think beyond linear models of argumentation. Having reassessed my negative response to students' experimentation, I began looking for ways to create "a safe and flexible environment" (Mead 89) in which students could learn from me while also teaching me about their innovative literate activities. With this purpose, I began reading scholarship in the use of computers in composition in order to see how flexible other teachers and institutions had become.

The first relevant text I found was published in 1992 by Curtis and Klem. They write that "it may well be from our students — less encumbered than we by old habits — that insights into the computer's potential for novel procedures *and even products* will come" (161–2). This phrase is followed by a note, part of which reads: "Hypertext shows that the products appropriate to reading as well as writing on computers may be indeed very different from those produced in traditional fashion and for traditional print" (170). Three years later this issue was raised as a query in an online discussion: "My first question about hypertext is how we will deal with these documents? Can we use them only for the writing process, or can we use the product in some way? Since most academic papers have a point, how can we use this kind of technology to count as an academic paper?" (qtd. in Gruber 66).

Intrigued by this query, I turned to Thomas J. DeLoughry's many fine articles on electronic communication in *The Chronicle of Higher Education* to see how other colleagues were embracing electronic writing. One article entitled "Term Papers Going High Tech" addresses the issues directly. The text begins with a celebratory tone, reporting that "Those who assign electronic term papers say the technology adds a new twist to their courses and the processes of developing the projects can teach students new communication skills and improve their comprehension of the subjects that they are studying" (A23). The celebration becomes qualified, however, as one instructor admits, "What will come of it, I'm not quite sure. . . . This may just be a total dud" (A25). Things become further qualified as DeLoughry tells us that students will not receive high grades for just putting photographs and movies in the computer. He includes another teacher's declaration that "the last thing I want them to do is create a collage" (A25).

Discussing hypertext in terms of a collage is understandable because both forms make use of readymade materials. Yet, dismissing collage as an intrinsically unsuitable model for academic discourse seems unwarranted. A fine collage may seem like a casual construction while being in fact a complex work of deliberate artistry representing the artist's ability to carefully recompose existing texts in thoughtful and persuasive ways. The artistry involved in composing an effective collage also reflects "a poetics of the *ready-made*" — one which suggests "that casual form is a work of art if we manage to imagine the shaping strategy of an author behind it" (Eco, *Six* 116).[4] The idea that a collage artist has a shaping strategy that informs all textual decisions is a good one to offer writers who may wish to create persuasive hypertexts. By showing students how a collage artist transforms found material (e.g., course readings and outside sources) into a persuasive collection, we can help them see that the act of selecting and linking texts is a challenging intellectual activity — one to which elements of western rhetoric pertain even when they are reconfigured by technology. My purpose is to use a specific poetics of collage to explore the parallels between artistic and written discourse. I hope to show that composing a persuasive collage or hypertext requires rhetorical skill, and also to show how this kind of skill is modeled in the work of the American collage artist Joseph Cornell (1903–72).[5]

Joseph Cornell, once called "'the Benvenuto Cellini of Flotsam and Jetsam'" (qtd. in Tashjian 15), did more than pick things up and put them in boxes. His boxes, models of informed selection and minimalist presentation, enact a poetics of collage that we can use to model the intelligence, complexity, and artistry of persuasive hypertexts. My aim is to suggest ways of using Cornell's art in order to create an appreciation of the ways that textual coherence can manifest itself, and to discern a shaping strategy that may help us support students' prefigurative literate activities. The specific features that pertain to Cornell's art and that can pertain to persuasive hypertexts are the minimalist use of readymade texts; the knowledgeable linking of disparate materials; and the creation of a critical commentary to illuminate the intellectual connections that motivate the links.[6] These features will inform my reading of Cornell's tribute to "Mad" King Ludwig of Bavaria. Before offering my reading of Cornell, though, I will review hypertext's central features — those of intertextuality and postmodern monumentality — and describe how they can complicate acts of interpretation.

Intertextuality and Postmodern Monumentality: Celebrations and Concerns

"Hypertext assumes a world of multiple texts" that coexist, via links, within one document (Perfetti 159). This coexistence gives hypertext its profound intertextuality. In 1992, Eldred and Fortune examined the metaphors used to describe hypertext's "intertextual aspects" (70). They found those metaphors to be "marked by their emphasis on connectivity" with stress on how texts "relate and interact" (70). Some scholars celebrate this interaction. George Landow writes that hypertext serves "to liberate us from the confinements of inadequate systems of classification and to permit us to follow [the mind's] natural proclivities for 'selection by association, rather than by indexing'" (*Hypertext* 15).[7] Umberto Eco adds that hypertext offers freedom of linkage: "One works on its pre-existing links and can navigate this labyrinth indefinitely by establishing (and inventing) personal connections" ("Texts" A4). More recently, Michael Joyce has argued that the connections become more fluid as they mutate. Consider his comparison of print and electronic writing:

> Print stays itself; electronic text replaces itself. If with the book we are always printing — always opening another text unreasonably composed of the same gestures — with electronic text we are always painting, each screen unreasonably washing away what was and replacing it with itself. (186)

The phenomenon of "washing away" allows hypertext to maintain its perpetual draft status.

In *The Electronic Word: Democracy, Technology, and the Arts*, Richard Lanham celebrates hypertext's evolving inscriptions. He cites the western visual arts as evidence that digital expression is the fulfillment of "postmodern monumentality" (46), which conceptualizes composing as an ongoing, perpetual project. Lanham describes "the postmodern critique" as a time of "outward frame-expanding" (50) when artists [read here as "writers"] are so committed to composing and revising texts that "our poetics will require some basic non-Aristotelian adjustments" (7). Lanham writes that digital expression supports interactive text. This interaction, which represents our wish to compose without end, takes many forms. It includes the video release of films with alternative endings and the multiplication of texts such as Warhol's *Thirty [Mona Lisas] Are Better Than One* (40). It also finds architectural precedent in buildings like Paris' Centre Pompidou (a.k.a. *Le Beaubourg*) whose facade reveals "the undisguised guts of the building and finely ornamented surface," thereby announcing the structure's deliberate "bi-stability" (72). This gesture motivates works like Oldenburg's "play/purpose reversals" where the everyday object receives a "scaling up" (42), and "gargantuan projects" (49) like Christo's *Running Fence,* which was soon dismantled and recomposed as another draft text. For Lanham, "The book for *Running Fence* is one kind of 'printout' among many, which, taken together, form a record of the artistic event" (49). In describing the desired reception of such texts, he writes that, "We will construe them not as absolute entities but as part of an expressive process both alphabetic and iconic, an entity whose physicality is manifest, whose rhetoric is perfectly self-conscious, that is to say whose place in a complex matrix of behavior forms a native part of its expression" (49).

While hypertext scholars are intrigued by this complex matrix of intertextuality and postmodern monumentality, they also realize that,

when it comes to written discourse, these same features can complicate acts of reading. One complication involves size. John Slatin argues that while a print text is often "winnowed out of a larger mass of
material," a "hyperdocument 'grows' by a process of accretion" (876).
Thus, "Thanks to the capability of creating nodes and links, material
not linearly related to the point . . . need not be thrown away . . . This
inclusiveness . . . means that the hyperdocument is in fact a collection
of possible documents" (876). Yet a rhetoric of endless growth conflicts
with the idea, endemic to academic prose, that persuasion is usually
predicated on focus, selection, and strategic presentation. "The writer's
job in this context is to contrive a sequence that will not only determine the reader's experience and understanding of the material but
will also seem to the reader to have been the only possible sequence for
that material; you want it to seem to have been somehow inevitable"
(Slatin 872). My concern, based on reading my students' hypertexts, is
that they may confuse the ability to link materials with intellectual
enrichment, subscribing to the idea that saying all that you know (or
linking as much as you can find) about a topic is better than selecting
your evidence based on an analysis of your reader's questions, knowledge, and needs. When Landow suggests that "Hypertext demands the
presence of many blocks of texts that can be linked to one another"
(1992, 187), he is not saying that texts will automatically become more
sophisticated as they increase in size. He realizes the difference between an artful and an ineffective "scaling up" (Lanham 42) — and
knows that the latter may consign the reader to " 'purposeless wandering'" (qtd. in Biemiller A55) as a result of the indiscriminate collection
of readymade materials.

The fact that hypertext can turn a reader into a wanderer constitutes another complication. Davida Charney notes that "Most people
conceive of *text* as a collection of ideas that a writer has carefully selected, framed, and organized into a coherent sequence or pattern in
hopes of influencing a reader's knowledge, attitudes, or actions" (238).
Yet, "the net effect of hypertext systems is to give readers much greater
control over the information they read and the sequence in which they
read it" (248). Another concern, then, is that the author's reliance on
the reader's ability to link texts in ways that stimulate important connections (remember my student's wish to keep meaning in "continuous
oscillation") can create unresolvable interpretive issues by overwhelming the reader with too much choice. Of course, hypertexts vary from
one another and many types can be discerned. Michael Joyce distinguishes between those texts where authors try to structure the reader's
response and those where authors invite readers to "compose" the text.
Charney talks mostly about hypertexts designed to structure reader
response, while Lanham celebrates a more "artistic" mode. Such texts
are aimed at different audiences and will serve different purposes. It is
understandable that students unschooled in hypertext composition
would choose a more inventive form because it allows for the exercise
of their creativity even in instances where a more structured hypertext

would be appropriate. My belief is that, whether in a print or electronic environment, students need to take the expectations of "coherence" on the part of the readers into consideration. As Gary Heba writes, students must create a "presentation environment" (34) that is "readable" (36) and coherent.[8]

This emphasis on coherence has caught the attention of several scholars. In "The Rhetoric of Hypermedia: Some Rules for Authors," George Landow warns against mere giganticism. He writes that "simply linking one text to another" fails to achieve coherence "and can even alienate the user" (81) who may resent having to navigate the text in order to find the desired material. Davida Charney details this alienation. Defining linking as an associative and potentially insular activity, she thinks that "hypertext may dramatically increase the burdens on both readers and writers" who are "purposively seeking" (241). She argues that, given the plurality and mutability of linkages, interpretation "may simply reduce itself to a guessing game, as the user figures out what the hypertext writer . . . had in mind when creating a link" (259). In this sense "the trails of associations in a hypertext may represent the ultimate in what Linda Flower calls 'writer-based prose,' prose that reflects the writer's process of coming to terms with a set of ideas but that may bear little relation to his or her final stance and none whatsoever to the readers' needs" (259).

Mutability and ambiguity have important consequences for composing and interpreting text. Landow and Delaney write that "Hypertext linking, reader control, and continual re-structuring not only militate against modes of argumentation to which we have become accustomed, but they have other, more general effects. The reader is now faced by a kind of textual randomness . . . [as] the text appears to break down, to fragment and atomize into constituent elements (the *lexia* or block of text), and these reading units take on a life of their own . . ." (9–10). Similarly, Catherine Smith reports on the readers' difficulties. She notes that the text "often appears to the user to have no large-grain structure" and that "All links and nodes seem accessible from any point in the graph and equally relevant" (275).[9] Smith reports such problems as readers "getting lost in multiperspectival space," becoming "baffled by being presented with three equally significant options," and feeling "no motivation to choose at all" (277). She calls this last problem "equipotentiality" — a condition in which "all the perspectives seem equally important or interesting" (279). Equipotentiality underscores the image of hypertext as an unfocused species of discourse — a kind of casual collage where texts are linked, but where the logic of the linkages can appear ambiguous and arbitrary.

Several scholars suggest ways that writers can specify the logic of their linkages. Yet while they describe "apparatuses designed to aid information retrieval" (Landow, *Hypertext* 66), they sometimes criticize cuing aids that merely emulate print-based prose.[10] These scholars resist "making do with what we know" (Mead 75), and seek models that envision coherence beyond the sequential arrangement of text.

This is where Cornell's work becomes valuable. Although Cornell, whose art has been called "a totem of the self" (Simic 62), is an unlikely purveyor of clarity, his work and ideas about composing suggest a shaping strategy that can help authors transform readymade material into coherent and persuasive nonsequential text. At this point, I wish to introduce the artist and move to a reading of one box.

Cornell and Hypertextual Artistry

Joseph Cornell is known for his "'shadow boxes,' small-scale box constructions in which pasted papers, reproductions, sand, pipes, and other found objects are assembled in a kind of collage with depth, framed in wood, and usually sealed with glass" (Waldman 7). Intrigued by enclosed spaces, he composed boxes that simulate ballet stages, bird cages, hotel rooms, jewel cases, and pinball machines. Devoted to the arts, he crafted tributes to writers (Emily Dickinson), celebrities (Hedy Lamarr), and monarchs (King Ludwig II of Bavaria) who captured his interest.

Cornell's credo was "'collage'=life" (qtd. in Caws 311). In *Dime Store Alchemy: The Art of Joseph Cornell,* the poet Charles Simic dignifies collage, declaring that "Only such an all-inclusive aesthetic could make sense of American reality" (23). Curator Diane Waldman suggests that Cornell's seemingly "illogical juxtapositions" enact "the Duchampanian concept of the Readymade, in the sense that the images are pre-existing, altered not by the hand of the artist but by the decision-making process of his mind and imagination" (17). Cornell's creative process led him to New York City bookstores, cafeterias, and record shops in order to collect "sightings" — images and texts — for his boxes (Caws 32). His collages link disparate texts, yet don't explain the precise logic of the linkages. Evoking what he called "that something no words can hold" (qtd. in Caws 231) — think here of previously cited evocations of hypertext's ambiguity and mutability — "each box works by the ineffable associations among its own objects . . ." (Caws 29). The interplay among these associations inspires Simic to call Cornell's work "A force illegible" (28).

Despite Simic's praise, Cornell's work on a first encounter resembles that of a glorified junk-monger — someone who is indiscriminate in his collections, recondite in his references, and arbitrary in his juxtapositions. The fact that Cornell is admired for his inscrutability distances him from student writers who, whether in hyper- or print-textual performances, are rarely rewarded for being mysterious. Yet Cornell is no accidental artist. His collages give evidence of close reading, purposeful selection, and strategic presentation. I hope to prove this, and to show how these elements can serve as a model for composing persuasive hypertexts, by engaging in a thought experiment — one that involves reading and responding to Cornell's King Ludwig tribute as if it were a hypertext draft. My experiment has two purposes — to show how an author can communicate and specify meaning hypertextually, and to suggest ways that teachers can use their knowledge of

rhetoric to help students refine their nonsequential, collagistic compositions.[11]

Opening the Box

Imagine that Cornell's assignment reads: "Please research and write a
persuasive hypertext about a historical figure with whom you identify.
Focus your discussion on key points of identification, and explain the
relevance of the passages you present and link." Like Cornell's text,
many drafts arrive untitled. Yet critics like Dickran Tashjian, whose
interpretation of Cornell's work I will treat as analogous to that of a
teacher reading a hypertext draft, refer to it as *The Life of King Ludwig
of Bavaria.* Unlike some of Cornell's collages, this tribute is not an actual "box." It is a valise that resembles, upon initial inspection, a cluttered briefcase, a freeform collage, or — pursuing my analogy between
collage and hypertext — a rough draft. This resemblance becomes more
explicit as we consider Tashjian's description of its contents:

> The interior cover of the valise reveals a sepia photograph of an outra-
> geously baroque **carriage** . . . Cornell left unadorned the rest of the
> interior, which compactly holds several small boxes of various shapes: a
> rectangular box advertising Henke's candy, a circular box for **Royal
> Swan** ribbons, and a blue packet containing photographs of the interi-
> ors of Herrenchiemsee Castle. Apart from their commercial labels,
> Cornell refrained from embellishing these boxes. The only exception is a
> small circular box within a box that has a marbled interior containing
> pieces of mica and a jeweled sash on marbled cardboard ("private
> garden fetes, etc. / for Richard Wagner"). (97/100)

I have highlighted the words **carriage** and **Royal Swan** to indicate
that, if this tribute were a hypertext, they could appear on screen as
marked links on which we could click and get more information.

Despite my superimposition of these hypothetical links, Cornell's
text seems "remarkably reticent" (Tashjian 97). The reader may wonder what Cornell has in common with Ludwig, and what these
readymade and juxtaposed texts could possibly mean. Yet Cornell is
lionized for his craftsmanship and coherence. Consider Tashjian's comment that

> Although this homage may seem more like an aggregate of elements
> than a sustained celebration of Ludwig, Cornell's elusiveness should not
> be mistaken for absence; his sensibilities and interests governed the
> subtleties of his gift to Ludwig — a resuscitation of the king as an
> extravagant patron of the arts, even, perhaps, as a conceptual artist,
> who commissioned others to carry out his ideas. (97)

It is important to see that, despite differences between rhetorical theory
and art history, in "reading" this tribute, Tashjian finds evidence of an
informed critical perspective, as well as a clear thesis. He believes that

Cornell portrays Ludwig as a conceptual artist, and identifies with him on several levels. Yet because such an appreciative reading is usually withheld from student texts, the question becomes: How does a reader who is not already persuaded of the text's merits achieve such a reading? My response is that the reader's perception of coherence hinges on the rhetorical moves that Cornell makes — namely the formation of a critical commentary to illuminate the rhetorical intentions behind the links, and the development of a minimalist aesthetic that encourages an author to link the minimum amount of text with maximum effectiveness.

Composing Coherence: Critical Commentary and Minimalist Linking

Several hypertext theorists have described the difficulty of achieving coherence in composing nonsequential text. In a volume entitled *Hypertext and Cognition,* Foltz suggests that, "Unlike preparing a single coherent set of arguments, the writer must determine the relationship

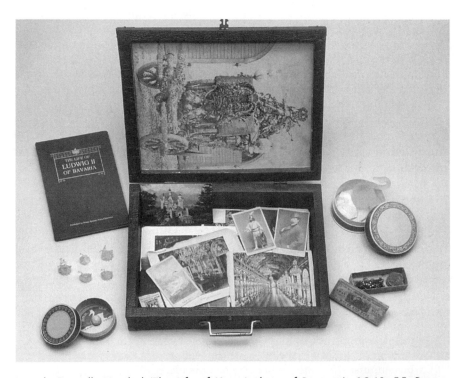

Joseph Cornell, *Untitled (The Life of King Ludwig of Bavaria),* 1940–55. Reproduced with permission of Philadelphia Museum of Art: Gift of The Joseph and Robert Cornell Memorial Foundation.
© The Joseph and Robert Cornell Memorial Foundation.

between all pieces of information and structure them in a much more complicated manner than the linear equivalent" (132). He claims that such structuring "would need to include information about what is contained in the text, what information a reader already knows, and what information the reader needs to know" (132). In the same volume, Britt, Rouet, and Perfetti say that in order "to integrate information across multiple texts, one must be able to locate relevant excerpts in lengthy texts, create a meaningful reading sequence for the passages, and establish crucial relations between different documents which may even be of various types . . ." (43–44). These theorists underscore the importance of conveying communicable relationships between texts, and ask authors to include "bridging inferences" (Foltz 116) in order "to represent between-document relationships" (Britt et al. 69). Such inferences help "hypertext to represent the argument model, that is, the global relationships (rhetorical, expository, and argumentative) among a set [of] documents" (Britt et al. 69). The task of establishing global relationships between linked texts — of conveying coherence through collage — mandates that the author give the reader enough "background knowledge" (Foltz 128) and contextual information to help her achieve a "coherent representation" (129) of the nonsequential text.

Cornell realizes that the viewer (reader) must have a specific knowledge base in order to appreciate the meaning of the seemingly disparate texts he has linked. He gives us that knowledge by including a copy of Hans Steinberger's 1930 biography entitled *The Life of Ludwig II of Bavaria* and a folder of photographs and clippings in the valise. Yet Cornell never insists that we must read the book in order to understand his tribute. Instead, he calls our attention to important excerpts from Steinberger's text by including paper markers that offer clues to points of relevance between his life and that of Ludwig. These markers (excerpts from Steinberger's text) illuminate the intellectual connections and rhetorical relations between the texts Cornell has collected and juxtaposed.

If we appreciate the idea that a hypertext author can use excerpts in order to provide a reader with contextual information, we can see how Cornell's first Steinberger excerpt, one which portrays Ludwig as "'full of romantic ideas'" and "'eager and ambitious as a boy to do great deeds'" (qtd. in Tashjian 100), could serve as a prefatory comment and contextualizing agent for a persuasive hypertext. This excerpt could appear on the first screen, along with a menu that could tell us where we could go in order to learn about the author's identification with, and appreciation of, Ludwig by clicking on the marked links **Steinberger, Royal Swan,** and **carriage.**

Clicking on **Steinberger** would activate the link in which the author tells of his identification with the king. Here, we would read that both author and monarch were unmarried, and that both had to care for their physically (in Cornell's case) and mentally (in Ludwig's case) ill brothers. Cornell also writes on the back of a photograph of Ludwig that he was nearing forty when he began composing this tribute, and that Ludwig was forty-two when he allegedly committed suicide. This annotation constitutes another kind of cue. It signifies a minimalist commentary on which we might ask the author to elaborate, but which nonetheless helps him communicate the depth of his connection to Ludwig while illuminating the global relationships of the more than juxtaposed texts in this collage. Having read the **Steinberger** links, we might click on **Royal Swan** in order to see why swan imagery figures so prominently in this text. Reading Steinberger excerpts would tell us that Ludwig took the swan as his personal symbol, displaying it on the royal crest of Bavaria. Other excerpts would link the subject of swans to Ludwig's patronage of the composer Richard Wagner. Here the link **Royal Swan** would become illustrated and enriched by its musical component; we would read of the swans that appeared in Wagner's operas *Parsifal* and *Lohengrin.* We would learn that Parsifal shot a swan and that, in *Lohengrin,* a swan was actually a man who was put under a spell.

Reading more Steinberger excerpts would tell us how Ludwig suffered for his patronage of Wagner — that the monarch was despised for diminishing state coffers in order to fund what were thought to be his and Wagner's excesses. The contextual information communicated by the excerpts Cornell has selected, coupled with our knowledge that Ludwig was ultimately disgraced and deposed, helps us understand why one of the swans is broken. Cornell has thus given us enough information to help us see the global relationships between, and critical perspective that informs, these linkages. The links' overall coherence suggests an image of swans as an endangered species in need of protection, and an understanding of Ludwig as their misunderstood (and ultimately endangered) protector. Armed with important contextual clues, we can read Cornell's comment "Ludwig in Central Park," which he inscribed on a news photograph of a black swan trapped in a snowy pond, as a sophisticated interpretive move — one in which readymade texts, cuing aids, and commentary collaborate to compose **Royal Swan** as an essential link that contains layers of personal significance for the artist and monarch.

Clicking on **carriage** would bring up Steinberger's accounts of the lavish castles, furnishings, and carriages that Ludwig commissioned. Here we would read a contemporary article about Ludwig's rooftop garden, which "gave credit for the garden to 'the ingenuity of the machinist and the magic art of the painter'" (qtd. in Tashjian 103). These links, and attendant contextual information, further support an image of Ludwig as a conceptual artist. Here one notices the internal coherence of Cornell's linkages; every link comprises texts relating to swans or architecture. Hence, Cornell's seemingly cluttered "draft" appears deeply focused and tightly structured. This depth of focus is informed by Cornell's minimalism — an aesthetic in which interpretive power emanates from the depth, rather than the variety, of the links presented. Cornell's minimalism, which avoids problems inherent in postmodern monumentality and equipotentality, finds its voice in the artist's reflections on effective written composition.

Cornell was an avid diarist who kept over a hundred journals and files. He used these texts as "a clearinghouse for dreams and visions" in order to screen material for effective inclusion in his boxes (qtd. in Simic 35). Cornell's diaries constitute a kind of *ars poetica* because they articulate his processes of selection, discrimination, and distillation. As a writer and artist, Cornell did not compose by purely "associate urgency" (Waldman 14). His journal entries show him to be judicious in selecting and employing readymade materials. For example, in wondering what he should include in a collage, he states that "Everything can be used." However, he follows this statement with an important question: "But of course one doesn't know it at the time. How does one know what a certain object will tell another?" (qtd. in Waldman 31). Cornell's question about the rhetorical issues surrounding inclusion informs his concerns about monumentality and equipotentality. Consider his confession to the poet Marianne Moore that, in composing, "There seems to be such a complexity, a sort of endless 'cross-indexing' of detail (intoxicatingly rich) in connection with what and how I feel that I never seem to come to the point of doing anything about it" (qtd. in Tashjian 23).

Whether composing a written or visual text, Cornell resists including every insight. Aware that an effective rhetor evinces restraint, he suggests that "A discipline will also be acquired against the habit of too much piling up of diverse material" (qtd. in Caws 108). Believing that persuasion involves the careful selection and strategic presentation of evidence in terms of audience knowledge and needs, he favors "consideration of 'the moment,' at time of pen to paper, clearance of conflicting elements coherence enough to attempt copy" (qtd. in Caws 413). Such clearance entails focus; the writer must pare down the links in order to capture "phenomena without getting lost in detail and/or in rambling" (qtd. in Caws 413). Cornell's ability to achieve this distillation (through careful reading, selective presentation, and minimalist linking) gives his Ludwig tribute its conceptual focus and interpretive edge.

While Cornell's Ludwig "draft" strikes me as a persuasive collection of purposeful links, I think that (were we to continue speculatively to treat it as a hypertext) its overall coherence could be enhanced by careful reconsideration and revision. Charney is right to say that, in envisioning models for hypertexts, "it is up to researchers, teachers, and software designers to ensure that these texts promote the work of writers and readers" (261). As teachers, we have pedagogical responsibilities that extend beyond applauding authors for composing intelligent and coherent hypertexts. We must help students improve their work. In order to understand the importance of this responsibility, we should revisit Mead's ideas about culture and community. Mead explains that "the child . . . represents what is to come" (88) by doing unprecedented things — in this case, I am suggesting by composing nonsequential texts that seek definition and recognition as academic discourse. She then warns us "Without adult care, the child will never learn" how to build upon what he has has already done (89). Mead asks community elders (teachers) to provide youngsters (students) with the kind of "imaginative, innovative, and dedicated adult care" (88) that will support and direct their innovative activities. Mead's charge is daunting. Yet I hope to show how a teacher can offer a hypertext author specific revision strategies that seek to honor the integrity of his rhetorical project while respecting the discourse features of hypertext.

Reopening the Box

In this imaginative scenario, Cornell remains cast as the student author of an untitled draft. As a teacher, I would work to appreciate what he has done and, if asked, offer him some revision suggestions. After complimenting the author on the creativity of his approach and the coherence of his linkages, I would ask if he had any questions. Imagine that the author wondered if he had relied too heavily on Steinberger's biography to support his interpretation of Ludwig. My response would be to enter into a discussion about the other texts he had read so that the author might clarify his selection criterion for giving Steinberger's book such prominence in his work. I would let the author know that his draft inspired me to read recent scholarship about Ludwig, including Greg King's 1996 biography, *The Mad King,* which draws a complex and sympathetic portrait of the ruler. In covering aspects of Ludwig's personal life, King identifies many swan-shaped objects that the monarch wore and commissioned. These include: "a swan-shaped pin studded with diamonds" that he received for his eighteenth birthday (45); "an enormous swan boat" on which he staged *Lohengrin* tableaus (111); a desk that "rested on two large gilded swans" (229); and a "silver-and-gilt-bronze washstand in the shape of a swan" that Ludwig ordered for one of his bedrooms (235). I might suggest that the writer consult, and perhaps refer to King's work, in order to enhance his "Royal Swan" link by delineating the pleasure that Ludwig apparently derived from this lavishly embellished personal symbol.

Next, the author might say that he is considering devoting a primary link to Ludwig's relationship with Richard Wagner, which would appear on the first screen along with the links to **Steinberger, carriage,** and **Royal Swan.** My response would be to suggest that, in opera history, Ludwig's role as Wagner's royal benefactor is considered to be of great significance. Here, I would refer the author to King's chapter entitled "Wagner," to King's contention that "without Ludwig's dedication and support, Tristan and Isolde might never have been produced" (103), to Wagner's public citation of Ludwig as "'co-creator' of the Ring" cycle (qtd. in King 215), and to the passionate correspondence between the monarch and composer.[12]

The author might then ask if any links need elaboration. Appreciative of his text's informed minimalism, I would not ask the author to expand every linkage. After sharing my perception that the "Architecture" link is not quite as evocative as that of the "Royal Swan," I would give him the option of making the meaning of this link more apparent to the general reader, or of possibly deleting it from his text. My purpose would be to show the author that he has already persuaded me that he has learned something important about Ludwig through his well-crafted **Royal Swan** link. Conversely, I could see myself apprising him of a potential lead. Greg King writes that, in 1866, Ludwig attended a performance of Schiller's *Mary Stuart* and began corresponding with Lila von Bulyowsky, the actor who portrayed Stuart. He adds that, "Along with Marie Antoinette, the doomed Mary, Queen of Scots, had always been one of Ludwig's greatest tragic heroines . . . he was so moved by the play that on leaving the theater just before midnight, he ordered that a church be specially opened so that he could say prayers for the martyred queen's soul" (171). I might ask the writer to consider researching Ludwig's sympathy for, and possible identification with, these royal figures since it may prove relevant to his evocation of the monarch's tragic sensibility.

At this point, I might ask some questions about the text's out-takes: What did he learn about Ludwig that was relevant to, yet somehow unworthy of, inclusion in his draft? Did he find any material that was important, but that did not cohere with the links he decided to compose? Is there any way that I could help him achieve that coherence? Finally, I would admit to my postfigurative sensibility, and confess that his text would strike me as even more effective and persuasive if it had a title. As a reader I need to know what specifically, in this rhetorical context, he is saying about the life of King Ludwig II of Bavaria.

Discerning Links

My thought experiment with Cornell's art has two purposes. The first is to suggest that his work and ideas about composing model intelligent ways of composing persuasive nonsequential text. Cornell's minimalist, yet communicative linkages underscore Smith's idea that "Hypertext, we may increasingly find, favors the prepared mind" (279). His work signals a careful rhetor who researches his subject, composes with specific communicative intentions, and endows his text with a discernible coherence.

My second purpose is to delineate some important pedagogical responsibilities and opportunities. Foltz writes that "Success for hypertexts lies in exploiting the powers of both the computer and the writer to generate better personalized texts." He adds that "the future of hypertext depends on improving both models of the user and models of the text" (132). If we consider Cornell's work to be a viable model for composing personalized and persuasive hypertexts, we might also consider the aforementioned revision comments to be a small step toward developing a model of a discerning, nonexpert hypertext reader. I say "discerning" because our service to students extends beyond just complimenting them for creating works whose coherence we can, at some level, immediately understand.

At this juncture, Mead's insights prove invaluable. She writes that, in nurturing the young's unprecedented activities, "We must create new models for adults who can teach their children not what to learn, but how to learn" (92). The meaning I take from her comment is that, as students begin composing persuasive hypertexts, we can strive to help them better conceptualize and refine the linkages they design. In this context, teaching students ways of composing well-crafted hypertexts could mean apprising them of the rhetorical complexity involved in creating an effective collage. We could show students that a sophisticated collage artist, like an effective hypertext author, does not indulge in the casual accumulation and juxtaposition of readymade materials. Instead, he engages in attentive reading in order to develop a solid knowledge base, meticulous craftsmanship to ensure that the linkages cohere, and careful revision in order to distill extraneous material from his work.

This cultivation of student artistry finds an eloquent voice in L. M. Dryden. In discussing hypertextual literacy environments, Dryden asks teachers "to put technology at the service of students, to encourage their most creative efforts in exploring the connections between literature, history, the arts and sciences, and — most important — their own lives" (302). I believe that Cornell's work — which makes incisive connections between literature, history, art, and the artist's life — models ways of encouraging students' creativity *and* effort. In his poem "The Magic Study of Happiness," Charles Simic honors Cornell's work for the ways it achieves persuasion through knowledge, focus, and distillation. Observing a Cornell box in the way that we might look at a hypertext screen, Simic states that "In the smallest theater in the world the breadcrumbs speak" (47). While most composition teachers will not face an avalanche of speaking breadcrumbs — or persuasive hypertexts — this afternoon, we may wish to develop a receptive, discerning, and anticipatory pedagogy so that, when our students do speak to us through new kinds of texts, we stand a reasonable chance of hearing and responding helpfully to whatever it is they have to say.

ACKNOWLEDGMENTS: I am very grateful to Diana George, Jamie Hagedorn, Patricia Harkin, Susan Miller, James Sosnoski, Farrell J. Webb, and an anonymous *CCC* reviewer for their thoughtful guidance and response. My friends and colleagues, Timothy R. Austin, Maria Carrig, Chris Castiglia, Allen J. Frantzen, and Steven Jones deserve thanks for sharing their wonderful insights with me on a regular basis. This essay is dedicated to Norma Deloris Egstrom and Yola Janangelo for their ongoing humanity.

Notes

1. The term "persuasive" is intended to signify a use of hypertext that goes beyond the way it is discussed in this essay. Student documents, designed to demonstrate learning, constitute one permutation of the persuasive

hypertext. What is important, I think, is the distinction between hypertexts that are designed to be mainly presentational (representing the fullness of information) and those in which links are obviously constructed and edited in order to foster a particular interpretation. In this second scenario, the hypertext evolves into a kind of rescript where found material is rewritten and transformed as it is linked. I use the term "persuasive" instead of "argumentative" in support of Olivia Frey's idea that academic writing need not be confrontational or monologic. Frey's idea seems consonant with Landow's claim that "hypertext does not permit a tyrannical, univocal voice" (*Hypertext* 11).

2. Susan Miller has written persuasively that instructors often believe all student texts to be in need of criticism and correction. I suspect that this belief contributed to my negative response to my students' hypertexts.

3. See *T.H.E. Journal (Technological Horizons in Education)* for interesting accounts of the many uses of hypertext in literacy and literature instruction taking place at the K–university levels. This journal is published monthly except July. Address: T.H.E. JOURNAL L.L.C., 150 El Camino Real, Suite 112, Tustin, CA 92780–3760.

4. The idea that there is a "poetics of the *ready-made*" can be traced to appreciations of the work of collage artist Michel Duchamp. In praising the artist, Calvin Tomkins refers to readymades as "common manufactured items that Duchamp promoted to the status of works of art simply by selecting and signing them." Tomkins defines readymades as "primary sources for the conceptual approach that has come to dominate art in the second half of the twentieth century: an approach that defines art primarily as a mental act" (94). Landow links the poetics of the readymade to composing through discussion of Derrida's "conception of hypertext as a vast assemblage" of preexisting texts. He notes that, "To carry Derrida's instinctive theorizing of hypertext further, one may also point to his recognition that such a montagelike textuality marks or foregrounds the writing process and therefore rejects a deceptive transparency" (*Hypertext* 9). Landow's review of Derrida's ideas helps me see how readers can appreciate authors who deftly recompose readymade texts in ways that simultaneously convey their "original" and "transformed" (for the current rhetorical situation) meanings.

5. I realize that my thought experiment has its limitations. By using a creative artifact as a "model" for student writing, I am minimizing the discourse discontinuity that permits art historians to applaud the very things that writing teachers must rail against (in the cartoon version). My purpose, however, is to diminish this discontinuity by elevating student hypertexts from the status of the casually enigmatic, to that of the complexly coherent. Also, the parallels I construct between visual and verbal discourse may appear to depict textuality as a universal essence, which is not my intention. Cornell is my chosen artist precisely because he is so insistent on, and adept at, incorporating print text into his work. Appreciating the complexity of a Cornell box (in which the iconic refers to, and often depends on, the alphabetic for its enriched meaning) almost always involves reading the texts that the artist has read (and often excerpted and appended) in order to recognize the work's intricate intertextuality.

6. There is a discrepancy between the features of collage technique enumerated here and my students' hypertexts. My hope is that this essay's concluding sections will offer a way of reconciling them.

7. Landow is quoting Vannevar Bush whose vision of the "memex" retrieval system is considered to be the first expression of hypertext theory. In "As We May Think," first published in the *Atlantic Monthly* in 1945, Bush describes a retrieval system that permits "selection by association, rather than by indexing" (102). He sees this system as both natural and desirable because "The human mind . . . operates by association. With one item in its grasp, it snaps instantly to the next that is suggested by the association of thoughts, in accordance with some intricate web of trails carried by the cells of the brain" (101). Analogy has already played a strong role in helping scholars theorize hypertext. For an excellent discussion of the ways in which hypertextual discourse has been linked to classical rhetoric, postmodern literary theory, and art criticism, see Hawisher et al.'s *Computers and the Teaching of Writing in American Higher Education, 1979–1994: A History.*

8. Heba writes that "the most important design feature of the presentation environment is an information map. This information map acts like a master menu or table of contents; it directs users' attention and guides them through the full range of information available and how to get to it" (34).

9. Other scholars have described the alienating effects of equipotentiality. In 1991, Moulthrop and Kaplan discussed the problems that students experienced while working with interactive hypertextual fiction. After confiding that "students found the interactive fictions perplexing and problematic" (15), they concluded that, "If it is to be anything other than a babble of randomness and subjectivity, an interactive fiction must impose some limiting principle on its collection of voices" (17).

10. Scholars appear divided over this issue. On the one hand, Raymond Smock claims that creating "documents that can take full advantage of the electronic media and provide researchers with a greater range of information requires . . . the use of 'hypertext' links, which make it possible to add new levels of explanatory matter to an existing document." Smock appreciates the fact that "Such links . . . serve many purposes, including those of conventional footnotes or annotations" (B2). This view of hypertext as a tool for maintaining the conventions of academic discourse runs counter to the vision of scholar George Landow, who speaks of "the new rhetoric needed for hypermedia," one that does not take print-based prose to be an inviable standard for textual coherence ("Rhetoric of Hypermedia" 82). This resistance to print-based epistemologies is found in Eldred's and Fortune's critique of " 'front ends' geared to compensate for the gap between the processing strategies suited to conventional books and the special challenges and opportunities implicit in the structure of a true hyperdocument." These scholars are disheartened that "the 'book' metaphor often even dominates the thinking that goes into the design of these front ends. That is, they often amount to no more than tables of contents or lists of topics characteristic of conventional books" (68).

11. My experiment is not intended to force Cornell's art, which makes brilliant use of contemporary sources, to answer questions it would never have asked itself. Instead, I am trying to foster a working interplay between composition pedagogy and the arts — one that applauds Cornell as a visionary whose artistic discourse and reflections on composing anticipate and nurture the teaching of hypertextual writing. In this essay, I will suggest ways that aspects of Cornell's art object could be revised for fur-

ther clarity. My intent is not to patronize the artist: In fact, I believe my suggestions to be in concert with Cornell's project of perpetual revision. Caws reports that Cornell was an avid revisor. He often gave correspondents, most notably Susan Sontag, boxes only to take them back for further revision (26). In "tinkering with earlier boxes" (Solomon 367), Cornell's revision goal was to restore the intensity of his work. My goal, in comparing his project of "'refurbishing'" (275) to pedagogies and processes of composing, is to identify and celebrate ways that Cornell's discerning craftsmanship can inform the writing and teaching of hypertext.

12. Surviving examples of Ludwig's correspondence with Wagner underscore the ruler's great enthusiasm for the composer's work. Greg King reports that, after a performance of *Tristan and Isolde,* Ludwig wrote Wagner "a letter of adoration," part of which reads "How glorious! Perfect! So full of Rapture!" (qtd. on 102). Ludwig's passion for Wagner's work informed even his most intimate communications. King reports that Ludwig "wrote frequent letters" to his cousin and fiancée Sophie, addressing her "as 'Elsa' and signing himself as 'Heinrich,' two of the principal characters from *Lohengrin*" (qtd. on 156).

Works Cited

Biemiller, Lawrence. "'Purposeless Wandering' Through L.A. Neighborhoods With a Pinhole Camera." *The Chronicle of Higher Education* 14 May 1995: A55.

Britt, M. Anne, Jean-François Rouet, and Charles A. Perfetti. "Using Hypertext to Study and Reason About Historical Evidence." Rouet, Levonen, Dillon, and Spiro 43–72.

Bush, Vannevar. "As We May Think." *From Memex to Hypertext: Vannevar Bush and the Mind's Machine.* Ed. James M. Nyce and Paul Kahn. Boston: Academic, 1991. 85–110.

Caws, Mary Ann, Ed. *Joseph Cornell's Theater of the Mind: Selected Diaries, Letters, and Files.* New York: Thames, 1993.

Charney, Davida. "The Effect of Hypertext on Processes of Reading and Writing." Selfe and Hilligoss 238–63.

Curtis, Marcia and Elizabeth Klem. "The Virtual Context: Ethnography in the Computer-Equipped Writing Classroom." Hawisher and LeBlanc 155–72.

Delaney, Paul and George P. Landow, Eds. *Hypermedia and Literary Studies.* Cambridge: MIT, 1991.

DeLoughry, Thomas J. "Term Papers Go High Tech: More and More Professors Assign Projects that Embrace New Electronic Technologies." *The Chronicle of Higher Education* 7 Dec. 1994: A23, A25.

Dryden, L. M., "Literature, Student-Centered Classrooms, and Hypermedia Environments." Selfe and Hilligoss 282–304.

Eco, Umberto. "The Texts to Boot." *The Observer Review* 18 June 1995: A4.

Eco, Umberto. *Six Walks in the Fictional Woods.* Cambridge: Harvard UP, 1994.

Eldred, Janet Carey and Ron Fortune. "Exploring the Implications of Metaphors for Computer Networks and Hypermedia." Hawisher and LeBlanc 58–73.

Foltz, Peter W. "Comprehension, Coherence, and Strategies in Hypertext and Linear Text." Rouet, Levonen, Dillon, and Spiro 109–36.

Frey, Olivia. "Beyond Literary Darwinism: Women's Voices and Critical Discourse." *College English* 52 (1990): 507–26.

Gruber, Sibylle. "Re: Ways We Contribute: Students, Instructors, and Pedagogies in the Computer-Mediated Writing Classroom." *Computers and Composition* 12 (1995): 61–78.

Hawisher, Gail E., Paul LeBlanc, Charles Moran, Cynthia L. Selfe, Eds. *Computers and the Teaching of Writing in American Higher Education, 1979–1994: A History.* Norwood: Ablex, 1996.

Hawisher, Gail E. and Paul LeBlanc, Eds. *Re-Imagining Computers and Composition: Teaching and Research in the Virtual Age.* Portsmouth: Boynton, 1992.

Hawisher, Gail E. and Cynthia L. Selfe. "Tradition and Change in Computer-Supported Writing Environments: A Call for Action." *Theoretical and Critical Perspectives on Teacher Change.* Ed. Phyllis Kahaney, Linda A. M. Perry, and Joseph Janangelo. Norwood: Ablex, 1993. 155–86.

Heba, Gary. "HyperRhetoric: Multimedia, Literacy, and the Future of Composition." *Computers and Composition* 14 (1997): 19–44.

Joyce, Michael. *Of Two Minds: Hypertext Pedagogy and Poetics.* Ann Arbor: U of Michigan P, 1995.

King, Greg. *The Mad King: The Life and Times of Ludwig II of Bavaria.* Secaucus: Birch Lane, 1996.

Landow, George P. "The Rhetoric of Hypermedia: Some Rules For Authors." Delaney and Landow 81–103.

———. *Hypertext: The Convergence of Contemporary Critical Theory and Technology.* Baltimore: Johns Hopkins UP, 1992.

Landow, George P. and Paul Delaney. "Hypertext, Hypermedia and Literary Studies: The State of the Art." Delaney and Landow 1991. 3–50.

Lanham, Richard A. *The Electronic Word: Democracy, Technology, and the Arts.* Chicago: U of Chicago P, 1993.

Mead, Margaret. *Culture and Commitment: A Study of the Generation Gap.* Garden City: Natural History, 1970.

Miller, Susan. "Writing Theory: Theory Writing." *Methods and Methodology in Composition Research.* Ed. Gesa Kirsch and Patricia A. Sullivan. Carbondale: Southern Illinois UP, 1992. 62–83.

Miller, Susan and Kyle Knowles. *New Ways of Writing: A Handbook for Writing with Computers.* Upper Saddle River: Blair, 1997.

Moulthrop, Stuart. "In the Zones: Hypertext and the Politics of Interpretation." *Writing on the Edge* 1 (1989): 18–27.

Moulthrop, Stuart and Nancy Kaplan. "Something to Imagine: Literature, Composition, and Interactive Fiction." *Computers and Composition* 9 (1991): 7–23.

Perfetti, Charles A. "Text and Hypertext." Rouet, Levonen, Dillon, and Spiro 157–61.

Rouet, Jean-François, Jarmo J. Levonen, Andrew Dillon, and Rand J. Spiro, Eds. *Hypertext and Cognition.* Mahwah: Erlbaum, 1996.

Selfe, Cynthia L. and Susan Hilligoss, Eds. *Literacy and Computers: The Complications of Teaching and Learning with Technology.* New York: MLA, 1994.

Selfe, Richard J. "What Are They Talking About? Computer Terms That English Teachers May Need to Know." Hawisher and LeBlanc 207–18.

Simic, Charles. *Dime Store Alchemy: The Art of Joseph Cornell.* Hopewell: Ecco, 1992.

Slatin, John M., "Reading Hypertext: Order and Coherence in a New Medium." *College English* 52 (1990): 870–83.

Smith, Catherine F. "Hypertextual Thinking." Selfe and Hilligoss 264–81.

Smock, Raymond W. "What Promise Does the Internet Hold for Scholars?" *The Chronicle of Higher Education.* 22 September 1995: B1–2.

Solomon, Deborah. *Utopia Parkway: The Life and Work of Joseph Cornell.* New York: Farrar, 1997.

Tashjian, Dickran. *Joseph Cornell: Gifts of Desire.* Miami Beach: Grassfield, 1992.

Tomkins, Calvin. "Duchamp and New York: What did he find here? The things that made art modern." *The New Yorker* (1996): 92–101.

Waldman, Diane. *Joseph Cornell.* New York: Braziller, 1977.

CHAPTER

3

Teaching Argument in the English Class

W riting teachers often find the teaching of argument one of their most challenging tasks because we have all been influenced by a culture that treats argument as a simplistic contest concerned primarily with winners and losers. Whether we like it or not, presidential debates and daytime talk shows often pass for argument in twenty-first-century culture. The presidential debates feature short, prepackaged responses to extremely complex questions about the national good. While somewhat formal in tone and highly important to our political culture, they typically emphasize form over substance and appeal to popular prejudice over in-depth engagement with ideas. In addition, many daytime talk shows, on the other hand, promote "argument" as a contest that can be resolved only through physical violence and/or appeals to our lowest cultural stereotypes.

As a result, student writers sometimes see classes or exercises in argumentation as the chance to write polemics with little depth, balance, or insight. They may also view class discussions as the opportunity to shout down other students and to belittle opposing ideas. Some students choose simply to be negative, doubting the potential value and truth of any argument they encounter, and, therefore, never "losing" any debate. Students who engage in such processes rarely learn anything new, while students not interested in discourses of aggression, dominance, and nihilism simply tune out the discord. Ultimately, classes based on a win-lose model (one, incidentally, that is only too easy for instructors to get caught up in) rarely produce productive learning environments.

Teaching argument is also difficult because argumentation demands exceptional communication, analytical, and research skills. While scholars rightly debate whether some forms of communication (such as argument or analysis) are more sophisticated than others, it is no accident that many first-year composition classes end with the argument or persuasive essay and that some spend a whole semester on the teaching of argument. This type of writing can be the most difficult for students to master because it builds from virtually all the other rhetorical skills traditionally taught in composition, including summary, comparison and contrast, analysis, and evaluation. Well-written arguments also demand that writers have an advanced understanding of audience and the ability to understand persuasion as a process that depends on context. Writers need subtle control over language and style and the ability to move beyond absolutes in order to explore controversial and complex subjects. These are high-level intellectual processes that students need to work on carefully and with expert guidance if they are to achieve proficiency in argumentation.

It is particularly important that students find the kind of guidance they need in departments of English and rhetoric because few other disciplines will give students the opportunity to study argument for its own sake. The teaching of argument in these disciplines can, and should, promote the free exchange of a wide variety of ideas both within and beyond the classroom. It should further promote responsible inquiry into personal, local, and national problems; critical self-examination; and better understanding of the historical power differentials that affect communication between individuals and communities. Advancing such ideals is critical if the academy is to compete with cultural models of "debate" that inhibit sustained and responsible engagement with ideas.

The essays in this section provide theoretically sound and practical models to help teachers and students move past the win-lose paradigm and to engage in alternative forms of argumentation. They provide a comprehensive yet teachable notion of argument that promotes a classical liberal education while drawing from theories of reading, writing as process, ethics, and classical notions of refutation. They address the special concerns of English instructors, who need to present argument as an intellectually demanding process with the potential to provide substantial rewards for individuals and their communities.

Rogerian Rhetoric: Ethical Growth through Alternative Forms of Argumentation

Doug Brent

Doug Brent's essay offers strong arguments for adapting Carl Rogers's ideas about communication and psychotherapy to the argument classroom. Originally published in Argument Revisited; Argument Redefined *in 1996, this piece suggests that Rogerian rhetorics can help students with the invention of ideas (rather than simply their arrangement). It also considers the ways Rogers's theories can help instructors create specific speaking, reading, and writing assignments adaptable to first-year writing classes and advanced courses. Through such assignments, Brent argues that students will learn more than techniques for understanding and composing arguments — they will also adopt new ways of thinking complementary to a liberal education.*

It may be useful to read Brent's essay in conjunction with the other essays in this collection concerning Rogers, in particular the excerpt from Young, Becker, and Pike's Rhetoric: Discovery and Change *(p. 97), which includes Rogers's own version of his communication theories. Other useful essays include James Baumlin's work on Rogerian rhetoric and imaginative play (p. 111) and Phyllis Lassner's critique of Rogerian rhetoric in a women's studies class (p. 406).*

As the introduction to this volume points out, all of the approaches to argumentation collected here offer some form of alternative to the "argument as war" metaphor. In each approach, "argument" is re-defined as one or another form of negotiated inquiry into common grounds for belief.

Rogerian rhetoric also moves away from a combative stance but is distinct from other models of argumentation in three ways. First, it goes even further than most other models in avoiding an adversarial approach. Second, it offers specific strategies based on nondirective therapy for building the cooperative bridges necessary for noncombative inquiry. Third, and in my opinion most important, it has the potential to offer students an opportunity for long-term cognitive and ethical growth.

Ever since Young, Becker, and Pike introduced the discipline of composition to Rogerian rhetoric in 1970, our profession has remained deeply divided over whether such a rhetoric is conceptually sound, useful in practice, or even possible. Some have argued that it is nothing but warmed-over Aristotelian rhetoric (Lunsford); others, that it is untrue to Carl Rogers's principles (Mader) or that it is a cumbersome welding together of persuasion and nondirective therapy, two fundamentally incompatible processes (Ede). All of these criticisms point to real problems with the model, problems that often reflect the way it has been conceptualized by its proponents. Nonetheless, the literature of composition studies reflects a continuing fascination with Rogerian principles.

Textbooks continue to suggest these principles as alternative methods of persuasion (Coe 1990; Flower), and a recent collection edited by Nathaniel Teich (1992) presents a wide variety of both philosophical and pedagogical investigations into Rogerian perspectives.

In this chapter I will try to account for this continuing fascination with Rogerian rhetoric and explain what it can offer that no other approach to argumentation can quite match. To do so I will briefly survey the history of Rogerian rhetoric and outline its basic principles. Then I will discuss some of the ways in which Rogerian principles can be used in practice to teach both a *technique* of inquiry and an *ethic* of inquiry.

Background: Rogerian Therapy and Rogerian Rhetoric

Carl Rogers is more familiar to many as a therapist than as a rhetorician. However, the goal of therapy, like the goal of rhetoric, can be broadly described as "attitude change." Whereas rhetoricians may want their audience to adopt certain specific beliefs, therapists may not — in fact, should not — have a clear model of specific behaviors that they want their clients to adopt in place of the dysfunctional ones that brought the clients into therapy in the first place. Rather, therapists aim for a broader change in the way their clients interact with the world. Nonetheless, the essence of both arts is to induce change through verbal means — Plato's "art of influencing the soul through words" (*Phaedrus* 48).

Rogerian therapy informs rhetoric by offering a new way of thinking about the means of inducing change. Rogers ("Communication") describes how, as a young practitioner, he quickly discovered that he could not change the attitudes or behavior of his clients by rational argument. The ideal rhetorical situation as described by Plato involves an audience that, like his hero Socrates, is "not less happy to be refuted than to refute" (*Gorgias* 17). Alas, this attitude is rare among real, vulnerable human beings who are not characters in a Platonic dialogue. Clients in therapy, at the peak of their vulnerability, are particularly unhappy to be refuted. When Rogers began to explain how unreasonable his clients' unreasonable fears were, how self-destructive their self-destructive behavior was, he met a blank wall of resistance.

The problem, he decided, was that rational argument of this type always implies a form of evaluation. Argument may convince a person to buy this kind of car or to vote for that politician, but the closer the subject of the argument comes to the beliefs that constitute the core of a person's sense of self, of identity, the more any attempt to change beliefs is perceived as a threat and met with walls of defense.

The way around these walls, Rogers discovered, was to change the role of the therapist. The therapist, in Rogers's view, is not a healer, but rather a *facilitator* of healing. Therapists do not explain their point of view to their clients, but instead listen actively to their clients as clients get in touch with their own thoughts and emotions and do their own healing.

For the art of rhetoric, the most immediately useful aspect of Rogerian therapy is the specific technique that Rogers developed to facilitate this self-healing process. This technique is called "restatement" or "saying back." Rogers is quite explicit that this is not simply a passive process (*Therapy* 27). Therapists continually repeat back their understanding of the clients' words in summary form to check their understanding of the clients' mental state. Thus the therapist might say, "It sounds as though what you are really saying is that you hate your father." The client might respond, "No, that's not quite it," and the therapist would continue with more probes such as, "Well, perhaps you were just angry with him at that moment." Always therapists must walk the fine line between giving their clients words to express hitherto inexpressible feelings and putting words in their mouths. As a therapeutic tool, Rogerian reflection is both difficult — it can quickly degenerate into an irritating echo chamber of voices — and breathtakingly successful when done well.[1]

In this "pure" form, Rogerian therapy is not "argument." Rogerian therapy is antiargument, a form of discourse in which the speaker must specifically *avoid* stating a point of view either directly or indirectly. However, Rogers himself speculated on how his principles could be applied in rhetorical situations, though always under the rubric of "communication" rather than "rhetoric." In his 1951 paper, "Communication: Its Blocking and Its Facilitation," Rogers proposes that the empathy and feedback model could be used to facilitate communication in emotion-laden situations outside the therapeutic relationship, such as political or labor negotiations. His formula is simple: "Each person can speak up for himself only *after* he has first restated the ideas and feelings of the previous speaker, and to that speaker's satisfaction" (332). In later articles he details Rogerian-style negotiation sessions that have produced astonishing results, including the Camp David negotiations conducted by Jimmy Carter, a conference involving health care providers and impoverished and embittered health care consumers, and even opposing sides in Northern Ireland (Rogers and Ryback).

This power to create an atmosphere of cooperation is what led Young, Becker, and Pike to propose an alternative form of rhetoric based on Rogerian principles.[2] Rogerian rhetoric as recreated by Young, Becker, and Pike is aimed at those situations in which more confrontational techniques are most apt to fail: that is, in highly emotional situations in which opposing sides fail to establish even provisional grounds for discussion. Young, Becker, and Pike recommend that rather than trying immediately to present arguments for their point of view and refute their opponents, writers should first undertake a task similar to that of the Rogerian psychotherapist. They should try to reduce the reader's sense of threat by showing that they have genuinely listened to the reader's position. This reduction of threat will in turn induce an "assumption of similarity": The reader will see the writer as a human being more or less like herself and therefore be more likely to listen to what the writer has to say.

Although they argue that it should not be reduced to a mechanical formula, Young, Becker, and Pike outline four basic stages through which a Rogerian argument should pass:

1. An introduction to the problem and a demonstration that the opponent's position is understood.

2. A statement of the contexts in which the opponent's position may be valid.

3. A statement of the writer's position, including the contexts in which it is valid.

4. A statement of how the opponent's position would benefit if he were to adopt elements of the writer's position. If the writer can show that the positions complement each other, that each supplies what the other lacks, so much the better. (283)

Not every version of Rogerian rhetoric emphasizes exactly these stages, but the common denominator among all versions is that writers must state the opposing viewpoint *first,* before stating their own, and do so honestly, with understanding, and without either overt or covert evaluation.

Rogerian Rhetoric in the Writing Classroom

Beginning with Maxine Hairston's seminal article, a number of writers have recommended Rogerian rhetoric as an alternative form of argument to be used, as Young, Becker, and Pike originally recommended, when emotions and a sense of threat preclude direct debate in the classical mode (Bator 1989, 1992; Coe 1992).

Lunsford and Ede, Gage [. . .], and others have argued that those who view classical rhetoric as inherently combative have been misled both by later misreadings of Aristotle and his contemporaries and by an incomplete understanding of the role of the enthymeme. They argue that the enthymeme, the heart of Aristotle's structure of argumentation, differs from the logical syllogism precisely in that it involves the rhetor in building an argument from the opinions of the audience. Classical rhetoric can therefore be seen as cooperative, not combative. This in fact is the basis for Lunsford's argument that a Rogerian "alternative" to traditional rhetoric is unnecessary.

Regardless of the merits of these arguments, the traditional conception of rhetoric still poses limitations. Traditional rhetoric as envisioned by Aristotle and by most modern textbooks on argument is typically triadic; that is, it is aimed at a third party who will judge the case on the basis of the arguments presented by competing advocates, politicians, researchers, advertisers, or other partisan arguers. In this case it matters little if one arguer threatens the beliefs and self-esteem of the other, for it is not the opponent the arguer is trying to convince, but the audience as third party. The process of inquiry claimed for the enthymeme creates cooperation between rhetor and audience, not between rhetor and opponent.

But what about the instances — far more common in everyday life — in which two parties are directly trying to convince each other? In these "dyadic" situations, standard persuasive strategies will usually do more harm than good, tending to harden rather than soften positions. In such cases of dyadic argument, a technique is required that will create the grounds for reasonable discussion that classical rhetoric presupposes. Rogerian rhetoric offers such a technique (Coe 1992).

The challenge for the composition teacher, of course, is how to teach students to put Rogerian principles into practice. Rogerian rhetoric is often tried and dismissed as impractical, too difficult for students to use, too difficult to teach, or too easy for students to misinterpret as a particularly sly form of manipulation.

I believe that some of these problems stem from a failure to recognize just what Rogerian rhetoric really is. The basic model of Rogerian argument, particularly when abstracted from the rich context of heuristic techniques in which Young, Becker, and Pike originally embedded it, looks like a form of *arrangement:* a recipe for what to say first. But arrangement is only part of the business of any rhetorical system. Logically prior to arrangement — and as I will argue, embedded in the process of arrangement, not separate from it — is the process of *invention.* In Rogerian terms, this means exploring an opposing point of view in sufficiently rich complexity to make it possible to reflect it back convincingly to an audience.

The problem of invention is accentuated by the written medium. A writer is in a much worse position than the therapist, for writing does not allow the back-and-forth movement of face-to-face conversation that makes possible the continual readjustment of the discourse. But if we are content to relax our standards somewhat, it is still possible for students to learn how to apply a form of Rogerian principles in writing. To do so, they must learn how to imagine with empathy and how to read with empathy.

By *imagining with empathy,* I mean more than teaching students to imagine another's views. This would be little different from classical audience analysis. I mean teaching students to think carefully about *how* another person could hold views that are different from one's own. This is what Young, Becker, and Pike mean by finding the contexts in which the opposing viewpoint is valid. Rather than simply imagining an isolated set of arguments for an opposing viewpoint, the writer must imagine the entire world view that allows those arguments to exist, and that makes them valid for the other.

By *reading with empathy,* I mean teaching students to use the printed words of another as a guide to this imagining process. In a sense, this is no more than what is usually known as *research.* When preparing any written argument it is useful to do one's homework. But whereas students often associate research with the mere looking-up of facts, *research* in a Rogerian context emphasizes the looking-up of facts in the context of the arguments that support them and looking at those arguments in the context of other world views, other ways of seeing.

This kind of imaginative reconstruction does not come easily. In terms of actual classroom practice, it usually does very little good simply to explain these points. Rather, the teacher must set up situations in which the students can practice Rogerian reflection and the Rogerian attitude long enough for it to sink in. For instance, the teacher can set up a dialectical situation in which students can practice on real, present people in a context more like the original therapeutic situations for which Rogerian principles were originally designed. The oral, face-to-face conversation serves as a bridge to the more difficult imaginative task of the distanced written conversation.

Though these tasks are in one sense designed to serve as preparation for another, they are in no sense mere warm-up drills or "prewriting" activities separate from the business of argument itself. They are integral parts of what Rogerian rhetoric understands by "argument": a process of mutual exploration that may culminate in a written text but that may also take oral and other pathways. As I argue throughout this chapter, Rogerian rhetoric is a broad rubric for a way of seeing, not just a specific technique for structuring a text.

Rogerian Rhetoric in Action: Some Close-Ups

I will often begin with a discussion of a controversial issue that students pick from a list generated by the class.[3] For this exercise I usually depend on the knowledge that students already possess on the subject, though in more advanced classes I ask students to research the topic beforehand. I get students to identify themselves with one side or the other. Then I will call on a volunteer from each side to engage in a public Rogerian discussion (since my disastrous first experience with this technique I am careful not to use the word "debate").

The discussion is organized according to Rogers's own rules as suggested in "Communication: Its Blocking and Its Facilitation." Neither person can mention their own view until they have restated the other person's *to that person's satisfaction.* Thus the first "round" would consist of student A stating an argument, student B *re*stating that argument in summary form, and student A either agreeing that the summary is accurate or attempting to correct it. This goes on until student A is happy with the summary; then student B gets a turn to state his or her own point of view (*not* to refute A).

The exercise often breaks down into a traditional debate in which one person either tries to refute the other's views or restates them in a way that will make them easier to attack. Emotional hot buttons get pushed and more straw men begin flying about than in the monkey attack from *The Wizard of Oz.*

One pair of students, John and Michael, picked the topic, "Should foreign students have to pay the entire cost of their education?" Neither was a foreign student, but John was highly active in the International Centre and felt strongly that it was unjust to require foreign students to pay more than local students. He stated his reasons, including basic principles of equity and the important contribution that foreign students make to the university. Michael opened his "restatement" along the lines of, "So, you think it's okay to make our taxpayers pay for the education of a student from Singapore who won't even stay in this country?"

Obviously, this is hardly Rogerian reflection. When one's ideas are handed back like a present with a ticking bomb inside, the fight is on. But this is exactly the point. I want students to see the difference between this sort of rebuttal and true Rogerian discussion. Sometimes I involve the entire class in discussing whether a particular response is genuinely "Rogerian" or is really just a sneak attack on the other's values. After some discussion and more prompting from John, Michael eventually worked himself around to identifying the values behind John's statement:

> So, if I understand you correctly, you don't think that the cost of education should be tied directly to the amount of money one's family has paid into a given educational system, or the obvious financial returns that a country can get from educating people. Rather, you think that a more general principle of equity applies and that we need to look at a more global good.

He still didn't agree, but at least he understood John's point of view. Only John's assent that Michael had in fact got it right gave Michael permission to go on to state the reasons for that disagreement.

The process is exhausting and usually the class is over before the first exchange of views is complete. But by the end of the process, students (and the teacher) have a greater appreciation of the difference between their own default mode of argument and the process of struggling toward a genuine understanding of another's point of view.

The point of this oral exchange is not so much to invent material for a particular piece of writing as to get the general feel of Rogerian discussion in its most native mode, face-to-face communication. Once I think students have got the hang of this, I move them on to the more difficult task faced by writers: recovering underlying values from other people's written texts. Again I pair them off and they begin by writing straight-ahead, univocal arguments for their own point of view on a controversial issue. Students exchange papers and try to write summaries that satisfy the original author, who in turn may write countersummaries that extend and correct the reflected image of their ideas.

Kathy, for instance, felt quite passionate about the Young Offenders Act, a controversial Canadian law that severely limits the sentencing of criminals under sixteen years of age even if they have committed violent crimes. Her statement began like this:

> I feel that we must dispose of the Young Offenders Act. It is a useless piece of legislation practically promoting crime. Hasn't our society enough evidence that the YOA doesn't work? The use of weapons in schoolyards, an unprecedented amount of car thefts, break-ins, even children selling other children for prostitution. A slap on the hand prevents nothing. If greater punishment, including *real* time in jail were a threat, I guarantee that our youth would be a little more reluctant.

And on and on, rehearsing in no uncertain terms the most common arguments leveled against the YOA in the media. Her partner, Tracey, began her restatement like this:

> You have expressed concern over the YOA. You are concerned that it actually encourages crime because of the lack of deterrence. You feel that a person under sixteen knows right from wrong and should be held responsible for his or her actions, regardless of the personal situation or background which might be used as an excuse for committing crimes. You believe that we should place the betterment of society above the protection of criminals, regardless of their age.

The important feature of this restatement is that it is not just a summary of the other's point of view, but, somewhat like Michael's, an attempt to get at underlying beliefs. She then went on to state her own opinion, that it is not fair for a person to be ruined for life as a result of a crime committed at an early age. But her response was moderate and had to deal with the delicate balance between protection of society and protection of individual youths that she had detected in Kathy's position. The effect of the restating process was not simply to soften up Kathy by putting her in the right frame of mind to receive Tracey's argument. Rather, it put Tracey in touch with the complexities of the matter, enabling her to see the matter from another's point of view rather than just her own.

Once students have begun to improve their ability to reflect the arguments of others who are physically present, I have them move on to Rogerian discussions of writers who are not present. One fruitful assignment is to have students reply to articles embodying world views that they do not share. Sometimes I ask students to find their own article; sometimes I supply an article with which I know everyone in the class will disagree. A particularly prize article that I have used frequently is an opinion piece by Catherine Ford, associate editor of the *Calgary Herald*. (The entire article is included as an appendix on pages 317–18.) Ford addresses teenage girls who, she feels, cut themselves from economic opportunities because they take "bubblegum courses" instead of science and math. She cites chilling statistics about how much time most women spend in the work force and how little most of them are paid, and equates science and math — which, she says, most girls have been "conned" into thinking are too difficult — with "one of the fastest ways to economic independence for women."

However, Ford begins by telling her audience that "the world is passing you by, while you're all out there spray-painting your hair purple and reading *People* magazine," and tries to get their attention by telling them, "You guys seem to have melted your brains with your stereo headphones." Ford clearly is not exactly a master of Rogerian rhetoric and the class usually has an entertaining few minutes raking her over the coals for her unsupported generalizations and unflattering portrayal of the very people she is supposedly trying to convert. Students taking a humanities course are particularly irritated by being accused, by implication, of having chosen a "bubblegum" course. Then I set my students a dyadic task: to write a letter *directly to Ford herself* that uses Rogerian techniques to convince her to moderate her position.

To do so, we discuss not only the areas of validity in Ford's argument, but also try to understand both the rhetorical situation — why she might decide to adopt such an aggressive tone to get her point across — and also who she is as a person. Nobody in the class ever knows much about her personally, but with a little exploratory discussion, we begin to think about the implications of being a woman in her forties — to judge by her picture — who has fought her way up to associate editor of the city's major newspaper. From this and experience with Ford's writing, we build up a picture of a woman who prides herself on pulling no punches, who is easily angered by behavior that she perceives as foolish, and whose feminism frequently takes the form of being disgusted by girls who cut themselves off from the opportunities that she herself fought so hard to make for herself. Her insistence on "economic independence" suggests someone with a fierce personal pride and a hard-nosed attitude to life, but not — judging by other columns in which she discusses government fiscal policy — someone who values money for its own sake. In short, the students are applying consciously the reader-response process of constructing both a text and the person behind the text. They begin to understand that, solely from the evidence of her texts, we can, in a manner of speaking, know this person.

None of these personal details need to find their way into the final written product, of course. There is not much to be served by presenting Ford with a detailed picture of herself that is not directly relevant to the issue and could very well be inaccurate. The object of this part of the exercise is simply to sensitize the students to the idea that arguments come from somewhere, and if you can understand where they are coming from, you can negotiate meaning more effectively.

Here is an example of the sort of texts students produce when they sit down to produce their actual written responses:

> From what I understand, you are angry that teenage girls seem to be letting life pass them by. They are playing into the roles society seems to have laid out for them, even though the deficiency of women in math

and science is an enormous myth. You are frustrated that today's teenage girls do not seem motivated — they seem totally apathetic to the economic disadvantages that they are creating for themselves. I see young girls in shopping malls who seem to be wasting their lives away, concerned more with buying the right kind of makeup than with insuring that they will have the resources to lead independent lives.

However, I have to ask you this — what about all the successful women in fields other than math and science? I think there are many opportunities in math and science — opportunities that many teenage girls overlook because they think that these fields are too difficult. But your own success in the field of journalism is a prime example of the fact that there are many other ways to achieve not only economic independence but also personal fulfillment.

I don't think we should make girls feel inferior because they have genuinely chosen to enter a non-science field. But I guess the point is that girls should not feel locked out of any profession, and they should take advantage of every strength they have and every opportunity life offers them. Otherwise they are going to end up being dependent on some guy because they don't have the skills they need to look after themselves.

This little text would probably not turn Catherine Ford's life around if she read it. But it would be more likely to engage her in honest debate than would a text that began "How dare you tell me that I'm lazy and ignorant because I'm majoring in the humanities!" More important, it reflects a new understanding on the student's part. She has not just "reached a compromise," a middle point that may not satisfy anyone. Rather, she has thought through what she and Catherine Ford might genuinely share on a subject that she has surely discussed before but perhaps not explored in this way.

The skills learned in this sort of reconstructive reading will, I hope, carry over from civil to academic discourse. As Booth long ago argued, and as rhetorics of science and rhetorics of academic disciplines increasingly make us aware, there is no field of knowledge in which "facts" emerge unencumbered by values. A history paper or even the literature review section of a laboratory report can be enhanced by a Rogerian belief that points of view come from somewhere, that the lenses other people choose to hold up to reality are worthy of honest, empathic understanding.[4]

One may ask, if Rogerian principles go so much beyond mere form, why is all of this Rogerian apparatus needed at all? My answer is that even if Rogerian rhetoric is best seen as fundamentally a matter of invention, this invention is driven by the Rogerian form. As Richard M. Coe contends ("Apology"), to choose any form, any pattern of arrangement, is automatically to impose an invention heuristic. If students are attempting to "fill in the form" of Rogerian rhetoric, they know that they must produce a statement of another's beliefs that the other person can recognize as his or her own and can take seriously. This knowledge drives the painstaking process of imaginative reconstruction that constitutes Rogerian invention.

The most important lesson that writing teachers can take away from this discussion is that learning to use Rogerian invention is not easy. This learning cannot be accomplished in a few classes as a coda to traditional argumentation, as one might think from textbooks that spare it only a few pages.

I don't mean to suggest that an entire composition course ought to be built around explicit instruction in Rogerian rhetoric from beginning to end. Dialogic communication is only one kind of communication, and Rogerian rhetoric is only one kind of dialogic communication. As a form of arrangement, Rogerian rhetoric may not always be appropriate; if communicative bridges are already in place, it may not be necessary to build them, and in some forms of triadic communication it may be desirable to underline only one's own point of view. Students therefore need to be taught a variety of rhetorical forms.

However, the general spirit of Rogerian invention should be woven into the fabric of the course through a variety of exercises that help students learn to understand others' points of view. Rogerian rhetoric is not so much a strategy as a habit of mind that must be built painstakingly over a period of months — or as I will argue, over a lifetime.

Criticisms of Rogerian Rhetoric

Rogerian rhetoric has been subject to a number of criticisms that shed light on its strengths and weaknesses. In particular, these criticisms illustrate the importance of treating Rogerian rhetoric as part of a larger system of knowing and valuing, not as an isolated "technique."

One criticism of Rogerian rhetoric is that it can be manipulative. In formal structure, it looks suspiciously like the often-described "indirect structure" in which a writer buffers unwelcome news or an unpalatable request by flattering the reader. (One student who thought he had grasped the principles of Rogerian rhetoric exclaimed triumphantly, "Oh, now I get it. First you get the reader on your side, then you hit 'em with your own ideas at the end.")

Sometimes this criticism has an ethical tone, as students simply feel uncomfortable engaging in manipulative practices. (In an interview with Nathaniel Teich, Rogers himself states that using his techniques to win an argument or change another's mind is "a perversion of my thinking" [Teich "Conversation" 55].) Sometimes it has a more practical tone. Students frequently protest that Rogerian rhetoric is too idealistic to be used in day-to-day life. People are too hostile, they say, have too often been burned by smooth talkers, to be moved into a more cooperative mindset by Rogerian techniques.

Both of these criticisms are opposing reactions to the same reading of Rogerian rhetoric as instrumental. When seen purely as a *techne*, a specific tool that a student can pull out like a rhetorical torque wrench when a certain job needs doing, Rogerian rhetoric is always open to the charge that it doesn't always turn the nut or that it turns one that should not be turned. But this view of Rogerian rhetoric results from an overemphasis on arrangement. When Rogerian arrangement becomes divorced from the therapeutic roots of Rogers's philosophy, it becomes little more than an updated version of the *benivolentiae captatio* (securing of good will) recommended in medieval and modern letter-writing practice. That structure is as inane now as it was then, and I have written elsewhere about how easily most readers see through it ("Indirect Structure"). Aside from the ethical issues, foregrounded flattery just doesn't work very well in an age in which readers have been inoculated by a lifetime of exposure to sales techniques that would have made Gorgias envious.

However, when Rogerian techniques are taught more as a matter of invention than of arrangement, the emphasis falls more on the underlying attitude rather than the form, the mutual exploration rather than the attempt to convince an "opponent." The goal of Rogerian rhetoric is to identify genuine grounds of shared understanding not just as a precursor to an effective argument but as a means of engaging in effective knowledge making. Rogerian rhetoric is a way of activating the Kantian imperative to pay as much attention to others' ideas as you would have them pay to yours. If the result sometimes looks manipulative to a cynical audience, this is simply the price we pay for living in an imperfect world in which we can never be sure of each other's intentions.

A deeper criticism comes from feminist approaches to language. On the surface, Rogerian rhetoric might appear to be an ideal instantiation of feminist discourse. Studies of women's language suggest that women in conversation tend to engage in more transactional and cooperative than linear and competitive behavior. "Through question-asking and affirming utterances, women's speaking promotes understanding" (Spitzack and Carter 411). Rogerian rhetoric, because it privileges cooperative construction of meaning over goal-directed persuasion, the building of relationships over the winning of an argument, seems to fit neatly into the feminist perspective.

However, Phyllis Lassner, Catherine Lamb, and other feminist rhetoricians have reported that their students and they themselves have felt extremely uncomfortable with Rogerian rhetoric. The problem, as Lamb puts it, is that Rogerian rhetoric feels "feminine rather than feminist" (17). Although studies of women in conversation frequently show them working harder than men at promoting understanding and maintaining relationships, the typical method of doing so, especially in gender-mixed groups, is through self-effacement (Lakoff). Their tendency to interrupt less than men, to ask more questions, and to avoid direct confrontation, can be seen not just as a "maternal" desire to focus on relationships, but also as a willingness to give in, to let the conversation be directed by men. "It has always been women's work to understand others," claims Lamb. "Often that has been at the expense of understanding self" (17).

For men, who have been brought up to value the individualist, goal-directed construction of self, the challenge is to connect with others.

For women, brought up to see themselves as socially constructed through their relationships with others, the challenge is to find ways of *having* a well-defined self without sacrificing that connectedness. Elizabeth Flynn's comparison of compositions by male and female students ("Composing as a Woman") dramatically illustrates these differences in orientation to self and other. In their important study *Women's Ways of Knowing,* Belenky, Clinchy, Goldberger, and Tarule also paint a powerful picture of women whose selves are not simply connected to, but all too often extinguished by, the more dominant selves (frequently but not always male) around them. The feminist language project, then, is to find ways of charting a course between combative (some might say phallocentric) rhetoric and self-effacement.

Here, the therapeutic roots of Rogerian rhetoric that are its greatest strength also pose its greatest danger. The role of the Rogerian therapist is precisely to efface the self to enable the client to use language as a tool of self-exploration. Even for the therapist, this is risky. Because the client in a therapeutic relationship is by definition dysfunctional in some way, the possibility of the therapist's personality being significantly changed by the client's is not necessarily an attractive prospect. "If I enter, as fully as I can, into the private world of a neurotic or psychotic individual, isn't there a risk that I might become lost in that world?" (Rogers "Communication" 333). The same danger confronts any student, male or female, who tries to use Rogerian exploration to enter another's world.

Moreover, as Lassner points out, the detached, unemotional tone recommended by standard Rogerian rhetoric goes against the grain of most women's preferred ways of knowing. As developed by Young, Becker, and Pike under the influence of General Semantics (by way of Anatol Rapoport's studies in conflict resolution), Rogerian rhetoric insists on a nonevaluative, neutral language of pure description that modern language theory, even without reference to feminist insights, rejects as impossible (Brent "Reassessment"). This privileging of rationalist objectivity, with its concomitant assumption that emotional involvement destroys the purity of reason, can be seen as yet another variant on the old theme that women make poor scientists, poor speakers, and poor leaders of society because they are inclined to be emotional.

Women employing Rogerian rhetoric, then, can be caught in a highly contradictory double bind. One tenet of Rogerian rhetoric, empathy, looks too much like feminine subservience; the other, suspension of judgment, looks too much like masculine detachment.

To deal with the first problem, it is important to keep in mind the differences and also the similarities between Rogerian rhetoric and Rogerian therapy. Rogerian rhetoric requires that rhetors suspend their tendency to judge *temporarily,* to make contact with other points of view. But the process does not end there; Rogerian rhetors, unlike Rogerian therapists, have their own point of view as well and put it forward in concert with the picture they have constructed of the other's view. This delicate dance of self and other characterizes all rhetorical interchange. If Rogerian rhetoric is to take its place as a means of participating in this dance, it must be a whole rhetoric, a rhetoric in which the rhetor's views and those of others collaborate in a dialectical process of meaning making.

When students use Rogerian reflection to understand other points of view, then, it is important that they use the glimpses of other selves not just to understand those other selves but also to gain a fuller understanding of their own beliefs and what has caused them to think differently from the others they take in. In classroom practice, this means that the teacher needs to direct discussion toward differences in addition to similarities, and toward understanding the roots of those differences. The students coming to grips with their first defensive reaction to Ford's article, for instance, explored not only what might have made Ford such an outspoken advocate of math and science but also their own experience of gender differences, the reasons for their varied choices of specialization, and their relationship with different forms of knowledge in their high-school years. As part of this process they use not only Rogerian reflection but group conversation, storytelling and freewriting — all methods of exploration that can be and have been used without a Rogerian context but that take on new depth in a Rogerian frame.

Possibly male students profit most from the connection with others entailed by this process whereas female students profit most by the strengthening of their understanding of self. I do not, however, wish to buy into the politics of separation by setting up Rogerian exercises differently for male and female students. Rather, I try to allow space for all differences in meaning making by emphasizing the connections between the two parts of the process — the exploration of self and the exploration of other.

To deal with the second problem, "neutral" language must be valued not as a pure good in itself, but in a dialectical relationship with emotional language and the connection with self that emotion entails. As previously noted, students get a chance to try out their first reactions to an opposing point of view, responding for instance to Ford's caricature of teenage girls with the derision that an overstated viewpoint deserves. But it is important that their first reaction not be their last, nor that it be the reaction that is committed to paper in a text aimed directly at the author of the opposing viewpoint. And even when they are passing through the most overt stage of Rogerian reflection, in which hostile language is to be avoided at all costs, I do not make them feel that avoiding overt hostility means adopting a tone of total detachment. We can strive for empathy, understanding, and the completest possible construction of the other, without supposing that language can ever be a fully neutral descriptor.

In short, most of the more problematic aspects of Rogerian rhetoric result from insufficiently complex uses of the technique and a failure to bring it into line with views of language, gender and politics appropriate to the nineties. Neither Rogers nor Young, Becker, and Pike ever pretended that their ideas were anything but a stage in the development of new paradigms of communication. To teach Rogerian rhetoric as if Young, Becker, and Pike's twenty-year-old formulation were the last word is to ignore the promptings of teacherly common sense and the work of Bator, Teich, Coe, and many others in constantly updating the spirit of nonadversarial rhetoric.

Rogers and the Ethics of Rhetoric

Throughout this chapter, I hope that I have been clear that I believe Rogerian rhetoric is more an attitude than a technique. The specific form of Rogerian discourse in which one must be able to reflect another's point of view before stating one's own is not just a technique to get someone else to listen to you. This form is a technique that helps students learn to connect with other points of view, explore them fully, and place them in a dialectical relationship with their own as part of a process of mutual discovery.

I believe, in consequence, that the benefits of Rogerian rhetoric go far beyond teaching students an alternative model of argument. An important goal of a liberal education is to create citizens who are fully equipped to take their place in society. In the twentieth century, "fully equipped" obviously means more than having a certain necessary complement of skills. "Fully equipped" should mean not only training in how to communicate, but also training in what communication is *for.*

Once people have fully internalized the process of inquiry into another's beliefs — not just the surface of those beliefs but the underlying experiences and values from which they spring — it will be proportionally more difficult for them to treat others as mere instruments for the fulfillment of their own desires. They will be in a better position to find, as Booth puts it, "ground for confidence in a multiplicity of ways of knowing" (see also Bator "Teaching of Rhetoric").

This growth in understanding of others is frequently placed under the heading of "cognitive" growth by developmental researchers such as William Perry. This name is certainly not inappropriate, for the ability to think through one's own position relative to those of others and to find grounds for at least provisional confidence in an intellectual position is certainly a cognitive act. But it is also an ethical act. Cognition is concerned with understanding and ethics is concerned with valuing, but the one presupposes the other. We do not have to value positively all those whom we understand — we may "understand" a Nazi prison guard, as Bruno Bettelheim does in one of Young, Becker, and Pike's examples, without adopting the guard's views. But we certainly cannot make informed ethical choices without being able to explore other points of view.

Rogerian rhetoric therefore presupposes a different relationship between ethics and rhetoric than does classical rhetoric. Quintilian, for instance, insists on virtue as a *precondition* to good rhetoric: Rhetoric is "a good man speaking well." If "virtue" includes being able to achieve understanding of other people, not only those with whom we must argue directly but also those countless others, alive and long dead, who contribute to the rhetorical building of our selves, then Rogerian rhetoric reverses the equation. Rogerian training in speaking well helps to create a "good" person by contributing to ethical and cognitive growth. Good rhetoric is a precondition to virtue.

This is a heavy burden and of course Rogerian rhetoric cannot be expected to carry it alone. The world will not become populated by caring and mutually supportive citizens simply because students are taught one particular method (even if it is, as I believe, a particularly powerful method) of exploring others' points of view. But we could certainly do worse than to take up Rogers's challenge to "take this small scale answer, investigate it further, refine it, develop it and apply it to the tragic and well-nigh fatal failures of communication that threaten the very existence of our modern world" ("Communication" 337).

Coda: Beyond Rogerian Rhetoric

Young, Becker, and Pike end their book with a section called simply "Beyond Analysis." With almost no comment they reproduce A. M. Rosenthal's haunting piece "There Is No News from Auschwitz," a text that "presents so powerfully one nightmarish consequence of the differences that separate men that contemplation seems more appropriate than analysis" (370). This text is an eloquent testimony to the need to develop and teach any textual practices, however imperfect and in need of continued development, that we can find which might help our students bridge such tragic differences.

I would like to end, with equally little comment, with an incident that suggests a more optimistic counterpart to Rosenthal's dark vision: a renewed faith in the healing power of language.

I had paired several sets of students for an oral Rogerian discussion as previously described. One pair decided to discuss drunk driving. They are not exactly on "opposing sides" — who would be *for* drunk driving? — but they had very different views of the problem and its consequences. Was that all right? I told them that it was; in reality, differences of opinion seldom divide along neat bipolar lines of cleavage that allow pat "yes/no" sides.

Lisa went first. Her initial "statement of position" was much fuller than usual. In somewhat abbreviated form, it went like this:

> The year I was born, my grandmother was killed by a drunk driver.
>   She was the stabilizing force in my grandpa's life, so when she died he became a bitter and miserable man. The only time I've ever spent with my grandpa is when he lived with our family after he was seriously injured in another drinking and driving incident. This time he was the drunk. This accident left him crippled and even more miserable.

I see my grandpa once a year. He is usually in his wheelchair complaining. All I think is, "You did this to yourself." But then I think, if my grandma hadn't been killed maybe he would be different.

The driver that killed her robbed me. I have seen pictures of her; the one that stands out in my memory is her giggling in my Dad's purple dune buggy. She was wearing a short skirt, had a beehive and was 50 years old. I never got to meet her.

My family does not dwell on what happened so many years ago. We never talk about what happened to the other driver. But we never drink and drive.

Gayleen went through the motions of reflecting back Lisa's statement, appreciating the pain and the anger contained within it. But there really wasn't much to uncover. Lisa's eloquent narrative hid little that needed to be dug out by Rogerian techniques, and they reached agreement very quickly that Gayleen had "got it."

Gayleen's opening statement was equally full:

I also learned a very hard lesson, but from a different perspective than you, Lisa. I too was the victim of a drunk driver, and I too lost something that day that I will never be able to regain. The difference is that a member of my family was not killed by a drunk driver — a member of my family *was* the drunk driver.

When I was nineteen years old, my fiancé went to a stag party one night. They all drank and then drove home. On the way home, he went through a stop sign and broadsided a car, killing a woman in the back seat.

From that day on, my life was never the same. While the court case dragged on, I was trying to plan a future. But since my fiancé was charged with four counts of criminal negligence causing death, jail was a real possibility. Several people who didn't feel comfortable confronting my fiancé said terrible, hurtful things to me, as if I condoned this act he had chosen. "Friends" dropped us as if we had a contagious disease, including the same guys my fiancé had grown up with and partied with that night, and who also drank and drove themselves home. I also grieved for the family of the woman who was killed, a woman about my mother's age — I kept thinking that it could have been her.

My fiancé was never able to talk about his feelings about that night. Though we got married and were together for twenty years, it set a pattern for him of avoiding difficult situations and emotions. He continued to drink and drive — perhaps ten times in twenty years, but it was ten times too many, and it was the one thing we argued about until our marriage fell apart.

I always wanted to tell the woman's family how truly sorry I was for their loss. I thought of her every day for many years, so that now the incident is a part of the fabric of my being. I don't drink and drive, yet I feel the same shame as if I had been behind the wheel that day.

What more could be said? What could be "reflected back"? Lisa repeated back the pain that Gayleen had expressed, but there was little need; Gayleen had said what needed to be said without benefit of quasi-

Rogerian questioning. And as for working through propositions to isolate areas of mutual validity — well, as you might imagine, we never got that far.

At the end of their "Rogerian discussion," they shared the background of their topic. Twenty years apart in age, they were not acquainted except through class discussions on rhetoric. Gayleen had recognized Lisa's name at the beginning of term, but they had not discussed the incident until they were paired by random number draw. At that time they decided to try discussing their beliefs on drunk driving because they shared far more than a general interest in the subject. The accidents they had discussed were actually the same accident. Gayleen's fiancé had killed Lisa's grandmother.

The class was left speechless by the courage they displayed in talking about this incident in front of people who until two months ago had been total strangers. They also had the courage to revisit the long-standing grief and anger with each other and with their families. Lisa, who had never really talked with her parents about the incident and what it had meant to her family, talked now, and gave a copy of Gayleen's speaking notes to her father. A renewed process of healing through language was begun.

Rogerian rhetoric is lauded for its power to build bridges. But in this instance, the elaborate scaffolding of Rogerian rhetoric was unnecessary because Gayleen and Lisa, through the most impossible of chances, had already found the opportunity to work through their long-separated feelings in both private and public rhetoric. The bridges were already in place when they stood to speak.

There is no news from Auschwitz, but there is news from Communications Studies 461. One news items is that Rogerian rhetoric is not always necessary if the conversants have the will to communicate. But the more important news is that the power of rhetoric, Rogerian or not, to heal is as powerful as its ability to persuade. It has a power that is beyond analysis.

Notes

1. To watch Rogers in action in films such as *Three Approaches to Psychotherapy, II: Dr. Rogers* is instructive. I do not necessarily suggest showing these films to a composition class, as they set up such a powerful image of Rogers's methods as therapy that it may be difficult for students to make the transition to written rhetoric. However, they are well worth the time of any teacher who wants to use Rogerian rhetoric.
2. For a more thorough critical analysis of the strengths and weaknesses of Young, Becker, and Pike's entire project and a more complete discussion of the criticisms that have been leveled at Rogerian Rhetoric over the years, see my article "Young, Becker and Pike's 'Rogerian' Rhetoric: A Twenty-Year Reassessment."
3. Nathaniel Teich recommends exactly the opposite. Because controversial arguments tend to produce intractable positions, Teich suggests avoiding them and concentrating on less emotionally taxing ones ("Rogerian Prob-

lem Solving" 57–58). I take his point, but because emotional situations are precisely the ones in which Rogerian rhetoric is most necessary, I tend to damn the torpedoes and let students argue about gun control, nuclear disarmament and such. Perhaps the main criterion for choosing between these paths is how long the course is — that is, how much time the instructor is able to spend on damage control.

4. In *Reading as Rhetorical Invention* (Urbana: NCTE 1992), I extend this argument to claim that all research, even into the most apparently "factual" information, is strongest when it consists of this sort of imaginative reconstruction of the person behind the text. That we can never do so perfectly — that all reading is fundamentally indeterminate — ought not to dissuade us from teaching our students to come as close as they can.

Works Cited

Bator, Paul. "Aristotelian and Rogerian Rhetoric." *College Composition and Communication* 31 (Dec. 1980): 427–32.

———. "Rogers and the Teaching of Rhetoric and Composition." *Rogerian Perspectives: Collaborative Rhetoric for Oral and Written Communication.* Ed. Nathaniel Teich. Northwood, NJ: Ablex, 1992. 83–100.

Belenky, Mary Field, Blythe McVicker Clinchy, Nancy Rule Goldberger, and Jill Mattuck Tarule. *Women's Ways of Knowing: The Development of Self, Voice, and Mind.* New York: Basic Books, 1986.

Booth, Wayne C. *Modern Dogma and the Rhetoric of Assent.* Chicago: University of Chicago Press, 1974.

Brent, Doug. "Indirect Structure and Reader Response." *Journal of the American Business Communication Association* 22 (Spring 1985): 5–8.

———. "Young, Becker and Pike's 'Rogerian' Rhetoric: A Twenty-Year Reassessment." *College English* 53 (Apr. 1991): 452–66.

———. "Reading as Rhetorical Invention." Urbana, IL: NCTE, 1992.

Coe, Richard M. "An Apology for Form, or, Who Took the Form Out of the Process?" *College English* 49 (Jan. 1987): 13–28.

———. *Process, Form, and Substance: A Rhetoric for Advanced Writers.* Englewood Cliffs, NJ: Prentice Hall, 1990.

———. "Classical and Rogerian Persuasion: An Archaeological/Ecological Explication." *Rogerian Perspectives: Collaborative Rhetoric for Oral and Written Communication.* Ed. Nathaniel Teich. Northwood, NJ: Ablex, 1992. 83–100.

Ede, Lisa S. "Is Rogerian Rhetoric Really Rogerian?" *Rhetoric Review* 3 (Sept. 1984): 40–48.

Flower, Linda. *Problem-Solving Strategies for Writers.* 4th ed. Fort Worth, TX: Harcourt Brace Jovanovich, 1993.

Flynn, Elizabeth. "Composing as a Woman." *College Composition and Communication* 39 (Dec. 1988): 423–35.

Ford, Catherine. "Science Courses Key to Future Jobs." *Calgary Herald* 20 Oct. 1983, A4.

Gage, John. "The Reasoned Thesis: The E-Word and Argumentative Writing as a Process of Inquiry." *Argument Revisited; Argument Redefined: Negotiating Meaning in the Composition Classroom.* Barbara Emmel, Paula Resch, and Deborah Tenney, Eds. Thousand Oaks, CA: Sage Publications, 1996. 1–33.

Hairston, Maxine. "Carl Rogers's Alternative to Traditional Rhetoric." *College Composition and Communication* 27 (Dec. 1976): 373–77.

Lakoff, Robin. *Language and Women's Place.* New York: Harper and Row, 1975.

Lamb, Catherine E. "Beyond Argument in Feminist Composition." *College Composition and Communication* 42 (Feb. 1991): 11–24.

Lassner, Phyllis. "Feminist Responses to Rogerian Argument." *Rhetoric Review* 8 (Spring 1990): 220–31.

Lunsford, Andrea A. "Aristotelian vs. Rogerian Argument: A Reassessment." *College Composition and Communication* 30 (May 1979): 146–51.

Lunsford, Andrea A., and Lisa S. Ede. "On Distinctions Between Classical and Modern Rhetoric." *Essays of Classical and Modern Discourse.* Ed. Robert J. Connors, Lisa S. Ede, and Andrea A. Lunsford. Carbondale and Edwardsville: Southern Illinois University Press, 1984. 37–49.

Mader, Diane C. "What Are They Doing to Carl Rogers?" *Et Cetera* 37 (Winter 1980): 314–20.

Plato. *Gorgias.* Trans. W. C. Helmbold. Indianapolis, IN: Bobbs-Merrill, 1951.

———. *Phaedrus.* Trans. W. C. Helmhold and W. G. Rabinowitz. Indianapolis, IN: Bobbs-Merrill, 1956.

Rogers, Carl R. "Communication: Its Blocking and Its Facilitation." 1951 Rpt. in *On Becoming a Person.* Boston: Houghton Mifflin, 1961. 329–37.

———. "This Is Me." Chapter 1 of *On Becoming a Person.* Boston: Houghton Mifflin, 1961.

———. *Client-Centered Therapy.* Boston: Houghton Mifflin, 1965.

Rogers, Carl R., and David Ryback. "One Alternative to Nuclear Planetary Suicide." *The Consulting Psychologist* 12 (1984): 3–12. Rpt. in *Rogerian Perspectives: Collaborative Rhetoric for Oral and Written Communication.* Ed. Nathaniel Teich. Northwood, NJ: Ablex, 1992. 83–100.

Spitzack, Carole, and Kathryn Carter. "Women in Communication Studies: A Typology for Revision." *Quarterly Journal of Speech* 73 (Nov. 1987): 401–23.

Teich, Nathaniel, Ed. *Rogerian Perspectives: Collaborative Rhetoric for Oral and Written Communication.* Northwood, NJ: Ablex, 1992.

———, Ed. "Conversation with Carl Rogers." *Rogerian Perspectives: Collaborative Rhetoric for Oral and Written Communication.* Northwood, NJ: Ablex, 1992. 55–64.

———. "Rogerian Problem Solving and Rhetoric of Argumentation." *Journal of Advanced Composition* 7 (1987): 52–61.

Three Approaches to Psychotherapy, II: Dr. Rogers. Psychological Films 1977. 50 min., sd., col., 16 mm.

Young, Richard E., Alton L. Becker, and Kenneth L. Pike. *Rhetoric: Discovery and Change.* New York: Harcourt, 1970.

Appendix: Science Courses Key to Future Jobs

Catherine Ford

Calgary Herald

Okay out there — all you teenage girls — listen up and don't turn the page. This is specifically for you.

You won't believe your parents, you won't pay any attention to your teachers and counselors, so I'll try. (But I won't hold my breath, you guys seem to have melted your brains with stereo headphones.)

The world is passing you by, while you're all out there spray-painting your hair purple and reading *People* magazine. About 10 or 15 years from now, you are going to be working at some menial, low-paying, miserable job and wondering what happened.

Allow me to tell you what is happening while it's happening and maybe you can do something about it. There's a whole great world out here waiting for you, if you have enough sense to prepare for it. Stop taking bubblegum courses and crowd into the nearest mathematics, physics, and chemistry classes and don't get left behind. Because you are being left behind even as you think that math and physics are too tough for you to take, and what difference will it make anyway?

It could make all the difference in the world to your future. Yes, you may well be married at 18. You may well meet Mr. Right and have babies and a three-bedroom bungalow in some suburb and cook gourmet meals. But please, for once in your life, listen: you will also work. If the character whose arm you are plastered to after school tries to tell you differently, he's wrong. He may say he will love and support you and let you stay at home and bring up babies, but the cold hard statistics call him a liar.

These days, having a career is not a choice, it's a necessity. You will work for about 30 years of your life and if you think that school is boring, you ain't seen nothing yet. When you graduate from high school, these are the facts you will face.

Over 80 percent of women spend up to 30 years in the workforce.

On average, women earn 40 percent less than men.

Half of Canada's families with two wage earners bring home less than $15,000 a year.

Most women work in clerical, secretarial or unskilled jobs.

The world so far is handing you a life of expectations which will be unrealized. We are in the midst of a technological revolution, and the science courses which are the foundation for jobs in that revolution are overwhelmingly populated with your boyfriends.

Why? Because you think that science and math are too difficult. You have been conned into thinking that. There is no difference between the brains of men and women. You think they're difficult because a society which tries to keep you in your place has led you to believe that.

You think that science and math are unfeminine. That is unadulterated nonsense. If you buy the "unfeminine" label you are condemning yourself to that ghetto reserved for women who still believe it's cute to be stupid. There is only one thing less attractive than stupidity, and that's being stuck in a boring job — or being unemployed, on welfare and seeking job retraining when you're 30.

Within a few years, many of the "traditional" jobs for uneducated women will not exist, as the computer takes over. By dropping science and mathematics, girls eliminate at least half of their job opportunities for the future, and if that isn't frightening, consider the economic implications.

Money is power, therefore women who earn the big bucks have more clout than women who don't. As Senator Bud Olson said last weekend at a conference on Women, The Law and The Economy: "Opportunities and freedoms flow from economic independence." Almost in the same breath he said that women are "discouraged" from entering science and math courses, yet those fields provide one of the fastest ways to economic independence for women.

It seems unfair to have to make lifetime decisions when you're only 14 years old and the most important thing is to have a date for the Grade 9 dance. But it's even more unfair to condemn yourself to always being treated as a 14-year-old, which is about the level of treatment that uneducated, unskilled workers are afforded.

Refutatio as a Prewriting Exercise

A. E. B. Coldiron

Coldiron's essay draws on a classical strategy promoted by Cicero and Quintilian to help students consider multiple points of view when forming arguments. First published in Teaching English in the Two-Year College *in 1991, this piece offers important strategies to help students understand the perspectives of a variety of audiences, deal effectively with opposing viewpoints, and reflect on the importance of context to argumentation. In addition, by actively involving students in their own learning about argumentation, Coldiron's strategies help students develop two particularly important things: a vocabulary of argument that makes sense within the academic world and beyond, and a method of questioning received truths.*

A prevalent problem in freshmen argument or position papers is a wealth of opinion without much factual support. Another frequent problem is the freshman writer's failure to understand that any argument worth arguing has at least two sides. And still another problem is the writer's failure to anticipate and address audience objections to a given position. I've developed an exercise based on a principle of classical rhetoric which helps alleviate all three problems by catching them early in the writing process. Instead of vapid incantations of "there ought to be a law," and instead of formulaic "X Must Be Stopped" essays, the exercise tends to produce papers in which a carefully narrowed claim is supported by appropriate facts and in which serious consideration has been given to the validity of an opposing view.

The exercise? Because it focuses on the section of oratory Cicero (*De Oratore* I.xxxi.143) and Quintilian (*De Institutione Oratoria* III.ix.1) called *refutatio,* I call it the refutatio exercise. I use the exercise as an in-class prewriting session in preparation for writing argument or position essays. After the students have read several argument or position essays and have chosen a topic about which they feel impassioned (or at least on which they have an opinion), I ask them to narrow their position and to bring to class a one-sentence claim statement. "Capital punishment should be abolished," "HOV commuter lanes are a good idea," and "English composition should not be a required course at this school" exemplify the kinds of student claims which can successfully open the refutatio exercise.

Clarifying Claim and Audience

I ask the students to fold a piece of paper lengthwise and to write their narrowed claim statement across the top left side. Then students have five or six minutes to write down all the reasons they feel the way they do. No order or formal construction is required at this point; I emphasize that students are merely jotting or brainstorming on the left side of the page the many reasons they have taken their position. After they've more or less filled the left side of the page, I ask them to select a partner and to trade papers.

Now students are to read the partner's claim and support and are to imagine audiences likely to oppose the claim. I ask students to "get radical" at this point and to imagine as many possible opposed audiences and as wide a range of opposition as they can. Students are to list at the top of the right side of the page as many groups or individuals as they can imagine who might oppose the first writer's claim. One student's claim, for example, was that marijuana should be legalized in the United States. The student who imagined audiences opposed to the originator's claim came up with a range of levels of opposition and reasons for opposition — from Jerry Falwell to William Bennett to concerned parents to inner-city drug dealers. Her reasons for potential opposition, of course, ranged from the moral and religious to the economic and practical. Our discussion of this claim and opposition led us into what were for the students some very new ways of viewing the drug problem. Conjuring opposed audiences can be productive when individual students have the opportunity to exercise imagination first on the right side of the page and then with the entire class.

Developing Opposition

Next the students are to extend their imaginative work by putting themselves in the shoes of those opposing audiences. I ask them to be suspicious, to be iconoclastic, to be downright contrary, and to fill the right side of the page with statements opposing each point their partner, the originating writer, has made. Very often students will protest, saying, "But I agree with everything's she's written here!" I remind students to pretend to be the most radically opposed audience possible and to think through what each opposed group might say in response to the first writer's claim.

Sometimes a role-playing conversation can help stimulate the less imaginative students to come up with opposing points. That can be fun, too — I remember one claim, that English composition classes should be abolished, and a future engineering student who agreed so deeply with the claim that he really couldn't imagine opposition. So we role-played on the spot: I played the student, and he played an English professor. Not only was it hilarious, not only did it lead us into serious consideration of why we were all there in the first place, but it was terrific for the class to follow our struggle through the unfamiliar territory of an opposing viewpoint. Once students have imagined opposing audiences and have begun to explore *why* there is opposition to a given claim, they have taken steps toward Perry-scheme relativism and multiplicity. This part of the exercise is most productive on several levels: Students get to record on the right-hand side of the page their point-by-point rebuttals, and I get to watch minds opening.

Examining Support and Development

To help students record points of opposition during the seven or eight minutes this part of the exercise usually takes, I remind them to look for logical fallacies in the left-side information. I tell them to think, "Maybe so, but what about . . ." and "Not necessarily . . ." I tell them to watch for generalizations, for faulty assumptions, and especially for claims unsubstantiated by facts. Naturally there are many of these; very few freshman writers have facts at their command in an in-class prewriting exercise. But the advantage of this is that it increases the students' capacity to spot flawed support, and it gives student writers a clear lead into the research they may need to back their positions. Simply having another student write something like "Oh yeah? Prove it — I heard that more accidents happen to older drunk drivers than to teenagers" can send students to the library to gather supporting data. At the very least, it engages students in the material and helps them practice identifying problems of logic, development, and support.

After the right side of the page has been filled with opposing statements and identification of weaknesses, I ask the students to return the papers to their originators. This is when the mêlée usually begins. The first writers are surprised and sometimes angry that anyone could be so unreasonable as to disagree, even hypothetically, with their position, or to ask for factual support for an opinion they've taken for granted as truth. At this point I allow several minutes for discussion, either as a class or writer to writer. Frequently students are unaware of possible sources for support, and both instructor and class can offer suggestions. Often discussion arises about the differences between fact, opinion, bias, and belief. This point in the exercise also permits review of appeal strategies. Students now have a focus for their new vocabularies: "Is an aesthetic appeal really convincing here?" or "You appeal to logic but you provide no facts for the audience to work with," and so on.

Technical Logic, Comp-Logic, and the Teaching of Writing

Richard Fulkerson

The following essay was first published in 1988 in College Composition and Communication. *Though it provides somewhat dated critiques of argument textbooks, Richard Fulkerson discusses issues still relevant to argument teachers. First, he provides a careful analysis of the limited ways in which writing instructors have integrated formal logic into argument instruction. Through such analysis, Fulkerson reminds instructors that we must be very careful with the way we define (and misdefine) terms such as "deductive logic" and "inductive logic." He also suggests that we look carefully at the applicability of both formal logic and the Toulmin model of informal logic to writing pedagogy. Finally, and maybe most significantly, Fulkerson provides methods for analyzing textbooks so that teachers and students can select texts that provide concrete strategies for the* process of *writing arguments. He concludes that too much argument theory ignores the process movement in composition and that argument texts can best take advantage of writing process theory by utilizing classical stasis theories.*

For further consideration of stasis theory, see Marie Secor and Jeanne Fahnestock's "The Stases in Scientific and Literary Argument" (p. 58). For further discussion of Stephen Toulmin's work, refer to the selection from Toulmin's The Uses of Argument *(p. 121) and to Gail Stygall's "Toulmin and the Ethics of Argument Fields: Teaching Writing and Argument" (p. 377). Readers interested in pursuing Richard Fulkerson's later work on argumentation should consult* Teaching the Argument in Writing *and "The Toulmin Model of Argument and the Teaching of Composition" in Barbara Emmel, Paula Resch, and Deborah Tenney's* Argument Revisited; Argument Redefined: Negotiating Meaning in the Composition Classroom.

Frederick Crews tells a story about teaching logic to composition students at U.C. Berkeley early in his career. He spent "two weeks drawing interlocked circles on the blackboard representing syllogisms and enthymemes" (11). The results, he said, were "stupefyingly irrefutable papers" built on syllogisms such as,

> My major premise is that all freshmen at Berkeley are eager to succeed in life.
>
> I am a freshman at Berkeley.
>
> It therefore follows that I am eager to succeed in life. (11)

One illustration of teaching gone awry proves almost nothing, but I find this anecdote revealing. Like Crews, many of us — encouraged by materials that pervade our textbooks — have attempted to introduce some features of what Walter Fisher calls "technical logic" into our classrooms. Rarely, I think, with success.

The rationale for including some technical logic in composition is simple and apparently impeccable. First, much of the writing we teach, even writing we label as exposition, involves argument because it involves the attempt to support some claims (such as theses and topic sentences) with other claims (such as details, examples, and quotations). That attempt is, by definition, argument (see Copi 6). Second, since logic is the intellectual discipline dedicated to analyzing and evaluating argument (Copi 3), then logic should be useful in teaching our students how to improve any writing that involves argument. As Fisher puts it, "argumentation is the theme in the rhetorical tradition that ties rhetoric to logic" (3).

Such borrowings from technical logic also have eminent classical sanction, since it was Aristotle who declared rhetoric to be the counterpart of dialectic and the enthymeme to be a rhetorical syllogism. But it is worth noticing that Aristotle's *Rhetoric*, unlike many current composition texts, includes no discussion of the syllogism.

A glance through current composition textbooks reveals a consequence of that "impeccable" rationale, an apparently accepted paradigm of how logic should be treated in composition, a paradigm I will call comp-logic. It is an attempt to borrow elements of technical logic and make them relevant to rhetorical logic (that term is also Fisher's). Comp-logic includes three parts: "induction," by which composition texts mean generalizing from evidence; "deduction," by which composition texts mean reasoning from general principle to specific case; and an array of material fallacies that students are to avoid. Almost always the paradigmatic materials are presented in a separate section or chapter of a larger text.

But the rationale for teaching the comp-logic paradigm is in fact dangerously flawed, and our common textbook presentations are frequently so confused and confusing as to be almost useless either for creating arguments or criticizing them. Furthermore, the goal of assisting students to produce effective argumentative discourse can probably be achieved more successfully by borrowing either from modern informal logic or from the mostly neglected classical stasis theory.

The Terms "Induction" and "Deduction" in Comp-Logic

When English textbooks borrow the technical terms "induction" and "deduction," more limited definitions are given to both terms than they have within technical logic. This would be perfectly reasonable: In rhetoric courses we do not need *all* the logician's baggage. But in addition, the definitions we use invite confusion, partly because they stress an ambiguous motion metaphor, and partly because we present the two terms as complementary and exhaustive (e.g., all arguments are supposed to be one or the other), when, in our usage, they are not.

Here are typical definitions from a 1985 composition textbook: "Reasoning by induction means *moving from* individual pieces of evidence to a conclusion" (Gere 185, emphasis added). The same textbook says that "reasoning by deduction means *moving from* a general statement to a conclusion about the particular case" (Gere 187, emphasis added).

I invite you to go with me now into a freshman class the morning after this material has been assigned. It is, let us say, 9:00 A.M. After checking the roll, collecting daily journals, answering a question or two, the teacher begins:

> *Teacher:* Now then, what was the main subject of the reading assignment for today?
>
> *Class in General:* Induction and deduction.
>
> *Teacher:* And what did your text say they were?
>
> *First Student (Reading):* "Inductive reasoning proceeds from a number of particular cases to a generalized conclusion; deductive reasoning proceeds from the application of a general principle to a particular case and then to a particular conclusion" (Adelstein and Pival 356).
>
> *Teacher:* O.K. That is *exactly* what it says. Now, in your own words, what does that mean?
>
> *Second Student:* It means that in induction you go from specific instances to a general conclusion, but in deduction you go from the general to the particular.

Our teacher finds herself at an impasse. She isn't sure of what the students actually understand or even of how to find out. She resists the temptation to resort to a minilecture, and finally inspiration strikes. She writes two, almost identical, paragraphs on the board. Both argue for the claim that "Even honors students are sometimes lazy." The first opens with the claim, then gives three examples. The other gives the same three examples, but puts the claim at the end.

> *Class in General:* Yeah, that's it. The first is deductive reasoning; the second is inductive.
>
> *Teacher:* That's what I suspected. You are confusing the *order* of presentation of an argument with the *type* of reasoning. The reasoning in these paragraphs is identical; both show induction.

Second Student: But that's what the book said! "Movement from the general to particulars is deductive; movement from particulars to the general is inductive" (Guinn and Marder 69). That's what the second paragraph does, but the first one is just the opposite. So the first *has* to be deduction.

For the rest of the period, in circles mostly, the conversation continues.

Ironically, the students have just reasoned very well from the textbook definitions. They have applied them to the teacher's sample paragraphs and come out with conclusions, in almost classical syllogistic form.

The fact that the conclusions are wrong, though validly derived, merely indicates the ambiguity of the definitions. Despite the frequent use of motion metaphors like "going from" in English textbooks, the order of presentation is irrelevant to the type of argument involved. Whether one "goes from" the premises first and follows with the conclusion or "goes from" the conclusion to the premises (or some other combination), the same set of premises and conclusions will always be the same argument.

In technical logic, the difference between an inductive argument and a deductive one involves neither the notion of movement nor the notion of general and specific. In technical logic any argument in which the premises purport to prove the conclusion (*entail* is the technical term) is a deduction. And all other arguments, those in other words in which the premises purport to make the conclusion highly probable, are induction (Copi 169 and 403: see also Hurley 491 and 494; and Kahane, *Logic and Philosophy* 12).

Let me illustrate. Here is an argument that in technical logic is inductive because the premises do not purport to guarantee the conclusion:

Most up-to-date writing teachers stress invention.

She seems from her discussion to be up-to-date.

So she probably emphasizes invention in her classroom.

But in comp-logic this is "deduction" because it "goes from" general to specific.

Comp-logic limits deduction to arguments in the form of the BARBARA syllogism (exemplified by the chestnut upon Socrates' mortality)[1] and structures similar to it like my example above. Comp-logic "deduction" thus leaves out most of what technical logicians mean when they use the term: categorical syllogisms that do not move from general premise to specific conclusion; other sorts of syllogisms (such as hypothetical); plus the entire modern corpus called symbolic logic. Similarly, comp-logic's "induction" excludes much of what logicians mean by induction: arguments from analogy, authority, and sign, for example.

There is nothing inherently wrong in using the terms to mean what we want them to mean. But we should be aware that our definitions differ so dramatically from those used in technical logic that we are not in actuality making much use of whatever that field has to offer. And we should be aware that many types of common arguments do not fit the comp-logic definition of either induction or deduction.

On the other hand, there is something wrong with using the terms in vague and confusing ways as our books do. Furthermore, as Michael Scriven has pointed out, since any inductive argument can be turned into a valid deductive argument by stating the "unstated" premises, "the distinction isn't one you would want to build very much on" (34).

"Induction" in Comp-Logic

Even though many logicians now restrict technical logic to deduction (see Kneale and Kneale), probably the most valuable borrowing in comp-logic is the treatment of what we call "induction." Typically, our texts define it as "the process of drawing a conclusion . . . from particular instances or evidence" (Gefvert 465). It would be more aptly named *argument by generalization*. Because much student writing *does* involve giving examples or details to support a general claim, including discussion of "induction" in this sense seems perfectly sensible.

To show students what makes a good induction, our texts borrow an evaluation system that can be summed up neatly with the acronym STAR. The STAR system requires that there be Sufficient, Typical, Accurate, and Relevant examples in order to support a generalization.

In comp-logic we make the STAR system serve our purposes by applying it contextually instead of logically. That is, instead of asking whether the evidence is extensive enough to justify logically a conclusionary leap, we ask "Are the examples sufficient to persuade a reader?" and "Will a reader perceive them as typical and accurate?" The concepts of generalizing from examples and of evaluating such inferences by a contextual use of the STAR system are useful in composition. Indeed, they are common sense.

"Deduction" in Comp-Logic

As explained above, comp-logic presents deduction as a syllogism or quasi-syllogism in which a general rule or principle, enunciated in the first or major premise, is applied to a specific case, identified in the second premise. But unlike borrowing the principle of argument by generalization, borrowing the BARBARA syllogism from traditional technical logic is of little use in teaching composition for three reasons.

First, writers rarely build full categorical syllogisms. Instead they use abbreviated forms phrased with noncategorical premises. Consequently, the structure of major, minor, and middle terms, and the distribution rules for validity, and the distinction between soundness and validity rarely fit even writing that does apply general principles to specific cases, such as a *Consumer Reports* product evaluation or a legal brief. So none of this material, which our textbooks frequently import from technical logic, *applies* to most written discourse.

Second, all valid syllogisms, including BARBARA, must have at least one universal premise (e.g., *all* humans have to be mortal). Not surprisingly, our texts do not discuss what sorts of universal, categorical premises students might build arguments on, especially arguments about contingent issues. So students told to write papers based on syllogisms are likely to use as their premises sweeping generalizations, such as "all teachers who give essay tests are unfair" or "all lies are bad." Or even, "all freshmen at Berkeley are eager to succeed."

Third, recall that in both comp-logic and technical logic a deduction is an argument in which the premises purport to entail the conclusion. In other words, in a properly carried out deduction (that is, in a valid one), the truth of the premises guarantees that the conclusion follows. (The most convenient illustration for many of us is a proof in geometry.) Writing, however, almost always deals with contingent issues, issues in which the evidence will never entail the conclusion. (Notice I felt compelled to make even *that* claim a contingent one by saying "almost always.") Given its contingent-ness, writing has little use for the certitudes of deductive reasoning. The moment we acknowledge the contingent nature of our conclusions, we leave the realm of deduction for what Chaim Perelman properly calls, in his book of that title, "the realm of rhetoric." Perelman reminds us, as Aristotle had also done, that most of the argumentation we are concerned about is in the realm of the probable rather than the certain. For that reason, Perelman and Olbrechts-Tyteca devote a long section of *The New Rhetoric* to "Quasi-Logical Arguments," arguments which look somewhat like syllogisms but really are not (193–95). Neither technical logic's broad view of deduction, nor comp-logic's more limited view, applies to real-world discourse.

William McCleary conducted a thoughtful empirical study about the effects on student writing of teaching technical deductive logic. A control group of community college freshmen studied composition without studying any logic, and two groups studied traditional syllogistic deduction in slightly different ways. All students were tested on gains in critical thinking, and upon improvements in writing argumentative essays on moral issues.

McCleary concluded, "There is no evidence that studying logic had a positive effect on students' written arguments. In fact, most evidence, though seldom statistically significant, points in the opposite direction" (196). His study found just what the theoretical analysis above would lead one to expect.

I cannot resist adding that since English teachers are not generally trained in syllogistic logic, comp-logic frequently includes bizarre remarks. If students' writing were genuinely affected by what they had studied, they would be in trouble. And if, God forbid, logicians were to read our textbooks, they would have fits, of either laughter or apoplexy.

I have collected a rogues' gallery of the more exotic remarks about the syllogism from our texts. Let me share three of them.

(1) Gerald Levin in *Writing and Logic* attempts to distinguish between validity and soundness, a standard and important distinction in technical logic, but one of little relevance to real discourse. He gives the following example:

> Mathematics is an exact science.
>
> Astrology is wholly based on mathematics.
>
> Therefore, astrology is an exact science. (93)

He remarks, "As we can see from the last argument, valid syllogistic reasoning has great persuasive force even when it is unsound" (93). That may be true, but we cannot see it from this syllogism, since the syllogism is neither valid nor sound. (In technical logic, a syllogism is called *valid* if it is in proper form; to be *sound* it must be valid and have true premises as well. But technical logic is not concerned with soundness beyond pointing out that validity does not guarantee it.) Levin's syllogism commits the four-term fallacy, since its categories are mathematics, exact sciences, astrology, and "things based on mathematics." Since it is formally fallacious it is invalid. And thus unsound as well.

(2) Miller and Judy, after expressing intuitive disdain for formal logic, nevertheless go on to discuss deductive reasoning and state a rule that "the same term cannot appear as the direct object of both major and minor premises" (117). Now, since all propositions in a categorical syllogism must be expressed with copula verbs, there are no direct objects in the premises. I assume Miller and Judy mean to say that the same term cannot appear as the *predicate* of both major and minor premises. Which is wrong. It would make invalid every syllogism of the figure two configuration (see note 1), when in fact at least four moods of that syllogism are valid (see Hurley 204–05).

The following syllogism, for example, with "scholars" as the predicate of both premises is perfectly valid:

> All composition teachers are scholars.
>
> No politicians are scholars.
>
> Therefore, no politicians are composition teachers.

(3) My nominee for the single most erroneous presentation comes from Daniel McDonald's *The Language of Argument,* 2nd ed. He claims that "commonly, 'valid form' means that the general subject or condition of the major premise must appear in the minor premise as well" (50). That's confusing, but it might be a mere slip of the pen. However, McDonald uses it to explain the following syllogism:

All thieves have ears.

All Presbyterians have ears.

All Presbyterians are thieves.

What makes this argument "unreliable syllogistically is that the major term 'thieves' does not appear in the minor premise" (51). Since it is impossible, by definition, for the major term to appear in the minor premise, this is nonsense. (The analysis is changed somewhat in the third edition of McDonald's text, made even worse in my view. See p. 71.)

I have found many other examples nearly as erroneous. But I will resist the temptation to multiply my inductive proof, and simply leap to the conclusion that our textbooks' presentations about deduction are full of errors. May God help the naive professor or graduate assistant who falls innocently into the pit of teaching from such a book and takes it seriously. It may be necessary for composition teachers to learn about deductive logic purely to defend themselves from such materials.

Since presentations about "deduction" are likely to be both confused and confusing, since deduction demands absolute entailment of the conclusion and universal premises, and since empirical evidence suggests that student writing is not improved by studying deduction even when presented accurately, our time could be better spent if we deleted the teaching of "deduction" from the comp-logic paradigm. (Now I ask you, does this paragraph involve an inductive argument or a deductive one?)

The Treatment of Material Fallacies in Comp-Logic

The third element of comp-logic involves teaching a list of common nonformal or material fallacies, argument types which though unsound are common enough and deceptive enough to have been given names and studied widely. Such presentations are an honored tradition, going all the way back to Aristotle's *On Sophistical Refutations*. They play a major role in the modern informal logic movement (led by such figures as Ralph Johnson and J. A. Blair, editors of *Informal Logic Quarterly*) as well as in a good number of English textbooks. Some composition authors such as Hartwell prefer a brief list of five or six, realizing that a great deal is left out. Others opt for thoroughness, at the risk of overkill: Barry's *Good Reason for Writing* indexes over thirty fallacies, and Spurgin's *The Power to Persuade* includes twenty-four. (The record number of fallacies discussed may be the more than 112 in David Fischer's *Historians' Fallacies: Toward a Logic of Historical Thought*.)

Teaching some fallacy theory in composition may be a good idea, although I know of no careful study of the question. But at least three problems have to be dealt with.

First, fallacy theory is inherently incomplete. As Horace Joseph put it in 1906, "truth may have its norms, but error is infinite in its aberrations" (569). The fewer fallacies a text presents, the more room for illogic the student is left. But the greater the number of fallacies presented, the greater the chances of confusion. And no matter how many fallacies are included, the list will always remain incomplete. Second, fallacy theory is inherently negative. It tells students some argumentative moves to avoid, but not how to reason well. Teaching fallacies is very much like concentrating on grammar errors as a means of improving sentence structure: It presumes that if all the fallacies/ errors are removed, the result is good argument/writing.

Third, and most important, even within the field of logic, material fallacies are not clearly defined and distinguished from each other. C. L. Hamblin noted, in what has become the standard full-length discussion *Fallacies,* that "nobody, these days, is particularly satisfied with this corner of logic. The traditional treatment is too unsystematic for modern tastes. . . . We have no *theory* of fallacy at all in the sense in which we have theories of correct reasoning" (11). A decade later, Maurice Finocchiaro, a member of the editorial board of the *Informal Logic Quarterly,* surveyed the ground again. Despite the growth of the informal logic movement, complete with many textbooks concentrating almost exclusively on fallacies, he concluded,

> [T]extbook accounts of fallacies are basically misconceived, partly because their concept of fallacy is internally incoherent, partly because the various alleged fallacious practices have not been shown to be fallacies, partly because their classification of fallacies is unsatisfactory, and partly because their examples are artificial. (18)

When such material becomes part of comp-logic, it rarely improves in the translation.

Some illustrations of the internal incoherence of fallacy theory: Every *post hoc* argument is also a hasty generalization. So is stereotyping. And a *non sequitur,* included in many texts, is any argument in which the conclusion does not follow from the premises — a definition that includes *post hoc,* hasty generalization, and stereotyping.

Since many fallacies parallel good arguments, definitions often seem to fit both a fallacy and its legitimate cousin. We tell students that they must not argue *ad populum,* because an appeal to the crowd's emotions is fallacious. Yet we simultaneously tell them that a good argument persuades through *pathos,* certainly an appeal to the emotions.

I tell my technical logic students that they must learn the difference between an irrelevant appeal to pity (such as a student's arguing for a better grade on the ground of having experienced a romantically disastrous semester) and a relevant appeal to pity (such as an argument that we should help save baby seals from being cruelly slaughtered for their pelts). And I tell them they must distinguish between a slippery slope fallacy and its cousin, the legitimate argument from negative consequences. In both cases, they find it difficult to tell the difference.

Many texts that present fallacies conclude with a name-that-fallacy exercise, a task which seems valuable *in a logic class* where there is time to study fallacies at length and where weaknesses in fallacy theory can be discussed. But such exercises are of dubious value in a writing course. Given the vague and overlapping definitions of the fallacies, especially in English texts, it is no wonder that I have frequently had to shepherd even bright graduate teaching assistants through these exercises. Without the teacher's manual to provide the "right" answers, they were often stumped by the questions. (See for example Rottenberg 192–94.)

In a new composition text, Wayne Booth and Marshall Gregory try to turn the definitional difficulty into a virtue. In a section entitled "From 'fallacies' to 'rhetorical resources,'" they analyze twenty-six fallacies and discuss how the same reasoning patterns can be used legitimately. Hasty generalization obviously pairs with generalization, poor analogy with analogy, authority with false authority. Bandwagon they match with tradition or folk wisdom, an ironic pairing since arguments from tradition have also been identified as fallacious (Kahane, *Logic and Contemporary Rhetoric* 56, and Rottenberg, 2nd ed. 198). Of the twenty-six fallacies, Booth and Gregory find only two that have no legitimate parallels, card stacking and the appeal to force (408–26). (But see Kielkopf, who argues that there are legitimate appeals to force.) This presentation is honest about the fuzziness of standards for determining an argument to be materially fallacious, but it may leave students even more confused about fallacies than our textbooks typically do.

Comp-Logic and Writing-as-Process

Comp-logic, like technical logic, provides criteria for judging existent argumentative texts. Writing-as-process, on the other hand, describes the complex sequence of recursive and interactive processes which generate and refine texts.

Almost never do the two paradigms meet in composition textbooks. No book that I have examined integrates the two by discussing the processes a student would use to build an argument satisfying the book's criteria. This isn't surprising: Logic and comp-logic are tools for criticizing arguments, not for generating them. Not since Peter Ramus have logicians concerned themselves with how arguments are created.

It is a revealing fact, I think, that most of the full-length argument texts for composition classes are actually argument anthologies with some accompanying apparatus presenting principles of logic. In other words, they stress critical analysis of already written (and usually professional) arguments in the hope that students can imitate what they have read (see Rottenberg, Spurgin, McDonald, Barry). But they do not discuss the procedures the authors went through to build their arguments, and they offer students virtually no advice about generating arguments.

The Toulmin Model of Argument

Recognizing the problems with the common comp-logic paradigm, a few English textbook authors, following the lead of Brockriede and Ehninger in speech, have adopted the six-part Toulmin model of argument first presented in *The Uses of Argument*. Most isolate the model in a single chapter or section, just as the comp-logic paradigm is usually presented (Hairston, Winterowd, Levin, Spurgin, Dodds, Gage, Hartwell). Only one book that I am aware of uses Toulmin as an informing principle with separate chapters on claim, data (or grounds), warrants, and backing — Rottenberg's *Elements of Argument*.

The Toulmin model is attractive in precisely the ways that traditional logic proved troublesome. It does away with any distinction between induction and deduction, rejecting both terms. It concerns both form and substance of an argument, and it raises the question of where one gets "warrants" (the Toulmin counterpart of universal premises). It explicitly deals with the contingent nature of conclusions, as well as with the existence of counterarguments. It continues to stress the STAR evaluation under its heading of "grounds," and it is consistent with any fallacy theory one wants, since all the traditional fallacies can be explained as involving defects in grounds, warrant, or backing.

Yet, there are significant difficulties in using the Toulmin model as it appears in our textbooks. Since Toulmin's model rejects the distinction between induction and deduction, a confusing overlap occurs whenever the model appears side by side with "induction," as in Hairston's *Contemporary Composition*. Within the Toulmin approach, induction is simply any argument with instances as grounds, and a warrant which says "what is true of a sample is very likely true of the group as a whole" (Toulmin, Rieke, and Janik 219).

Presenting Toulmin side by side with traditional deduction, as Levin and Winterowd do, is even more theoretically inconsistent, since Toulmin developed his model as an alternative after a scathing attack on traditional concepts of the syllogism. One of his British colleagues, in fact, continually referred to *A Theory of Argument* as "Toulmin's anti-logic book" (cited by Toulmin, "Logic and the Criticism of Arguments" 392).

A second problem arises whenever an author assumes as some books seem to, that the Toulmin model applies to an entire discourse. The Toulmin model, like traditional deduction and induction, fits only a single argument, that is, any move from grounds to claim. Thus, as Charles Kneupper has argued, it rarely fits full essays, but can be used, with some strain, to explicate any single argumentative move. Kneupper, for example, uses it to explicate the first paragraph of "Civil Disobedience" (293–40).

A third problem is that while the model provides a framework for analyzing an argument, for seeing its various parts and how they interrelate, unlike traditional logic it does not provide a means of evaluation. The fact that an argument has or lacks one or several of the six parts does not make it a good argument or a bad one. Evaluation must come from other sources, and since Toulmin maintains that arguments can be evaluated only within a discourse field according to the canons of that field, evaluating argument in a nondisciplinary writing course becomes problematic.

And finally, Toulmin logic, like traditional logic, is a tool for analyzing existing arguments, rather than a system for creating them. It shares with the more traditional technical logic and comp-logic paradigms difficulties in being integrated into a course attempting to teach a generative process.

Here, however, may be a unique potential of the Toulmin model. Conceivably the six parts could be converted into heuristic questions in a way that comp-logic cannot be. The student would ask the following sequence of questions:

1. "What is my claim?"

2. "What grounds do I have to support it?" (using STAR again).

3. "What statement could warrant my move from the grounds to the claim?"

4. "How can I back up that warrant?"

5. "How much must I qualify my conclusion as contingent?"

6. "What counterarguments that would weaken my conclusion do I need to acknowledge?"

No book currently available turns Toulmin's model into an invention scheme, although Rottenberg makes some gestures in this direction, as does Winterowd, who says the "model provides a guide to *prewriting* the persuasive essay" (248).

John Gage's *The Shape of Reason* fuses parts of Toulmin logic with some traditional syllogistic logic and with classical rhetoric's theory of the enthymeme into the closest thing I have found to an integration of logical concepts and writing as a process. Gage advocates that students learn to phrase each thesis first as a complex enthymeme, consisting of the claim plus the major line of support, and then to add the necessary unstated assumption (or Toulmin warrant) connecting the two. He uses the example of a student who creates the following framework for a paper: "Scientific education should include the issue of moral responsibility so that scientists will learn to consider the harmful effects of their research and weigh them against the potential good, because harmful effects are always possible" (89). In Toulmin's terms we have,

CLAIM: Scientific education should include the issue of moral responsibility.

GROUNDS: Scientists would then learn to consider the harmful effects of their research.

WARRANT: Harmful effects are always possible.

This is obviously not a strong argument. The grounds are not givens already accepted by both arguer and opponents, and the "warrant" does not in fact connect the grounds to the claim. But Gage supplements Toulmin by proposing several standards for evaluating such a frame (87) and shows the student criticizing this initial formulation and creating a more sophisticated one: "Ethics classes for scientists will teach them to weigh the potential harmful effects of their research against the potential good, because raising questions of right and wrong in relation to science will confront them with their compassionate feelings for other people" (103). Notice that not only has the support been changed; the claim is different as well. It has been transformed from a policy assertion to a causal one.

But whether the student can actually make the causal connection plausible, and sustain the implied claim that without such courses scientists will not weigh potential harmful effects of their research, is doubtful. So far the student has only a general framework, a sort of outline; the real ground for this argument, the evidence, has yet to be generated. And neither the Toulmin model, nor comp-logic, nor technical logic tells him how to do that.

In his research, McCleary examined the effects on freshman writing of studying the Toulmin model of argument. Again the students who studied Toulmin logic improved their argumentative writing no more than those who studied no logic at all.

However, because of the complexity of the Toulmin model, and the various ways it might conceivably be presented to a class, including the heuristic possibility above, the McCleary study is less convincing on this matter than on classical deduction.

The verdict on the Toulmin model in composition is still out. And several doctoral dissertations probably are hiding in the jury room.

Stasis Theory: A Nonlogical Approach to Argumentation?

Despite all the above, our students *do* need to learn to write effective arguments. And a precondition of that skill is being able to judge when an argument is effective and when it isn't. If neither comp-logic nor technical logic will help, where are we to look? My answer is that we should look to stasis theory, developed in classical rhetoric but expanded and adapted by several composition theorists in the last fifteen years.

In the rhetorics of Aristotle and Cicero, among others, stasis theory was mainly a system of possible courtroom defenses, but modern adaptations are more inclusive.

Two current composition textbooks are based on stasis theory, *A Rhetoric of Argument* by Fahnestock and Secor and *Real Writing* by Walter Beale. Several others refer to it in passing.

This is not the place for a full-blown discussion of stasis theory. Interested readers should consult the articles by Fahnestock and Secor and by Eckhardt and Stewart in the bibliography. But I do want to outline the essence of stasis theory and to suggest how it achieves the goals of comp-logic yet avoids most of the problems.

Stasis theory classifies arguments in a wholly different way from logic, not by their form (such as categorical or hypothetical syllogism) or by the type of premises used (such as argument from authority or argument from analogy) or even the relationship between premises and conclusions (deductive demonstration or inductive probability), but by the ontological status of the reality claim the conclusion asserts. In stasis theory, an argument of fact differs from an argument of value, and both differ from an argument of policy. In stasis theory, any argument for a policy conclusion is called a policy argument. It is appropriate to use the phrase "stasis of policy" to describe either the conclusion reached or the entire argument.

In no traditional sense is stasis theory a part of technical logic, since it classifies arguments by the substance of the conclusion. But if one considers that the goal of logic is the evaluation of argument strength, then stasis theory can provide at least as strong a methodology as traditional induction or the Toulmin model, through the mechanism of the *stasis-specific prima facie case.*

The notion of a *prima facie* case comes from both law and competitive debate. It means that the case (extended argument) made for a claim is structurally and substantively complete so that if no countercase were presented then the claim would stand. For each type of *stasis* being argued, certain elements must be present before the case can be regarded as complete and in need of evaluating. As an example, in a court of law, a *prima facie* case for the charge of battery must normally include four items:

There must have been a touching by the defendant,

The touching must have been either offensive or harmful,

The touching must have been unconsented,

And it must have been intentional rather than accidental.

If anything is lacking, the prosecution has presented a "bad" argument, and the case will be dismissed without any defense being necessary. Handling all four, however, does not mean that the prosecution will win. It merely means that an argument of sufficient strength has been presented to necessitate some response. The *prima facie* case is thus a minimum but crucial criterion for a satisfactory argument.

In this illustration, the *stasis* can reasonably be called substantiation (Eckhardt and Stewart's term) or interpretation (Beale's term). The defense attorney might counter the case and remain in the same stasis by pointing out that the touching was "privileged" (as when a boxer strikes another boxer, or a parent spanks a child). On the other hand, the defense might choose to shift the stasis to one of value, by admitting that the defendant's acts do indeed fit the definition of battery but were nevertheless proper in terms of some greater good. This was Brutus's defense for murdering Caesar, and it is the standard defense of civil protesters tried on such charges as trespassing on government property. In "Toward a Modern Version of Stasis," Fahnestock and Secor refer to opponents in a federal inquiry chasing "one another up and down the stases" (218).

Books built around stasis theory divide the types of claims a student might need to argue for and then discuss what is required to create a *stasis specific prima facie* case for each one. The presentations vary, but all are consistent, differing mainly in terminology and the number of major stases presented. In *Real Writing,* Beale presents three: interpretation, value, and policy. Fahnestock and Secor present four in *A Rhetoric of Argument:* "What is it?" "How did it get that way?" "Is it good or bad?" and "What should we do about it?"

Stasis theory does not exclude other potentially useful portions of comp-logic. In every stasis, a rhetor must generalize from evidence, that is, reason "inductively" in the comp-logic sense, and the STAR evaluation system still applies. In fact, the STAR criteria are almost identical to traits of a good argument of the first stasis (interpretation or substantiation). In every stasis a fallacious argument is still fallacious. And every stasis can be fitted into the Toulmin model (see Brockriede and Ehninger), although no composition text that I know of has integrated stasis theory and Toulmin. Furthermore, unlike comp-logic, stasis theory does provide an invention system, because the elements of the *prima facie* case immediately translate into heuristic questions.

Unlike both technical logic and Toulmin logic, stasis theory applies to full discourses rather than single arguments within a discourse. And it can include evaluative principles for each stasis.

In addition, stasis theory provides two extra-argumentative advantages. First, it creates an easily applied discourse taxonomy with increasing levels of complexity as one moves from substantiation to evaluation to policy. Second, it includes concepts of what constitutes effective *arrangement* of an argument in each stasis.

Unfortunately, the textbooks currently built on stasis theory do not integrate stasis theory into a process approach to writing. Each book presents writing as a process in a separate section and then devotes single sections to each stasis. Moreover, these texts are complex and relatively dry and difficult to read. Thus they are not well suited for most freshman classes, although in my experience Beale's *Real Writing* has worked well with honors students.

Conclusion

Based on what our textbooks typically provide, Kaufer and Neuwirth's conclusion seems correct: "Students typically come away from their writing course with a hodgepodge of information about syllogism, Aristotelian topics, fallacy, evidence, and warrants, but they have little idea how to put this information to use when actually composing" (388).

That occurs because our textbook transmutations of technical logic into comp-logic are both ambiguous and ill-conceived to begin with. Even if adapted well, much of what can be borrowed from technical logic is unlikely to be helpful to writers because it describes products not processes and because the absolute nature of deduction ill suits the contingent nature of argumentative discourse. Toulmin logic does suit such contingency, but it has a wealth of unresolved problems of its own.

For contingent arguments, stasis theory can provide heuristic questions leading to sensible procedures for writing each stasis. It also provides criteria for judging arguments of the same stasis, and a progressive taxonomy upon which courses can be built. Thus can a borrowing from classical rhetoric do what our borrowings from technical logic cannot, provide systematic and useful approaches to teaching written argument.

Note

1. In fact, BARBARA is a mnemonic code to indicate that the syllogism has three Universal Affirmative or type-A propositions.

   The vowels *A, E, I,* and *O* were used in medieval times to designate the four types of propositions. The vowels supposedly come from the Latin verbs *affirmo* and *nego*. Thus *A* and *I* designate affirmative propositions, such as "All teachers are hard workers" and "Some teachers are hard workers" respectively. *E* and *O* designate negative propositions of the forms "No teachers are lazy" and "Some teachers are not lazy." The medieval logicians gave personal names to each valid syllogistic form, names in which the three vowels represent the types of propositions in the syllogism. Thus CELARENT refers to a valid syllogism with an *E* major premise, an *A* minor premise, and an *E* conclusion.

   But there are four possible syllogisms with that configuration of propositions, depending on the position of the middle term in the two premises. CELARENT is specifically a syllogism in which the middle term appears as the subject of the major premise and the predicate of the minor premise, or what is called Figure 1. If the middle term appears as the predicate of both premises, we have Figure 2. The Figure 2 syllogism with the same types of propositions (EAE) is CESARE. In more modern technical logic these two valid forms are designated simply EAE-1 and EAE-2. EAE-3 and EAE-4 also exist, but both are invalid. Thus they lack medieval names.

   The medieval logicians were ingenious; not only did all the valid syllogisms have names whose vowels represented the propositions, but a mnemonic rhyming jingle was used to teach the valid syllogisms for each of the four figures. In Figure 1 these are BARBARA, CELARENT, DARII, and FERIOQUE. Moreover, the consonants in each name represent complex ways by which syllogisms of the second, third, and fourth figures can be transformed into equivalent syllogisms of the first figure (see McCall 157–69).

Works Cited

Textbooks are indicated with asterisks.

*Adelstein, Michael, and Jean G. Pival. *The Writing Commitment*. New York: Harcourt, 1976.

Aristotle. *On Sophistical Refutations*. Trans. E. S. Forster. Cambridge: Harvard UP, 1955.

*Barry, Vincent. *Good Reason for Writing*. Belmont: Wadsworth, 1983.

*Beale, Walter H. *Real Writing*. 2nd ed. Glenview: Scott-Foresman, 1986.

*Booth, Wayne, and Marshall Gregory. *The Harper & Row Rhetoric*. New York: Harper, 1987.

Brockriede, Wayne, and Douglas Ehninger. "Toulmin on Argument: An Interpretation and Application." *Quarterly Journal of Speech* 46 (Feb. 1960): 44–53. Rpt. in *Contemporary Theories of Rhetoric: Selected Readings*. Ed. Richard Johannesen. New York: Harper, 1971. 241–55.

Copi, Irving. *Introduction to Logic,* 7th ed. New York: Macmillan, 1986.

Crews, Frederick. "Theory for Whose Sake?" *CCTE Studies* 51 (Sept. 1986): 9–19.

*Dodds, Jack. *The Writer in Performance*. New York: Macmillan, 1986.

*Eckhardt, Caroline, and David Stewart. "Towards a Functional Taxonomy of Composition." *CCC* 30 (Dec. 30): 338–42. Rpt. in *The Writing Teacher's Sourcebook*. Ed. Gary Tate and Edward P. J. Corbett. New York: Oxford, 1981. 100–06.

———. *The Wiley Reader: Brief Edition*. New York: John Wiley & Sons, 1979.

*Fahnestock, Jeanne, and Marie Secor. *A Rhetoric of Argument*. New York: Random House, 1982.

———. "Teaching Argument: A Theory of Types." *CCC* 34 (Feb. 1983): 20–30.

———. "Toward a Modern Version of Stasis." *Oldspeak/Newspeak Rhetorical Transformations*. Ed. Charles W. Kneupper. Arlington: Rhetoric Society of America, 1985. 217–26.

Finocchiaro, Maurice A. "Fallacies and the Evaluation of Reasoning." *American Philosophical Quarterly* 18 (Jan. 1981): 13–22.

Fischer, David Hackett. *Historians' Fallacies: Toward a Logic of Historical Thought*. New York: Harper, 1970.

Fisher, Walter. "Technical Logic, Rhetorical Logic, and Narrative Rationality." *Argumentation* 1 (1987): 3–21.

*Gage, John. *The Shape of Reason*. New York: Macmillan, 1987.

*Gefvert, Constance. *The Confident Writer: A Norton Handbook*. New York: Norton, 1985.

*Gere, Anne Ruggles. *Writing and Learning*. New York: Macmillan, 1985.

*Guinn, Dorothy M., and Daniel Marder. *A Spectrum of Rhetoric*. Boston: Little, Brown, 1987.

*Hairston, Maxine. *Contemporary Composition*. Short ed. New York: Houghton-Mifflin, 1986.

Hamblin, C. L. *Fallacies*. London: Methuen, 1970.

*Hartwell, Patrick. *Open to Language: A New College Rhetoric*. New York: Oxford, 1982.

Hurley, Patrick. *A Concise Introduction to Logic*. 2nd ed. Belmont: Wadsworth, 1985.

Johnson, Ralph, and J. A. Blair. *Logical Self-Defense*. 2nd ed. Toronto: McGraw-Hill Ryerson, 1983.

Joseph, Horace William Brindley. *An Introduction to Logic,* 2nd rev. ed. Oxford: Clarendon Press, 1906.

Kahane, Howard. *Logic and Contemporary Rhetoric: The Use of Reason in Everyday Life.* 4th ed. Belmont: Wadsworth, 1984.

———. *Logic and Philosophy.* 5th ed. Belmont: Wadsworth, 1986.

Kaufer, David S., and Christine M. Neuwirth. "Integrating Formal Logic and the New Rhetoric: A Four-Stage Heuristic." *College English* 45 (April 1983): 380–89.

Kielkopf, Charles. "Relevant Appeals to Force, Pity, and Popular Pieties." *Informal Logic Newsletter* 2 (April 1980): 2–5.

Kneale, William, and Martha Kneale. *The Development of Logic.* Oxford: The Clarendon Press, 1962.

Kneupper, Charles W. "Teaching Argument: An Introduction to the Toulmin Model." *CCC* 29 (Oct. 1978): 237–41.

*Levin, Gerald. *Writing and Logic.* New York: Harcourt, 1982.

McCall, Raymond J. *Basic Logic: The Fundamental Principles of Formal Deductive Reasoning.* 2nd ed. New York: Barnes & Noble, 1952.

McCleary, William James. "Teaching Deductive Logic: A Test of the Toulmin and Aristotelian Models for Critical Thinking and College Composition." Diss. U of Texas at Austin, 1979.

*McDonald, Daniel. *The Language of Argument.* 2nd ed. New York: Harper, 1975.

*———. *The Language of Argument.* 3rd ed. New York: Harper, 1980.

*Miller, James E., and Stephen Judy. *Writing in Reality.* New York: Harper, 1978.

Munson, Ronald. *The Way of Words: An Informal Logic.* Boston: Houghton-Mifflin, 1976.

Perelman, Chaim. *The Realm of Rhetoric.* Trans. William Kluback. Notre Dame: U of Notre Dame P, 1982.

Perelman, Chaim, and L. Olbrechts-Tyteca. *The New Rhetoric: A Treatise on Argumentation.* Trans. John Wilkinson and Purcell Weaver. Notre Dame: U of Notre Dame P, 1969.

*Rottenberg, Annette T. *Elements of Argument.* New York: St. Martin's, 1985.

*Rottenberg, Annette T. *Elements of Argument.* 2nd ed. New York: St. Martin's, 1988.

Scriven, Michael. *Reasoning.* New York: McGraw-Hill, 1976.

Sharvy, Robert Lee. "The Treatment of Argument in Speech Text Books." *Central States Speech Journal* 13 (Autumn 1962): 265–69.

*Spurgin, Sally DeWitt. *The Power to Persuade.* Englewood Cliffs: Prentice, 1985.

Toulmin, Stephen. "Logic and the Criticism of Arguments." *The Rhetoric of Western Thought.* 3rd ed. Ed. James Golden, Goodwin F. Berquist, and William E. Coleman. Dubuque: Kendall/Hunt, 1983. 391–401.

———. *The Uses of Argument.* Paperback ed. Cambridge, England: Cambridge UP, 1963.

Toulmin, Stephen, Richard Rieke, and Allan Janik. *An Introduction to Reasoning.* 2nd ed. New York: Macmillan, 1984.

Weddle, Perry. "Inductive, Deductive." *Informal Logic* 22 (Nov. 1979): 1–5.

*Winterowd, W. Ross. *The Contemporary Writer.* 2nd ed. New York: Harcourt, 1981.

Starkweather and Smith: Using "Contact Zones" to Teach Argument

Robin Muksian-Schutt

The following essay, originally published in Teaching English in the Two-Year College *in 1998, provides a way to help students argue from a point of view that recognizes the complexity of issues such as capital punishment. Drawing on the highly influential idea of "contact zones," a term first coined by Mary Louise Pratt and promoted in composition by Patricia Bizzell and others, Robin Muksian-Schutt's pedagogical scheme avoids looking at themes such as capital punishment in a general, decontextualized way. Instead, her classes look at specific court cases where capital punishment is an issue. Muksian-Schutt finds that asking her students to analyze multiple accounts (found court documents, news accounts, fictionalized accounts, and music) of one case helps them see the importance of genre to making arguments. Students also begin to understand the ways the media, the government, and other institutions with power help to construct the cultural assumptions that inform our thinking. Muksian-Schutt argues that more argument classes should ask students to investigate and write about "those social spaces where cultures meet, clash and grapple with each other, often in contexts of highly asymmetrical relations of power" (Pratt 34). Teaching argument in this way, she believes, will give meaning to students' writing and help students move past a simple pro/con stance on important social issues.*

Introduction

After six years of teaching argument sections of introductory composition courses, perhaps my most memorable section was one which I taught at the University of Rhode Island in 1992. The course (one of the two sections field tested at URI) was E306, Linda Brodkey's controversial course questioned by some administrators at the University of Texas for its potential to be indoctrinating (Fowler and Penticoff). Critics feared that composition instructors, who would be teaching from a text composed primarily of court cases, would use the course as a forum to promote their ideology. Not surprisingly, E306 showed no more potential to be indoctrinating than any other argument section since an instructor with a subversive agenda can promote personal ideals regardless of the text choices. But what I failed to realize at the time was that the course offered a broader ground for students to enter a conversation since it dealt with specific cases rather than themes.

The benefits of specific cases as text seem to have resurfaced recently with the emerging concept of "contact zones," defined by Mary Louise Pratt as "those social spaces where cultures meet, clash and grapple with each other, often in contexts of highly asymmetrical relations of power" (34). In the case of E306, those social spaces were American courtrooms. But in many argument courses, no particular social spaces (or events) can be "grappled" with since often none are clearly defined, creating confusion for students as to where they can enter a conversation.

Often, students confuse expressing a belief with "taking a side," thereby forcing themselves into a "left/right" dichotomy which does not offer a comfortable conversation entry on moderate ground. As I watched students struggle in trying to determine "their side," I realized that sometimes their discomfort was not the result of a poor self-examination, but, in fact, was caused by a great awareness that some issues are best addressed from this moderate ground. As a result of having many students who were unaware that nonpolar views in many cases represent a position, I was searching for a new way to approach a "Writing Arguments" course.

Contact Zone

In June 1996, I attended a rhetoric and composition conference at the University of Rhode Island. An early roundtable discussion led to a conversation about the polarization of students and a study of textbooks that tried to limit that format. Later in the day, in a workshop session, Pat Bizzell discussed the idea of "contact zones" where one or two particular situations are the focus of the course, and the students are required to research a multitude of mediums to learn about the issues and from there possibly consider the thematic implications. In a related article, Bizzell addresses the result of contact zones in terms of an approach to "negotiating difference," which she defines as "studying how various writers in various genres have grappled with the pervasive presence of difference in American life and developed virtues out of necessity" (168). Using contact zones as a pedagogical method dictates that the student must review a variety of texts (Bizzell 168).

I was intrigued by the use of multiple forms of "text" as a way to help students access their positions. It seems only logical that since art forms such as musical lyrics impact students, using these art forms in an argument class might provide students with the tools to study and express their positions and perhaps even to understand their positions better. For a summer 1996 quarter, I decided to pursue this "contact zone" method of teaching argument, though in a modified form appropriate for an argument course. Bizzell's subject matter involves issues of "difference." For my argument course, I wanted to use a subject or theme from past sections so that I could compare student performance in this new course to student performance in previous courses. Also, I needed a subject which would allow me to focus on some very specific cases represented in a multitude of genres. The issue of capital punishment fit well into my plans.

Charles Starkweather and Susan Smith

For this course, I chose two cases involving the death penalty. The first case was that of Charles Starkweather, who was executed in 1958, and the second was that of Susan Smith, who received a sentence for life imprisonment (eligible for parole in thirty years). Particularly interesting (and a focus of the course) is the variety of mediums (from newspaper accounts, to biographies, to Bruce Springsteen's song, "Nebraska") that addresses Starkweather's late 1950's killing spree:

> I saw her standing on her front lawn
> Just a twirling her baton,
> Me and her went for a ride, sir
> and ten innocent people died.
> ("Nebraska" 1982)

The students viewed several documents early in the quarter including photographs of Starkweather, autobiographical and biographical accounts of his crimes, newspaper clippings, excerpts from accomplice Caril Ann Fugate's biography, and the Springsteen lyrics.

Since the Susan Smith case was more recent, I asked each student to bring to class some source of information on Smith's crime in an effort to promote collaborative research. These sources and the documents on Starkweather provided the primary readings for the course. And while I wanted to stay away from thematic essays as much as possible, I later did provide essays by Coretta Scott King and H. L. Mencken, among others. These essays were not used to study views on capital punishment; rather, they provided rhetorical models of how writers package such views. One reading we did use was composed of chapters from former warden and "executioner" Donald Cabana's book, *Death at Midnight*. This book compellingly expresses the inner conflicts many feel when they consider the death penalty.

The ultimate goal was to help students become more adept at studying why courts and society make certain decisions and to provide them with the tools necessary to connect what they have read to their own set of values, allowing them, then, to be capable of making a formal, Toulmin style argument for their position.

Contact Zone in the Classroom

Class time included lecture on the basic elements of argument and their applications, discussion of the cases, and several group activities. Some of the most beneficial activities were exercises that asked the students to consider how they personally determined the value of a person's life. One that was particularly effective asked students to rank the rescue order of six people trapped in a cave. I provided students with a brief biography of the trapped people as their only determining factors. Most of the students felt that this exercise helped them to realize the types of judgments that people make when they are looking at someone else's life situations. This information helped them when they had to balance the issues of human rights, criminal rights, and victim rights.

Student Writing

My biggest challenge after the initial organization process was to create assignments that focused on these cases while still working to improve students' argument skills. I believe that argument analysis is extremely beneficial to a budding writer. Consequently, the first of the students' papers required them to read critically a document and comment on its success as an argument (Figure 1).

Assignment I served to illuminate for students the importance of clear claims and adequate and varied support. Yet, because I wanted to study less thematic material and more specific media information, the assignment immediately following their analysis asked students to look at an alternate form of media, the film *Dead Man Walking* and consider how Hollywood can masterfully play both sides of an issue in one production (Figure 2).

From the film assignment, students gained an understanding of how society is bombarded with potentially leading images through fictionalized accounts of situations. One student responded to the issues in the film in a positive light. She believed that in this case Hollywood's portrayal of the death penalty was balanced: "While watching *Dead Man Walking* my opinion swayed back and forth. I believe that the movie accomplished its goal. It showed how people's opinions are diverse, and how complicated the issue still is."

After addressing thematic overviews and fictionalized accounts of capital punishment, students began to focus on some very real cases. The final short essay for the course required students to analyze the

---

Figure 1. Assignment for Learning to Critique an Argument

English 102 Assignment I

Read the two handouts discussing the death penalty as a deterrent to crime. Keep in mind that both essays take the same stand — that capital punishment helps to prevent crime. Your job is to decide which author presents a stronger argument. Consider the elements of good writing. Which essay makes a clearer claim? Which writer uses support with the greatest impact? Which essay is more interesting/enjoyable to read?

No correct response exists. In other words, you may choose whichever essay you prefer without penalty. You must, however, defend your choice. Consider which of the qualities of writing are important to you as a reader, and identify the essay that fulfills your expectations.

Your paper will have an introductory paragraph that includes the names of both essays, the names of both authors, a brief statement of the main idea of the essays, and a claim stating which of the two essays you prefer. The remainder of your paper will focus on the reasons why you chose that particular essay supported by direct quotations from the piece. You may also include, not only positive points of your choice, but negative aspects of the other essay as support. Your concluding paragraph should leave the reader thinking about why one approach to this argument works better than the other.

Figure 2. Assignment Using a Film to Study a Position

EN 102 Worksheet for Assignment II

You have viewed the film *Dead Man Walking*. People both for and against capital punishment believe that the film supports their side. Considering your own views on the subject, write a paper showing how the movie supports your view. You can point to specific scenes and characters, filming techniques, settings and scenery, and overall characterization of the situation.

---

media's portrayal of our specific cases. The discourse surrounding both the Starkweather and Smith cases was clearly leading. For this last essay, I wanted the students to consider how journalists help to create an attitude toward a public figure or event through their writing (Figure 3).

This last assignment was, perhaps, the most empowering to the students since it encouraged them to question what is presented to the public as "fact." Student papers reflected the resulting strength of conviction. In reference to an article which included dialogue between a mother and a child regarding the Smith case, a group of students wrote the following: "This dialogue is clearly an emotional ploy by the author to influence the opinion of the reader. The author shows one of the many ways that the media paints a biased picture." Even more encouraging was that this student team could see the media influence in rhetoric that was seemingly simple fact-based reporting: "In addition to emotional rhetoric, the media has other ways of influencing public opinion. The most widely used way, in the articles we reviewed, was negatively describing the actions and details of the Susan Smith case." These student writers pointed out lines from articles that included words such as "depravity" and "incomprehensible savagery."

Figure 3. Assignment for Studying Media Control and Bias

Starkweather/Smith Cases
EN 102 Assignment III

You have studied many accounts of the Susan Smith and Charles Starkweather cases including newspaper reports of Smith's crime and sentencing and biographical accounts of Starkweather's crime from *Compulsive Killers: The Story of Modern Multiple Murder,* by Elliott Leyton. In a short paper, analyze the different attitudes that the writers have toward their subject. For example, in what light does the writer from *Newsweek* present Susan Smith? Is he neutral in his account? Is Leyton's chapter on Starkweather a biased account? If so, what view does the author have of Starkweather? If not, provide examples from the text as evidence to support that the writer has provided his reader with an unbiased view of the criminal. Consider the quotations from Starkweather's autobiography, the accounts of his school teachers, etc.

At this point, after studying how other writers presented their points regarding Starkweather and Smith, students were required to consider their own reactions to these criminals. The final paper for the course needed to draw on all of the short essays and allow the students to express their views on the decisions made in the Starkweather and Smith cases. Students who seemed to have come to a polar conclusion about capital punishment because of the variety of material they examined could express such a view. For students who were still not sure if they could stand in the "pro" or "con" camp, the notion of "sometimes" or "maybe" still existed. I hoped at this point, students understood that what they had perceived as lack of position was very much a position, one rooted in moderate ground (Figure 4).

One student's reaction to the decisions in the cases was rooted in the concept of society's acceptance of certain behaviors:

> If you were on trial for murder, the difference between living and dying may lie within the decade in which you were tried. While reviewing the cases of Susan Smith and Charles Starkweather, I was compelled to ask this question: "If Charles Starkweather were tried today, would he get the death penalty?"

She brings this concept full circle in the concluding sections of her essay:

> The world has been desensitized to violence, and now it would seem that murder is an everyday occurrence. In 1957, however, the world was still innocent and the same crimes that [society] found so profoundly awful might very well be the thing that would earn a slot on Dateline or 20/20 or even a 15 minute blurb on the 6 o'clock news.

Figure 4. Final Paper Assignment

EN 102 Final Paper Assignment

Throughout the quarter we have studied a variety of documents focusing on both the Charles Starkweather case and the Susan Smith case. Using these documents as references (along with other sources on these cases or on capital punishment), decide if you agree or disagree with both decisions — that of Starkweather receiving death and Susan Smith receiving life imprisonment instead of death as a punishment.

Write a paper that explains your position regarding these two criminals. Include your reasons for your position as well as your beliefs as to why Starkweather received "death" and Smith received "life." What factors contributed to this? Do the same factors help to determine your position?

You are required to cite several of these sources in your paper. You may paraphrase or use direct quotations. The sources are simply there to provide you with a picture which can then be used to help justify your position for this paper.

The paper should be four to five pages long and have a separate "works cited" page as well as a cover page which includes the title of your paper, your name, and the date of presentation.

This student's willingness to consider her era as a possible explanation for her views shows a strong sense of self-awareness along with a perception that beliefs are often deeply rooted within society. This realization becomes a first step for a writer in creating stronger arguments.

Conclusion

That they were not forced to choose sides when they stood somewhere in the middle validated the moderate ground where so many students stand. Even more importantly, these students realized that some of the confusion they feel toward public figures is a result of the media's portrayal. This realization seemed to make students more critical readers and stronger writers.

Finally, this validation of student views and improvement of critical reading worked well together to emphasize further the basic elements of argument — claim, support, and warrant. The concept of warrants as generalizations or assumptions is often difficult for students to grasp. By studying journalistic and fictional documents that surrounded a particular case, students began to notice the assumptions that underlie much of the public's thinking.

I continue to teach sections of this course with success, having added some original court transcripts from the cases so students can examine the argument techniques of the lawyers and judges. Focusing on specific contact zones has helped me show students how arguments are constructed and how they can analyze them and form valid opinions of their own.

Works Cited

Bizzell, Patricia. "'Contact Zones' and English Studies." *College English* 56 (1994): 163–69.

Cabana, Donald A. *Death at Midnight*. Boston: Northeastern UP, 1996.

Fowler, Shelli, and Richard Penticoff. "The National Debate on Multiculturalism: Revising the English 306 Syllabus at the U of Texas." *Notes in the Margins,* Stanford University, May 1991.

King, Coretta Scott. "The Death Penalty Is a Step Back." *Arguing in Communities,* Ed. Gary Layne Hatch. Mountain View: Mayfield, 1996. 428–29.

Leyton, Elliott. *Compulsive Killers: The Story of Modern Multiple Murder.* New York: Washington Mews, 1986.

Mencken, H. L. "The Penalty of Death." *A Mencken Chrestomathy.* 1926. New York: Knopf, 1954.

Pratt, Mary Louise. "Arts of the Contact Zone." *Profession 91,* New York: MLA, 1991. 33–40.

Robbins, Timothy. Writer/Dir. *Dead Man Walking.* Polygram, 1995.

Springsteen, Bruce. "Nebraska." *Nebraska.* Columbia Records, 1982.

The "Argument of Reading" in the Teaching of Composition

Mariolina Salvatori

Mariolina Salvatori's essay, first published in Argument Revisited; Argument Redefined: Negotiating Meaning in the Composition Classroom *in 1996, asks writing instructors to explicitly teach students the very complex and often misunderstood set of processes that inform the reading-writing connection. Salvatori argues that helping students see the connection between the reading and writing processes will help them understand a form of academic argument that requires deep understanding rather than direct opposition.*

Salvatori's work promotes what she calls critical reflexivity (students' analysis of their own reading, writing, and thinking processes), and the assignments she proposes help students understand their own cognitive processes better. Such an understanding, she suggests, will provide students with a range of reading strategies and the ability to gain greater distance from their own texts. With this self-conscious distance, they will be able to carefully analyze the audiences they are trying to reach and, therefore, will revise their arguments effectively and with a reader in mind. Salvatori recognizes that such critical reflexivity on the part of students requires that instructors also be reflexive about their own teaching, and she makes clear that the task she is proposing will be challenging for students and teachers alike. She believes, however, that difficulty should not determine how we teach, and that the rewards of learning academic argument will be substantial if we translate theories of reading and writing as interactive, recursive, and observable processes into effective classroom praxis.

For other essays in this collection on the relationship between reading, writing, and argument, see Patrick J. Slattery's "The Argumentative, Multiple-Source Paper: College Students Reading, Thinking, and Writing about Divergent Points of View" (p. 361) and Jean-François Rouet, M. Anne Britt, Robert A. Mason, and Charles A. Perfetti's "Using Multiple Sources of Evidence to Reason About History" (p. 417).

T he art of dialectic is not the art of being able to win every argument. . . . Dialectic, as the art of asking questions, proves itself only because the person who knows how to ask questions is able to persist in his questioning. . . . The art of questioning . . . i.e., the art of thinking . . . is called "dialectic," for it is the art of conducting a real conversation. . . . To conduct a conversation means to allow oneself to be conducted by the object to which the partners in the conversation are directed. It requires that one does not try to out-argue the other person, but that one really considers the weight of the other's position. . . .

Hans-Georg Gadamer
Truth and Method

Here Gadamer is writing about face-to-face conversations, but he does so to articulate the rules and the workings of other inaudible conversations, those that readers make happen as they read. Gadamer theorizes reading as a "hermeneutical conversation with a text" — a conversation that can only begin and be sustained if and when the reader/interlocutor reconstructs and critically engages the "question" or the argument that the text itself might have been occasioned by or be an answer to.[1] He writes, "Texts . . . have to be *understood,* and that means that one partner in the hermeneutical conversation, the text, is expressed only through the other partner, the interpreter" (349, emphasis added). This view of reading enables us to imagine a text's argument not as a position to be won and defended by one interlocutor at the expense of another, but rather as a "topic" about which interlocutors generate critical questions that put them in a position to think what it means to know, to understand, and to reflect on different processes of knowledge formation (of which the argument can be seen as an example). Thus, a text's argument can function as a fulcrum that brings parties (reader[s] and text) together. But for this to happen, a reader must accept and carry out the tremendous responsibility of giving a voice, and therefore a sort of life, to the text's argument. Although Gadamer does not point it out explicitly, a corollary to a reader's responsibility is a writer's responsibility, that is, the responsibility to write a text that asks (rather than answers) questions, that proposes (rather than imposes) arguments, and that therefore makes a conversation possible. And although Gadamer's subjects are expert readers and writers, what he has to offer to those of us who teach as yet inexperienced readers and writers is, I believe, very valuable. The preceding quotation, "Texts . . . have to be understood," for example, makes me think of the tremendous and delicate responsibility I have as reader of my students' arguments. But it also makes me think of the corollary to my responsibility, students' responsibility to write argument in ways that allow their readers to converse with it. To teach students to assume and to exercise this responsibility is indeed very difficult. Nevertheless, I will suggest, they can learn to exercise this sophisticated practice of writing while, if, and when they learn to understand and to appreciate the effects of this writing on themselves as readers.

What follows is an argument on behalf of the theoretical and practical appropriateness of using *reading* as a means of teaching *writing.*[2] Throughout this essay, I will be using the phrase *the argument of reading* to refer to the debate about the presence of reading in the composition classroom.[3] But I will also be using the phrase *the argument of reading* as a descriptor of the particular understanding of reading and the teaching of reading that I am proposing here.

In 1974, in *Teaching Composing: A Guide to Teaching Writing as a Self-Creating Process,* William E. Coles argued against the use of reading in the composition classroom. He wrote,

> So we decided to get rid of everything that teachers and students alike are tempted to look at writing from behind or through or under. The anthology went; so did the standard plays, novels, poems. (2)

I remember, when I read these lines for the first time in the early 1980s, how struck I was by what I considered a peculiar and arbitrary decision. In 1992, in the process of composing a paper to be delivered at 4Cs, I returned to Coles's text and for reasons that have to do with the kind of work I had done in the interim — mainly, my historical research in pedagogy and my work with hermeneutics and the phenomenology of reading — I was able to read and to respond to this quotation differently. In that paper I returned to a subject that, though central to my intellectual formation as a compositionist and central to my undergraduate and graduate teaching, I had not written about for some time. The paper was my attempt to understand which theoretical and institutional forces had led first to the separation and subsequently to the integration of the activities of reading and writing in the composition classroom. Focusing on the juncture of the theoretical and the institutional gave me a vantage point from which I was able to conjecture and to reconstruct the "argument" that had led Coles to make what had seemed to me such an iconoclastic gesture. This time, rather than judging Coles's statement as a blanket and arbitrary indictment of the presence of reading in composition classrooms, I began to see in Coles's gesture a specific denunciation of what reading had been reduced to within *the teaching of composition* (but also within the teaching of literature, which was and remains the model for much of the teaching of reading done in composition classrooms). I began to see that what Coles was indicting was a particularly enervated, atrophied kind of reading. A reading immobilized within textbooks and reduced therein to sets of disparate simplifying practices that, separated from the various theories that motivate them, turn into meaningless and arbitrary *exercises:* reading for *the main idea,* for *plot,* for *argument,* for *point of view,* for *meaning,* for *message* — interchangeably and without knowing why. Or reading texts as inscrutable and unquestionable "models" of style or rhetorical strategies. Or as "blueprints" for linguistic theories, political programmes, or philosophies of language. I began to see, *through* Coles, the effects of practices that restrain students and teachers from asking questions of a text other than the ones the textbooks have already "gridded." I began to see, *with* Coles, why the kind of writing that these texts and their "facilitating" questions would foster could be nothing but "canned" or "theme" writing. This I understood to be the "problem" of reading that Coles was attacking and for which he proposed, as a *pharmakon,* "get[ting] rid of" anthologies, plays, novels, and poems, and replacing them with the text of the assignments and of the writing that students did in response to them.

Considering the position of composition in the academy in 1974 — both within and without departments of English; considering the available work force of teachers of composition at the time; considering that the services of composition were in ascending demand; considering the perceived need for compositionists to define their discipline on their own terms, Coles's apparent "disciplinarian" act can be read, perhaps, as a stern act of self-discipline. That act, set in motion by a confluence of institutional needs, theoretical positions, and programmatic divisions, had its lasting influence. That act, moreover, in a complex sort of way, led to, encouraged, hastened or catalyzed other compositionists' felt need for a theory and practice of the reading-writing relation that had the potential to construct a teacher's respectful attentiveness to a student's writing as an issue of theoretical responsibility and rigor.

In the 1980s, Coles's move seemed to be challenged, if not reversed, by some compositionists who shared his concern that student writing would not hold the center of attention in the composition classroom. Rather than turning away from reading, however, these compositionists turned to theories of reading that seemed to make it possible to obviate that problem.

A 1985 essay by John Clifford and John Schilb, "Composition Theory and Literary Theory," reviewed the work of literary theorists who made it possible to imagine and to justify the teaching of literature and composition, reading and writing, as interconnected disciplines and activities. In their article, Clifford and Schilb assessed the influence of reader-response theories, post-structuralist theories, and examined the work of those compositionists and literary critics (to name a few: Susan Miller, Richard Lanham, Ross Winterowd, Wayne Booth, Nancy Comley and Robert Scholes, and Terry Eagleton) who, they argued, offered ways of thinking about reading and writing that would elide programmatic and disciplinary separations. In the 1980s, then, it seems that the argument about the reading and writing connection was constructed in terms antithetical to those of the 1970s. Rather than seen as an impingement onto the field of composition or as a pretext and a justification for paying attention to something other than students' writing, reading, reseen through some of the new theories and practices being disseminated, was now appealed to as a means of "bridging the gap" between the two activities and disciplines; a way of paying attention to "reading and writing *differently*." But, I wish to argue, to set the two arguments side by side is to realize what either position unwittingly ended up obscuring and deflecting attention from: that "the argument of reading in the teaching of composition" is not merely an argument about whether reading should or should not be used in the composition classroom. The argument is about *which kind of reading* gets to be theorized and practiced. To be more precise, that argument cannot be critically and reflexively engaged apart from the following interconnected questions: (1) Which theories of reading are better suited to teaching reading and writing as interconnected activities? (2) What is the theoretical justification for privileging that interconnectedness? (3) How can one teach that interconnectedness?

Q.1 (a). In response to the first question, I will argue that *not all* theories of reading are suited to uncovering and enacting the interconnectedness of reading and writing. Among those least suited to doing so are those that construct writers as visionary shapers of meanings and their works as venerable repositories for those meanings;[4] theories that construct as mysterious and magical the complicated and farraginous processes of thinking on which writing imposes provisional order and stability;[5] and theories that subject texts to unquestioned and unquestionable interpretive frames thereby reducing texts to various thesis statements — cultural, political, religious, and so forth. What I find objectionable about these theories is that they make it possible to cover over the processes by which knowledge and understanding are produced. By invalidating the possibility of recapturing, recuperating, and learning from the complex processes that have given a written text its particular shape, these theories, in different ways and for different reasons, simultaneously glorify reading and proclaim its unteachability. In classrooms where these theories of reading are unreflexively performed *for* students, where reading materials are used as mere pretexts for writing exercises, a *student's* reading of those materials may become *secondary* in at least two ways: It may become less important than and not necessarily accountable for the writing it produces or it may be constructed as needing to rely on a series of simplifications which, although meant to help inexperienced readers understand the materials in question, inevitably expose the assumption that such understanding can only be promoted through somebody else's simplifying practices. In these cases, the use of reading as a means of teaching writing can indeed be arbitrary, questionable, and even counterproductive.

Q.1 (b). In contrast with these notions about reading, theories that posit the possibility and the advantages of exploring the complex processes by which "reading" gives a voice to an otherwise mute "writing"; theories that turn both texts and readers into "interlocutors" of each other; theories that interrogate rather than mystify the "naturalness" and the mystery and the interpretive "framing" both of the reading and of the writing processes, make it possible not only to claim that reading can be taught but also that it can be taught as an opportunity to reflect on, investigate, and intervene in at least some of the processes that produce the knowledge that shapes and is shaped by one's understanding of a text. Rather than divining a text's meaning or making a text subservient to preestablished significations, such theories construct reading as an activity by means of which readers potentially engage texts responsibly and critically.[6] Responsibly, that is, in ways that will as much as possible make *those* texts speak, rather than speak *for* them or make them speak *through* other texts. And *critically* in ways that demand that readers articulate a reflexive critique both of the argument they attribute to those texts and of the argument they compose as they respond to those texts. However, it does not follow from what I just said that these theories automatically and necessarily lead to their own rigorous enactment (see section Q.3). A case in point: Two of the texts that in the 1980s advocated a programmatic and theoretical rapprochement of reading and writing and their attendant domains of expertise and performance — literature and composition —

demonstrate what I would call a perplexing inattentiveness to moving from theorizing the interconnectedness of reading and writing to making it visible and to teaching it. The texts I am referring to are *Bridging the Gap,* edited by Winifred Bryan Horner, and *Writing and Reading Differently,* edited by Douglas Atkins and Michael Johnson. With a few notable exceptions (the essays by Sharon Crowley, Barbara Johnson, and Jasper Neel) *the teaching* of reading and writing as interconnected activities, in these volumes, is constructed as something that teachers either do *to* and *for* their students or for themselves and for equally enlightened others, rather than something teachers do *with* their students to open up the areas of investigation that this particular focus makes possible. The interconnectedness of reading and writing (that virtual, provisional transaction of two extremely complex, invisible, imperceptible processes that can nevertheless be used to test and to foreground each other's moves) tends to be constructed as something either obvious or authorized by such an illustrious tradition — from Plato to Derrida — as not to require much explanation or articulation. The advantages for the teaching of writing that this understanding of reading promises are ultimately invalidated. Teaching the reading/writing interconnectedness becomes another kind of hermetic performance, one that covers over, one that hides rather than reveals, the processes of cognition that ought to be the subject of investigation and reflection. Paradoxically, these two texts end up reconfiguring the very problem that Coles was trying to excise — approaching students' writing and reading "from behind or through or under" something else. In this case, the theory calls for the teaching of a "differently" conceived interconnectedness between reading and writing, literature and composition, critical theory and composition theory. Perhaps, though, what I perceive as a regrettable shortcoming of otherwise encomiable projects can serve an important function: To remind us that although certain theories of reading *are* more conducive than others to teaching reading and writing as interconnected activities, to foreground and to teach — rather than just to understand — that interconnectedness is a highly constructed, unnatural, obtrusive activity — one that requires a particular kind of training that, historically, U.S. educational systems and traditions have neither made available nor valorized.

Q.2. What is the theoretical justification for focusing on the interconnectedness of reading and writing?

I wish to suggest at least two reasons. (1) Insofar as reading is a form of thinking (Gadamer calls it "an analogue for thinking"), written accounts of it, however approximate, can provide us with valuable insights into the ways we think. (2) To learn to recapture in one's writing that invisible, imperceptible moment when our reading of a text began to attribute to it — began to produce — a particular "meaning" makes possible to consider again, and to reconsider, what leads us to adopt and to deploy certain interpretive practices. In other words, although the processes that constitute our reading and writing are essentially invisible, those processes are, in principle, accessible to analysis, scrutiny, and reflection. The ways we think need neither be *kept* imperceptible, *shrouded* in mystery, nor be *reduced* in the interest of demystifying the reading process, to a bunch of technocratic, predictive, or authoritarian formulas. To learn to gain access to these processes by no means implies that they can be completely controlled, contained, or managed. Nor should they. But to learn to gain access to these processes does mean, I believe, that one might learn to account for, however approximately, and to understand, however imperfectly, how certain meanings, certain stories, certain explanations, and certain interpretive frames get to be composed or adopted. Expert readers/writers have developed and have learned to summon a kind of *introspective reading* of their own and of others' readings that allows them to decide — as they read and as they write — when to pursue, when to revise, when to abandon this or that line of argument, and when to start afresh. Part of the challenge confronting us as teachers is to learn how to make it possible — within the time and institutional constraints that bind us — for students to learn to perform this kind of introspective reading. To think about reading and the teaching of reading in these terms — to think of reading, that is, as an analogue for thinking about one's own and others' thinking, about how one's thinking ignites and is ignited by the thoughts of others, justifies the presence of reading in composition classrooms not as a pretext but as a context for writing.

Q.3. How can we teach this interconnectedness?

To say that, even to articulate how, reading and writing are interconnected (as most of the authors featured in *Bridging the Gap* and *Writing and Reading Differently* do) is one thing; and it is another to imagine and to develop teaching practices that both enact and benefit from that interconnectedness. This approach to teaching, one that requires teachers' and students' relentless attention and reflexivity, is difficult both to initiate and to sustain.[7] Over the years, both as a teacher of composition and of literature, I have learned to deploy certain teaching strategies that simultaneously enable and force me and my students to reflect on the moves we make as readers, writers, and thinkers. I do not consider these strategies mere *applications* or *implementations* of somebody else's theories, and as I proceed to describe some of them, I certainly do not intend to offer them as such. Rather I think of these strategies as means teachers have of exposing (i.e., of making visible and of making available to reflection and critique — their own and others') the *nexus* between the theory they espouse and the practices that theory demands.[8] To foreground and to exploit the interconnectedness of reading and writing, I make a point of framing reading and writing activities (formal assignments, in-class writings, journals) that ask students to write their response to a text, to construct a reflective commentary on the moves they made as readers and the possible reasons for them, and to formulate an assessment of the particular writing their reading produced. By means of this triadic (and recursive) sequence, I try to teach readers to become conscious of their mental moves, to see what such moves produce, and to learn to revise or to complicate those moves as they return to them in light of their newly constructed awareness of what those moves did or did not make possible.[9] Initially, my assignments generate considerable resistance on the part of students, mainly because they are not accustomed to performing this kind of introspective reading. When I ask of a point they made, "Why did you think so?" or "What made you think that?" or "How did you come to such a conclusion?" they often hear reproach in my questions despite my concerted efforts to explain, in the course description and repeatedly in class, my rationale for such an approach. Occasionally students do readily learn to hear my questions as I intend for them to be heard, but often they don't. In that case I try to be extremely sensitive to any clues they offer that might make it possible for me to develop a strategy that answers the need of the moment. Here is an example. Several years ago, one of the first times I taught "The Yellow Wallpaper," I was temporarily silenced by a female student's defense of the doctor. She was very articulate about all that the doctor had said and done and had come to the conclusion that the text made an argument for men's (versus women's) inclination for science (medicine), and for what women had to lose when they did not abide by men's counsels. As I tried to collect myself enough to formulate a question that might make her reflect on what she had just said and why, the book in front of her caught my attention. The text was highlighted, rather sparsely. I picked it up, flipped through it, and in a rare moment of extraordinary clarity, I noticed that what she had marked in the text, what she had chosen to pay attention to, was all that in the text had to do with the doctor. She had paid little or no attention to anything else. I asked to be shown how other students had marked the text. The rest of the period was spent first discussing the marks in the text as correlatives for what readers choose to be attentive to as they read a text and then focusing on three representative samples: one by the student who mainly paid attention to the character of the doctor; one by a student who chose to focus on the narrator; and one by a student who after an initial rather random system of marking the text focused on the various characters' responses to the wallpaper. That class made it possible for me to turn a rather mechanical study habit — the highlighting of a text — into a strategy, one that can make visible the number and the intricacy of strands in a text's argument that a reader (or an interlocutor) pays attention to and that can show how the selection, connection, and weaving of those strands affects the structuring of the argument a reader constructs as/in response to a text.[10] As any strategy, this strategy is not effective in and by itself — it is a tool to be used at the appropriate moment, more as a commentary on an incipient awareness of what it means to read a text's (or an interlocutor's) argument than as a means of instructing a reader about how to pay attention to somebody else's argument. A less local strategy, one less contingent on a particular context, is the assignment of what I call the "difficulty paper."[11] Before we discuss a text collectively, I ask students to write a detailed one-page description of any difficulty the text they have been assigned to read might have set up for them.[12] I select and photocopy what I consider a representative paper and I distribute it for class discussion. What I try to do is to guide the discussion toward an assessment of the kind of reading that names a particular feature of a text as "difficult" — is it because readers' expectations do not make them pay attention to a text's clues? Is it because inexperienced readers tend to assume that difficulties are an indictment of their abilities rather than characteristic features of a text? Is it because the method of reading a reader is accustomed to performing will not work with this particular text? I have repeatedly relied on this kind of assignment not as a means to expose my students' inadequacies but as a reflexive strategy that eventually allows them to recognize that what they perceive as "difficult" is a feature of the text demanding to be critically engaged rather than ignored. What is remarkable about this approach is that students' descriptions of difficulties almost inevitably identify a very crucial feature of the text they are reading and contain *in nuce* the interpretive move necessary to handle them. They might say for example that they had difficulty with a text because it presented different and irreconcilable positions on an issue — their difficulty being an accurate assessment of that text's argument.

The focus on difficulty can also be profitably used as a means of fostering students' attention to the assignments by means of which many teachers suggest a possible reading of a text. In this case, students can be asked to reflect on the kind of argument that the assignment's frame simultaneously makes and does not make possible to construct about the assigned text. Thus, the focus will be on the assignment simultaneously as an example of the difficulty of doing justice to a complex text and of the difficulty of adequately representing the complexity of one's response to a complex text. This exercise can be useful to foster habits of rigorous attention to one's reading of others' positions and to one's representations of them, and it can teach students to read (and to remind teachers to think of) assignments as more than sets of injunctions.

There are many ways of putting students in a position to practice recursive and self-monitoring readings, and they will vary according to different contexts, the rapport that different teachers can establish with their students, the configuration of the group, the "feel" of the classroom. The ones I am partial to are those that contribute to making what is imperceptible — thinking — at least dimly perceptible. Let's assume, for example, that student writers have begun to compose a reading of a text (whether in response to an assignment, to the "difficulty paper" instructions, or as a response of their own) that their teacher thinks might benefit from a second, more attentive reading. Let's assume, in other words, that the students have produced a hasty generalization, an inaccurate conclusion, or an overbearingly biased and unexamined preunderstanding that makes them oblivious to a text's argument. To ask those students to account for the steps they took to compose that reading, to ask them to actually *mark* which places in the text they "hooked up with" and which they merely skimmed, can serve as a dramatic visualization of how much of a text's argument can be ignored (erased) because of preestablished conclusions or inattentiveness to that argument's construction. Another way of putting students in a position to "see" the limits and the possibilities of how one chooses to structure an argument is to set up a comparative analysis of two or three different papers. Focusing on the papers' introductory moves as simultaneous points of entry into a text (reading) and tentative beginnings for the arguments they will formulate (writing) helps one consider what difference it makes for one's argument to begin a (written or oral) discussion of a text *there* rather than *elsewhere,* or to begin with a question rather than an evaluative comment. This exercise also helps to avoid interventions and discussions that focus on mistakes, on deficiencies, and on what is wrong with this or that way of thinking.

The strategies I have cursorily described here represent some of the ways I choose to participate in and to respond to my students' reading/thinking/writing activities. What should be noticed about these strategies is that they function simultaneously as heuristic devices (through them I teach my students how to perform certain reflexive moves) and as constant reminders to me that as a teacher I must demonstrate in my reading of my students' comments, questions, interventions, and arguments the responsiveness and the responsibility with which I expect them to engage texts. (Which does not mean, unfortunately, that I will always be successful in doing so.) What should also be noticed is that they deliberately go to "moments of reading" to foreground how those moments determine the writing they produce and that they tend to privilege — for the purpose of discussion — places or occasions in a student's text that can serve as points of critical reflection on the connection between reading and writing.

In the concluding section of this essay, I want to turn to and acknowledge what in my experience are two of the most frequently articulated academic objections to the theory and practice of the reading/writing interconnectedness I have outlined. I find these objections compelling and challenging, so much so that I keep returning to them to assess how they can help me better to understand the assumptions about and the preunderstandings of reading that subtend them. Insofar as for the past ten years these objections have consistently complicated and forced me to reexamine my position on reading, on writing, on teaching, and on education, I cannot exclude them from an argument of which they are such an integral part.

Using the names of the programs in my department whose theoretical orientations and proclivities these objections could be said to represent, I will call them the "creative writing" and the "culture studies" positions. What follows is a composite sketch of these objections that I glean from three graduate courses I teach — the "Seminar in the Teaching of Composition," "Literacy and Pedagogy," and "Reception Theories." These are courses that lend themselves extremely well to engaging the issue of the intellectual and programmatic division of which the argument of reading in the teaching of composition, in the two senses I have discussed, is both a cause and a consequence. Some of the representatives of the "creative writing" position articulate their opposition to the rigorous introspection that the interconnectedness of reading and writing requires in the name of (a version of) creativity that is constructed as *being,* and *needing to remain,* beyond analysis. When as a group we discuss the need and we grope for ways of describing not only *what* happens when we read but also *how* it is that we tend to construct one and not another critical response to a text, some of the graduate students who align themselves with the "creativity" position seem willing to engage the first but not the second line of inquiry. Their descriptions of reading are often magical, mysterious. They recollect, lyrically and convincingly, scenes of instruction within which — as children or adolescents — they taught themselves to read with passion and imagination as their motives and guides. In response to questions about the context that favored their autodidacticism, some will describe households replete with books and talks about books — a kind of oasis of family discourse that "naturally" fostered a love of reading and writing. Others, however, will describe settings that are exactly the opposite, within which they performed a sort of heroic, individually willed — and therefore "natural" in quite a different sense of the word — form of self-education.

My aim in interrogating these poignant accounts of education is not to devalue or discredit their veracity. My aim is to point out that these notions of reading may lead to approaches to teaching that are potentially elitist and exclusionary.[13] What happens when students show little cultural, emotional, and intellectual predisposition to this mythical love for reading? What kinds of responses will they write to a text they did not *love* reading? How can teachers teach their students to perform a kind of reading that they have themselves learned to perform mysteriously and magically? I think it is significant that when some of the readers who describe their reading processes as dreamlike or intuitive are asked to read back those processes so as to gain insight into their habitual cognitive strategies, they often declare their anxiety about or suspicion of a process they call "critical dissecting."

The "culture studies" position, on the other hand, objects to the focus on critical self-reflexivity as a nostalgic, reactionary, humanistic, and ultimately ineffective educational practice. Such a focus, this position claims, can foster, on the one hand, the illusion of human beings as independent, self-relying subjectivities and it can, on the other hand, disseminate a pernicious account of knowledge formation that exploits self-reflexivity or a focus on method as a tactic of avoidance, derailment, or deflection. A teacher's commitment to enacting ways of reading that make it both possible and necessary for readers to reflect on and to be critically aware of how arguments — one's own and others' — are constructed becomes within this critique a structured avoidance of more substantial issues. According to this critique, to focus, for example, on *how* John Edgar Wideman in "Our Time," Alice Walker in "In Search of Our Mothers' Gardens," or Gloria Steinem in "Ruth's Song (Because She Could Not Sing It)" construct their narratives is potentially a way of avoiding an ideological argument of race, class, and gender issues.

Insofar as it does not reduce critical reflexivity to an intentionally depoliticizing attention to form or to deadening pigeonholing, the culture studies position provides a salutary warning. Insofar as it does not reduce it to a version of necrophilia, the creative writing position on critical self-reflexivity as a potential blockage to action — creative or political — is compelling. But why is it that at their most oppositional, these and other critiques of self-reflexivity are predicated on a construction of it that turns it into an unnecessary, arbitrary, or stultifying practice?

What is so disturbing and uncomfortable about critical reflexivity? Why do the critical questioning and the introspective analysis it requires generate such suspicion and anxiety? How are we to read these responses? Do they indicate that the project of teaching reading and writing as interconnected activities is unreasonable, utopian, and oblivious to the material circumstances within which it is to be carried out? Should we decide, as Coles did in the 1970s, that it might be opportune to scale down this project of reading in the composition classroom from reading the interconnectedness of reading and writing to reading the assignments and student papers? (What does this suggest about teachers' and students' ability to engage in this task?) Does my critique of the ways most "integrationists" carried out in the 1980s the project of eliding the schism between reading and writing, literature and composition, suggest, indeed underscore, the wisdom of Coles's solution?

I see how it might be possible to answer all these questions in the affirmative and I become despondent. My current historical work in pedagogy, work that I undertook to understand what as a foreigner I found here puzzling and disturbing, namely the separation of reading from writing, the proliferation of specialized programs within departments, the reduction of pedagogy from a philosophical science to a repertoire of "tips for teaching," shows that our educational system has consistently opted for simplifying solutions every time it has been confronted with the inherent and inescapable complexity of educational issues. What I find disturbing is that decisions often made for teachers, without the participation of teachers, are subsequently read as indictments of teachers' inadequate intellectual and professional preparation. (One of the most frequently voiced reservations to my project is that "it is too difficult" to carry it out without sacrificing writing to reading.) We cannot afford not to come to terms with the consequences of these streamlining interventions. We need to acknowledge that, for reasons the complexity of which we cannot deny but we can certainly call into question, our scheme of education has consistently and repeatedly skirted the responsibility of nurturing one of the most fundamental human activities — critical self-reflexivity.

Every time I teach reading and writing as interconnected activities I begin by declaring, by making visible, my teaching strategies and exposing their rationale. And yet every time it takes considerable time for students to see this approach to teaching not as a cynical tendency to tear apart and to discredit the ways they read and write, as an exercise in dissection or a paralyzing threat, but rather as it is meant, as an attempt to promote engagement in the kind of self-reflection and self-awareness that they are so often expected to demonstrate but are seldom given an opportunity to learn.

In *On Literacy,* Robert Pattison argues that the project of developing the critical mind requires "another kind of training not generally available in the American scheme of education" (176). I agree with him and I believe that we can and we must find ways of providing that kind of training even within institutional environments that are opposed to it. Let me suggest that teaching reading and writing as interconnected activities, teaching students how to perform critically and self-reflexively those recuperative acts by means of which they can conjecture a text's, a person's, argument and can establish a responsible critical dialogue with it, as well with the text they compose in response to it, might be an approach appropriate to developing the critical mind — an approach that might mark the difference between their partaking in, and their being passively led through their own education.

AUTHOR'S NOTE: This essay is a revision of a lecture I delivered at the University of Oregon's Annual Conference on Composition and Rhetoric (April 1992). That lecture was itself a revision of a talk I had given at the Conference on College Composition and Communication the previous year. I would like to take this opportunity to thank John Gage, Jim Crosswhite, and their graduate students for being interested in my work. I would also like to thank Dave Bartholomae for the ways in which he "understands my texts," and the editors of [*Argument Revisited, Argument Redefined*] for their insightful comments and suggestions.

Notes

1. For the purpose of this essay, I use the term *argument* to replace, or interchangeably with, *question* which is Gadamer's word. Since I wrote this piece, I have found it useful to work with both terms in my continuing attempts to theorize and to practice a transactional understanding of reading with undergraduates. The two terms — used together, overlapped, or in a relation of adjacency — have made it easier for students to interrogate common preunderstandings of them as "cozy, fireside talk" and "high-pitched debate or quarrel."
2. The teaching of argumentative writing has a strong and respected tradition in composition that I have no intention to challenge. My understanding of argumentative writing is only indirectly related through Gadamer

to classical rhetoric. But I am pleased to notice possible points of contact between, for example, John Gage's approach to argumentative writing as "reasoned inquiry" and mine.

3. For a revival of this debate, see Erika Lindemann ("Freshman Composition," "Three Views") and Gary Tate ("A Place for Literature," "Notes").

4. These theories of reading generally discourage or consider as inappropriate a reader's (particularly an inexperienced reader's) critical response to a text. See, for example, Wilson Knight's *The Wheel of Fire,* especially the difference he sets up between *interpretation* and *criticism.*

5. I am thinking here of critics and theorists as different from one another as Benedetto Croce and Georges Poulet.

6. Among the theorists of reading who, in different ways, provide such possibilities are Hans-Georg Gadamer (especially *Truth and Method* and *Philosophical Hermeneutics*); Wolfgang Iser (*The Act of Reading* and *The Fictive and the Imaginary: Charting Literary Anthropology*); M. M. Bakhtin (*The Dialogic Imagination*); and Paul DeMan (*Allegories of Reading*).

7. One of the reasons why this approach to teaching is often met with considerable resistance and skepticism (by students, teachers, administrators, and the public) is that it can be said, and rightly so, that such an approach does not aim at producing a body of knowledge and is not efficient in terms of immediate and quantifiable results. Both resistance and skepticism need to be taken into serious consideration. Clearly, they indicate a widespread appreciation of at least one version of the aims of education, that is, education as the accumulation of a cultural capital that can be weighed and used as currency. To mock these assumptions, to underestimate how they regulate much of our lives, would be unwise. But equally unwise would be to suggest that the two approaches to and understanding of knowledge formation are antithetical to one another. To do so might amount to denying students and teachers the possibility to acquire certain bodies of knowledge and at the same time to learn to assess and to critique the processes that make the formation of certain knowledge possible and to understand the rules that regulate how and which kind of knowledge gets to be included, valued, and circulated, and correspondingly, which kind of knowledge gets to be excluded, devalued, even ostracized.

8. Let me enter an important caveat. The strategies I describe here, as *all* strategies, make sense, that is, are plausible and justifiable, within the particular approach to teaching that my understanding of the act of reading and its connections with writing calls for. They cannot and they should not be lifted out of the theoretical framework that I have articulated here, and be offered as transportable tips or prescriptives.

9. This "frame" is my attempt to imagine strategies that enact what Gadamer sees as the three pivotal and interconnected phases of reading — *kennen, wiederkennen,* and *herauskennen.* Important to notice is that this frame is not a "grid." Insofar as readers bring to the texts they read, the situations they find themselves in, and the experiences they live, their own "presuppositions of knowledge," and insofar as those presuppositions of knowledge will vary from one person to another, readers' readings of a text will vary accordingly.

10. The strategy consists of asking students to reproduce two or three marked pages of their texts and to articulate the system that determines their marks as interventions in the text and the connections among them. This

is one way of approximating, though very inadequately, the otherwise imperceptible moves that readers make as they read a text. This is one way to begin a conversation about and a critical assessment of reading practices.

11. In *Ways of Reading,* Dave Bartholomae and Anthony Petrosky have developed a sequence of assignments ("The Problems of Difficulty") around the generative force of difficulty.

12. In "Towards a Hermeneutics of Difficulty," Salvatori articulates a theoretical framework for such an assignment.

13. Salvatori develops this argument in "Pedagogy and the Academy: 'The Divine Skill of the Born Teacher's Instincts,'" and more fully in *Pedagogy: Disturbing History,* forthcoming.

Works Cited

Atkins, Douglas G., and Michael L. Johnson, Eds. *Writing and Reading Differently: Deconstruction and the Teaching of Composition and Literature,* Lawrence: U of Kansas P, 1985.

Bakhtin, M. M. *The Dialogic Imagination: Four Essays by M. M. Bakhtin.* Ed. Michael Holquist. Trans. Caryl Emerson and Michael Holquist. Austin: U of Texas P, 1981.

Bartholomae, David, and Anthony Petrosky. *Ways of Reading: An Anthology for Writers.* 2nd ed. Boston: Bedford/St. Martin's, 1990.

Clifford, John, and John Schilb. "Composition Theory and Literary Theory." *Perspectives on Research and Scholarship in Composition.* Ed. Ben W. McClelland and Timothy R. Donovan. New York: Modern Language Association, 1985.

Coles, William E. *Teaching Composing: A Guide to Teaching Writing as a Self-Creating Process.* Rochelle Park: Hayden, 1974.

DeMan, Paul. *Allegories of Reading: Figural Language in Rousseau, Nietzsche, Rilke, and Proust.* New Haven: Yale UP, 1979.

———. *Blindness and Insight: Essays in the Rhetoric of Contemporary Criticism.* Minneapolis: U of Minnesota P, 1983.

Gadamer, Hans-Georg. *Truth and Method.* New York: Continuum, 1975.

———. *Philosophical Hermeneutics.* Trans. and Ed. David E. Linge. Berkeley: U of California P, 1976.

Gilman, Charlotte Perkins. "The Yellow Wallpaper." *The Charlotte Perkins Gilman Reader.* Ed. Ann J. Lane. New York: Pantheon, 1950.

Horner, Winifred Bryan, Ed. *Composition and Literature: Bridging the Gap.* Chicago: U of Chicago P, 1983.

Iser, Wolfgang. *The Act of Reading: A Theory of Aesthetic Response.* Baltimore: Johns Hopkins UP, 1978.

———. *The Fictive and the Imaginary: Charting Literary Anthropology.* Baltimore: Johns Hopkins UP, 1993.

Knight, Wilson. *The Wheel of Fire.* London: Methuen, 1930.

Lindemann, Erika. "Freshman Composition: No Place for Literature." *College English* 55 (Mar. 1993): 311–16.

———. "Three Views of English 101." *College English* 57 (Mar. 1995): 287–302.

Pattison, Robert. *On Literacy: The Politics of the Word From Homer to the Age of Rock.* New York: Oxford UP, 1982.

Salvatori, Mariolina. "Towards a Hermeneutics of Difficulty." *Audits of Meaning: A Festschrift in Honor of Ann E. Berthoff.* Ed. Louise Z. Smith. Portsmouth: Boynton/Cook, 1988.

———. "Pedagogy and the Academy: 'The Divine Skill of the Born Teacher's Instincts.'" *Pedagogy in the Age of Politics: Writing and Reading (in) the Academy.* Ed. Patricia A. Sullivan and Donna J. Qualley. Urbana: NCTE, 1994.

———. *Pedagogy: Disturbing History.* U of Pittsburgh P, forthcoming.

Steinem, Gloria. "Ruth's Song (Because She Could Not Sing It)." *Ways of Reading: An Anthology for Writers.* 2nd ed. Ed. David Bartholomae and Anthony Petrosky. Boston: Bedford/St. Martin's, 1990.

Tate, Gary. "A Place for Literature in Freshman Composition." *College English* 55 (Mar. 1993): 319–21.

———. "Notes on the Dying of a Conversation." *College English* 57 (Mar. 1995): 303–09.

Walker, Alice. "In Search of Our Mothers' Gardens." *Ways of Reading: An Anthology for Writers.* 2nd ed. Ed. David Bartholomae and Anthony Petrosky. Boston: Bedford/St. Martin's, 1990.

Wideman, John Edgar. "Our Time." *Ways of Reading: An Anthology for Writers.* 2nd ed. Ed. David Bartholomae and Anthony Petrosky. Boston: Bedford/St. Martin's, 1990.

The Argumentative, Multiple-Source Paper: College Students Reading, Thinking, and Writing about Divergent Points of View

Patrick J. Slattery

Patrick J. Slattery's essay, first published in the Journal of Teaching Writing *in 1991, builds from the developmental theories of William Perry and others to argue for a developmental scheme that is especially applicable to research papers. Though Slattery notes the inherent limitations of applying a universal developmental standard — separate from cultural and political influences — to all students, he offers significant evidence for what he sees to be the more common perspectives among writing students: the dogmatic, the noncommittal, and the analytical.*

In many ways these perspectives parallel the categories developed by Perry and others. They suggest that students often begin their university education with a desire for absolute knowledge, then move to an uncritical acceptance of many perspectives, and finally settle on a version of critical relativism.

Slattery's scheme offers a framework that can help teachers understand how and why students use sources, particularly conflicting sources on the same issue, in their arguments. Slattery demonstrates, for example, that a misreading of sources may have less to do with students' lack of reading skills than with their reluctance or inability to let go of a dogmatic perspective. Slattery's work reminds writing instructors that, while an overreliance on developmental theories can be problematic, developmental taxonomies can help teachers interpret students' written arguments.

Readers interested in exploring the relationship between argument and reading should consult Mariolina Salvatori's (p. 346), and Jean-Francois Rouet, M. Anne Britt, Robert A. Mason, and Charles A. Perfetti's (p. 417) essays in this volume. Additional work on the strengths and weaknesses of developmental theories can be found in the section in the bibliography titled "Developmental Theory and Argument" (p. 456).

Many college writing assignments, especially in the humanities and social sciences, call for students to use multiple — and often contradictory — sources of information. For example, a history teacher might ask students to evaluate several competing accounts of a battle in Vietnam. A psychology teacher might require students to analyze a complicated case study from the perspectives of Sigmund Freud's and Carl Jung's theories of psychology. And an English teacher might have students compare several critics' interpretations of Robert Frost's "Stopping by Woods on a Snowy Evening." This type of assignment, what I call the "argumentative, multiple-source paper," emphasizes skills such as summarizing, quoting, paraphrasing, and documenting. It also emphasizes thinking processes such as analyzing several authors' perspectives, reaching an informed judgment about them, and justifying it to a reader. In my experience, however, college students have had much less difficulty with the skills than with the thinking processes; therefore, in an attempt to learn more about how college students intellectually approach divergent points of view, I investigated the reading, thinking, and writing of several freshmen who had taken a course I taught on argumentative, multiple-source writing. In this essay I explain the investigation and some of its pedagogical implications.

Several composition studies (e.g., Russell Durst, Mary Lynch Kennedy, Carol Sherrard) and numerous textbooks (e.g., Charles Bazerman, Laurence Behrens and Leonard J. Rosen, Mary Lynch Kennedy and Hadley Smith, Laurie G. Kirszner and Stephen R. Mandell, Robert K. Miller, Brenda Spatt) focus on the source-related skills I have mentioned. More importantly, however, a few studies in developmental psychology (e.g., William Perry, Karen Kitchener and Patricia King, Blythe Clinchy and Claire Zimmerman) focus on how college students make and justify decisions about complex topics. According to the developmentalists, as students attend classes, write papers, and participate in dormitory discussions, their implicit metaphysical and epistemological assumptions become increasingly complex to accommodate the diversity of values and opinions found in most college environments. Developmentalists further suggest that as students' assumptions about knowledge and reality grow more sophisticated, so do their ways of thinking about multiple perspectives and reaching and justifying judgments about them. Even though their theoretical models have different emphases, Perry, Kitchener and King, and Clinchy and Zimmerman agree in their description of undergraduates' conceptual development as an evolution from an early period of authority-centered and dualistic thinking, through a middle state of uncritical and sometimes skeptical thought, to a final stage of critical relativism.

Although I have argued elsewhere that schemes of intellectual development have limitations ("Applying Intellectual Development Theory to Composition"; "Encouraging Critical Thinking: A Strategy for Commenting on College Papers"), I do believe that students approach diversity of opinion from various interpretive frameworks and that these frameworks can be described by broad categories like those used by Perry, Kitchener and King, and Clinchy and Zimmerman. In fact, I planned and conducted my investigation with these assumptions in mind, but because I was interested not only in how students think about contradictory positions towards a topic, but also in how they read and write about them, I devised my own descriptive categories, which I discuss and illustrate later.

My study involved twelve students who were taking a section of freshman composition I taught at Indiana University-Bloomington. I required students in the class to use preselected sources to write two argumentative essays on assigned topics — the "Cinderella" fairy tale and Stanley Milgram's famous experiment on obedience to authority — and to find their own sources to write three argumentative papers on topics of their choice. The assignment on "Cinderella" asked students to summarize, analyze, and evaluate a Freudian and a feminist interpretation of the fairy tale, and the assignment on the Milgram experiment asked them to do the same with three articles that expressed different viewpoints on the experiment's ethics and scientific validity. I chose to determine the sources for the first two papers, reasoning that if the same readings were used by all the students, I could work more closely with them on the skills and thinking processes I have already mentioned. For the last three papers, I continued to instruct students in these areas, but also introduced them to choosing their own topics and conducting research in the library. At the end of the semester, I solicited volunteers for my investigation, and twelve students (nine women and three men between the ages of seventeen and nineteen) agreed to participate. I collected all five papers from and conducted interviews with these students, using the interview transcripts to help me analyze their essays.

Because I was involved first as teacher and then as investigator, my study does not neatly fit the paradigm of scientific inquiry. I believed, however, that my involvement provided a very good opportunity to analyze students' argumentative, multiple-source papers: Because I taught the course, I understood the students' assignments, was familiar with some of their sources, and had already read and thought about their essays. I further believed that my own involvement could lead to more humane and fruitful interviews: Since I knew the participants well, they felt comfortable talking to me about their writing and could therefore more easily provide the rich and detailed types of responses that I hoped to receive.

Each interview consisted of three sections. For the first part, participants answered the question, "Does anything stand out in your mind about the papers you have written over the past semester?" The purpose of this opening question was to ask students to comment on what they found most salient in their own experience with writing from sources. The next two sections of the interview, however, were more structured. For the second part, participants read three abbreviated student papers — argumentative, multiple-source essays about using animals in laboratory experiments, watching soap operas, and fighting terrorism (see Appendix A) — ranked the papers, and gave reasons for their rankings. I chose these essays because they seemed to reflect the three major intellectual orientations described by developmentalists; by asking participants to respond to the papers, I hoped to learn what they liked and disliked about how students write about competing opinions. The last section of the interview required participants to read several statements about the relative/absolute nature of authors' knowledge (see Appendix B); to arrange the statements, which were typed on cards, into meaningful groups; and to explain their groupings. This exercise served as an opportunity for students to explain how they themselves evaluated the contradictory stances represented in sources. To elicit detailed explanations without overdirecting participants' comments during the interview, I limited myself to responses such as "I think I see what you mean, but could you give me an example?"

Although all of the interviews and essays were different, the ways in which students read, thought, and wrote about divergent points of view tended to fall into three very broad categories — what I will call the "dogmatic," "noncommittal," and "analytical" approaches.

The Dogmatic Approach

When students took a dogmatic approach, they unreflectively reached argumentative positions before reading any sources about their topics. Responding to the opening interview question, Kathy commented, "Everyone already has set opinions" and "when I read the sources, and I see a weak argument, and then there's a better one, I pick the [better] one, because I've already decided how I feel, what makes more sense to me." Bob responded similarly to the first question:

> When we were asked to write about something we could choose, a certain topic, I, uh, chose something that I knew about, like cars or sports for instance. And I would base what I was gonna write on as to how much I knew about the subject. I would say, "Well, can I relate this to automobiles? Yes. So, I'll write about that." And I used a lot of the knowledge I had before. Sometimes, I knew exactly what I was gonna say, and I wrote the paper before looking at, at any sources. But then I knew where to get the sources because sometimes I have some of the magazines in my room. I'd say, "I remember this article," and I'd look through that and use that, document that. So I was always, well, half the time, I probably wrote a good percentage of the paper before looking at any sources.

For the open-topic assignments, Bob usually wrote his essays without reading any sources, relying on views he already had, and then "looked through" articles to find evidence to support what he had written. Kathy, on the other hand, read sources before writing her papers; but nonetheless she, too, based argumentative stances on preconceived ideas rather than on an analysis of the positions presented in her sources. Because they relied heavily on their own opinions, students who took a dogmatic approach sometimes based their evaluations on personal experience. For example, when Kathy ranked the abbreviated student essay on animal experimentation used during the second part of the interview, she thought "back to my perspective and my beliefs, what I thought originally," which she had based on her own experiences with animals:

> Personally, I'm allergic to every animal. I can't even be near an animal without my eyes watering. I can't go to the circus. I can't go to the zoo. I get shots every week because I'm so allergic to them. I have no affection for them. It says right here that it was ethically and morally right, but for me there was no question in my mind to start with. I mean I've been through all these biology classes, and we cut up animals and it doesn't bother me, skin cats and look at their brains.

As Kathy's response to the animal experimentation essay suggests, when students demonstrated a dogmatic approach, they tended to think about diversity in absolutist terms — to believe that experts who agreed with their ideas were "right" and that those who disagreed with them were "wrong." Notice how she responded to the card-sorting task:

> By this time in my life, I've decided what I think is right and wrong. If something will just hit me, like "You're crazy!" you just totally think they're crazy, you're like "No!" — then that'll start me, and I'll find anything and everything to go against them. Or if they're right, I totally agree with them and try to support them.

Like Bob, who tended first to write his papers and then to skim his sources in search of information to support what he had written, Kathy, too, read with the purpose of finding information to support the "right" viewpoint.

The reading and writing strategies associated with the dogmatic approach sometimes led students to misunderstand sources and to misrepresent them in their papers. As Bob mentioned during his interview, he chose to write about cars and sports in the open-topic papers; and in one of these essays, a paper on trends in the automobile industry, Bob misrepresented several authors' arguments. Describing "flush-mounted glass in relation to body sheet metal, lower and more sloped hoods, spoilers located on the trunk or underneath bumpers and also new aerodynamic headlights," he argued, "The only reason for designing aerodynamic cars is to reduce the amount of fuel used." To support his assertion, Bob cited a specific article, paraphrasing its author as saying, "The aerodynamic cars give far better fuel efficiency than those of the seventies." The article to which he referred, however, actually attributes the recent changes in automobile bodies not to a demand for fuel economy but to the public's taste in styling and the industry's desire to sell cars. Furthermore, Bob suggested that the search for fuel efficiency has led automobile makers to use new materials such as aluminum, plastic, and high-strength steel for making engine parts, but the source to which he attributed this information credits the development of these new materials to a desire not only for better mileage but also for engines with stronger parts, lower weight, better heat tolerance, reduced noise level, and especially lower manufacturing cost. Although we might assume that Bob purposely — even maliciously — misrepresented his sources, I question whether this was the case. If Bob were eager to find information to back up what he had already written, he might well have misinterpreted some of the information in his sources unintentionally.

In some essays that reflected the dogmatic approach, students represented alternative perspectives accurately, but in these cases the absolutist thinking associated with the approach seemed to lead them to dismiss the viewpoints prematurely. For example, in a paper about the fifty-five-mile-per-hour speed limit, Bob acknowledged an alternative position but then immediately dismissed it without explaining why. In this essay, in which he argued that "there is no justifiable reason to keep the speed limit," Bob claimed that it "simply wastes time and money." To support his assertion, he paraphrased an expert who favors raising the limit as saying, "The average American spends seven additional hours per year in his car as a result of the 55 [mile-per-hour limit]." Bob then admitted that "the government says the 55 [limit] is still in effect to save lives," but without analyzing this view, he labeled it "ludicrous," concluding "What I suggest, since Congress seems to keep the states' holding on to the 55 [limit], is that everyone vote with their right foot":

> Many states' legislatures are now seeing the point, and trying to pass bills which abolish the 55 [mile-per-hour speed limit]. They are seeing an increase in motorists not obeying it and people speaking up for what's right, and Congress now knows it has an issue on its hands which has to be decided. Naturally, they will go with what the people want; no 55 [limit].

Perhaps Bob represented opinions accurately in this second paper because the expert to which he referred agrees that the speed limit wastes time. If Bob read his sources to find evidence to support his argument and therefore tended to interpret them as reflecting his own stance, when authors did in fact agree with him Bob would have less chance of misunderstanding them. Furthermore, the alternative perspective to which he referred — that the speed limit reduces the number of automobile injuries and deaths — is common knowledge, and therefore Bob would have had less tendency to misinterpret it. But even though Bob represented the government's viewpoint correctly, he unreflectively assumed that it was "wrong" and that he was "right." In fact, he even believed that "everyone" would agree with him, again illustrating the absolutist thinking that typified the dogmatic approach.

The Noncommittal Approach

When students took a noncommittal approach, they read sources to explore rather than to judge divergent points of view. Responding to the opening question, Roberta commented:

> We used a variety of sources, a wide variety. . . . You get more knowledge. You get more than one person's point of view. It gives you a better understanding of the topic you're trying to talk about. I could get a better understanding of different points of view. Basically, it just seemed to, it just helped me understand that, that there wasn't just one set thing, that what one guy said wasn't gospel.

Unlike Bob and Kathy, who read sources in search of evidence to support their own opinions, Roberta valued multiplicity, reading about different perspectives in order to understand her topic more fully. Moreover, the first two students assumed that the experts who agreed with them were "right," but Roberta did not believe that any one authority had access to the truth.

Because students who demonstrated a noncommittal approach accepted diversity, they typically ranked the abbreviated student paper on soap operas highest. James, for example, explained, "I kinda like, like that one article I read, let's see, about, what was that, where they left it up — soap operas. Yeah, I wouldn't mind writing an article like that, where you know, you don't have to agree to an issue." Whereas Kathy preferred the paper on animal experimentation because it took the same stance she did, James liked the essay about soap operas because it was nonjudgmental. But while explaining his preference for this paper, James also commented that college teachers often expect students to make a judgment, comparing his freshman composition course to a debate class:

> It's just like I remember in high school. We had to do speeches, and we had to take sides, you know. We did them in the auditorium, and like the whole school would come and sit down for different periods. It was kinda hard, 'cause I didn't really, I kinda didn't want to take sides, ya know. Capital punishment was the other one, that's the one we had to do, abortion, and euthanasia. I didn't really want to, but she like wanted us to take a side. Life for capital punishment, I remember there was a lot of different things for each side.

James found it difficult, even painful, to take a stand because, at least in some cases, he thought two competing positions could both be valid.

Doug responded somewhat similarly to the abbreviated papers. Initially, he ranked the essay on soap operas above the one on animal experimentation, saying, "I'd probably put the soap opera paper ahead just because, uh, the amount of information for each side is equal." Critiquing the paper on animal experimentation, he explained:

> It just seems like it would be biased [because] it says, "The antivivisectionists, who say that using animals in experimentation is wrong, apparently do not have enough information to understand the issue," which basically, you know, is saying that they're wrong.

But then he commented that because " 'soap operas' leaves it up to you, it doesn't make a point really" and that the paper on animal experimentation "made a point." Doug liked the essay about soap operas because, unlike the other papers, it presented conflicting perspectives in a balanced, nonjudgmental fashion. Yet he was troubled that the soap opera essay did not argue a point, apparently realizing that academic writing often has an argumentative edge. Doug's confusion surfaced even more when he puzzled to himself about how to evaluate multiple viewpoints:

> Two different people are going to have two different views, or are more than likely going to have two different views on something, so it just depends on, like it would depend on my point of view to decide which is right, when more than likely they are both right.

Doug believed contradictory opinions could be equally "right," but he, like James, was also concerned about the conventions of argumentative, multiple-source writing, according to which a paper should take a stand.

Essays that reflected the nonjudgmental thinking associated with this approach typically presented but did not evaluate different arguments. For example, in response to the "Cinderella" assignment, Roberta first summarized the feminist interpretation of Cinderella's role:

> In Kolbenschlag's article, she claims that Cinderella is placed in what used to be considered a "woman's" world of menial work. She also claims that in the past it was believed that Cinderella spent her time grieving the loss of her loving mother and did not mind the work. It was also thought that if Cinderella was allowed any free time, she would learn to enjoy it and not want to return to her work.

Then, explaining that "the Freudians view Cinderella's place as natural," Roberta stated their perspective on her role:

> Bettelheim claims children, when growing, go through the oedipal complex. In this complex, the child wants the parent of the same sex to die in order to have a sexual relationship with the other parent. Because of this complex, Cinderella feels inferior to her siblings and thinks

she is supposed to do all the work. Cinderella believes she is being punished because of the "dirty" thoughts she has.

After this balanced presentation, Roberta summarized the feminist and the Freudian positions toward several other elements of the fairy tale, similarly reporting but not evaluating the critics' opinions. Finally, she concluded with "The fairy tale 'Cinderella' can be considered universal because of the many different meanings associated with the major motifs used in the tale," a nonjudgmental statement reflecting the appreciation of diversity that characterizes the noncommittal approach and differentiates it from the dogmatic approach.

Although most papers suggestive of the noncommittal approach concluded after explaining different points of view, some writers presented various arguments and then, apparently out of a concern for the conventions of academic writing, made a perfunctory judgment about them. For example, in his essay on the Milgram experiment, Doug first focused on the moral debate, stating Diana Baumrind "feels that the experiment was unethical because people were hurt":

> In her response to Milgram's experiment, she says, "I am not speaking of physical discomfort, inconvenience, or experimental deception per se, but of permanent harm, however slight." She feels that the experiment was harmful because "it could easily affect an alteration in the subject's self-image or ability to trust adult authorities in the future."

"On the other hand," he then wrote, "Stanley Milgram . . . believes that the experiment is totally ethical":

> After the experiment was completed, everyone was told what had happened. The person also got to meet the unharmed "subject." In addition, a survey was handed out after the experiment to all participants involved. Eighty-four percent of the subjects were glad to be in the experiment, fifteen percent were neutral, and 1.3 percent wished that they had not participated.

After evenly presenting Baumrind's and Milgram's positions, Doug took a stand and attempted to justify it, claiming, "The experiment was ethical for the reasons just mentioned." At the conclusion of this discussion, his paper turned to the issue of scientific validity, one paragraph reporting Baumrind's perspective, another explaining Milgram's. After he summarized the authors' views, Doug again asserted and attempted to justify his own stance: "In my opinion the experiment was valid because of the points mentioned above." Doug did not analyze the scientists' arguments or express an authentic commitment to either one of them, but he tried to make his paper comply with the conventions of academic writing by using phrases — "because of the points mentioned above" and "for the reasons just stated" — that suggest a sense of logical inquiry and evaluation. Despite the fact that Doug made a judgment, in tone and organization his paper resembled Roberta's noncommittal essay much more than it did Bob's dogmatic papers.

The Analytical Approach

When students took an analytical approach, they based evaluations on an analysis of divergent perspectives. Responding to the abbreviated student essays, Toni explained that the terrorism paper, which she ranked highest, states that "the two [proposals] together would be good, and military retaliation should not be used, so they, you know, thought it out, and they had the advantages and disadvantages" of each proposal, whereas "other papers did not comment on what was there." Toni preferred the essay on terrorism because, unlike the other two papers, it analyzed different positions and thus justified its argument.

In her response to the card-sorting task, Toni specified that evaluations should be based on comparison, suggesting, "If you wanna form an opinion on it . . . you have to look at a situation from different people's point of view. You can't just have your own and say, 'Mine's right.' You gotta look at their point of view and look at your point of view." According to Toni, students who use comparison to evaluate sources "don't say what is right but what is the most, um, likely to be or what they feel now is most likely to be the way why it is that way." Clarifying her point, she summed up, "You're saying that one [perspective] is better but not that one is right and one is wrong." Unlike students who took a dogmatic approach, Toni relied on comparison to make relativistic judgments — that is, to determine which perspectives are probably better, rather than which ones are "right."

Some student papers illustrated this relativistic type of evaluation to which Toni referred in her interview. For example, in one of her open-topic essays, Paula considered the "6 million illegal immigrants in the United States," analyzing proposals that address this issue. Pointing out that "the solutions to the problem vary," she wrote, "Some [experts] believe that we should stabilize the migration flow by stiffening the border control," and "others feel that we should allow the immigrant traffic to continue and just accept the fact that we need the cheap labor." But according to Paula's paper, a disadvantage of the first proposal is that it would sacrifice the United States' "good foreign relationship with our neighbor Mexico," and a disadvantage of the second is that "the American job market will be adversely affected by the increasing number of illegal aliens holding jobs." Suggesting a reasonable compromise that addresses both of these drawbacks, Paula argued for passing a bill that would grant citizenship to aliens who arrived in the United States before 1983 and deport those who arrived after that date. She reasoned, "We cannot afford the $3 billion the aliens send home, to educate their children," but "it is a good idea to legalize those aliens already in the country since they have established homes." Thus, Paula compared different viewpoints, analytically reaching and persuasively justifying a moderate, rather than absolutist, position.

The papers that suggested an analytical approach always compared various experts' arguments, but in some of these essays, students also compared statements made by the same author. For example, in her essay on the Milgram experiment, Toni asserted, "After analyzing both sides of the argument whether experiments such as Stanley Milgram's should continue, I have concluded, as Diana Baumrind does, that . . . Milgram's experiment was unethical." To justify her position, Toni compared the account of the experiment that Milgram gives in his initial report to that which he provides in his response to Baumrind's critique, arguing that the two versions contradict each other:

> Milgram states in his response to Baumrind's article that there were no "injurious effects resulting from participation." He states that the experiment would have been terminated "at once" if the subjects were harming themselves in any way. This contradicts Milgram's study of the experiment that reports people having "seizures" from "nervous laughter" and "digging their fingers into their flesh."

After pointing out the inconsistency of Milgram's own accounts of the experiment, Toni summarized, analyzed, and finally evaluated additional comments that he and two other scientists make about the psychological harm subjects might have experienced. Proponents of the experiment, she explained, argue that the harm was only short-term:

> Robert Hernstein, a supporter of Milgram's experiment, believes that the "temporary" discomfort of the subjects is worth the information that it provides us. Milgram describes this discomfort as "momentary excitement" and he believes that it is worth the knowledge gained.

But Baumrind, Toni wrote, "is more concerned about the potentially permanent harm that may have resulted from this experiment":

> Baumrind believes that the subjects experience a "loss of dignity" after participating in the experiment. She also believes that the emotional trauma of the experiment could diminish the trust that one has with adults in control.

To evaluate these conflicting opinions, Toni again analyzed Milgram's response to Baumrind's critique, explaining that he "give[s] the results of a psychiatrist's examination of the subjects that were 'most likely to have suffered consequences from participation.'" Although she acknowledged that the results showed no indication of long-term harm, Toni claimed:

> This particular statement confirms my assumption of Milgram's uncertainty of the long term effects of the experiment. If there was even a chance that someone could have "suffered consequences," Milgram should have discontinued the experiment.

Reasoning that if Milgram could identify the participants who were "most likely to have suffered consequences," then he must have been at least somewhat unsure of their well-being, Toni concluded, "Because of the uncertainty of the long-term effects of the experiment on its subjects, I feel experiments such as this one should not be conducted." Both Paula and Toni relied on comparison for their analysis, but Toni compared specific statements made by the same author as well as the more general views expressed by different experts.

Pedagogical Implications

When students in this investigation demonstrated a dogmatic approach to writing argumentative, multiple-source papers, they unreflectively took stances towards their topics before reading any sources. Because these students assumed they were absolutely "right," they read with the purpose of finding information to support their own views and did not accommodate diversity of opinion in their essays. As we saw in Bob's interview statements and papers, the dogmatic approach can be associated with problems in interpreting, representing, and evaluating divergent perspectives. It seems very important, therefore, to have students identify and examine their own points of view on the topics about which they are writing. Before my students even begin researching or reading sources for a particular paper, I ask them to write informal, exploratory answers to a series of simple, but very challenging, questions designed to help them probe assumptions and biases:

> What is your current position toward the topic of your paper?
>
> How did you reach this position?
>
> Does it reflect your religious beliefs, political affiliation, or personal experiences?
>
> Does it reflect what you have heard your family or friends say, what you have read, or what you have seen on television?

Students cannot, and should not, will their beliefs and values out of existence; but if they explicitly acknowledge their preconceptions about a topic, they have a better chance of recognizing and understanding arguments that challenge their opinions.

Students in the study who demonstrated a noncommittal approach did not read sources to find evidence for their own opinions, but rather to explore various positions. As Roberta's interview comments and paper suggested, these students read empathetically — that is, with a sense of receptivity and a spirit of good will — and therefore were more successful at understanding and representing different interpretations. Therefore, it seems reasonable to have students read their sources initially with the purpose of acknowledging, even appreciating, authors' viewpoints. To help my students read with empathy, I teach them to annotate texts in a nonjudgmental fashion. Students do not have to make annotations such as "I don't believe this" or "the writer contradicts himself here" to read actively. I believe they can more fully engage themselves with a text, in fact, by using underlinings and marginal annotations that focus on questions such as:

> What is the author's primary argument?
>
> What are his or her supporting points and ideas?
>
> What key terms and definitions does the writer use?

When students read with these nonevaluative questions and an awareness of their own preconceptions in mind, they find it easier to understand their sources fully and to represent them accurately.

The participants who demonstrated an analytical approach not only understood but also successfully analyzed and evaluated sources. As Toni's interview comments and essay suggested, these students relied on comparison to reach and justify their own relativistic stances. After students have read and annotated their sources empathetically, we can help them compare several authors' reasoning, evidence, and expertise, by leading them through a series of evaluative questions:

> If the authors present original research, what are the differences in the designs and executions of their studies?
>
> What facts do the writers present?
>
> How authoritative are the experts to whom authors refer?
>
> Do some writers claim more than their evidence can support?
>
> Can you find contradictions in any of their arguments?
>
> Do some authors make you choose between two extreme positions? If so, why?
>
> Do any of the writers use ambiguous or "loaded" terms that could lead you to make incorrect assumptions?
>
> What are the writers' professional experiences?
>
> In what fields are their educational degrees?
>
> What other articles or books, if any, have they published on your topic?
>
> What are the authors' biases and assumptions?

These questions can help students thoughtfully evaluate which argumentative positions are more rational and fully supported than others.

Something this investigation indicates, then, is that we need to help students balance ambiguity with certainty — that is, the need to explore, understand, and appreciate different points of view with the need to compare, analyze, and judge them. But because argumentative, multiple-source writing ultimately calls for a critical response, composition teachers typically tend to focus only on the latter set of thinking processes. To argue that teachers should emphasize empathetic reading and critical analysis equally might even seem counterproductive, for as Peter Elbow asserts in *Writing Without Teachers,* the tradition of Western rationalism privileges the "doubting game" over the "believing game." Elbow, adds, however, that "the believing game needs to be legitimized if only for the sake of the doubting game" (150).

Appendix A

Using Animals for Laboratory Testing

There is much disagreement about the use of lab animals in research. Antivivisectionists feel that animals should not be used for testing because it is cruel and inhumane, whereas scientists and theologians feel that animals must be used in order to make medical advances.

Animal welfare groups suggest that scientific experiments "inflict pain on research animals." The president of one of these antivivisectionist groups explains that "animals are burned, injected with heroin, and forced to incure diseases ranging from pneumonic plague to cancer." Furthermore, says the president, "There is little evidence to indicate that a single animal experiment has been of benefit to humans."

All of these tests, however, benefit mankind. One scientist indicates that he used experiments with cats and monkeys to show that "vision involves a hierarchy of brain cells." A theologian says these tests are performed for the benefit of mankind and should, therefore, be performed. "Animals were put forth on earth by God in order to serve man," says the scholar of theology.

To sum up, as scientists and theologians indicate, using animals in laboratory experiments is ethically and morally right since all of these experiments benefit mankind. The antivivisectionists, who insist that using animals in experimentation is wrong, do not have enough information to understand the issue.

Soap Operas

Some authorities believe that watching soaps is detrimental, and other experts think it is beneficial.

One expert who argues against watching soap operas suggests that teenagers "are likely to misjudge the amount of sex between unmarried partners and married partners." He indicates that "the major concern with college students watching soap operas is that they tend to overestimate significantly the number of unfaithful spouses, divorces, illegitimate children, and abortions in the real world." Even adults have trouble distinguishing reality from fantasy; once, when a character was kidnapped on a daytime soap, an older viewer "placed a long distance telephone call to the network station and told them where they could find the missing character."

On the other hand, some studies have shown that it may be beneficial to watch soaps. It has been concluded by one authority that "teens who watch soaps tend to take fewer drugs because the soaps serve as the same kind of an escape as drugs do." Some older viewers, in fact, "may even be prescribed to watch a soap opera if there is a character dealing with the same problem the patient is." One psychologist believes, "It gives the person another way of thinking about the problem, and in most cases, the more alternatives one has for solutions, the easier the problem will be to solve."

In conclusion, whether you should watch soap operas or not seems left up to your own judgment. I think it all depends on your own view of soap operas.

Terrorism: Protecting U.S. Embassies and Diplomats

Experts set forth three different solutions to the problem of terrorist attacks against U.S. embassies and diplomats abroad — increased security, increased intelligence, and military retaliation.

Increasing security by using "less glass and fewer windows, blast-resistant walls, and better electronic monitoring systems," says one expert, will help embassies and ambassadors' homes "become better able to resist substantial damage from terrorist attacks." The problem with increasing security, however, is that this plan will not curtail the attacks themselves. If intelligence is increased, suggests another expert, "as information about a terrorist attack is obtained, the U.S. can activate such preventive strikes as arresting terrorists before they can attack or moving military forces to the threatened area." The drawback of this measure, however, is that although increased intelligence reduces the number of terrorist attacks, it cannot curtail the effects of attacks when they do happen.

Some officials argue that military force is "the only solution," but other experts point out that such retaliation will cause many problems. One such problem is that U.S. retaliation will fuel anti-Americanism and thus result in even more terrorist attacks against U.S. embassies.

Therefore, to better defend U.S. embassies abroad, increased intelligence must be used in conjunction with better security, and military retaliation, which has risks, should not be used.

Appendix B

Although the authors of scholarly books sometimes argue, we can count on the qualified experts to agree.

In articles about literature, critics often interpret the same poem differently, but one point of view isn't necessarily better than another.

When two articles contradict each other, they can't both be right.

When authors of newspaper articles disagree about something, one author's point of view is better than the other's.

Since events in the past either happened or didn't happen as a historian recorded them, historical accounts of the past are either right or wrong.

I wouldn't say that one author's argument is right and one author's argument is wrong, but I might like one argument better than another.

We will never have total knowledge in areas like psychology, and in these areas one author's point of view is as valid as another's.

Works Cited

Bazerman, Charles. *The Informed Writer: Using Sources in the Disciplines.* Boston: Houghton Mifflin, 1989.

Behrens, Laurence, and Leonard J. Rosen. *Writing and Reading Across the Curriculum.* Boston: Little, Brown, 1985.

Clinchy, Blythe, and Claire Zimmerman. "Epistemology and Agency in the Development of Undergraduate Women." *The Undergraduate Woman.* Ed. Pamela J. Perun. Lexington, MA: Lexington Books, 1982. 161–181.

Durst, Russell K. "Monitoring Processes in Analytic and Summary Writing." *Written Communication* 6.3 (1989): 340–363.

Elbow, Peter. *Writing Without Teachers.* New York: Oxford University, 1973.

Kennedy, Mary Lynch. "The Composing Process of College Students Writing from Sources." *Written Communication* 2.4 (1985): 434–456.

Kennedy, Mary Lynch, and Hadley Smith. *Academic Writing: Working with Sources Across the Curriculum.* Englewood Cliffs, NJ: Prentice-Hall, 1986.

Kirszner, Laurie G., and Stephen R. Mandell. *The Writer's Sourcebook: Strategies for Reading and Writing in the Disciplines.* New York: Holt, Rinehart and Winston, 1987.

Kitchener, Karen Strohm, and Patricia M. King. "Reflective Judgment: Concepts of Classification and Their Relationship to Age and Education." *Journal of Applied Developmental Psychology* 2 (1981): 89–116.

Miller, Robert K. *The Informed Argument.* San Diego: Harcourt Brace Jovanovich, 1989.

Perry, William G. *Forms of Intellectual and Ethical Development in the College Years: A Scheme.* New York: Holt, 1970.

Sherrard, Carol. "Summary Writing: A Topographical Study." *Written Commu-nication* 3.3 (1986): 324–343.

Slattery, Patrick J. "Applying Intellectual Development Theory to Composi-tion." *Journal of Basic Writing* 9 (1990): 54–65.

———. "Encouraging Critical Thinking: A Strategy for Commenting on Col-lege Papers." *College Composition and Communication* 41 (1990): 332–335.

Spatt, Brenda. *Writing from Sources.* New York: St. Martin's, 1987.

Toulmin and the Ethics of Argument Fields: Teaching Writing and Argument

Gail Stygall

Gail Stygall's essay questions a common binary in argument theory: the idea that Carl Rogers's work helps students create ethical forms of argumentation while Stephen Toulmin provides students a relatively value-free alternative to formal syllogistic logic. Stygall's analysis of the importance of fields, disciplines, and discourse communities to Toulmin's work, however, suggests that teaching students about Toulmin's notions of warrants and backing is also an effective way to teach them about argumentative ethics in argument.

Such instruction will help students see the impact of context on argumentative styles and content. Argument instructors following Stygall's suggestions will also encourage students to see that multiple and conflicting viewpoints are both likely and potentially productive in any argument. They will urge students to explore the multiple forms of rationality that shape arguments and the discourses which frame them, and to consider the values that inform all arguments and all argumenta-tive styles.

It may be useful to read Stygall's work, first published in the Journal of Teaching Writing *in 1987, in conjunction with the excerpt from Stephen Toulmin's* The Uses of Argument *(p. 121) and with the critique of Toulmin found in Richard Fulkerson's "Technical Logic, Comp-Logic, and the Teaching of Writing" (p. 321).*

George Lakoff and Mark Johnson begin their work *Metaphors We Live By* with a description of

> ... what it means for a metaphorical concept, namely, ARGUMENT IS WAR, to structure what we do and how we understand what we are doing when we argue. The essence of metaphor is understanding and experiencing one kind of thing in terms of another. It is not that argu-ments are a subspecies of war. Arguments and wars are different kinds of things — verbal discourse and armed conflict — and the actions performed are different kinds of actions. But ARGUMENT is partially structured, understood, performed and talked about in terms of war. ... Moreover, this is the ordinary way of having an argument and talking about one. (5)

For writing instructors who are involved in the teaching of argument, particularly those who recognize and articulate their profession within a tradition of the humanities, the dilemma is one of conflicting metaphors. On one hand, those of us who teach writing through a process approach may structure our teaching through a growth or benevolent nature metaphor. On the other hand, we cannot deny the tenacity of the argument as war metaphor. We need only listen to our own voices and those of our students in the argumentative writing classroom:

> If you don't provide adequate support, your argument will fall.
>
> Your strategy should provide an excellent defense.
>
> Your line of attack should include better evidence.

Our students are often more to the point:

> If he uses that study, I'll blow him away.
>
> When she uses Hart's article, I'll just bring in my big gun authorities.
>
> We'll shoot him down if he tries that approach.

Lakoff and Johnson suggest that these metaphoric concepts are a major component of how human beings structure and understand their experience, making the argument as war metaphor even more pervasive. To break the war metaphor suggests that ethics must become a major consideration in teaching written argument. Analysis of Rogerian persuasion is one way of turning argument to a more ethical dimension. Though Toulmin's informal logic model is often perceived as just an alternative to formal logic, I would like to suggest that Stephen Toulmin's model of argument provides another way of moving argument to ethical considerations.

Many composition scholars have adopted Toulmin's model of argument as a reasonable alternative to the teaching of classical syllogistic deduction. My own experience with syllogisms and writing students was only sometimes successful. My students did understand all the elaborate formalisms, but when the time came to write a paper based on deduction, something was missing. The world view that syllogistic logic encompasses encircled my students as well. Classical deduction presumes an acceptance of a single, objective truth, precluding much discussion about how that major premise came to be viewed as truth. My students furiously resisted the concept that a syllogism could be valid without being true. Moreover, great chasms opened up in my students' papers. If I had a student arguing that "voluntary prayer in the schools is constitutionally acceptable" as a major premise, followed by "a moment of silence is a form of voluntary prayer" as a minor premise, that student might write a paper with what amounted to two separate, unrelated sections. The first section would trace the legal history of voluntary prayer in this country, the second would trace the history of moments of silence, and the two might never connect in the appropriate categorical fashion. The form dictated the substance and content of the paper, not the student's own sense of the weight of the argument. Instead, the student had "might and right" on her side, the compelling force of the obligatory deductive conclusion derived from two valid premises, never having to consider "truth" once a workable syllogism was found. The student often would not consider counterarguments, alternative syllogisms, once her own syllogism was in place.

Ralph Johnson, evaluating textbook approaches to nonformal argument, in *Teaching Philosophy,* confirms our sister disciplines' concern with the same issue. After substantial critiques of philosophy's array of textbook approaches, Johnson nevertheless concludes in favor of nonformal argument analysis.

> Logicians, as a breed, are not markedly different from other teachers. We teach as we were taught — at least until experience forces us to change. Most of us were taught in graduate school the elements of formal logic. When we found ourselves in front of a classroom full of students, we did what we had been trained to do. For reasons too numerous to mention here, it didn't work. It didn't satisfy. . . . All of this activity falls under the rubric of breaking the spell cast by formal logic, freeing ourselves from the bondage to it, and helping informal logic along into the mainstream of logical inquiry. I am convinced that we will all be better off as a result: our students, our colleagues, the general public. (142)

Though Johnson does not consider Toulmin directly in this article, his analysis of the failure of formal logic to connect with our students supports a movement to informal logic in the writing classroom. When formal logic is encompassed by the structuring war metaphor, our failure as humanists is even more complete. Taught alone, as the "right," "best," or "most intellectually demanding" approach to argument, we teach in formal logic, by implication, that there is one "right" answer, one truth, one valid approach. We foreclose the other options allowing our students to ignore the reasoning and values that lead to other nonformal arguments and conclusions. Comprehending and producing arguments in the real world has much to do with being able to envision underlying assumptions, the criterion Johnson calls "supplying missing premises" (137), and little to do with mastering the given categorical syllogism.

In short we foreclose our students' growth. If William Perry accurately describes our arriving male college students, then we stall the necessary insights for movement from dualism to relativism. How? By providing the right answer through formal logic, we allow our students' dualism to remain unchallenged and the views of others to remain unknown. If Carol Gilligan is correct about our women students' development, then we provide a too easy solution to the problems of how to value self within a community, a critical stage for further ethical development. Why? Because when we offer a structure to preclude further consideration of the issue, we close another door of opportunity. Academically, we may also stall growth, by pretending when we teach formal logic that we have all the right answers, our certain and valid conclusions, allowing that product model we exorcised out of beginning composition back in the door for a higher level writing class.

Toulmin's approach does suggest a reasonable alternative to classical deductive argument. And we should explore that alternative. I have included a diagram (Figure 1) on which the basic model is demonstrated. A Toulmin structure, at the college level, demands a minimum of four parts, data, warrant, backing and claim. The claim is the part that the arguer seeks to prove, in this case that "John was at fault in this automobile accident." The data is simply the evidence, in this case that Marg had the right-of-way, confirmed by two witnesses; that there were no tire marks; that John appeared to be intoxicated by his weaving walk, his slurred speech and flushed face; that the police officer on the scene required John to take a blood test; and that the blood test indicated a blood alcohol level of .13. Warrant is the third dimension of the model and the key element of difference from an ethical perspective. How do we view that data? How do we put it together? The warrant becomes the frame through which the data is viewed. As Toulmin states, using another metaphor, "warrants are hypothetical bridge-like statements" (105). The warrant here is "Since an intoxicated driver will generally be presumed to be at fault in an accident" and the backing for such a warrant is the Code of the State of Indiana, with statutes on fault in accidents, and those on definition of intoxication at .10 as drunk driving.

What is intriguing about the Toulmin model, however, is that if you change the argument field from which the backing and warrant arise, you change the data available to support the claim. In the case of the accident, an entirely different frame operates when the claim is medical, even though the incident itself is the same. Unfortunately, though, the concept of the argument field has received but little attention from most composition researchers. Its most apparent application would be in those writing courses in which students are reading and writing among several disciplines. Its other application, perhaps more important, however, is in its ethical dimension. Toulmin suggests that criteria for evaluation of arguments will vary from field to field. He says:

> . . . the criteria or sorts of ground required to justify such a conclusion vary from field to field. In any field, the conclusions that "cannot" be the case are those we are required to rule out. (36)

Toulmin further suggests that through the examination of field-dependent criteria we may eventually arrive at field-invariant criteria for all disciplines, all claims in all areas. But until we have carefully examined the form, structure and differences among fields, we may have trouble imposing outside structural evaluations. Toulmin further de-

Figure 1

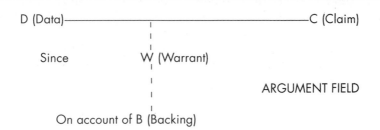

D (Data)————————————————————————C (Claim)

Since   W (Warrant)

                                ARGUMENT FIELD

On account of B (Backing)

Data:
Marg had the right-of-way
Two witnesses saw the accident.
No brake-tire marks on pavement.
Marg was unconscious.
John's speech was slurred.
John's walk was uncertain and
   his face was flushed.
The police officer required John
   to take a blood test.
John's blood alcohol level
   was .13.
Marg was bleeding around her
   face and her right leg was
   twisted in an unnatural position.
Witnesses estimated John's speed
   at 50 mph.

Claim 1: John caused the accident.
Claim 2: Marg was seriously hurt.

Argument Field Claim #1: Law
Argument Field Claim #2: Medicine

Warrant 1:   Since an intoxicated driver is generally presumed
to be at fault in an accident . . .

Warrant 2:   Since the impact of a 2000 lb. auto moving at 50
mph on a human will generally cause serious injury . . .

Backing 1:   *Indiana Code:* drunk driving at .10 blood alcohol
and common law doctrine of negligence per se

Backing 2:   Emergency medical records at Wishard Hospital
in Indianapolis, Indiana, indicate this type of collision will result in serious condition.

velops the concept of intellectual disciplines and their development in his work *Human Understanding*. Here, the conception of argument field is developed in relation to intellectual disciplines.

Toulmin defines a discipline, a field, even a near-discipline, at least partially by its agreement on common goals and conceptions of its purpose. Why then should the teaching of this particular model, applied to academic disciplines, enhance students' tolerance? After all, we demonstrate through a preliminary analysis that the individual disciplines have their own coherence of thought, and, thus, formal logic could be expected to apply. Toulmin makes two distinctions in *Human Understanding* that clarify this apparent problem. First, not all disciplines are, as he called it, "compact," those disciplines of the natural sciences in which goal and conceptions are agreed upon and explicitly known and discussed. We must thus reason that apart from these narrowly defined "hard" sciences other disciplines may require informal logic. Toulmin also suggests that the social sciences do not have the necessary compactness. Subdisciplines and subspecialties, each with separate warrants and backing, are, he posits, far more likely outside of natural science. Second, Toulmin also suggests there is a qualitative change in the dimension of the argument when ethical questions enter.

> In any culture and generation men [and women] acknowledge the authority of a dozen inherited approaches to ethical questions. Each of these approaches has its own rubric — "as a matter of self respect/morality/loyalty/etiquette/integrity/equity/religious commitment/simple humanity . . ." — and each defines a particular set of issues, considerations, and modes of argument. In any chosen culture and generation, furthermore, men [and women] do not merely continue applying all these different considerations and arguments in exactly the same way as their forefathers; they also attempt to refine their application, and to reorder their relative priorities, in light of the changing needs and conditions of life. (410)

How we best prepare our students to enter argument ethically, "the multivalued character of concrete ethical issues" (410), is through learning to use Toulmin's model as a tool of analysis of discipline-oriented issues, to come to know why and how a member of a discipline, a resident of a field, arrived where he or she did. A fact then is not just a fact. A fact is constrained by its context, its designated field. What facts are considered in determining a legal case are not necessarily the same to be considered in a medical case. What a linguist considers to be a fact of language an English teacher might reject. When a sociologist looks at families at risk, she sees a group with defined characteristics; when the psychologist looks at a family at risk, he sees a problem to be resolved. What happened to facts? Are we thus prevented from evaluating arguments? Toulmin's model suggests the answer is no, but we must first determine the argument field and its corresponding warrants and backing, before we have facts, or salient data.

This negotiability of facts and data between disciplines leaves an opening for developing our students' consciousness of the differences among the disciplines and the "backing," the reasons why some facts are considered and others are not. Rarely do our students receive explicit instruction in the philosophical backing of a discipline. The very idea may seem ridiculous in the late high school or early college years. History is history; those who aren't included weren't important is typical analysis. The rules of English grammar have always been the rules of English grammar is another typical analysis. Our students' perceptions of fields remain at the right and wrong, dualistic level.

When teaching argument and research, we have the opportunity to make these differences in analysis by field part of our students' analytical tools. Moreover, this expansion in their repertoire also leads to a greater tolerance for multiple perspectives on a topic. They may not be so quick to reject a point of view as "wrong" if they first must examine the view from the backing of the argument field from which the view comes. Further, as Charles Kneupper suggests, "people are participants in multiple fields"; thus, our students also have this aspect, a field grounding their knowledge. Our students may have already declared an academic field, but they are also participants in religious, political, athletic, and avocational fields. Kneupper elaborates by stating:

> Such a person may not advance the knowledge in any of these fields, but will still utilize the knowledge and constructs provided by these fields. Further, such a person may gradually increase in personal knowledge as he or she gains more experience in, more constructs from, a fuller comprehension of each of these fields. Fields focus upon, capture and emphasize some limited aspect or feature of human experience in the world. They enable and expedite common understanding and problem solving within that sphere. (83)

In the teaching of argumentative writing where the conflict of value systems may be explicit, we may use that surfacing of the ethical systems, the value systems behind fields of inquiry, to expand our students' world knowledge and more importantly to increase tolerance for the views of others.

So how might we teach the ethics of argument in conjunction with the Toulmin model? First, we need to come to a definition of ethics. Previously my discussion contrasting categorical deduction with informal logic defined ethics in argument only implicitly, as "not war," not just two opposing sides, from which only one can emerge as valid. Ethics in the argumentative writing classroom has further dimensions as a part of a liberal education. To become participants in the college experience, our students must come to understand the conventions of our discussion. Those conventions include a preference for the logical and the rational over the purely emotional and dramatic, a predilection for thorough analysis over the stereotype or hasty generalization, and the acknowledgment of the possibility of a number of points of view. Though this description is, of course, ideal, many observers suggest these are some of the underlying values of the liberal undergraduate education. Moreover, in reexamining William Perry's scheme of moral and ethical development, we can find a correspondence between acknowledging the possibility of many points of view and his stage of multiplicity. Students of college age move beyond dualism, or simple right and wrong, into discovery of multiple perspectives. From knowledge of these perspectives, Perry asserts these students will reach a stage of commitment. While most students experience multiplicity in unplanned settings — sheer contact with other students and coursework in various disciplines — it is possible to focus students' attention on multiplicity of viewpoint within an academic context. This focus on multiplicity of viewpoint then becomes the key to ethics in the argumentative writing classroom.

Let me offer an example of what this focus on multiplicity might mean in actual classroom practice. One approach I have found useful is to present an overview of the Toulmin model at the same time I provide a set of apparently contradictory facts. I ask my students to attempt to account for how the "facts" came to be, in spite of their contradictions. Figure 2, a sample exercise, illustrates an issue presented in such a way as to highlight the necessity of analyzing multiple perspectives. The topic in this exercise was the policy question of whether or not English should be made the official language of the United States. Students had been asked to read a variety of materials including the 1984 California ballot initiative on requesting the U.S. Congress to make English the official national language, various editorials appearing in newspapers, and Rudolph Troike's review "Synthesis of Research on Bilingual Education." After reading these materials, students compiled a list of data from the various sources. Their lists were compiled and made a part of the exercise.

Figure 2

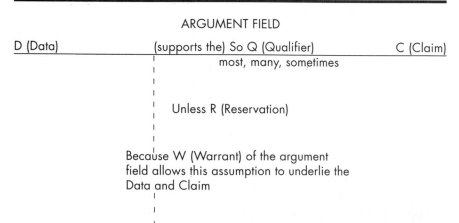

ARGUMENT FIELD

D (Data)   (supports the) So Q (Qualifier)   C (Claim)

most, many, sometimes

Unless R (Reservation)

Because W (Warrant) of the argument
field allows this assumption to underlie the
Data and Claim

On account of B (Backing) of the argument field in its official documents and records, laws, agreements, etc. provides evidence of the warrant.

DATA:
English speakers cannot do business with speakers of Spanish only.
In Miami, Tuscon, El Paso and Los Angeles more than 30 percent of elementary grades instruction is carried out in Spanish.
Bilingual education is more costly than monolingual education and thus requires federal aid to local schools.

Bilingual ballots cost more to print.

Bilingual ballots have been available in New Mexico since 1912.

Bilingual ballots have been required in federal elections since 1975.

Foreign language ballots are unnecessary because all immigrants must pass an English language literacy test.

Twenty million citizens of the United States were born in households in which English was not the first language.

All other major immigrant populations to the United States have mastered English.

Dade County, Florida, declared itself officially bilingual in 1975.

A ballot proposition in California in 1986 enforcing English as the official language of California won 73 percent voter approval.

In Los Angeles County, bilingual ballots account for only 2 percent of costs.

The language of the home is the dominant language of any speaker.

In areas of language contact, most speakers know enough of the two (or more) languages to communicate minimally.

Students who begin their elementary education in their native language and then transfer it to a second language test better on standardized examinations of language ability and aptitude.

Students who are forced to be educated in a completely nonnative language environment are more likely to become drop-outs.

Argument Field #1: Language Purists
Probable Warrants:

> A single language is a unifying element of a country.

> Other immigrant groups have been capable.

> Bilingualism allows students to be lazy and undisciplined.

> English is the best world language, now the language of international business and commerce.

> Bilingualism is costly.

> Anyone born in the United States speaks English.

Argument Field #2: Linguists
Probable Warrants:

> All speakers of any language have at least minimal language learning aptitude.

> Language learning which makes use of previous language experience is most effective.

> Language learning alienation occurs when the speaker's first language is institutionally banned.

> The language of the home is the native language.

> All languages are roughly equivalent in complexity, and no one language is superior to any other language.

> Social and economic factors provide their own motivations to learn prestige languages and dialects.

What claims can you develop for each of the two argument fields?

List at least four claims, allowed by the warrants, and supported by at least part of the data. List four claims below. Include the necessary warrants and the data relevant to each claim.

Initially, the mere compiling of the data had little effect on students' perspectives on the issue. Central Indiana being a place of little linguistic variation, students generally saw no problem in adopting English as an official national language. They knew only those who spoke some intelligible dialect of American English, so the original claims they generated simply reiterated that English should be the official U.S. language. By providing some probable underlying warrants to the argument, I was able to suggest that the problem was more complex than it appeared on the surface. In being asked to link warrants with appropriate data, students were able to see what data they were forced to reject when they selected one set of warrants over another. For example, many of my students selected the claim that English should be the official language by using "language purist" warrants of a single language being unifying and that other immigrants have been capable of learning English. But troublesome to many of these students was the realization that they had to reject all the data on bilingual education and they had to ignore the significant number of American citizens, born in this country, who did not use English as a first language. Alternatively, students who had selected the "linguist" warrants were forced to reject the possibility that a single language could be a unifying factor and that there were very real governmental costs involved in providing multilingual services and functions. Such dissonance required some resolution and students were to return to the original packet of readings and attempt to synthesize the conflicting points of view, generating new claims. Four collaborative groups responded in the following ways:

> One side wants English to be the official language while the other believes bilingualism should be available in the educational system. The two are not necessarily opposites. Maybe the U.S. English law could be written so bilingual services are still available.

> The cost and education sides are not really in opposition. The educators believe students should learn English, but on a gradual basis. The people concerned with other bilingual costs in government and business could eliminate the problem through bilingual education.

> The bilingual educators' approach describes ways to teach English to non-English speakers by gradually introducing English, along with using their own language as they study. English is still the goal for both groups. Those who are bilingual will have the advantage of being able to communicate in more than one setting.

> Bilingual education could be a less expensive alternative in the long run as its intent is to move the student from one language to another. In this way, every speaker is looked on as a potential resource instead of as a burden. Though both articles leaned toward English as the main language, the U.S. English position abandons all attempts to support speakers of other languages, while bilingual educators have a more thoughtful approach.

Even if the students remained steadfast in their support of English as an official language, they were now ready to qualify that stand, to acknowledge the viewpoints of linguists and educators experienced in the problem. Upon reconsidering the California ballot initiative, many remarked on the value of having voters understand what they were voting on, difficult if language was a barrier. Further, many were particularly concerned with the image of a six-year-old child entering school and finding himself or herself in a totally foreign language setting. Were they accommodating multiple perspectives? I would suggest that the answer must be yes, and by the previous definition of ethics in this context, they were beginning to meet the components of the definition. They were considering the issue from a logical and rational point of view rather than "but I don't want to learn to speak Spanish" being the guiding principle. Their analysis was now more thorough, less stereotypical, recognizing that not everyone born in the United States speaks English in the home. And they were able to encompass more than a single perspective while taking a position.

Had this particular issue been taught within the categorical, deductive approach, my experience tells me the syllogisms would have demonstrated little, if any, accommodation to multiple perspectives. I suspect I would have received many essays guided by the following syllogism: Linguistic accommodation is too costly for the United States; bilingual education is linguistic accommodation; therefore, bilingual education is too costly for the United States. Though far more sophisticated syllogisms are possible, rarely does the beginning student of written argumentation make them. By seeking a categorical form, the student must necessarily assert oppositions: One is either in a category or not in the category. And we are left once again with the war metaphor: for or against.

Let me offer a final example of this movement from one of my own students last year. The particular student in question was male, early twenties, a very articulate conservative. His strong rejection of socialist or Marxist analysis of historical events precluded his use of some of the typical analytical tools of his field, history. He had decided that any economic analysis of historical events was indicative of a left-wing approach. Thus, in a previous history class, when this student attempted to analyze a situation he posits in his paper — that the Russian officer corps was in part responsible for the Russian Revolution of 1917 — he was unable to make his case. What had previously precluded success was that he did not want to use social or economic analysis to clarify the historical context, feeling that to do so would violate his personal conservatism. Two aspects of the argumentative writing class using Toulmin came into play. First, his fellow history majors in class read his work, commenting on how his analysis differed from theirs, correctly identifying the lack of a warrant in his work allowing him to use social and economic factors. Second, his use of Toulmin to study his own intended field allowed him to see that social and economic context provided him the necessary warrant to make his case, this time successfully. He no longer believes his professor was critiquing him on the basis of his politics and he knows how to warrant his own arguments from his home field. He had taken a first step toward toleration, my claim for the benefits of using this approach.

Finally, rather than structuring our conception of argument through the war metaphor, we might want to use a growth metaphor. The act of arguing can then form around cycles, growth, fertilizing, flowering, seeding, and weeding. With the growth metaphor, argument can be seen as flowering and bearing seeds, rather than as destroying and dominating. Disagreements no longer need to be battlefield sites; sites may be fields where ecological balance may be achieved. The dark side of the war metaphor — the stark, ashen, lifeless place of battle — is sterile. We need to replace this sterile metaphor with a productive one. Battlefields have their brief moment of glory in time; gardens may be timeless.

Works Cited

Gilligan, Carol. *In A Different Voice: Psychological Theory and Women's Development.* Cambridge: Harvard UP, 1982.

Johnson, Ralph H. "The New Logic Courses: The State of the Art in Non-Formal Methods of Argument Analysis." *Teaching Philosophy* 4.2 (1981): 123–143.

Kneupper, Charles. "Argument Fields: Some Social Constructivist Observations." *Dimensions of Argument: Proceedings of the Second Summer Conference on Argumentation.* George Ziegelmueller and Jack Rhodes, Eds. Annandale, Virginia: Speech Communication Association, 1981.

Lakoff, Gregory and Mark Johnson. *Metaphors We Live By.* Chicago: U of Chicago P, 1980.

Perry, William G. Jr. *Forms of Intellectual and Ethical Development in the College Years: A Scheme.* New York: Holt, Rinehart and Winston, 1970.

Toulmin, Stephen E. *Human Understanding.* Princeton: Princeton UP, 1972.

———. *The Uses of Argument.* Cambridge: Cambridge UP, 1958.

Troike, Rudolph. "Synthesis of Research on Bilingual Education. *Educational Leadership* (March, 1981): 498–503.

4

Teaching Argument across the Curriculum

When first-year composition became a required subject at most universities around the turn of the twentieth century, it was paradoxically one of the most taught and least respected classes in the curriculum. Few recognized the class's intellectual roots in rhetoric, and the writing class was viewed by many as a service course responsible for preparing less-than-fully-literate students to succeed in the "real," content-based disciplines and in the workplace. Today's composition professionals still struggle with questions about composition's role as a "service course" and its relationship to other disciplines.

The writing across the curriculum (WAC) movement has also raised new and, for many scholars, more important issues. WAC programs began to grow in the 1970s and marked the first time in recent U.S. history that an institutionalized rhetorical sensibility connected composition with disciplines such as history, psychology, and philosophy. Since that time, writing across the curriculum theory has drawn from a wide range of sources, including classical Greek rhetoric, twentieth-century philosophers such as Stephen Toulmin and Chaim Perelman; and contemporary composition scholars such as Susan McLeod, Barbara Walvoord, Art Young, and Toby Fulwiler. Currently scholars in many fields, including but not limited to those fields represented in this section (history, women's studies, and business), are exploring the relationship between writing and learning in the disciplines. These and other scholars emphasize that although writing instructors may never be able to fully "train" students to write effectively in every discipline (and should not even take on such an impossible task), we can help students understand the contextualized nature of all writing.

First-year university students, that is, often need to be shown that although some writing standards seem universal, each writing experience is unique and draws on both general principles and specific, context-bound "rules." WAC specialists point out that students need to be given strategies for determining how to balance their knowledge of general writing principles with the specific needs of individual writing episodes. This kind of balance can only be achieved if students are taught to explore how all communication must respond to the needs of the writer, the needs of the audience, the social context in which the text is being written, and the technology available to readers and writers.

Such work is difficult but critical if students are to understand writing as a living, breathing process. Written argument, in particular, often seems like a static form, with some students feeling stuck writing endless variations of the five-paragraph theme and wondering what the point is to having a thesis or to going to the library (or, more likely, the Internet) to find "expert" support for their own ideas. At the same time, teachers often feel as if there is little creativity in teaching argument and that the ideas of "support" and "thesis" should be self-explanatory.

Approaching writing in the disciplines and in composition classes as a rhetorical activity, however, demands creativity on the part of students and teachers. Instructors *can* give students a general sense of what kinds of things constitute "support," for example, of an argument, but we will serve our students better if we also encourage them to recognize that the idea of support is a contingent one. Even more, we need to help students analyze fields of study so that they are comfortable determining the different means of support appropriate to the many disciplines they will encounter at the university.

This work is critical because it asks writers to understand how knowledge is socially constructed in accordance with disciplinary ways of knowing — as well as with social and cultural norms. With this knowledge, which recognizes the close connection between philosophy and rhetoric, student writers will have the ability to adapt to the multiple writing contexts they encounter and, just as important, to adapt these disciplines to their needs and interests.

The Figures of Speech, *Ethos,* and Aristotle: Notes toward a Rhetoric of Business Communication

Craig Kallendorf and Carol Kallendorf

In this essay, originally published in The Journal of Business Communication *in 1985, Craig and Carol Kallendorf suggest that we examine business communication in light of classical rhetoric, particularly the work of Aristotle. Arguing that all business writing is persuasive in nature, the Kallendorfs analyze a number of documents in order to propose a rhetoric of business communication derived from practice. The*

*authors note that the rhetorical figures of speech that textbooks often
assume to be antithetical to "clear" and "concise" business writing actually contribute to effective persuasion in the business world. More specifically, they link the rhetorical figures (which some consider to be linguistic
devices for use by poets rather than business writers) to Aristotle's notions
of ethos, pathos, and logos.*

*For Aristotle, ethos refers to the ability of a rhetor to project a positive
image to an audience; pathos refers to rhetors' appeals to an audience's
emotions and values; and logos refers to rhetors' appeals to logic. The
connection between business communication and Aristotle's appeals
provides the basis for a comprehensive rhetoric of business communication, one that respects business writing as a complex interaction that
depends on much more than short, clear sentences and hard logic. Given
the significance of corporate life in today's world and the omnipresence of
business communication, the Kallendorfs finally suggest that we add
business rhetoric to the three major types of rhetoric — deliberative
(political), forensic (legal), and epideictic (ceremonial) — that Aristotle
proposed over two thousand years ago.*

*Readers interested in considering classical rhetoric further should
consult the section in this book titled "Some Classical Influences on
Rhetoric" (p. 1), particularly the excerpt from Aristotle's Rhetoric (p. 4).
The bibliography in this text also lists a number of readings on classical
rhetoric as well as readings on the rhetoric of business and technical
writing.*

As interest in the discipline of business communication has grown
in recent years, the number of textbooks and handbooks in the
field has quickly multiplied. A glance along the appropriate library
shelf will flush out a whole covey of books which promise to tell the
reader how to write better business letters and reports, how to write
for managers and for hourly workers, how to write for internal consumption and for the general public.

What is more striking than the sheer number of such books, however, is their almost unanimous agreement on one point: the appropriate style for business communication. In advocating shorter sentences,
economical phrasing, and logical constructions, the authors return again
and again to *clarity* as a guiding principle for business prose.[1] This is
as it should be, for all the obvious reasons. But as these writers struggle
to describe clear writing, a certain ambivalence creeps into the discussion. On the one hand, most of the authors recognize that clarity does
not happen by itself, that we must work at our writing in order to express ourselves clearly.[2] On the other hand, the guides to business communication restrict themselves to a much more limited range of
stylistic strategies than most other writing manuals, since business
communicators seem to believe that any signs of artifice in the finished product inevitably interfere with comprehension. For example,
Menning, Wilkinson, Clarke, and Wilkinson contend that evidence of a
conscious attention to style can only come between writer and reader,
that style is best when it is most inconspicuous.[3] They even go so far as

to condemn the deliberate cultivation of style as a "mark of immaturity."[4] No stylistic devices have suffered more from this bias than the figures of speech, which threaten almost by definition to draw attention to themselves. Brought into disrepute by such accusations of artificiality and burdened down with forbiddingly polysyllabic Greek names, the figures have never found a place in business writing texts.[5] Many of the people who write *about* business prose seem to feel that the figures are at best distracting and worst confusing, that clear writing cannot strive for obvious stylistic polish as well. But what of the people who actually *write* business prose?

As the advance guard of sales promotion, advertising reaches more people than internal memos, reports, letters, and other less public company documents. A close look at the slogans and the prose of advertising copy reveals an unexpected interest in the figures of speech. From epistrophe, such as "If you're on the phone a lot, the calling cards help a lot," to antimetabole, such as "You can take Salem out of the country, but you can't take the country out of Salem," many ads use one or more of the figures of speech with varying degrees of skill. The following table illustrates the use of some of the more common figures in advertising.[6]

Name of Figure and Definition	Example
ANAPHORA: Repetition of the same word at the beginning of successive clauses	TWA's Ambassador Class to Europe. More room to sit. More room to work. More room to relax.
ANASTROPHE: Unusual arrangement of words or clauses within a sentence	One ad does not a survey make. (Peugeot)
ANTIMETABOLE: Inverting the order of repeated words	You can take Salem out of the country, but you can't take the country out of Salem.
ANTITHESIS: Conjoining contrasting ideas	For men, they created retirement plans, medical benefits, profit sharing, and gold watches. For women, they created Mother's Day. (Older Women's League)
ASYNDETON: Omission of conjunctions	Waterford pours forth memories. It conjures up fantasies, evokes poetic imagery, provokes the creative spirit, celebrates life's mysteries.
ELLIPSIS: Omission of a word easily understood from context	There are newer homes we insure. But none more important. (The Travelers)
EPISTROPHE: Repetition of a closing word or words at the end of several clauses, sentences, or verses	If you're on the phone a lot, the calling card helps a lot. (AT&T)
HYPERBOLE: Exaggerated or extravagant terms used for emphasis and not intended to be understood literally	Scientific breakthroughs have always been met with hysteria from the conservative and nostalgic. And Bill Blass has always stood proudly among the hysterics. Bill, observing the polyester business suit, felt it might well mean the end of civilization as we know it.

METAPHOR: Assertion of identity rather than, as with a simile, likeness	Buick Skyhawk comes by its name very honestly. Hawks are known, after all, for their power and maneuverability.
METONYMY: Drawing a suggestive expression from a closely associated object or idea	The nation's finest names in banking invite you to join the nation's first name in ATM networks. (Plus System)
PARALLELISM: Repetition of phrases of equal length and usually corresponding structure	Fast talk gets you in a corner. Straight talk gets you out. (InterFirst Banks)
PERSONIFICATION: An animal or an inanimate object is represented as having human attributes	Make filing come alive! (Pendaflex)
RHETORICAL QUESTION: Question implying strong affirmation or denial	Is it possible for someone with three kids, a mortgage, and hefty orthodontia bills to drive a car he actually likes? (Saab)
SIMILE: One thing is likened to another.	Cars, like people, respond to tender loving care. (Car Care Council)

We could multiply examples almost without limit, but the few advertising slogans cited here are enough to show that advertising does indeed use the figures and that, in fact, it uses a wide range of them.[7]

The appearance of such stylistic devices in advertising does not by itself prove that business writers in general use them. The purpose of advertising and its formal considerations require greater reliance on the epigrammatic, the visual, and the allusive than most business prose. Therefore, our survey of business communication, defined broadly as all of a company's internal and external documents and oral presentations, should include some more routine examples as well, such as letters, speeches, business plans, and annual reports.

A letter which the president of a large health insurance company sent to his customers after the highly publicized loss of a large contract blends several figures of speech in what amounts to an exercise in confidence-building. Using parallelism, the president writes: "I feel certain the information conveyed in this letter will both *allay whatever fears* you might have *about our financial position* and *bolster your confidence in our company* as a competitive and progressive carrier."[8] Toward the end of the letter he combines parallelism with anaphora to reassure his readers: "*We have thoroughly evaluated the potential impact of this loss on our organization and found* it to be manageable. *We have thoroughly evaluated the impact on our groups and found* that it is not significant."

TIMEBASE, Inc., a publisher of computer software, uses a variety of figures of speech in its business plan to capture the company's entrepreneurial vigor. The bold use of parallelism and anaphora in the following statement communicates the company's vitality and self-confidence: "TIMEBASE is a company *with the right ideas and the right people at the right time.*" Since to succeed, a young company must be savvy as well as energetic, TIMEBASE uses antimetabole, anastrophe, and parallelism to underscore the sophistication it uses in analyzing the software market:

> *The days are gone when a handful of young designers could get* a stranglehold on the production of new programs. *Gone, too, are the days when a covey of software companies published* virtually everything on the market.

The artful use of the figures of speech gives what could be a prosaic document considerable persuasive force and helps it establish a company image.

The following excerpt from Beatrice Foods' 1979 annual report illustrates a genre of business writing we often think of as pedestrian:

> The economies of scale, innovation, productivity and efficiency of the *"Great American Food Machine,"* and the diversified companies which comprise it, offer the American consumer the broadest variety of food, *of the finest quality, in the greatest abundance, and at the lowest costs* anywhere in the world.

Metonymy and a simple parallelism enliven this passage and in doing so, raise it above the pedestrian.

Business communication includes speaking as well as writing, and the following example demonstrates that business speakers also use the figures. This passage is taken from a speech that Wes Poriotis, president of Wesley-Brown Enterprises, delivered to the American Society for Hospital Public Relations in 1982.

> *I don't think I'm* the only one for whom your industry is *like a kaleidoscope* bursting with confusing fragments. *I don't think Americans know* there's a big merger movement going on in the health-care industry — with profit-minded and non-profit-minded *circling each other warily like IBM and AT&T. I don't think Americans buy* the idea that medical costs are *not* [authors' emphasis] one of the principal driving forces behind inflation.

Poriotis marshals a whole regiment of figures to critique the health care industry. Parallelism and anaphora drive his point home and give it urgency, while simile and personification make what could be an arid topic concrete and immediate.

According to Menning, Wilkinson, Clarke, and Wilkinson, the modern period of business prose began at the turn of the century.[9] Did business writers in the early part of this period make such ready use of the figures as their later counterparts? In a speech to the students of Cornell University, John D. Rockefeller, Jr. developed an extended simile between labor relations and sex:

> Like knowledge of the problems of sex, than which no department of life is more sacred, vital, or deserving of full and ennobling instruction, an understanding of this subject [labor relations] is left to be acquired by

experience, often costly or bitter, or through chance information, gleaned too frequently from ignorant and unreliable sources.[10]

Rockefeller makes his point, and, through a witty use of the figures, he makes it memorable. Later in that same speech he uses a series of elegant parallelisms, an antithesis, and a rhetorical question to emphasize the importance of healthy human relationships:

> After all is it not the personal relations with one's fellows which, *when rightly entered into, bring joy and inspiration into our lives and lead to success,* and which, on the other hand, *if disregarded or wrongly interpreted, bring equally sorrow and discouragement, and lead to failure?*[11]

While Rockefeller's style is clear and urbane, even elegant, his contemporary W. R. Heath developed a style which combined clarity with aphoristic punch. In a speech entitled "The Demands of the Business World for Good English," Heath uses parallelism, anastrophe, and ellipsis to state his problem:

> *One difficulty we encounter* in our work. We write English well. *Our display is striking and sloganish; our text fascinating and pregnant with selling talk; our letters appreciative of commendation,* yet withal modest; *our answers to complaints generous, sincere, and adequate.* Our difficulty is, we are not understood.[12]

Heath uses anaphora, parallelism, and asyndeton to help define what he means by "good English": "Good English to the business man is simple English, *English that is listened to, English that is read, English that is understood, English that produces.*"[13] He closes his speech with an epigrammatic use of antimetabole: "Belittle *'big business'* if you will, but magnify *business bigness.*"[14] Thus Heath uses good English to call for good English. And it is worth noting that Heath and Rockefeller have styles which are equally effective and equally dependent on the figures, but totally different.

Our final illustration is offered — as it was written — with tongue firmly in cheek.

> To the gas company
> Hartford, February 1, 1891
>
> Dear Sirs:
>
> *Some day you will move me almost to the verge of irritation* by *your chuckle-headed Goddamned* fashion of shutting *your Goddamned* gas off without giving any notice to *your Goddamned* parishioners. Several times you have come within an ace *of smothering half of this household* in their beds and *blowing up the other half* by this idiotic, not to say criminal, custom of yours. And it has happened again to-day. *Haven't you a telephone?*
>
> Ys
>
> SL Clemens[15]

Samuel Clemens uses irony, anaphora, parallelism, and a rhetorical question to help communicate his frustration. A disclaimer of sorts is obviously in order here, since Clemens is well known as a literary figure with a carefully fashioned public image to preserve. Nevertheless, the circumstances which prompted this letter are private rather than public, and this complaint letter, like any other, can be placed in the realm of business correspondence.

This review of advertising slogans and more common genres of routine business writing from the present and the recent past reveals a puzzling contradiction. In their emphasis on clarity, most textbooks of business communication ignore — or even condemn — stylistic devices such as the figures of speech. The prose that business people actually write, however, shows that the figures of speech are used quite often and are entirely compatible with the goal of clarity, with the common sense drive to shorten sentences and simplify phrasing to what is logically essential. Indeed, it is even arguable whether prose which is devoid of the figures can be clear. A computer software manual, for example, is a type of writing which, if any, might be thought to have clarity and clarity alone as its goal. The manual to WordStar, a widely used and rather expensive word processing program, is written in such a lifeless style and in such burdensome detail that many consumers find it difficult or impossible to learn the program from it. These people then feel compelled to purchase a book like Arthur Naiman's *Introduction to WordStar,*[16] which is much easier to understand than the manual, because the simple, lively style in which it is written relies heavily on the figures of speech we have been looking at. Such books are able to have even technological *tabulae rasae* happily processing their words in a matter of minutes precisely because the engaging style carries and clarifies the necessary content.

Thus, we recommend the figures of speech as an aid, not an alternative, to clarity. But are there perhaps other reasons, reasons even more fundamental than clarity, which might lead business writers to figures of speech and explain why these figures prove so effective in business prose?

Ever since antiquity, one common approach to the figures has associated them with ornamentation for its own sake, with a stylistic polish and embellishment that is more or less divorced from the message.[17] This is the tradition against which the writers of many business communication texts seem to have reacted. There is, however, another tradition that integrates the figures quite thoroughly with the content and purpose of the message.

A survey of the basic sources in the history of rhetoric shows that for two thousand years, the figures have been associated with the passions. As Quintilian put it, "there is no more effective method of exciting the emotions [*pathos*] than an apt use of figures."[18] Brian Vickers has followed this association from Greek and Roman authors through Renaissance rhetoricians like Peacham, Sidney, and Puttenham to the eighteenth century theorists, leading him to conclude that the emotional power of rhetoric derives from the figures.[19] This point becomes obvious when we consider how our speech betrays our feelings when we are angry: Connectives are passed over in asyndeton, key words are emphatically repeated in anaphora, clauses become shorter and more direct through parallelism, and so forth, as we saw above in Clemens's letter to the gas company.

Obviously, there are many other circumstances in which business prose aims at least in part to rouse the reader or listener to action. Advertising comes to mind here, as do business plans designed to attract potential investors, letters of application for licenses or loans, and so forth. Though we like to think that our case stands or falls on its rational merits, most people are more likely to act when their emotions are engaged. And if we pursue this line of reasoning a little further, we can think of a number of corporate situations from which we cannot remove the emotional element. Retirement banquets, citations of recognition for meritorious service, and even a speech delivered at a plant closing benefit from an awareness of what the people involved must feel. And when business meets the public, it has to contend with the people's feelings as well as their ideas, as any public utility company in search of a rate increase well knows. The appeal to the emotions carried by the figures is certainly not the primary function of business prose, perhaps not even its secondary function, but under certain circumstances it can help to create a bond between writer and reader that leads to shared goals and shared action — and that is considerably more substantive than "ornamentation."

The figures have also been associated with logic and reasoning at various points in the history of rhetoric. In *Shakespeare's Use of the Arts of Language,* Sister Miriam Joseph has shown that over 60 percent of the figures commonly used in Renaissance England are related to the topics of invention and the principles of argumentation, so that logical division of a subject, for example, and the figure of diaeresis are similar.[20] Frank D'Angelo has recently developed this idea in *A Conceptual Theory of Rhetoric,* where he argues that the topics of invention and the figures of speech reflect the same underlying thought processes. That is, the conceptual structure that we call "the topic of difference in kind" when it serves a heuristic function involves the same mental processes as the figures of contrast, antithesis, antimetabole, chiasmus, and oxymoron.[21] This association offers immediate promise to the business communicator as a subtle means of reinforcing the logical reasoning [*logos*] on which most of us instinctively rely these days. The simile of sex and labor relations that John D. Rockefeller, Jr. used, for example, is not primarily ornamentation, but an effort to explain the unknown in terms of the known. Most good writers intuitively turn to the figure of parallelism to underscore the logical equivalence among items in an enumerated series. Since we have to rely on shared, basic thought processes in order to reach a common understanding with our readers, the ability of the figures to reinforce these thought processes also helps explain the association between the figures of speech and stylistic clarity.

Outside the area of business writing, *pathos* and *logos* have long been associated with the figures of speech. As many readers will undoubtedly have observed, they are also two-thirds of an important triad in Aristotelian rhetoric. Can the third member of that triad, *ethos,* perhaps contribute even more substantively to our understanding of the use of figures in business prose? Although it has not received much development, Quintilian among ancient theorists and Sister Miriam Joseph among modern scholars provide some justification for pursuing this relationship.[22]

The rhetorical notion of *ethos* refers to the image a writer or speaker projects to an audience; as commonly understood, it does not really involve questions of ethics as we use the term today.[23] This distinction is especially true of Aristotle; an Aristotelian rhetorician need not actually *be* a good person, but must only be *perceived* as one. According to Aristotle, a speaker or writer communicates a credible *ethos* when intelligence, upright character, and goodwill are projected to the audience.[24]

Business people seem to have an innate understanding of the importance of image. Although they would hardly describe their actions as building *ethos,* that is precisely what male executives do when they appear before important groups of investors in three-piece pin-striped suits, conservative silk ties, and neatly groomed hair. Many top salespeople understand this principle so well that they adapt the style of their dress to fit the backgrounds of their customers. When it comes to the words they use, business people also seem to appreciate, at least instinctively, the importance of conveying the proper image. Francis Weeks and Daphne Jameson imply this when they state that business people use jargon because they want their words to sound impressive.[25] Since jargon usually accomplishes the opposite, this choice of technique is regrettable, but the principle remains sound, as Weeks and Jameson note: "Also, we want our readers to have favorable impressions of us so that they will be motivated to believe what we tell them, agree with us, and want to cooperate with us."[26]

Aristotle argues for the importance of *ethos,* and business people seem to be in *de facto* agreement with him. But what do the figures of speech have to do with *ethos?* The figures of speech, as we have already seen, enable a writer to balance similar or contrasting ideas, to frame thoughts in epigrammatic expressions, to add a sense of drama or urgency to a message. The figures, in short, enable a writer to arrange, shape, and present ideas in a way that projects the image of a thoughtful and analytical person whose ideas deserve to be taken seriously. They provide the tools for communicating the intelligence, goodwill, and upright character which Aristotle said must be projected. Much as the pin-striped suit, conservative tie, and well groomed hair enable the business person to convey a certain visual *ethos,* the figures of speech are the tools for building an effective verbal *ethos.* In fact, while the visual *ethos* may win the initial attention or empathy of an audience, it is this verbal *ethos* which makes a substantive contribution to the impression of intelligence, goodwill, and character.

But why, precisely, is *ethos* such an important aspect of communication? For ancient theorists from Aristotle to Quintilian, the answer lay in its persuasive power. One writes and speaks, according to the classical sources, in order to persuade.[27] One persuades in large part by being or appearing to be a credible person. And one appears credible by conveying intelligence, character, and goodwill. Most business communication specialists are aware that business prose has a similarly persuasive function. Business is a social organization, and like any other social organization it must achieve consensus, win approval, compel obedience. It must, in short, *persuade* its various constituencies on a host of issues. An annual report not only states facts but also — and arguably foremost — persuades stockholders and the public to have confidence in the company. A proposal not only outlines the services or products a company can provide, but also persuades its readers — perhaps overtly, perhaps subtly — that this company's proposal is the most advantageous for the customer. And memos not only report opinions and directives, but also persuade their recipients that these opinions are sound and these directives are by all means to be followed.

Not surprisingly, traditional rhetoric associates the appeal to logic and the appeal to emotion with persuasion as well. Over two thousand years ago, Aristotle identified three kinds of persuasion supplied by the prose itself:

> The first kind resides in the character of the speaker; the second consists in producing a certain attitude in the hearer; the third appertains to the argument proper, in so far as it actually or seemingly demonstrates.[28]

"The character of the speaker," of course, is *ethos;* "producing a certain attitude in the hearer," as Aristotle notes elsewhere, involves the appeal to the audience's emotions;[29] and "argument proper" is the appeal to logic. It is precisely because business writing is so strongly persuasive that writers of advertising copy and annual reports find themselves unconsciously using the same basic rhetorical strategies today that Aristotle used under very different circumstances centuries ago. These persuasive strategies depend at least in part on the figures — and this point becomes crucial in a business setting. W. R. Heath and Beatrice Foods were not interested in stylistic embellishment for its own sake, nor did they necessarily consider the theoretical relationship between style and substance. What did interest them was effective, persuasive prose, and that is what drew them instinctively to the figures.

Our study of the figures thus far has moved us a long way toward bringing business communication within the realm of Aristotelian thought, since the figures have shown us that business prose aims to persuade using the same three appeals as other kinds of rhetoric. What is more, we have reached this conclusion by first observing what good business writers actually do and then asking what principles account for their success, principles of which the writers themselves have probably remained unaware. In moving from practice to underlying principles we have followed the procedure that Aristotle himself used when he observed the oratory of the Athenian law courts and political assemblies in order to abstract the art behind it:

> All make some attempt to sift or support theses, and to defend or attack persons. Most people do so, of course, either quite at random, or else merely with a knack acquired from practice. Success in either way being possible, the random impulse and the acquired facility alike evince the feasibility of reducing the processes to a method; for when the practised and the spontaneous speaker gain their end, it is possible to investigate the cause of their success; and such an inquiry, we shall admit, performs the function of an art.[30]

Thus, although much successful business prose has undoubtedly resulted from a "random impulse," art becomes a more efficient, surer guide to what works, so that the practice of business communication will surely benefit if we can continue "reducing the process to a method" as Aristotle would undoubtedly do if he were brought back to life today.

To accomplish this, we must also recognize that times have changed and that the demands of contemporary rhetoric are not in every way like those of fourth-century Athens. In examining who practiced oratory in his day, Aristotle divided rhetoric into three kinds: deliberative, or speeches of counsel and advice, particularly in a political setting; judicial, or speeches of prosecution and defense in the courts; and epideictic, or ceremonial and display speeches.[31] This division worked well in the culture of Aristotle's time, but in the intervening centuries business people have improved their social and economic positions considerably,[32] presenting opportunities for writing and speaking that did not exist in ancient Athens. The corporation is also a modern innovation, and we cannot expect Aristotle to have provided a rhetorical model for a social and economic structure whose development he could not have foreseen. Thus we need a fourth kind of rhetoric for business, to be constructed along the lines of the three traditional ones.[33]

At this point we can only sketch the broad outlines of this new rhetoric, but these outlines at least are fairly clear. According to Aristotle, the deliberative speaker recommends one course of action as preferable, and does so on the grounds of expedience, so that the end of deliberative rhetoric is "advantage" and "injury." Similarly, the end or aim of judicial rhetoric is "justice" and "injustice," and the epideictic speaker works toward the end of "honor" and "dishonor."[34] Other aims may be present as well, but they must remain subordinate to the principal goals of their respective rhetorical genres. What is the ultimate end of business rhetoric, the end to which other aims must defer? Obviously, the ultimate aim of every business is making a profit,[35] or in other words, "gain" and "loss." Thus, "profitability" becomes the counterpart of advantage, justice, and honor. Accordingly, a business plan is designed to attract the capital a new firm needs to begin profitable operation, a memo is designed to regularize a company's internal operations for maximum profitability, a speaker's bureau is designed to generate goodwill among those who might buy the company's product, and so forth. After all, W. R. Heath's simple, aphoristic style favors, as he put it, "English that produces," and we know immediately what he meant by that.

Aristotle also identifies key elements or means with which rhetoricians achieve their ends. The deliberative speaker looks toward advantage and injury and forms his arguments using "exhortation" and "dissuasion." Similarly, judicial rhetoric relies on "accusation" and "defense," while epideictic uses "praise" and "blame."[36] At first glance we may have difficulty in clarifying the relationship between profitability and language, since profitability may seem to be restricted to finance and production. However, a brief review of some of the basic genres of business communication suggests an appropriate element or means for it as well. An annual report is designed to renew confidence in a company and its ability to make a profit. The letter we cited from the president of the health insurance company was designed to reassure its policyholders after the well-publicized loss of a substantial part of the company's business. Corporate speakers serve as highly visible representatives of their companies, representatives whose intelligence, character, and goodwill are designed to attract customers and investors alike. In other words, effective business prose makes its contribution to a company's profitability by developing what we might call "assurance," or confidence in the company, its products, and its personnel.

Just as the changing times have forced us to reexamine Aristotle's division of rhetoric into kinds, so we must also reexamine the relationship of rhetoric to other fields of study in the context of business communication. While Aristotle's method led him to isolate whatever area he was studying until he could identify and describe its salient features, he never lost sight of the interdependence of all knowledge; thus the logical function of Aristotelian rhetoric associated it with dialectic, the political content of deliberative oratory drew it toward political science and ethics, and so forth.[37] Similarly, the nature of our fourth kind of rhetoric has practical and theoretical consequences for what the business writer needs to know. If he could pursue the point himself, Aristotle would undoubtedly say that business writers need to know a fair amount about their businesses: the products their companies make, the organizational structure of their firms, the markets in which their products must compete, the general financial condition of their industries, and so forth. This does not require a degree in business; in fact, one could argue that the specialized knowledge of the technician can interfere with clear and persuasive communication. Effective reasoning and a convincing *ethos* can only come from sound, broad knowledge.

What is more, Aristotle would also remind us that in the final analysis, rhetoric is one of the liberal arts, and this includes the rhetoric of business as well. "Business" may conjure up images of ledger sheets and computers, but "communication" involves people, and Aristotle never lets us forget that. His discussion of emotion, for instance, turns into one of the earliest extant treatments of human psychology, while study of the enthymeme and the rhetorical topics moves logic from the abstract to the terms that people actually use in reasoning with one another.[38] Aristotelian rhetoric ultimately involves people persuading people, and this is precisely what business writing does when it sells products, builds investor confidence, and generates community goodwill. For this reason, effective business writing also rests on a sound knowledge of people, the kind of knowledge gleaned from the study of literature, history, foreign languages, and so forth. When solid business knowledge is reinforced by broad reading in the humanities, business communication can become truly persuasive in a way that a reincarnated Aristotle would immediately recognize and support.

Such a vision of business writing is not for the faint of heart. Admittedly, we do not usually define business communication so broadly, nor for that matter do we customarily bring something like classical rhetoric to bear on the production of business plans and annual reports. In consolation, we can note that although Aristotle's program for deliberative, judicial, and epideictic rhetoric is also intimidating at first, it has inestimably enhanced the practice of political, forensic, and ceremonial oratory for those who have chosen to grapple with it. In addition, we can also console ourselves by recalling that this is not just theory for theory's sake. Our discussion has been abstracted from what effective business writers have already done, and we have every right to assume that these tentative steps toward an Aristotelian theory of business communication will in turn enrich the practice of business writing today and in the future.

Notes

The authors would like to thank *JBC*'s anonymous referee for his or her helpful comments and Dr. Gina Burchard for her encouragement with this project and for her careful reading of an earlier version of this essay.

1. Raymond V. Lesikar, *Basic Business Communication,* revised ed. (Homewood, IL, 1982), pp. 48–69 discusses the historical development of this emphasis on clarity. He explains that the business prose of the late nineteenth century was stilted and artificial because it borrowed heavily from the language of law and the aristocracy. Thus, according to Lesikar, the style of twentieth-century business writing aims at a conversational clarity in reaction to this earlier prose.

2. For a representative sampling of the recommendations these textbooks make for improving clarity, see Lesikar, *Basic Business Communication,* pp. 6–69; J. H. Menning, C. W. Wilkinson, Peter B. Clarke, and Dorothy C. M. Wilkinson, *Communicating through Letters and Reports,* 6th ed. (Homewood, IL, 1976), pp. 9–35; and Norman B. Sigband and David N. Bateman, *Communicating in Business* (Glenview, IL, 1981), pp. 35–73.

3. Menning, et al., *Communicating through Letters and Reports,* pp. 26–27.
4. *Ibid.,* p. 27.
5. The exception proving the rule is Thomas P. Johnson, *Analytical Writing: A Handbook for Business and Technical Writers* (New York, 1966), pp. 223–31, which favors a limited use of the figures in business prose. Johnson discusses several figures of speech under the rubric of metaphor, recommending them for their ability to enliven prose and explain complex ideas economically. The figures are also out of favor in many freshman composition textbooks. Texts which resist using any but the most common of figures (e.g. metaphor) are the norm, but again there are exceptions; E. P. J. Corbett's *Classical Rhetoric for the Modern Student,* 2nd ed. (New York, 1971), pp. 459–95 is perhaps the best known example of a writing text which relies heavily on the figures of speech. Sheridan Baker, *The Complete Stylist and Handbook,* 3rd ed. (New York, 1976), pp. 520–32 also provides a list of the figures which he encourages students to use.
6. The definitions used in this table are based on those found in Richard A. Lanham, *A Handlist of Rhetorical Terms: A Guide for Students of English Literature* (Berkeley, CA, 1968); some of these examples are taken from Corbett, *Classical Rhetoric,* pp. 463–93, where a fuller list may be found. Further information on the figures may be found in Warren Taylor, *Tudor Figures of Rhetoric* (Chicago, 1937); Leonid Arbusow, *Colores rhetoric: Eine Auswahl rhetorischer Figuren und Gemeinplätze als Hilfsmittel für akademische Übungen an mittelalterlichen Texten* (Göttingen, 1948); Heinrich Lausberg, *Handbuch der literarischen Rhetorik,* 2 vols. (Munich, 1960); and Lee A. Sonnino, *A Handbook to Sixteenth-Century Rhetoric* (New York, 1968).
7. To further illustrate the practical value of the figures of speech in advertising, an example of how an advertising slogan was actually developed might prove instructive. One of the authors was asked to suggest an advertising slogan for TIMEBASE, a publisher of computer software. The slogan had to communicate the idea that TIMEBASE publishes useful software programs at low prices, in fact in the price range of most computer games. Therefore, the author decided the slogan should have two contrasting members: one referring to the software's practicality and the other to its price. She began with the alliterative idea "serious software" and realized that the figure of alliteration should be repeated in the second member as well. A second figure, antithesis, seemed to hold promise as a way to convey the surprisingly low price of the programs. Within just a few minutes she had developed the finished slogan: "Serious software at a playful price."
8. In this and subsequent excerpts of business prose, the figures of speech are italicized for easy identification.
9. Menning, et al., *Communicating through Letters and Reports,* p. 6.
10. *The Literature of Business,* ed. Alta Gwinn Saunders and Herbert LeSourd Creek (New York, 1920), pp. 158–59.
11. *Ibid.,* p. 159.
12. *Ibid.,* pp. 290–91.
13. *Ibid.,* p. 291.
14. *Ibid.,* p. 298.
15. Quoted in John J. Fielden, " 'What Do You Mean You Don't Like My Style?'" *Harvard Business Review,* 60 (May–June, 1982), 138, an article which addresses the need to adapt style and tone to specific business situations

and to a manager's particular goals. This concept is, obviously, closely related to *ethos*.

16. (Berkeley, CA, 1982).

17. *Rhetorica ad Herennium,* ed. Harry Caplan, Loeb Classical Library (Cambridge, MA, 1954), p. 255 (4.8.11). Basic information on the history and theory of classical rhetoric may be found in Corbett, *Classical Rhetoric,* pp. 594–630 and George A. Kennedy, *Classical Rhetoric and Its Christian and Secular Tradition from Ancient to Modern Times* (Chapel Hill, NC, 1980). Bibliographical resources for the study of particular authors and subjects from classical rhetoric include *Historical Rhetoric: An Annotated Bibliography of Selected Sources in English,* ed. Winifred B. Horner (New York, 1980); *The Present State of Scholarship in Historical and Contemporary Rhetoric,* ed. Winifred B. Horner (Columbia, MO, 1983); *Index to Journals in Communication Studies through 1979,* compiled by Ronald J. Matlon (Annandale, VA, 1980); *L'Année philologique,* the annual bibliography in classical studies; and the occasional bibliographical surveys that appear in the *Rhetoric Society Quarterly.* Bibliographical resources for the study of style include Richard W. Bailey and Sister Dolores M. Burton, *English Stylistics: A Bibliography* (Cambridge, MA, 1968); Louis T. Milic, *Style and Stylistics: An Analytical Bibliography* (New York, 1967); George Miller, "Stylistic Rhetoric and the Analysis of Style: An Annotated Bibliography," *Style,* 14 (1980), 75–102; and the "Annual Bibliography on Style" in *Style.*

18. *Institutio oratoria,* ed. H. E. Butler (Cambridge, MA, 1976), vol. 3, p. 359 (9.1.21).

19. *Classical Rhetoric in English Poetry* (New York, 1970), pp. 85–121.

20. (New York, 1947), pp. 308–85, 398.

21. (Cambridge, MA, 1975), pp. 28–29, 106.

22. Quintilian hints at a relationship between *ethos* and the figures when he writes, "But, above all, *figures* serve to commend what we say to those that hear us . . . [when] we seek to win approval for our character as pleaders" (*Inst. orat.,* p. 359 [9.1.21]). Sister Miriam Joseph examines some two hundred figures used in Shakespeare's time and tries to organize them according to their affinities to the Aristotelian *ethos, logos,* and *pathos,* but she is only able to find four figures associated primarily with *ethos* (*Shakespeare's Use,* pp. 396–7). Further development of this point thus seems necessary.

23. This distinction has troubled some scholars; George E. Yoos, for instance, has proposed putting "ethics back into the concept of ethical appeal," in "A Revision of the Concept of Ethical Appeal," *Philosophy and Rhetoric,* 12 (1979), 42. Nevertheless, the distinction is especially important here, since an analysis of "ethics" in business communication is a completely different problem.

24. *The Rhetoric of Aristotle,* trans. Lane Cooper (New York, 1960), pp. 8–9 (1356a), 91–92 (1378a). Edward L. Pross, "Practical Implications of the Aristotelian Concept of Ethos," *Southern Speech Journal,* 17 (1957), 257–64 and William M. Sattler, "Conceptions of Ethos in Ancient Rhetoric," *Speech Monographs,* 14 (1947), 55–65 summarize and comment on the basic features of Aristotelian *ethos.* The standard commentaries on Aristotle's *Rhetoric* are those by E. M. Cope, *An Introduction to Aristotle's Rhetoric: With Analysis, Notes, and Appendices* (London, 1867) and for Book I, William M. A. Grimaldi, *Aristotle's Rhetoric I: A Commentary* (New York,

1980), to be supplemented by the essays collected by Keith W. Erickson, *Aristotle: The Classical Heritage of Rhetoric* (Metuchen, NJ, 1974). A thorough bibliography has been prepared by Erickson, *Aristotle's Rhetoric: Five Centuries of Philological Research* (Metuchen, NJ, 1975) and brought up to date by the same author in "A Decade of Research on Aristotle's *Rhetoric:* 1970–1980," *Rhetoric Society Quarterly,* 12 (1982), 62–66.

25. *Principles of Business Communication,* 2nd ed. (Champaign, IL, 1979), pp. 72–76, 86.
26. *Ibid.,* p. 107. Not surprisingly, researchers in the field of speech communication have confirmed the importance of *ethos* for modern rhetoric; see K. Andersen and T. Clevenger, Jr., "A Summary of Experimental Research in Ethos," *Speech Monographs,* 30 (1963), 59–78.
27. This bias toward persuasion runs all through Greek and Roman rhetoric; see Corbett, *Classical Rhetoric,* p. 3.
28. *Rhetoric,* p. 8 (1356a).
29. *Ibid.,* p. 9 (1356a).
30. *Ibid.,* p. 1 (1354a).
31. *Ibid.,* pp. 16–17 (1358a–b).
32. On the social and economic position of the business person in ancient Greece, see Marcus N. Tod, "The Economic Background of the Fifth Century," *Cambridge Ancient History* (Cambridge, England, 1940), V.5, 15–16. For Aristotle's reservations about the value of commerce and business, see *Politics,* 1.3.23–1.4.4.
33. Wayne Brockriede, "Toward a Contemporary Aristotelian Theory of Rhetoric," *Quarterly Journal of Speech,* 52 (1966), 34–37, suggests applying Aristotle's approach to the special situations of twentieth-century rhetoric, and some useful general observations appear in H. W. Hildebrandt, "Aristotelian Views of the Twentieth Century," *The Journal of Business Communication,* 21 (1984), 45–53. Weeks and Jameson, *Principles,* pp. 18–20, mention Aristotle along with Isocrates and Quintilian in their survey of theorists whose work they feel is applicable to business writing, but they do not develop this association in any detail. A number of writers have recently begun to stress the potential offered by this line of research; see the short pieces by Jack Selzer, *The Journal of Business Communication,* 18 (1981), 51–53 and Mohan Limaye, *The Journal of Business Communication,* 18 (1981), 3. For a specific, practical example of where this approach leads, see Craig Kallendorf and Carol Kallendorf, "A New Topical System for Corporate Speechwriting," *The Journal of Business Communication,* 21 (1984), 3–14.
34. *Rhetoric,* p. 18 (1358b).
35. We should probably note here that our use of the term "business" is grounded in a nonsocialist system, as we presently have it in the United States. A socialist system would probably present a somewhat different set of communication problems, but those problems are beyond the scope of this essay.
36. *Rhetoric,* p. 17 (1358b).
37. For rhetoric as the counterpart of dialectic, *ibid.,* p. 9 (1356a); on the association of rhetoric with politics and ethics, *ibid.,* pp. 46–47 (1366a–b).
38. On the emotions, *ibid.,* pp. 92–131 (1378a–1388b); on the enthymeme, *ibid.,* pp. 5 (1355a), 10–12 (1356b–1357a); on the topics, *ibid.,* pp. 143–72 (1392a–1400b).

Feminist Responses to Rogerian Argument

Phyllis Lassner

Though the common emphasis on empathy and a person-centered approach would seem to make feminist and Rogerian values compatible, Phyllis Lassner finds the fit to be problematic. Specifically, she and her students in a women's studies class discovered that a Rogerian approach to argument emphasized objectivity and detachment, traits dominant in a masculinist tradition that has not often recognized women's voices. They also discovered that a Rogerian approach assumes a level playing field between all writers and readers, an ideal simply not applicable to our stratified culture. The women in Lassner's class believed that their ability to establish strong female voices was limited by the Rogerian necessity of tending equally and objectively to the sides of others, since such a necessity undermined women's ability to invent oppositional voices to patriarchal dominance.

First published in Rhetoric Review *in 1990, Lassner's essay asks writing teachers to consider how we equate argumentation with objectivity and fairness and how such an equation is affected by the history of domination from which we have emerged. Ultimately, she suggests (with James Kastely and others) that conceiving of argument as a neutral, ahistorical tool will limit our ability to work toward a more equitable academic and national culture. Instead, we must continually redefine argument as a contextualized process often taking place between individuals and groups with differing positions of power. Through such analysis, the teaching of argument becomes not only more relevant in the classroom but also relevant to the "real world," where the history of power can never be ignored in the search for democratic ideals.*

When Rogerian argument was introduced in the 1970s, it was hailed as a heuristic which would "break the stalemate" that occurs when writers close themselves off from feeling the validity of an opposing argument (Hairston, "Carl Rogers's Alternative to Traditional Rhetoric" 373). Young, Becker, and Pike presented Rogerian argument as an alternative to traditional argument on the grounds that instead of using logic to destroy the opponent's case and legitimize your own, "Rogerian argument . . . serves an exploratory function, helping you to analyze the conditions under which the position of either side is valid" (*Rhetoric: Discovery and Change* 282). In more recent years, the bloom has been fading from those enthusiastic claims, and yet Rogerian argument is still very appealing to those who want to teach writing as "real communication with people, especially about sensitive or controversial issues" (Hairston, "Using Carl Rogers" 50). Particularly because there are contradictions in teaching academic literacy while showing sensitivity to students' various cultural backgrounds, Carl Rogers's "humane rhetoric" is attractive (Hairston, "Alternative" 373). Rogers encourages empathy instead of opposition, dialogue instead of argument. These are views that reflect the experiences of teachers who have found that traditional argumentation only inhibits self-reflection and the willingness to engage with the critical argument of another.[1] Likewise, the criticisms of Rogerian Rhetoric have come from teachers.

Any attempt to translate Carl Rogers's theories into practice must base its claims on his assumptions. To use his "person-centered approach," based on "empathic understanding" of another's feelings and experience, teachers would have to consider how the assignment affected, not only themselves, but the students who write Rogerian argument.[2] While we teachers can wax poetic over Rogers's humanistic escape from more authoritarian models of discourse, we return to our position on high so long as we prescribe what is good for our students without challenging our own assumptions and his.

My purpose here is to attempt such a challenge by exploring the responses of students in my "Women and Writing" course to writing Rogerian argument. I don't claim that their responses can be universalized. But in the very specific nature of what they have to say, these students present an authentic individual response to the affective claims made on behalf of Rogers's empathetic theories of communication.[3] In no way is this an objective, scientific study, but rather an effort to understand the conditions and contexts which shaped an almost entirely negative response.

When I asked this group of sixteen women students how they liked writing a Rogerian argument, I was greeted with jeers, boos, and this statement:

> I hated it. The Rogerian model is male, masculinist, and denialist. It leaves no space to be persuasive with anger. It denies that women have a right to be angry at being left out of most methods of persuasion and that anger is worthwhile listening to, even if it's threatening, because for women to be recognized, everyone needs to know how they feel.

I reeled with disappointment. I had viewed this assignment as a perfect opportunity to bring together the student-centered values of Composition and Women's Studies in a course which fulfills a University-of-Michigan graduation requirement for upper-level writing. Readings and discussions of composition and feminist theory would become more "real," I felt, in the experience of arguing about issues that were central in these students' lives. In turn, I assumed that arguing on behalf of both sides of an issue would test their own assumptions and claims and "humanize" their opponents'. Turning my dismay into a call for inquiry and action, I responded with a challenge: "OK, your next writing assignment is to tell me why."

As I try to understand both the substance and the passion of my students' denouncement, I look at the assumptions of those who promoted the application of Rogers's theories to composition, some critiques of his theories and their application, and then weave together my students' statements with my analysis of their implication for teaching writing.

Maxine Hairston and Young, Becker, and Pike introduced Carl Rogers's theories to composition studies.[4] Hairston extrapolated guidelines from Rogers's thought to develop a self-reflective method of argumentation which encourages writers to be as self-critical as they would become empathetic with the positions of the other. Rogerian argument would thus provide a heuristic by which students come to understand the assumptions and biases on which their positions are based, as well as the positions, attitudes, and values of those who differ from them. Paul Bator summarizes Young, Becker, and Pike's goal as learning to sense "when it is appropriate to confront 'opponents' and when it is more advantageous to strive for change through mutual acceptance and understanding by each party of the other's view" ("Aristotelian and Rogerian Rhetoric" 427).

The assumptions of Rogerian argument have been challenged by a growing awareness of the political implications of all rhetorics. In "Rhetoric and Ideology in the Writing Class," James Berlin observes that the structure of a rhetoric will "favor one version of economic, social, and political arrangements over other versions" and is therefore never "a disinterested arbiter of the ideological claims of others because it is always already serving certain ideological claims" (477). As Michael Awkward reminds us, no writing can be empathetic unless it considers the reader's ideological assumptions as "a politics of interpretation that is determined by race . . . and gender" ("Race, Gender, and the Politics of Reading" 5). For what constitutes understanding and communication is shaped by the ways we experience our cultural identities as we relate to each other and formulate "sensitive or controversial issues."

Rogers's person-centered communication is designed to enable us to learn to live with new knowledge about others, but as James P. Zappen points out, this can lead to manipulation ("Carl Rogers and Political Rhetoric" 107). For even though Rogers's psychology validates both the "independence and integration of the individual" and questions "any presupposition of social cohesion," it also presumes a definition of "the unity and integrity of the individual" (Zappen 102, 106, 105).[5] This definition in turn is socially constructed on a foundation of cultural hegemony and one towards which the client or reader is being guided to accept. In order to avoid manipulation, the "politics of interpretation" deeply embedded in the ideology of humanist therapy must be considered. Only then can we begin to understand, much less accept, the goal "of facilitating change by striving for mutual understanding and cooperation with the audience" (Bator 429).

If the threat of manipulation is present in nondirective therapy, where clients are encouraged to shape the terms and structure of their treatment, it becomes highlighted in writing. Lisa Ede points out that Rogers's wish to have the therapist's empathy replace judgment and guidance requires active dialogue; this is impossible in writing.[6] In Rogerian argument the writer's stance looks nondirective and active because it states the opposition's position, but in fact guides the reader to accept the writer's arguments as fair and empathetic. As Ede and Nathaniel Teich observe, to translate Rogers's humanistic therapy into a "formula" or "rhetoric" may be a contradiction in terms, since written argumentation still assumes that one side will win (Teich, "Rogerian Problem-Solving and the Rhetoric of Argumentation" 53). Ede notes that "Young, Becker, and Pike consistently call the reader 'the opponent'" and constantly refer to "winning as a strategy to gain the reader's attention" ("Is Rogerian Argument Really Rogerian?" 45). If writers of Rogerian argument are out to win, they are clearly very different from the therapist who submerges her own needs and adapts to the client's ego by changing her style of discourse in response to the client's needs.

For those who do not recognize themselves as worthy opponents with a fair chance of winning, Rogerian rhetoric can be as inhibiting and as constraining as any other form of argumentation. As Jim Corder shows, before we can build bridges between opponents, we must "face the flushed, feverish, quakey, shakey, angry, scared, hurt, shocked, disappointed, alarmed, outraged ... condition that a person comes to when his or her narrative is opposed by a genuinely contending narrative" ("Argument as Emergence" 21). Feminist scholars have shown how far women have to go before they can even face that contending narrative. This is because women feel they must capitulate to the values of the majority culture in which they live. Engaging in a person-centered dialogue fails to acknowledge women's ambivalent relations to culture, the fact that although the language of the majority culture does not always fit their experiences, they often behave as though it does. Because women and other marginalized people don't always see themselves represented either at all or accurately in their culture, they often find language to be inhibiting rather than expressive. Hairston's claim that neutral language improves communication is therefore problematic because in the experience of many no language is neutral, nondirective, or nonjudgmental.

Historically, some women writers have resisted being coerced into accepting the claims of traditional rhetorical forms by concealing their feelings. In order to even find an audience, they expressed their experiences in a rhetoric of disguise.[7] Women's writing has been suppressed, according to Joanna Russ, because their concerns are judged as too limited because too personal, and their emotions as interfering with rational discourse.[8] This is as true today as it was in the writing of Mary Wollstonecraft and Charlotte Brontë. Pamela Annas observes that when her women students internalize "a sense of audience — the academic establishment," there is a struggle in "sensing that their truth, because it is new, because it challenges old beliefs, can't be contained inside the bounds of traditionally defined objectivity" ("Style as Politics" 364).

We now understand that argumentative forms are governed by different historical and psychological experiences. In academic writing women students have said that they feel assumptions about objectivity, evidence, even subject matter, do not address their experiences and in fact present them with a double bind. They must write about subjects in which women are invisible. They must use linguistic and rhetorical conventions which invalidate the logic of their experiences. And all this turns out to be for the purpose of educating women to identify with those who ignore or dismiss their concerns.

In their studies of women's responses to classroom activity and women's "ways of knowing," feminist teachers show that women do not respond to language as though it generically represents their experience.[9] Radical feminists have argued that as long as language represents white, middle-class, patriarchal culture as the norm, women will have to create a language of their own in order to express their experiences as they feel them. If the feelings and experiences of women neither translate readily into conventional academic language nor can be expected to be received with "unconditional acceptance" (Ede 44), then what is the experience of women students writing Rogerian argument? In "Women and Writing," students read and write about feminist and composition theories while questioning old and new assumptions about the ways women think. In this course as in many Women's Studies courses, gender and race become categories of analysis as students explore the social construction of gender and the differing sense of self which grows out of the experiences of women of different cultures. Students are encouraged to question ideological assumptions in their readings and assignments in order to understand how learning itself is politically charged. Having read Carol Gilligan's study of women's moral choices, *In A Different Voice,* the class of winter 1987 wrote a Rogerian argument on a moral dilemma to which they felt particularly committed.

These students also kept journals in which they recorded how they felt about presenting both sides of the dilemma fairly, empathetically, and yet as objectively as they could, and finally about how they experienced their composing processes as liberated or constrained by this exercise. The results showed that the whole notion of communication is highly charged, that what we see ordinarily as negative, that is "communication breakdown" (Hairston, "Alternative" 374), may imply a positive move for some writers and that "acceptance and understanding" may sometimes be constraining. Of fourteen students in the class, ten felt in varying degree that Hairston's form was "easy to follow" and easy to revise once they had figured out how to "quell emotions" in order to produce the "detached writing" Hairston interprets Rogerian argument as demanding.

The steps these women writers felt it necessary to take in order to be "fair and present both sides impartially" were experienced by everyone as "unnatural." Although the writers admitted it was a worthwhile effort to try to understand the values of their opposition, they also felt that "fair" was a judgment already biased in its suppositions. It impelled them to present the other side as equally valid in its need for recognition and protection as their own, and in a sincere voice. They said they felt out of sync with their adopted voice. Several students reported that as a result of disguising their feelings they felt powerless and isolated from those who stood on different sides of the issues they chose for argument. Hairston identifies this problem as "rhetorical stance," and suggests projecting "a personal voice that inspires trust and acceptance" ("Alternative" 376). For these students, the rhetorical problem expressed, but also concealed and disguised an underlying one. They needed to figure out how to be comfortable in the role of "an equal" in relation to those on the other side of the issues who had failed to regard them as such. They wondered how they could be "impartial," a frame of mind which assumes one is partial to, that is, comfortable in the style and form of the debate.

The students' papers showed attempts in every step to recognize and understand the positions of those who oppose abortion on demand, who vote against the right to private consent of homosexuals, who will not include language expressing women's experience in prayer, who will not consider pornography a civil offense, and several other positions of concern to women today. The statements made by these students in discussion and in their journals show a conjunction between their experiences and the problems studied by Ede and Zappen.

One writer turns an assumption of Rogerian argument into a question that can be applied to all the moral dilemmas the students chose to explore: "How can you really know what others feel?" Those whose experiences are marginal or run counter to the assumptions of cultural norms understand how difficult it is to recognize another when her own needs have been misunderstood, ignored, and sometimes even condemned. For a gay couple who wishes to adopt a child or for women who feel alienated from the language and ritual of religious service, the values in question on both sides of the issue legitimate the sense of self at such a basic level that each side is experienced as a threat to the other's sense of wholeness and integrity. Hairston's interlocking claims about the ability of Rogerian communication to diminish threat disregards the depth of this sense.[10]

How can those who feel marginalized by the social, legal, and educational institutions that structure their lives be expected to "establish an atmosphere of trust and suspend judgment" (Hairston, "Using" 51–52)? Not only do they not trust, but they feel they are not trusted. Moreover, they feel oppressed by their own experience — where they have had to trust and suspend judgment in an adversarial situation and have found their trust betrayed. As one student argued on the issue of gay couple adoption, "Even to express the 'natural' joy of parenthood is threatened when you know the social worker is, with the best intentions, holding back feelings of revulsion in order to be fair." Even if one consciously chooses nonemotional language for the discussion, emotions crop up in the tone of the empathetic voice the writer tries to assume. For anyone who has prior experience of total rejection, who feels, in the words of one student, "as if my very identity is going to push me over the edge . . . to be empathetic means I'm also going to be pretty defensive." Defensiveness will not be masked; it will show through an unconsciously deployed irony or unexpected humor, the choice of metaphor, or in ambiguous language.

As the writer feels the feelings of the other, her own position is threatened by knowing she is using language that both disguises and exposes her vulnerability. For neutral language is really the provenance of those social institutions, such as education and social welfare, in which she feels marginalized. What these students experienced as "detached writing" implies once again detaching women's needs from the concerns of a dominant culture. As one student wrote:

> Because I feel it's so necessary to eliminate violence against women from our society, it is very easy to overstate my point through sheer emotion. Although the con side may be covered clearly and factually, it is overpowered by the overwhelming emotion coming through from me. I guess the trick is to try to find and represent the emotion of those on the con side. The choices are: divorce all emotion or charge both sides with equal emotion.

The ironic result of either choice is that the woman writer loses her voice.

To detach her emotion means, in effect, to deny her sense of herself. While this detachment, in one writer's words, "is more civilized," it relies on a notion of rationality which dismisses emotion as nonrational and disruptive and insists on distinctions between feeling and thinking. As Ann Berthoff has shown repeatedly, this dichotomy derives from reliance on positivist assumptions. Despite the claim of positivists that their assumptions are scientific because they observe categories of difference, philosophers such as Suzanne K. Langer have shown how these assumptions are unscientific because they create categories which discriminate against kinds of knowing which include emotion. To continue to insist that rationality can be exercised without emotion is to protect a system of thought which is exclusionary, despite the imperative from Rogerian argument that under all circumstances the other side has to be recognized on the part of both sides. For as Susan McLeod observes, we have "ignored the affective domain in our research on and speculation about the writing process. This is partly due to our deep Western suspicion of the irrational, the related scientific suspicion [of] anything which cannot be observed and quantified . . . and the simple fact that we lack a complete theoretical perspective and common vocabulary with which to carry on a cogent academic discussion of affect" ("Feelings" 426). The impact on women writers of dismissing the affective domain is revealed by another student:

> Rogerian argument feels like a model of mock democracy — too sweet, pretending to accept the minority view but writing in a way that makes women ignore how they feel. If they ignore how they feel no one else has to pay attention to them.

For this writer, Rogerian rhetoric manipulates women into feeling that they must change their way of thinking in order to be part of the majority culture. Zappen observes that it is not Rogers's "intention to change people but to assist them in changing themselves, with a full understanding of the process" (107). For the student quoted above, that would simply mean that women will repress their authentic feeling and comply with values and expectations of what others wish them to be, not with what they feel themselves to be. Such manipulation reflects the way our cultural institutions also pressure women into complying with their own exclusion. To understand the process simply legitimizes the process of suppression in the woman writer's mind. One student wrote how her insecurity about arguing for female inclusive language in the Bible and in Christian liturgy was exacerbated by her "fear of those in the powerful positions of deciding what was the language of God and gospel":

> Presenting the position of church leaders and traditional congregations
> meant a confrontation for me that made me feel fearful because I was
> ambivalent. I still wanted to be part of the church while I realized I had
> been excluded and I was afraid if I challenged their language and
> rituals they would find reasons for excluding me. The reason I felt
> ambivalent and fearful of my opposition was that not long before I wrote
> my paper, I had actually sided with my opposition.

To present the position of those in authority created a situation for this writer which did not allow her to feel safe in self-reflection, a primary goal of Rogerian argument. To be convinced by the opposition would mean giving up her insights about experiences which put her in opposition to authority in the first place. Her newly discovered, still fragile views were threatened by the certainty of beliefs legitimized by deeply entrenched tradition. The very act of presenting the views of those she opposed reinstated their validity in her experience. Her ability to fulfill the Rogerian contract was affected by her anxieties and lack of confidence. She overstated the cause of the church. She knew its terms so well, in their logical system, in their rhetoric, and perhaps most significantly, in the history of the church's need to consolidate an otherwise pluralistic and secular community. Having won its struggle, the church could rely on a united, unchallenged voice. Indeed, its language joined a community together with words whose familiarity and certitude overwhelmed their individual differences. To question the language of prayer, sermon, and liturgy was to underline uncertainties in the student's own argument. If there was no historical evidence or even question that God was man or woman, if many women who served the church out of their belief in its importance to their lives accepted and even enjoyed identification with patriarchal power, on what basis could the religious needs of this woman challenge her own community to integrate her experience into theirs?

What is the rhetorical solution to the experience of feeling anxious and threatened by a neutralized presentation of a message which denies otherness? As these students discovered, neutralizing an inherently threatening position exacerbates the danger because they felt it as disguised and concealed and therefore manipulative and disingenuous. Empathy requires acceptance of the other. For many, there are no social, religious, or legal structures that even recognize their needs, much less affirm them as legitimate. The presentation of women's needs, even in nonevaluative language, cannot conceal the threat to self and community experienced by those opposing abortion on demand or the decriminalization of prostitution. In one small group discussion of a paper, a student reader made the point that "even if I sympathize with the economic plight of prostitutes, and feel empathy for their situation, I understand, from the point of view of being a woman, that others would not want their daughters to know that prostitution was in any way legitimate, even if the women on the street were protected. I would be afraid of prostitution becoming an attractive profession." Here, precisely because empathy was real, not an assumed voice, the writer felt the strength of her own position eroding. Hairston argues that people "stop listening [to a threatening message] in order to reduce anxiety and protect the ego" ("Using" 52). The writing experiences of my students testify that they might stop listening to their own messages because they are a threat to themselves and to their opponents. For them, writing to achieve mutual understanding would have to begin with a plea for recognition, knowing that mutual empathy was many writing tasks away.

In the third step Hairston directs the writer as follows:

> The writer must present his own side of the issue with such restraint and tact that the person reading the argument will not feel threatened by either the information or the language. Doing this requires using descriptive rather than evaluative language and stating one's points as hypotheses or opinions rather than as assertions. Young, Becker, and Pike suggest "provisional writing," using a tentative, unassertive tone. ("Alternative" 376).

If we substitute *her* for *his,* we must consider that for women using a "tentative, unassertive tone," is, in effect, self-effacing; to validate the position of the other replicates a history of suppression.[11] According to Carol Gilligan, as caretakers of patriarchal worlds, women have acted out a morality of concern for others to the point of neglecting their own needs. The insecurities and anger of the students in "Women and Writing" expressed the fear that they were reinscribing, indeed underwriting, their own neglect.

Because we are so concerned with students' ability to learn the conventions of writing academic prose, it may seem counterproductive to question and perhaps undermine heuristics that facilitate the teaching and learning of argumentation. No matter how much we urge freewriting and create assignments which sequence the process of self-discovery in the social contexts in which students live and work, no matter how much we work against the production of "theme-writing," we are all aware, as David Bartholomae and others have observed, that students must adjust their self-expression to the requirements of academic coursework. How do the critical assumptions of a Woman's Studies curriculum accord with these purposes?

Hairston claims that Rogerian argument makes students more aware of what and how they are achieving by challenging students to replace "conventional pieties" with careful reflection about the values embedded in their writing ("Alternative" 377). A principal method in Women's Studies is the examination of ideological assumptions behind the language of men and women, and of the institutions which govern their lives. In their own writing, therefore, Women's Studies students are encouraged to explore their own biases in order to see themselves in relation to others. What is felt to be natural or unnatural comes to be seen as a cultural construct and not a matter of one's essential nature. By the same token, we discuss what it means to be a member of a community and how we must recognize the social and psychological forces that marginalize people and how we become complicit in our own oppression by internalizing social and cultural pressures.

Through this process of recognition, we try to figure out what values we share with our home communities and about which so much anger has been generated. Instead of presenting a persona that is trustworthy because it expresses empathy, a student might present a self that is ambivalent about the position of the other and is uncomfortable presenting her own position. There are no conventional pieties here, but rather an honest attempt to see what keeps self and other apart, but mutually respectful. As Geoffrey Chase reminds us, "writing needs to be seen as an ideological process whose aims should include teaching students to write as a part of a larger project in which they can affirm their own voices, learn how to exercise the skills of critical interrogation, and, finally, exercise the courage to act in the interests of improving the quality of human life" ("Accommodation" 22).

From the writing experiences of these women students, it is possible to imagine a form of argumentation that also works as inquiry into the ideological constructs of self in relation to other. Exploring the anxieties that writer and reader might bring to an issue would be a first step towards demystifying a subject whose object remains unknowable until looked at as real human beings living in a culture of its own and with its own values, and yet very much a part of the more dominant culture with which it is at loggerheads. No matter how alien, how repugnant those values might be to the writer or reader, recognition that they share the same world might very well be the bridge on which argumentation can begin.

Notes

1. See, for example, Patricia Bizzell. Andrea Lunsford points out that Aristotelian rhetoric does presuppose difficulties in communication and begins at the point where communication becomes possible.

2. Nathaniel Teich discusses the evolution and purpose of Rogers's term ("Rogerian Problem-Solving and the Rhetoric of Argumentation" 52–3).

3. For example, see Zappen (104–05), Young, Becker, and Pike (275), and Jim W. Corder for discussion of the affective components of Rogers's theory of empathy.

4. See Maxine Hairston and Richard Young, Alton Becker, and Kenneth Pike.

5. Paul Bator observes that Rogers's psychological model "questions the classical ideology of man as a rational animal living in a relatively homogeneous society" (428).

6. Teich notes that Rogers never saw his communication theory applicable to writing (52).

7. See Sandra M. Gilbert and Susan Gubar.

8. Cora Kaplan shows how women's written arguments which express their "need, demand and desire . . . exceed social possibility and challenge social prejudice" (*Pandora's Box* 169).

9. See *Women's Ways of Knowing,* ed. Mary Field Belenky et al.

10. For this group of women writers, Teich's recommendation to draw topics from students' "own experiences," but to avoid such "potentially loaded topics as abortion" is contradictory (57).

11. For James S. Baumlin, "understanding requires . . . a temporary negation or effacement of self" (37). For these students, this would be a double bind. In the same vein, Helen Rothschild Ewald warns against Rogers's mission to change as "adversarial" (174). To change is to yield one's sense of self to another's.

Works Cited

Annas, Pamela J. "Style As Politics: A Feminist Approach to the Teaching of Writing." *College English* 47 (April 1985): 360–70.

Awkward, Michael. "Race, Gender, and the Politics of Reading." *Black American Literature Forum* 22 (Spring 1988): 6–27.

Bator, Paul. "Aristotelian and Rogerian Rhetoric." *College Composition and Communication* 31 (1980): 427–32.

Baumlin, James S. "Persuasion, Rogerian Rhetoric, and Imaginative Play." *Rhetoric Society Quarterly* 7 (1987): 33–44.

Belenky, Mary Field, et al. *Women's Ways of Knowing.* NY: Basic Books, 1986.

Berlin, James. "Rhetoric and Ideology in the Writing Class." *College English* 50 (September 1988): 477–94.

Bizzell, Patricia L. "The Ethos of Academic Discourse." *College Composition and Communication* 29 (1978): 351–55.

Chase, Geoffrey. "Accommodation, Resistance and the Politics of Student Writing." *College Composition and Communication* 39: 13–22.

Corder, Jim W. "Argument as Emergence, Rhetoric as Love." *Rhetoric Review* 4 (September 1985): 16–32.

Ede, Lisa. "Is Rogerian Rhetoric Really Rogerian?" *Rhetoric Review* 3 (September 1984): 40–47.

Ewald, Helen Rothschild. "The Implied Reader in Persuasive Discourse." *Journal of Advanced Composition* 8 (1988): 167–78.

Gilbert, Sandra M., and Susan Gubar. *The Madwoman in the Attic: The Woman Writer and the Nineteenth-Century Literary Imagination.* New Haven: Yale UP, 1979.

Hairston, Maxine. "Carl Rogers's Alternative to Traditional Rhetoric." *College Composition and Communication* 27 (December, 1977): 373-77

———. "Using Carl Rogers's Communication Theories in the Classroom." *Rhetoric Review* 1 (September 1982): 50–55.

———. *A Contemporary Rhetoric*. 3rd ed. Boston: Houghton Mifflin, 1982.

Kaplan, Cora. "Pandora's Box: Subjectivity, Class and Sexuality in Socialist Feminist Criticism." *Making A Difference*. Ed. Gayle Greene and Coppelia Kahn. London: Methuen, 1985. 146–76.

Lunsford, Andrea. "Aristotelian vs. Rogerian Argument: A Reassessment." *College Composition and Communication* 30 (May 1979): 146–51.

McLeod, Susan. "Some Thoughts About Feelings." *College Composition and Communication* 38 (December 1987): 426–34.

Rogers, Carl R. *On Becoming A Person*. Boston: Houghton, 1961.

———. *Client-Centered Therapy*. Boston: Houghton, 1951.

Russ, Joanna. *How To Suppress Women's Writing*. Austin: U of Texas P, 1983.

Teich, Nathaniel. "Rogerian Problem-Solving and the Rhetoric of Argumentation." *Journal of Advanced Composition* 7 (1987): 52–61.

Young, Richard E., Alton L. Becker, and Kenneth L. Pike. *Rhetoric: Discovery and Change*. NY: Harcourt, 1970.

Zappen, James P. "Carl R. Rogers and Political Rhetoric." *PRE / TEXT* 1 (Spring–Fall 1980): 95–113.

Using Multiple Sources of Evidence to Reason about History

Jean-François Rouet, M. Anne Britt, Robert A. Mason, and Charles A. Perfetti

This essay, first published in the Journal of Educational Psychology *in 1996, uses empirical data to examine how students read and argue about history when they encounter a variety of documents on the same event (in this case, textbooklike accounts, participant accounts, historians' analyses, and primary documents). The authors note, for example, that students who read primary historical documents along with more traditional "school" readings (such as textbooks or scholarly essays) provide more textual references in their arguments than those who simply read the traditional texts. Equally important, the authors note clear differences in the ways the students read and think about the different texts.*

This study holds clear implications for teaching students to write arguments in any discipline. Whether in a literature, composition, or biology class, teachers and scholars need to consider how the types of texts we offer students contribute to their ability to write effective arguments on a subject. Composition classes in particular are prime sites for understanding the relationship between reading a variety of texts and writing arguments because writing instructors often ask students to read long and short texts, works from a variety of fields, fiction and nonfiction.

Finally, this essay advocates the use of computer technology — hypertext in particular — to teach and study the practice of arguing from sources. Students are often very comfortable with computers, and

*hypertext can easily facilitate empirical studies of students' reading
processes. Implicit in this call for hypertext readings in the classroom is
the idea that we will also have to consider how students assign credibility
or authority to electronic texts, and how reading these kinds of texts
affects their ability to write arguments.*

*For more discussion of the relation between reading and writing
arguments, see Mariolina Salvatori's "The 'Argument of Reading' in the
Teaching of Composition" (p. 346) and Patrick J. Slattery's "The Argumentative, Multiple-Source Paper: College Students Reading, Thinking,
and Writing about Divergent Points of View" (p. 361). For further consideration of hypertext documents in the classroom, see Joseph Janangelo's
"Joseph Cornell and the Artistry of Composing Persuasive Hypertexts"
(p. 272).*

S tudents in most areas of schooling are expected to learn from texts
and apply what they learn to reasoning and problem-solving tasks.
In history courses, for instance, college students are often expected to
read about characters and events in several documents and then write
an essay explaining why some event occurred. Although cognitive research on text processing has contributed much to our understanding
of how students represent and learn textual information (Mandl, Stein,
& Trabasso, 1985; Mandler & Johnson, 1977; Rumelhart, 1975; Stein &
Glenn, 1979; Thorndyke, 1977; Trabasso & van den Broek, 1985; van
Dijk & Kintsch, 1983), we know very little about how students coordi-
nate what they learn from multiple texts and how they become able to
use what they learn on reasoning tasks. This article addresses how
students use document information when reasoning about history problems.

Reasoning in History Learning

The study of history depends largely on a student's ability to reason
about complex, often controversial issues using various types of texts
and documents. History students cannot simply combine the contents
of several documents into a single representation. Instead, they must
carefully select information from documents and evaluate it in the context of who wrote the document, what type of document it is, and how
the document relates to other documents on the same topic (cf.
Wineburg, 1991b). Thus, in addition to constructing representations of
individual texts, a student studying a historical problem must coordi-
nate representations of several texts, resolve any inconsistencies among
texts, and weigh a text's information in light of its source.

The ability to manage multiple text representations requires that
a student possess specific knowledge about document characteristics
and use this knowledge when reading and when reasoning. We distinguish between two types of reasoning in which a history student must
engage: reasoning *about* documents and reasoning *with* documents.

Reasoning about Documents

When learning from multiple documents, a student needs to be able to evaluate each piece of information on the basis of the type of document it is. We refer to this activity as *reasoning about documents*. Proficiency at reasoning about documents is an important element of expertise in many disciplines, especially history.

As research on expertise has shown, experts differ from novices not so much in the cognitive processes they use as in the domain-specific knowledge they bring to bear on a problem (Chi, Feltovitch, & Glaser, 1981; Lesgold, Feltovitch, Glaser, & Wang, 1981; Spilich, Vesonder, Chiesi, & Voss, 1979; Wineburg, 1991a). In the context of reading, domain-specific knowledge can affect the way readers hierarchize textual information (Dee Lucas & Larkin, 1988). Domain experts have a deep knowledge of text structures, and they use this knowledge to build sophisticated reading strategies (Dillon, 1991). Thus, knowledge about domain-related discourse types is an important component of a reader's domain expertise.

Wineburg (1994) suggested that historians have special representations of history texts that enable them to integrate information across texts and evaluate information within a text (e.g., source and content). In a study comparing expert historians and high school students, Wineburg (1991a) found that expert historians consistently granted varying degrees of privilege to different types of documents. The historians tended to rank primary sources, such as an excerpt from a soldier's diary, as highly trustworthy, and secondary sources, such as an excerpt from a textbook, as less trustworthy. In contrast, several of the high school students ranks the textbook as most trustworthy. Thus, high school students appear to lack the ability to reason appropriately about documents when studying history problems.

Reasoning with Documents

An additional component of learning from multiple documents is the ability to use document information when solving a problem. We refer to this activity as *reasoning with documents*. Reasoning with documents is especially critical when writing an opinion essay based on multiple sources. Students must refer to source information and then organize and relate this information in their essays (McGinley, 1992; Nash, Schumacher, & Carlson, 1993; Spivey & King, 1989).

With respect to history, students may be asked to integrate information from multiple sources that disagree in their interpretations of a historical event. We refer to these cases as *controversies*. When a student encounters a contradictory account of a series of events, he or she must first recognize that there is a conflict (i.e., that not all of the authors are giving the same account of the events) and then reconcile the disparate accounts. This task includes remembering the specific arguments used to support the various positions and correctly attributing each argument to its respective author. Providing evidence, which includes citing information sources along with appropriate context information, is critical when writing about history. Yet it is unclear how well students can remember and refer to information sources, and how document type (e.g., primary sources vs. second-hand accounts) may influence their ability to do so.

How Exposure to Multiple Documents Affects Students' Reasoning

Work by Kuhn (1991) has demonstrated that people who have received a college education tend to produce more complex theories as explanations, often mentioning multiple causes for events or situations. They appear to be more capable of reflecting on their theories and acknowledge that evidence could be presented that would disconfirm their theory. These changes in reasoning are produced by activities associated with attending college and are not due to maturation alone.

There are several reasons why college experiences might produce a change in a student's reasoning ability. One of these reasons is that college offers students many opportunities to learn from varying types of documents (e.g., academic journals, scholarly essays, official reports). In high school, students learn mostly from textbooks (Ravitch & Finn, 1987) that generally avoid controversial issues and focus instruction on well-established facts (Crismore, 1984). College is often the first time that students are exposed to controversial topics and diverse sources of information. Exposure to multiple documents may partially explain college graduates' ability to engage in complex reasoning.

Evidence from previous research also supports the view that exposing students to multiple documents changes how they reason. Perfetti, Britt, and Georgi (1995) studied a small group of college students over an eight-week period as they sequentially read lengthy excerpts from scholarly and popular books describing the U.S. negotiations to build the Panama Canal. Each week the students read an average of thirty pages and then produced written summaries and answered knowledge and reasoning questions about the material. An analysis of their responses revealed two findings relevant to learning and reasoning from documents. First, students initially learned the basic narrative and gradually elaborated it. From their first reading, the students learned the main characters and major events and little else. After reading subsequent texts covering the same subject, they learned other, less central, events and details. Second, as students acquired more events and details, they engaged in more complex reasoning. They began to give more supporting reasons for their claims, more qualifiers, and used longer causal chains. It is possible that this increase in the students' quality of reasoning was due to an increase in domain-specific knowledge as well as exposure to multiple documents.

The main purpose of the study we report here is to examine students' ability to reason about different types of documents. In addition, we investigate students' ability to reason with multiple documents in an essay task and whether their propensity to do so is influenced by the type of documents they study. We presented two groups of undergraduate students with a description of a series of controversial issues and a set of documents that argued opposing sides of the issue. One group was given a textbooklike passage, historian essays, retrospective participant accounts, and critical primary documents (which were cited in other documents). The other group was given the passage, historian essays, and participant accounts, but no primary documents. We asked the students to read the documents with the purpose of writing a short essay expressing their opinions concerning the controversy. In addition to the essay task, we also had the students rank order the documents with regard to their trustworthiness and usefulness.

We expected that this manipulation would affect students' responses in two ways. First, having primary documents should influence how students reason *about* documents by sensitizing them to differences in document types. We expected this to be reflected in students' evaluations of the documents (e.g., use of different criteria to justify evaluations). Second, having primary documents should influence how students reason *with* documents by increasing their awareness of the importance of supporting arguments with documentary evidence. This should appear in the use of document information in the students' essays (e.g., citations of documents as evidence).

Method

Participants

Twenty-four undergraduate students at the University of Pittsburgh (seventeen male, seven female) participated in the experiment for course credit and cash. All students were native speakers of American English between the ages of seventeen and thirty-one years (average age was twenty). One student was replaced because of his failure to comply with the task requirements. Fourteen of the students had taken no college-level history classes, eight had taken one, and two had taken more than one.

Materials

The topic we selected was the history of the Panama Canal. On the basis of our study of this topic, we identified four controversial questions concerning the Panamanian revolution and the U.S.–Panama Canal treaty. A *controversy,* as we use the term here, is a description or interpretation of an event over which historical accounts disagree. We presented each controversy to the students by giving them a statement of the controversy, a chronologically ordered list of basic facts, and a document set. The controversies were stated so as to encourage argumentative reasoning (e.g., "To what extent was the U.S. military intervention in the Panamanian revolution justified?"). The list of basic facts stated the events and details that were agreed on by the majority of the sources we had studied. This fact list provided an overview of the story without commenting on the controversy itself. The document set consisted of seven documents that, with the exception of the textbooklike excerpt, were all selected from the available literature. The only modifications we made were to edit them to approximately equal length (171 words on average) and number of arguments. The complete document set for Controversy 2 is presented in the Appendix, along with a listing of the controversies and the sources used for each.

Each document set consisted of seven documents made up from the following document types:

HISTORIAN ESSAYS.　These accounts were written by historians or politicians commenting on, but not participating in, the events. Historian essays argued opposing interpretations of the controversy, citing other documents as support. For instance, one historian essay for Controversy 2 argued that the U.S. military intervention was justified and cited the 1846 treaty. We gave each historian essay a fictitious author name, credentials, and date of publication, to control for any influences of these factors across problems.

PARTICIPANT ACCOUNTS.　These were accounts written by characters directly involved in the events. These accounts argued opposite positions on the controversy. For Controversy 1, for instance, U.S. President Theodore Roosevelt wrote in his autobiography that his government had no contact with the revolutionaries prior to the revolution. The opposing document was an excerpt from Philippe Bunau-Varilla's (an ally of the Panamanian revolutionaries) memoirs stating quite clearly that Roosevelt indeed had met with him before the revolution.

TEXTBOOKLIKE EXCERPTS.　These texts were written by the experimenters based on several accounts found in the literature. They were presented as excerpts from a college-level textbook and gave clear and concise descriptions of the major events. They did not contain any arguments pertaining to the controversy.

PRIMARY DOCUMENTS.　In the context of the present study, the notion of a primary document corresponds to three criteria. First, primary documents were written before or during the events (e.g., the 1846 treaty between the United States and Colombia). Second, they did not contain arguments or take a position regarding the controversy. Third, they were explicitly cited in the historian essays and in some of the participant accounts to support their arguments.[1]

By design, all seven documents in each document set were relevant and useful. The historian essays provided arguments for the students' main task — essay writing — and provided interpretations of the primary documents. The participant accounts served a similar function, but did so from the perspective of relevant characters in the story. The textbook provided an overview of the main agreed-on events. Finally, the primary documents enabled the students to evaluate the accuracy of the historians' and participants' interpretations by giving the students the opportunity to read exactly what was being used as evidence for a specific argument.

To assess the influence of primary documents on students' reasoning, we also selected two additional historian essays to replace the primary documents in the control condition. The additional historian essays were selected according to the guidelines previously described for the historian essays. One essay argued for one side of the controversy, and the other argued for the opposing side.

Design

We manipulated the composition of the document set that two student groups received. For each of the four controversies, both groups received the statement of the controversy, the basic list of facts, and five shared documents. These shared documents consisted of two historian essays, two participant accounts, and a textbooklike excerpt. Each group also received two additional documents as part of their respective document sets. The *primary group* received two primary documents; the *secondary group* received two additional historian essays.

Apparatus

The experiment was run using a Macintosh IIsi computer and the Claris Hypercard software. A hypertext presentation (e.g., Nielsen, 1990) of the four document sets was designed as follows: The first page displayed the problem statement. It was followed (after a mouse-click) by a page showing the list of main facts on the left and a blank window on the right.[2] A click on the blank window uncovered a menu of the seven available documents. The list of facts and menu page for Controversy 2 are shown in Figure 1.

The screen order of the documents was historian essays, participant accounts, textbooklike excerpt, and primary documents (or additional historian essays in the secondary group). Selecting an item in the menu brought up a description of the document, including the date written, author information, document information, and a brief summary of the content (see the Appendix for examples). The student could then read the actual document or go back to the menu. As the documents were selected, they were marked in the menu, to remind the student which documents remained to be selected (see Documents 2, 4, and 5 in Figure 1). The most recently selected document was marked differently to facilitate task management (see Document 5 in Figure 1). At any time the students could look back at the problem statement.

Figure 1. List of facts (left) and document menu (right) for Problem 2 (the marked items have been previously selected).

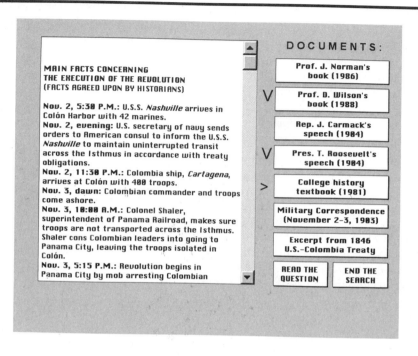

Procedure

The experiment lasted for a total of 4 hours over three sessions. The first session was used to assess the students' reading ability and history knowledge and to introduce them to the canal story. The introduction was a 2,184-word noncontroversial text on the history of Panama based on a report by the Center for Strategic Studies (1967). Students studied this text for 20 minutes and were asked about their opinions on the four controversies.

The second session took place one to five days after the first session. On the basis of their gender and performance on the reading and history tests, students were paired and then randomly assigned to either the primary or secondary conditions. Students were then trained to use the hypertext presentation system with a training set of documents about an unrelated historical controversy. Following their training, the students engaged in Controversies 1 and 2.

The third session took place 1 or 2 days after the second session and within six days of the first session. The directions were briefly restated, and then the students engaged in Controversies 3 and 4.

The procedure for all four controversies was identical and consisted of three phases: studying, essay writing, and document evaluation. The study phase took place in front of the computer and began with an initial screen stating the controversy. Then students were given 15 minutes to study the list of facts and the set of documents using the hypertext program. The 15-minute time limit was set based on a pilot study. Students were told that they could select the documents in any order and as many times as they wished but that they should make their selections wisely because of the limited amount of study time. The students were free to stop studying before the 15-minute limit if they had selected each document description at least once and felt that they had arrived at an informed opinion about the controversy.

After the students had completed the study phase, a screen restating the controversy appeared. The students were given ten minutes to write a 1-page essay expressing their opinions about the controversy. The documents were not available to them, but the students were given the document descriptions and a list of the important names mentioned in the document set. The students were told, however, that they were not expected to quote verbatim from the various documents.[3]

After finishing each essay, the students were given a sheet listing the seven document descriptions and were asked to rank order the documents according to their usefulness (i.e., "to the extent they helped you build up an informed opinion during the study period") and to write a sentence justifying the rank given to each document. Then the students were given the same document descriptions again and asked to rank order the documents according to their trustworthiness (i.e., "to the extent you trust what the author says"). Again they were asked to justify each document's ranking. Finally, students were asked whether there were any additional documents they would like to have read as part of the document set.

Results

Reasoning about Documents

WHAT KIND OF DOCUMENTS DID STUDENTS TRUST MOST? Figure 2 shows the median ranking of document trustworthiness for each type of document collapsed across the four controversies. For statistical analysis, documents of the same type were combined, resulting in four categories of document type. Using Friedman's test (with correction for ties), we found a significant difference in the trustworthiness rankings of the different documents in both the primary group, $X^2(3, N = 12) = 74.86, p < .001$, and the secondary group, $X^2(3, N = 12) = 80.69, p < .001$. A series of Wilcoxon pairwise comparisons with correction for ties (six tests for each group at $\alpha = .008$) showed that students in the secondary group ranked the textbook as more trustworthy than historian essays, participant accounts, and the additional historian essays. Students in the primary group also ranked the textbook as more trustworthy than the historian essays and participant accounts, but they considered the additional primary documents just as trustworthy as the textbook and more trustworthy than the other two document types.

HOW DID STUDENTS JUSTIFY THEIR TRUSTWORTHINESS RANKINGS?
The statements students gave to justify their trustworthiness rankings were segmented into units and classified according to four features: content, author, document, and opinion. *Content justifications* referred to the content of a document. These included mentions of specific content (e.g., "cites precedent of guarding railroad, but not of interdicting Colombian troops") or evaluations of content (e.g., "just contained opinion, no facts"). *Author justifications* referred to characteristics of a document's author, including his or her credentials, motivations, or participation in the events (e.g., "the President would say anything to keep from being impeached"). *Document type justifications* referred to the characteristics of the document type or genre (e.g., "college text would not print false facts"). *Opinion justifications* were statements of a student's personal view of a document (e.g., "I don't believe it was a good deal so I don't believe him"). Six percent of the justifications could not be scored according to this framework. In these cases, students usually just restated the task (e.g., justifying a document as trustworthy "because it was trustworthy").

Table 1 gives the average number of justifications of each type that students in each group made for the different document and justification types. The values reported in the table are averaged over students and problems. Separate 2 (groups) × 4 (justification types) repeated measures analyses of variance (ANOVAs) were performed for each document type.

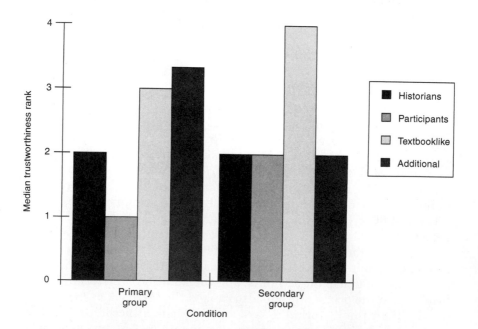

Figure 2. Median ranking of trustworthiness for each document type and group.

Table 1. Mean Number of Trustworthiness Justifications for Each Justification Type, Document Type, and Group

	Justification type			
			Document	
Group	Content	Author	type	Opinion
Historian essays				
Primary group	2.08	1.58	0.46	0.25
Secondary group	1.88	0.96	0.46	0.83
Participant accounts				
Primary group	0.96	2.96	0.25	0.17
Secondary group	0.92	2.92	0.33	0.08
Textbook				
Primary group	2.42	0.58	1.08	0.17
Secondary group	2.75	0.00	1.33	0.17
Additional documents				
Primary group	1.04	0.29	2.79	0.00
Secondary group	1.63	1.08	0.29	0.88

For the historian essays only the main effect of justification type was significant, $F(3, 66) = 8.81, p < .001, MSE = 1.380$. A Tukey honestly significant difference (HSD) post hoc test revealed that the students made significantly more content justifications than document type or opinion justifications (critical difference of 0.882 at $\alpha = .05$).

For participant accounts, an ANOVA again revealed only a significant main effect of justification type, $F(3, 66) = 76.44, p < .001, MSE = 0.524$. A Tukey HSD post hoc test indicated that more author justifications were given than all other types and more content justifications were given than document type or opinion justifications (critical difference of 0.544 at $\alpha = .05$).

For the textbooklike excerpts, the main effect of justification type was once again the only significant effect, $F(3, 66) = 22.04, p < .001, MSE = 1.354$. A Tukey HSD post hoc test indicated that more content justifications were given than all other types and more document type justifications were given than author or opinion justifications (critical difference of 0.874 at $\alpha = .05$).

Finally, for additional documents, an ANOVA revealed a significant main effect of justification type, $F(3, 66) = 7.87, p < .001, MSE = 0.832$, and a significant interaction of Justification Type × Group, $F(3, 66) = 19.15, p < .001, MSE = 0.524$. A Tukey HSD post hoc test on the interaction revealed that the students in the secondary group made significantly more content justifications than document type justifications, whereas students in the primary group made more document type justifications than all other types and more content than opinion justifications. Primary-group students also made more document type justifications than all types of justifications made by the secondary group (critical difference of 1.021 at $\alpha = .05$, pooled $df = 88$, pooled MSE = 0.659).

These results show that students evaluated the trustworthiness of the different document types according to different criteria. Historian essays were evaluated most often by the content of the document. Participant accounts were evaluated most often according to characteristics of the author and the content of the account. The textbook was evaluated most often by its content and, to a lesser extent, its document type. For the additional documents, the secondary group, which received more historian essays, again appeared to use document content as an evaluation criterion, just as they had for the other historian essays they had received. The primary group, which received primary documents, evaluated the primary documents' trustworthiness mostly by the documents' type. Thus, the students were well aware that primary documents are different from other document types and that this difference is relevant to evaluating the trustworthiness of a document's content.

WHAT KIND OF DOCUMENTS DID STUDENTS FIND MOST USEFUL? Usefulness rankings varied across document types in a pattern similar to that found for trustworthiness. Using Friedman's test, we found that the usefulness rankings varied across documents for both primary, $X^2(3, N = 12) = 9.43, p < .05$, and secondary, $X^2(3, N = 12) = 15.39, p < .01$, groups. A series of Wilcoxon pairwise comparisons with correction for ties (6 tests for each group at $\alpha = .008$) was conducted. For the primary group, primary documents appear to be ranked as more useful than the historian essays, though the difference did not reach statistical significance (median ranks of 3.5 compared to 1.0, $p = .010$). For the secondary group, students found the participant accounts more useful than the historian essays (median ranks of 2.5 compared to 1.5). Additionally, they found the textbook to be more useful than the historian essays (median ranks of 4.0 compared to 1.5). The additional documents were not ranked statistically higher or lower than any of the other documents.

HOW DID THE STUDENTS' RANKINGS COMPARE WITH THOSE OF EXPE-RIENCED HISTORY STUDENTS? To determine how reasonable this pattern of evaluation was, we had three University of Pittsburgh graduate students in history perform the students' task. Two of them participated in the primary group, and one participated in the secondary group. The secondary-group graduate student did not consider the textbook to be more trustworthy than other documents. Instead, he ranked the participant accounts as more trustworthy than all other documents. This contrasts with the undergraduates' strong trust in the textbook. The graduate student also justified his ranking differently than the undergraduates, basing them more often on the document type (46 percent) than on content or author characteristics. The two primary-group graduate students ranked the primary documents as most trustworthy, followed by the textbook (a pattern of rankings similar to the undergraduates' rankings). The graduate students' pattern of justifications, however, was not similar to those of the undergraduates. Like the secondary-group graduate student, the two primary-group graduate students based their justifications predominantly on the document type (44 percent) rather than on content or author. The primary-group undergraduates showed this pattern only for primary documents.

The graduate students' evaluation of usefulness was similar to those of the undergraduates. The only major difference was that the secondary-group graduate student did not find the textbooklike excerpt useful, whereas the secondary group undergraduates did.

As a further indication of perceived document usefulness, we evaluated the students' selections of additional information or documents that they would like for each controversy. The secondary-group students were less satisfied with their document set, asking for additional information 60 percent of the time compared to only 35 percent of the time for primary-group students. The most frequently requested information for both groups was primary documents (e.g., "the 1846 treaty which was referred to numerous times"). Primary documents accounted for 43 percent of secondary group requests and 44 percent of primary group requests.

DOCUMENT SELECTION.   We also performed an analysis of online document selection. Although there was a tendency to select the documents in their screen order, 75 percent of the students (8 in the primary group, 10 in the secondary group) selected the documents in an order different from the screen order on at least one of the four controversies.

Looking at only the cases in which students used a nonmenu order (23 cases in the primary group and 36 cases in the secondary group), we classified patterns of selection based on the type of document that was selected first. A pattern was scored if all of the documents of a certain type were selected before selecting any of the other document types. For example, a pattern would be scored as *primary and textbook* selection if both primaries and the textbooklike excerpt were selected, in any combination, as the first three documents read. A *primary and participant account* selection would be scored if both primaries and both participant accounts were selected prior to the selection of any other documents.

The selection patterns showed an interesting influence of document set. Fifty-seven percent of the primary group's nonmenu order selections were either *primary and textbook* (10 of 23 occasions) or *primary and participant account* (3 of 23 occasions) selections. The secondary group's selections, in contrast, were predominantly *participant account and textbook* (67 percent, 24 of 36 occasions) selections — an uncommon pattern for the primary group (3 percent, 1 of 23 occasions). Thus, the composition of the document set influenced students' selection order. In both groups, the documents selected first tended to be the ones students preferred in terms of trustworthiness and usefulness.

Reasoning with Documents

We analyzed students' essays in three ways. First, we analyzed students' claims and types of arguments; second, we analyzed students' references to documents; and third, we analyzed the relation between the documents cited and the type of arguments stated.

CLAIMS AND ARGUMENTS IN STUDENTS' ESSAYS.   An analysis of the students' essays revealed a diversity of information types (e.g., facts, evaluations, claims). We defined a scoring framework in order to segment each essay into claims and supporting arguments.[4] A reliability test based on one third (32 out of 96) of the essays indicated an interrater agreement of 85 percent. Discrepancies were resolved through discussion. We also identified references to the documents read. A sample essay for a student in each group, parsed into claims and arguments, is presented in Tables 2 and 3.

In the essay presented in Table 2 (secondary-group student), the student claimed that the U.S. intervention was justified (Units 1 and 2). She justified a controversial fact (the landing of 50 Marines at Colon) by the need to protect the railroad (Units 3–5). Although admitting that other motivations might have been at work (Units 6 and 7), the student linked them to the issue of transit protection (Unit 8). Two other arguments were presented: the small number of Marines involved (Units 9 and 13) and the aggressiveness of Colombian troops (Unit 12).

The student's reasoning scheme consisted of a list of selected facts, together with evaluations (i.e., interpretations in favor of the pro-intervention thesis). Another salient feature of the essay was the total lack of explicit reference to any of the documents read. All the arguments were expressed on behalf of the student's opinion.

The second essay (Table 3, primary group student) also started with a claim, which took the opposite stance on the controversy (Unit 1). The student summarized the provisions of the treaty excerpt (Units 2–4), thus introducing an explicit reference in his argument. Then he made another explicit reference (Prof. Norman, Unit 5) to evoke a scenario that illustrates the bias in the U.S. intervention (Unit 6). Like the previous one, this essay included a counterargument (Unit 7), which was immediately rebutted (Units 8 and 9). Two broad evaluations concluded the essay (Units 10 and 11), as if to "wrap up" the argument.

The second essay differed from the previous one in two major respects: the explicit use of references that supported most of the arguments, and a meaningful top-level structure in which the student used facts taken from the documents to support his evaluations, which in turn were used to support a general claim. We checked whether differences in argument structure and use of references could be generalized across groups.

HOW DID STUDENTS ORGANIZE THEIR ESSAYS? With respect to argument structure, we did not find any differences between groups. Most students took an explicit stance on the controversy, as evidenced by the presence of a "claim" statement in 86 percent of the essays. For each controversy we found essays supporting opposite positions (e.g., the intervention was vs. was not justified). In a majority of the cases (75 percent), the claim was expressed in the first, last, or both, sentences of the essay (see examples in Table 2). Forty-one percent of the supporting arguments were evaluations (e.g, the Panamanian revolution was in the best interests of the United States), 34 percent were facts (e.g., Dr. Amador came to the United States), and 25 percent were psychological events, including communications between characters (e.g., the United States wanted a canal). The analysis of claims and arguments showed that most students were able to select information from the documents and to combine it with their own opinions into a coherent essay.

HOW DID STUDENTS REFER TO THE DOCUMENTS? We identified two types of references to the documents: general (e.g., "according to the texts I have read") and specific references (e.g., "according to Prof. Norman's essay"). Fifty-two percent of the essays contained at least one specific reference (see examples in Tables 2 and 3). Furthermore, all the students explicitly referred to a document in at least one of their four essays. Only one student, however, included references in all

Table 2. A Sample Protocol Segmented Into Argumentation Units for Student 1 in the Secondary Group

Argumentation unit	Claim and supporting argument
1	The United States military intervention in Panama was necessary
2	and justified
3	When the 50 Marines landed
4	they had a simple job
5	Colonel Shaler must protect shipping lanes
6	It's obvious he had other orders
7	because he conned the leaders of the 500 man Colombian force at Colon to go to Panama City
8	In doing this, however, he was protecting shipping
9	The Marines at Colon were outnumbered
10	with a simple job:
11	Protect the American Railroad
12	If that means not letting 500 Colombian soldiers, who threatened to kill our civilians, on a railroad, that's what must be done
13	The force was large
14	[and] the railroad was ours

Table 3. A Sample Protocol Segmented Into Argumentation Units for Student 6 in the Primary Group

Argumentation unit	Claim and supporting argument
1	Legally, the intervention of U.S. military forces in the Panama Revolution was totally unjustified.
2	According to the Bidlack Treaty,
3	the U.S. promised to recognize the sovereignty of the Colombian government over the territory
4	and guarantee free passage to all.
5	Prof. Norman was correct in stating that
6	If Hubbard had received his telegram earlier, he would not have even allowed Colombian troops to land in their own nation.
7	It is true that Shaler was instructed to deny use of the railroad to both sides,
8	but the revolutionaries did not need the railroad,
9	the Colombians did.
10	Thus U.S. actions were prejudiced against Colombia
11	and contrary to the terms of the Bidlack Treaty.

four essays. The primary-group students cited a document in significantly more essays than did secondary-group students (2.6 vs. 1.6; $t[22]$ = 3.66, $p < .01$). Sixty-five percent of the primary-group essays contained at least one document reference, compared to only 39 percent of the secondary-group essays. Thus, studying primary documents as part of a document set promoted the use of references in the essays.

Figure 3 shows the number of times each type of document was cited by students in each group. References to the additional documents were classified as either historian essays or primary documents. As the figure shows, primary documents were referred to quite frequently by primary-group students, and even by some secondary-group students who knew of these documents only indirectly and did not actually read them. No references were made to the textbook in the essays despite the earlier finding that students ranked it among the most trustworthy and useful documents.

Although the three graduate students did cite documents slightly more often (67 percent of the essays), they did not do so in every essay. Like the undergraduates, primary documents were the most frequently cited (47 percent), followed about equally by secondary sources (27 percent) and general references (20 percent).

WHAT STATEMENTS DID REFERENCES SUPPORT? Explicit references were used in the essays to support a variety of statements such as facts, claims, or evaluations. For each type of document referred to, we

Figure 3. Number of references to documents by type of document (collapsed across problems).

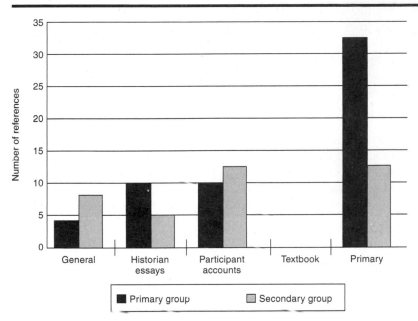

determined the type of statement it was used to support. Table 4 shows the percentage of each type of reference by the type of statement supported.

General references were used most often (58 percent) to support claims. Of the 15 times historian essays were referred to, they were most often used to support evaluations. Participant accounts were used to support statements concerning psychological events and also to support evaluations. Finally, primary documents were most often cited to support statements of fact and, to a lesser extent, evaluations.

Table 4. Percentage of Each Type of Statement Supported by Type of Reference Collapsed Across Groups and Controversies

		Type of statement		
Type of reference	*Claim*	*Evaluation*	*Psychological event*	*Fact*
General (n = 12)	67	8	0	25
Historian (n = 15)	27	53	13	7
Participant (n = 23)	13	39	39	9
Primary (n = 45)	9	33	11	47

In summary, the analysis of students' essays yielded three main results: Most students expressed an opinion and supported it by using arguments drawn from the documents. Studying primary documents, as opposed to learning about them through other documents, enabled students to cite primary documents more often in their essays; students tended to cite each type of document for specific argumentative purposes.

Discussion

The main purpose of this study was to investigate students' ability to reason about and with documents when learning about historical controversies. We focused on two aspects of document-based reasoning: students' awareness or literacy about document types and students' application of document information in an essay writing task.

Students' Reasoning about Documents

The ranking and justification results showed that students were aware of the characteristics of different document types. Students tended to trust the textbook most, a result observed in previous studies (e.g., Wineburg, 1991a). However, when given relevant primary documents, the students trusted those documents as much as the textbook. Furthermore, the students' justifications of their trustworthiness rankings varied across groups and document types. Content characteristics were critical for evaluating textbooks and historian essays, whereas source characteristics (document type, author) were critical for primary documents and participant accounts. Thus, evaluation criteria differed across document types, demonstrating students' ability to reason about documents.

From these results, it appears that when evaluating the trustworthiness of a document, students use information at two levels: the discourse level and the content level. At the discourse level, students recognize the document as belonging to a certain discourse category (e.g., textbooks). As an exemplar of a category, the document inherits the properties of that category. For instance, a particular excerpt from a treaty will be judged trustworthy just because, as one student put it, "as a treaty, it has no bias." However, this process is not sufficient for all categories of documents. For instance, historian accounts do not necessarily correspond to predefined levels of trustworthiness. Hence, the student must shift to a second level of evaluation. At the content level, students analyze the specific features of the document, source features, as well as semantic content. Content-based evaluation can be conducted on various grounds. Does the document take a position on the issue? Are alternate points of view considered? Is some information purposefully omitted? Rhetorical features also can be used. Does the author use colorful, slanted language as opposed to a neutral, expository style? The results of this experiment suggest that these two levels of evaluation exist. Future work, however, is needed to isolate the influence of discourse type and discourse content on students' evaluation of documents.

The pattern for usefulness rankings was similar to that of trustworthiness. However, the differences across documents were smaller, probably because all the documents were selected for their relevance to the controversy. Most usefulness justifications referred to content, although students also used document type to evaluate primary documents, and author characteristics to evaluate participant accounts.

Compared to the undergraduates, the three graduate students tended to dismiss the textbook and to rely on document type as their main evaluation criterion. This suggests that discipline experts may develop a greater sense of the value of primary evidence as well as more sophisticated knowledge about discipline-related discourse genres (Wineburg, 1994).

The analysis of online data was a useful complement to the ranking task. When students departed from the screen order of presentation, their selections coincided globally with the usefulness and trustworthiness ranking. This suggests that some of the knowledge that students demonstrated in the ranking task was also used during the study period. It is still unclear, however, what information critically determined students' selections. Each document was identified by a short phrase, including author name, document type, and date (see Figure 1). Any of these parameters, or a combination of them, might have been responsible for the observed selection patterns.

In sum, the analysis of document evaluation and selection patterns indicates that students are able to reason *about* different types of documents. This contrasts with Wineburg's (1991b) conclusion that inexperienced history students "cannot distinguish among different types of historical evidence, and . . . they look to a textbook for the 'answer' to historical questions" (p. 84). Several differences between the two studies may explain the discrepant conclusions. First, our participants were college students, as opposed to high school students in Wineburg's study. However, because our students were mostly average freshmen, and Wineburg's students were bright Advanced Placement history students, it is doubtful that differences in populations would entirely account for the discrepancy.

Second, in our study there was an overlap between document type and content. For instance, all historian essays and participant accounts took a stance on the controversy (i.e., they were explicitly "biased"), whereas primary documents and the "textbook" did not (i.e., they were apparently "neutral"). Students ranked the neutral documents as more trustworthy than the biased ones. One might argue that it was this neutrality — bias difference, not document type per se — that influenced students' evaluations in our study. However, students' justifications revealed important differences among document types within these neutral and biased categories. Document type mattered much more for primary documents (66 percent of the justifications) than for the textbook (25 percent), and author characteristics mattered much more for participant accounts (67 percent and 68 percent of the justifications) than for the historian essays (36 percent and 20 percent). Thus, although students did rank neutral documents more trustworthy than biased documents, the neutrality — bias dimension alone cannot account for students' ability to distinguish among document types. We suggest that increasing the diversity within the document set may have helped the students take into account discourse features as well as content.

Finally, in the present study the controversial nature of the problems was made explicit from the beginning, and students were asked to develop an informed opinion. This may have forced students to focus their attention on the claims and arguments and hence on source characteristics. Indeed, Wineburg and Wilson (1991) presented a case study (the "invisible teacher") in which having to play a role and defend a position seemed to promote students' understanding of a history problem. Thus, when given an explicit controversy and diverse document types, average college students will demonstrate some ability to reason about the documents.

Students' Reasoning with Documents

The analysis of our essay data showed that the students were also able to reason *with* documents. Most essays contained a claim supported by different types of arguments and at least one reference to a document. The arguments included a combination of facts, psychological events, and evaluations drawn from the documents or proposed by the student. Most (91 percent) of the references to specific documents were accurate. Moreover, students referred to historian essays, participant accounts, or primary documents to support different types of arguments. For instance, they referred to primary documents to support factual statements. Thus, students were able to reason with the different types of information contained in the various document types.

The primary-group students were more likely to include references in their essays, and they referred mostly to primary documents. Some secondary-group students also referred to primary documents, although they knew about the primary documents only through other documents (e.g., historian essays). The high proportion of references to primary documents, compared to other types of documents, suggests that students understand that primary documents are central to the structure of the controversy. Primary documents contain facts on which participants and historians can draw conflicting interpretations. Citing primary documents is an effective way to support one's arguments. The results suggest that having primary documents directly available for study (as opposed to having them cited in other documents) helped students reason with these documents.

It is also interesting that the textbook, which was consistently ranked as highly trustworthy and useful, was never referred to in the essays. This is a further indication that students possess a sense of how different sources can be used. Textbooks are useful to learn a basic version of the story. Students expect them to contain only "true" facts and reliable explanations (Wineburg, 1991a). However, textbooks are usually not a good source of arguments when one is reasoning about a controversial issue.

Mental Representation of Multiple Documents

On the basis of the results of this study, we suggest a tentative description of how information from multiple sources is represented in memory. Understanding multiple documents involves the same levels of representation as understanding single passages. For each document, the reader has to understand the literal meaning of the text and to build a situation model (van Dijk & Kintsch, 1983), in which both events and their causal-temporal connections are represented (Trabasso & van den Broek, 1985). However, the situation models of different documents must interact in several ways: They may overlap (e.g., tell the same basic story), a document may be part of the situation model of another document (e.g., a letter may play a role in a story episode), and different documents may yield incompatible situation models (e.g., offer conflicting interpretations of what happened). We suggest that when learning from multiple documents, readers build an additional level of representation, where both sources and contents of the document set are represented (Britt, Rouet, Georgi, & Perfetti, 1994). This *argument model* serves various purposes. First, it accounts for argumentative relations between documents (e.g., "Prof. Norman used the 1846 Treaty to argue against the U.S. intervention"). Second, it allows the students to maintain contradictory statements in a coherent representation (e.g., "Norman claims that the United States was not justified in its actions when Wilson claims it was justified"). When indexed under different source entries, antagonistic assertions can coexist. Third, it may serve as a retrieval structure.

Although the primary purpose of the present study was not to prove that argument models are built during multiple document reading, several results are consistent with this view. Most students were able to remember content information accurately when evaluating document trustworthiness or usefulness. The students were also able to refer to documents when writing an argument. This is evidence that source information is closely associated with content information in students' memory for document information.

It should be pointed out that the results were consistent across four different controversies, although these controversies took place in a single historical context. Moreover, the documents used in this study were taken directly from the available literature, with only minor alterations. These features of the present study make generalization to real life situations easier.

To conclude, we believe the results of the present study show that college students with little previous experience in history can learn from and reason with multiple documents. Our students were able to gather different types of information on the controversy and to integrate that information in a coherent essay. They were able to keep track of the sources of information and to refer to these sources in an appropriate way. Studying primary documents influenced students' evaluation of document usefulness and trustworthiness and promoted the use of references in the essays. Thus, using multiple and varied documents can be a valuable activity as part of a history curriculum (see also Perfetti et al., 1995). The use of contradictory historical accounts may improve students' awareness of the uncertainties of history, and reading relevant primary sources may highlight the role of evidence in historical accounts.

As a means of presenting students with multiple historical documents, a simple hypertext environment proved useful and easy to master. In fact, students often mentioned liking this type of presentation format. Thus, hypertext seems appropriate for the experimental study of historical reasoning and may also have some potential as an instructional medium (Britt, Rouet, & Perfetti, 1996). However, as demonstrated by Wineburg (1991a), using multiple documents requires appropriate study strategies (e.g., corroboration), which students may not master spontaneously. Further work is needed to determine the instructional conditions under which these strategies may be acquired.

Notes

1. Although there may be other definitions for primary documents, we have restricted our definition to this particular set of criteria in order to examine students' sensitivity to the role of documents as evidence.
2. It has been shown that nonlinear text presentation can be confusing for inexperienced users (Rouet, 1992). Consequently, a pilot study was conducted to assess the usability of the hypertext system. Five graduate students and faculty members of the University of Pittsburgh were asked to study two document sets using the hypertext system. The participants were asked to report any difficulty or suggestion about the system. All the participants managed to select and read the documents, and no major difficulty was reported. However, minor aspects of the hypertext interface (e.g., location of buttons) were improved following participants' reports.
3. Although it may have been more ecologically valid to have participants compose the essay with the documents available, we opted not to do so because we wanted to use the essay as a measure of how documents (source and content) were represented in memory.
4. A description of the types of units and scoring rules may be found in Rouet, Marron, Mason, and Perfetti (1993).

References

Britt, M. A., Rouet, J.-F., Georgi, M. C., & Perfetti, C. A. (1994). Learning from history texts: From causal analysis to argument models. In G. Leinhardt, I. Beck, & C. Stainton (Eds.), *Teaching and learning in history* (pp. 47–84). Hillsdale, NJ: Erlbaum.

Britt, M. A., Rouet, J.-F., & Perfetti, C. A. (1996). Using hypertext to study and reason about historical evidence. In J.-F. Rouet, J. J. Levonen, A. P. Dillon, & R. J. Spiro (Eds.), *Hypertext and cognition* (pp. 43–72). Mahwah, NJ: Erlbaum.

Center for Strategic and International Studies. (1967). *Panama: Canal issues and treaty talks.* Washington, DC: Georgetown UP.

Chi, M. T. H., Feltovitch, P. J., & Glaser, R. (1981). Categorization and representation of physics problems by experts and novices. *Cognitive Science, 5,* 121–152.

Crismore, A. (1984). The rhetorics of textbooks: Metadiscourse. *Journal of Curriculum Studies, 16,* 279–296.

Dee Lucas, D., & Larkin, J. H. (1988). Novice rules for assessing importance in scientific texts. *Journal of Memory and Language, 27,* 288–308.

Dillon, A. (1991). Readers' models of text structure: The case of academic articles. *International Journal of Man-Machine Studies, 35,* 913–925.

Kuhn, D. (1991). *The skills of argument.* New York: Cambridge University Press.

Lesgold, A., Feltovitch, P. J., Glaser, R., & Wang, Y. (1981). *The acquisition of perceptual diagnostic skill in radiology* (Technical Report No. PDS-1). Pittsburgh, PA: University of Pittsburgh, Learning Research and Development Center.

Mandl, H., Stein, N., & Trabasso, T. (1985). *Learning and comprehension of text.* New York: Erlbaum.

Mandler, J. M., & Johnson, N. S. (1977). Remembrance of things parsed: Story structure and recall. *Cognitive Psychology, 9,* 111–151.

McGinley, W. (1992). The role of reading and writing while composing from sources. *Reading Research Quarterly, 27,* 227–248.

Nash, J. G., Schumacher, G. M., & Carlson, B. W. (1993). Writing from sources: A structure-mapping model. *Journal of Educational Psychology, 85,* 159–170.

Nielsen, J. (1990). *Hypertext and hypermedia.* San Diego, CA: Academic Press.

Perfetti, C. A., Britt, M. A., & Georgi, M. C. (1995). *Text-based learning and reasoning: Studies in history.* Hillsdale, NJ: Erlbaum.

Ravitch, D. R., & Finn, C. E. (1987). *What do our 17-year-olds know? A report on the first national assessment of history and literature.* New York: Harper & Row.

Rouet, J.-F. (1992). Cognitive processing of hyperdocuments: When does nonlinearity help? In D. Lucarella, J. Nanard, M. Nanard, & P. Paolini (Eds.), *Proceedings of the 4th ACM Conference on Hypertext* (pp. 131–140). New York: ACM Press.

Rouet, J.-F., Marron, M. A., Mason, R. A., & Perfetti, C. A. (1993). *Claims and arguments: A framework for analyzing history argumentative essays.* Unpublished manuscript, University of Pittsburgh, Learning Research and Development Center, PA.

Wineburg, S. S. (1991a). Historical problem solving: A study of the cognitive processes used in the evaluation of documentary and pictorial evidence. *Journal of Educational Psychology, 83,* 73–87.

Wineburg, S. S. (1991b). On the reading of historical texts: Notes on the breach between school and academy. *American Educational Research Journal, 28,* 495–519.

Wineburg, S. S. (1994). The cognitive representation of historical texts. In G. Leinhardt, I. Beck, & C. Stainton (Eds.), *Teaching and learning in history* (pp. 85–135). Hillsdale, NJ: Erlbaum.

Wineburg, S. S., & Wilson, S. M. (1991). Student-matter knowledge in the teaching of history. *Advances in Research on Teaching, 2,* 305–347.

Appendix

Study Set for Controversy 2

Problem Statement

There has been much controversy about the U.S. role in the Panamanian Revolution. To what extent was the U.S. military intervention in the Panamanian Revolution justified?

List of Main Facts

MAIN FACTS CONCERNING THE EXECUTION OF THE REVOLUTION (FACTS AGREED UPON BY HISTORIANS)

Nov. 2, 5:30 P.M.: U.S.S. *Nashville* arrives in Colón Harbor with 42 marines.

Nov. 2, evening: U.S. Secretary of Navy sends orders to American consul to inform the U.S.S. *Nashville* to maintain uninterrupted transit across the Isthmus in accordance with treaty obligations.

Nov. 2, 11:30 P.M.: Colombia ship, *Cartagena,* arrives at Colón with 400 troops.

Nov. 3, dawn: Colombia commander and troops come ashore.

Nov. 3, 10:00 A.M.: Colonel Shaler, superintendent of Panama Railroad, makes sure troops are not transported across the Isthmus. Shaler cons Colombian leaders into going to Panama City, leaving the troops isolated in Colón.

Nov. 3, 5:15 P.M.: Revolution begins in Panama City by mob arresting Colombian officers.

Nov. 3, 6:00 P.M.: Independence of Panama declared.

Nov. 3, evening: *Nashville* commander, Hubbard, receives order to maintain uninterrupted transit. Hubbard orders Shaler not to transport Colombian troops on the railroad and informs the acting Colombian leaders that the troops will not be permitted on the railroad.

Nov. 4, 12:00 P.M.: Acting Colombian leader left in control of troops threatens to kill all Americans in Colón if superiors are not released by the Panamanians.

Nov. 4, 1:00 P.M.: U.S. troops land and take all American women and children to the ship. All male civilians are taken to Railroad warehouse.

Nov. 5, 4:00 P.M.: Panamanians persuaded acting Colombian leader and troops to leave Colón on a British steamer with money.

Nov. 6: United States telegrams Colombia that they will officially recognize Panama.

Nov. 6, 12:00 P.M.: United States recognizes the Republic of Panama.

Historian Essay 1

Excerpt from Prof. J. Norman's book *America and the Canal Title* (1986, p. 192). The author argues that the U.S. military intervention in the Panamanian revolution was not justified.

If Commander Hubbard of the *Nashville* had had the telegram sent him on November 2, the troops and administrative officers on the *Cartagena* would not have been allowed to land. In short, Colombia would have been prevented from landing troops on a part of her territory when there was no disturbance whatsoever. And that is called protecting the transit and maintaining order! It is the only interruption of the transit and of the peace there was.

As already stated, there was no revolution, there was no uprising. Certain interested persons merely volunteered to organize a civil government in the Province of Panama, independent of that of Colombia, if assured of protection by the United States. The protection was assured and was given. The purpose was to enable the one to grant and the other to receive title to the Canal Zone. Colombia was to be barred from interfering by the display of overwhelming force.

That is what was planned, and that is what eventuated.

The military forces of Colombia arrived at Colón in fulfillment of her obligations under the Treaty of 1846 and in the performance of the most elementary duty of a sovereign state. Those of the United States were there to interrupt in its most sacred use. It was the sovereign right of Colombia to secure transit from Colón to Panama for her troops, and the duty of the Railroad, under its charter, to supply it. The United States did interfere without a scintilla of right and in violation of the Treaty of 1846.

Historian Essay 2

Excerpt from Prof. D. Wilson's book *A History of Panama* (1988, p. 48). The author argues that the U.S. military intervention in the Panamanian revolution was justified.

It was on the basis of this 1846 treaty with Colombia that, on nine different occasions during the period 1856–1902, United States armed forces intervened in Panama to quell disorders that threatened transit across the Isthmus. Thus, for over 50 years before the events of 1903, United States warships had been steaming in and out of Colombia's Panamanian harbors and U.S. troops had been landing at Colombia's Panamanian ports in the legitimate fulfillment of U.S. treaty obligations.

Anyone who was surprised in November 1903 when two U.S. warships and a small force of Marines showed up in the harbor of Colón during the first few days of a widely heralded Panamanian revolution either had failed to observe past events, or had forgotten them.

Participant Account 1

Excerpt from Senator J. Carmack's speech to Congress (January 4, 1904). The author argues that the U.S. military intervention in the Panamanian revolution was not justified.

We have protected the transit again and again, but never before was the claim that we had a right to exclude Colombia from her own dominions. Never before was the claim made that we had the right under the Treaty of 1846 to support an insurrection against the authority of Colombia. You do not have to read the Treaty of 1846 to know that it contains no such preposterous provision. No nation on earth ever surrendered the right to protect its own soil and the integrity of its own domain with its own troops or surrendered to another government the right to prevent or to suppress an insurrection against its authority. No such thing can be found in the Treaty of 1846.

Participant Account 2

Excerpt from U.S. President T. Roosevelt's speech to Congress (January 4, 1904). The author argues that the U.S. military intervention in the Panamanian revolution was justified.

I have already adverted to the Treaty of 1846, by the thirty-fifth article of which the United States secured the right to a free and open transit across the Isthmus of Panama, and to that end agreed to guarantee to New Granada her rights of sovereignty and property over that territory. The article is sometimes discussed as if the latter guarantee constituted its sole object and bound the United States to protect the sovereignty of New Granada against domestic revolution. Nothing, however, could be more erroneous than this supposition. That our wise and patriotic ancestors, with all their dread of entangling alliances, would have entered into a treaty with New Granada solely or even primarily for the purpose of enabling that remnant of the original Republic of Colombia, then resolved into the State of New Granada, Venezuela and Ecuador, to continue from Bogotá to rule over the Isthmus of Panama, is a conception that would in itself be incredible, even if the contrary did not clearly appear. It is true that since the treaty was made the United States has again and again been obliged forcibly to intervene for the preservation of order and the maintenance of an open transit, and that this intervention has usually operated to the advantage of the titular Government of Colombia, but it is equally true that the United States in intervening, with or without Colombia's consent, for the protection of the transit, had disclaimed any duty to defend the Colombian Government against domestic insurrection or against the erection of an independent government on the Isthmus of Panama.

Textbooklike Passage

Excerpt from *One Land, One Flag,* a U.S. college history textbook (1981, p. 110). The author describes the execution of the Panama revolution.

> A United States warship, the U.S.S. *Nashville,* steamed into the Pana-
> manian port of Colón on November 2, 1903. Hours later a Colombian
> ship arrived with 400 troops sent to stop the revolt. Encouraged by this
> display of American support, the Panamanians immediately revolted.
> The presence of the United States naval forces prevented the Colombian
> army from taking action. Furthermore, the railroad refused to transport
> the Colombian troops to Panama City where the Panamanians declared
> their independence on November 3. Three days later the United States
> officially recognized the new nation.

Primary Document 1

Official correspondence between U.S. leaders (November 2–3, 1903). The correspondence concerns U.S. military action during the Panama-nian revolution.

1. To Hubbard, commander of the U.S.S. *Nashville,* from the Secre-tary of the Navy (Nov 2, 1903): Maintain free and uninterrupted tran-sit. If interruption threatened by armed force, occupy the line of rail-road. Prevent landing of any armed force with hostile intent, either Government or insurgent, either at Colón, Porto Bello, or other point. Send copy of instructions to the senior officer present at Panama City upon arrival of Boston. Have sent copy of instructions and have tele-graphed Dixie to proceed with all possible dispatch from Kingston to Colón. [Colombian] Government force reported approaching the Isthmus in vessels. Prevent their landing if in your judgment this would precipitate a conflict. Acknowledgement is required.

2. Reply from Hubbard to Secretary of Navy (Nov 3, 1903): Receipt of your telegram of November 2 is acknowledged. Prior to receipt this morning about 400 men were landed here by the Government of Co-lombia from Cartagena. No revolution has been declared on the Isthmus and no disturbances. Railway company have declined to transport these troops except by request of the governor of Panama. Request has not been made. It is possible that movement may be made tonight at Panama City to declare independence. Situation is most critical if revo-lutionary leaders act.

3. Loomis (U.S. Asst. Secretary of State), after failing to hear from Hubbard, sends another memo (Nov 3, 8:45 P.M.): The troops which landed from the *Cartagena* should not proceed to Panama City.

4. Secretary of State Hay adds instructions to Hubbard (Nov 3, 10:30 P.M.): If dispatch to *Nashville* has not been delivered inform her captain immediately that she must prevent Government troops depart-

ing for Panama City or taking any action which would lead to bloodshed, and must use every endeavor to preserve order on the Isthmus.

5. Hubbard to Shaler, Superintendent of the railroad (Nov 3, 10:00 P.M.): Sir: The condition of affairs at Panama being such that any movement of troops in the neighborhood must inevitably produce a conflict and interrupt the transit of the Isthmus which the United States Government is pledged to maintain uninterrupted, I am obliged to prohibit the carrying of troops of either party or in either direction by your railroad, and hereby notify you that I do so prohibit it.

Primary Document 2

Excerpt from the Bidlack Treaty between the United States and Colombia (1846, Article 35). The article concerns transit and defense in the Isthmus of Panama.

[. . .] The Government of New Granada guarantees to the Government of the United States that the right of way or transit across the Isthmus of Panama upon any modes of communication that now exist, or that may be hereafter constructed, shall be open and free to the Government and citizens of the United States, and for the transportation of any articles of produce, manufactures or merchandise, belonging to the citizens of the United States; [. . .] And, in order to secure to themselves the tranquil and constant enjoyment of these advantages, [. . .] the United States guarantee, positively and efficaciously, to New Granada, the perfect neutrality of the before mentioned Isthmus, with the view that the free transit from the one to the other sea may not be interrupted or embarrassed in any future time while this treaty exists; and, in consequence, the United States also guarantee, in the same manner, the right of sovereignty and property which New Granada has and possesses over the said territory [. . .]

Additional Historian Essay 1

Excerpt from Rep. D. Myers's book *Adventures in American Diplomacy* (1984, p. 57). The author argues that the U.S. military intervention in the Panamanian revolution was not justified.

We have seen how the American government prevented Colombia from restoring her control on the Isthmus when the revolt occurred. The argument that this action was justified under the Treaty of 1846 is not convincing. There was certainly little basis for the assertion that the treaty obligated Colombia to permit the United States to build a canal. [. . .] The purpose of the treaty was to facilitate the construction of a canal, or a railroad, but it hardly required Colombia to permit a canal to be built.

The intervention of North American forces to prevent fighting along the transit route was not in itself unusual or improper. The United States had repeatedly taken similar action in the past under the treaty

[. . .] What was difficult to justify was the use of force to prevent Colombia from suppressing a revolt. It would be hard to imagine that the makers of the Treaty of 1846 had contemplated that it would ever be invoked in a way that caused Colombia to lose the territory. [. . .]

The revolution would probably not have occurred, however, if the United States had attempted to discourage it. [. . .]

On the whole, in the light of hindsight, both the interests and the reputation of the United States might have been better served if Roosevelt had persisted in an effort to reach an agreement with Colombia.

Additional Historian Essay 2

Excerpt from Rep. P. Smith's book *The Great Adventure of Panama* (1988, p. 5). The author argues that the U.S. military intervention in the Panamanian revolution was justified.

The unvarnished truth is that Panamanian independence was the work of a small group of wealthy, influential Panamanians and foreign commercial interests, not the United States government. The bloodless coup owed its success to a handful of local conspirators who, working with officials of the Panama Railway Company, managed to talk the two officers commanding Colombia's ragtag, 500 man security force into a train ride to the other side of the isthmus, where they were briefly jailed and subsequently paid off to salve their wounded pride. While an offshore American naval presence lent credibility to U. S. support of Panamanian independence, the only official American "intervention" consisted of a landing party of forty-two marines; far from facing a hostile reception from the natives, the marines went through their brief paces without firing a shot in anger. The United States had, moreover, a perfectly legal right to land troops in Colombia to protect the rights of transit across the existing railroad — a right granted by Article 35 of the Bidlack Treaty of 1846. The whole coup had been carried out by a group smaller than a professional football team, and without a drop of blood spilled.

Problem Statement and List of Documents for the Other Three Controversies: Controversy 1

Problem Statement

The question of whether or not the U.S. government participated in the planning of the Panama revolution is still controversial. To what extent did the U.S. government influence the planning of the Panama revolution?

Historian Essay 1

Excerpt from Prof. G. Martin's book, *The Land Divided* (1984, p. 459). The author argues that the United States influenced the planning of the revolution.

Historian Essay 2

Excerpt from Prof. G. Brown's book, *Latin America and the United States* (1983, pp. 84–85). The author argues that the United States did not influence the planning of the revolution.

Participant Account 1

Excerpt from P. Bunau-Varilla's book, *Panama: The Creation, the Destruction, the Resurrection* (1913, pp. 310–318). The author describes his contacts with U.S. officials during the planning of the revolution.

Participant Account 2

Excerpt from U.S. President T. Roosevelt's *Autobiography* (1913, pp. 521–522). The author argues that his government had no contact with the revolutionaries.

Textbook

Excerpt from *One Land, One Flag*, a U.S. college history textbook (1981, p. 110). The author describes the planning of the revolution.

Primary Document 1

Excerpt of a personal letter from U.S. President T. Roosevelt to A. Shaw, writer (October 10, 1903). The author discusses the situation in Panama.

Primary Document 2

Excerpt of a personal letter from U.S. President T. Roosevelt to J. Bigelow, writer (January 6, 1904). The author discusses his relations with Bunau-Varilla.

Additional Historian Essay 1

Excerpt from Prof. D. McCall's book *Intervention and the Dollar Diplomacy in the Caribbean, 1900–1921* (1984, p. 57). The author argues that the United States influenced the planning of the revolution.

Additional Historian Essay 2

Excerpt from Prof. D. Evans's books *Theodore Roosevelt* (1982, p. 121). The author argues that the United States did not influence the planning of the revolution.

Controversy 3

Problem Statement

There has been controversy about Bunau-Varilla's actions in signing a treaty on his own. To what extent were Bunau-Varilla's actions in signing a treaty on his own fair to Panama?

Historian Essay 1

Excerpt from Prof. C. Stanton's book *New Light on the Panama Canal Treaty* (1985, p. 52). The author argues that Bunau-Varilla was acting unfairly to Panama.

Historian Essay 2

Excerpt from Prof. G. Price's book *Philippe Bunau-Varilla: The Man Behind the Panama Canal* (1986, p. 81). The author argues that Bunau-Varilla was acting in Panama's best interests.

Participant Account 1

Excerpt from a comment of P. Drake, a Panama Railroad executive (1903). The author argues that Bunau-Varilla's actions were unfair to Panama.

Participant Account 2

Excerpt from P. Bunau-Varilla's book *Panama: The Creation, the Destruction, the Resurrection* (1913, p. 367). The author argues that his actions were in Panama's best interests.

Textbook

Excerpt from *One Land, One Flag,* a U.S. college history textbook (1981, p. 110). The author describes the treaty negotiations.

Primary Document 1

Correspondence between the Panamanian provisional government and Bunau-Varilla (November 4–6, 1903). The messages concern Bunau-Varilla's appointment as minister to the United States.

Primary Document 2

Correspondence between the Panamanian provisional government and Bunau-Varilla (early November, 1903). The messages concern Bunau-Varilla's role in treaty negotiation.

Additional Historian Essay 1

Excerpt from Prof. W. Lewis's book *The Fight for Panama* (1928, p. 34). The author argues that Bunau-Varilla acted unfairly to Panama.

Additional Historian Essay 2

Excerpt from Prof. G. Lindt's book *The Story of Panama* (1924, p. 461). The author argues that Bunau-Varilla was acting in Panama's best interests.

Controversy 4

Problem Statement

The content of the Hay–Bunau-Varilla treaty has been subject to much debate among historians and politicians. Given the circumstances, was the Hay–Bunau-Varilla treaty a good deal for Panama?

Historian Essay 1

Excerpt from Prof. P. Moore's book *Victory in Panama* (1986, p. 41). The author argues that the Hay–Bunau-Varilla treaty was a good deal for Panama.

Historian Essay 2

Excerpt from Prof. R. Williams's book *The Panama Canal: The Crisis in Historical Perspective* (1988, pp. 35–36). The author argues that the Hay–Bunau-Varilla treaty was a bad deal for Panama.

Participant Account 1

Excerpt from P. Bunau-Varilla's book *Panama: The Creation, the Destruction, the Resurrection* (1913, p. 368). The author argues that the Hay–Bunau-Varilla treaty was a good deal for Panama.

Participant Account 2

Excerpt from U.S. Secretary of State J. Hay's papers (1903). The author argues that the Hay–Bunau-Varilla treaty was a bad deal for Panama.

Textbook

Excerpt from *One Land, One Flag,* a U.S. college history textbook (1981, p. 111). The author describes the Hay–Bunau-Varilla treaty.

Primary Document 1

Excerpt from the Hay-Herran treaty, signed by U.S. and Colombian diplomats (January 22, 1903). The treaty concerns the building of a canal by the United States in the province of Panama.

Primary Document 2

Excerpt from the Hay–Bunau-Varilla treaty, signed by U.S. and Panamanian diplomats (November 18, 1903). The treaty concerns the building of a canal by the United States in Panama.

Additional Historian Essay 1

Excerpt from Rep. D. Kohn's book *The History of the Panama Canal* (1928, p. 58). The author argues that the Hay–Bunau-Varilla treaty was a good deal for Panama.

Additional Historian Essay 2

Excerpt from Rep. C. Ewing's book *The U.S. and the Republic of Panama* (1925, p. 52). The author argues that the Hay–Bunau-Varilla treaty was a bad deal for Panama.

Acknowledgments *(continued from page ii)*

Kevin Michael DeLuca, "Unruly Arguments: The Body Rhetoric of Earth First!, ACT UP, and Queer Nation." *Argumentation and Advocacy* 36 (Summer 1999): 9–21. Reprinted with permission of the American Forensic Association.

Jeanne Fahnestock and Marie Secor, "The Stases in Scientific and Literary Argument," *Written Communication* 5.4, October 1988, 427–43. Reprinted by permission of Sage Publications, Inc.

Catherine Ford, "Science Courses Key to Future Jobs." *Calgary Herald,* October 20, 1983, A4. Reprinted by permission of the Calgary Herald.

Richard Fulkerson, "Technical Logic, Comp-Logic, and the Teaching of Writing," *College Composition and Communication,* December 1988. ©1988 by the National Council of Teachers of English. Reprinted with permission.

Alan Gross, "A Theory of Rhetorical Audience: Reflections on Chaim Perelman." *Quarterly Journal of Speech* 85.2 (May 1999): 203–11. Reprinted with permission of the National Communication Association.

R. Allen Harris, "Assent, Dissent, and Rhetoric in Science," *Rhetoric Society Quarterly* 20 (Winter 1990). Reprinted with permission of Rhetoric Society Quarterly.

Gary Layne Hatch, "Logic in the Black Folk Sermon: The Sermons of C. L. Franklin," *Journal of Black Studies,* 26.3, January 1996, 227–44. Reprinted by permission of Sage Publications, Inc.

Joseph Janangelo, "Joseph Cornell and the Artistry of Composing Persuasive Hypertexts," *College Composition and Communication* 49.1, February 1998. ©1998 by the National Council of Teachers of English. Reprinted with permission. Joseph Cornell, "Untitled (Ludwig II of Bavaria)." Philadelphia Museum of Art: Gift of the Joseph and Robert Cornell Memorial Foundation.

Craig Kallendorf and Carol Kallendorf, "The Figures of Speech, *Ethos,* and Aristotle: Notes Toward a Rhetoric of Business Communication" as it appeared in *The Journal of Business Communication* 22:1, 1985. Reprinted with the permission of Craig Kallendorf.

James Kastely, "From Formalism to Inquiry: A Model of Argument in *Antigone," College English* 62.2 (November 1999): 222–41. ©1999 by the National Council of Teachers of English. Reprinted with permission.

Catherine E. Lamb, "Other Voices, Different Parties: Feminist Responses to Argument." In Deborah Berrill (Ed.), *Perspectives on Written Argument* (pp. 257–269). ©1995. Hampton Press, Cresskill, NJ. Reprinted with permission.

Phyllis Lassner, "Feminist Responses to Rogerian Argument" from *Rhetoric Review,* 8.2, Spring 1990. Reprinted with permission of Lawrence Erlbaum Associates, Inc.

Julie Lindquist, "Class Ethos and the Politics of Inquiry: What the Barroom Can Teach Us about the Classroom," *College Composition and Communication* 51.2, December 1999: 225–47. ©1999 by the National Council of Teachers of English. Reprinted with permission.

Robin Muksian-Schutt, "Starkweather and Smith: Using 'Contact Zones' to Teach Argument," *TETYC* 25.2 (May 1998): 126–31. ©1998 by the National Council of Teachers of English. Reprinted with permission.

Chaim Perelman and Lucie Olbrechts-Tyteca, excerpt from *The New Rhetoric.* ©1969 University of Notre Dame Press. Used by permission.

Karen A. Redfield, "Opening the Composition Classroom to Storytelling: Respecting Native American Students' Use of Rhetorical Strategies." In Deborah Berrill (Ed.), *Perspectives on Written Argument* (pp. 241–256). ©1995. Hampton Press, Cresskill, NJ. Reprinted with permission. "Linguistic and Cultural Factors in Rhetorical Forms" (diagram) from *Linguistic and Written Discourse: Contrastive Rhetoric* by Diane B. Houghton and Michael M. Hoey. From *Annual Review of Applied Linguistics,* Volume 2 (1982). Reprinted with permission of Cambridge University Press.

Jean-François Rouet, M. Anne Britt, Robert A. Mason, and Charles Perfetti, "Using Multiple Sources of Evidence to Reason about History" as it appeared in *Journal of Educational Psychology* 8.3 (1996): 478–93. ©1996 by the American Psychological Association. Reprinted (or Adapted) with permission.

Mariolina Salvatori, "The 'Argument of Reading' in the Teaching of Composition" from *Argument Revisited, Argument Redefined.* Edited by Emmel, Resch, and Tenney. ©1996 Sage Publications, Inc. Reprinted by permission of Sage Publications, Inc.

Fan Shen, "The Classroom and the Wider Culture: Identity as a Key to Learning English Composition," *College Composition and Communication* 40.4, December 1989: 459–66. ©1989 by the National Council of Teachers of English. Reprinted with permission.

Patrick J. Slattery, "The Argumentative, Multiple-Source Paper" from *Journal of Teaching Writing* 10 (Fall/Winter 1991): 181–99. Reprinted with permission of the Journal of Teaching Writing.

Gail Stygall, "Toulmin and the Ethics of Argument Fields" from *Journal of Teaching Writing* 6 (1987): 93–108. Reprinted with permission of the Journal of Teaching Writing.

Stephen Toulmin, excerpt from *The Uses of Argument.* Copyright ©1958 by Cambridge University Press. Reprinted with permission of Cambridge University Press.

Barbara Warnick, "Judgment, Probability, and Aristotle's *Rhetoric.*" *Quarterly Journal of Speech* 9 (1989): 299–311. Reprinted with permission of the National Communication Association.

Richard E. Young, Alton L. Becker, Kenneth L. Pike. *Rhetoric: Discovery and Change.* NY: Harcourt, 1970. Used by permission. Carl R. Rogers, "Communication: Its Blocking and Facilitation." Originally published in *ETC: A Review of General Semantics,* Vol. IX, No. 2. Copyright 1952 by the International Society for General Semantics.

Bibliography

Argument in Business and Technical Fields

Bronn, Carl. "Applying Epistemic Logic and Evidential Theory to Strategic Arguments." *Strategic Management Journal* 19.1 (January 1998): 81–96.

Butler, Marilyn S. "The Persuasive Use of Numerical Data in Influential Business Periodicals." *Bulletin of the Association for Business Communication* 54 (March 1991): 13–16.

Gilsdorf, Jeanette W. "Write Me Your Best Case For . . ." *Bulletin of the Association for Business Communication* 54 (March 1991): 7–12.

Horevitz, Ann Marie, and John F. McCarthy. "Appraisal Writing, Aristotle, and the Art of Persuasion." *The Appraisal Journal* 65 (July 1997): 242–46.

Infante, Dominic A., and William I. Gorden. "Argumentativeness and Affirming Communicator Style as Predictors of Satisfaction/Dissatisfaction with Subordinates." *Communication Quarterly* 37.2 (Spring 1989): 81–90.

Infante, Dominic A., and William I. Gorden. "How Employees See the Boss: Test of an Argumentative and Affirming Model of Supervisors' Communicative Behavior." *Western Journal of Speech Communication* 55.3 (Summer 1991): 294–304.

Infante, Dominic A., and William I. Gorden. "Superiors' Argumentativeness and Verbal Aggressiveness as Predictors of Subordinates' Satisfaction." *Human Communication* 12.1 (Fall 1985): 117–25.

Jacobi, Martin J. "Using the Enthymeme as a Heuristic in Professional Writing Courses." *JAC* 7 (1987): 41–51.

Jacobi, Martin J. "Using the Enthymeme to Emphasize Ethics in Professional Writing Courses." *Journal of Business Communication* 27 (Summer 1990): 273–92.

Keough, Colleen M. "The Nature and Function of Argument in Organizational Bargaining Research." *Southern Speech Communication Journal* 53 (Fall 1987): 1–17.

La Duc, Linda. "Infusing Practical Wisdom Into Persuasive Performance: Hermeneutics and the Teaching of Sales Proposal Writing." *Journal of Technical Writing and Communication* 21 (1991): 155–64.

Little, Joseph. "Confusion in the Classroom: Does Logos Mean Logic?" *Journal of Technical Writing and Communication* 29.4 (1999): 349–53.

Michael, Catherine. "The Persuasive Letter from Start to Finish." *Bulletin of the Association for Business Communication* 54 (March 1991): 28–29.

Mulvihill, Peggy. "So That's Who You Are: An Exercise that Moves Students from "I" to "You" in Persuasive Writing." *Bulletin of the Association for Business Communication* (September 1990): 57–59.

Possin, Kevin. "Ethical Argumentation." *Journal of Technical Writing and Communication* 21 (1991): 65–72.

Powell, Melissa L. "The Language of Letters: A History of Persuasive and Psychological Strategies in American Business Letters from 1905 through 1920." *Iowa State Journal of Business and Technical Communication* 5 (January 1991): 33–47.

Sawyer, Thomas M. "Argument." *Journal of Technical Writing and Communication* 17 (1987): 253–63.

Sawyer, Thomas M. "The Argument about Ethics, Fairness, or Right and Wrong." *Journal of Technical Writing and Communication* 18 (1988): 367–75.

Secor, Marie. "Recent Research in Argumentation Theory." *Technical Writing Teacher* 14.3 (Fall 1987): 337–54.

Sellnow, Timothy L., and Robert L. Ulmer. "Ambiguous Argument as Advocacy in Organizational Crisis Communication." *Argumentation and Advocacy* 31.3 (Winter 1995): 138–50.

Shapiro, B. P. "Toward a Normative Model of Rational Argumentation for Critical Accounting Discussions." *Accounting Organizations and Society* 23.7 (October 1998): 641–64.

Classical Argumentation — And Its Updates

Aristotle. *On Rhetoric*. Ed. George A. Kennedy. New York: Oxford University Press, 1991.

———. *Complete Works*. Ed. Jonathan Barnes. Princeton, NJ: Princeton University Press, 1984.

Bator, Paul. "Aristotelian and Rogerian Rhetoric." *College Composition and Communication* 31 (1980): 427–32.

Bitzer, Lloyd. "Aristotle's Enthymeme Revisited." *Quarterly Journal of Speech* 45 (1960): 399–408.

Bizzell, Patricia, and Bruce Herzberg, Eds. *The Rhetorical Tradition: Readings from Classical Times to the Present*. Boston: Bedford/St. Martin's, 2001.

Bracci, Sharon Blinn, and Mary Garrett. "Aristotelian Topoi as a Cross-Cultural Analytical Tool." *Philosophy and Rhetoric* 26 (Spring 1993): 93–112.

Braet, Antoine. "The Classical Doctrine of *Status* and the Rhetorical Theory of Argumentation." *Philosophy and Rhetoric* 20 (1987): 79–93.

Brinton, Alan. "Cicero's Use of Historical Examples in Moral Argument." *Philosophy and Rhetoric* 21 (1988): 169–84.

Cicero. *Ad Herennium*. Trans. H. Caplan. The Loeb Classical Library. Cambridge, MA: Harvard University Press, 1949.

Corbett, Edward P. J., and Robert J. Connors. *Classical Rhetoric for the Modern Student*. 4th Ed. New York: Oxford University Press, 1998.

Corbett, Edward P. J., James L. Golden, and Goodwin F. Berquist, Eds. *Essays on the Rhetoric of the Western World*. Dubuque, IA: Kendall/Hunt, 1990.

Craig, Christopher P. *Form as Argument in Cicero's Speeches: A Study of Dilemma*. Atlanta, GA: Scholars Press, 1993.

Cross, Mary. "Aristotle and Business Writing: Why We Need to Teach Persuasion." *Bulletin of the Association for Business Communication* 54 (March 1991): 3–6.

Devet, Bonnie. "Rewriting Classical Persuasion as Rogerian Argument." *Exercise Exchange* 33 (1988): 8–10.

Emmel, Barbara A. "Toward a Pedagogy of the Enthymeme: The Roles of Dialogue, Intention, and Function in Shaping Argument." *Rhetoric Review* 14 (Fall 1994): 132–49.

Fahnestock, Jeanne, and Marie Secor. "Toward a Modern Version of Stasis." *Oldspeak / Newspeak: Rhetorical Transformations*. Ed. Charles W. Kneupper. Arlington, TX: Rhetoric Society of America, 1985. 217–26.

Gage, John T. "Teaching the Enthymeme: Invention and Arrangement." *Rhetoric Review* 1 (September 1983): 38–50.

Garver, Eugene. "Aristotle's *Rhetoric* on Unintentionally Hitting the Principles of the Sciences." *Rhetorica* 6 (1988): 381–93.

Gates, Rosemary L. "Causality, Community, and the Canons of Reasoning: Classical Rhetoric and Writing across the Curriculum." *JAC* 8 (1988): 137–45.

Gilbert, Michael A. "The Enthymeme Buster: A Heuristic Procedure for Position Exploration in Dialogic Dispute." *Informal Logic* 13 (Fall 1991): 159–66.

Kennedy, George A., *The Art of Persuasion in Greece*. Princeton: Princeton University Press, 1963.

Lunsford, Andrea. "Aristotelian vs. Rogerian Argument: A Reassessment." *College Composition and Communication* 30 (May 1979): 146–51.

Lunsford, Andrea A., and Lisa S. Ede. "Classical Rhetoric, Modern Rhetoric, and Contemporary Discourse Studies." *Written Communication* 1 (1984): 78–100.

Mercadente, Richard A. "Classical Dialectic and Philosophy in the English Classroom." *Leaflet* 87 (1988): 2–31.

Miller, Carolyn R. "Aristotle's 'Special Topics' in Rhetorical Practice and Pedagogy." *Rhetoric Society Quarterly* 17 (1987): 61–70.

Moline, John M. "Plato on Persuasion and Credibility." *Philosophy and Rhetoric* 21 (1988): 260–78.

Mulgan, R. "Aristotle, Ethical Diversity, and Political Argument." *Journal of Political Philosophy* 7.2 (1999): 191–208.

Murphy, James J., Ed. *The Rhetorical Tradition and Modern Writing*. New York: Modern Language Association of America, 1982.

Newstead, Stephen E. "Interpretational Errors in Syllogistic Reasoning." *JMC* 28 (February 1989): 78–91.

O'Banion, John. "Narration and Argumentation: Quintilian on *Narratio* as the Heart of Rhetorical Thinking." *Rhetorica* 5 (1987): 325–51.

Porter, James E. "*Divisio* as Em-/De-Powering the Topic: A Basis for Argument in Rhetoric and Composition." *Rhetoric Review* 8 (Spring 1990): 191–205.

Poster, Carol. "A Historicist Recontextualization of the Enthymeme." *Rhetoric Society Quarterly* 22 (Spring 1992): 1–24.

Quintilian. *Institutio Oratoria*. Trans. H. E. Butler. Loeb Classical Library. Cambridge, MA: Harvard University Press, 1920–22.

Smith, P. Christopher. *The Hermeneutics of Original Argument: Demonstration, Dialectic, Rhetoric*. Evanston, IL: Northwestern University Press, 1998.

Sutton, Jane. "Rereading Sophistical Arguments: A Political Intervention." *Argumentation* 5 (May 1991): 141–57.

Timmerman, David M. "Ancient Greek Origins of Argumentation Theory: Plato's Transformation of Dialegesthai to Dialectic." *Argumentation and Advocacy* 29.3 (Winter 1993): 116–24.

Vega Renon, Luis. "Aristotle's Endoxa and Plausible Argumentation." *Argumentation* 12.1 (1998): 95–114.

Walker, Jeffrey. "The Body of Persuasion: A Theory of the Enthymeme." *College English* 56 (January 1994): 46–65.

Worman, Nancy. "The Body as Argument: Helen in Four Greek Texts." *Classical Antiquity* 16.1 (April 1997): 151–200.

Developmental Theory and Argument

Berrill, Deborah P. "Anecdote and the Development of Oral Argument in Six-teen-Year-Olds." *Oracy Matters.* Eds. M. MacLure, T. Phillips, and A. M. Wilkinson. Milton Keynes, UK: Open University Press, 1988.

Berrill, Deborah P. "What Exposition Has To Do with Argument: Argumenta-tive Writing of Sixteen-Year-Olds." *English in Education* 24.1 (1990): 77–92.

Crowhurst, M. "Cohesion in Argument and Narration at Three Grade Levels." *Research in the Teaching of English* 21.2 (1987): 185–201.

Dimant, Rose J., and David J. Bearison. "Development of Formal Reasoning During Successive Peer Interactions." *Developmental Psychology* 27 (March 1991): 277–84.

Dinitz, Sue, and Jean Kiedaisch. "Persuasion from an 18-Year-Old's Perspec-tive: Perry and Piaget." *Journal of Teaching Writing* 9 (Fall–Winter 1990): 209–21.

Dixon, J., and L. Stratta. "Argument and the Teaching of English." *The Writing of Writing.* Ed. A. Wilkinson. Milton Keynes: Open University Press, 1986. 8–21.

Fox, C. "The Genesis of Argument in Narrative Discourse." *English in Educa-tion* 24.1 (1990): 23–31.

Hays, Janice N. "Socio-Cognitive Development and Argumentative Writing: Issues and Implications from One Research Project." *Journal of Basic Writing* 7 (1988): 42–67.

Hays, Janice N., Kathleen M. Brandt, and Kathryn H. Chantry. "The Impact of Friendly and Hostile Audiences on the Argumentative Writing of High School and College Students." *Research in the Teaching of English* 22 (1988): 391–416.

Kline, Susan L. "Social Cognitive Determinants of Argument Design Features in Regulative Discourse." *Argumentation and Advocacy* 25.1 (Summer 1988): 1–12.

Kline, Susan L., and Barbara L. Clinton. "Developments in Children's Persua-sive Message Practices." *Communication Education* 47.2 (April 1998): 120–36.

Kline, Susan L., and Dee Oseroff-Varnell. "The Development of Argument Analy-sis Skills in Children." *Argumentation and Advocacy* 30.1 (Summer 1993): 1–15.

Knudson, Ruth E. "The Development of Written Argumentation: An Analysis and Comparison of Argumentative Writing at Four Grade Levels." *Child Study Journal* 22.3 (September 1992): 167–84.

Lunsford, Andrea A. "The Content of Basic Writers' Essays." *College Composi-tion and Communication* 31 (1980): 278–90.

McCann, T. M. "Student Argumentative Writing: Knowledge and Ability at Three Grade Levels." *Research in the Teaching of English* 23.1 (1989): 62–76.

Mosenthal, P., R. Davidson, and V. Krieger. "How Fourth-Graders Develop Points of View in Classroom Writing." *Research in the Teaching of English* 15.3 (1981): 197–214.

Perry, William G. *Forms of Intellectual and Ethical Development in the College Years: A Scheme.* New York: Holt, Rinehart, & Winston, 1970.

Stein, N. L., and C. A. Miller. "I Win — You Lose: The Development of Argu-mentative Thinking." *Conversational Organization and Its Development.* Ed. B. Dorval. Norwood, NJ: Ablex, 1990. 265–309.

van Eemeren, Frans H., Kees de Glopper, Rob Grootendorst, and Ron Oostdam. "Identification of Unexpressed Premises and Argumentation Schemes by Students in Secondary School." *Argumentation and Advocacy* 31.3 (Winter 1995): 151–62.

White, J. "Children's Argumentative Writing: A Reappraisal of Difficulties." *Writing In Schools: Reader*. Ed. F. Christie. Geelong, Victoria: Deakin University Press, 1989. 9–23.

Diversity and Argumentation

Allen, Julia M., and Lester Faigley. "Discursive Strategies for Social Change: An Alternative Rhetoric of Argument." *Rhetoric Review* 14 (Fall 1995): 1142–72.

Andrews, Patricia. "Gender Differences in Persuasive Communication and Attribution of Success and Failure." *Human Communication Research* 13 (1987): 372–85.

Berrill, Deborah P., Ed. *Perspectives on Written Argument*. Cresskill, NJ: Hampton Press, 1995.

Bizzell, Patricia. "The Fourth of July and the 22nd of December: The Function of Cultural Archives in Persuasion, as Shown by Frederick Douglass and William Apess." *College Composition and Communication* (February 1997): 61–85.

Bruner, M. Lane. "Producing Identities: Gender Problematization and Feminist Argumentation." *Argumentation and Advocacy* 32.4 (Spring 1996): 185–99.

Campbell, Karlyn Kohrs. *Man Cannot Speak for Her, v. 1: A Critical Study of Early Feminist Rhetoric*. Contributions in Women's Studies, no. 101. Westport, CT: Greenwood Press, 1989.

———. *Man Cannot Speak for Her, v. 2: Key Texts of the Early Feminists*. Contributions in Women's Studies, no. 102. Westport, CT: Greenwood Press, 1989.

Corbett, Edward P. J. "The Rhetoric of the Open Hand and the Rhetoric of the Closed Fist." *College Composition and Communication* 20 (1969): 288–96.

de Beaugrande, Robert. "In Search of Feminist Discourse: The Difficult Case of Luce Irigaray." *College English* 50 (1988): 253–72.

Easley, Alexis. "Toward a Feminist Theory of Teaching Argumentative Writing." *Feminist Teacher* 11.1 (Spring/Summer 1997): 30–39.

Emmel, Barbara, Paula Resch, and Deborah Tenney. *Argument Revisited; Argument Redefined*. Thousand Oaks, CA: Sage Publications, 1996.

Foss, Sonja K., and Cindy L. Griffin. "Beyond Persuasion: A Proposal for an Invitational Rhetoric." *Communication Monographs* 62.1 (March 1995): 2–18.

Fulkerson, Richard. "Transcending Our Conception of Argument in Light of Feminist Critiques." *Argumentation and Advocacy* 32.4 (Spring 1996): 199–218.

Garrett, Mary M. "Classical Chinese Conceptions of Argumentation and Persuasion." *Argumentation and Advocacy* 29.3 (Winter 1993): 105–16.

Grimshaw, A., ed. *Conflict Talk: Sociolinguistic Investigations of Arguments in Conversation*. New York: Cambridge University Press, 1990.

Jan Mohamed, Abdul R. and David Lloyd, eds. *The Nature and Context of Minority Discourse*. New York: Oxford University Press, 1991.

Kochman, Thomas. "Classroom Modalities: Black and White Communicative Styles in the Classroom." *Language in School and Community*. Ed. N. Mercer. London: Edward Arnold, 1981. 96–114.

Kraemer, Don. "Enthymemes and Feminist Discourse: Mediating Public and Private Identity." *Freshman English News* 18 (Fall 1989): 37–40.

Lamb, Catherine E. "Beyond Argument in Feminist Composition." *College Composition and Communication* 42.1 (February 1991): 11–24.

Maier, R., ed. *Norms in Argument*. Dordrecht, The Netherlands: Foris, 1971.

Mao, Lu Ming. "Persuasion, Cooperation, and Diversity of Rhetorics." *Rhetoric Society Quarterly* 20 (Spring 1990): 131–42.

Marback, Richard. "Corbett's Hand: A Rhetorical Figure for Composition Studies." *College Composition and Communication* 47.2 (May 1996): 180–98.

Moore, Vincent. "Using Role Playing in Argument Papers to Deconstruct Stereotypes." *Teaching English in the Two-Year College* 22 (October 1995): 190–96.

Osborn, Susan. "Revisioning the Argument: An Exploratory Study of Some Rhetorical Strategies of Women Student Writers." *Praxis* 1 (1987): 113–33.

Palczewski, Catherine. "Argumentation and Feminism: An Introduction." *Argumentation and Advocacy* 32.4 (Spring 1996): 161–70.

Powers, Lloyd D. "Chicano Rhetoric: Some Basic Concepts." *Southern Speech Communication Journal* 38.4 (Summer 1973): 340–46.

Purves, Alan C. "Writing Across Languages and Cultures: Issues in Contrastive Rhetoric." *Written Communication Annual*, v. 2. Eds. Charles R. Cooper and Sidney Greenbaum. Newbury Park, CA: Sage, 1988.

Argument in Group and Collaborative Settings

Canary, Daniel J., Brent G. Brossman, and David R. Seibold. "Argument Structures in Decision-Making Groups." *Southern Speech Communication Journal* 53 (1987): 18–37.

El-Shinnawy, Maha, and Ajay S. Vinze. "Polarization and Persuasive Argumentation: A Study of Decision Making in Group Settings." *MIS Quarterly* 22.2 (June 1998): 165–99.

Pavitt, Charles. "Another View of Group Polarizing: The Reasons for One-Sided Oral Argumentation." *Communication Research* 21.5 (October 1994): 625–43.

General Argumentation Theory

Allen, Mike, and Nancy A. Burrell. "Resolving Arguments Accurately." *Argumentation* 4 (May 1990): 213–21.

Benoit, William L. "Argumentation and Credibility Appeals in Persuasion." *Southern Speech Communication Journal* 52 (1987): 191–97.

Bensley, Alan D., and Cheryl Haynes. "The Acquisition of General Purpose Strategic Knowledge for Argumentation." *Teaching in Psychology* 22.1 (February 1995): 41–5.

Berg, Jonathan. "The Point of Interpreting Arguments." *Informal Logic* 14 (Spring/Fall 1992): 119–30.

Bjork, Rebecca S. "Argument: Theory and Practice." *Argumentation and Advocacy* 31.1 (Summer 1994): 47–50.

Bohner, Gerd, and Norbert Schwartz. "Mood States Influence the Production of Persuasive Arguments." *Communication Research* 20 (October 1993): 696–722.

Bowles, George. "Evaluating Arguments: The Premise Conclusion Relation." *Informal Logic* 13 (Winter 1992): 1–20.

Brockriede, Wayne, and Douglas Ehninger. *Decision by Debate*. New York: Dodd, Mead, 1963.

Bruxelles, Sylvie, Oswald Ducrot, and Pierre-Yves Raccah. "Argumentation and Lexical Topical Fields." *Journal of Pragmatics* 24.1–2 (1995): 99–114.

Chandler, James, Arnold I. Davidson, and Harry D. Haroofunian, Eds. *Questions of Evidence: Proof, Practice, and Persuasion across the Disciplines*. Chicago: The University of Chicago Press, 1994.

Cohen, Robin. "A Processing Model for the Analysis of One-Way Arguments in Discourse." *Argumentation* 4 (November 1990): 431–46.

Cushman, Donald P. "A Window of Opportunity Argument." *Communication Monographs* 57 (December 1990): 328–32.

Elhadad, Michael. "Using Argumentation in Text Generation." *Journal of Pragmatics* 24.1–2 (1995): 189–220.

Fleming, David. "Can Pictures Be Arguments?" *Argumentation and Advocacy* 33.1 (Summer 1996): 11–23.

Govier, T. *Problems in Argument Analysis and Evaluation*. Dordrecht, The Netherlands: Foris, 1987.

Grize, Jean Blaise, and Gilberte Piéraut-Le Bonniec. "The Use of Contradiction in Argumentative Discourse." *Journal of Pragmatics* 24.1–2 (1995): 17–34.

Gronbeck, Bruce E. "The Alta Conference: Negotiating the Disciplinary and Cross-Disciplinary Study of Argumentation." *Argumentation and Advocacy* 34.1 (Summer 1997): 46–50.

Holmquest, Anne. "The Rhetorical Strategy of Boundary Work." *Argumentation* 4 (August 1990): 235–58.

Jensen, J. Vernon. "Bibliography of Argumentation." *Rhetoric Society Quarterly* 19 (Winter 1989): 71–82.

Johannesen, Richard L., Ed. *Contemporary Theories of Rhetoric: Selected Readings*. New York: Harper & Row, 1971.

Kazoleas, Daen. "The Impact of Argumentativeness on Resistance to Persuasion." *Human Communication Research* 20 (September 1993): 118–37.

Lee, David A., and Jennifer J. Peck. "Troubled Waters: Argument as Sociability Revisited." *Language in Society* 24 (March 1995): 29–52.

Liddicoat, Anthony. "Argumentation as an Interactional Process in Conversation." *Australian Review of Applied Linguistics* 18.2 (1995): 85–104.

Morley, Donald Dean. "Subjective Message Constructs: A Theory of Persuasion." *Communication Monographs* 54 (1987): 183–203.

O'Keefe, Daniel J. *Persuasion: Theory and Research*. Current Communication: An Advanced Text Series, v. 2. Newbury Park, CA: Sage, 1990.

Oostdam, R. J. "Empirical Research on the Identification of Singular, Multiple, and Subordinate Argumentation." *Argumentation* 4 (May 1990): 223–34.

Raccah, Pierre-Yves. "Modeling Argumentation and Modeling *with* Argumentation." *Argumentation* 4 (November 1990): 447–83.

Reinard, John C. "The Empirical Study of the Persuasive Effects of Evidence: The Status After 50 Years of Research." *Human Communication Research* 15 (1988): 3–59.

Rowland, Robert C. "On Defining Argument." *Philosophy and Rhetoric* 20 (1987): 140–57.

Sillince, J. A. "Shifts in Focus and Scope During Argumentation." *Journal of Pragmatics* 24.4 (1995): 413–31.

Sprott, Richard A. "On Giving Reasons in Verbal Disputes: The Development of Justifying." *Argumentation and Advocacy* 29.2 (Fall 1992): 61–77.

Spurgin, Sally Dewitt. *The Power to Persuade*. Englewood Cliffs, NJ: Prentice-Hall, 1985.

Trapp, Robert, and Pamela J. Benoit. "An Interpretive Perspective on Argumentation: A Research Editorial." *Western Journal of Speech Communication* 51 (1987): 417–30.

van Eemeren, F. H., and R. Grootendorst. *Argumentation, Communication and Fallacies*. Hillsdale, NJ: Erlbaum, 1992.

van Eemeren, Franz H., Rob Grootendorst, Sally Jackson, and Scott Jacobs. *Reconstructing Argumentative Discourse*. Studies in Rhetoric and Communication. Eds. E. Culpepper Clarke, Raymie E. McKerrow, and David Zarefsky. Tuscaloosa, AL: University of Alabama Press, 1993.

Voss, James F., Rebecca Fincher-Kiefer, Jennifer Wiley, and Laurie Ney Silfies. "On the Processing of Arguments." *Argumentation* 7 (1993): 165–81.

Walton, Douglas N. *The Place of Emotion in Argument*. University Park, PA: The Pennsylvania State University Press, 1992.

Wangerin, Paul T. "A Multidisciplinary Analysis of the Structure of Persuasive Arguments." *Harvard Journal of Law and Public Policy* 16.1 (Winter 1993): 195–240.

Argument in History and the Social Sciences

Haslett, Diane C. "The Education Task Group: Teaching Proposal Writing to Social Work Students." *Social Work with Groups* 20.4 (1997): 55–67.

Hersch, Charles. "The Quote Analysis: Teaching Political Science Students to Read with Focus." *PS, Political Science and Politics* 28 (September 1995): 523–24.

Karras, Ray W. "Let's Teach More than Stories." *OAH Magazine of History* 14.1 (Fall 1999): 52–56.

Kassiola, Joel J. "Rationally Persuasive Writing Is Like House Painting: It's All in the Preliminaries." *PS, Political Science and Politics* 25 (September 1992): 534–37.

Argument and the Law

Benoit, William L. "Argumentation in *Miranda v. Arizona*." *Communication Studies* 42 (Summer 1991): 129–40.

Bruschke, Jon. "Deconstructive Arguments in the Legal Sphere: An Analysis of the Fischl/Massey Debate about Critical Legal Studies." *Argumentation and Advocacy* 32.1 (Summer 1995): 16–29.

Lempereur, Alain. "Logic of Rhetoric in Law?" *Argumentation* 5 (August 1991): 283–97.

Marouf, Jr., Hasian. "The Domestication of Legal Argumentation: A Case Study of the Formalism of the Legal Realists." *Communication Quarterly* 46.4 (Fall 1998): 430–46.

Prott, Lyndel V. "Argumentation in International Law." *Argumentation* 5 (August 1991): 299–310.

Argumentation and Literature

Anderson, Chris. *Style as Argument: Contemporary American Nonfiction.* Carbondale, IL: Southern Illinois University Press, 1987.

Andrews, R. *Narrative and Argument.* Milton Keynes, UK: Open University Press, 1989.

Ewald, Helen Rothschild. "The Implied Reader in Persuasive Discourse." *JAC* 8 (1988): 167–78.

Helotes, Lynnette. "Responding to Literature via the Essay of Persuasion." *Exercise Exchange* 35 (Spring 1990): 28–31.

Hershey, Lewis. "The Performance of Literature as Argument." *Southern Speech Communication Journal* 53 (1988): 259–78.

Olson, Gary A. "Literary Theory, Philosophy of Science, and Persuasive Discourse: Thoughts from a Neo-PreModernist." *JAC* 13 (Fall 1993): 283–310.

Rains, Charleen. "'You Die for Life': On the Use of Poetic Devices in Argumentation." *Language in Society* 21 (June 1992): 253–76.

The "New Rhetoric"

Crosswhite, James. "Being Unreasonable: Perelman and the Problem of Fallacies." *Argumentation* 7 (1993): 385–402.

———. "Universality in Rhetoric: Perelman's Universal Audience." *Philosophy and Rhetoric* 22 (1989): 157–73.

Dearin, Ray D., Ed. *The New Rhetoric of Chaim Perelman: Statement and Response.* Lanham, MD: University Press of America, 1989.

Frank, David A. "Dialectical Rapprochement in the New Rhetoric." *Argumentation and Advocacy* 34.3 (Winter 1998): 11–26.

Perelman, Chaim. *The Realm of Rhetoric.* Trans. William Kluback. Notre Dame, IN: University of Notre Dame Press, 1982.

Perelman, Chaim, and Lucie Olbrechts-Tyteca. *The New Rhetoric: A Treatise on Argumentation.* Trans. J. Wilkinson and P. Weaver. South Bend, IN: Notre Dame University Press, 1969.

Sharrat, Peter. "Introduction: Ramus, Perelman, and Argumentation: A Way through the Wood." *Argumentation* 5 (November 1991): 335–45.

Tordesillas, Alonso. "Chaim Perelman: Justice, Argumentation, and Ancient Rhetoric." *Argumentation* 4 (February 1990): 109–24.

van Eemeren, Franz H., and Rob Grootendorst. "Perelman and the Fallacies." *Philosophy and Rhetoric* 28.2 (1995): 122–33.

Warnick, Barbara, and Susan L. Kline. "The New Rhetoric's Argument Schemes: A Rhetorical View of Practical Reasoning." *Argumentation and Advocacy* 29.1 (Summer 1992): 1–15.

Argumentation in Mathematics

Douek, Nadia. "Argumentation and Conceptualization in Context: A Case Study on Sunshadows in Primary School." *Educational Studies in Mathematics* 39.1–3 (1998): 89–111.

Merriam, Allen H. "Words and Numbers: Mathematical Dimensions of Rhetoric." *Southern Communication Journal* 55 (Summer 1990): 337–54.

Wood, Terry. "Creating a Context for Argument in Mathematics Class." *Journal for Research in Mathematics Education* 30.2 (March 1999): 171–92.

Yackel, Erna, and Paul Cobb. "Sociomathematical Norms, Argumentation, and Autonomy in Mathematics." *Journal for Research in Mathematics Education* 27.4 (July 1996): 458–78.

Zack, Vicki. "Everyday and Mathematical Language in Children's Argumentation about Proof." *Educational Review* 51.2 (June 1999): 129–47.

Philosophy, Rhetoric, and Argument

Barton, Ellen L. "Contrastive and Non-Contrastive Connectives: Metadiscourse Functions in Argumentation." *Written Communication* 12.2 (April 1995): 219–39

———. "Evidentials, Argumentation, and Epistemological Stance." *College English* 55.7 (November 1993): 745–69.

Birdsell, David S. "Kenneth Burke at the Nexus of Argument and Trope." *Argumentation and Advocacy* 29.4 (Spring 1993): 178–86.

Bitzer, Lloyd F. "The Rhetorical Situation." *Philosophy and Rhetoric* 1 (1968): 1–14.

Booth, Wayne C. *Modern Dogma and the Rhetoric of Assent.* Chicago: University of Chicago Press, 1974.

Brookey, Robert Alan, and Edward Schiappa. "The Epistemic View, Thirty Years Later." *Argumentation and Advocacy* 35.1 (Summer 1998): 1–2.

Bybee, Michael D. "Logic in Rhetoric — and Vice Versa." *Philosophy and Rhetoric* 26 (1993): 169–90.

Canary, Daniel, Jeanette E. Brossman, Brent G. Brossman, and Harry Weger Jr. "Toward a Theory of Minimally Rational Argument: Analyses of Episode-Specific Effects of Argument Structures." *Communication Monographs* 62.3 (September 1995): 183–213.

Clausen, Christopher. "Moral Inversion and Critical Argument." *Georgia Review* 42 (1988): 9–22.

Coe, Richard. "Defining Rhetoric — And Us: A Meditation on Burke's Definitions." *Composition Theory for the Postmodern Classroom.* Gary A. Olson and Sidney I. Dobrin, Eds. Albany: SUNY Press, 1995.

Cox, J. R., and C. A. Willard. *Advances in Argumentation Theory and Research.* Carbondale: Southern University Press, 1982.

Crosswhite, James. "Is There an Audience for This Argument? Fallacies, Theories, and Relativism." *Philosophy and Rhetoric* 28.2 (1995): 134–45.

———. "Mood in Argumentation: Heidegger and the Exordium." *Philosophy and Rhetoric* 22 (1989): 28–41.

———. *The Rhetoric of Reason: Writing and the Attractions of Argument.* Madison: University of Wisconsin Press, 1996.

Davson-Galle, Peter. "Arguing, Arguments, and Deep Disagreements." *Informal Logic* 14 (Spring/Fall 1992): 146–56.

Disson, George. "Argumentation and Critique: College Composition and Enlightenment Ideals." *Into the Field.* Ed. Anne Ruggles Gere. New York: MLA, 1993.

Finocchiaro, M. A. "The Port-Royal Logic's Theory of Argument." *Argumentation* 11.4 (November 1997): 393–410.

Foss, Sonja K., Karen A. Foss, and Robert Trapp. *Contemporary Perspectives on Rhetoric.* 2nd ed. Prospect Heights, IL: Waveland Press, 1991.

Freeman, James B. *Dialectics and the Macrostructure of Arguments: A Theory of Argument Structure.* New York: Foris, 1991.

Gehrke, Pat J. "Teaching Argumentation Existentially: Argumentation Pedagogy and Theories of Rhetoric as Epistemic." *Argumentation and Advocacy* 35.2 (Fall 1998): 76–87.

Gilbert, Michael A. "Multi-Modal Argumentation." *Philosophy of the Social Sciences* 24.2 (June 1994): 159–178.

Goldman, Alvin I. "Argumentation and Social Epistemology." *Journal of Philosophy* 91.1 (January 1994): 27–50.

Greene, Ronald Walter. "The Aesthetic Turn and the Rhetorical Perspective." *Argumentation and Advocacy* 35.1 (Summer 1998): 19–30.

Horne, Janet S. "Rorty's Circumvention of Argument: Redescribing Rhetoric." *Southern Communication Journal* 58 (Spring 1993): 169–81.

Jacquette, Dale. "The Hidden Logic of Slippery Slope Arguments." *Philosophy and Rhetoric* (1989): 59–70.

Jamison, David. "Michael Meyer's Philosophy of Problematology: Toward a New Theory of Argumentation." *Argumentation* 5 (February 1991): 57–68.

Kelman, Mark. "Reasonable Evidence of Reasonableness." *Critical Inquiry* 17 (Summer 1991): 798–817.

Kienpointer, Manfred. "Rhetoric and Argumentation — Relativism and Beyond." *Philosophy and Rhetoric* 24 (1991): 43–53.

Klinger, Geoffrey D. "The Philosophy and Rhetoric of Argumentation Theory." *Argumentation and Advocacy* 31.2 (Fall 1994): 111–14.

Levasseur, David G. "Edifying Arguments and Perspective by Incongruity: The Perplexing Argumentation Method of Kenneth Burke." *Argumentation and Advocacy* 29.4 (Spring 1993): 195–204.

Lyne, John. "Social Epistemology as a Rhetoric of Inquiry." *Argumentation* 8 (May 1994): 11–24.

Madsen, Arnie J. "The Comic Frame as a Corrective to Bureaucratization: A Dramatistic Perspective on Argumentation." *Argumentation and Advocacy* 29.4 (Spring 1993): 164–78.

McKerrow, Raymie E. "The Ethical Implications of a Whatelian Rhetoric." *Rhetoric Society Quarterly* 17 (1987): 321–27.

Meiland, Jack. "Argument as Inquiry and Argument as Persuasion." *Argumentation* 3 (1989): 185–96.

Pieretti, A. "The Argumentative Reason in Johnstone." *Philosophy and Rhetoric* 27 (1994): 121–42.

Prado, Jr., Plinio Walder. "Argumentation and Aesthetics." *Philosophy Today* 36.4 (Winter 1992): 351–67.

Raccah, Pierre-Yves. "Argumentation and Natural Language: Presentation and Discussion of Four Foundational Hypotheses." *Journal of Pragmatics* 24.1–2 (1995): 1–15.

Reboul, Olivier. "Can There Be Nonrhetorical Argumentation?" *Philosophy and Rhetoric* 21 (1988): 220–33.

Ricoeur, Paul. "History and Rhetoric." *Diogenes* 42.4 (1994): 7–25.

Roberts, Patricia, and Virginia Pompei Jones. "Imagining Reasons: The Role of the Imagination in Argumentation." *JAC* 15.3 (1995): 527–41

Rowland, Robert C. "In Defense of Rational Argument: A Pragmatic Justification of Argumentation Theory and Response to the Postmodern Critique." *Philosophy and Rhetoric* 28.4 (1995): 350–64.

Rudinow, Joel. "Argument-Appreciation/Argument-Criticism: The Aesthetics of Informal Logic." *Informal Logic* 13 (Spring 1991): 89–97.

Shapiro, Irving David. "Fallacies of Logic: Argumentation Cons." *ETC: A Review of General Semantics* 53.3 (Fall 1996): 251–66.

Simons, Herbert W., ed. *The Rhetorical Turn: Invention and Persuasion in the Conduct of Inquiry*. Chicago: University of Chicago Press, 1990.

Thaden, Barbara Z. "Derrida in the Composition Class: Deconstructing Arguments." *Writing Instructor* 7 (1988): 131–37.

Tiles, J. E. "Logic and Rhetoric: An Introduction to Seductive Argument." *Philosophy and Rhetoric* 28.4 (1995): 300–15.

Tindale, Christopher W., and James Gough. "The Use of Irony in Argumentation." *Philosophy and Rhetoric* 20 (1987): 1–17.

van Eemeren, Frans H., Rob Grootendorst, and Tjark Kruiger. *Handbook of Argumentation Theory: A Critical Survey of Classical Backgrounds and Modern Studies*. Dordrecht, Holland/Providence, RI: Foris, 1987.

Verene, Donald Phillip. "The Limits of Argument: Argument and Autobiography." *Philosophy and Rhetoric* 26 (Winter 1993): 1–8.

Walton, Douglas N. "Alethic, Epistemic, and Dialectical Modes of Argument." [Response to Johnson, *Philosophy and Rhetoric* 23 (1990).] *Philosophy and Rhetoric* 26 (1993): 302–10.

———. *Argumentation Schemes for Presumptive Reasoning*. Hillsdale, NJ: Lawrence Erlbaum Associates, 1995.

———. *Begging the Question: Circular Reasoning as a Tactic of Argumentation*. New York: Greenwood Press, 1991.

———. "Rethinking the Fallacy of Hasty Generalization." *Argumentation* 13.2 (1999): 161–83.

Wilkinson, A. M. "Argument as a Primary Act of Mind." *Educational Review* 38.2 (1986): 127–38.

Yoos, George E. "Rhetoric of Appeal and Rhetoric of Response." *Philosophy and Rhetoric* 20 (1987): 107–17.

Zarefsky, David, ed. "Special Issue: Critical Social Theory of Jurgen Habermas and Its Implications for Argumentation Theory and Practice." *Journal of the American Forensic Association* 16.2 (Fall 1979).

Argument in Popular and Public Cultures

Aldridge, Heather. "The Rap on Violence: A Rhetorical Analysis of Rapper KRS-One." *Communication Studies* 44.2 (Summer 1993): 102–16.

Branham, Robert James. "'I Was Gone on Debating': Malcolm X's Prison Debates and Public Confrontations." *Argumentation and Advocacy* 31.3 (Winter 1995): 117–37.

Brossman, Brent G., and Daniel G. Canary. "An Observational Analysis of Argument Structures: The Case of 'Nightline.'" *Argumentation* 4 (May 1990): 199–212.

Chappell, Virginia A. "Expert Testimony, 'Regular People,' and Public Values: Arguing Common Sense at a Death Penalty Trial." *Rhetoric Review* 13.2 (Spring 1995): 301–308.

Condit, Celeste Michelle. "Democracy and Civil Rights: The Universalizing Influence of Public Argumentation." *Communication Monographs* 54 (March 1987): 1–18.

Davy, George Alan. "Argumentation and Unified Structure in 'Notes on the State of Virginia.'" *Eighteenth Century Studies* 26.4 (Summer 1993): 581–94.

Dennis, Valerie Cryer, Lynda Lee Kaid, and Sandra Ragan. "The Impact of Argumentativeness and Verbal Aggression on Communication Image: The

Exchange Between George Bush and Dan Rather." *Western Journal of Speech Communication* 54 (Winter 1990): 99–112.

Doxtader, Erik. "Learning Public Deliberation through the Critique of Institutional Argument." *Argumentation and Advocacy* 31.4 (Spring 1995): 185–203.

Gauthier, Gilles. "Referential Argumentation and Its Ethical Considerations in Televised Political Advertising." *Argumentation and Advocacy* 31.2 (Fall 1994): 96–111.

Gustainis, J. Justin, and Dan F. Hahn. "While the Whole World Watched: Rhetorical Failures of Anti-War Protest." *Communication Quarterly* 36 (1988): 203–216.

Hartnett, Stephen. "'A Plain Public Road': Evaluating Arguments for Democracy in a Post-Metaphysical World." *Argumentation and Advocacy* 35.3 (Winter 1999): 95–115.

Jowett, Garth S., and Victoria O'Donnell. *Propaganda and Persuasion.* 2nd ed. Newbury Park: Sage, 1992.

Lake, Randall A. "Argumentation and Self: The Enactment of Identity in *Dances With Wolves.*" *Argumentation and Advocacy* 34.2 (Fall 1997): 66–90.

Mitchell, Gordon R. "Simulated Public Argument as a Pedagogical Play on Worlds." *Argumentation and Advocacy* 36.3 (Winter 2000): 134–50.

Morello, John T. "The 'Look' and Language of Clash: Visual Structuring of Argument in the 1988 Bush-Dukakis Debates." *Southern Communication Journal* (Spring 1992): 205–18.

Myers, Frank. "Political Argumentation and the Composite Audience: A Case Study." *Quarterly Journal of Speech* 85.1 (February 1999): 55–72.

Popkin, Samuel L. *The Reasoning Voter: Communication and Persuasion in Presidential Campaigns.* Chicago, IL: University of Chicago Press, 1991.

Sayer, Cathy. "Writing to Change Community." *The Writing Instructor* 15 (Fall 1995): 35–42.

Wells, Susan. "Rogue Cops and Health Care: What Do We Want from Public Writing?" *College Composition and Communication* 47.3 (October 1996): 325–41.

Argument and Religion

Janowitz, Naomi, and Andrew J. Lazarus. "Rabbinic Methods of Inference and the Rationality Debate." *Journal of Religion* 72.4 (October 1992): 491–512.

Vos, Johan S. "Paul's Argumentation in Galatians 1–2*." *Harvard Theological Review* 87.1 (January 1994): 1–17.

Voth, Ben. "A Case Study in Metaphor as Argument: A Longitudinal Analysis of the Wall Separating Church and State." *Argumentation and Advocacy* 34.3 (Winter 1998): 127–40.

Rogerian Argumentation

Bator, Paul. "Aristotelian and Rogerian Rhetoric." *College Composition and Communication* 31 (1980): 427–32.

Brent, Doug. "Young, Becker, and Pike's Rogerian Rhetoric: A Twenty-Year Reassessment." *College English* 53 (April 1991): 452–66.

Ede, Lisa. "Is Rogerian Rhetoric Really Rogerian?" *Rhetoric Review* 3 (September 1984): 40–47.

Hairston, Maxine. "Carl Rogers's Alternative to Traditional Rhetoric." *College Composition and Communication* 27 (December 1976): 373–77.

———. "Using Carl Rogers's Communication Theories in the Composition Classroom." *Rhetoric Review* (September 1982): 50–55.

Lassner, Phyllis. "Feminist Response to Rogerian Argument." *Rhetoric Review* 8 (Spring 1990): 220–31.

Lunsford, Andrea. "Aristotelian vs. Rogerian Argument: A Reassessment." *College Composition and Communication* 30 (May 1979): 146–51.

Mader, Diane C. "What Are They Doing to Carl Rogers?" *ETC: A Review of General Semantics* 37.4 (Winter 1980): 314–20.

Pounds, Wayne. "The Context of No Context: A Burkean Critique of Rogerian Argument." *Rhetoric Society Quarterly* 17 (1987): 4⌐ ⌐⌐

Rogers, Carl R. *On Becoming a Person*. Boston: Houg.___ ___ifflin, 1961.

Teich, Nathaniel, ed. *Rogerian Perspectives: Collaborative Rhetoric for Oral and Written Communication*. Northwood, NJ: Ablex, 1992.

Teich, Nathaniel. "Rogerian Problem Solving and the Rhetoric of Argumentation." *JAC* 7 (1987): 52–61.

Zappen, James P. "Carl R. Rogers and Political Rhetoric." *PRE / TEXT* (Spring–Fall 1980): 95–113.

Science, Technology, and Argumentation

Bacig, Thomas D., Robert H. Evan, Donald W. Larmouth, and Kenneth C. Risdon. "Beyond Argumentation and Comparison/Contrast: Extending the Socrates CAI Design Principles of Classroom Teaching and the Production of Other Forms of Discourse." *Computers and the Humanities* (February–April 1990): 15–41.

Ballenger, Cynthia. "Social Identities, Moral Narratives, Scientific Argumentation: Science Talk in a Bilingual Classroom." *Language and Education* 11.1 (1997): 1–15.

Borillo, Mario. "A Logical Argumentation Model of Computer-Assisted Reasoning." *Argumentation* 4 (1990): 397–414.

Crain, Jeanie C., and Roy Kunkle. "Classroom Presentations Using Aldus Persuasion: Professional and Impressive." *Computers and the Humanities* 27.4 (August 1993): 299–304.

Dear, Peter, ed. *The Literary Structure of Scientific Argument*. Philadelphia, PA: University of Pennsylvania Press, 1991.

Driver, Rosalind, Paul Newton, and Jonathan Osborne. "Establishing the Norms of Scientific Argumentation in Classrooms." *Science Education* 84.3 (2000): 287–313.

Dubois, Betty Lou. *Persuasive Scientific Discourse: A Selective Analysis of Biomedical Journal Articles*. Norwood, NJ: Ablex, 1995.

Evans, John C., John Mark Dean, and Scott Chapal. "Expert Witness or Advocate: Developing Oral Argument Skills in the Marine Science Student." *Journal of College Science Teaching* 21 (December 1991/January 1992): 149–53.

Fogg, B. J. "Persuasive Technologies." *Communications of the ACM* 42.5 (May 1999): 26–29.

Grabau, Larry J. "Jumping on Thin Ice: Values Argument Writing Assignment for a Large Enrollment Plant Science Class." *Journal of Natural Resources and Life Sciences Education* 24.2 (Fall 1995): 185–89.

Gross, Alan G. "Does Rhetoric of Science Matter? The Case of the Floppy-Eared Rabbits." *College English* 53 (December 1991): 933–43.

———. *The Rhetoric of Science.* Cambridge, MA: Harvard University Press, 1990.

Harris, R. Allen. "Argumentation in Chomsky's Syntactic Structures: An Exercise in Rhetoric of Science." *Rhetoric Society Quarterly* 19 (Spring 1989): 105–30.

Harris, R. Allen. "Rhetoric of Science." *College English* 53 (March 1991): 282–305.

Hashim, Safaa H. "WHAT: An Argumentative Groupware Approach for Organizing and Documenting Research Activities." *Journal of Organizational Computing* 1 (Fall 1991): 275–302.

Kaufer, David, and Cheryl Geisler. "Structuring Argumentation in a Social Constructivist Framework: A Pedagogy with Computer Support." *Argumentation* 4 (November 1990): 379–96.

Keith, William. "Rhetorical Criticism and the Rhetoric of Science: Introduction." *Southern Communication Journal* 58 (Summer 1993): 255–57.

Lyne, John. "Knowledge and Performance in Argument: Disciplinarity and Proto-Theory." *Argumentation and Advocacy* 35.1 (Summer 1998): 3–10.

Marttunen, Miika. "Electronic Mail as a Pedagogical Delivery System: An Analysis of the Learning of Argumentation." *Research in Higher Education* 38.3 (June 1997): 345–64.

O'Neill, John. "Rhetoric, Science, and Philosophy." *Philosophy of the Social Sciences* 28.2 (June 1998): 205–25.

Prelli, Lawrence J. "Rhetorical Logic and the Integration of Rhetoric and Science." *Communication Monographs* 57 (December 1990): 315–22.

Ravenscroft, Andrew. "Designing Argumentation for Conceptual Development." *Computers and Education* 34.3 (2000): 241–257.

Roberts, R. H., and J. M. M. Good, eds. *The Recovery of Rhetoric: Persuasive Discourse and Disciplinarity in the Human Sciences.* Charlottesville, VA: University Press of Virginia, 1993.

Sellnow, Timothy L. "Scientific Argument in Organizational Crisis Communication: The Case of Exxon." *Argumentation and Advocacy* 30.1 (Summer 1993): 28–43.

Shelley, Cameron. "Rhetorical and Demonstrative Modes of Visual Argument: Looking at Images of Human Evolution." *Argumentation and Advocacy* 33.2 (Fall 1996): 53–69.

Warnick, Barbara. "Persuasion and Privacy in Cyberspace: The Online Protests Over Lotus Marketplace and the Clipper Chip." *Quarterly Journal of Speech* 84.3 (August 1998): 389–90.

Weinstein, Mark. "Towards an Account of Argumentation in Science." *Argumentation* 4 (August 1990): 269–98.

Stephen Toulmin's Theory of Argument

Brockriede, Wayne, and Douglas Ehninger. "Toulmin on Argument: An Interpretation and Application." *Quarterly Journal of Speech* 46 (February 1960): 44–53.

Fairbanks, A. Harris. "The Pedagogical Failure of Toulmin's Logic." *The Writing Instructor* 12 (Spring/Summer 1993): 103–14.

Hart, Roderick P. "On Applying Toulmin: The Analysis of Practical Discourse." *Explorations in Rhetorical Criticism.* Eds. G. P. Mohrmann, Charles J.

Stewart, and Donovan J. Ochs. University Park: Pennsylvania State University Press, 1973. 75–95.

Karbach, Joan. "Using Toulmin's Model of Argumentation." *Journal of Teaching Writing* 6 (1987): 81–92.

Kneupper, Charles W. "Teaching Argument: An Introduction to the Toulmin Model." *College Composition and Communication* 29 (October 1978): 237–41.

Tanner, William E., and Betty Kay Seibt, eds. *The Toulmin Method: Exploration and Controversy.* Arlington, TX: Liberal Arts Press, 1991.

Toulmin, Stephen. *Human Understanding.* Princeton, NJ: Princeton University Press, 1972.

———. *The Uses of Argument.* Cambridge: Cambridge University Press, 1958.

———, R. Rieke, and A. Janik. *An Introduction to Reasoning.* New York: Macmillan, 1979.

Argument in the Writing and Communications Class

Adams, Katharine, and John Adams, eds. *Teaching Advanced Composition: How and Why.* Portsmouth: Heinemann, 1991.

Allen, Mike, and Sandra Berkowitz. "A Meta-Analysis of the Impact of Forensics and Communication Education on Critical Thinking." *Communication Education* 48.1 (January 1999): 18–31.

Bartholomae, David. "Inventing the University." *When a Writer Can't Write: Studies in Writer's Block and Other Composing Process Problems.* Ed. Mike Rose. New York: Guilford Press, 1985.

Beason, Larry. "Textbooks on Argumentative Writing Display Much Agreement, Though Each Has Own Slant." *Composition Chronicle* 8.2 (March 1995): 1–4.

Berrill, Deborah P. "What Exposition Has To Do With Argument." *English in Education* 24.1 (1990): 77–92.

Black, Kathleen. "Audience Analysis and Persuasive Writing at the College Level." *Research in the Teaching of English* 23 (October 1989): 231–53.

Brent, Doug. *Reading as Rhetorical Invention: Knowledge, Persuasion, and The Teaching of Research-Based Writing.* Urbana, IL: NCTE, 1992.

Carrell, Patricia L., and Ulla Connor. "Reading and Writing Descriptive and Persuasive Texts." *The Modern Language Journal* 75 (Autumn 1991): 314–24.

Chapman, David W. "Forming and Meaning: Writing the Counterpoint Essay." *JAC* 11 (Winter 1991): 73–81.

Costello, Patrick J. M., and Sally Mitchell, Eds. *Competing and Consensual Voices: The Theory and Practice of Argument.* Avon, England: Multilingual Matters, 1995.

Crowhurst, M. "Interrelationships Between Reading and Writing Persuasive Discourse." *Research in the Teaching of English* 25.3 (1991): 314–38.

Durst, Russel, Chester Laine, Lucille M. Schultz, and William Vilter. "Appealing Texts: The Persuasive Writing of High School Students." *Written Communication* 7 (April 1990): 232–55.

Fahnestock, Jeanne, and Marie Secor. "Teaching Argument: A Theory of Types." *College Composition and Communication* 34 (1983): 20–30.

Freedman, A., and I. Pringle. "Why Students Can't Write Arguments." *English in Education* 18.2 (1984): 73–84.

Fulkerson, Richard. *Teaching the Argument in Writing*. Urbana, Illinois: NCTE, 1996.

Gleason, Mary M. "The Role of Evidence in Argumentative Writing." *Reading and Writing Quarterly* 15.1 (January–March 1999): 81–107.

Kaufer, David S., and Cheryl Geisler. "A Scheme for Representing Written Argument." *JAC* 11 (Winter 1991): 107–22.

Kroll, Barry M. "Broadening the Repertoire: Alternatives to the Argumentative Edge." *Composition Studies* 28.1 (Spring 2000): 11–27.

Lynch, Dennis A., Diana George, and Marilyn M. Cooper. "Moments of Argument: Agonistic Inquiry and Confrontational Cooperation." *College Composition and Communication* 48.1 (February 1997): 61–85.

Mitchell, Gordon R. "Pedagogical Possibilities for Argumentative Agency in Academic Debate." *Argumentation and Advocacy* 35.2 (1998): 41–61.

Moxley, Joseph M. "Reinventing the Wheel or Teaching the Basics: College Writers' Knowledge of Argumentation." *Composition Studies* 21 (Fall 1993): 3–15.

Robertson, Elizabeth. "Moving from Expressive Writing to Academic Discourse." *Writing Center Journal* 9 (1988): 21–28.

Sanders, Judith A. "Does Teaching Argumentation Facilitate Critical Thinking?" *Communication Reports* 7.1 (Winter 1994): 27–36.

Schmudde, Carol. "Teaching Accommodation in Argument through Negotiations Roleplay." *Exercise Exchange* 36 (Spring 1991): 17–20.

Shermis, Michael. "Research, Activities, and Writing Assignments in Persuasion." *Composition Chronicle* 3 (December 1990): 8–9.

Tindell, John H. "Argumentation and Debate Textbooks: An Overview of Content and Focus." *Argumentation and Advocacy* 35.4 (Spring 1999): 185–92.

To-Dutka, Julia. "Developing Self-Monitored Comprehension Strategies through Argument Structure Analysis." *Journal of Reading* 35.3 (November 1991): 200–05.

Trail, George Y. "Teaching Argument and the Rhetoric of Orwell's 'Politics and the English Language.'" *College English* 57.5 (September 1995): 570–83.

Wyandotte, Annette. "Participatory Action Research: Bringing Student Arguments up to PAR." *Journal of Teaching Writing* 15.2 (1996): 211–33.